QUICKBOOKS® DESKTOP 2018: A COMPLETE COURSE

QUICKBOOKS® DESKTOP 2018:
A COMPLETE COURSE

Janet Horne, M.S.

 Pearson

New York, NY

Vice President, Business, Economics, and UK Courseware: Donna Battista
Director of Portfolio Management: Adrienne D'Ambrosio
Director, Courseware Portfolio Management: Ashley Dodge
Senior Sponsoring Editor: Neeraj Bhalla
Editorial Assistant: Elisa Marks
Vice President, Product Marketing: Roxanne McCarley
Product Marketing Assistant: Marianela Silvestri
Manager of Field Marketing, Business Publishing: Adam Goldstein
Executive Field Marketing Manager: Nayke Popovich
Vice President, Production and Digital Studio, Arts and Business: Etain O'Dea
Director, Production and Digital Studio, Business and Economics: Ashley Santora
Managing Producer, Business: Melissa Feimer
Content Producer: Sugandh Juneja

Operations Specialist: Carol Melville
Design Lead: Kathryn Foot
Manager, Learning Tools: Brian Surette
Content Developer, Learning Tools: Sarah Peterson
Managing Producer, Digital Studio and GLP: James Bateman
Managing Producer, Digital Studio: Diane Lombardo
Digital Studio Producer: Mary Kate Murray
Digital Studio Producer: Alana Coles
Digital Content Team Lead: Noel Lotz
Digital Content Project Lead: Martha LaChance and Elizabeth Geary
Project Manager: Nicole Suddeth, SPi Global
Interior Design: Janet Horne
Cover Design: Laurie Entringer
Cover Art: Sergiy Molchenko/123RF.com
Printer/Binder: LSC/Menasha
Cover Printer: Phoenix Color/Hagerstown

Library of Congress Cataloging-in-Publication Data
Names: Horne, Janet, author.
Title: QuickBooks Desktop 2018 : A Complete Course/Janet Horne, M.S.
Description: New York : Pearson Education, [2019]
Identifiers: LCCN 2018022570 | ISBN 9780134743813 (pbk.)
Subjects: LCSH: QuickBooks. | Small business--Accounting--Computer programs.
 | Small business--Finance--Computer programs.
Classification: LCC HF5679 .H66384 2019 | DDC 657/.9042028553--dc23
LC record available at https://lccn.loc.gov/2018022570

1   18

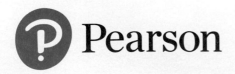

ISBN 10:   0-13-474381-4
ISBN 13: 978-0-13-474381-3

To my family

BRIEF TABLE OF CONTENTS

TABLE OF CONTENTS

Chapter 2—Sales and Receivables: Service Business

Chapter 3 — Payables and Purchases: Service Business

Chapter 4—General Accounting and End-of-Period Procedures: Service Business

Chapter 7—General Accounting and End-of-Period Procedures: Merchandising Business

Chapter 6—Payables and Purchases: Merchandising Business

Contents

Practice Set 1—Service Business Your Name's Concierge for You ....

Chapter 5—Sales and Receivables: Merchandising Business

Chapter 9—Create a Company in QuickBooks Desktop

Practice Set 2—Merchandising Business Your Name's Desert Golf

Chapter 8—Payroll

Contents

Appendix A—QuickBooks Desktop: Program Integration

Appendix B—QuickBooks Desktop: Additional Features

Appendix C—QuickBooks Desktop: Online Features

Index

PREFACE

QuickBooks 2018: A Complete Course is a comprehensive instructional learning resource. The text provides training using the *QuickBooks Premier Accountant 2018* accounting program (for simplicity, the program is referred to as *QuickBooks 2018* throughout the text). Even though the text was written using the 2018 Accountant version of QuickBooks Premier, it may be used with the Pro version of the program as well. (Because of the many differences between the Windows and Mac versions of QuickBooks, this text should not be used for training using QuickBooks for the Mac.)

NEW TO THIS EDITION

Each version of QuickBooks comes with changes, enhancements, and new features. Many of these changes are incorporated into the text; while others may or may not be mentioned. Some of the features are only available on a subscription basis. Since the companies in the text are fictitious, the dates used are not current, and the subscriptions are not free, these features are not explored in the greatest detail.

Some of the new features of QuickBooks and changes in the 2018 text include:

- Use an Access Code Card and instructions for downloading QuickBooks 2018 Educational Trial Version of the program
- Use of complex passwords to protect data
- QuickBooks onscreen report formatting has been changed to show details more clearly
- Use of Accrual and Cash report basis toggle in report
- Explore enhanced report filters and custom fields in reports
- Use the Show/Hide filter feature in reports
- Create, memorize, and use Custom Reports
- Explore and use Commented Reports feature
- Use Enhanced Search features including:
  - Smart Search
  - Amount Range Search
  - Search by Customer and Vendor Type
  - ?rch in Chart of Accounts
  - Ins?? to company files
  - Cust?any files
  - Statem?ome Page
  - Passwor? Methods List
  - Batch Dele?
  - Add Credit C?
  - ??tions
  - ?ividual customers

- Auto copy Ship To Address
- Select Preferred Delivery and Payment Methods for customers
- Use Past Due stamp on invoices
- Merge Vendors
- Use of more secure Webmail and e-invoicing
- Use of Bill Tracker to manage bills
- Add additional information to Employees including:
  - Marital Status
  - U.S. Citizen
  - Ethnicity
  - Disability
- New Business Checklist
- File Manager
- Send and Import General Journal Entries

DISTINGUISHING FEATURES

Throughout the text, emphasis has been placed on the use of QuickBooks' innovative approach to recording accounting transactions based on a business form rather than using the traditional journal format. This approach, however, has been correlated to traditional accounting through adjusting entries, end-of-period procedures, and use of the "behind the scenes" journal. The text uses a tutorial-style training method to guide the students in the use of QuickBooks in a step-by-step manner and is designed to help students transition from training to using *QuickBooks 2018* in an actual business.

The text provides:

- Comprehensive exploration of QuickBooks
- Reinforcement of accounting concepts
- Exploration of error correction and resulting ramifications
- Introduction to and use of many QuickBooks features
- Experience in recording transactions for service and merchandising businesses
- Transactions ranging from simple to complex that simulate real-world occurrences
- Use of Manual Payroll and comparison of Payroll Subscriptions
- Creation of companies for use in QuickBooks
- Printing of business forms and reports
- Opportunity to learn how to customize QuickBooks:
  - Forms
  - Preferences
  - Reports
- Screen shots used liberally to show:
  - QuickBooks screens
  - Completed transactions
  - Reports

- Extensive assignment material including:
  - Tutorials
  - End-of-chapter questions (true/false, multiple-choice, fill-in, and essay)
  - End-of-chapter reinforcement problem
  - Practice sets

COURSES

QuickBooks 2018: A Complete Course is designed for a one-term course in microcomputer accounting. This text covers using QuickBooks in a service business, a merchandising business, a sole proprietorship, and a partnership. Preparing payroll and creating a new company are also included. When using the text, students should be familiar with the accounting cycle and how it is related to a business. No prior knowledge of or experience with computers, Windows, or QuickBooks is required; however, an understanding of accounting is essential to successful completion of the coursework.

SOLVING TEACHING AND LEARNING CHALLENGES

Many studies have been done that identify requirements for job skills in business. These include critical thinking, problem solving, oral and written communications, professionalism and work ethics, teamwork and collaboration, self-management/initiative and mindset, creative thinking, information/technology application, leadership, and social responsibility.

If you're not an accounting major, you may be thinking that this course or these job skills are not relevant to you. Let me assure you that they are. Whether or not you plan on a career in accounting or bookkeeping, the concepts, procedures, and job skills you learn and apply in this course will help you in business and/or in your life. Moreover, it is only through the aggregate of your educational experience that you will have the opportunity to develop many of the skills that employers have identified as critical to success in the workplace. In this course, and specifically in this text you'll have the opportunity to develop job skills and practice using QuickBooks Desktop to keep the financial records of companies. You will analyze business transactions, prepare and analyze financial reports, understand the process of using computerized accounting versus pencil and paper accounting and bookkeeping, and, find and correct errors, among others.

ORGANIZATIONAL FEATURES

QuickBooks 2018: A Complete Course is designed to present accounting concepts and their relationship to *QuickBooks 2018*. While completing each chapter, students will

- Learn underlying accounting concepts
- Receive hands-on training using QuickBooks 2018
- Analyze and record transactions for service and merchandising businesses

Area of Organization	Organization Features
Text	<ul><li>Divided into Sections<ul><li>Section 1: Accounting for a Service Business</li><li>Section 2: Accounting for a Merchandising Business</li><li>Section 3: Payroll and Creating a Company</li><li>Practice Sets for Sections 1 and 2</li><li>Comprehensive Practice Set for entire text</li><li>Three Appendices:<ul><li>QuickBooks Program Integration</li><li>QuickBooks Features (not covered in chapters)</li><li>QuickBooks Online Features</li></ul></li></ul></li></ul>
Chapters	<ul><li>A single company is used within the chapters for a full business cycle</li><li>A second company is used for the end of chapter problem for a full business cycle</li><li>End of chapter materials reinforce concepts and applications learned in the chapter and include:<ul><li>True/False questions</li><li>Multiple-Choice questions</li><li>Fill-in questions</li><li>Essay questions</li></ul></li></ul>

INSTRUCTOR AND STUDENT RESOURCES

Pearson Education maintains a Web site, **www.pearsonhighered.com/horne**, for the online resources. Students can download Data and Solution files for their classroom use. Instructors can download all the following materials:

Supplement	Features of the Supplement
Data & Solution Files	<ul><li>Master company files:<ul><li>Used for each company in the text</li><li>Same as student files</li></ul></li><li>Backup company files:<ul><li>Used to restore a QuickBooks Company file</li></ul></li><li>Logos<ul><li>Used when students create a company</li></ul></li></ul>
Instructor's Resource Manual	<ul><li>Appendix with instructions to<ul><li>Download, Install, and Register QuickBooks</li><li>Open a company file</li><li>Backup and restore company files</li></ul></li><li>Answers to end-of-chapter questions</li><li>Excel files of all reports prepared in text</li><li>Instructor's Manual<ul><li>Assignment sheets</li><li>IM Preface for instructors</li><li>IM Table of Contents</li><li>Teaching suggestions</li></ul></li><li>Transmittal sheets with totals</li></ul>
PowerPoint Presentations	<ul><li>Presentation and notes for each chapter</li><li>Additional presentation for installing and registering QuickBooks Desktop Trial Version</li></ul>
Instructor's Solutions Manual	<ul><li>Adobe .pdf files for all printouts prepared in text</li></ul>
Test Bank	<ul><li>Written exams and keys for<ul><li>Every chapter in text</li><li>Four section exams (Chapters 1-4, 5-7, and 8-9)</li><li>Final exam</li></ul></li><li>Computer exams and solutions<ul><li>Exam for each chapter</li><li>Exam for each Practice Set</li></ul></li></ul>

If you need assistance with QuickBooks, go to www.QuickBooks.Com/Support and click on one of the Resource Centers for help. The Resource Centers include: Install Center, Download & Updates, Support Tools, and others. For specific information when installing the trial version of the software, please go to the Intuit Install Center at: http://support.quickbooks.intuit.com/Support/InstallCenter/default.aspx

ERRATA AND INSTRUCTOR COMMENTS

While I strive to write an error-free textbook, it is inevitable that some errors will occur. As I become aware of any errors, they will be added to an errata sheet that is posted in the Instructor's Resource Center on the Pearson Web site at **www.pearsonhighered.com/horne**. Once an errata is posted, instructors should feel free to share that information with their students and to check back periodically to see if any new items have been added. If you or your students discover an error, or have suggestions and/or concerns, I would appreciate it if you would contact me and let me know what they are. My email address for instructors is also shown in the Instructor's Resource Center.

ACKNOWLEDGMENTS

I wish to thank my colleagues for testing and reviewing the manuscript, the professors who use the text and share their thoughts and suggestions with me, and my students for providing me with a special insight into problems encountered in training. All of your comments and suggestions are greatly appreciated. A special thank you goes to Cheryl Bartlett for her proofreading and comments. In addition, I would like to thank Neeraj Bhalla and the production team at Pearson Education for their editorial support and assistance.

Janet Horne

Janet Horne received her Master of Science in Business Administration and Bachelor of Science in Business Education from California State University, Long Beach and has spent her educational career teaching business and computer applications courses. The majority of her teaching career has been at Los Angeles Pierce College. Where, in addition to being a full-time professor, she was the Computer Applications and Office Technologies Department Chairperson, served on many committees, and developed new programs. Janet has been a presenter at many educational meetings and seminars and has been involved with a variety of professional organizations.

Janet's quest to find a textbook to use in teaching QuickBooks led her to write one of the first texts for QuickBooks Desktop. QuickBooks Desktop has long been and still is a very popular and powerful computerized accounting program that is widely used in businesses today. In addition to this book, Janet's texts include: QuickBooks Online Plus: A Complete Course 2017 several previous editions of QuickBooks: A Complete Course (uses QuickBooks Desktop Accountant software), QuickBooks Pro: Simplified, QuickBooks Pro: An Introduction, Peachtree Complete Accounting, Getting Started with QuickBooks Pro, and Computerized Accounting with CA-Simply Accounting. Janet is also the author of Runners Corporation and A-1 Photography accounting practice sets.

INTRODUCTION TO QUICKBOOKS DESKTOP 2018 AND COMPANY FILES

LEARNING OBJECTIVES

At the completion of this chapter, you will be able to:

1.01.   Identify versions of QuickBooks.
1.02.   Apply, install and activate QuickBooks Accountant Desktop 2018 Student Trial Version.
1.03.   Update QuickBooks Desktop.
1.04.   Open a company.
1.05.   Distinguish program features including the Menu Bar, Menus, Icon Bar, Centers, Home Page, and Insights.
1.06.   Understand keyboard conventions.
1.07.   Use onscreen Help and keyboard shortcuts.
1.08.   Recognize business forms, form terms, form menus, and form icons.
1.09.   Use Lists, Registers, and QuickZoom.
1.10.   Prepare Reports, Graphs, and QuickReports.
1.11.   Use QuickMath and Windows Calculator.
1.12.   Download and use QuickBooks Accountant Desktop Company Files.
1.13.   Review QuickBooks Accountant Desktop opening screens.
1.14.   Verify an open company and add your name to the company name.
1.15.   Create a company backup file.
1.16.   Change account names.
1.17.   Restore a company backup file.

MANUAL AND COMPUTERIZED ACCOUNTING

The work performed to keep the books for a business is the same whether you use a manual or a computerized accounting system. Transactions need to be analyzed, recorded in a journal, and posted to a ledger. Business documents such as invoices, checks, bank deposits, and credit/debit memos need to be prepared and distributed. Reports to management and owners for information and decision-making purposes need to be prepared. Records for one business period need to be closed before recording transactions for the next business period.

In a manual system, each transaction that is analyzed must be entered by hand into the appropriate journal (the book of original entry where all transactions are recorded) and posted to the appropriate ledger (the book of final entry that contains records for all the accounts used in the business). A separate business document such as an invoice or a check must be prepared and distributed. To prepare a report, the accountant or bookkeeper must go through the journal or ledger and look for the appropriate amounts to include in the report. Closing the books must be done item by item via closing entries. The closing entries are recorded in the journal and posted to the appropriate ledger accounts. After the closing entries are recorded, the ledger accounts must be ruled, and balance sheet accounts must be reopened with Brought Forward Balances being entered.

When using a computerized system and a program such as QuickBooks Desktop, the transactions must still be analyzed and recorded. QuickBooks Desktop operates from a business document point of view. As a transaction occurs, the necessary business document (an invoice or a check, for example) is prepared. Based on the information given on the business document, QuickBooks Desktop records the necessary debits and credits behind the scenes in the Journal. If an error is made when entering a transaction, QuickBooks Desktop allows the user to return to the business document and make the correction. QuickBooks Desktop will automatically record the changes in the debits and credits in the Journal. If you want to see or make a correction using the actual debit/credit entries, QuickBooks Desktop allows you to view the transaction register and make corrections directly in the register. You may also make the correction in the General Journal. Reports and graphs are prepared by simply clicking "Report" on the menu bar.

DEVELOPING SKILLS FOR YOUR CAREER

If you're not an accounting major, you may be thinking that this course and the job skills you will learn are not relevant to you. Please be assured that they are. Whether or not you plan on a career in accounting or bookkeeping, the concepts, procedures, and job skills you learn and apply in this course will help you in business and/or in your life. Moreover, it is only through the aggregate of your educational experience that you will have the opportunity to develop many of the skills that employers have identified as critical to success in the workplace. In this course, and specifically in this text you'll have the opportunity to develop job skills and practice using QuickBooks Desktop to keep the financial records of companies. You will analyze business transactions, prepare and analyze financial reports, understand the process of using computerized accounting versus pencil and paper accounting and bookkeeping, and find and correct errors, among others. Because learning about and using QuickBooks Desktop has so many job skills incorporated into the training, the text will not point out each individual skill.

VERSIONS OF QUICKBOOKS

This text focuses on training using the Accountant edition of QuickBooks Premier Desktop 2018. For simplicity in the text, the program may be referred to as QuickBooks Accountant Desktop, QuickBooks Desktop, QuickBooks DT, or QBDT. The Educational Trial Version of the program is QuickBooks Accountant Desktop 2018.

QuickBooks Accountant Desktop is part of the Premier version of the program. In QuickBooks Premier Desktop, you may toggle to General Business, Accountant, Contractor, Manufacturing & Wholesale, Nonprofit, Professional Services, Retail, and QuickBooks Pro. The Accountant version used in the text offers some additional enhancements not available in the Pro version, but the basics are the same. QuickBooks Pro may also be purchased as a standalone program that is not part of the Premier program suite.

In addition to QuickBooks Premier Desktop and QuickBooks Pro Desktop, there is also QuickBooks Enterprise Desktop, which is designed for larger businesses that want a great deal of customization and have more complex accounting requirements. At the time of writing, QuickBooks Enterprise Desktop has three different subscription plans beginning with Silver, and then upgrading to Gold, and finally Platinum. Pricing is set based on the number of users—from one to thirty—and the subscription level.

There are several Online Editions of QuickBooks: While some of the QuickBooks Online programs contain many of the same features as QuickBooks Desktop, there are other QuickBooks Desktop features that are not available in QuickBooks Online. For businesses, available programs include QuickBooks Self Employed, Simple Start, Online Essentials, and Online Plus. For Accountants there is Online Accountant. All the online editions are sold on a monthly subscription basis. There are also QuickBooks Apps available for iPhone, iPad, Mac, and Android.

The last QuickBooks Desktop program for Macs was released in 2016. Now, Mac users work in QuickBooks Online.

For a comparison of features available among the different versions of the QuickBooks programs, access Intuit's Web site at www.quickbooks.intuit.com.

WINDOWS

All computers use an operating system in conjunction with the software applications. Windows 10 is the operating system used in the text. Various screen shots will show procedures using Windows 10.

BEGIN COMPUTER TRAINING

 When you see this arrow, it means you will be performing a computer task. Sometimes the computer task will have several steps. Continue until all steps listed are completed.

QUICKBOOKS ACCOUNTANT DESKTOP 2018 STUDENT TRIAL VERSION

If you use your school's computers to complete the training in the text, you may omit this step. However, if you purchased the *QuickBooks Desktop 2018: A Complete Course* text, you are eligible for a free five-month Student Trial Version of QuickBooks Premier Desktop Accountant Edition 2018 for Windows. You may install the software on your home or laptop computer.

If you already have any version of QuickBooks Desktop 2018 on your home computer, you may not install the Trial Version for 2018. For example, if you have QuickBooks Pro Desktop 2018, you may not install the Student Trial Version of QuickBooks Accountant Desktop 2018 on the same computer. Installing QuickBooks Desktop 2018 has no effect on earlier versions of QuickBooks Desktop.

The free educational trial version of the QuickBooks Desktop 2018 program may be installed on your computer and used for 30 days. You must activate the program within 30 days of installation. When you activate the program, **your** trial period will be extended to five-months.

Depending on your version of windows, your storage location, your Internet security system, and a variety of other variables, your screens may not always match those shown in the text. In addition, at the time of this writing, Intuit was in the process of implementing an instant verification program for obtaining the Educational Trial Version. Because of this, some of the screens may change slightly when the process becomes live. If you find differences and are not sure if you are proceeding correctly, check with your instructor or go to the Intuit Install Center.

Use the following the instructions to apply, install, and activate QuickBooks Desktop 2018 Trial Version.

APPLY FOR STUDENT TRIAL VERSION

The first step in obtaining your Student Trial Version of QuickBooks Accountant Desktop 2018, is to complete an application process with Intuit. The following information describes the procedures for college and university students. High school students should check with their instructors to determine the procedures to be followed.

  Apply for your Student Trial Version of QuickBooks Accountant Desktop 2018

Enter **www.intuiteducationprogram.com** in the URL of your Web browser
Press **Enter**
- You will see the screen describing the Intuit Education Program.

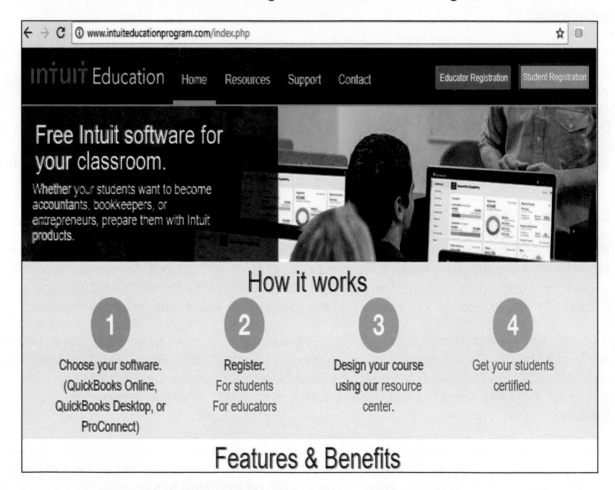

Click the **Student Registration** button
Complete the registration form by entering your information
- Be sure to select **2018** for the QuickBooks Desktop Version.

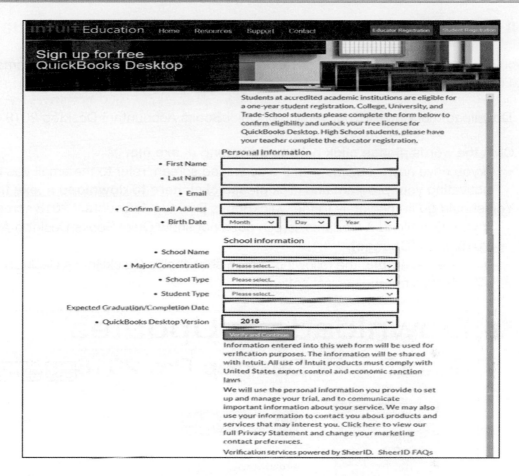

Click **Verify and Continue**

If the verification is successful, you will see the following screen

- You will also receive a confirmation email that contains the same information as shown on the screen below.

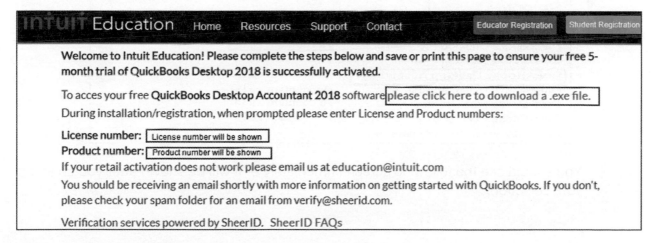

Write down your License number and Product number

- They are required when you install the program.
- The steps for downloading, installing, and registering the software are provided as you work through the chapter. Do not install or register without following the step-by-step instructions provided.

DOWNLOAD AND INSTALL QUICKBOOKS ACCOUNTANT DESKTOP 2018

Once you see the Welcome to Intuit Education! Screen or receive your verification email, you are ready to download the program.

 Download the Student Trial Version of QuickBooks Accountant Desktop 2018

Click the words **please click here to download a .exe file.**
- If you have any problems with the download screen, refer to the email you received for activating your program and click **please click here to download a .exe file.**

You should go immediately to the QuickBooks Desktop Accountant 2018 screen
- If your Download & Updates screen does <u>not</u> show QuickBooks Desktop Accountant 2018, click **[Change]**.
    - As an **example**, the following screen shot shows QuickBooks Desktop Pro 2018, which is not the correct software.

- If you had to click Change, you will get a Select screen. Click **QuickBooks Desktop Accountant** in the Product list; then, in the Version list, click **Accountant 2018**.

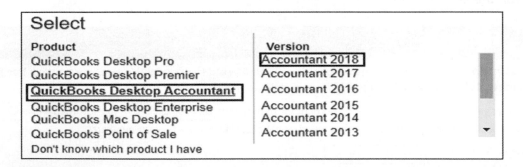

- You should see the following screen immediately or it will be shown after you changed your selection.

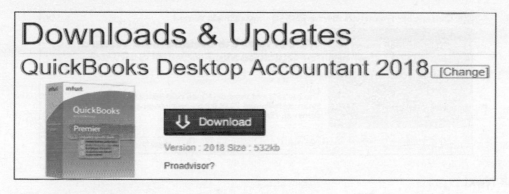

When the Download & Updates screen for QuickBooks Desktop Accountant 2018 is shown, click **Download**

Difficulties with the installation? Use either of the following links to find help at the Intuit Install Center.

www.quickbooks.com/support
http://support.quickbooks.intuit.com/Support/Install/Center/InstallCenter.aspx

In the lower-left portion of your browser, you will see the status of the download, when it is finished, click the drop-down list arrow for **Setup_QuickBooks....exe**
- The text demonstration is using Google Chrome. The process would be very similar if you use a different browser.

Click **Open**

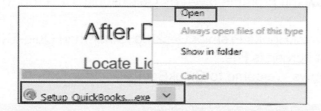

An Intuit Download Manager will appear on the screen for a short time

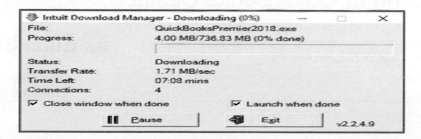

You will see the screen for QuickBooks Financial Software 2018 R5 – InstallShield Wizard
- The R5 may not be the number you see as it changes with QuickBooks Desktop updates.

Click **Next**
- You may see another screen or two briefly on the screen.
- If you get a message asking if you want to make changes to your computer, click **Yes**.

You will see **Intuit QuickBooks Desktop Installer**

You should see the QuickBooks Desktop screen briefly
- As QuickBooks Desktop is updated by Intuit, the screens you see may change. If they do, simply follow the prompts given by QuickBooks Desktop to complete the installation.
- You may see QuickBooks Premier Desktop rather than QuickBooks Accountant Desktop. Either screen is fine.

The first screen shows Welcome to QuickBooks Desktop

Click **Next**

Scroll through and read the License Agreement. After reading, click the checkbox for **"I accept the terms of the license agreement"**

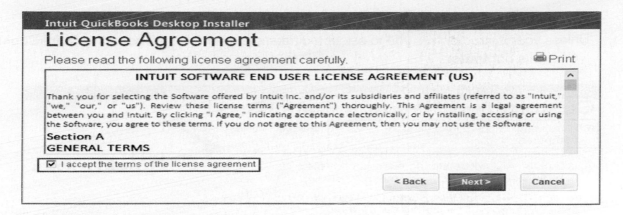

Click **Next**

Enter the **License Number** and **Product Number** that was on the Intuit screen for
successful verification or in your verification email

- You will not need to enter any hyphens or tab between sections. QuickBooks Desktop
automatically jumps from the License Number to the Product Number as well.
- No license or product numbers are shown below because each copy of the software
has a unique number.

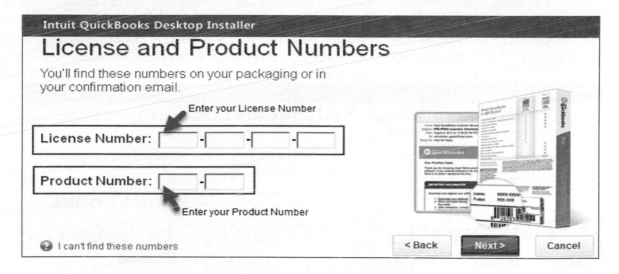

Click **Next**

Use the **Custom and Network options** for the installation type

- If you do not have another version of QuickBooks on your computer and do not care
where the program is stored, you may use the Express installation type.

Click **Next**

Unless your instructor tells you to select a different answer, click **I'll be using QuickBooks on this computer**

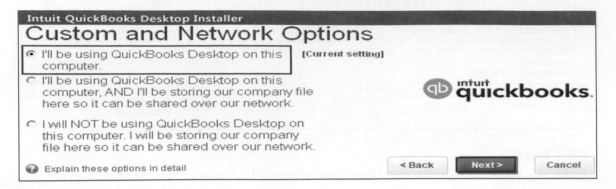

Click **Next**

To choose the installation location for the program, make sure **Change the install location** is selected

- If you are satisfied with the storage location shown, you do not make any changes.
- If you want to change the location shown, click the Browse button and scroll through the locations shown; then click your selection, and click the OK button.
- If you have another version of QuickBooks Desktop installed on your computer, you will see a text box asking if you want to replace a previous version of QuickBooks.

Click **Next**

The screen will show your license number, product number, and program location

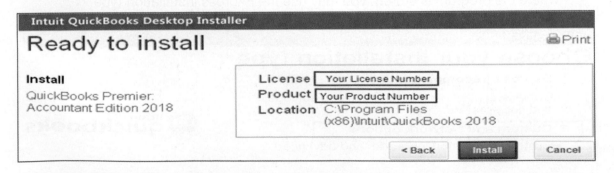

Click **Install**
- During the program installation you will see the Intuit QuickBooks Desktop Installer screens. At the top of the screen, is a status area where you can track the QuickBooks Desktop installation. This can take up to 20 minutes to complete, so be patient.

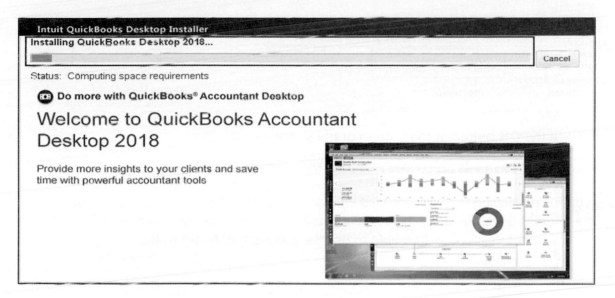

After a successful installation, you will get a congratulations screen

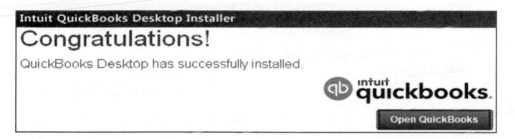

Click the **Open QuickBooks** button on the Congratulations! Screen
- QuickBooks Accountant Desktop 2018 will be opened and on your screen.

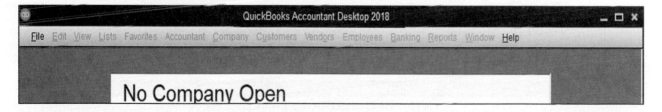

VERIFY PRODUCT INFORMATION AND ACTIVATION STATUS

Once the program has been installed, it is important to verify the Product Information and to determine its activation status.

 Verify Product Information and Activation Status

With the No Company Open screen showing, press the function key **F2**

- The Product Information window displays either NOT ACTIVATED or ACTIVATED based on the registration status. In addition, this screen tells you which QuickBooks Desktop Accountant Release you are using, your License Number, Product Number, and other information about the program.

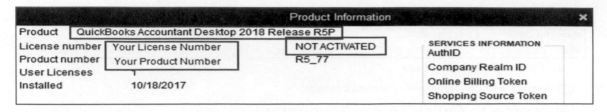

Click the **OK** button at the bottom of the screen

ACTIVATE INSTALLED STUDENT TRIAL VERSION

Once you have installed the Student Trial Version of QuickBooks Accountant Desktop 2018, you may use it for 30 days. Because this is an education version of the program, if you register it within the first 30 days of use, you will be able to use the program for five-months.

 Activate QuickBooks Desktop

You should get the following screen, click **Activate**

If not, click the **Help** menu; then click **Activate QuickBooks Desktop...**
- The following screen shot shows this alternate method.

- As QuickBooks Desktop is updated by Intuit, the screens you see may change. Most of the registration information required is the same. If the screens you see are different from the ones displayed in the text, complete the information in the order presented by QuickBooks Desktop.

Click the **Begin Activation** button

The first step of Activation is to create an account with Intuit

Enter your email address, your first name, your last name, a password, and then re-enter your password again

- You need to use a strong password for QuickBooks Desktop. It must be eight or more characters, use both upper and lowercase letters, use a number, and use a symbol.

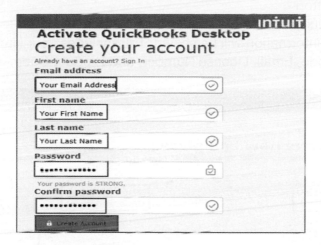

Click the bright-blue **Create Account** button

Complete the information to Review your Customer Account

- If the order sequencing or the questions change from the list below, answer everything that appears with your actual information.

Enter the information for the fields with an asterisk as follows:

Company Information:

　　Country: **United States** from the drop-down list

　　Company name: **Student**

　　Industry: **Other** from the drop-down list

　　Address 1: Enter your actual street address

　　City: Enter your city

　　State: Enter your state

　　Zip/Postal Code: Enter your Zip or Postal Code

　　Business Phone: Enter your phone number

Primary Contact:

　　First Name: Your first name

　　Last Name: Your last name

　　Job Title: Other

　　Work Phone: Your phone number

　　Email Address: Enter your email address again

In the next section, click the drop-down list arrow and then click on the appropriate answer:

　　Tell us about your company:

　　1. Is this your company's first version of QuickBooks? **Yes** (If you own a previous version of QuickBooks, then click **No**.)

　　2. Where did you get this copy of QuickBooks? **Online from QuickBooks.com or Intuit.com**

　　3. Number of full & part-time employees on your payroll? **None, just myself**

4. Does your company
   a. Accept credit cards? **No, but want to**
   b. Print checks? **Yes**
   c. Use a payroll service or payroll software? **No**

For Accountants, Intuit ProAdvisors, and Intuit Solution Providers:

Are you an Accountant, Intuit ProAdvisor, or Intuit Solution Provider? **No**

Click the **Next** button

You will see the QuickBooks Registration – Confirmation screen

- Your account information will be shown. This includes your Name, User ID, Business Phone, Zip Code, Email, License Number, and Product Code.

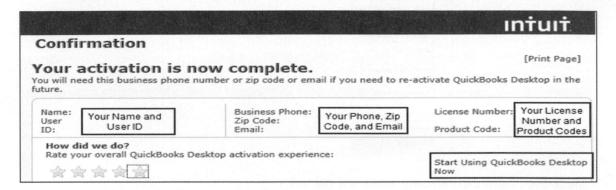

Click **Start Using QuickBooks Desktop Now** under your Product Code

 Verify that QuickBooks Desktop is activated

Press the **F2** key when QuickBooks Desktop is open

- The Product Information window displays either ACTIVATED or NOT ACTIVATED based on the registration status. In addition, this screen tells you which QuickBooks Desktop Release you are using, your License Number, Product Number, and other information about the program.

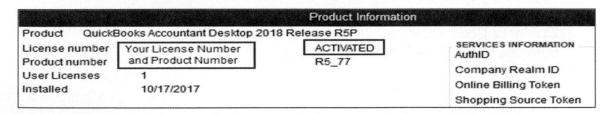

After verifying that you program is ACTIVATED, click **OK** to close the Product Information Window

UPDATE QUICKBOOKS DESKTOP (OPTIONAL)

QuickBooks Desktop is setup to automatically update the program whenever Intuit releases new features, maintenance files, or other enhancements to the program. You may also update the program manually. This is especially important to do if you install a trial version of the software.

Update QuickBooks Desktop

Click the **Help** menu and click **Update QuickBooks Desktop**
There are three tabs shown on Update QuickBooks: Overview, Options, and Update Now
Read the information shown on the **Overview** tab
- There is a button on the Overview tab that you may also click to Update Now; however, if you click this button, you will not see information about the updates.
Click the **Update Now** tab
Click **Get Updates**

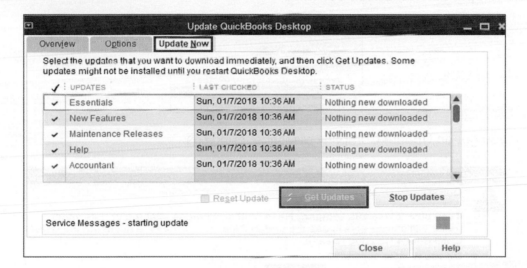

- The dates shown are the computer dates of the author's computer when different updates were performed. The dates will not match your dates.
- After updating is complete, verify the STATUS. If new files have been installed, STATUS will say "New files installed." If nothing new was installed, STATUS will say "Nothing new downloaded."
- Occasionally, after an update, a QuickBooks Desktop Information screen will appear telling you that QuickBooks Desktop needs to close to install updates. If this occurs, click **OK**.
When the update is complete, click the **Close** button at the bottom of the Update QuickBooks screen

NEW FEATURE TOUR

Whenever a new version of QuickBooks Desktop is released, and a company is opened, a new feature tour showing changes from the previous edition of QuickBooks Desktop is included. It may be on the screen when a company is opened. If it is not shown, click the Help menu, point to New Features, and click New Feature Tour to display the information. To get more detailed information about each feature, click Learn more at the bottom of the New Feature Tour screen. To close the new feature Tour, click the Close icon on the title bar. ▨

OPEN SAMPLE COMPANY

To explore some of the features of QuickBooks Desktop, you will work with a sample company that comes with the program. The company is Larry's Landscaping & Garden Supply and is stored on the hard disk (C:) inside the computer.

 Open a sample company

Click the **Open a sample file** button on the "No Company Open" screen
Click **Sample service-based business**

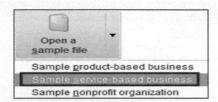

- If you get an Update Company message, click **Yes**.

- When using the sample company for training, a warning screen will appear. This is to remind you NOT to enter the transactions for your business in the sample company. It will show a date that is several years into the future.

Click **OK** to accept the sample company data for use
If the Accountant Center appears, click the checkbox for **Show Accountant Center when opening a company file** at the bottom of the screen to remove the check mark
Click the Close icon on the title bar

VERIFY OPEN COMPANY

It is important to make sure you have opened the data for the correct company. Always verify the company name in the title bar. The title bar is located at the top of the screen and will tell you the name of the company and the program.

Verify an open company

Check the **title bar** at the top of the QuickBooks Desktop screen to make sure it includes the company name. The title bar should show the company name, program name, and program year:

Sample Larry's Landscaping & Garden Supply - QuickBooks Accountant Desktop 2018

PROGRAM DESKTOP FEATURES

Once you have opened a company, the title bar displays the **Company Name - QuickBooks Accountant Desktop 2018.** (The following example shows the title bar for Sample Larry's Landscaping & Garden Supply.) Beneath the Title Bar, you will see the Menu Bar. Each menu is for a separate area of the program and is used to give commands to QuickBooks Desktop.

Sample Larry's Landscaping & Garden Supply - QuickBooks Accountant Desktop 2018

File Edit View Lists Favorites Accountant Company Customers Vendors Employees Banking Reports Window Help

Title Bar and Menu Bar

MENU BAR

The first line displayed beneath the title bar is the **Menu Bar**. By pointing and clicking on a menu or using the keyboard shortcut of Alt+ the underlined letter in the menu item you will give QuickBooks Desktop the command to display the drop-down menu. For example, the File menu is used to open and close a company and may also be used to exit QuickBooks Desktop.

QUICKBOOKS DESKTOP MENUS

Each menu focuses on a different area in QuickBooks Desktop. Menus can be the starting point for issuing commands in QuickBooks Desktop. Many commands will be the same as the ones you can give when using the QuickBooks Desktop Home Page (detailed later in the chapter). To use a menu, click the desired menu, then click the command you want to use. Notice that available keyboard shortcuts are listed next to the menu item. If a menu item has a ▶, it means there is a submenu that may be accessed. To close a menu, click outside of it.

 Access each of the menus by clicking or pointing to each menu item

File menu is used to access company files and perform several other functions—New Company, New Company from an Existing Company File, Open or Restore Company, Open Previous Company, Open Second Company, Back Up Company, Create Copy, Close Company, Switch to Multi-user Mode, Utilities, Send Company File, Print, Save as PDF, Print Forms, Printer Setup, Send Forms, Shipping, Update Web Services, Toggle to Another Edition, and Exit.

Several options on the File menu have submenus. These are accessed by clicking at the right edge of the option. For example, Utilities on the File menu contains a submenu that allows Import, Export, Synchronize Contacts, Convert, Copy Company File for QuickBooks Mac, Copy Company File for QuickBooks Online, Repair File and Network Problems, Host

Multi-User Access, Verify Data, Rebuild Data, Condense Data, Restore Backup for Earlier QuickBooks Version.

Edit menu is used to make changes such as: Undo, Revert, Cut, Copy, Paste, Copy Line, Paste Line, Use Register, Use Calculator, Find, Search, and Preferences.

View menu is used to select things to view. They include: Open Window List, Switch to Multi-monitor Mode, Top Icon Bar, Left Icon Bar, Hide Icon Bar, Search Box, Customize Icon Bar, Add Home to Icon Bar, Favorites Menu, One Window, and Multiple Windows.

Lists menu is used to show lists used by QuickBooks Desktop. These lists include: Chart of Accounts (the General Ledger), Item List, Fixed Asset Item List, Price Level List, Billing Rate Level List, Sales Tax Code List, Payroll Item List, Payroll Schedule List, Class List, Workers Comp List, Other Names List, Customer & Vendor Profile Lists, Templates, Memorized Transaction List, and Add/Edit Multiple List Entries.

Favorites menu is used to place your favorite or most frequently used commands on this list. It is customized with your selected commands.

Accountant menu is used to access the Accountant Center, Chart of Accounts, and Fixed Asset Item List. It is also used to Batch Enter Transactions, Batch Delete/Void Transactions perform a Client Data Review, Make General Journal Entries, Send General Journal Entries, Reconcile (an account), prepare a Working Trial Balance, Set Closing Date, Condense Data, Manage Fixed Assets, QuickBooks File Manager, use QuickBooks Desktop Statement Writer, participate in the ProAdvisor Program, and use Online Accountant Resources.

Company menu is used to access company information. This includes the Home Page, Company Snapshot, Calendar, Documents, and Lead Center. It is also used to access My Company (this contains information about the company), Set Up Users and Passwords, Customer Credit Card Protection, Set Closing Date, Bulk Enter Business Details, Planning & Budgeting, To Do List, Reminders, Alerts Manager. You may also display the Chart of Accounts, Make General Journal Entries, Manage Currency, Enter Vehicle Mileage, Prepare Letters with Envelopes, and Export Company File to QuickBooks Online.

Customers menu is used to access information about customers and prepare customer specific transactions. This includes access to the Customer Center, Create Sales Orders, prepare Sales Order Fulfillment Worksheet, Create Invoices, Create Batch Invoices, Enter Sales Receipts, Enter Statement Charges, Create Statements, Assess Finance Charges, Receive Payments, Create Credit Memos/Refunds, use the Income Tracker, and use the Lead Center. In addition, you may Add Credit Card Processing and Link Payment Service to Company File. It is also used to access the Item List and to Change Item Prices.

Vendors menu is used to access information about vendors and prepare vendor specific transactions. This includes access to the Vendor Center and Bill Tracker. In addition, this menu may be used to Enter Bills, Pay Bills, Sales Tax, Create Purchase Orders, Receive Items and Enter Bill, Receive Items, Enter Bill for Received Items, Inventory Activities, Print/E-file 1099s, and access the Item List.

Employees menu is used to access information about employees and prepare employee specific transactions. This includes access to the Employee Center, the Payroll Center, Pay Employees, have Payroll done for you, prepare After-the-Fact Payroll, Add or Edit Payroll Schedules, Edit/Void Paychecks, process Payroll Taxes and Liabilities, access Payroll Tax Forms & W-2s, offer Labor Law Posters, access Workers Compensation, perform My Payroll Service activities, Pay with Direct Deposit, Payroll Setup, Manage Payroll Items, Get Payroll Updates, and access the Billing Rate Level List.

Banking menu is used to perform functions relating to bank account transactions; including Write Checks, Order Checks & Envelopes, Enter Credit Card Charges, Use Register, Make Deposits, Transfer Funds, Reconcile accounts, access Bank Feeds, use the Loan Manager, and access the Other Names List.

Reports menu is used for report preparation. You may access the Report Center and use it to prepare reports. In addition, you may access and prepare Memorized Reports, Scheduled Reports, Commented Reports, Company Snapshot, Process Multiple Reports, and QuickBooks Desktop Statement Writer. In addition, it is used to prepare reports in the following categories: Company & Financial; Customers & Receivables; Sales; Jobs, Time & Mileage; Vendors & Payables; Purchases; Inventory; Employees & Payroll; Banking; Accountant & Taxes; Budgets & Forecasts; List; and Industry Specific. You may also create and access Contributed Reports, Custom Reports, QuickReport, Transaction History, and Transaction Journal.

Window menu is used to organize the screens/windows that you view in QuickBooks Desktop. You may Arrange Icons, Close All, Tile Vertically, Tile Horizontally, or Cascade open windows. You may also switch among open windows.

Help menu is used to get assistance with QuickBooks Desktop. Features available include QuickBooks Desktop Help, Ask Intuit, New Features, Support, Find a Local QuickBooks Desktop Expert, and Send Feedback Online. The Help menu includes topics such as: Internet Connection Setup, New Business Checklist, Year-End Guide, Add QuickBooks Services, App Center: Find More Business Solutions, Update QuickBooks Desktop, Manage My License, Reset Intuit ID Settings, QuickBooks Desktop Privacy Statement, About Automatic Update, QuickBooks Desktop Usage & Analytics Study, and About QuickBooks Accountant Desktop 2018. If QuickBooks Desktop has not been activated, you will also see Activate QuickBooks Desktop.

ICON BAR

An icon bar contains small picture symbols that may be clicked to give commands to QuickBooks Desktop. These small picture symbols are called icons. By default, QuickBooks Desktop comes with a Left Icon Bar (shown below).

If Insights displays when you open the company, click the tab for **Home Page**
If you see a yellow tab for WHAT'S NEW, click the **X** on the tab to close it.

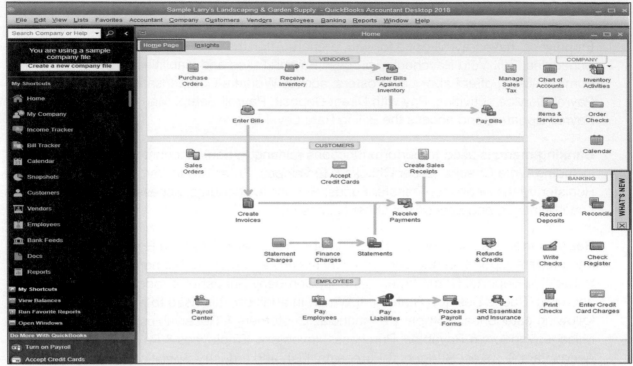

Home Page and Partial Left Icon Bar

You may change the placement of the Icon Bar from the left of the screen to the top of the screen just below the Menu Bar. Throughout the text, the Left Icon bar has been changed to a Top Icon Bar. This is done to save screen space and to focus on tasks rather than shortcuts and Do More With QuickBooks Desktop. Once the Top Icon bar is selected, it will appear below the Menu bar and the Left Icon bar will not be seen. The Top Icon bar may be shown in color and it may be customized. The standard icon bar is divided into four specific areas: Home; Snapshots and Command Centers; Command Icons; Services and Search. Depending on the screen size of your computer, not all the icons may be displayed.

 Change to a Top-Icon Bar and display it in color

To change to the top-icon bar, Click the **View Menu**, and click **Top Icon Bar**
- If you already have the Top Icon Bar showing, there is no need to change it.

To change to a colored icon bar, click the **Edit** menu, click **Preferences**, click **Desktop View**, click the **My Preferences** tab, click **Switch to colored icons/light background on the Top Icon Bar**, click **OK**

First Section of the Top Icon Bar:

Home is the first icon shown below the Menu bar and is used to go to the Navigator screen, also known as the Home Page.

My Company displays Company Information, which may be edited. It informs you of Product Information; allows you to manage apps, services, and subscriptions; and makes recommendations for you.

Income Tracker allows you to view Unbilled Sales Orders, Unbilled Time & Expenses, Unpaid, Overdue, and Paid Invoices. You may view individual customers or all customers. You may perform Batch Actions; such as, Batch Email or Print Selected Invoices, Sales Orders, Sales Receipts, and Credit Memos/Refunds. Manage Transactions enables you to Create New Sales Orders, Invoices, Sales Receipts, Statement Charges, Receive Payments, Credit Memos/Refunds, and Edit Highlighted Row.

Bill Tracker summarizes and simplifies the information needed to manage bills on one screen. You may view information for Unbilled Purchase Orders, Unpaid Open Bills, Overdue Bills, and Paid Bills. You may perform Batch Actions; such as, Print Selected Purchase Orders, Pay Bills, and Close Purchase Orders. Manage Transactions is a shortcut to Create New: Purchase Orders, Bills, CC Charges, and/or Checks. You may also Edit Highlighted Row. Group By (on the line for Vendor, Type, Status, and Date) enables you to group information so it is displayed by vendor.

Calendar is used to maintain a monthly calendar and contains information for the To Do List, Upcoming: Next 7 days, and Due: Past 60 days.

Second Section of the Top Icon Bar:

QuickBooks Desktop Snapshots is next to the Calendar icon. When you click this icon, you may click on one of three tabs to get information about the Company, Payments, and Customer. The information displayed on each tab may be customized by selecting a variety of options.

QuickBooks Desktop Command Centers Next to the Company Snapshot icon there are icons for Centers. Each center goes to a specific list within the program. The centers are: Customers, Vendors, Employees, Bank Feeds, Docs, Reports, User Licenses, and Order Checks.

Third Section of the Top Icon Bar:

Command Icons are used to give commands to QuickBooks Desktop by pointing to a picture and clicking the primary mouse button. Depending on the size of your monitor, you may or may not see the command icons. If they do not appear, click the `>>` to show them. Command icons are discussed in more detail later in the chapter and throughout the text.

Fourth Section of the Top Icon Bar:

Services takes you to a QuickBooks Desktop Products and Services link where you will be able to add recommended services.

Add Payroll takes you to an Intuit page for QuickBooks Smarter Business Tools for the World's Hardest Workers. You may add services and apps from this screen.

Credit Cards allows you to sign up for Intuit QuickBooks Payments, so your company can accept credit card payments and bank transfers using QuickBooks Desktop.

QuickBooks Search is used to search through QuickBooks Desktop Help for information or through the Company file for various transactions, accounts, items, customers, vendors, employees, etc.

COMPANY SNAPSHOTS

QuickBooks Desktop has an icon that allow access to Snapshots that focus on providing detailed information about the Company, Payments and Customers.

 Access Snapshots

Click the **Snapshots** icon on the Icon bar

Snapshots provides three tabs: Company, Payments, and Customer. To display information about one of the sections, you click the appropriate tab. Each Snapshot may be customized by clicking Add Content and selecting from among different options.

To see how your business is doing, click the **Company** tab. When you click Add Content, there are 12 different items that may be displayed for the company. These options include listings or graphs for Account Balances, Previous Year Income Comparison, Income Breakdown, Previous Year Expense Comparison, Expense Breakdown, Income and Expense Trend, Top Customers by Sales, Best-Selling Items, Customers Who Owe Money, Top Vendors by Expense, Vendors to Pay, and Reminders.

When you click the **Payments** tab, you get information about the company revenues. You may select from among seven options on Add Content to display information about your company revenue. These include Recent Transactions, Receivables Reports, A/R by Aging Period, Invoice Payment Status, Customers Who Owe Money, QuickLinks, and Payment Reminders.

To view information regarding individual customers, click the **Customer** tab to select from among four items to display on Add Content. These are Recent Invoices, Recent Payments, Sales History, and Best-Selling Items.

CENTERS

The icons for Customers, Vendors, Employees, Bank Feeds, Docs, Reports, User Licenses, and Order Checks all open different centers. A Center groups information together regarding a specific section of the company. The Centers are:

 Access each of the centers by clicking the appropriate icon beneath the menu bar and close each Center before opening the next.

Customers shows information about the company's customers. The Customer Center has two tabs: Customers & Jobs and Transactions. In addition to the information displayed on tabs, icons at the top of the Customers Center may be used to perform different tasks depending on the tab selected.

The **Customers & Jobs** tab is the default tab and displays a list of all your customers and their balances. When you click on an individual customer, Customer Information and Transactions are displayed for that customer. When you click on the icon for New Customer & Job at the top of the Customer Center, you may add a New Customer, a New Job, or Multiple Customer:Jobs. If you click the icon for New Transactions, you may enter Sales Orders, Invoices, Sales Receipts, Statement Charges, Receive Payments, and Credit Memos/Refunds. Clicking the Print icon enables you to print the Customer & Job List, Customer & Job Information, and a Customer & Job Transaction List. Clicking the Excel icon allows you to Export Customer List and Export Transactions. You may also Import from Excel and Paste from Excel information about customers. Clicking the Word icon allows you to Prepare a Letter to the customer whose information is displayed, Prepare Customer Letters, Prepare Collection Letters, and Customize Letter Templates. Click the Income Tracker icon to see which customers have Overdue and Almost Due balances.

Clicking the **Transactions** tab displays transaction categories and allows you to get information about transaction groups. These may include Sales Orders, Invoices, Statement Charges, Sales Receipts, Received Payments, Credit Memos, and Refunds. When the Transactions tab is selected, the icons will allow you to add a New Customer, enter New Transactions, Print transaction reports, display Customer & Job Info, and Export the transaction reports to Excel.

Vendors shows information about the company's vendors. The Vendor Center has two tabs: Vendors and Transactions. In addition to the information displayed on tabs, icons at the top of the Vendors Center may be used to perform different tasks depending on the tab selected.

The default tab is **Vendors**. It allows you to display a list of vendors and their balances. You may also select a vendor and get Vendor Information and Transactions for that vendor. When the Vendors tab is selected, you may use the New Vendor icon to add New Vendors or Multiple Vendors. When you click the New Transactions icon, you may

Enter Bills, Pay Bills, prepare Purchase Orders, Receive Items and Enter Bill, Receive Items, and Enter Bill for Received Items. Clicking the Print icon enables you to print the Vendor List, Vendor Information, and Vendor Transaction List. When the Excel icon is clicked, the Vendor List and Vendor Transactions may be exported to Excel and vendor information may be imported and or pasted from Excel. When the Word icon is clicked, you may Prepare Letter to the vendor whose information is displayed, Prepare Vendor Letters, and Customize Letter Templates.

The Vendor Center includes an icon for Bill Tracker. Click the Bill Tracker icon to see which vendors have Purchase Orders, Open Bills, and Overdue Bills. You may also view transactions organized by Purchase Order, Bill, Item Receipt, Credit, Unapplied Payments, CC Charge, CC Payments, Bill Pmt-Checks, Bill Pmt-CCard, and Checks.

Clicking the **Transactions** tab displays transaction categories and allows you to get information about transaction groups; such as, Purchase Orders, Item Receipts, Bills, Bill Payments, Checks, Credit Card Activities, and Sales Tax Payments. When the Transactions tab is selected, the icons will allow you to add a New Vendor; enter New Transactions for Enter Bills, Pay Bills, prepare Purchase Orders, Receive Items and Enter Bill, Receive Items, and Enter Bill for Received Items. Clicking the Print icon allows you to Print transaction reports. The View Vendor Info icon displays the vendor information for a selected transaction, and the Export icon sends a report for All Purchase Orders or Open Purchase Orders to Excel.

Employees shows information about the company's employees. The Employee Center has three tabs: Employees, Transactions, and Payroll. In addition to the information displayed on the tabs, there are icons that may be used.

The default tab **Employees** allows you to display a list of all employees. You may select an individual employee and see Employee Information and Transactions for that employee. On the Employees tab, you may use the New Employee icon to add an employee. The Manage Employee Information icon allows you to Add/Edit Sales Rep and to Change New Employee Default Settings. The Print icon allows you to print Paychecks, Print/Send Paystubs, Employee List, Employee Information, and the Employee Transaction List. The Excel icon exports the Employee List, Transactions, Client-Ready Payroll Reports and Summarized Payroll Data to Excel. The Word icon may be used to Prepare Letter to the highlighted employee, Prepare Employee Letters, and Customize Letter Templates.

Clicking the **Transactions** tab displays transaction categories and allows you to get information about transaction groups, such as: Paychecks, Liability Checks, Liability Adjustments, Year-To-Date Adjustments, and Non-Payroll Transactions. The Transactions tab has an icon to add a New Employee. The Manage Employee Information icon enables you to Add/Edit Sales Rep and to Change New Employee Default Settings. The Print icon enables you to print a Transaction Report, and the Excel icon is clicked to Export Transactions, Client-Ready Payroll Reports, and Summarize Payroll Data in Excel to Excel.

After clicking the **Payroll** tab, you will see information for Create Paychecks, and Recent Payrolls. There are tabs to Pay Employees, Pay Liabilities, and File Forms. The

Payroll tab icons pertain to My Payroll Service and allow you to get Payroll Updates, add Payroll Items, complete the Payroll Setup, change Preferences, get Support, and access Help.

Bank Feeds shows information about your Bank Accounts, allows you to Download Transactions, and Send Items to your bank. By clicking Create New, you may prepare Online Checks, Pay Bills, Transfer Funds, Messages, Inquire About Payments, and Cancel Payments. In addition, you may click icons to Add Account and display Rules.

Docs displays the Doc Center that is used to keep track of documents you use with QuickBooks Desktop. It allows you to Add a Document to the Doc Center from your computer or scanner. You may attach documents, view and add document details, search for documents, detach documents, and remove documents from the Doc Center. Documents may be items such as receipts, spreadsheets, bills, invoices, etc.

Reports opens a Report Center that allows you to prepare all the Reports available in QuickBooks Desktop. There are several tabs available. The Standard Tab lists reports by category. The categories are: Company & Financial; Customers & Receivables; Sales; Jobs, Time & Mileage; Vendors & Payables; Purchases; Inventory; Employees & Payroll; Banking; Accountant & Taxes; Budgets & Forecasts; List; Contractor; Mfg & Wholesale; Professional Services; Retail; and Nonprofit. The available reports in each category may be displayed in a carousel view, a list view, or a grid view. The Memorized tab allows the use of report formats that have been customized and saved for reports for Accountant, Banking, Company, Customers, Employees, and Vendors. The Favorites tab shows reports that you have marked as favorites. The Recent tab tells you which reports have been viewed recently. The Contributed tab displays customized shared report formats that have been created and are available to be downloaded.

User Licenses connects you to a link that will allow you to add multiple users to QuickBooks Desktop. You may purchase QuickBooks Desktop for a single user (1 individual) or multiple users (5 individuals). Multi-user access to QuickBooks Desktop allows up to five individuals to work in a QuickBooks Desktop company file at the same time.

Order Checks takes you to Checks, Business Cards & More screen where you may place orders for QuickBooks Checks and Supplies.

COMMAND ICON BAR

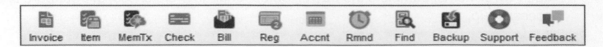

In addition to giving commands to QuickBooks Desktop via Menus, they may be given by clicking command icons on the icon bar. The command section of the icon bar has a list of buttons (icons) that may be clicked to enter transactions. Additional icons to use Find, prepare a Backup, get Support, and give Feedback are shown as well. The icon bar may be turned on or off and it may be customized. If there is a double >> at the edge of the icon bar, that means that there are more icons available for use. The command icons will be discussed in more detail during training.

ACCOUNTANT CENTER

The Accountant Center is accessed by clicking the Accountant menu and then clicking Accountant Center. The Center has Tools that may be customized and used for transactions, reports, and activities completed by accountants. In the Accountant Center you may select an account for Reconciliation, select Memorized Reports, and get Accountant Updates. You may also select "Show Accountant Center when opening a company file" and the Center will be shown whenever you open QuickBooks Desktop.

HOME SCREEN

The QuickBooks Desktop Home screen has two tabs: Home Page and Insights.

HOME PAGE

The Home Page allows you to give commands to QuickBooks Desktop according to the type of transaction being entered. The Home Page tasks are organized into logical groups (Vendors, Customers, Employees, Company, and Banking). Each of these areas on the Home Page is used to enter different types of transactions. When appropriate, the Home Page shows a flow chart with icons indicating the major activities performed. The icons are arranged in the order in which transactions usually occur. Depending on the type of company in use, the icons on the Home Page may change.

Information regarding Account Balances, Do More with QuickBooks Desktop, and Backup Status is displayed on the right side of the Home Page and may be expanded or minimized.

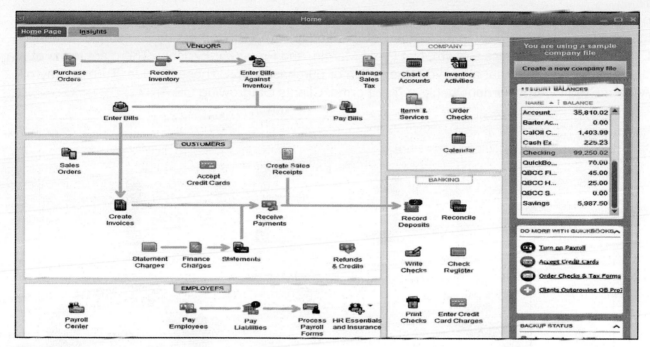

 View the five command areas on the Home Page:

Vendors allows service and merchandising businesses to enter bills and record the payment of bills. Companies with inventory can create purchase orders, receive inventory items, enter bills against inventory, and manage sales tax.

Customers allows you to record transactions associated with Invoices (sales on account or credit sales), Create Sales Receipts (cash sales), Receive Payments (for sales recorded on invoices), Refunds & Credits. Accept Credit Cards enables you to subscribe to QuickBooks Payments, which allows you to accept payments made by debit card, credit card, online, and e-payments. If you want to use Sales Orders, issue Statement Charges, charge Finance Charges, or prepare Statements, these are entered in this section as well.

Employees allows access to the Payroll Center (if you subscribe to a payroll service), Pay Employees, Pay Liabilities, Process Payroll Forms, and HR (human resources) Essentials and Insurance information that enables you to produce labor law posters and use Workers' Comp Payment Service.

Company allows you to display information about your company. There are graphic icons used to display the Chart of Accounts, Inventory Activities, Items & Services, Order Checks, and Calendar.

Banking allows you to Record Deposits, Write Checks, Print Checks, Reconcile (Balance Sheet Accounts), access the Check Register, and Enter Credit Card Charges.

INSIGHTS

The Insights tab on the Home Screen displays information and data about the company. The company name, logo, and date along with icons for Print, Refresh, and Customize are shown. The default is to display information about Profit & Loss, Income, and Expenses. There are gray arrows on the right and left sides of the Profit & Loss data that you may click to access other selected information; such as, Prev Year Income Comparison and Top Customers by Sales Income and Expense Trend, Business Growth, Net Profit Margin, and Prev Year Expense There are icons at the bottom of the screen that allow you to enroll in or purchase items. These include: Turn on Payroll, Accept Credit Cards, Order Checks & Tax Forms, Clients Outgrowing QB Pro?

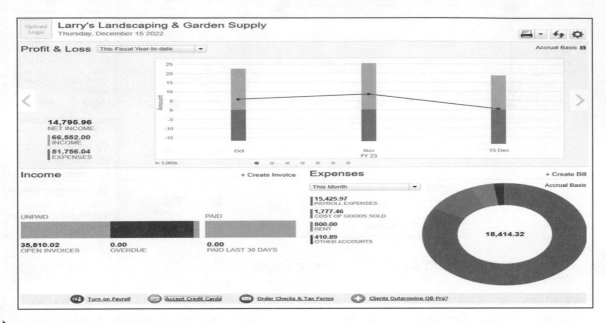

 View the Insights tab and click the gray arrows to see the default reports

When finished, click the **Home Page** tab

KEYBOARD CONVENTIONS

When using Windows, there are some standard keyboard conventions for the use of certain keys. These keyboard conventions also apply to QuickBooks Desktop and include:

Alt key is used to access the drop-down menus on the menu bar. Rather than click on a menu item, press the Alt key and type the underlined letter in the menu item name. Close the menu by simply pressing the Alt key.

Tab key is used to move to the next field or, if a button is selected, to the next button.

Shift+Tab is used to move back to the previous field.

Esc key is used to cancel an active window without saving anything that has been entered. It is equivalent to clicking the Cancel button.

 Practice using the keyboard conventions:

Access **Customers** menu: **Alt+U**
Access **Create Invoices**: type **I**

- Note: Ctrl + I is shown on the menu. This is a keyboard shortcut that may be used to open an invoice without using the Customer menu or the Home Page icon.

Press **Tab** key to move forward through the invoice, press **Shift+Tab** to move back through the invoice, press **Esc** to close the invoice

ON-SCREEN HELP

QuickBooks Desktop has on-screen help, which is like having the QuickBooks Desktop reference manual available on the computer screen. Help can give assistance with a function you are performing. QuickBooks Desktop Help also gives you information about the program using an on-screen index. Help may be accessed to obtain information on a variety of topics, and it may be accessed in different ways:

To find out about the window in which you are working, press F1, click on the list of relevant topics displayed and read the information given; or enter the topic you wish to view, and then click the 🔍 Start Search button. When the topic for Help has been located, a list of results will be shown. Click the result that best describes the information you want. The information is either displayed on the same Have a Question? screen or in a Help Article. If there is more information than can be shown, scroll bars will appear on the right side of the screen(s). A scroll bar is used to show or go through information. As you scroll through Help, information at the top of the Help screen disappears while new information appears at the bottom of the screen.

Sometimes words appear in blue in the QuickBooks Desktop Help screen. Clicking on the blue word(s) will give you more information or will take you to other topics. Often, the onscreen help provides links to an external Web site. To visit these links, you must have an Internet connection and be online. The Have a Question? Screen will show Answers in Help and Answers from Community.

If you want to see a different topic, you may type in different key words at the top of the Have a Question? Screen and then click the Search button. Information will be provided on the new topic.

If you want to print a copy of the QuickBooks Desktop Have a Question? or Article screen(s), click the Printer icon at the top of the Have a Question? screen. You may close a QuickBooks Desktop Help Article or Have a Question? by clicking the Close button ☒ in the upper right corner of the Help screen.

To get additional information on how to use QuickBooks Desktop or to enter a question and get immediate answers drawn from the QuickBooks Desktop Help system and the technical support database, click the Help menu and click Support.

USE HELP SEARCH TO FIND KEYBOARD SHORTCUTS

Frequently, it is faster to use a keyboard shortcut to give QuickBooks Desktop a command than it is to point and click the mouse through several layers of menus or icons. The list of common keyboard shortcuts may be obtained by using Help.

　Use Help

Click **Help** on the Menu bar
Click **QuickBooks Desktop Help**
Type **keyboard shortcuts** in the text box
Click the **Search** button
Look at the list of topics provided

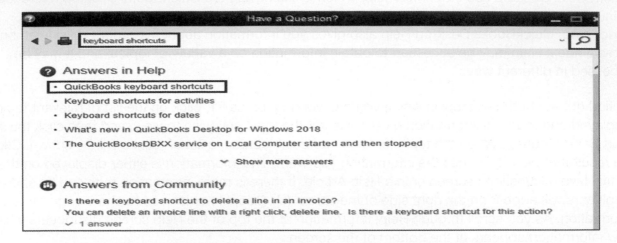

Click **QuickBooks keyboard shortcuts** and view the results

- You may see the results in a Help Article <u>or</u> on the Have a Question? screen.

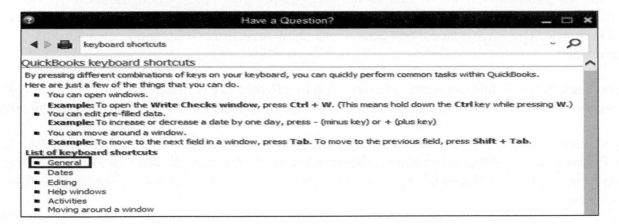

Click <u>**General**</u> in the list of keyboard shortcuts to see the General keyboard shortcuts

General keyboard shortcuts

General action	Shortcut
To start QuickBooks without a company file	Ctrl (while opening)
To suppress the desktop windows (at Open Company window)	Alt (while opening)
Display product information about your QuickBooks version	F2 or Ctrl + 1
Close active window	Esc or Ctrl + F4
Save transaction	Alt + S
Save transaction and go to next transaction	Alt + N
Record (when black border is around OK, Save and Close, Save and New, or Record)	Enter
Record (always)	Ctrl + Enter

Click the **Close** button in the upper right corner of the Have a Question? screen; and, if shown, the Help Article screen

FORMS

The premise of QuickBooks Desktop is to allow you to focus on running the business, not deciding whether an account is debited or credited. Transactions are entered directly onto the business form that is prepared based on the transaction. Behind the scenes, QuickBooks Desktop enters the debit and credit to the Journal and posts to the individual accounts. To view the transactions in the Journal, you prepare a Journal report.

QuickBooks Desktop has several types of forms for use in recording your daily business transactions. They are divided into two categories: forms you want to send or give to people and forms you have received. Forms to send or give to people include invoices, sales receipts, credit memos, checks, deposit slips, and purchase orders. Forms you have received include payments from customers, bills, credits for a bill, and credit card charge receipts.

You may use the forms as they come with QuickBooks Desktop, you may change or modify them, or you may create your own custom forms for use in the program.

 Examine the following invoice and note the terms, icons, and buttons listed as they apply to invoices. These terms will be used throughout the text when giving instructions for entries.

Click the **Create Invoices** icon on the Home Page
* This will open a blank invoice.

Compare the invoice on your screen with the following information:

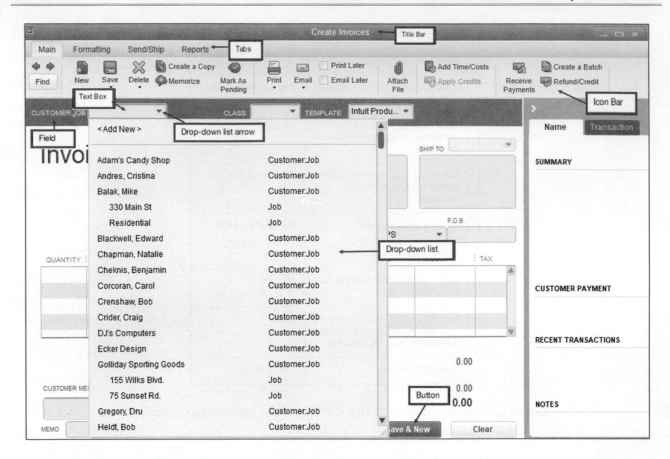

Title bar at the top of the form indicates what you are completing. In this case, it says **Create Invoices**. The title bar also contains some buttons on the right side. They include:

> **Minimize button** 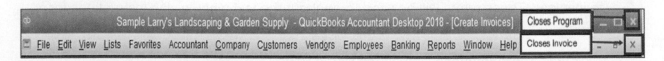 clicking this will remove the form from the screen but still leave it open. You may click the form on the Taskbar to re-display it.
>
> **Maximize** or **restore button** enlarges the form to fill the screen or restores the form to its previous size.
>
> **Close button** closes the current screen.

- If the Create Invoices screen is maximized, the task for Create Invoices will be shown on the QuickBooks Desktop title bar. (See below) If this happens, the buttons on the title bar are applicable to the program. Clicking on the Close button on the title bar will close QuickBooks Desktop, which could result in the loss of data. Clicking on the separate Close button located on the menu bar just below the one for QuickBooks Desktop will close the invoice.

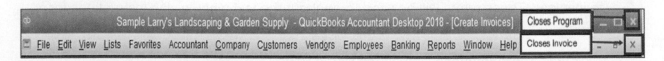

Field is an area on a form requiring information. Customer:Job is a field.

Text box is the area within a field where information may be typed or inserted. The area to be filled in to identify the Customer:Job is a text box.

Drop-down list arrow appears next to a field when there is a list of options available. On the invoice for Larry's Landscaping & Garden Supply, clicking the drop-down list arrow for Customer:Job will display the names of all customers who have accounts with the company. Clicking a customer's name will insert the name into the text box for the field.

Buttons on the bottom of the invoice are used to give commands to QuickBooks Desktop.

> **Save & Close button** is clicked when all information has been entered for the invoice and you are ready for QuickBooks Desktop to save the invoice and exit the Create Invoices screen.

> **Save & New button** is clicked when all information has been entered for the invoice and you want to save the current invoice and then complete a new invoice.

> **Clear button** is clicked if you want to clear the information entered on the current invoice.

Icon Bar a group of commands shown as small pictures (icons) that may be given to QuickBooks Desktop. The Icon Bar for an invoice is just below the Create Invoices Title Bar. It has four tabs containing icons that are used to give commands to QuickBooks Desktop or to get information regarding linked or related transactions. If an icon has an arrow at the bottom, it means that there are choices/commands that may be selected.

Tabs show choices of activities. On an Invoice the tabs enable you to select different Icon Bars.

> **Main** Tab Icons include:

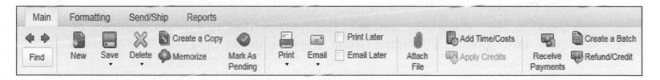

> **Previous** ◀ is clicked to go back to the previous invoice. This is used when you want to view, print, or correct the previous invoice. Each time the Previous icon is clicked, you go back one invoice. You may click the Previous icon until you go all the way back to invoices with opening balances.

> **Next** ▶ is clicked to go to the next invoice after the one you entered. If the invoice on the screen has not been saved, this saves the invoice and goes to the next one. The next invoice may be one that has already been created and saved or it may be a blank invoice.

> **Find** is used to find invoices previously prepared.

New is clicked to create a new invoice.

Save is clicked to save the invoice and leave it on the screen. The arrow at the bottom of the Save icon means you can save it in more than one way. An invoice may be saved as a QuickBooks Desktop invoice or a PDF file.

Delete will delete the invoice. To void the invoice, click the arrow below Delete and then click Void.

Create a Copy allows you to make a copy of the invoice using a new number. This invoice may be edited and saved.

Memorize allows QuickBooks Desktop to save an invoice as a template for future use.

Mark As Pending saves the invoice but doesn't record the accounting behind the scenes. Later, the invoice may be marked as Final to record the accounting.

Print is used to print the invoice. The arrow beneath Print may be clicked so you can preview an invoice. Other choices include printing an invoice, a batch of invoices, packing slips, shipping labels, and envelopes. You may also save the invoice as a PDF file. There is also checkbox on the Icon bar that may be clicked so the invoice may be printed later.

Email is used to e-mail an invoice or a batch of invoices. The arrow below Email allows you to email an invoice, an invoice and its attached files, and to email a batch of invoices. Email also has a checkbox on the Icon bar that may be clicked so the invoice is emailed later.

Attach File attaches a file or a scanned document to this invoice.

Add Time/Costs adds any costs you marked as billable to this Customer:Job.

Apply Credits is used to apply an existing credit for this Customer:Job to this invoice. A credit for a return or overpayment must be recorded as a Credit Memo prior to clicking this Icon and linking the Credit Memo to the Invoice.

Receive Payments is used to record the receipt of payment for this invoice.

Create a Batch creates one invoice to send to multiple customers.

Refund/Credit enables you to create a Credit Memo using the items and prices on this invoice. It may be edited and saved and is an alternate method to prepare a Credit Memo in Refunds & Credits.

Formatting Tab Icons include:

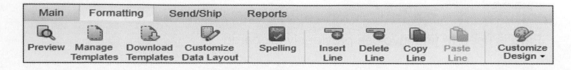

Preview allows you to see how the printed invoice will look

Manage Templates allows you to view a list of standard forms available in QuickBooks Desktop. These may be copied, edited, and customized.

Download Templates allows you to download preformatted forms that are customized.

Customize Data Layout allows you to customize the information that appears and the location where it appears on the form your customer sees.

Spelling is used to check the spelling in the item descriptions.

Insert Line will insert a blank line above the selected item, so additional text may be added, extra space may be created, or a new line item may be inserted.

Delete Line is used to delete a selected line item.

Copy Line is used to duplicate a selected line item.

Paste Line is used to "paste" the copied line onto a new line.

Customize Design allows online form customization and requires an online Intuit account to save your designs.

Send/Ship Tab Icons include:

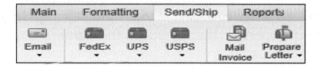

Email is used to email the current invoice and a batch of invoices.

FedEx, UPS, and **USPS** allow you to send/ship packages, find drop off locations, schedule pickups, track or cancel a shipment, and setup accounts for shipping, among other things.

Mail Invoice uses QuickBooks Billing Solutions to mail invoices.

Prepare Letter uses Microsoft® Word to create letters and envelopes for customers using templates provided by QuickBooks Desktop. These templates may be edited and/or customized.

Reports Tab Icons include:

QuickReport is used to display transactions for the Customer:Job on this invoice.

Transaction History is a report that lists all transactions that are linked to this invoice.

Transaction Journal displays a report showing the journal entry that QuickBooks Desktop makes behind the scenes for this invoice.

View Open Invoices displays a report containing information about unpaid invoices, when they are due, and unapplied refunds/credits.

Sales by Customer Detail displays the sales to each customer and shows the totals of every line item on sales and refunds/credits.

Average Days To Pay Summary analyzes the payment history for each customer and displays the average number of days it takes each customer to pay.

Click the **Close** button on the Create Invoice screen to close the invoice

LISTS

To expedite entering transactions, QuickBooks Desktop uses lists as an integral part of the program. Customers, vendors, sales items, and accounts are organized as lists. In fact, the chart of accounts is a list in QuickBooks Desktop. Frequently, information can be entered on a form by clicking on a list item.

Most lists have a maximum. However, it's unlikely that you'll run out of room on your lists. With so many entries available, there is room to add list items "on the fly" as you work. The vendors, customers, and employees lists are all provided in the related Centers. If you open the Customer Center, the Customer List will appear on the left side of the Center.

 Examine several lists following the instructions given below:

There are several ways in which to access Lists

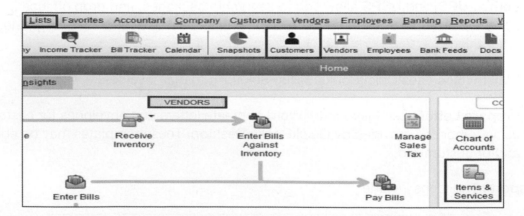

Click the **Customers** icon on the Top Icon Bar. On the left side of the Customer Center, the list of customers is shown; click the **Close** button to exit

- In accounting concepts, the Customers list would be referred to as the Accounts Receivable Subsidiary Ledger.

Click the **Lists** menu, click **Chart of Accounts** to view the Chart of Accounts, click the **Close** button to exit

Click the **Vendors** icon at the top of the Vendors section of the Home Page, view the list of vendors on the left side of the Vendor Center; click the **Close** button to exit

- In accounting concepts, the Vendors list would be referred to as the Accounts Payable Subsidiary Ledger.

Click the **Items & Services** icon in the Company Section of the Home Page to view the list of items for sale and services performed by the company, click the **Close** button to exit

REGISTERS

QuickBooks Desktop prepares a register for every balance sheet account. An account register contains records of all activity for the account. Registers provide an excellent means of looking at transactions within an account. For example, the Accounts Receivable register maintains a record of every invoice, credit memo, and payment that has been recorded for credit customers (in accounting concepts this is the Accounts Receivable account).

 Examine the Accounts Receivable Register

Chart of Accounts

Click **Chart of Accounts** in the Company section of the Home Page
Click **Accounts Receivable**
Click the **Activities** button at the bottom of the screen
Click **Use Register**
Scroll through the register
Look at the **Number/Type** column
Notice the types of transactions listed:
    INV is for an invoice
    PMT indicates a payment received from a customer

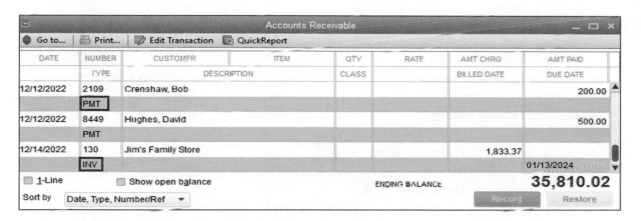

Click the **Close** button on the Register
Click the **Close** button on the Chart of Accounts

REPORTS

Reports are an integral part of a business. Reports enable owners and managers to determine how the business is doing and to make decisions affecting the future of the company. Reports can be prepared showing the profit and loss for the period, the status of the Balance Sheet (assets equal liabilities plus owner's equity), information regarding accounts receivable and accounts payable, and the amount of sales for each item. QuickBooks Desktop has a wide range of reports and reporting options available. Reports may be customized to better reflect the information needs of a company. Reports may be generated in a variety of ways.

Reports menu may be used to access the Report Center, Memorized Reports, Scheduled Reports, Commented Reports, Company Snapshot, Process Multiple Reports, and QuickBooks Desktop Statement Writer. In addition, it includes a complete listing of the reports available in QuickBooks Desktop and is used to prepare reports in the following categories: Company & Financial; Customers & Receivables; Sales; Jobs, Time & Mileage; Vendors & Payables; Purchases, Inventory, Employees & Payroll, Banking; Accountant & Taxes; Budgets & Forecasts; List; Industry Specific, Contributed Reports, Custom Reports, Quick Report, Transaction History, and Transaction Journal.

Report Center includes a complete listing of the reports available in QuickBooks Desktop. Reports may be shown in a Carousel view, a Grid view, and a List view.

 Prepare reports from the **Reports** menu

Click **Reports** on the menu bar
Point to **Company & Financial**
Click **Profit & Loss Standard**
Scroll through the Profit and Loss Statement for Larry's Landscaping & Garden Supply
- Notice the Net Income for the period.
Click the **Close** button to exit the report

 Prepare reports using the **Report Center**

Click **Reports** on the Icon Bar
Click **Company & Financial** in the list of reports on the left side of the navigator if it is not already highlighted
Explore the report list view options by clicking the following buttons in the upper-right corner of the Report Center:
Click the button for **Carousel View**
- Sample reports revolve when clicked and are shown in the correct format.
Click the button for **Grid View**
- Sample reports are shown in a side-by-side grid.
Click the button for **List View**
- Reports and a brief description are listed.
Scroll through the list of reports available until you see Balance Sheet Standard
Click **Balance Sheet Standard**
Click the green **Run** button to display the report

Balance Sheet Standard
What is the value of my company (its assets, liabilities, and equity), showing me the individual balances for each account?

Run   Info   Fave   Help | Dates: This Fiscal Year-to-date   ▾   10/1/2022   12/15/2022

Scroll through the report
- Notice that Total Assets equal Total Liabilities & Equity.

Do not close the report

QUICKZOOM

QuickZoom allows you to view transactions that contribute to the data in reports or graphs.

   Use QuickZoom

Scroll through the Balance Sheet on the screen until you see the fixed asset **Truck**
Position the mouse pointer over the amount for **Total Truck**
- The mouse pointer turns into .

Double-click the mouse to see the transaction detail for the Total Truck
Click the **Close** button to close the **Transactions by Account** report
Click the **Close** button to close the **Balance Sheet**
Do <u>not</u> close the Report Center

GRAPHS

Using bar charts and pie charts, QuickBooks Desktop gives you an instant visual analysis of different elements of your business. You may obtain information in a graphical form for Income & Expenses, Sales, Accounts Receivable, Accounts Payable, Net Worth, and Budget vs. Actual. For example, using the Report Center and Company & Financial as the type of report, double-clicking Net Worth Graph allows you to see an owner's net worth in relationship to assets and liabilities. This is displayed on a bar chart according to the month. To obtain information about liabilities for a given month, you may zoom in on the liabilities portion of the bar, double-click, and see the liabilities for the month displayed in a pie chart.

   View a Graph

Report Center should be on the screen
Company & Financial is the **Type of Report**
Click the **Carousel View** button
As you use the bottom scroll bar to scroll through the reports you will see samples
    displayed
Scroll through the list of reports, click **Net Worth Graph**
Click **Run**

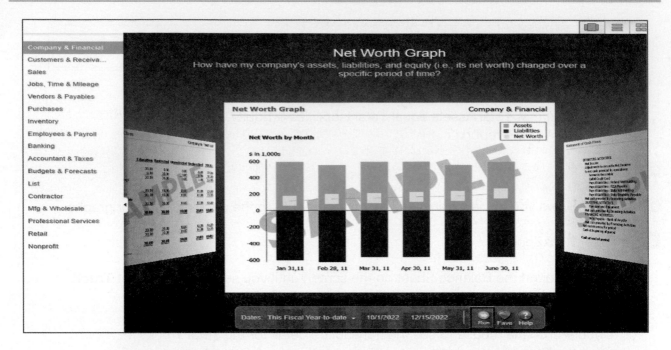

View the Net Worth Graph

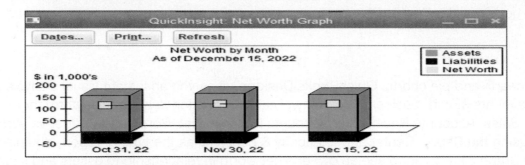

Zoom in on the Liabilities for October by pointing to the liabilities portion of the graph (brown color) and double-clicking

View the pie chart for October's liabilities

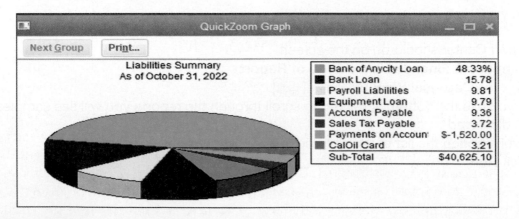

Click the **Close** button to close the pie chart

Zoom in on the **Net Worth** (yellow) for **December** and double-click

View the pie chart for **December's Net Worth Summary**

Use the keyboard shortcut **Ctrl+F4** to close the pie chart

Click the **Close** button to close the Net Worth graph
Close the **Report Center**

QUICKREPORT

QuickReports are reports that give you detailed information about Items you are viewing. They look just like standard reports that you prepare but are considered "quick" because you don't have to go through the Reports menu or Report Center to create them. For example, when you are viewing the Chart of Accounts, clicking an account, clicking the Reports button, and selecting QuickReports from the menu will show details about the individual account.

 View a QuickReport

Click **Lists** on the menu bar
Click **Chart of Accounts**
Click **Prepaid Insurance**
Click **Reports** button at the bottom of the Chart of Accounts List
Click **QuickReport: Prepaid Insurance**

Click the **Close** button to close the **QuickReport**
Click the **Close** button to close the **Chart of Accounts**

USE QUICKMATH

QuickMath is available for use whenever you are in a field where a calculation is made. Frequently, QuickBooks Desktop will make calculations for you automatically; however, there may be instances when you need to perform the calculation. For example, on an invoice, QuickBooks Desktop will calculate an amount based on the quantity and the rate given for a sales item. If for some reason you do not have a rate for a sales Item, you may use QuickMath to calculate the amount. To do this, you tab to the amount column, type an = or a number and the +. QuickBooks Desktop will show an adding machine tape on the screen. You may then add, subtract, multiply, or divide to obtain a total or a subtotal. Pressing the enter key inserts the amount into the column.

Use QuickMath

Click the **Create Invoices** icon on the Home Page
Click in the **Amount** column on the Invoice

Enter the numbers: 123+
                     456+
                     789

	123.00
+	456.00
+	789

Press **Enter**
The total **1,368** is inserted into the Amount column
Click the **Clear** button to remove the total amount of **1,368**, do not close the invoice

USE WINDOWS CALCULATOR

Windows includes accessory programs that may be used to complete tasks while you are working in QuickBooks Desktop. One of these accessory programs is Calculator. Using this program gives you an on-screen calculator. To use the Calculator in Windows, click the Windows Start button, scroll through the list, and click Calculator. A calculator appears on your screen. The Windows calculator is also accessible through QuickBooks Desktop.

  Access Windows Calculator through QuickBooks Desktop

Click **Edit** on the menu bar
Click **Use Calculator**
To view available Windows Calculations: click the List icon on Calculator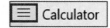
- In addition to Standard and Scientific, you may also select Programmer or Data Calculation.

Click **Standard** to return to the calculator
Numbers may be entered by:
    Clicking the number on the calculator
    Keying the number using the numeric keypad
    Typing the keyboard numbers
    Enter the numbers: 123+
                      456+
                      789=

The amount is subtotaled after each entry
After typing 789=, the answer 1368 appears
- Note: Using the Windows Calculator does not insert the amount into a QuickBooks Desktop form.

To clear the answer, click the **C** button on the calculator
Using the cursor, click the keys for the following: **55 x 6**
- You may also key in: **55 * 6**

Press **Enter** or click = to get the answer 330
- Again, note that answer is not inserted into the invoice.

Click the **Close** button to close the **Calculator**
Click the **Close** button on the Invoice to close the invoice without saving

CLOSE COMPANY AND CLOSE QUICKBOOKS DESKTOP

The sample company—Larry's Landscaping & Garden Supply—will appear as the open company whenever you open QuickBooks Desktop. To discontinue the use of the sample company, you must close the company. In a classroom environment, you should always back up your work and close the company you are using at the end of a work session. If you use different computers when training, not closing a company at the end of each work session may cause your files to become corrupt, your disk to fail, or leave unwanted .qbi (QuickBooks In Use) files on your storage location.

 Close a company

Click **File** on the Menu bar, click **Close Company**
Click the **Close** button to exit and close **QuickBooks Desktop**
- If you get a message regarding Exiting QuickBooks, click the check box for **"Do not display this message in the future,"** and then click **Yes.**

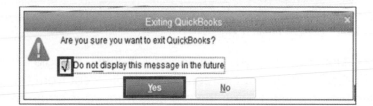

Click the Close button on the QuickBooks Desktop title bar

COMPANY FILES

When working in QuickBooks Desktop, you will use files that contain data for companies that are in the text. Before beginning to use the program, you need to get a working copy of the company files. This may be done by accessing the Pearson Education Web Site. Instructions follow for downloading and extracting files.

DOWNLOAD COMPANY FILES

The company files for the text are available on the Pearson Web site. Depending on your internet browser, your version of windows, your storage location, and a variety of other variables, your screens may not always match those shown in the text. If you find differences and are not sure if you are proceeding correctly, check with your instructor. All screen shots are given for QuickBooks Desktop 2018. Google Chrome is used as the browser.

 Download company files

Insert your USB drive into your computer or ask you professor for specific directions to be used at your school
Open **Google Chrome** or whatever browser you use
Enter the address **http://www.pearsonhighered.com/horne/**
- Sometimes it is difficult to read "horne" so, remember the name is HORNE.

- When completing the following steps, be sure to use the section for the QuickBooks Desktop 2018 edition of the text.
- Check with your instructor to determine if you will use a different procedure.

Click **Student Download Page**

- You will be downloading the files for Tech_2018, Oasis_2018, and Concierge_2018 at this time. These are the company files that will be used in Chapters 1, 2, 3, 4, and Practice Set 1.
- When you get to Chapter 5, you will download the remaining company and logo files.

- <u>IMPORTANT</u>: Depending on your version of Windows, Google Chrome, Internet Explorer, or other browser your screens may be different from the examples shown. If so, complete the download using the prompts from your program. Ask your instructor for assistance if you are not using Google Chrome.

Click **Tech_2018** in the QuickBooks Master Company Files section of the Student Resources screen

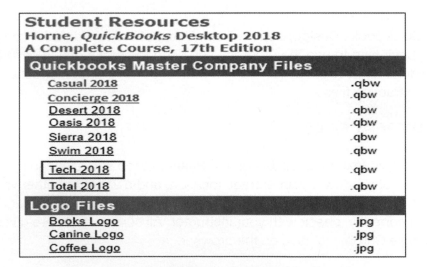

You will see a download message at the bottom of the screen
When the file has finished downloading, click the drop-down list arrow and click **Show in folder**

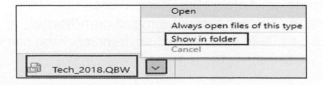

The Download Folder should open in the File Explorer
Scroll through the list of downloaded files until you see Tech 2018, then click
   Tech_2018
 * All the company files may or may not have the underline between the company and year. Either way the file name is shown is fine. So, Tech_2018 and Tech 2018 are both the same company.

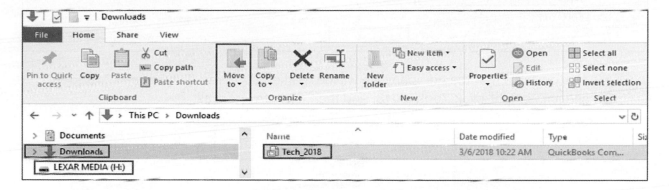

Tech_2018 will be highlighted and the icons will now be bold
Click **Move to**
Scroll through the list of storage locations, click **Choose location**

When the **Move Items** screen appears, scroll through the list of storage locations, then click your USB drive
 * In the example, LEXAR MEDIA (H:) is used.

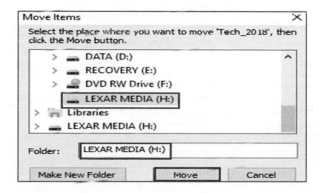

Click **Move**
 * Tech_2018 has been moved to your USB drive. (Lexar Media (H:) in the example.)
Scroll through the list of storage locations on the left side of the File Explorer, click your
   USB drive location
 * The example uses Lexar Media (H:) as the location.

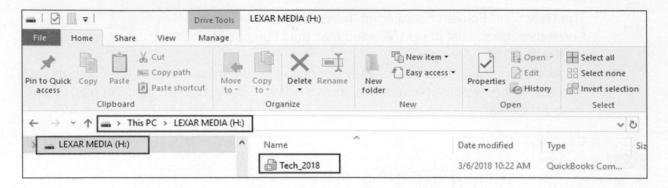

- It is possible that the company file will be marked as "Read Only" and/or "**Hidden.**" To see if it is, right-click **Tech_2018**; and then, click **Properties**

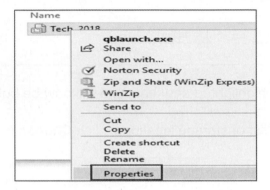

If there is a check mark next to **Read Only** and/or **Hidden**, click the check box to remove the mark

- Your Properties for Tech_2018 may show a different storage location and different dates. This should not be of any concern.

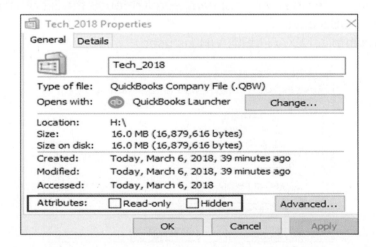

If you had to deselect Read only or Hidden, click the **Apply** button

To exit the file properties, click **OK**

- The file is now ready for use.

Repeat the procedures given and download Oasis_2018 and Concierge_2018

When you are finished, you will see all three companies listed in your USB drive

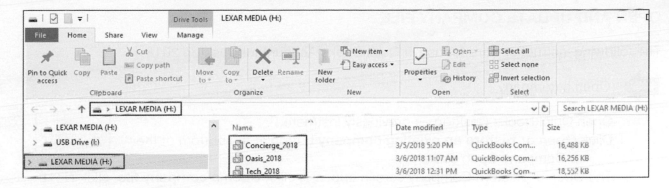

Close all screens

COMPANY DESCRIPTION

In the text you will be recording transactions for a fictional company that specializes in technology services. The company provides program installation, training, and technical support for today's business software as well as helping clients learn how to go online and giving instruction in the use of the Internet. In addition, Your Name's Tech Services will set up computer systems and networks for customers and will install basic computer components, such as: memory, modems, sound cards, hard drives, and CD/DVD drives.

This fictitious, small, sole proprietorship company will be owned and run by you. You will be adding your name to the company name and equity accounts. This company will be used for training while completing Chapters 1 through 4.

OPEN QUICKBOOKS DESKTOP 2018

Now that the company files have been downloaded, you will need to open QuickBooks Desktop 2018 to be able to record information in the company file.

 Open QuickBooks Desktop 2018

There are several ways to open QuickBooks Desktop
Click the **Start** button, scroll through the list of programs, click the drop-down list arrow for **QuickBooks**, then click **QuickBooks Premier – Accountant Edition 2018**

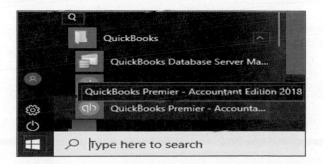

OR
Click the **QuickBooks Premier Accountant Edition 2018** shortcut on the Desktop

OPEN AND UPDATE COMPANY FILE

The following instructions are for use in QuickBooks Accountant Desktop 2018.

 Open a company

Open QuickBooks Desktop as previously instructed
Click **Open or restore an existing company** button at the bottom of the
   No Company Open screen
The Open or Restore Company screen appears, click **Open a company file**, click **Next**

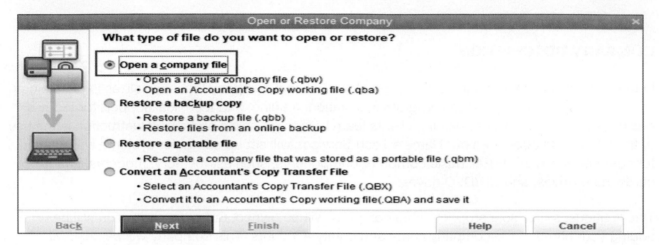

Click the drop-down list arrow for **Look in**
Click **USB Drive (USB Drive Letter:)**
Click **Tech_2018**
- The File name: text box now shows **Tech_2018**
- Notice the Files of type: is **QuickBooks Files (*.QBW, *QBA).**
    - **.QBW** stands for QuickBooks Working file and is used to record all transactions for a company.
    - **.QBA** is the copy of the company file used by the company's accountant.
Click **Open**

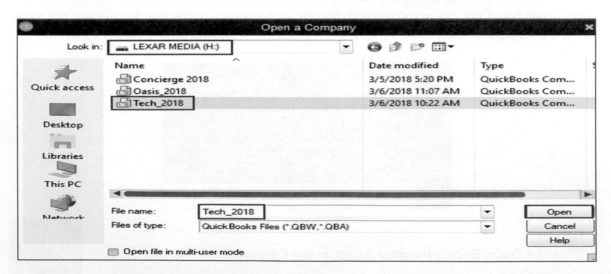

You should see a screen to enter your password

ENTER PASSWORD AND UPDATE COMPANY FILE

Before working in a company file, you will need to enter the company password. Tech_2018 uses the password **QBDT2018**. For security reasons, QuickBooks Desktop requires that passwords are updated every 90 days. If you get a message to do this, update to the password 2018QBDT.

➡ Enter the password for Tech_2018

On the QuickBooks Desktop Login screen, enter **QBDT2018**, then click **OK**
- For security reasons, passwords are not shown on the login screen.

- Sometimes a company file will need to go through an update procedure when it is first opened. Other times you will be able to open the company and go right to work.

If you get a message to Update Your QuickBooks Company File screen, follow the steps shown to update your company
- If QuickBooks Desktop has received some program changes, you may see the Update Company screen.
- If you do not see the Update Company screen after you enter the password for Tech_2018 or you show a screen for Update Your QuickBooks Company File, simply read the following information.

If you get an Update Company screen, click **Yes**

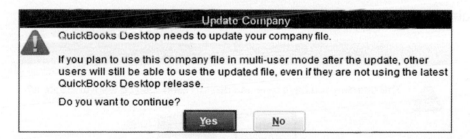

- If the backup file location does <u>not</u> show your USB drive or you are saving to a different location or folder, click **Change this default location** below the suggested storage area, and continue the update.

UPDATE COMPANY FILE FOR NEW QUICKBOOKS EDITION—INFORMATION ONLY

Sometimes, QuickBooks Desktop will require a more extensive update of your company file. This usually happens when you purchase a new version of QuickBooks Desktop. For example, when you upgrade from QuickBooks Desktop 2017 to QuickBooks Desktop 2018 or QuickBooks Desktop 2019, you may be required to go through the following steps.

If you get an Update Your QuickBooks Desktop Company File message, you would follow the steps shown below to backup and update your company

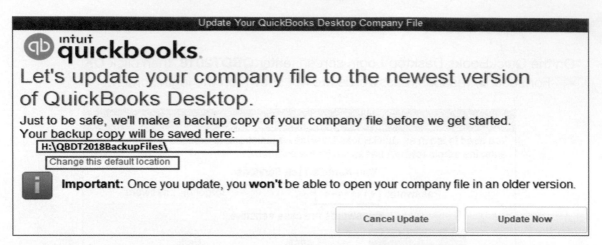

Enter your file location **USB location:\QBDT2018BackupFiles**
Click **OK**
- Remember the USB drive location (H:) is shown in the text.

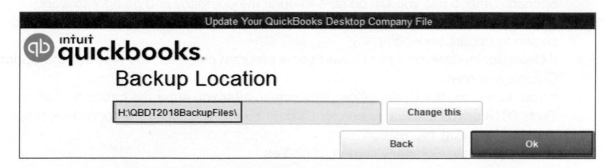

If you get a Backup message, click **Yes**

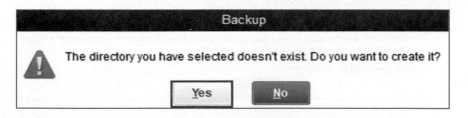

- The backup storage location should be shown correctly.
  If it is, click the **Update Now** button

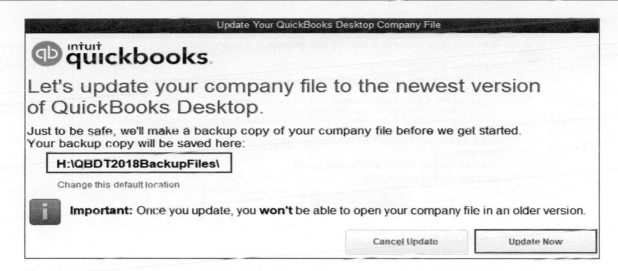

- Your company file will be updated to the latest version of QuickBooks Desktop.

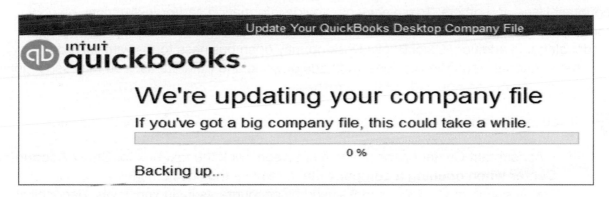

When the update is complete, click **Done** on the message that says: You're all set!

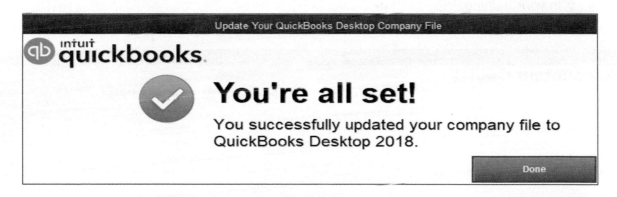

If you get a screen to Set Up an External Accountant User, click the check box to mark **Don't show this again**, then click **No**

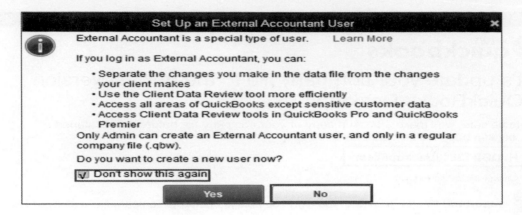

QUICKBOOKS DESKTOP OPENING SCREENS

Sometimes company files open with screens such as Update Company, Accountant Center, New Feature Tour, QuickBooks Products and Services, QuickBooks Alerts, Set Up an External Accountant User, and others. These screens provide information and/or instructions on how to use QuickBooks Desktop, how to subscribe to optional services, or give information regarding reminder alerts. In addition, QuickBooks Desktop may open business forms with wizards, questions, or tutorials regarding options, methods of work, and other items. You may see a gold "What's New" tab on the right side of the screen.

 If you receive any opening screens, read them and select an appropriate answer.

If the Accountant Center opens as the first screen, click the text box for **Show Accountant Center when opening a company file** to remove the check mark
- The Accountant Center has tasks used by accountants including Tools, Reconciliation, Memorized Reports, and Accountant Updates. You will use the Accountant Center later in your training.
Click the **Close** button at the top of the Accountant Center

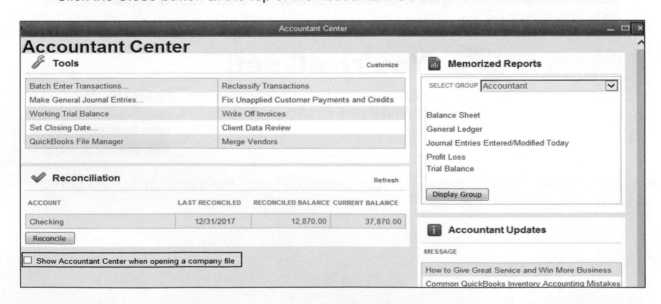

If you get a New Feature Tour, click the **Close** button to close it
- This screen shows you the new features available in this edition of the software. These are things that you will be learning during your training.

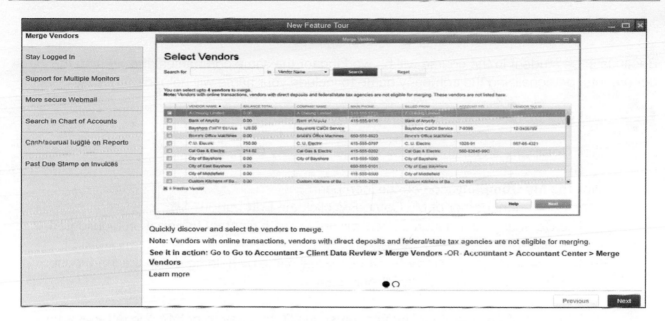

If you see the "What's New" message, click the **Close** button to close it
- What's New provides yellow highlight boxes to show what's new on each screen where you are working.
- You may turn on the New Feature Tour or What's New by clicking Help on the Menu bar and then clicking either New Features or What's New.

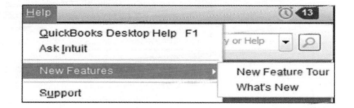

VERIFY OPEN COMPANY

Unless you tell QuickBooks Desktop to create a new company, open a different company, or close the company, Your Name's Tech Services will appear as the open company whenever you open QuickBooks Desktop. However, when you finish a work session, you should always close the company to avoid problems with the file in a future work session.

      Verify the title bar heading:

- Remember, throughout the text the program is referred to as QuickBooks Desktop rather than QuickBooks Premier or QuickBooks Accountant Desktop, etc. No distinction will be made regarding Premier or Accountant from this point forward in the text.

ADD YOUR NAME TO COMPANY NAME

Because each student in the course will be working for the same companies and printing the same documents, personalizing the company name to include your name will help identify your work.

 Add your name to the company name and legal name

Click **Company** on the menu bar, and then click **My Company**
> **OR**

Click the **My Company** icon on the Icon bar.
In the upper-right corner of My Company, click the **Edit** button
- The Company Information screen will appear with Contact Information highlighted, if not click it.

Replace the words **Your Name's** with your real name by holding down the left mouse button and dragging through "Your Name's" to highlight
> **OR**

Click in front of the Y in Your Name's; press the **Delete** key to delete one letter at a time
Replace the words Your Name's with your_actual name, for example, Janet Horne would type **Janet Horne's**
- Because each student's name will be different, the text will show the company name as Your Name's Tech Services.

Click **Legal Information** on the left side of Company Information
Repeat the steps to change the legal name to **Your Name's Tech Services** (Remember to enter your actual name—not the words "Your Name")
Click **OK**
- Note the change on My Company.

Click the **Close** button for My Company
- The title bar now shows **Your Name's Tech Services – QuickBooks Accountant Desktop 2018**.

> Your Name's Tech Services - QuickBooks Accountant Desktop 2018   — ☐ ✕

- Remember your actual name is now part of the company name and will be on the title bar. In the text, however, the title bar will show the words **Your Name's**.

CREATE COMPANY BACKUP FILE

As you work with a company and record transactions, it is important to back up your work. This allows you to keep the information for a period separate from current information. A backup also allows you to restore information in case your data file or storage location becomes damaged. QuickBooks Desktop has a feature to make a backup copy of your company file. A condensed file is created by QuickBooks Desktop. The file contains the essential transaction and account information. This file has a **.qbb** extension and is <u>not</u> usable unless it is restored to a company file that has a **.qbw** extension. This can be an existing company file or a new company file.

In this text, you will make a backup file at the end of each chapter. It will contain the transactions entered up until the time you made the backup. *Future transactions will not be part of the backup file unless you make a new backup file*. For example, Chapter 1 backup will not contain any transactions entered in Chapter 2. However, Chapter 2 backup will contain all the transactions for both Chapters 1 and 2. Chapter 3 backup will contain all the transactions for Chapters 1, 2, and 3, and so on.

In many classroom configurations, you will be storing your backup files onto the same USB drive that you use for the company file. In actual business practice, you should save the backup to a different location. Most likely, you will store your company file on the hard disk of the computer and the backup file will be stored on a USB drive, a network drive, the Cloud, or some other remote location. Check with your instructor to see if there are any other backup file locations you should use in your training.

 Make a QuickBooks Desktop backup of the company data for Your Name's Tech Services.

Click **File** on the Menu Bar
Click **Back Up Company**
Click **Create Local Backup**
- Make sure the Create Backup screen has Local backup selected. If not, click **Local backup** to select.

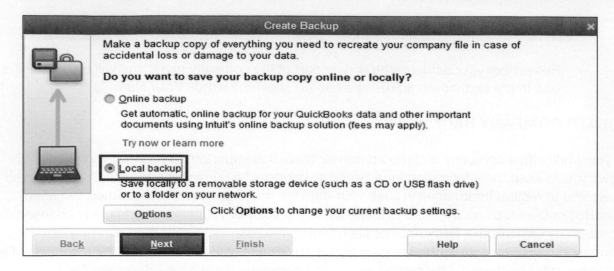

Click the **Next** button
- It is possible that you will need to tell QuickBooks Desktop more detailed information about where you want to save your backup file. This typically happens the first time you backup a file.
- Since you downloaded the company file to your USB drive, QuickBooks Desktop may recognize that location for saving your backup file and you will not need to go through the more detailed Backup Options screen.
- **Note:** If you do not get a screen for Backup Options, read the next few lines of instruction and resume training with **Continue Here**.

If you get the Backup Options screen, complete the following:

Click the **Browse** button next to "Tell us where to save your backup copies (required)"

Scroll through the list of folders, click the location of your USB drive (or designated storage area)
- The text uses (H:\).

Click **OK**

Click the checkboxes for **Add the date and time of the backup to the file name** and **Remind me to back up when I close my company file** to remove the check marks

Keep **Complete verification**, click **OK**

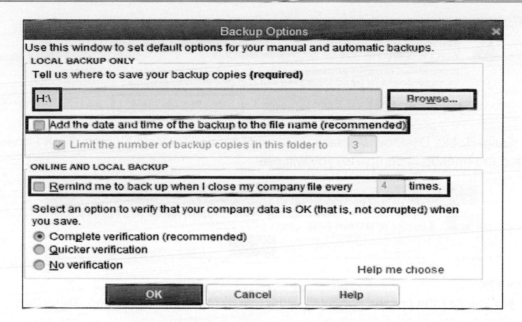

Continue Here whether you read or completed the Backup Options

> To complete the **Create Backup** screen, make sure **Save it now** is selected, then click the **Next** button
> On the Save Backup Copy screen, **Save in:** should be **USB Drive Location**
> - If necessary, click the drop-down list arrow next to Save in: and click the USB Drive Location.
> Change the File Name to **Tech 2018 (Backup Ch. 1)**
> Save as type: **QBW Backup (*.QBB)**

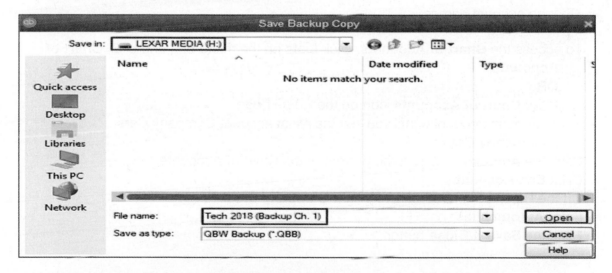

> - Do not worry if the Date modified shown above does not match the date of your file. Remember the date modified is the date of your computer when you created the backup file and will be different from the text.
> Click the **Save** button
> If you are saving the backup file to the same location that you are using to store the company file, you <u>may</u> get the following screen
> If you do, click **Use this Location**

- QuickBooks Desktop will back up the information for Your Name's Tech Services. When the backup is complete, you will see

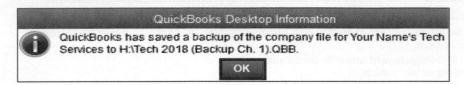

Click **OK**
- Notice that the company name on the title bar still has your name. This change was saved in the backup.

CHANGE ACCOUNT NAME

QuickBooks Desktop makes it easy to set up a company using the Easy Step Interview. You will learn how to create a company in Chapter 9 of the text. When creating a company using the QuickBooks Desktop EasyStep Interview, account names are assigned automatically. They might need to be changed to names more appropriate to the individual company. Even if an account has been used to record transactions or has a balance, the name can still be changed.

   Change account names

To access the **Chart of Accounts**, click **Lists** on the menu bar, and click **Chart of Accounts**
OR
Click the **Chart of Accounts** icon on the Home Page
Scroll through accounts until you see the asset account Company Cars
Click **Company Cars**
Click the **Account** button at the bottom of the Chart of Accounts
Click **Edit Account**
On the **Edit Account** screen, highlight **Company Cars**
Enter **Automobiles**
Click the **Save & Close** button

- The account name has been changed to Automobiles.

Close the **Chart of Accounts**

VIEW REPORT

To see the change in the account name in use, you may view a report.

 Open the Report Center and view a Trial Balance for January 1, 2018

Click **Reports** on the icon bar to open the Report Center
Click the **List View** icon
Click **Accountant & Taxes** on the left side of the screen
Scroll through the reports
Click **Trial Balance** in the Account Activity section
Click **Run**

At the top of the screen, Dates should show Last Month
- Since your computer will show a different date than the example in the text you will need to insert the date used for the report.

Press the **Tab** key to highlight the **From** date
Key in the date **01/01/2018**
Press the **Tab** key to highlight the **To** date
When the **To** date is highlighted, enter **01/01/2018**
Press **Tab** two times to generate the Trial Balance for January 1, 2018

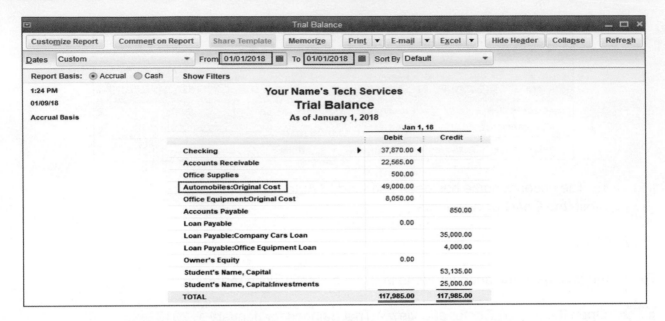

- In the upper-left corner of the report you will see the time and date the report was prepared along with the report basis. Since the date and time of your computer is current, it will not match the dates shown above.
- Notice that the asset account Company Cars is now Automobiles: Original Cost. (The subaccount Original Cost is combined with the master account Automobiles.)
- The changes you made to account names are shown in this report.

Click the **Close** button to close the report

- If you get a Memorize Report screen, click **No**.

Click the **Close** button to close the Report Center

RESTORE COMPANY BACKUP FILE

If you make an error in your training, you may find it beneficial to restore your .qbb backup file. The only way in which a .qbb backup file may be used is by restoring it to a .qbw company file. Using QuickBooks' Open or Restore Company… command on the File menu restores a backup file.

IMPORTANT: A restored backup file replaces the current data in your company file with the data in the backup file, so any transactions recorded after the backup was made will be erased. In this chapter, the backup was made after you added your name to the company name but before you changed the name of Company Cars to Automobiles. After restoring the Tech 2018 (Backup Ch. 1.qbb) backup file to Tech_2018.qbw, the name of the asset account Automobiles will revert back to Company Cars; but the company name will still contain your name.

 Restore a backup file after a change has been made in the company file

Click **File** on the menu bar
Click **Open or Restore Company**

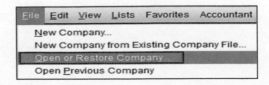

Click **Restore a backup copy**, then click the **Next** button

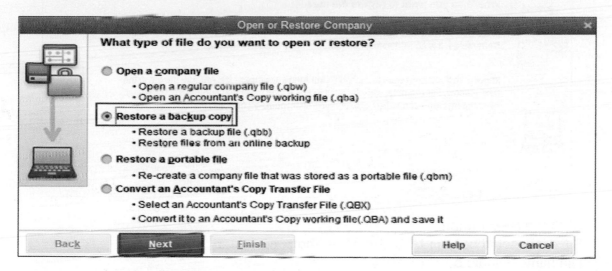

Click **Local backup**, then click the **Next** button

On the Open Backup Copy screen, make sure that Look in: shows the name of your **USB Drive** location

The File name: should be **Tech 2018 (Backup Ch. 1)**, if necessary, click the file name to insert it

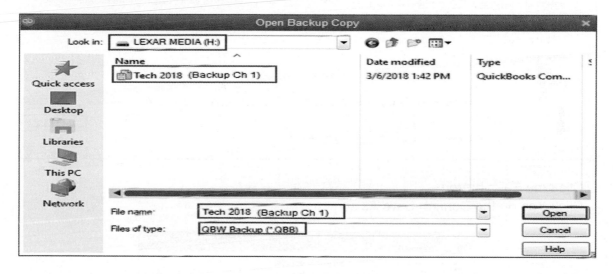

Click the **Open** button

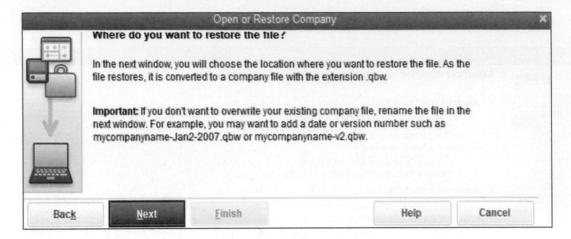

Click the **Next** button
Save in: should be your **USB Drive Location**
File name: should be **Tech 2018**

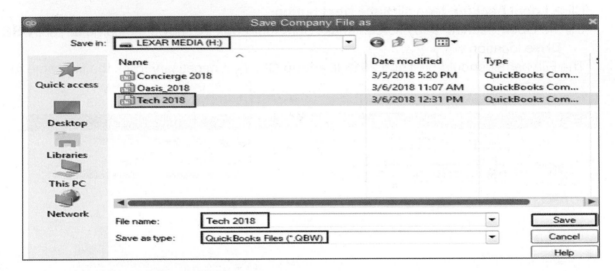

Click the **Save** button
Click **Yes** on the Confirm Save As screen

You will get a **Delete Entire File** warning screen
Enter the word **Yes** and click **OK**

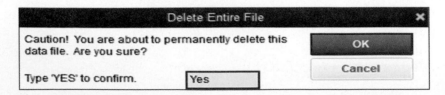

- When you restore a file to an existing company file, all the data contained in the company file will be replaced with the information in the backup file.

You will return to the QuickBooks Desktop Login

Enter the Password: **QBDT2018**, click **OK**

- Remember that the password is case sensitive.
- When the file has been restored, you may see the following QuickBooks Information screen. If so, click **OK**.

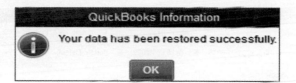

 Verify that Your Name's Tech Services is still on the Title bar and that Company Cars rather than Automobiles is the account name

Look at the Title bar to verify the company name

- The company name was changed before you made the backup. Thus, your name remains in the company name.

Click **Chart of Accounts** on the Home Page

Scroll through the Chart of Accounts until you find the asset account Company Cars

- Automobiles no longer shows as the account name because the company information was restored from the backup file created <u>before</u> changing the account name.

Close the Chart of Accounts

VIEW REPORT AFTER RESTORING BACKUP FILE

To see the change in the asset account name after the company file was restored, prepare a Trial Balance.

 Open the Report Center and view a Trial Balance for January 1, 2018

Click **Reports** on the icon bar to open the Report Center
Click the icon for **List View**
Click **Accountant & Taxes** on the left side of the screen
Scroll through the reports
Click **Trial Balance** in the Account Activity section
Click **Run**
At the top of the screen, **Dates** should show Last Month

- Since your computer will show a different date than the example in the text you will need to insert the date used for the report.

Press the **Tab** key to highlight the **From** date

Key in the date **01/01/18**

Press the **Tab** key to highlight the **To** date

When the **To** date is highlighted, enter **01/01/18**

Press **Tab** two times to generate the Trial Balance for January 1, 2018

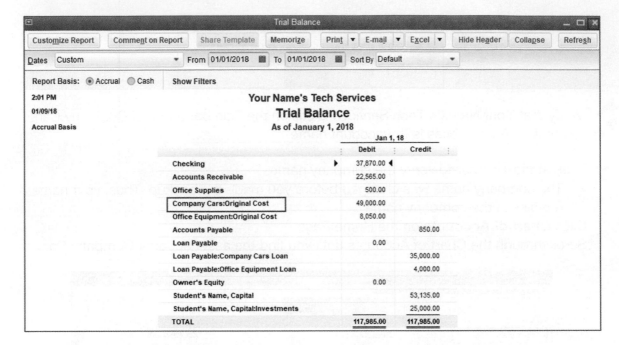

- Notice that the company name in the title of the report shows Your Name's Tech Services. This is because the company name was changed before you made your backup file.
- The asset account in the report shows Company Cars: Original Cost. This is because the account name was changed from Company Cars to Automobiles after the backup file was created. When the backup file was restored, it erased all the changes made after the backup was created.

Click the **Close** button to close the report

- If you get a Memorize Report screen, click **No**.

Click the **Close** button to close the Report Center

CREATE DUPLICATE USB DRIVE

In addition to making a backup of the company file, you should always have a duplicate of the USB drive you use for your work. Follow the instructions provided by your instructor to copy your files to another USB drive or to a different storage location.

EXIT QUICKBOOKS DESKTOP AND REMOVE USB DRIVE (CRITICAL!)

When you complete your work, you need to exit the QuickBooks Desktop program. If you are saving work on a USB drive, you must <u>not</u> remove your drive until you exit the program. Once

QuickBooks Desktop has been closed, your USB drive must be removed properly. Following the appropriate steps to close and exit a program and to remove a USB drive is extremely important. There are program and data files that must be closed in order to leave the program and company data so that they are ready to be used again. If a USB drive is simply removed from the computer, damage to the drive and its files may occur. It is common for a beginning computer user to remove the USB drive or to turn off the computer without closing the company file and exiting a program. This can cause corrupt program and data files and can make a USB drive or the program unusable.

 Close the company file, Your Name's Tech Services; close QuickBooks Desktop; eject the USB

To close the company file, click **File** on the Menu bar, click **Close Company**
Once you see the No Company Open screen, close QuickBooks Desktop by clicking the
    Close button in upper right corner of title bar
If you get a message box for Exiting QuickBooks, click **Do not display this message in**
    the future so you will not see the Exiting QuickBooks screen again; and then, click **Yes**

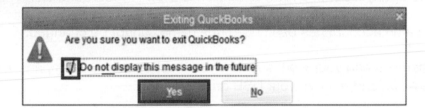

Click the icon for the USB drive in the lower right portion of the Taskbar
Click on the drive location where you have your USB drive

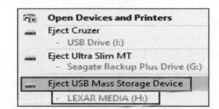

- Your Open Devices and Printers will be different from the example above. Make sure to click on the location for your USB.
When you get the message that it is safe to remove hardware or when the light goes out on your USB drive, remove your USB

SUMMARY

Chapter 1 provides general information regarding QuickBooks Desktop. In this chapter, the request to receive, install, and activate the Student Trial Version of QuickBooks Desktop was completed. Master Company files were downloaded, and various QuickBooks Desktop features were examined. A company file was opened, your name was added to the company name, and an account name was changed. QuickBooks Desktop backup files were made and restored. Companies were closed, QuickBooks Desktop was closed, and USB drives were removed.

END-OF-CHAPTER QUESTIONS

TRUE/FALSE

ANSWER THE FOLLOWING QUESTIONS IN THE SPACE PROVIDED BEFORE THE QUESTION NUMBER.

_____ 1.01.   In a computerized accounting system, each transaction that is analyzed must be entered by hand into the appropriate journal and posted to the appropriate ledger.

_____ 1.02.   There are various methods of giving QuickBooks Desktop commands, including use of QuickBooks Desktop Home Page, icon bar, menu bar, and keyboard shortcuts.

_____ 1.03.   When you use QuickBooks Desktop to make a company backup file, QuickBooks Desktop creates a condensed file that contains the essential transaction and account information.

_____ 1.04.   A company file with a .qbw extension is used to record transactions.

_____ 1.05.   Once an account has been used, the name cannot be changed.

_____ 1.06.   When you end your work session, you must close your company, close QuickBooks Desktop, and remove your USB drive properly.

_____ 1.07.   A Student Version of QuickBooks is automatically registered once the program download is complete.

_____ 1.08.   QuickBooks Desktop Home Page appears beneath the title bar and has a list of drop-down menus.

_____ 1.09.   You must complete the New Feature Tour to activate new features for QuickBooks Desktop.

_____ 1.10.   Transactions entered today will be erased after a backup from an earlier date is restored.

MULTIPLE CHOICE

WRITE THE LETTER OF THE CORRECT ANSWER IN THE SPACE PROVIDED BEFORE THE QUESTION NUMBER.

_____ 1.11.   A (n) ___ is a list in QuickBooks Desktop.
          A. Invoice
          B. Chart of Accounts
          C. Company
          D. none of the above

_____ 1.12. The extension for a company file that may be used to enter transactions is___.
   A. .qbi
   B. .qbb
   C. .qbw
   D. .qbc

_____ 1.13. QuickBooks Desktop Home Page ___.
   A. allows you to give commands to QuickBooks Desktop according to the type of transaction being entered
   B. are icons shown in a row beneath the menu bar
   C. appears above the menu bar
   D. appears at the bottom of the screen

_____ 1.14. QuickBooks Desktop keyboard conventions ___.
   A. are not available
   B. use the mouse
   C. use certain keys in a manner consistent with Windows
   D. incorporate the use of QuickBooks Desktop Company Center

_____ 1.15. Icons on the Invoice Icon Bar of an invoice are used to ___.
   A. give commands to QuickBooks Desktop
   B. add Customers
   C. prepare reports
   D. show graphs of invoices prepared

_____ 1.16. A way to find out the keyboard shortcuts for various commands is to look them up using ___.
   A. the Internet
   B. Help
   C. the File menu
   D. a Keyboard icon

_____ 1.17. QuickBooks Desktop QuickMath displays ___.
   A. a calculator
   B. an adding machine tape
   C. a calculator with adding machine tape
   D. none of the above

_____ 1.18. An icon is ___.
   A. a document
   B. a picture
   C. a chart
   D. a type of software

_____ 1.19. A .qbb extension on a file name means that the file is ___.
   A. open
   B. the working file
   C. a restored file
   D. a backup file

_____ 1.20.   To verify the name of the open company, look at ___.
            A.   the icon bar
            B.   QuickBooks Desktop Home Page
            C.   the menu bar
            D.   the title bar

FILL-IN

IN THE SPACE PROVIDED, WRITE THE ANSWER THAT MOST APPROPRIATELY COMPLETES THE SENTENCE.

1.21.   The _____ menu is used to open and close a company and may also be used to exit QuickBooks Desktop.

1.22.   In QuickBooks Desktop you may change the company name by clicking My Company on the _____ menu.

1.23.   Whether you are using a manual or a computerized accounting system, transactions must still be _____, _____, and _____.

1.24.   The Report Center has three different views available to display reports. They are _____ view, _____ view, and _____ view.

1.25.   The _____ organizes tasks into logical groups (Vendors, Customers, Employees, Company, and Banking).

SHORT ESSAY

Describe the importance of making a backup of a company file and explain what will happen to transactions entered today if a backup from an earlier date is restored.

_____
_____
_____
_____
_____
_____
_____
_____

END-OF-CHAPTER PROBLEM

YOUR NAME'S POOL & GARDEN OASIS

At the end of each chapter, you will work with a different company and enter transactions that are similar to the ones you competed in the text. Follow the instructions given for transaction entry and printing. You may refer to the chapter for assistance.

Your Name's Pool & Garden Oasis is owned and operated by you. Vicki Turner and Tomas Perez also work for the company. Vicki manages the office and keeps the books for the business. Tomas provides lawn maintenance and supervises the lawn maintenance employees—Diego Vargas and Scott Evans. You provide the pool maintenance. The company is in Santa Barbara, California.

INSTRUCTIONS

- ► Open the company file **Oasis_2018**, as instructed in the chapter
  - You may need to backup and/or update the company file. Follow the instructions provided in Chapter 1.
- ► Enter the Password: **QBDT2018**
- ► Change the company name and the legal name from **Your Name's Pool & Garden Oasis** to your real name's Oasis. (Type your actual name, *not* the words *Your Name's*. Do this whenever you are instructed to add *Your Name's*.)
- ► Unless your instructor directs you to a different storage location for your backup file, create a local backup of the Oasis.qbw file to **Oasis 2018 (Backup Ch. 1)** on the same USB drive where you have your company file
- ► Change the name of the asset account Office Supplies to **Office & Sales Supplies**
- ► Use the Report Center to prepare a Trial Balance
- ► Verify the asset account name change; then close the report and the Report Center
- ► Restore the **Oasis 2018 (Backup Ch. 1)** file
  - The account Office & Sales Supplies reverted back to Office Supplies because the company information was restored from the backup file that was made before the account name was changed.
- ► Use the Report Center to prepare a Trial Balance
- ► Verify that the asset account name is once again Office Supplies; then close the report and the Report Center

SALES AND RECEIVABLES: SERVICE BUSINESS

2

LEARNING OBJECTIVES

At the completion of this chapter, you will be able to:

2.01.   Enter, correct, edit, and print a sale on account.
2.02.   Analyze transactions in the Journal report.
2.03.   Prepare and print the Customer Balance Summary report.
2.04.   Use QuickZoom in a report.
2.05.   View and analyze a QuickReport.
2.06.   Void and delete sales forms.
2.07.   Use Search and Find.
2.08.   Prepare Credit Memos.
2.09.   Prepare and print the Customer Balance Detail report.
2.10.   Add a new account, new sales items, and customer.
2.11.   Prepare a daily backup of the company file.
2.12.   Modify customer records.
2.13.   Create Sales Receipts to record cash sales.
2.14.   Correct and print Sales Receipts.
2.15.   Prepare and print Sales by Customer Detail.
2.16.   View and analyze a QuickReport.
2.17.   Analyze sales by preparing the Sales by Item Summary report.
2.18.   Record full and partial customer payments on account.
2.19.   Prepare Transaction List by Customer report.
2.20.   Deposit Checks.
2.21.   Analyze and print the Journal and Trial Balance reports.
2.22.   Prepare Accounts Receivable and Sales Graphs.

ACCOUNTING FOR SALES AND RECEIVABLES

Rather than use a traditional Sales Journal to record sales on account using debits and credits and special columns, QuickBooks Desktop records sales by preparing invoices, cash receipts, or statements.

If your customer doesn't pay you in full at the time you provide your service or sell your product, an invoice is prepared. QuickBooks Desktop uses an invoice to record sales transactions for accounts receivable in the Accounts Receivable Register. When a sale is "on account" this means that the customer owes you money and Accounts Receivable is used as the account.

Statements are prepared if you need to track how much your customers owe you and don't want to send an invoice each time you perform a service for a customer. Statements are useful if you want to accumulate charges before requesting payment or if you assess a regular monthly charge.

When preparing a statement, you would enter statement charges one by one as you perform services for a customer; and then, once a month send out a statement requesting payment. Statements also use Accounts Receivable to record sales on account.

When a customer pays the amount due on an invoice, the payment is recorded in Receive Payments. Behind the scenes, QuickBooks Desktop will debit Cash or Checking and will credit Accounts Receivable.

Because cash sales do not involve accounts receivable and would be recorded in the Cash Receipts Journal in traditional accounting, the transactions are recorded on a Sales Receipt. However, all transactions, regardless of the activity, are placed in the General Journal behind the scenes. Rather than using the Accounts Receivable account for the debit part of the transaction, Cash or Checking is used because you received payment at the time the sale was made or the service was performed.

QuickBooks Desktop puts the money received from a cash sale and from a customer's payment on account (payment for an existing invoice or statement) into the Undeposited Funds account. When a bank deposit is made the Undeposited Funds are placed in the Checking or Cash account.

A new customer can be added on the fly as transactions are entered. In QuickBooks Desktop, error correction is easy. A sales form may be edited, voided, or deleted in the same window where it was created. Customer information may be changed by editing the Customer in the Customer Center. Once the change to a customer's account information is saved, existing transactions are updated with the change automatically.

A multitude of reports are available when using QuickBooks Desktop. Accounts receivable reports include Customer Balance Summary, Customer Balance Detail, and Transaction Reports by Customer, among others. Sales reports provide information regarding the amount of sales by customer, by sales item, and others are available as well as the traditional accounting reports such as Trial Balance, Profit and Loss, and Balance Sheet. QuickBooks Desktop also has graphing capabilities that enable you to see your accounts receivable and sales at the click of a button.

TRAINING TUTORIAL

The following tutorial is a step-by-step guide to recording sales (both cash and credit), customer payments, bank deposits, and other transactions for receivables for a fictitious company with fictional employees. (As a note, the employee names are given in transactions; however, they are not added to the company file. In Chapter 8 employees will be added to a company file.) The company used in this chapter was also used in Chapter 1. It is called Your Name's Tech Services (remember, the company name has your real name *not* the words Your Name's). In addition to recording transactions using QuickBooks Desktop, we will prepare several reports and graphs for the company. The tutorial for Your Name's Tech Services will continue in Chapters 3 and 4, where accounting for payables, customizing a chart of accounts, bank reconciliations, financial statement preparation, and closing an accounting period will be completed.

This text focuses on training using QuickBooks Accountant Desktop 2018. For simplicity in the text, the program is referred to as <u>QuickBooks Desktop</u>, <u>QB Desktop</u>, <u>QuickBooks DT</u>, or <u>QBDT</u>.

TRAINING PROCEDURES

To maximize the training benefits, you should:

1. Read the entire chapter *before* beginning the tutorial within the chapter.
2. Answer the end-of-chapter questions.
3. Be aware that transactions to be entered are given within a **MEMO**.
4. Complete all the steps listed for the Your Name's Tech Services tutorial in the chapter. (Indicated by: ➡)
5. When you have completed a section, put a check mark next to the final step.
6. If you do not complete a section, put the date in the margin next to the last step completed. This will make it easier to know where to begin when training is resumed.
7. You may not finish the entire chapter in one computer session. At the end of your work session, make a backup file that will contain the work you completed from Chapter 1 through the current day. Name this file **Tech 2018 (Daily Backup)**.
8. In addition to the daily backup, always use QuickBooks Desktop to back up your work at the end of the chapter as described in Chapter 1. The name of the chapter backup for Chapter 2 is **Tech 2018 (Backup Ch. 2)**. Make a duplicate copy of your USB drive as instructed by your professor.
9. As you complete your work, proofread carefully and check for accuracy. Double-check amounts of money, the accounts, items, and dates used.
10. If you find an error while preparing a transaction, correct it. If you find the error after the Invoice, Sales Receipt, Credit Memo, Receive Payments, or Customer:Job List is complete, follow the steps indicated in this chapter to correct, void, or delete transactions.
11. Print as directed within the chapter. (Check with your instructor to see if you should print everything listed or if there is printing that you may omit.)
12. There is a checklist at the end of the chapter that lists everything that is printed when working through the chapter. There is a blank line next to each document listed so you can mark it when it has been printed and/or completed.
13. When you complete your computer session, always close your company. If you use a computer where a previous student did not close the company, QuickBooks Desktop may freeze when you start to work. If you do not close the company as you leave, you may have problems with your company file, your USB drive may be damaged, and you may have unwanted .qbi (QuickBooks In Use) files that cause problems when using the company file.

DATES

Throughout the text, the year used for the screen shots is 2018, which is the year of the program version. Check with your instructor to verify the use of 2018 as the year for the transactions. If your instructor wants you to use the current year, that is fine. Just make sure that you are consistent with the year throughout the text.

Pay special attention to the dates when recording transactions. It is not unusual to forget to enter the date that appears in the text and to use the date of the computer for a transaction. This can cause errors in reports and other entries. There will be times when you can tell QuickBooks Desktop which date to use such as, business documents and some reports. There will be other instances when QuickBooks Desktop automatically inserts the date of the computer, and it cannot be changed. This will occur later in the chapter when you print the bank deposit summary. When this happens, accept the QuickBooks Desktop printed date.

PRINTING

Throughout the text, you will be instructed when to print business documents and reports. Everything that is to be printed within the chapter is listed on the chapter checklist. The end-of-chapter problem printouts are also on the chapter checklist. In some instances, your instructor may direct you to change what you print. Always verify items to be printed with your instructor.

COMPANY FILE

In Chapter 1, you began using Your Name's Tech Services. You changed the company name from Your Name's Tech Services to Your Name's Tech Services (your real name). A backup of the file was made. An account name was changed. The backup file was restored, and you learned that the account name change had been replaced with the original account name that was in the backup file. During Chapters 2-4, you will continue to use the Tech 2018.qbw file originally used in Chapter 1 to record transactions. In Chapter 4, you will customize your chart of accounts.

If you did not complete the work in Chapter 1, you will need to download the company file from the Pearson Web site. Refer to Chapter 1 for step-by-step procedures to do this. You will also need to refer to Chapter 1 to add your name to the company name. If you plan to install the trial version of QuickBooks Desktop and want to use step-by-step instructions to install and register the program, refer to Chapter 1. You should refer to the **www.Pearsonhighered.com/Horne** Web site periodically for updates, new material, and errata.

COMPANY PROFILE

As you learned in Chapter 1, Your Name's Tech Services is a company specializing in technology services. The company provides program installation, training, and technical support for today's business software, Web Site design, setting up company networks, providing instruction in the use of the Internet, and assistance in using the Internet. In addition, Your Name's Tech Services will set up computer systems for customers and will install basic computer components, such as memory, modems, sound cards, graphics cards, etc.

Your Name's Tech Services is in Southern California and is a sole proprietorship owned by you. You are involved in all aspects of the business and have the responsibility of obtaining clients. There are three employees: Emily Edwards, who is responsible for software training; Jacob Katz, who handles hardware and network installation, Web Design, Cloud services, and technical support; and Sofia Sanchez, whose duties include being office manager and bookkeeper and providing technical support.

Your Name's Tech Services bills by the hour for training, hardware and software installation, and network setup. Each of these items has a minimum charge of $95 for the first hour and $80 per hour thereafter. Web Design and Cloud Services are offered to clients at the rate of $150 per hour. Clients with contracts for technical support are charged a monthly rate for service.

BEGIN QUICKBOOKS DESKTOP TRAINING

As you continue this chapter, you will be instructed to enter transactions for Your Name's Tech Services. As you learned in Chapter 1, you must boot up or start your computer, open the QuickBooks Desktop program, and open the company.

 Refer to Chapter 1 to Open QuickBooks Desktop

OPEN COMPANY

In Chapter 1, Your Name's Tech Services was opened, and a backup of the company file was made using QuickBooks Desktop. Your Name's Tech Services should have been closed in Chapter 1. To open the company for this work session you may click the Open an Existing Company button on the No Company Open screen or by clicking File on the Menu bar and Open or Restore Company. Verify this by checking the title bar.

 Open **Your Name's Tech Services**

> Click **Open or Restore an Existing Company** button at the bottom of the No Company
> > Open screen
> > **OR**
> Click **File** on the Menu bar and click **Open or Restore Company**

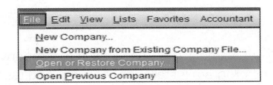

> On the Open or Restore Company screen, **Open a Company File** should be selected, click
> > **Next**.
> Click the drop-down list arrow for **Look in**
> Click **Removable Disk (USB Drive Location:)**
> - The screen shot shows (H:) as the USB location. Your location may be different.
> Click **Tech 2018** (in the Name section under the Look in text box)
> - Your company file may have an extension of **.qbw.** This is the file extension for your "QuickBooks Working" file. This is the company file that may be opened and used. As you learned in Chapter 1, you may not use a .qbb (backup) file for direct entry. A backup file must be restored to a .qbw (company) file.
> - The files shown below are the company files for Chapters 1-4. If you downloaded the files for Chapters 5-8 you will have additional company files on the USB drive.

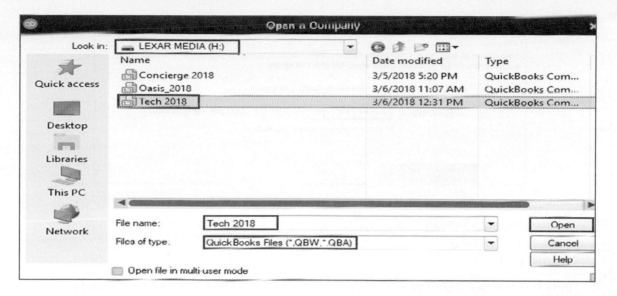

- Since this company was used in Chapter 1, when you see the Open a Company screen, you may see other QuickBooks Desktop files and/or folders associated with that company. QuickBooks Desktop will create them as you use a company file. Some of these files may have extensions of QBW.ND or .QBW.TLG. Folders that say QuickBooksAutoDataRecovery, Restored, or .QBW.SearchIndex are common. For the most part, you do not use or change any of these files or folders, simply click the company file and click the Open button.

Click **Open**

- Remember, this is the same file you used in Chapter 1.
- If you try to open a company file by double-clicking the company file name, QuickBooks Desktop will give you an error message.
- Sometimes, when switching from one company to the next; i.e., Tech 2018 to Oasis 2018 and then back to Tech 2018, QuickBooks Desktop might mark your company file as read only. If this happens, right-click the company name on your USB drive, click Properties, click to remove the check from Read Only and/or Archive, click the Apply button, and then click OK.

If you get a screen to Update Company, click **Yes**

- If necessary, refer to Chapter 1 to review Update Company procedures.

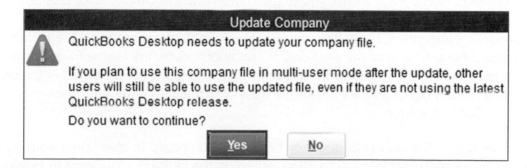

Enter the Password **QBDT2018** on the QuickBooks Desktop Login

- The Password is case sensitive so be sure to enter it exactly as shown.
- Notice that, for security reasons, the Password is shown as ●●●●●●●●
- The Password must be entered every time you open the company.

Click **OK**

VERIFY OPEN COMPANY

     Verify the title bar heading:

- The title bar should show **Your Name's Tech Services** as the company name. (Remember you will have your actual name in the title.)
- If your title bar shows QuickBooks Premier Accountant Desktop 2018, that is fine. There is no difference in the program since QuickBooks Accountant Desktop is part of the Premier version of QuickBooks Desktop.
- Remember, throughout the text the program is referred to as QuickBooks Desktop rather than QuickBooks Premier Desktop or QuickBooks Accountant Desktop, etc.
- Note: Unless you tell QuickBooks Desktop to create a new company, open a different company, or close the company, Your Name's Tech Services will appear as the open company whenever you open QuickBooks Desktop. However, when you finish a work session, you should always close the company to avoid problems with the file in a future work session.

QUICKBOOKS DESKTOP HOME PAGE AND TOP ICON BAR

The QuickBooks Desktop Home Page allows you to give commands to QuickBooks Desktop according to the type of transaction being entered. The Home Page tasks are organized into logical groups (Vendors, Customers, Company, and Banking). Each of the areas on the Home Page is used to enter different types of transactions. When appropriate, the Home Page shows a flow chart with icons indicating the major activities performed. The icons are arranged in the order in which transactions usually occur and are clicked to access screens to enter information or transactions in QuickBooks Desktop.

You may also choose to use the menu bar, the icon bar, or the keyboard to give commands to QuickBooks Desktop. For more detailed information regarding the QuickBooks Desktop Home Page and the Top Icon Bar, refer to Chapter 1. Instructions in this text will be given primarily using the QuickBooks Desktop Home Page. However, the menu bar, the Top Icon bar, and/or keyboard methods will be used as well.

If the Top Icon Bar is not showing, click the **View** menu, and then click **Top Icon** Bar; if the Home Page is not showing, click the **Home** icon, and, if necessary, click the **Home Page** tab to display it

BEGIN TUTORIAL

In this chapter you will be entering accounts receivable transactions, cash sales transactions, receipts for payments on account, and bank deposits. Much of the organization of QuickBooks Desktop is dependent upon lists. The two primary types of lists you will use in the tutorial for receivables are a Customers & Jobs List and a Sales Item List.

The names, addresses, telephone numbers, credit terms, credit limits, and balances for all established credit customers are contained in the Customer & Jobs List in the Customer Center. To conform with GAAP (Generally Accepted Accounting Principles), the Customer Center may also be referred to as the Accounts Receivable Ledger. QuickBooks Desktop does not use this term; however, the Customer Center does function as the Accounts Receivable Subsidiary Ledger. A transaction entry for an individual customer is posted to the customer's account in the Customer Center just as it would be posted to the customer's individual account in an Accounts Receivable Ledger.

The balance of the Customer & Jobs List in the Customer Center will be equal to the balance of the Accounts Receivable account in the Chart of Accounts. The Chart of Accounts would be referred to as the General Ledger when using GAAP standards. Invoices and accounts receivable transactions can also be related to specific jobs you are completing for customers.

You will be using the following Customers & Jobs List in the Customer Center for established credit customers.

Customers & Jobs	Transactions	
Active Customers ▼		>
🔍		
NAME	BALANCE TO...	ATTACH
◦ Ahmad Imports	300.00	
◦ Allen, Elaine	0.00	
◦ Baker and Martinez	0.00	
◦ Brooks, Stark, and Thompson	3,685.00	
◦ Chiang, Young, and Lee	1,915.00	
◦ Clark, Hill, and Scott	0.00	
◦ Collins & Day, CPA	0.00	
◦ Distinctive Creations	3,230.00	
◦ Garcia, Juan Esq.	150.00	
◦ Innovative Products	1,295.00	
◦ Johnson, Leavitt, and Moraga	3,680.00	
◦ McBride, Matt CPA	475.00	
◦ Morris, Ray CPA	0.00	
◦ Research Corp.	815.00	
◦ Taylor Illustrations	3,830.00	
◦ Wagner Productions	3,190.00	

Note: When you display the Customers & Jobs list in the Customer Center, customer names may not be displayed in full. The lists shown in the text have been formatted to show the names in full.

Sales are often made up of various types of income. In Your Name's Tech Services, there are several income accounts. To classify income based on the type of sale, the sales account may have subaccounts. When recording a transaction for a sale, QuickBooks Desktop requires that a Sales Item be used. When the sales item is created, a sales account is required. When the sales item is used in a transaction, the income is credited to the appropriate sales/income account. For example, Training 1 is a sales item and uses the account Training Income, a subaccount of Sales, when a transaction is recorded.

In addition, there are categories within an income account. For example, Your Name's Tech Services uses Training Income to represent revenues earned by providing on-site training. The sales items used for Training Income are Training 1 for the first or initial hour of on-site training and Training 2 for all additional hours of on-site training. As you look at the Item List, you will observe that the rates for the two items are different. Using lists for sales items allows for flexibility in billing and a more accurate representation of the way in which income is earned. The following Item List for the various types of sales will be used for the company.

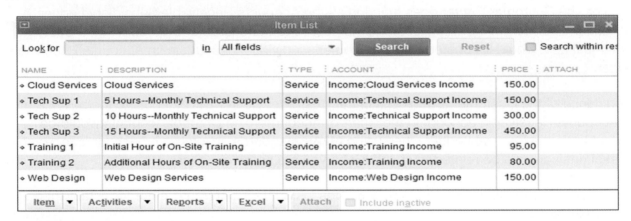

In the tutorial all transactions are listed in memos. Unless otherwise specified within the transaction, the transaction date will be the same date as the memo date. Always enter the date of the transaction as specified in the memo. By default, QuickBooks Desktop automatically enters the current date of the computer or the last transaction date used. In many instances, this will not be the same date as the transaction in the text. Customer names, when necessary, will be given in the transaction. All terms for customers on account are Net 30 days unless specified otherwise. If a memo contains more than one transaction, there will be a visual separation between transactions.

MEMO

DATE: Transaction date is listed here

Transaction details are given in the body of the memo. Customer names, the type of transaction, amounts of money, and any other details needed are listed here.

Even when you are given instructions on how to enter a transaction step by step, you should always refer to the memo for transaction details. Once a specific type of transaction has been entered in a step-by-step manner, additional transactions will be made without having instructions provided. Of course, you may always refer to instructions given for previous transactions for ideas or for the steps used to enter those transactions. Again, always double-check the date and the year used for the transaction. QuickBooks Desktop automatically inserts the computer's current date, which will be different from the date in the text. Using an incorrect date will cause reports to have different totals and show transactions that are different from those shown in the text.

ENTER SALE ON ACCOUNT

Because QuickBooks Desktop operates on a business form premise, a sale on account is entered via an invoice. You prepare an invoice, and QuickBooks Desktop records the transaction in the Journal and automatically posts it to the customer's account in the Customer Center.

MEMO

DATE: January 2, 2018

Invoice 1: Juan Garcia has many questions regarding his new computer system. He spoke with you about this and signed up for 10 hours of technical support (Tech Sup 2) for January. Bill him for this and use Thank you for your business. as the message.

 Record the sale on account shown in the memo above.

Click the **Create Invoices** icon on the Home Page
- A blank invoice will show on the screen.

Click the drop-down list arrow next to **CUSTOMER:JOB**

Click **Garcia, Juan Esq.**

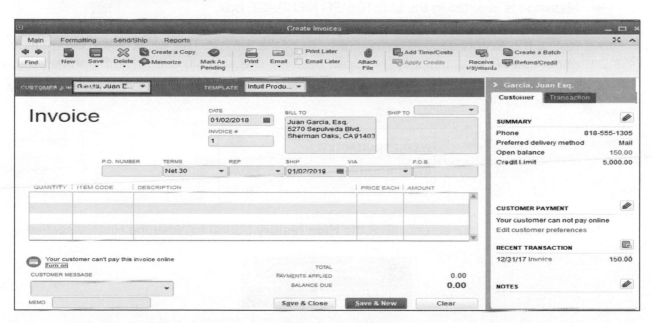

- His name is entered as CUSTOMER:JOB, and Bill To information is completed automatically.

Click the drop-down list arrow for **TEMPLATE**, click **Intuit Service Invoice**
- Intuit Service Invoice is the appropriate invoice to use for this company since only services are sales items. Always check the template. QuickBooks Desktop likes to use the Product Invoice and will frequently revert to it rather than use the Service Invoice.

Press the **Tab** to tab to and highlight the date in the **DATE** field

Type **01/02/18** as the date

- This should replace the date shown in the field. If you did not tab to the date, drag through the date to highlight and then type 01/02/18.

Invoice 1 should be showing in the **INVOICE #.** box

- The INVOICE #. should not have to be changed.

There is no PO No. (Purchase Order Number) to record

TERMS should be indicated as **Net 30**

- If not, click the drop-down list arrow next to **TERMS** and click **Net 30**.

Tab to or click in the first line beneath **ITEM**

Click the drop-down list arrow that appears in the first line

- Refer to the memo above and the Item List for appropriate billing information.

Click **Tech Sup 2** to bill for 10 hours of technical support

- Tech Sup 2 is entered as the Item.

Tab to or click **QUANTITY**

Type **1**

- The quantity is one because you are billing for 1 unit of Tech Sup 2. As you can see in the description, Tech Sup 2 is for 10 hours of support. The total for the item and for the invoice is automatically calculated when you tab to the next item or click in a new invoice area. If you forget to tell QuickBooks Desktop to use a quantity, it will automatically calculate the quantity as 1.

Click in the text box for **CUSTOMER MESSAGE**

Click the drop-down list arrow next to **CUSTOMER MESSAGE**

Click **Thank you for your business.**

- Message is inserted in the CUSTOMER MESSAGE box.

Click the **Save** icon on the Main Invoice Icon Bar at the top of the invoice

- Notice the History section on the right side of the invoice. This will give you information about Juan Garcia. Including his Open balance, Credit Limit, and Recent Transactions.

In the Recent Transaction section, you will see 01/02/18 Invoice of 300.00 and the 12/31/17 Invoice for 150.00

RECENT TRANSACTION	
01/02/18 Invoice	300.00
12/31/17 Invoice	150.00

To save space on your screen, click the **Hide history** button to close the History section

- You may wish to resize the invoice to make it smaller, if so, point to the right side of the invoice, when you get a double arrow ⟷ , hold down the primary mouse button and drag to the left until the invoice is the size you want.
- If the Invoice is maximized, you will not be able to use the sizing handle (double-arrow) to resize the form. If that is the case, click the **Restore** button; and then resize as instructed above.

If you wish to view the history later, simply click the Show History button

View the completed invoice:

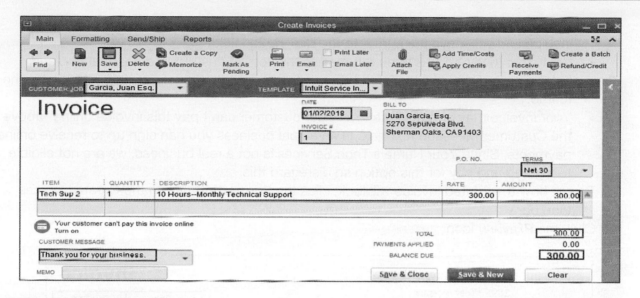

EDIT AND CORRECT ERRORS

If an error is discovered while entering invoice information, it may be corrected by positioning the cursor in the field containing the error. You may return to the field with the error by clicking in the field, tabbing to move forward through each field, or pressing Shift+Tab to move back to the field. If the error is highlighted, type the correction. If the error is not highlighted, you can correct the error by pressing the backspace or the delete key as many times as necessary to remove the error, and then typing the correction. (Alternate method: Point to the error, highlight by dragging the mouse through the error, then type the correction or press the Delete key to remove completely.)

 Practice editing and making corrections to Invoice 1

Click the drop-down list arrow next to **CUSTOMER:JOB**
Click **McBride, Matt CPA**
- Name is changed for CUSTOMER:JOB and BILL TO information.
Click to the left of the first number in the **DATE**—this is **0**
Hold down primary mouse button and drag through the date to highlight.
Type **10/24/18** as the date
- This removes the 01/02/2018 date originally entered.
Click to the right of the **1** in **QUANTITY**
Backspace and type a **2**
Press **Tab** to see how QuickBooks Desktop automatically calculates the new total
To eliminate the changes made to Invoice 1, click the drop-down list arrow next to
    Customer:Job
Click **Garcia, Juan, Esq.**
Tab to the **DATE** text box to highlight the date
Type **01/02/18**
Click to the right of the **2** in **QUANTITY**
Backspace and type a **1**
Press the **Tab** key

- This will cause QuickBooks Desktop to calculate the amount and the total for the invoice and will move the cursor to the Description field.
- Verify that Invoice 1 has been returned to the correct customer, date, quantity, and balance due. Compare the information you entered with the information provided in the memo.
- Your invoice may or may not show "Your customer can't pay this invoice online" above the Customer Message text box. In an actual business you can sign up to receive online payments. Since Your Name's Tech Services is not a real business, we are not eligible to sign up and pay for this option so disregard this.

To see how the printed invoice will look, click the **Formatting** tab on the Create Invoices Icon bar

Click the **Preview** icon

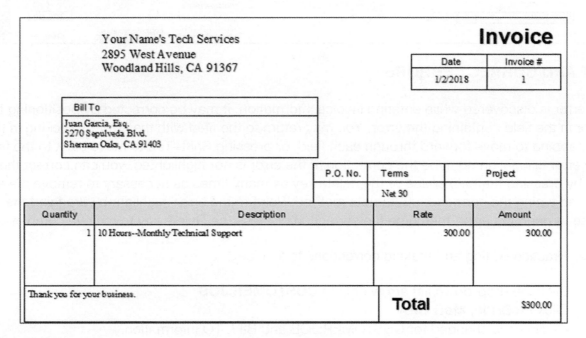

- Notice that the column for ITEM (Tech Sup 2) does not show.
- The ITEM column does not appear on a printed Service Invoice.

Click the **Close** button on the Preview to return to Invoice 1

PRINT INVOICE

 With Invoice 1 on the screen, print the invoice immediately after entering information

Click the **Main** tab on the Create Invoices Icon bar
- This will save the invoice.
- Because your computer date will not be for January 2018, you will see that invoices are marked Past Due once they are saved. Past Due is not shown in the screen shots in the text.

Click the **Print** icon (looks like a printer) on the Main icon bar for Create Invoices
- If you click the drop-down list arrow for the Print button, you will get a list of printing options. Click the **Invoice** option.

Because you made changes to the original Invoice 1, click **Yes** on the Recording Transaction message box

Check the information on the **Print One Invoice Settings** tab:

Printer name: (should identify the type of printer you are using)

- This may be different from the printer identified in this text.

Printer type: Page-oriented (Single sheets)

Print on: Blank paper

- The circle (radio button) next to this should be filled. If it is not, click the circle to select.

Click **Do not print lines around each field** to insert a check mark in the check box

- If a check is not in the box, lines will print around each field.
- If there is a check in the box, lines will <u>not</u> print around each field.

Number of copies: should be 1

- If a number other than 1 shows: click in the box, drag to highlight the number, and then type **1**.

Collate may or may not show a check mark

- Since the invoice is only one-page in length, you will not be using the collate feature.

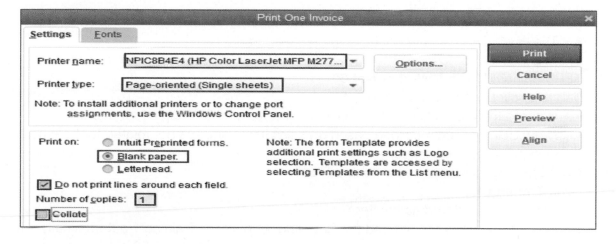

Click the **Print** button

- This initiates the printing of the invoice through QuickBooks Desktop. However, because not all classroom configurations are the same, check with your instructor for specific printing instructions.
- If QuickBooks Desktop prints your name on two lines, do not be concerned. This will be changed later.
- If you print to a pdf file, save the document as **1-Your Name Inv 1 Garcia Ch2**. (Use your real name. Note that the document name suggested will be different from the Chapter Checklist. For this document the checklist will show 1-Inv 1 Garcia.)

Click the **Save & New** button to save Invoice 1 and go to a new invoice

ENTER TRANSACTION WITH TWO SALES ITEMS

MEMO
DATE: January 3, 2018

Invoice 2: Matt McBride, CPA, spoke with you regarding the need for on-site training to help him get started using the Internet. Bill him for a 5-hour on-site training session with Emily Edwards. Use <u>Thank you for your business.</u> as the message. (Remember to use Training 1 for the first hour of on-site training and Training 2 for the four additional hours of training.)

 Record a transaction on account for a sale involving two sales items

On Invoice 2, click the drop-down list arrow next to **CUSTOMER:JOB**
Click **McBride, Matt, CPA**
- Name is entered as CUSTOMER:JOB. BILL TO information is completed automatically.
- Make sure that <u>Intuit Service Invoice</u> is shown as the TEMPLATE; if not, click the drop-down list arrow and select it.

Tab to or click **DATE**
Delete the date
- Refer to instructions for Invoice 1 editing practice if necessary.

Type **01/03/18** as the date
Make sure that **2** is showing in the **INVOICE #** text box
- The INVOICE #. should not have to be changed.

There is no PO No. to record
TERMS should be indicated as **Net 30**
Tab to or click the first line beneath **ITEM**
- Refer to the Memo and to the Item List for appropriate billing information.
- *Note:* Services are recorded based on sales items and are not related to the employee who provides the service.

Click the drop-down list arrow next to **ITEM**
Click **Training 1**
- Training 1 is entered as the Item.
- QuickBooks Desktop entered the Rate and Amount for Training 1 automatically. This is based on an assumed quantity of 1. Notice the amount of $95.00.

Tab to or click **QUANTITY**
Type **1**
- Even though QuickBooks Desktop always assumes a quantity of 1, it is wise to enter the quantity as 1. This proves that you did record the correct quantity. This can be helpful when preparing reports and other documents.

Tab to or click the second line for **ITEM**
Click the drop-down list arrow next to **ITEM**
Click **Training 2**
Tab to or click **QUANTITY**
Type **4**, press **Tab**
- The total amount of training time is five hours. Because the first hour is billed as Training 1, the remaining four hours are billed as Training 2 hours.
- The total amount due for the Training 2 hours and the total for the invoice were automatically calculated when you pressed the Tab key.

Click **CUSTOMER MESSAGE**
Click the drop-down list arrow next to **CUSTOMER MESSAGE**
Click **Thank you for your business.**
- Message is inserted in the CUSTOMER MESSAGE box.

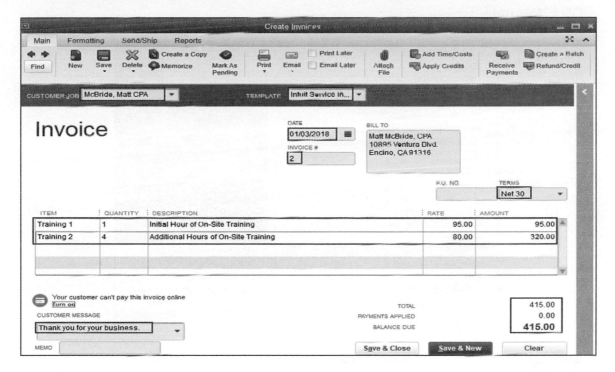

PRINT INVOICE

 With Invoice 2 on the screen, print the invoice immediately after entering invoice information

Click the **Print** button on the **Create Invoices** screen
- If you click the drop-down list arrow for the Print button, you will get a list of printing options. Click the **Invoice** option.
Check the information on the **Print One Invoice Settings** tab:
   Printer name: (should identify the type of printer you are using)
Printer type: Page-oriented (Single sheets)
Print on: Blank paper
Do not print lines around each field: check box should have a check mark
Click the **Print** button
- If you print to a pdf file, save the document as **2-Your Name Inv 2 McBride Ch2**.
After the invoice has printed, click the **Save & Close** button at the bottom of the **Create Invoices** screen to record Invoice 2 and exit Create Invoices

ANALYZE TRANSACTIONS IN THE JOURNAL REPORT

Whenever a transaction is recorded on an invoice or any other business form, QuickBooks Desktop enters the transactions into the Journal in the traditional Debit/Credit format.

View the Journal report and verify the transaction entries

    Click **Reports** on the Menu bar
    Point to **Accountant & Taxes**
    Click **Journal**

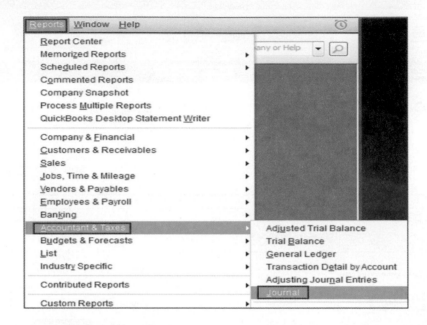

    Click **OK** on the Collapsing and Expanding Transactions dialog box

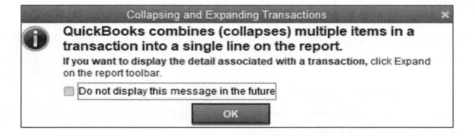

- Reports may be prepared for a range of dates by clicking the drop-down list arrow for Dates. Choices will include All, Today, This Week, This Week-to-date, This Month, This Month-to-date, This Fiscal Quarter, This Fiscal Quarter-to-date, This Fiscal Year, This Fiscal Year-to-last month, This Fiscal Year-to-date, Yesterday, Last Week, Last Week-to-date, Last Month, Last Month-to-date, Last Fiscal Quarter, Last Fiscal Quarter-to-date, Last Fiscal Year, Last Fiscal Year-to-date, Next Week, Next 4 Weeks, Next Month, Next Fiscal Quarter, Next Fiscal Year, and Custom.

To prepare a report for specific dates, tab to the **From** text box
Enter the date **01/01/18**
Tab to the **To** text box
Enter the date **01/03/18**
Press Tab twice to generate the report

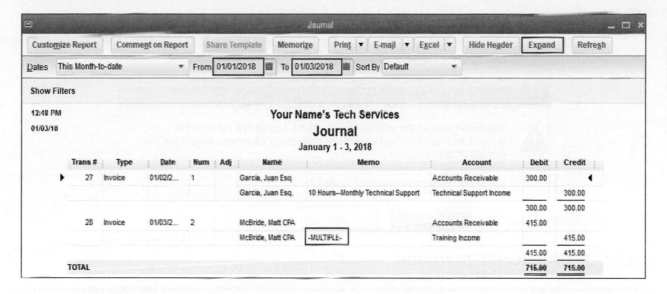

- Your report may not have account names, memos, or other items shown in full. Each example in the text, will have all items displayed in full when possible. You will learn how to do this later in the chapter.
- Notice the word –MULTIPLE- in the Memo section for Invoice 2. This appears because the report is in the collapsed format and has more than one sales item.
Click the **Expand** button at the top of the screen to show all the entries
- The Memo column shows the item description for each sales item used.

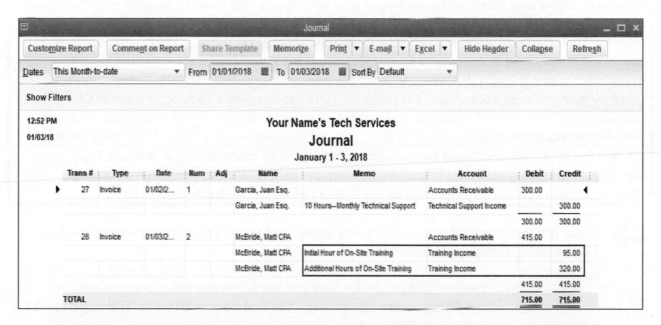

- Notice the debit to Accounts Receivable for both Invoice 1 and 2.
- The credit for each invoice is to an income account. The income accounts are different for each invoice because the sales items are different. Technical Support Income is the account used when any Tech Sup sales item is used. Training Income is the account used when any Training sales item is used.
- In the upper-left corner of the report is the date and time the report was prepared. Your date and time will be the actual date and time of your computer. It will not match the illustration.

Click the **Close** button to close the report
- Make sure you click the Close button for the report and not for QuickBooks Desktop.
- If you get a Memorize Report dialog box, click **No**.

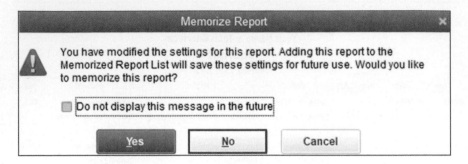

PREPARE ADDITIONAL INVOICES

> ### MEMO
> **DATE**: January 5, 2018
>
> Invoice 3: Elaine Allen needed to have telephone assistance to help her set up her Internet connection. Prepare an invoice as the bill for 10 hours of technical support for January. (Remember customers are listed by last name in the Customers & Jobs List. Refer to Item List to select the correct item for billing.)
>
> Invoice 4: Baker and Martinez have several new employees that need to be trained in the use of the office computer system. Bill them for 40 hours of on-site training from Emily Edwards. (Your Name's Tech Services does not record a transaction based on the employee who performs the service. It simply bills according to the service provided.)
>
> Invoice 5: Collins & Day, CPA, need to learn the basic features of QuickBooks Desktop, which is used by many of their customers. Bill them for 10 hours of on-site training, 1 hour of Cloud Services, and 10 hours of technical support for January so they may call and speak to Jacob Katz regarding additional questions. (Note: You will use four sales items in this transaction.)
>
> Invoice 6: Clark, Hill, and Scott have a new assistant office manager. Your Name's Tech Services is providing 40 hours of on-site training for Beverly Wilson. To obtain additional assistance, the company has signed up for 5 hours technical support for January.

 Enter the four transactions in the memo above. Refer to instructions given for the two previous transactions entered

- Always check the Template to make sure you are using the Intuit Service Invoice.
- Remember, when billing for on-site training, the first hour is billed as Training 1, and the remaining hours are billed as Training 2.
- If you forget to enter the quantity, QuickBooks Desktop calculates the amount based on a quantity of 1.
- Always use the Item List to determine the appropriate sales items for billing.
- Use **Thank you for your business.** as the message for these invoices.
- If you make an error, correct it.
- Print each invoice immediately after you enter the information for it.

- If you print to a pdf file, save the documents as **3-Your Name Inv 3 Allen Ch2,** **4-Your Name Inv 4 Baker and Martinez Ch2, 5-Your Name Inv 5 Collins & Day Ch2,** and **6-Your Name Inv 6 Clark, Hill, and Scott Ch2.**
- To go from one invoice to the next, click the **Save & New** button.
- Click **Save & Close** after Invoice 6 has been entered and printed.

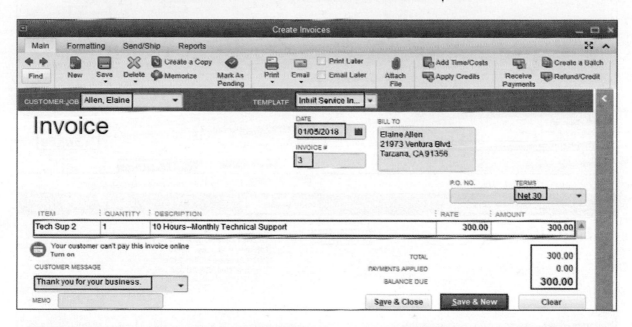

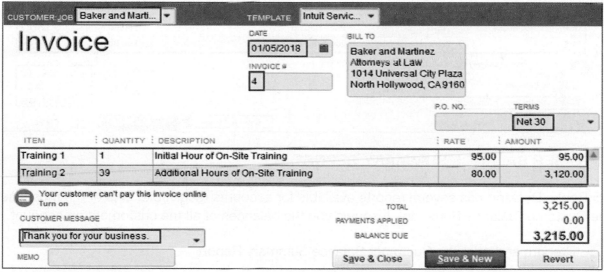

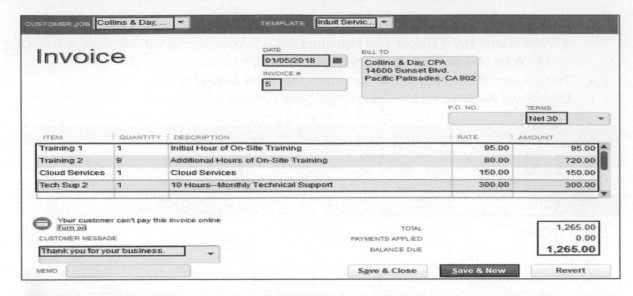

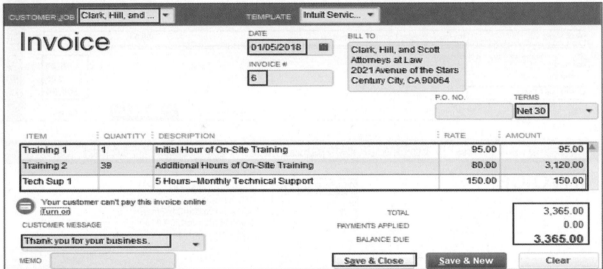

CUSTOMER BALANCE SUMMARY REPORT

QuickBooks Desktop has several reports available for accounts receivable. One of the most useful is the Customer Balance Summary. It shows you the balances of all the customers on account.

 Prepare and print the Customer Balance Summary Report

Click **Reports** on the menu bar
Point to **Customers & Receivables**
Click **Customer Balance Summary**
- The report should appear on the screen.
- The current date and time will appear on the report. Since the dates given in the text will not be the same date as the computer, it may be helpful to remove the date and time prepared from your report.
Remove the date prepared and the time prepared from the report:
Click **Customize Report**
Click the **Header/Footer** tab

Click the check box next to **Date Prepared** to deselect this option

Click the check box next to **Time Prepared** to deselect this option

- *Note:* Some reports will also have a Report Basis—Cash or Accrual. You may turn off the display of the report basis by clicking the check box for this option.
- Check with your instructor to see if you should turn off the Date and Time Prepared.
- To avoid confusion, all reports will <u>not</u> have the Date Prepared, Time Prepared or Report Basis on the screen.

Click **OK** on the **Modify Report** screen

- The Date Prepared and Time Prepared are no longer displayed on the report.
- The modification of the header is only applicable to this report. The next time a report is prepared, the header must once again be modified to deselect the Date Prepared and Time Prepared.

Change the Dates for the report:

Click in or tab to **From**, enter **01/01/18**

Tab to **To**, Enter **01/05/18**

Press the Tab key

- After you enter the date, pressing the tab key will generate the report.
- This report lists the names of all customers with balances on account. The amount column shows the total balance for each customer. This includes opening balances as well as current invoices.

Your Name's Tech Services **Customer Balance Summary** As of January 5, 2018	Jan 5, 18
Ahmad Imports	300.00
Allen, Elaine	300.00
Baker and Martinez	3,215.00
Brooks, Stark, and Thompson	3,685.00
Chiang, Young, and Lee	1,915.00
Clark, Hill, and Scott	3,365.00
Collins & Day, CPA	1,265.00
Distinctive Creations	3,230.00
Garcia, Juan Esq.	450.00
Innovative Products	1,295.00
Johnson, Leavitt, and Moraga	3,680.00
McBride, Matt CPA	890.00
Research Corp.	815.00
Taylor Illustrations	3,830.00
Wagner Productions	3,190.00
TOTAL	**31,425.00**

Click the **Print** button at the top of the Customer Balance Summary Report

To select between printing a Report or Save as PDF, click **Report**

Complete the information on the **Print Reports Settings** tab:

Printer To: **Printer**: (should identify the type of printer you are using)

- This may be different from the printer identified in this text.

Orientation: Should be Portrait. If it is not, click **Portrait** to select Portrait orientation for this report

- Portrait orientation prints in the traditional 8 ½- by 11-inch paper size.

Page Range: **All** should be selected; if it is not, click **All**

Make sure **Page Breaks**: **Smart page breaks (widow/orphan control)** is selected; if not, click to select

Number of copies: should be **1**

Collate is not necessary on a one-page report, it may be left with or without the check mark

If necessary, click on **Fit report to 1 page(s) wide** to deselect this item

If necessary, click on **Fit report to 1 page(s) High** to deselect this item

- When selected, the printer will print the report using a smaller font, so it will be one page in width or one-page high.

Leave **Print in color** without a check mark

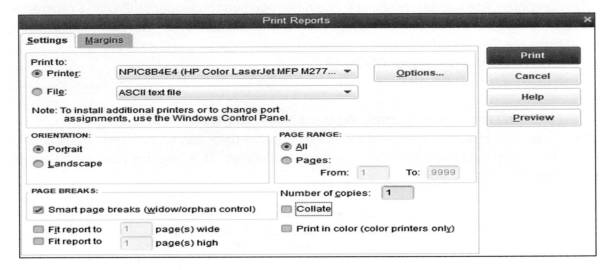

Click **Print** on the **Print Reports** screen

- If you print to a pdf file, save the document as **7-Your Name Cust Bal Sum Ch2**.

Do not close the **Customer Balance Summary Report**

QUICKZOOM

You ask the office manager, Sofia Sanchez, to obtain information regarding the balance of the Baker and Martinez account. To get detailed information regarding an individual customer's balance while in the Customer Balance Summary Report, use the QuickZoom feature. With the individual customer's information on the screen, you can print a report for that customer.

 Use QuickZoom

Point to the balance for **Baker and Martinez**

- Notice that the mouse pointer turns into a magnifying glass with a **Z** in it.

Click once to mark the balance **3,215.00**

- Notice the marks on either side of the amount.

Double-click to **Zoom** in to see the details

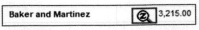

The report dates used should be from **01/01/18** to **01/05/18**

Remove the Date Prepared and Time Prepared from the header

- Follow the instructions previously listed for removing the date and time prepared from the header for the Customer Balance Summary Report.

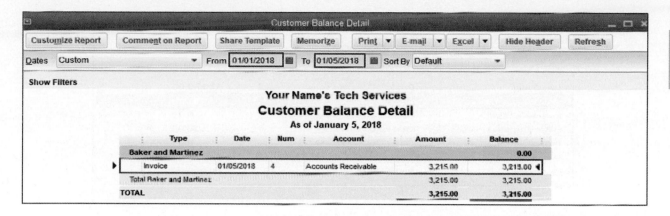

- Notice that Invoice 4 was recorded on 01/05/2018 for $3,215.00.
- To view Invoice 4, simply double-click on this transaction, and the invoice will be shown on the screen.

To exit Invoice 4 and return to the Customer Balance Detail Report, click the **Close** button on the title bar of the **Create Invoices** screen for Invoice 4

Print the **Customer Balance Detail Report** for Baker and Martinez

- Follow the steps previously listed for printing the Customer Balance Summary Report.
- If you print to a pdf file, save the document as **8-Your Name Cust Bal Detail Ch2**.

Click **Close** to close **Customer Balance Detail Report**

- If you get a screen for Memorize Report, always click **No**.

Click **Close** to close **Customer Balance Summary Report**

- If you get a screen for Memorize Report, always click **No**.

CORRECT AND PRINT INVOICE

Errors may be corrected very easily with QuickBooks Desktop. Because an invoice is prepared for sales on account, corrections may be made directly on the invoice or in the Accounts Receivable account register. We will access the invoice via the register for the Accounts Receivable account. The account register contains detailed information regarding each transaction that used the account. Therefore, anytime an invoice is recorded, it is posted to the Accounts Receivable register.

MEMO

DATE: January 7, 2018

The actual amount of time spent for on-site training at Collins & Day, CPA increased from 10 hours to 12 hours. Change Invoice 5 to correct the actual amount of training hours to show a total of 12 hours.

 Correct an error in Invoice 5 using the Accounts Receivable Register and print the corrected invoice

Click the **Chart of Accounts** icon in the Company Section of the Home Page
In the Chart of Accounts, click **Accounts Receivable**

Chart of Accounts

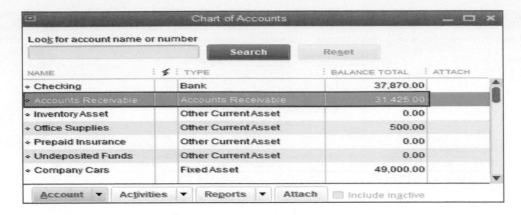

Click the **Activities** button and click **Use Register**

> **OR**

Double-click **Accounts Receivable** in the Chart of Accounts

- The Accounts Receivable Register appears on the screen with information regarding each transaction entered in the account.
- *Note:* This is the same as the Accounts Receivable General Ledger Account.

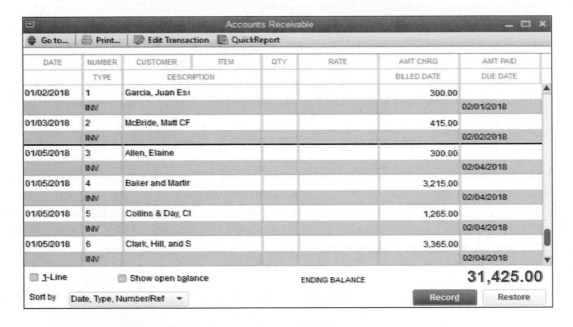

- Look at the **NUMBER/TYPE** column to identify the number of the invoice and the type of transaction.
- When the NUMBER line shows an invoice number, the TYPE line will show INV.
- If the NUMBER line shows a check number, the TYPE line will show PMT. This indicates that a payment on account was received.

If necessary, scroll through the register until the transaction for **Invoice 5** is on the screen

- When scrolling through the register, you may see some opening balances that are dated 12/31/2017. These amounts are balances from the previous year.

Click anywhere in the transaction for **Invoice 5** to Collins & Day, CPA

Click **Edit Transaction** at the top of the register   ![Edit Transaction]

- Invoice 5 appears on the screen.

Click the line in the **QUANTITY** field that corresponds to the **Training 2** hours

Change the quantity from 9 hours to 11 hours

Position cursor in front of the 9
Press **Delete**
Type **11**
Press **Tab** to generate a new total

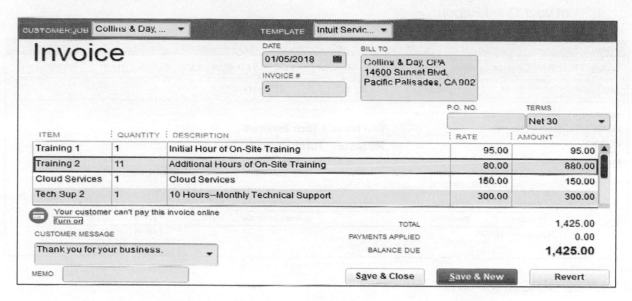

- Notice that the date remains 01/05/2018.

Click the **Print** button on the **Create Invoices** screen to print a corrected invoice

If you get the Recording Transaction dialog box at this point, click **Yes**

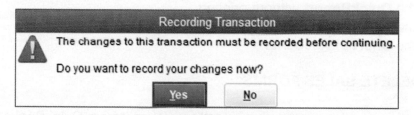

Check the information on the **Print One Invoice Settings** tab
Click **Print**

- If you print to a pdf file, save the document as **9-Your Name Inv 5 Collins & Day Corrected Ch2**.

Click **Save & Close** to record changes and close invoice

- If you did not get the Recording Transaction dialog box before printing and you see it now, click **Yes**.

After closing the invoice, you return to the register

VIEW QUICKREPORT

After editing the invoice and returning to the register, you may get a detailed report regarding a customer's transactions by clicking the QuickReport button.

View a QuickReport for Collins & Day, CPA

Make sure that your cursor is on one of the lines for Invoice 5

Click the **QuickReport** button at the top of the Register to view the **Cooper & Cranston** account

Verify the balance of the account. It should be **$1,425.00**

* *Note:* You will get the date prepared, time prepared, and the report basis in the heading of your QuickReport.

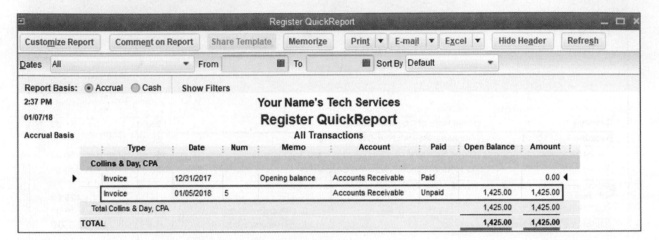

ANALYZE QUICKREPORT

 Analyze the QuickReport for Collins & Day, CPA

Notice that the total of Invoice 5 is $1,425.00
Close the **QuickReport** without printing
Close the **Accounts Receivable Register**
Close the **Chart of Accounts**

VOID AND DELETE SALES FORMS

Deleting an invoice or sales receipt permanently removes it from QuickBooks Desktop without leaving a trace. If you would like to correct your financial records for the invoice that you no longer want, it is more appropriate to void the invoice. When an invoice is voided, it remains in the QuickBooks Desktop system with a zero balance. QuickBooks Desktop allows you to void or delete transactions in batches. You may do this instead of voiding or deleting individual transactions this will be explored in more detail in Chapter 5.

VOID INVOICE

When an invoice is voided, it will still be in the company records and the balance will be zero.

MEMO

DATE: January 7, 2018

Elaine Allen called to cancel the 10 hours of technical support for January. Since none of the technical support had been used, you decide to void Invoice 3.

Void Invoice 3 by going directly to the original invoice
Use the keyboard shortcut **Ctrl+I** to open the Create Invoices screen
- Remember I stands for Invoice.

Click the **Previous** or **Back** arrow on the Invoice icon bar ◄ until you get to **Invoice 3**
With Invoice 3 on the screen, click **Edit** on the QuickBooks Desktop Menu bar below the title bar
Click **Void Invoice**

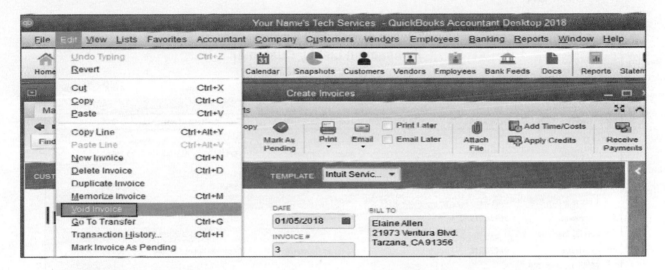

- Notice that the amount and total for the invoice are no longer 300. They are both **0.00**.
- Find the Memo text box at the bottom of the invoice and verify that **VOID:** appears as the memo.

Click **Save & Close** on the **Create Invoices** screen
Click **Yes** on the **Recording Transaction** dialog box
Click the **Reports** button on the Icon bar
Click **Customers & Receivables** as the Type of Report
- The report categories are displayed on the left side of the Report Center. To prepare a report, click the desired type of report.

Click the **List View** button to select the report list
- Remember there are three ways to view a report list—Carousel, List, and Grid.

After selecting List view, scroll through the list of reports, and click **Transaction List by Customer** in the Customer Balance section
Click the **Run** button

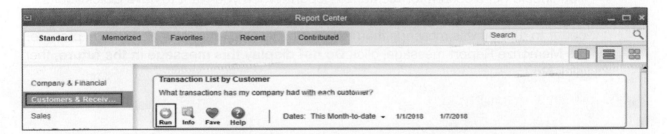

Tab to or Click in **From**
Remove the current date; if it is not highlighted, and enter **010118**
- Using a **/** between the items in a date is optional.

Tab to or click in **To**

Remove the current date; if it is not highlighted, and enter **010718**, press **Tab**

Remove the date prepared and the time prepared from the report heading:

Click **Customize Report**

Click **Header/Footer** tab

Click the check box next to **Date Prepared** and **Time Prepared** to deselect these options

Click **OK**

Your Name's Tech Services
Transaction List by Customer
January 1 - 7, 2018

Type	Date	Num	Memo	Account	Clr	Split	Debit	Credit
Allen, Elaine								
Invoice	01/05/2018	3	VOID:	Accounts Receivable	✓	Technical Support Income	0.00	◀
Baker and Martinez								
Invoice	01/05/2018	4		Accounts Receivable		-SPLIT-	3,215.00	
Clark, Hill, and Scott								
Invoice	01/05/2018	6		Accounts Receivable		-SPLIT-	3,365.00	
Collins & Day, CPA								
Invoice	01/05/2018	5		Accounts Receivable		-SPLIT-	1,425.00	
Garcia, Juan Esq.								
Invoice	01/02/2018	1		Accounts Receivable		Technical Support Income	300.00	
McBride, Matt CPA								
Invoice	01/03/2018	2		Accounts Receivable		-SPLIT-	415.00	

- This report gives the amount for each transaction with the customer.
- Notice that Invoice 3 is marked VOID in the Memo column and has a √ in the **Clr** (Cleared) column.
- The SPLIT column tells you which account was used to record the income. If the word **-SPLIT-** appears in the column, this means the transaction amount was split or divided among two or more sales items.

Print the **Transactions List by Customer Report** in Landscape orientation following printing instructions provided earlier in the chapter

Click **Landscape** to use Landscape Orientation (11 wide by 8 ½ long)

- Do not use the option to fit the report to one-page wide.
- If you print to a pdf file, save the document as **10-Your Name Trans List by Cust Ch2**.

Close the **Transaction List by Customer Report**

- You should get a screen for Memorize Report. When you want to have QuickBooks Desktop memorize a report, there are several ways to tell it to do so. At this point, it is better to turn off this message than to have to click No after every report you prepare.

On the Memorize Report message, click **Do not display this message in the future**, then click **No**

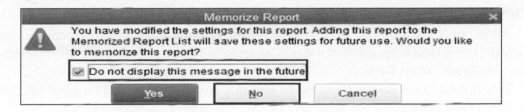

Close the **Report Center**

USE FIND

When an invoice is deleted, it is permanently removed from QuickBooks Desktop. It will no longer be listed in any reports or shown as an Invoice.

Find is useful when you have a large number of invoices and want to locate an invoice for a particular customer. Using Find will locate the invoice without requiring you to scroll through all the invoices for the company. For example, if customer Jimenez's transaction was on Invoice 3 and the invoice on the screen was Invoice 1,084, you would not have to scroll through 1,081 invoices because Find would locate Invoice 3 instantly. QuickBooks Desktop has two methods for finding transactions: Simple Find and Advanced Find.

Simple Find allows you to do a quick search using the most common transaction types. Transaction Types include Invoice, Estimate, Sales Receipt, Credit Memo, Bill, Check, Credit Card, Purchase Order, Sales Order, and Journal. The search results are displayed in the lower portion of the window. You can view an individual transaction by highlighting it and clicking Go To, you can view a Find Report on the search results by clicking Report, and you can click Export to the export the Find results to Excel.

Advanced Find is used to do a more detailed search for transactions than you can do using Simple Find. Advanced Find allows you to apply filters to your search criteria. When you apply a filter, you choose how you want QuickBooks Desktop to restrict the search results to certain customers, for example. QuickBooks Desktop will exclude any transactions that don't meet your criteria. You can apply filters either one at a time or in combination with each other. Each additional filter you apply further restricts the content of the search. The search results are displayed in the lower portion of the window. You can view an individual transaction by highlighting it and clicking Go To, you can view a Find Report on the search results by clicking Report, and you can click Export to export the Find Report to Excel.

MEMO
DATE: January 7, 2018

Because of the upcoming tax season, Matt McBride has had to reschedule his 5-hour training session with Emily Edwards three times. He finally decided to cancel the training session and reschedule it after April 15. Delete Invoice 2.

 Use Find to locate Invoice 2 to Matt McBride,

Use Simple Find by clicking **Edit** on the menu bar, clicking **Find** on the Edit menu, and clicking the **Simple Find** tab

The Transaction Type should be **Invoice**
- If it is not, click the drop-down list arrow for Transaction Type and click Invoice.

Click the drop-down list arrow for **Customer:Job**

Click **McBride, Matt CPA**
- This allows QuickBooks Desktop to find any invoices recorded for Matt McBride.

Click the **Find** button

Click the line for **Invoice 2**
- Make sure you have selected Invoice 2 and not the invoice containing the opening balance.

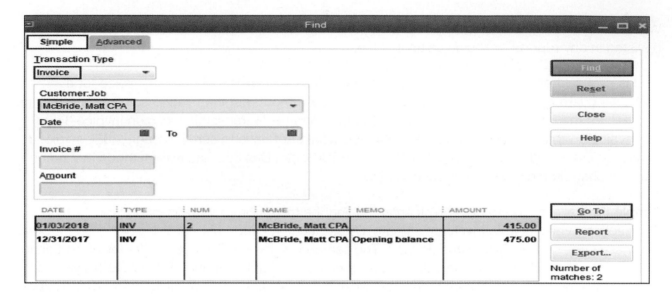

Click the **Go To** button
- Invoice 2 appears on the screen.

DELETE INVOICE

 With the Invoice 2 on the screen, click **Edit** on the QuickBooks Desktop menu bar

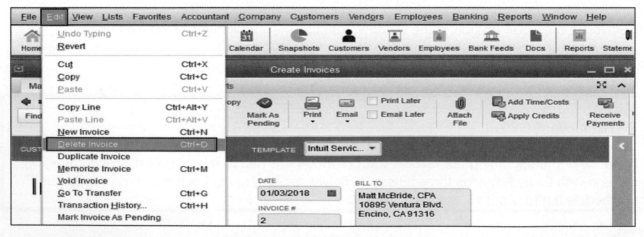

Click **Delete Invoice**

Click **OK** in the **Delete Transaction** dialog box

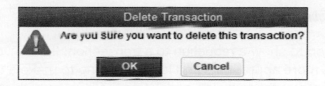

- Notice that the cursor is now positioned on Invoice 3.

Click the **Save & Close** button on the **Create Invoices** screen to close the invoice

- Notice that Invoice 2 no longer shows on **Find**.

Click the **Close** button to close **Find**

Click **Reports** on the menu bar

Point to **Customers & Receivables**

Click **Customer Balance Detail**

Remove the **Date Prepared** and **Time Prepared** from the report header as previously instructed

Dates should be **All**

Print the report in Portrait orientation as previously instructed

- If you print to a pdf file, save the document as **11-Your Name Cust Bal Detail Ch2**.
- To save space, only a partial report is displayed below.

Your Name's Tech Services
Customer Balance Detail
All Transactions

Type	Date	Num	Account	Amount	Balance
McBride, Matt CPA					
Invoice	12/31/2017		Accounts Receivable	475.00	475.00
Total McBride, Matt CPA				475.00	475.00
Research Corp.					
Invoice	12/31/2017		Accounts Receivable	815.00	815.00
Total Research Corp.				815.00	815.00
Taylor Illustrations					
Invoice	12/31/2017		Accounts Receivable	3,830.00	3,830.00
Total Taylor Illustrations				3,830.00	3,830.00
Wagner Productions					
Invoice	12/31/2017		Accounts Receivable	3,190.00	3,190.00
Total Wagner Productions				3,190.00	3,190.00
TOTAL				30,870.00	30,870.00

Partial Report

- Look at the account for Matt McBride. Notice that Invoice 2 does not show up in the account listing. When an invoice is deleted, there is no record of it anywhere in the report.
- Notice that the Customer Balance Detail Report does not include the information telling you which amounts are opening balances.
- The report does give information regarding the amount owed on each transaction plus the total amount owed by each customer.

Click the **Close** button to close the **Customer Balance Detail Report**

PREPARE CREDIT MEMO

Credit memos are prepared to show a reduction to a transaction. If the invoice has already been sent to the customer, it is more appropriate and less confusing to make a change to a transaction by issuing a credit memo rather than voiding or deleting the invoice and issuing a new one. A credit memo notifies a customer that a change has been made to a transaction.

MEMO

DATE: January 8, 2018

Credit Memo 7: Baker and Martinez did not need 5 hours of the training billed on Invoice 4. Issue a Credit Memo to reduce Training 2 by 5 hours.

 Prepare a Credit Memo

Click the **Refunds and Credits** icon in the Customers area of the Home Page
Click the drop-down list arrow next to **CUSTOMER:JOB**
Click **Baker and Martinez**
- Notice that the History for Baker and Martinez is shown on the right side of the invoice.
The **TEMPLATE** text box should say **Custom Credit Memo**
- If not, click the drop-down list arrow and click **Custom Credit Memo**.
Tab to or click **DATE**
Type in the date of the credit memo: **01/08/18**
The **Credit No.** field should show the number **7**
- Because credit memos are included in the numbering sequence for invoices, this number matches the number of the next blank invoice.
There is no PO No.
Tab to or click in **ITEM**
Click the drop-down list arrow in the Item column
Click **Training 2**
Tab to or click in **QTY**
Type in **5**
Click the next blank line in the DESCRIPTION column
Type **Deduct 5 hours of unused training. Reduce the amount due for Invoice 4.**
- This will print as a note or explanation to the customer.
Click the drop-down list arrow next to **CUSTOMER MESSAGE**
Click **It's been a pleasure working with you!**

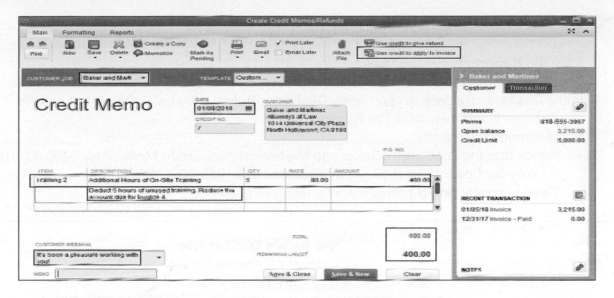

To apply the credit to an invoice, click **Use credit to apply to invoice** on the Create Credit Memos/Refunds Icon bar

> **Use credit to apply to invoice**

- Make sure there is a check mark for Invoice 4 on the Apply Credit to Invoices screen.

Apply Credit to Invoices

CREDIT MEMO

Customer:Job	Baker and Martinez				
Ref. No.	7		Original Amt.		400.00
Date	01/08/2018		Remaining Credit		0.00

✓	DATE	JOB	NUMBER	ORIG. AMT.	AMT. DUE	AMT. APPLIED
✓	01/05/2018		4	3,215.00	3,215.00	400.00
			Totals	3,215.00	0.00	400.00

Clear Selections   Done   Cancel

Click **Done**

- Notice the Recent Transactions section in the History pane. It includes the Credit Memo.

RECENT TRANSACTION	
01/08/18 Credit Memo	400.00
01/05/18 Invoice	3,215.00
12/31/17 Invoice - Paid	0.00

Click the **Print** button on **Create Credit Memos/Refunds**

Click **Print** on the **Print One Credit Memo** screen

- Make sure that there <u>is</u> a check mark for "Do not print lines around each field."
- If you print to a pdf file, save the document as **12-Your Name CM 7 Baker and Martinez Ch2**.

Click the **Save & Close** button

CUSTOMER BALANCE DETAIL REPORT

Periodically viewing reports allows you to verify the changes that have occurred to accounts. Information for customers with an account may be shown on reports prepared from the Customers & Receivables reports. For example, the Customer Balance Detail report shows all the transactions for each credit customer. Cash customers information must be prepared through Sales reports.

View the Customer Balance Detail Report

Click the **Reports** button on the Icon bar

Click **Customers & Receivables** as the report type

In the Customer Balance section, click **Customer Balance Detail** on the list of reports displayed; and then, click the **Run** icon

Scroll through the report

- Notice that the account for Baker and Martinez shows Credit Memo 7 for $400.00. The total amount owed was reduced by $400 and is $2,815.00.
- To save space, only a partial report is displayed below.

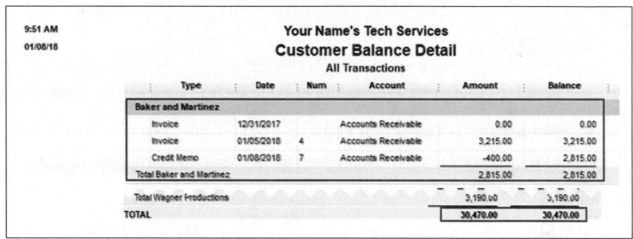

Partial Report

Click the **Close** button to close the report without printing

Close the **Report Center**

ADD NEW ACCOUNT

Because account needs can change as a business is in operation, QuickBooks Desktop allows you to make changes to the chart of accounts at any time. Some changes to the chart of accounts require additional changes to lists.

You have determined that Your Name's Tech Services has received a lot of calls from customers for assistance with hardware and network installation. Even though Your Name's Tech Services does not record revenue according to the employee performing the service, it does assign primary areas of responsibility to some of the personnel. Jacob Katz will be responsible for installing hardware and setting up networks for customers. Because you have created another area of income, you will be adding another income account. It will be used when revenue from hardware or network installation is earned. In addition to adding the account, you will add two new sales items to the Item list that will be used for hardware and network installation.

> **MEMO**
> **DATE**: January 8, 2018
>
> Add a new account, Installation Income. It is a subaccount of Income.

Add a new income account for Hardware and Network Installation

Click the **Chart of Accounts** icon in the Company section of the Home Page
* Remember that the Chart of Accounts is also the General Ledger.
Click the **Account** button at the bottom of the Chart of Accounts screen
Click **New**

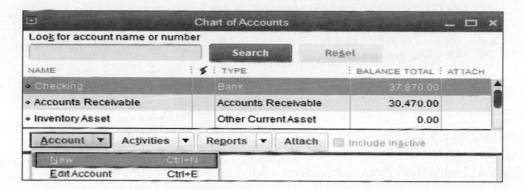

Click **Income** to choose one account type

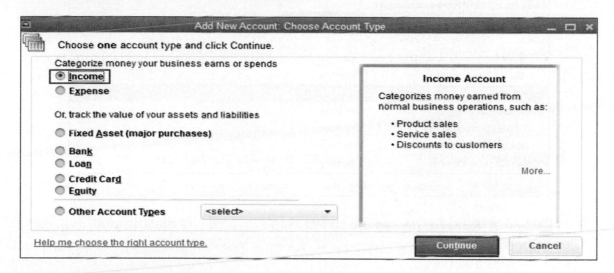

Click the **Continue** button.
If necessary, tab to or click in the text box for **Account Name**
Type **Installation Income**
Click the check box for **Subaccount of**
Click the drop-down list arrow for **Subaccount of**
Click **Income**
Tab to or click **Description**
Type **Hardware and Network Installation Income**

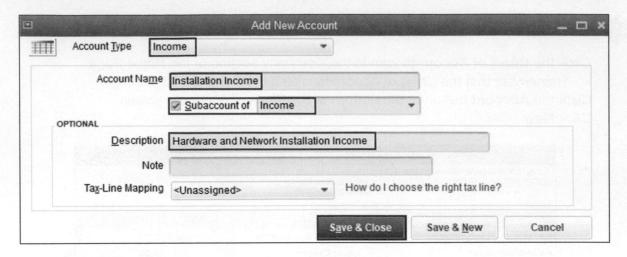

Click the **Save & Close** button

Scroll through the Chart of Accounts

Verify that Installation Income has been added as a subaccount of Income

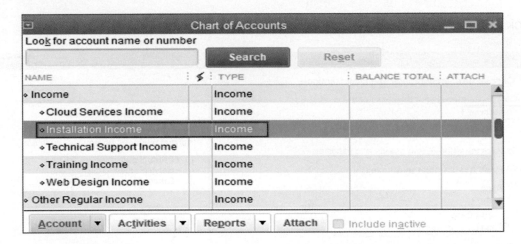

- Notice that the subaccounts are shown below Income and are indented.

Close **Chart of Accounts**

ADD NEW ITEMS

To accommodate the changing needs of a business, all QuickBooks Desktop lists allow you to make changes at any time. The Item List stores information about the services Your Name's Tech Services provides. Items are sometimes called Sales Items because an item is identified when recording a cash or credit sale.

To use the new Installation Income account, two new items need to be added to the Item List. When these items are used in a transaction, the amount of revenue earned in the transaction will be posted to the Installation Income account.

MEMO
DATE: January 8, 2018

Add two Service items to the Item List:

Name: Install 1, Description: Initial Hour of Hardware/Network Installation, Rate: 95.00, Account: Installation Income.
Name: Install 2, Description: Additional Hours of Hardware/Network Installation, Rate: 80.00, Account: Installation Income.

 Add two new items

Click the **Items & Services** icon in the Company section of the Home Page
Click the **Item** button at the bottom of the **Item List** screen
Click **New**
TYPE is **Service**
Tab to or click **Item Name/Number**
Type **Install 1**
Do not enable UNIT OF MEASURE
* UNIT OF MEASURE is used to indicate the quantities used for calculation of prices, rates, and costs. For example, a quantity of 4 for installation could mean four hours, four days, or four weeks. Setting the unit of measure would clarify this.
Tab to or click **Description**
Type **Initial Hour of Hardware/Network Installation**
Tab to or click **Rate**
Type **95**
To indicate the general ledger account to be used to record the sale of this item, click the drop-down list arrow for **Account**
Click **Installation Income**

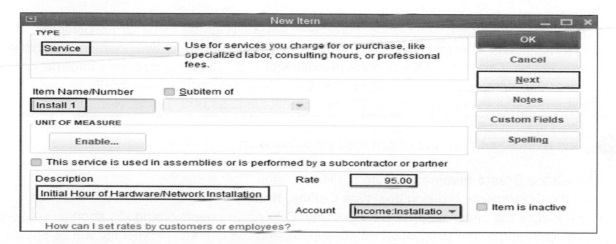

Click **Next** on the New Item dialog box
Repeat the steps above to add **Install 2**
The description is **Additional Hours of Hardware/Network Installation**
The rate is **80.00** per hour
The account is **Installation Income**

When finished adding Install 2, click **OK** to add new items and to close the **New Item** screen

- Whenever hardware or network installation is provided for customers, the first hour will be billed as Install 1, and additional hours will be billed as Install 2.

Verify the addition of Install 1 and Install 2 on the Item List

- If you find an error, click on the item with the error, click the **Item** button, click **Edit**, and make corrections as needed.

Close the **Item List**

ADD NEW CUSTOMER

Because customers are the lifeblood of a business, QuickBooks Desktop allows customers to be added "on the fly" as you create an invoice or a sales receipt. You may choose Quick Add (used to add only a customer's name) or Set Up (used to add complete information for a customer).

MEMO
DATE: January 8, 2018

Invoice 8: A new customer, Ken Collins, purchased several upgrade items for his personal computer. He needs assistance with the installation. Jacob Katz spent two hours installing the hardware. Bill Mr. Collins for 2 hours of hardware installation. Enter his customer information: Address: 20985 Ventura Blvd., Woodland Hills, CA 91371. Telephone: 818-555-2058. Fax: 808-555-8502. E-mail: KCollins@123.com. Credit Limit: $1,000; Terms: Net 30.

 Add a new customer and record the sale on account

Click the **Create Invoices** icon on the Home Page
In the Customer:Job dialog box, type **Collins, Ken**

- Notice the suggestion for Collins & Day, CPA as you begin typing. As soon as you key the comma, the suggestion will disappear, and the entire Customer list will be shown.

Press **Tab**

- You will see a message box for **Customer:Job Not Found** with buttons for three choices:

  Quick Add (used to add only a customer's name)
  Set Up (used to add complete information for a customer)
  Cancel (used to cancel the **Customer:Job Not Found** message box)

Click the **Set Up** button

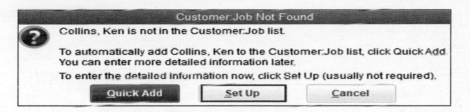

Complete the **New Customer** dialog box
- The name **Collins, Ken** is displayed in the CUSTOMER NAME field and as the first line of INVOICE/BILL TO in the ADDRESS DETAILS section on the Address Info tab.

There is no Opening Balance, so leave this field blank
- An opening balance may be given only when the customer's account is created. It is the amount the customer owes you at the time the account is created. It is not the amount of any transaction not yet recorded.
- Since there is no opening balance, you do not need to change the AS OF date to 01/08/2018.

Complete the information for the **Address Info** tab

Tab to or click in the text box for **First** in the line for Full Name, type **Ken**

Tab to or click in text box for **Last** in the line for Full Name, type **Collins**

Tab to or click in text box for **Main Phone**

Type the phone number **818-555-2058**

Tab to or click in text box for **Main E-mail**, enter **KCollins@123.com**

Tab to or click in text box for **Fax**, enter **818-555-8502**

Tab to or click the first line for **INVOICE/BILL TO**

If necessary, highlight **Collins, Ken**

Type **Ken Collins**
- Entering the customer name in this manner allows for the Customer:Job List to be organized according to the last name, yet the bill will be printed with the first name, then the last name.

Press **Enter** or click the second line of the billing address

Type the address **20985 Ventura Blvd.**

Press **Enter** or click the third line of the billing address

Type **Woodland Hills, CA 91371**

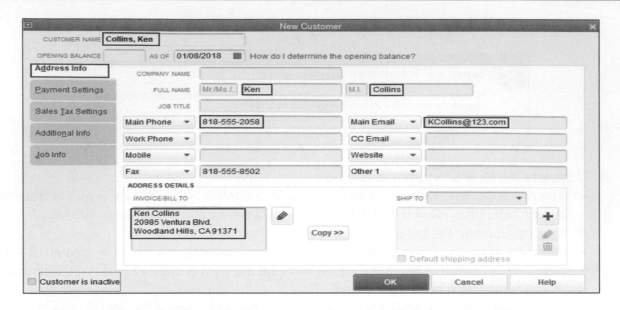

Click the **Payment Settings** tab on the left-side of the New Customer screen

Tab to or click in the **PAYMENT TERMS** text box

Click the drop-down list arrow

Click **Net 30**

Tab to or click in the **CREDIT LIMIT** text box

Type the amount **1000**, press **Tab**

- Do not use a dollar sign. QuickBooks Desktop will insert the comma and decimal point.

Click the drop-down list arrow for **PREFERRED DELIVERY METHOD**, click **None**

- You may or may not see the ONLINE PAYMENTS section on the Payment Settings screen.

Click **OK** to return to the Invoice

Enter Invoice information as previously instructed

DATE is **01/08/18**

INVOICE # is **8**

The bill is for 2 hours of hardware installation
- Remember to bill for the initial or first hour, then bill the other hour separately.
- Make sure you are using the Intuit Service Invoice.

The message is **Thank you for your business.**

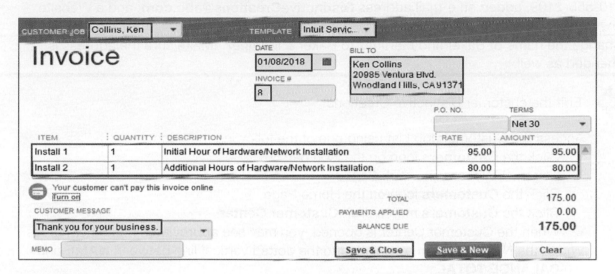

Print the invoice as previously instructed
- If you print to a pdf file, save the document as **13-Your Name Inv. 8 Collins Ch2**.

Click **Save & Close** on the invoice to record and close the transaction

PREPARE DAILY BACKUP

A backup file is prepared as a safeguard in case you make an error. After several transactions have been recorded, it is wise to prepare a backup file. In addition, a backup should be made at the end of every work session. The Daily Backup file is an appropriate file to create for saving your work as you progress through a chapter.

If you have created a daily backup file while you are working in a chapter and make an error later in your training and cannot figure out how to correct it, you may restore the backup file. Restoring your daily backup file will restore your work from the previous training session and eliminate the work completed in the current session. By creating the backup file now, it will contain your work for Chapter 1 and up through entering Invoice 8 in Chapter 2.

 Prepare the Tech 2018 (Daily Backup).qbb file

Follow the steps presented in Chapter 1 for creating a backup file
Name the file **Tech 2018 (Daily Backup)**
The file type is **QBW Backup (* .QBB)**

MODIFY CUSTOMER RECORDS

Occasionally, information regarding a customer will change. QuickBooks Desktop allows you to modify customer accounts at any time by editing the Customer:Job List.

MEMO

DATE: January 8, 2018

Update the following account: Distinctive Creations has changed its fax number to 310-555-2109, added an e-mail address **DistinctiveCreations@abc.com**, and a Website **www.DistinctiveCreations**.

Change the name of Baker and Martinez to Baker & Martinez. (Make sure the address is changed as well.

 Edit the customer Distinctive Creations:

Access the Customer:Job List using one of the following methods:
>   Click the **Customers** icon on the icon bar.
>   Use the keyboard shortcut: **Ctrl+J**
>   Click the **Customers** icon on the Home Page
>   Click the **Customers** menu, click **Customer Center**
- When the Customer Center is opened, you may see abbreviated customer names .

Widen the **NAME** column by pointing to the dotted vertical line between **NAME** and **BALANCE TOTAL**

When you get a double arrow, hold down the primary mouse button and drag to the right until the full customer name appears for all the customers

Click **Distinctive Creations** in the Customers & Jobs list in the Customer Center

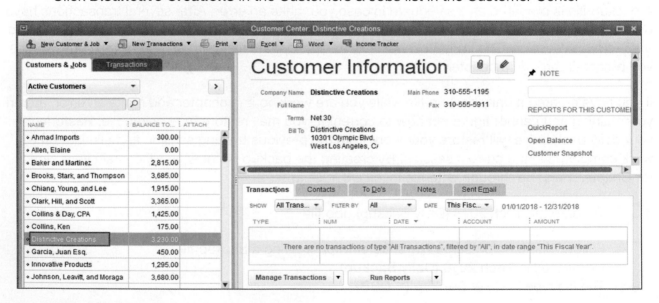

Edit the customer in one of three ways:
>   Click the **Edit** button
>   Use the keyboard shortcut **Ctrl+E**
>   Double-click **Distinctive Creations** on the **Customer:Job List**
- The Address Info tab should be shown; if not, click it.

To change the fax number to **310-555-2109**: Click at the end of the fax number, backspace to delete **5911**, type **2109**

Tab to or click in the text box for **Main E-mail**, enter the e-mail address
DistinctiveCreations@abc.com

Tab to or click in the text box for **Website**, enter the Web address
www.DistinctiveCreations

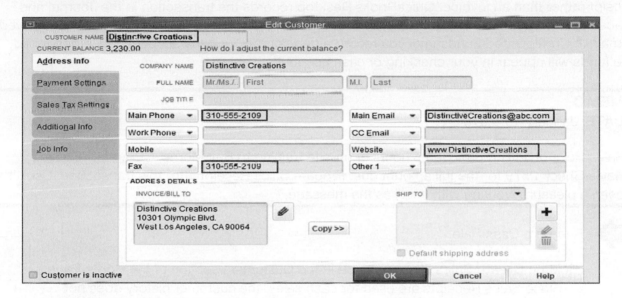

- Note the change to the Fax, Email, and Website.

Click **OK**

Click **Baker and Martinez**

Use the keyboard shortcut **Ctrl+E** to edit the customer

Change the Customer Name, Company Name, and Invoice/Bill To address to **Baker & Martinez**

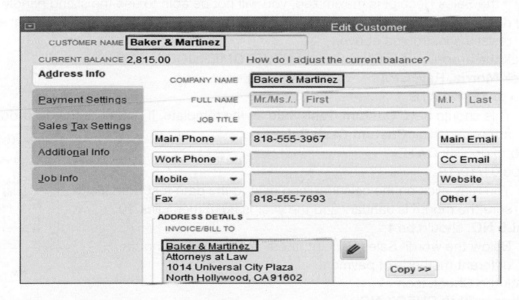

Click **OK**, close the **Customer Center**

RECORD CASH SALES

Not all sales in a business are on account. In many instances, payment is made at the time the service is performed and is entered as a cash sale. When entering a cash sale, you prepare a sales receipt rather than an invoice. QuickBooks Desktop records the transaction in the Journal and places the amount of cash received in an account called Undeposited Funds. The funds received remain in Undeposited Funds until you record a deposit to your bank account. Once deposited, the funds will appear in your checking or cash account.

MEMO
DATE: January 10, 2018

Sales Receipt 1: You provided 5 hours of on-site training to Ray Morris, CPA, and received Ray's Check 2579 for the full amount due. Prepare Sales Receipt 1 for this transaction. Use "It's been a pleasure working with you!" as the message.

   Record a Cash Sale

Click the **Create Sales Receipts** icon in the Customers section of the Home Page
- Since Sales Receipts are used for cash sales, the customer history does not need to be displayed on the right side of the screen each time you create a Sales Receipt.

To remove the History, click the **Hide History** button

Resize the form by pointing to the right edge of the Sales Receipt

When your cursor turns into a double arrow [icon], hold down the cursor and drag to the left to make the form smaller
- If the Sales Receipt is maximized, you will not be able to use the sizing handle (the double arrow) to resize the form. If that is the case, click the **Restore** button; and then resize as instructed above.

Click the drop-down list arrow next to **CUSTOMER:JOB**

Click **Morris, Ray, CPA**

Tab to **TEMPLATE**
- This should have **Custom Cash Sale** as the template. If not, click the drop-down list arrow and click **Custom Cash Sale**.

Tab to or click **DATE**

Type **01/10/18**
- You may click on the calendar icon next to the date text box. Make sure the month is January and the year is 2018 then click **10**.

SALE NO. should be **1**
- Below the words Sales Receipt, there are icons showing the different methods of payment.

Click the **Check** icon

Tab to or click **CHECK NO.**

Type **2579**

Tab to or click the first line for **ITEM**

Click the drop-down list arrow next to **ITEM**

Click **Training 1**

- If you need to widen the text box, follow the procedures that were used when you were in the Customer Center.

Tab to or click **QTY**

- Notice that the QTY column is after the DESCRIPTION column. This is different from an Invoice.

Type **1**

Tab to or click the second line for **ITEM**

Click the drop-down list arrow next to **ITEM**

Click **Training 2**

Tab to or click **QTY**

Type **4**

- The amount and total are automatically calculated when you go to the CUSTOMER MESSAGE or tab past QTY.

Click **CUSTOMER MESSAGE**

Click the drop-down list arrow for **CUSTOMER MESSAGE**

Click **It's been a pleasure working with you!**

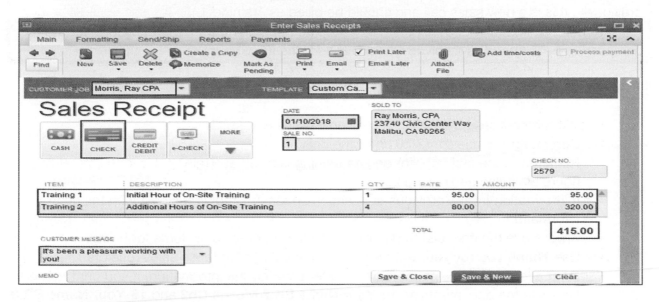

Do not close the Sales Receipt

PRINT SALES RECEIPT

 Print the sales receipt

Click the **Print** button on the **Enter Sales Receipts** Icon bar

Check the information on the **Print One Sales Receipt Settings** tab:

Printer name: (should identify the type of printer you are using)

Printer type: Page-oriented (Single sheets)

Print on: Blank paper

Click **Do not print lines around each field** to insert a check mark

Number of copies: should be **1**

Click **Print**

- This initiates the printing of the sales receipt through QuickBooks Desktop. However, since not all classroom configurations are the same, check with your instructor for specific printing instructions.
- If you print to a pdf file, save the document as **14-Your Name SR 1 Morris Ch2**.
  Once the Sales Receipt has been printed, click **Save & New** on the bottom of the **Enter Sales Receipts** screen
- If you get a Recording Transaction message, click **Yes**.

ENTER ADDITIONAL CASH SALES

> <u>**MEMO**</u>
> **DATE**: January 12, 2018
>
> Sales Receipt 2: Ray Morris needed additional on-site training to correct some error messages he received on his computer. You provided 1 hour of on-site training for Ray Morris, CPA, and received Check 2599 for the full amount due. (Even though Mr. Morris has had on-site training previously, this is a new sales call and should be billed as Training 1.)
>
> Sales Receipt 3: You provided 4 hours of on-site Internet training for Research Corp. for the company to be online. You received Check 1258 for the full amount due.

    Record the two January 12, 2018 transactions listed above

Use the procedures given when you entered Sales Receipt 1:
- Don't forget to use 01/12/2018 for the date.
- Remember, the <u>first hour for on-site training</u> is billed as <u>Training 1</u> and the <u>remaining hours</u> are billed as <u>Training 2</u>.
- If information from a previous transaction appears, simply replace it with the new information.
- Always use the Item List to determine the appropriate sales items for billing.
- Use **Thank you for your business.** as the message for these sales receipts.
- **Print** each sales receipt immediately after entering the information. If you print to a pdf file, save the documents as **15-Your Name SR 2 Morris Ch2** and **16-Your Name SR 3 Research Corp. Ch2.**
- If you make an error, correct it.
- To go from one sales receipt to the next, click the **Save & New** button on the bottom of the **Enter Sales Receipts** screen.
- Click **Save & Close** after you have entered and printed Sales Receipt 3.

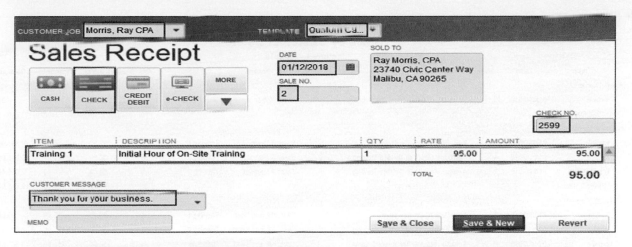

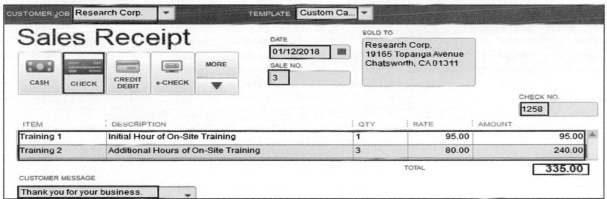

SALES BY CUSTOMER DETAIL REPORT

QuickBooks Desktop has reports available that enable you to obtain sales information about sales items or customers. To get information about the total amount of sales to each customer during a specific period, print a Sales by Customer Detail Report. The total shown represents both cash and/or credit sales.

 Prepare and print a Sales by Customer Detail Report

> Click **Reports** on the menu bar
> Point to **Sales**
> Click **Sales by Customer Detail**
> To remove the **Date Prepared**, **Time Prepared**, and **Report Basis** from the report, click the **Customize Report** button and follow the instructions given previously for deselecting the date prepared, time prepared, and report basis from the Header/Footer
> Change the dates to reflect the sales period from **01/01/18** to **01/12/18**
> Tab to generate the report
> - Notice that the report information includes the type of sales to each customer, the date of the sale, number of the business document, the transaction Memo that includes sales items descriptions, the sales item(s), the quantity for each item, the sales price, the amount, and the balance.
> - The report does not include information regarding opening or previous balances due.
> - The scope of this report is to focus on sales.

Your Name's Tech Services
Sales by Customer Detail
January 1 - 12, 2018

Type	Date	Num	Memo	Name	Item	Qty	Sales Price	Amount	Balance
Allen, Elaine									
Invoice	01/05/2018	3	10 Hours--Monthly Technical Support	Allen, Elaine	Tech Sup 2	0	300.00	0.00	0.00 ◄
Total Allen, Elaine						0		0.00	0.00
Baker & Martinez									
Invoice	01/05/2018	4	Initial Hour of On-Site Training	Baker & Martinez	Training 1	1	95.00	95.00	95.00
Invoice	01/05/2018	4	Additional Hours of On-Site Training	Baker & Martinez	Training 2	39	80.00	3,120.00	3,215.00
Credit Memo	01/08/2018	7	Additional Hours of On-Site Training	Baker & Martinez	Training 2	-5	80.00	-400.00	2,815.00
Total Baker & Martinez						35		2,815.00	2,815.00
Clark, Hill, and Scott									
Invoice	01/05/2018	6	Initial Hour of On-Site Training	Clark, Hill, and Scott	Training 1	1	95.00	95.00	95.00
Invoice	01/05/2018	6	Additional Hours of On-Site Training	Clark, Hill, and Scott	Training 2	39	80.00	3,120.00	3,215.00
Invoice	01/05/2018	6	5 Hours--Monthly Technical Support	Clark, Hill, and Scott	Tech Sup 1	1	150.00	150.00	3,365.00
Total Clark, Hill, and Scott						41		3,365.00	3,365.00
Collins & Day, CPA									
Invoice	01/05/2018	5	Initial Hour of On-Site Training	Collins & Day, CPA	Training 1	1	95.00	95.00	95.00
Invoice	01/05/2018	5	Additional Hours of On-Site Training	Collins & Day, CPA	Training 2	11	80.00	880.00	975.00
Invoice	01/05/2018	5	Cloud Services	Collins & Day, CPA	Cloud Services	1	150.00	150.00	1,125.00
Invoice	01/05/2018	5	10 Hours--Monthly Technical Support	Collins & Day, CPA	Tech Sup 2	1	300.00	300.00	1,425.00
Total Collins & Day, CPA						14		1,425.00	1,425.00
Collins, Ken									
Invoice	01/08/2018	8	Initial Hour of Hardware/Network Installation	Collins, Ken	Install 1	1	95.00	95.00	95.00
Invoice	01/08/2018	8	Additional Hours of Hardware/Network Installation	Collins, Ken	Install 2	1	80.00	80.00	175.00
Total Collins, Ken						2		175.00	175.00
Garcia, Juan Esq.									
Invoice	01/02/2018	1	10 Hours--Monthly Technical Support	Garcia, Juan Esq.	Tech Sup 2	1	300.00	300.00	300.00
Total Garcia, Juan Esq.						1		300.00	300.00
Morris, Ray CPA									
Sales Receipt	01/10/2018	1	Initial Hour of On-Site Training	Morris, Ray CPA	Training 1	1	95.00	95.00	95.00
Sales Receipt	01/10/2018	1	Additional Hours of On-Site Training	Morris, Ray CPA	Training 2	4	80.00	320.00	415.00
Sales Receipt	01/12/2018	2	Initial Hour of On-Site Training	Morris, Ray CPA	Training 1	1	95.00	95.00	510.00
Total Morris, Ray CPA						6		510.00	510.00
Research Corp.									
Sales Receipt	01/12/2018	3	Initial Hour of On-Site Training	Research Corp.	Training 1	1	95.00	95.00	95.00
Sales Receipt	01/12/2018	3	Additional Hours of On-Site Training	Research Corp.	Training 2	3	80.00	240.00	335.00
Total Research Corp.						4		335.00	335.00
TOTAL						103		8,925.00	8,925.00

Click the **Print** button on the **Sales by Customer Detail** screen

Click **Report** to select between printing a Report or Save as PDF

On the **Print Report** screen, check the Settings tab to verify that **Print to**: Printer is selected and that the name of your printer is correct

If necessary, click **Landscape** to change the **Orientation** from Portrait

- Landscape changes the orientation of the paper, so the report is printed 11-inches wide by 8½-inches long.

Verify that the **Page Range** is **All**

Make sure **Smart page breaks** have been selected

Preview the Report

If necessary, select **Fit report to 1 page(s) wide**.

On the **Print Report** screen, click **Print**

- If you print to a pdf file, save the document as **17-Your Name Sales by Cust Detail Ch2**.

Close the **Sales by Customer Detail Report**
- If you get a Memorize Transaction dialog box, click **No**.

CORRECT AND PRINT SALES RECEIPT

As previously shown on invoices, QuickBooks Desktop makes correcting errors user friendly. When an error is discovered in a transaction such as a cash sale, you can simply return to the form where the transaction was recorded and correct the error. Thus, to correct a sales receipt, you would open Sales Receipts, click the Previous button until you found the appropriate sales receipt, and then correct the error. Because cash or checks received for cash sales are held in the Undeposited Funds account until the bank deposit is made, you can access the sales receipt through the Undeposited Funds account in the Chart of Accounts as well. Accessing the receipt in this manner allows you to see all the transactions entered in the account for Undeposited Funds.

When a correction for a sale is made, QuickBooks Desktop not only changes the form, it also changes all journal and account entries for the transaction to reflect the correction. QuickBooks Desktop then allows a corrected sales receipt to be printed.

> ### MEMO
> **DATE**: January 14, 2018
>
> After reviewing transaction information, you realize the date for the Sales Receipt 1 to Ray Morris, CPA, was entered incorrectly. Change the date to 1/9/2018.

 Correct the error indicated in the memo, then print the corrected sales receipt

Click the **Chart of Accounts** icon on the Home Page
Click **Undeposited Funds**

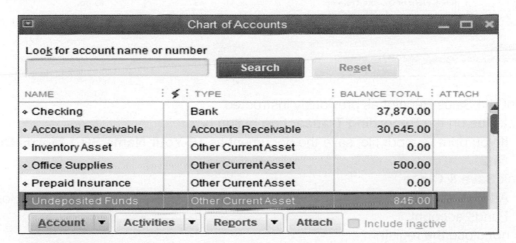

Click the **Activities** button
Click **Use Register**
- The register maintains a record of all the transactions recorded within the Undeposited Funds account.

Click anywhere in the transaction for **RCPT 1** to Ray Morris, CPA
- Look at the REF/TYPE column to see the type of transaction.

- The number in the REF line indicates the number of the sales receipt or the customer's check number.
- TYPE shows RCPT for a sales receipt.

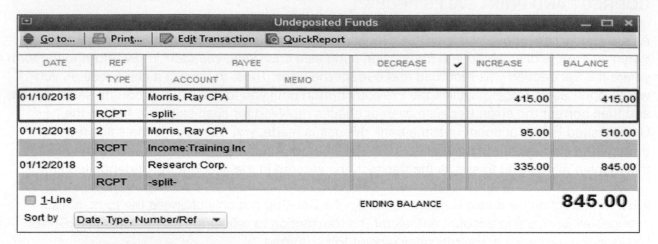

Click the **Edit Transaction** button at the top of the register
- The sales receipt appears on the screen.

Tab to or click in the **DATE** field

Change the Date to **01/09/18**, press Tab to enter the date

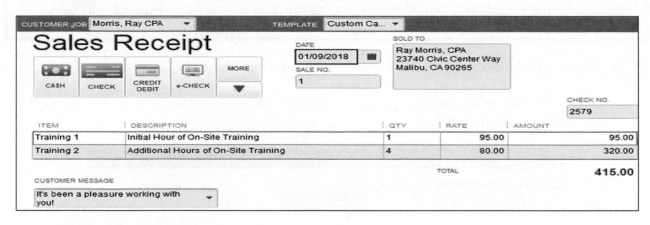

Print the Sales Receipt as previously instructed

Click **Yes** on the **Recording Transaction** dialog box
- If you print to a pdf file, save the document as **18-Your Name SR 1 Morris Corrected Ch2**.

Click **Save & Close**
- After closing the sales receipt, you are returned to the register for the Undeposited Funds account.

Do not close the register

VIEW QUICKREPORT

After editing the sales receipt and returning to the register, you may prepare a detailed report regarding the customer's transactions by clicking the QuickReport icon.

 Prepare a QuickReport for Ray Morris

Click the **QuickReport** icon to display the Register QuickReport for Ray Morris, CPA

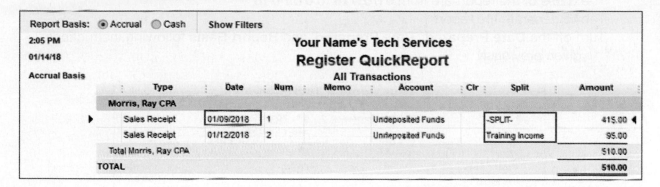

Type	**Date**	**Num**	**Memo**	**Account**	**Clr**	**Split**	**Amount**
Morris, Ray CPA							
Sales Receipt	01/09/2018	1		Undeposited Funds		-SPLIT-	415.00
Sales Receipt	01/12/2018	2		Undeposited Funds		Training Income	95.00
Total Morris, Ray CPA							510.00
TOTAL							510.00

ANALYZE QUICKREPORT

 Analyze the QuickReport for Ray Morris

Notice that the date for Sales Receipt 1 has been changed to **01/09/2018**
- You may need to use the horizontal scroll bar to view all the columns in the report.

The account used is Undeposited Funds

The Split column contains the other accounts used in the transaction
- For Sales Receipt 2, the account used is **Training Income**.
- For Sales Receipt 1, you see the word **Split** rather than an account name. Split means that more than one sales item or account was used for this portion of the transaction.

View the sales items or accounts used for the Split by using QuickZoom to view the actual Sales Receipt

Use QuickZoom by double-clicking anywhere on the information for Sales Receipt 1
- You will see Sales Receipt 1.
- The sales items used are Training 1 and Training 2.

Close the **Sales Receipt**

Close the **Register QuickReport** without printing

Close the **Register for Undeposited Funds**

Close the **Chart of Accounts**

ANALYZE SALES

To obtain information regarding the amount of sales by item, you can print or view sales reports. Sales reports provide information regarding cash and credit sales. When information regarding the sales according to the Sales Item is needed, a Sales by Item Summary Report is the appropriate report to print or view. This report enables you to see how much revenue is being generated by each sales item. This provides important information for decision making and managing the business. For example, if a sales item is not generating much income, it might be wise to discontinue that sales item.

 Print a summarized list of sales by item

Click the **Reports** icon to open the Report Center

Click **Sales** as the type of report

Double-click **Sales by Item Summary** in the Sales by Item report list
The dates of the report are from **01/01/18** to **01/14/18**
Tab to generate the report
Turn off the **Date Prepared**, **Time Prepared**, and **Report Basis** following instructions
given previously

Your Name's Tech Services
Sales by Item Summary
January 1 - 14, 2018

	Qty	Amount	% of Sales	Avg Price
▼ **Service**				
Cloud Services ▶	1 ◀	150.00	1.7%	150.00
Install 1	1	95.00	1.1%	95.00
Install 2	1	80.00	0.9%	80.00
Tech Sup 1	1	150.00	1.7%	150.00
Tech Sup 2	2	600.00	6.7%	300.00
Training 1	6	570.00	6.4%	95.00
Training 2	91	7,280.00	81.6%	80.00
Total Service	103.00	8,925.00	100.0%	86.65
TOTAL	103	8,925.00	100.0%	86.65

Click the **Print** button, click **Report**
The Orientation should be **Portrait**
Click **Print** on **Print Reports** dialog box
• If you print to a pdf file, save the document as **19-Your Name Sales by Item Sum Ch2**.
Close the report, do <u>not</u> close the Report Center

 View a Sales by Item Detail report to obtain information regarding which transactions apply
to each sales item

Double-click **Sales by Item Detail** in the Sales reports list
The dates of the report are from **01/01/18** to **01/14/18**
Tab to generate the report
Scroll through the report to view the types of sales and the transactions that occurred
within each category
• Notice how many transactions occurred in each sales item.

2:17 PM			**Your Name's Tech Services**						
01/14/18			**Sales by Customer Detail**						
Accrual Basis			January 1 - 14, 2018						
Type	Date	Num	Memo	Name	Item	Qty	Sales Price	Amount	Balance
Allen, Elaine									
Invoice	01/05/2018	3	10 Hours—Monthly Technical Support	Allen, Elaine	Tech Sup 2	0	300.00	0.00	0.00
Total Allen, Elaine						0		0.00	0.00
Baker & Martinez									
Invoice	01/05/2018	4	Initial Hour of On-Site Training	Baker & Martinez	Training 1	1	95.00	95.00	95.00
Invoice	01/05/2018	4	Additional Hours of On-Site Training	Baker & Martinez	Training 2	39	80.00	3,120.00	3,215.00
Credit Memo	01/08/2018	7	Additional Hours of On-Site Training	Baker & Martinez	Training 2	-5	80.00	-400.00	2,815.00
Total Baker & Martinez						35		2,815.00	2,815.00
Clark, Hill, and Scott									
Invoice	01/05/2018	6	Initial Hour of On-Site Training	Clark, Hill, and Scott	Training 1	1	95.00	95.00	95.00
Invoice	01/05/2018	6	Additional Hours of On-Site Training	Clark, Hill, and Scott	Training 2	39	80.00	3,120.00	3,215.00
Invoice	01/05/2018	6	5 Hours—Monthly Technical Support	Clark, Hill, and Scott	Tech Sup 1	1	150.00	150.00	3,365.00
Total Clark, Hill, and Scott						41		3,365.00	3,365.00
Collins & Day, CPA									
Invoice	01/05/2018	5	Initial Hour of On-Site Training	Collins & Day, CPA	Training 1	1	95.00	95.00	95.00
Invoice	01/05/2018	5	Additional Hours of On-Site Training	Collins & Day, CPA	Training 2	11	80.00	880.00	975.00
Invoice	01/05/2018	5	Cloud Services	Collins & Day, CPA	Cloud Services	1	150.00	150.00	1,125.00
Invoice	01/05/2018	5	10 Hours—Monthly Technical Support	Collins & Day, CPA	Tech Sup 2	1	300.00	300.00	1,425.00
Total Collins & Day, CPA						14		1,425.00	1,425.00
Collins, Ken									
Invoice	01/08/2018	8	Initial Hour of Hardware/Network Installation	Collins, Ken	Install 1	1	95.00	95.00	95.00
Invoice	01/08/2018	8	Additional Hours of Hardware/Network Installation	Collins, Ken	Install 2	1	80.00	80.00	175.00
Total Collins, Ken						2		175.00	175.00
Garcia, Juan Esq.									
Invoice	01/02/2018	1	10 Hours—Monthly Technical Support	Garcia, Juan Esq.	Tech Sup 2	1	300.00	300.00	300.00
Total Garcia, Juan Esq.						1		300.00	300.00
Morris, Ray CPA									
Sales Receipt	01/09/2018	1	Initial Hour of On-Site Training	Morris, Ray CPA	Training 1	1	95.00	95.00	95.00
Sales Receipt	01/09/2018	1	Additional Hours of On-Site Training	Morris, Ray CPA	Training 2	4	80.00	320.00	415.00
Sales Receipt	01/12/2018	2	Initial Hour of On-Site Training	Morris, Ray CPA	Training 1	1	95.00	95.00	510.00
Total Morris, Ray CPA						6		510.00	510.00
Research Corp.									
Sales Receipt	01/12/2018	3	Initial Hour of On-Site Training	Research Corp.	Training 1	1	95.00	95.00	95.00
Sales Receipt	01/12/2018	3	Additional Hours of On-Site Training	Research Corp.	Training 2	3	80.00	240.00	335.00
Total Research Corp.						4		335.00	335.00
TOTAL						103		8,925.00	8,925.00

Close the report without printing
Close the **Report Center**

PREPARE DAILY BACKUP

As you learned earlier in the chapter, creating a backup file saves your work up to that point. The daily backup prepared earlier contains all of Chapter 1 and the portion of Chapter 2 where invoices were entered. By creating the backup file now and using the same file name, it will contain your work for Chapter 1 and all the work completed through entering Sales Receipts in Chapter 2.

 Prepare the Tech 2018 (Daily Backup).qbb file

Follow the steps presented in Chapter 1 for creating a backup file
Name the file **Tech 2018 (Daily Backup)**

The file type is **QBW Backup (* .QBB)**
- This backup is using the same backup file that you prepared earlier in the chapter.
- The daily backup will now contain all of Chapter 1 and Chapter 2 up through entering sales receipts.

RECORD CUSTOMER PAYMENT ON ACCOUNT

Since a sale on account is originally recorded on an invoice, Receive Payments is used when a customer pays you what is owed on an invoice. Frequently, new users of QuickBooks Desktop will try to record a payment receipt using a Sales Receipt, which is used only for cash sales not for payments on account.

When you start to record a payment made by a customer who owes you money for an invoice, you see the customer's balance, any credits made to the account, and a complete list of outstanding invoices. QuickBooks Desktop automatically places a check in the check mark column for the invoice that has the same amount as the payment. If there isn't an invoice with the same amount, QuickBooks Desktop marks the oldest invoice and enters the payment amount in the Payment column for the invoice being paid. When customers make a full or partial payment of the amount they owe, QuickBooks Desktop places the money received in the Undeposited Funds account. The money stays in this account until a bank deposit is made.

MEMO
DATE: January 15, 2018

Record the following cash receipt: Received Check 846 for $815 from Research Corp. as payment on account.

 Record the receipt of a payment on account

Receive Payments

Click the **Receive Payments** icon in the Customers section of the Home Page
- Notice the flow chart line from Create Invoices to Receive Payments. The icons are illustrated in this manner because a payment for an invoice (a sale on account) is recorded as Receive Payments. This is <u>not</u> a cash sale.

Click the drop-down list arrow for **RECEIVED FROM**

Click **Research Corp.**
- Notice that the current date or the last transaction date shows in the **DATE** column and the total amount owed appears as the CUSTOMER BALANCE.
- Also note that previous cash sales to Research Corp. are not listed. This is because a payment receipt is used only for payments on account.

Tab to or click **PAYMENT AMOUNT**
- If you click, you will need to delete the 0.00. If you tab, it will be deleted when you type in the amount.

Enter **815**
- QuickBooks Desktop will enter the **.00** when you tab to or click **DATE**.
- When you press Tab, QuickBooks Desktop automatically places a check in the check mark column for the invoice that has the same amount as the payment. If there isn't an invoice with the same amount, QuickBooks Desktop marks the oldest invoice and enters the payment amount in the Payment column for the invoice being paid.

Tab to or click in the **DATE** text box
- If you click, you will need to delete the date. If you tab, the date will be replaced when you type 01/15/18.
- You may also click the calendar icon and then click 15 for the month of January.

Type date **01/15/18**

Click the **CHECK** icon to indicate the method of payment

Tab to or click in the text box for **CHECK #**

Enter **846**

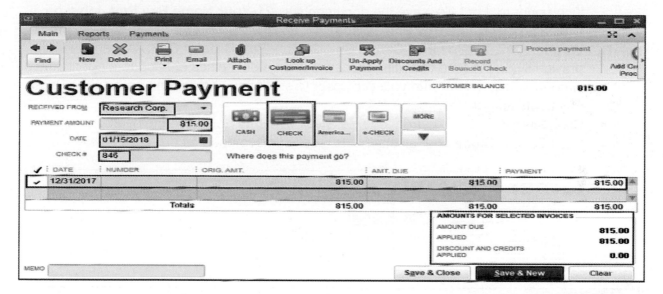

Click the **Print** button and print a copy of the Payment Receipt following steps presented earlier for printing other business forms
- If you print to a pdf file, save the document as **20-Your Name Rcv Pmt Research Corp. Ch2**. Please note that at the time of writing, there were some difficulties printing to a pdf file. If you encounter this, check with your professor to see if you should omit printing the Receive Payments as a pdf file.

When the Receive Payment has been printed, click **Save & New**

RECORD ADDITIONAL PAYMENTS ON ACCOUNT

> **MEMO**
>
> **DATE:** January 15, 2018
>
> Received Check 1952 from Johnson, Leavitt, and Moraga for $3,680.
>
> Received Check 8925 for $2,000 from Taylor Illustrations in partial payment of account. Receipt requires a Memo: Partial Payment. Make sure "Leave as an underpayment" is selected in the lower portion of the Customer Payment.
>
> Received Check 39251 from Matt McBride, CPA for $475.
>
> Received Check 2051 for $2,190 from Wagner Productions as a partial payment. Enter a Memo: Partial Payment. Leave as an underpayment.
>
> Received Check 5632 from Juan Garcia, Esq. for $150 to pay his opening balance. Since this is payment in full for the opening balance, no memo is required.
>
> Received Check 80195 from Brooks, Stark, & Thompson for $3,685.

Enter the above payments on account; if necessary, refer to the previous steps listed

- If an invoice is not paid in full, enter the amount received, enter a Memo of **Partial Payment**, and make sure **Leave as an underpayment** is selected in the lower portion of the screen.
- Remember, an invoice may be paid in full, but an account may still have a balance (refer to the payment for Juan Garcia).
- Print a Payment Receipt for each payment received.
- If you print to a pdf file, save the documents as **21-Your Name Rcv Pmt Johnson. Ch2**, **22-Your Name Rcv Pmt Taylor Ch2**, **23 Rcv Pmt McBride Ch2**, **24-Rcv Pmt Wagner Ch2**, **25-Rcv Pmt Garcia Ch2**, **26-Rcv Pmt Brooks Ch2**. As mentioned previously, at the time of writing there were some difficulties printing to a pdf file. If you encounter this, check with your professor to see if you should omit printing the Receive Payments as pdf files.
- Click **Save & New** to go from one Receive Payments Screen to the next.
- Click **Save & Close** after all payments received have been recorded.

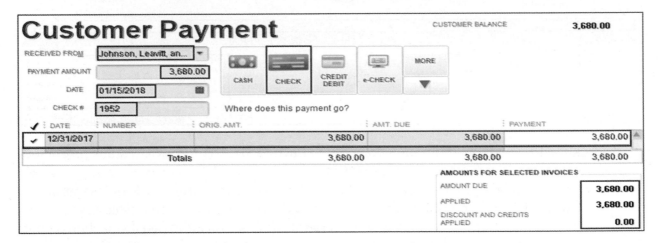

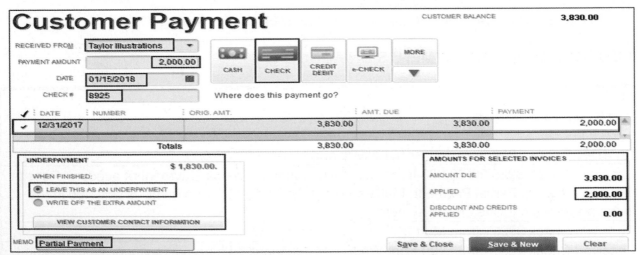

- Note: The UNDERPAYMENT of $1,830.00, the selection of LEAVE THIS AS AN UNDERPAYMENT, and the. MEMO of "Partial Payment."
- Note the AMOUNT DUE of 3,830 and the APPLIED of 2,000.

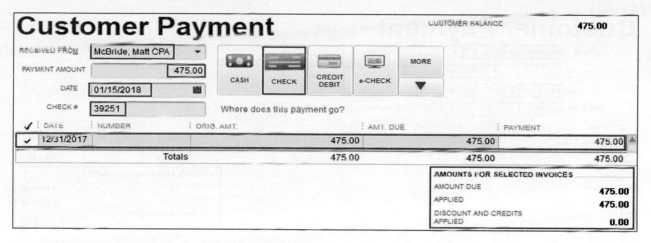

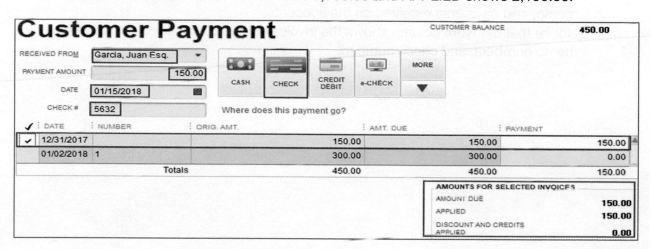

- Verify the underpayment of $1,000 by Wagner Productions.
- Note that the AMOUNT DUE shows 3,190.00 and APPLIED shows 2,190.00.

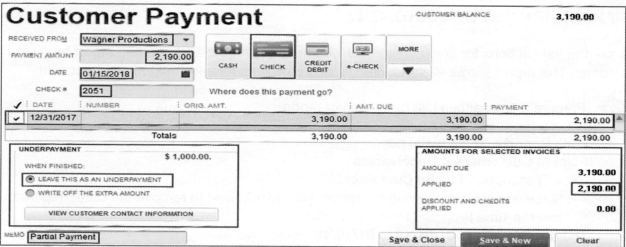

- Note: The 12/31/2017 Opening Balance was marked for the payment—the amount paid is a match to the amount due.
- Note that the marked transaction is the oldest.
- Invoice 1 was not paid. It remains unmarked.
- The AMOUNTS FOR SELECTED INVOICES of $150.00 are shown for the 12/31/2017 transaction that is marked.

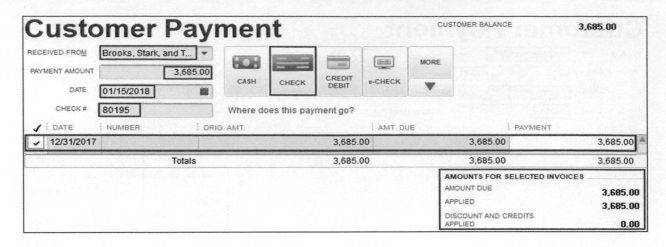

TRANSACTION LIST BY CUSTOMER

To see the transactions for credit customers, you need to prepare a transaction report by customer. This report shows all sales, credits, and payments for each customer on account.

  Prepare a Transaction List by Customer report

> Click **Reports** on the menu bar
> Point to **Customers & Receivables**
> Click **Transaction List by Customer**
> * Since you are only viewing the report, you do not need to remove the Date Prepared and the Time Prepared from the header.
> The dates are From **01/01/18** to **01/15/18**
> Tab to generate the report
> Scroll through the report
> * Notice that information is shown for the invoices, sales receipts (cash sales), credit memo, and payments received on the accounts.
> * Notice that the **Num** column shows the invoice numbers, sales receipt numbers, credit memo numbers, and check numbers.

11:00 AM			**Your Name's Tech Services**					
01/15/18			**Transaction List by Customer**					
			January 1 - 15, 2018					
Type	Date	Num	Memo	Account	Clr	Split	Debit	Credit
Allen, Elaine								
Invoice	01/05/2018	3	VOID: VOID:	Accounts Receivable	✓	Technical Support Income	0.00	
Baker & Martinez								
Invoice	01/05/2018	4		Accounts Receivable		-SPLIT-	3,215.00	
Credit Memo	01/08/2018	7		Accounts Receivable		-SPLIT-		400.00
Brooks, Stark, and Thompson								
Payment	01/15/2018	80195		Undeposited Funds		Accounts Receivable	3,685.00	
Clark, Hill, and Scott								
Invoice	01/05/2018	6		Accounts Receivable		-SPLIT-	3,365.00	
Collins & Day, CPA								
Invoice	01/05/2018	5		Accounts Receivable		-SPLIT-	1,425.00	
Collins, Ken								
Invoice	01/08/2018	8		Accounts Receivable		-SPLIT-	175.00	
Garcia, Juan Esq.								
Invoice	01/02/2018	1		Accounts Receivable		Technical Support Income	300.00	
Payment	01/15/2018	5632		Undeposited Funds		Accounts Receivable	150.00	
Johnson, Leavitt, and Moraga								
Payment	01/15/2018	1952		Undeposited Funds		Accounts Receivable	3,680.00	
McBride, Matt CPA								
Payment	01/15/2018	39251		Undeposited Funds		Accounts Receivable	475.00	
Morris, Ray CPA								
Sales Receipt	01/09/2018	1		Undeposited Funds		-SPLIT-	415.00	
Sales Receipt	01/12/2018	2		Undeposited Funds		Training Income	95.00	
Research Corp.								
Sales Receipt	01/12/2018	3		Undeposited Funds		-SPLIT-	335.00	
Payment	01/15/2018	846		Undeposited Funds		Accounts Receivable	815.00	
Taylor Illustrations								
Payment	01/15/2018	8925	Partial Payment	Undeposited Funds		Accounts Receivable	2,000.00	
Wagner Productions								
Payment	01/15/2018	2051	Partial Payment	Undeposited Funds		Accounts Receivable	2,190.00	

Click the **Close** button to exit the report without printing

DEPOSIT CHECKS RECEIVED

When you record cash sales and the receipt of payments on accounts, QuickBooks Desktop places the money received in the Undeposited Funds account. Once the deposit has been made at the bank, it should be recorded. When the deposit is recorded, the funds are transferred from Undeposited Funds to the account selected when preparing the deposit (usually checking). This is important because, until the money is deposited, it does not show as being available for use.

> **MEMO**
> **DATE:** January 15, 2018
>
> Deposit all checks received for cash sales and payments on account.

➡️ Deposit checks received

Click the **Record Deposits** icon in the Banking section of the Home Page

- Notice that the icon indicates how many receipts are available for deposit.
- **Payments to Deposit** window shows all amounts received for cash sales and payments on account that have not been deposited in the bank.
- The column for **TYPE** contains RCPT, which means the amount is for a Sales Receipt (Cash Sale), and PMT, which means the amount received is for a payment on account.
- Notice that the √ column to the left of the DATE column is empty.

Click the **Select All** button

- Notice the check marks in the √ column.

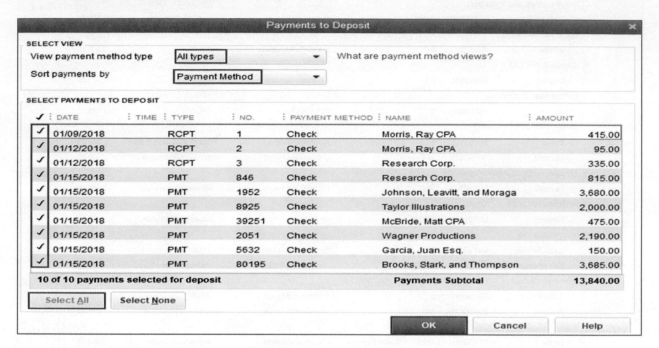

Click **OK** to close **Payments to Deposit** screen and open **Make Deposits** screen
On the **Make Deposits** screen, **Deposit To** should be **Checking**
Date should be **01/15/2018**

- Tab to date and change if not correct.

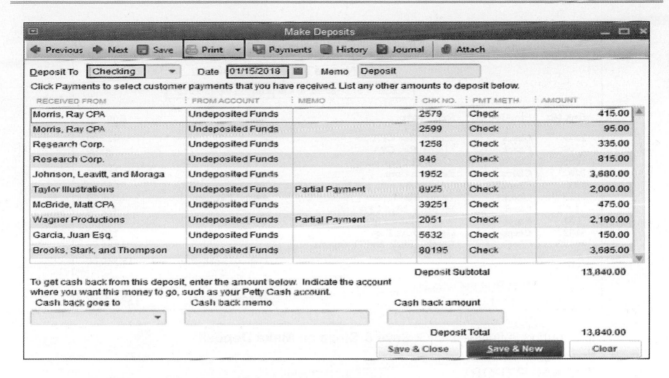

Click the **Print** button to print **Deposit Summary**
Select **Deposit summary only** on the **Print Deposit** dialog box, click **OK**

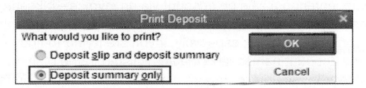

Check the **Settings** for **Print Lists**, click **Print**
- If you print to a pdf file, save the document as **27-Your Name Deposit Sum Ch2**. If you get an error message when trying to print this to a pdf file, you may print the Deposit slip and deposit summary instead.
- *Note:* QuickBooks Desktop automatically prints the company name and the date that the Deposit Summary was printed on the report. It is the current date of your computer and cannot be changed; therefore, it will not match the date shown in the following screen shot.

Deposit Summary   1/15/2018

Your Name's Tech Services

Summary of Deposits to Checking on 01/15/2018

Chk No.	PmtMethod	Rcd From	Memo	Amount
2579	Check	Morris, Ray CPA		415.00
2599	Check	Morris, Ray CPA		95.00
1258	Check	Research Corp.		335.00
846	Check	Research Corp.		815.00
1952	Check	Johnson, Leavitt, and Moraga		3,680.00
8925	Check	Taylor Illustrations	Partial Payment	2,000.00
39251	Check	McBride, Matt CPA		475.00
2051	Check	Wagner Productions	Partial Payment	2,190.00
5632	Check	Garcia, Juan Esq.		150.00
80195	Check	Brooks, Stark, and Thompson		3,685.00
			Deposit Subtotal:	13,840.00
			Less Cash Back:	
			Deposit Total:	13,840.00

When printing is finished, click **Save & Close** on **Make Deposits**

PRINT JOURNAL REPORT

Even though QuickBooks Desktop displays registers and reports in a manner that focuses on the transaction—for example, entering a sale on account via an invoice—it keeps a Journal. The Journal report shows each transaction and lists the accounts and the amounts for debit and credit entries. The Journal report is very useful; especially, if you are trying to find errors. Always check the transaction dates, the account names, and the items listed in the Memo column. If a transaction does not appear in the Journal report, it may be due to using an incorrect date. Remember, only the transactions entered within the report dates will be displayed. In many instances, going through the Journal report entries will help you find errors in your transactions.

In your concepts course, you may have learned that the General Journal was where all entries were recorded in debit/credit format. In QuickBooks Desktop, you do record some non-recurring debit/credit transactions in the General Journal and then display all debit/credit entries no matter where the transactions were recorded in the Journal report. (At times in the text Journal and General Journal are used synonymously to represent the report).

 Print the Journal report

Open the **Report Center** as previously instructed
Click **Accountant & Taxes** as the Report type
Double-click **Journal**
- If you get the Collapsing and Expanding Transactions dialog box, click **OK**.
When the Journal report is displayed, click the **Expand** button
The dates are from **01/01/18** to **01/15/18**
Customize the Report to change the **Header/Footer** so the **Date Prepared** and **Time Prepared** are not selected, click **OK**
Scroll through the report to view the transactions

- You may find that your Trans # is not the same as shown in the following report. QuickBooks Desktop automatically numbers all transactions recorded. If you have deleted and re-entered transactions more than directed in the text, you may have different transaction numbers. Do not be concerned with this.
- Many of the columns do not display in full. To see important information; such as, the account used in the transactions, the columns need to be resized.

Resize the width of the Account column so the account names are displayed in full

Position the cursor on the sizing diamond between **Account** and **Debit**

- The cursor turns into a plus with arrows pointing left and right.

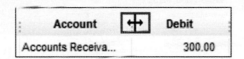

Hold down the primary (left) mouse button

Drag the cursor from the diamond between **Account** and **Debit** to the <u>right</u> until you have the account names displayed in full

- You will see a dotted vertical line while you are dragging the mouse and holding down the primary mouse button.

Look at the other columns, if any have … to represent information not shown, point to the sizing diamond and drag until the information is shown

- You may make columns smaller by pointing to the sizing diamond and dragging to the <u>left</u>.

Point to the sizing diamond between the **Debit** and **Credit** columns

Drag to the left to make the Debit column smaller

- If you make the column too small, the numbers that cannot be displayed will be shown as ******. If this happens, make the column larger.

Resize the remaining columns to eliminate extra space and to display names, memos, and accounts in full

Once the columns have been resized, click the **Print** button, click **Report**

Click **Preview**

- You will be able to see how the report will appear when it is printed. If the report prints two-pages wide, you may want to resize the columns until you can get it to print on one-page wide. If you need to hide a few words in the Memo column to reduce the report to one-page wide, that is acceptable. For example, you may need to hide the word Installation for Initial Hour of Hardware/Network Installation in the Memo column.

Click **Close** to close the **Preview**

Once you have the column widths adjusted so the report is one-page wide, click the **Print** button, click **Report**

On the **Print Reports** screen, the settings will be the same used previously except:

Click **Landscape** to select Landscape orientation

- If you cannot get the report to print on one-page even after resizing the columns, click on **Fit report to one page wide** to select this item.
- The printer will print the Journal report using a smaller font, so the report will fit across the 11-inch width.

Click **Print**

- If you print to a pdf file, save the document as **28-Your Name Journal Ch2**.
- The Journal report will be several pages in length so only a partial report is shown.

Your Name's Tech Services
Journal
January 1 - 15, 2018

Trans #	Type	Date	Num	Adj	Name	Memo	Account	Debit	Credit
44	Payment	01/15/2018	80195		Brooks, Stark, and Thompson		Undeposited Funds	3,685.00	
					Brooks, Stark, and Thompson		Accounts Receivable		3,685.00
								3,685.00	3,685.00
45	Deposit	01/15/2018				Deposit	Checking	13,840.00	
					Morris, Ray CPA	Deposit	Undeposited Funds		415.00
					Morris, Ray CPA	Deposit	Undeposited Funds		95.00
					Research Corp.	Deposit	Undeposited Funds		335.00
					Research Corp.	Deposit	Undeposited Funds		815.00
					Johnson, Leavitt, and Moraga	Deposit	Undeposited Funds		3,680.00
					Taylor Illustrations	Partial Payment	Undeposited Funds		2,000.00
					McBride, Matt CPA	Deposit	Undeposited Funds		475.00
					Wagner Productions	Partial Payment	Undeposited Funds		2,190.00
					Garcia, Juan Esq.	Deposit	Undeposited Funds		150.00
					Brooks, Stark, and Thompson	Deposit	Undeposited Funds		3,685.00
								13,840.00	13,840.00
TOTAL								36,560.00	36,560.00

Partial Report

Close the report, do <u>not</u> close the Report Center

TRIAL BALANCE

When all sales transactions have been entered, it is important to prepare and print the Trial Balance and verify that the total debits equal the total credits.

 Print the Trial Balance

Click **Trial Balance** on the Report Center list of Accountant & Taxes reports
Click the **Run** icon
Enter the dates from **010118** to **011518**
- Shortcut: You do not have to use **/** to separate the date into month, day, year.

Click the **Customize Report** button and change **Header/Footer** so **Date Prepared**, **Time Prepared**, and **Report Basis** do not print
Print the report in **Portrait** orientation following instructions presented earlier in the chapter
- If necessary, click on **Fit report to one page wide** to deselect this item.
- If you print to a pdf file, save the document as **29-Your Name Trial Bal Ch2**.

Your Name's Tech Services
Trial Balance
As of January 15, 2018

	Jan 15, 18	
	Debit	**Credit**
Checking	51,710.00	
Accounts Receivable	17,650.00	
Office Supplies	500.00	
Undeposited Funds	0.00	
Company Cars:Original Cost	49,000.00	
Office Equipment:Original Cost	8,050.00	
Accounts Payable		850.00
Loan Payable	0.00	
Loan Payable:Company Cars Loan		35,000.00
Loan Payable:Office Equipment Loan		4,000.00
Owner's Equity	0.00	
Student's Name, Capital		53,135.00
Student's Name, Capital:Investments		25,000.00
Income:Cloud Services Income		150.00
Income:Installation Income		175.00
Income:Technical Support Income		750.00
Income:Training Income		7,850.00
TOTAL	**126,910.00**	**126,910.00**

Close the report
Do <u>not</u> close the Report Center

GRAPHS

Once transactions have been entered, transaction results can be visually represented in a graphic form. QuickBooks Desktop illustrates Accounts Receivable by Aging Period as a bar chart, and it illustrates Accounts Receivable by Customer as a pie chart. For further details, double-click on an individual section of the pie chart or chart legend to create a bar chart analyzing an individual customer. QuickBooks Desktop also prepares graphs based on sales and will show the results of sales by item and by customer.

ACCOUNTS RECEIVABLE GRAPHS

Accounts Receivable graphs illustrate account information based on the age of the account and the percentage of accounts receivable owed by each customer.

 Create Accounts Receivable Graphs

Click **Customers & Receivables** in the Report Center list to select the type of report
Scroll through the list of reports; and then, double-click **Accounts Receivable Graph** to select the report
Click **Dates** on the QuickInsight: Accounts Receivable Graph screen
On the **Change Graph Dates** change **Show Aging As of** to **01/15/18**
Click **OK**
- QuickBooks Desktop generates a bar chart illustrating Accounts Receivable by Aging Period and a pie chart illustrating Accounts Receivable by Customer.

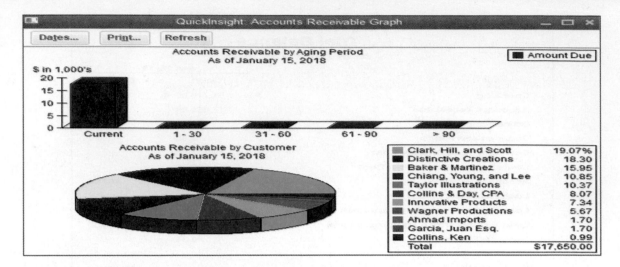

Printing is not required for this graph

- If you want a printed copy, click **Print** and print in Portrait mode.

Click the **Dates** button

Enter **02/15/18** for the **Show Aging As of** date

Click **OK**

- Notice the difference in the aging of accounts.

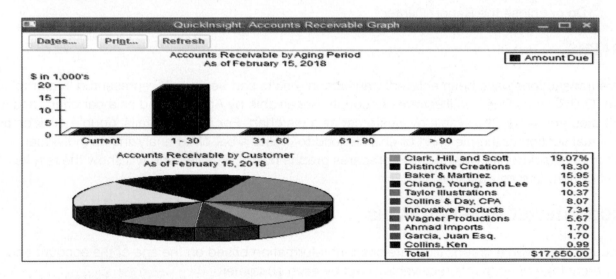

Click **Dates**

Enter **01/15/18**

Do not close the graph

QUICKZOOM FOR INDIVIDUAL CUSTOMER DETAILS

It is possible to get detailed information regarding the aging of transactions for an individual customer by using the QuickZoom feature of QuickBooks Desktop.

    Use QuickZoom to see information for Clark, Hill, and Scott

- The color in the ledger shows you that the customer Clark, Hill, and Scott is represented in lime green.

Double-click on the section of the pie chart for **Clark, Hill, and Scott**
- You get a bar chart aging the transactions of the customer.

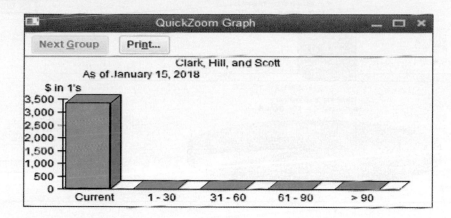

Printing is not required for this graph
Close the **QuickZoom Graph** for Clark, Hill, and Scott
Close the **Accounts Receivable Graph**
Do <u>not</u> close the Report Center

SALES GRAPHS

Sales graphs illustrate the amount of cash and credit sales for a given period as well as the percentage of sales for each sales item.

 Prepare a Sales Graph

Click **Sales** in the Report Center
Scroll through the list of reports until you find Sales Graph
Double-click **Sales Graph**
Click the **Dates** button
Click in **From**, enter **01/01/18**
Tab to **To**, enter **01/15/18**
Click **OK**
The **By Item** button should be selected
- You will see a bar chart representing Sales by Month and a pie chart displaying a Sales Summary by item.

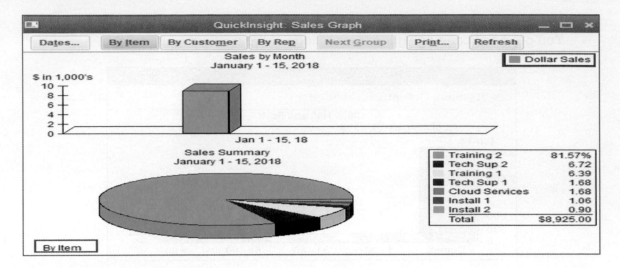

- If the **By Customer** button is indented, you will see the same bar chart, but the pie chart and chart legend will display a Sales Summary by Customer.
- If the **By Rep** button is indented, you will see the same bar chart, but the pie chart and chart legend will display a Sales Summary by Sales Rep.

Printing is not required for this graph

Do <u>not</u> close the graph

QUICKZOOM TO VIEW ITEM

It is possible to use QuickZoom to view details regarding an individual item's sales by month.

  Use QuickZoom to see information for Install 1

Since Install 1 is such a small area in the pie chart, double-click **Install 1** In the chart legend

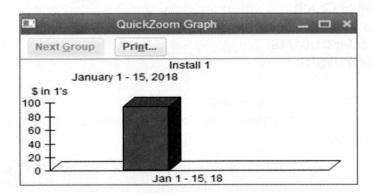

You will see the Sales by Month for Install 1

Close the **QuickZoom Graph** and the **Sales Graph** without printing

Close the **Report Center**

CREATE CHAPTER BACK UP

As you learned in Chapter 1, when you use QuickBooks Desktop to make a backup file, the program creates a condensed file that contains all the data for the entries made up to the time of the creation of the backup file. This file has a **.qbb** extension and cannot be used to record transactions. When new transactions are recorded, a new backup file must be made. In training, it is wise to make a daily backup, as you did while working in the chapter, and an end-of-chapter backup. If errors are made in training, the appropriate backup file can be restored. For example, if you back up Chapter 2 and make errors in Chapter 3, the Chapter 2 backup may be restored to a company file with the **.qbw** extension. The data entered for Chapter 3 will be erased and only the data from Chapters 1 and 2 will appear.

A duplicate copy of the file may be made using Windows. Instructions for this procedure should be provided by your professor. You may hear the duplicate copy referred to as a backup file. This is different from the QuickBooks Desktop backup file.

 Back up the company

Follow the instructions provided in Chapter 1 to make your backup
Name for the Chapter 2 backup file should be **Tech 2018 (Backup Ch. 2)**
* Tech 2018 (Backup Ch. 1) file contains all work from Chapter 1.
* Tech 2018 (Backup Ch. 2) file contains all work from Chapters 1 and 2.
* Tech 2018 (Backup Ch. 2) will not contain any Chapter 3 transactions.
* Keeping a separate backup file for each chapter is helpful for those times when you have made errors and cannot figure out how to correct them. Restoring your Chapter 2 back up file will restore your work from Chapters 1 and 2 and eliminate any work completed in Chapter 3. This will allow you to start over at the beginning of Chapter 3. If you do not have a backup file for Chapter 2, you would need to restore the Chapter 1 backup and then re-enter all the transactions for Chapter 2 before beginning Chapter 3.
* Your Daily Backup file will contain your work up to the point where you created the daily backup file. It does not need to be redone at this point since the Tech 2018 (Backup Ch. 2) contains the work for both Chapters 1 and 2.

CLOSE COMPANY AND EXIT QUICKBOOKS DESKTOP

 After the backup file has been made, close the Company and QuickBooks Desktop

Follow the procedures given in Chapter 1 to close a company and to close QuickBooks Desktop

SUMMARY

In this chapter, cash and credit sales were prepared for Your Name's Tech Services, a service business, using sales receipts (cash sales) and invoices (sales on account). Credit memos were issued. Customer accounts were added and revised. Invoices and sales receipts were edited, deleted, and voided. Customer payments for invoices were received. Bank deposits were made. The bank deposit included all receipts from cash sales and receive payments. All the transactions entered reinforced the QuickBooks Desktop concept of using the business form to record transactions rather than enter information in journals. However, QuickBooks Desktop does not disregard traditional accounting methods. Instead, it performs this function in the background. The Journal report was accessed and printed. The fact that the Customer:Job List functions as the Accounts Receivable Ledger and the Chart of Accounts functions as the General Ledger in QuickBooks Desktop was pointed out. The importance of reports for information and decision-making was illustrated. Exploration of the various sales and accounts receivable reports and graphs allowed information to be viewed from a sales standpoint and from an accounts receivable perspective. Sales reports emphasized both cash and credit sales according to the sales item generating the revenue. Accounts Receivable reports focused on amounts owed by credit customers. The traditional trial balance emphasizing the equality of debits and credits was prepared.

END-OF-CHAPTER QUESTIONS

TRUE/FALSE

ANSWER THE FOLLOWING QUESTIONS IN THE SPACE PROVIDED BEFORE THE QUESTION NUMBER.

_____ 2.01. A new customer can be added to a company's records on the fly.

_____ 2.02. QuickZoom allows you to print a report instantly.

_____ 2.03. An Item List stores information about products you purchase.

_____ 2.04. Credit memos are prepared to record a reduction to a sale on account.

_____ 2.05. The QuickBooks backup (.qbb) file is used to record transactions.

_____ 2.06. When a correction for a transaction is made, QuickBooks Desktop not only changes the form used to record the transaction, it also changes all journal and account entries for the transaction to reflect the correction.

_____ 2.07. Once transactions have been entered, modifications to a customer's account may be made only at the end of the fiscal year.

_____ 2.08. Graphs allow information to be viewed from both a sales standpoint and from an accounts receivable perspective.

_____ 2.09. Checks received for cash sales are held in the Undeposited Funds account until the bank deposit is made.

_____ 2.10. A customer's payment on account is immediately recorded in the cash account.

MULTIPLE CHOICE

WRITE THE LETTER OF THE CORRECT ANSWER IN THE SPACE PROVIDED BEFORE THE QUESTION NUMBER.

_____ 2.11. When an invoice is deleted, ___.
   A. the amount is changed to 0.00
   B. the word "Deleted" appears as the Memo
   C. it is removed without a trace
   D. an invoice cannot be deleted

_____ 2.12. To obtain information about sales by item, you can view ___ report(s).
   A. the Profit & Loss
   B. the Trial Balance
   C. Receivables reports
   D. Sales reports

_____ 2.13.   Two primary types of lists used in this chapter are ___.
A. Receivables and Payables
B. Invoices and Checks
C. Registers and Navigator
D. Customers and Items

_____ 2.14.   While in the Customer Balance Summary Report, it is possible to get an individual customer's information by using ___.
A. QuickReport
B. QuickZoom
C. QuickGraph
D. QuickSummary

_____ 2.15.   Undeposited Funds represents ___.
A. cash or checks received from customers but not yet deposited in the bank
B. all cash sales
C. the balance of the Accounts Receivable account
D. none of the above

_____ 2.16.   When you enter an invoice, an error may be corrected by ___.
A. backspacing or deleting
B. tabbing and typing
C. dragging and typing
D. all the above

_____ 2.17.   QuickBooks Desktop uses graphs to illustrate information about ___.
A. the Chart of Accounts
B. Sales
C. the Cash account
D. Supplies

_____ 2.18.   When a bank deposit is made, the amounts for cash and checks received are removed from ___ and deposited into ___.
A. Accounts Receivable, Checking
B. Payments Received, Checking
C. Checking, Cash
D. Undeposited Funds, Checking

_____ 2.19.   To enter a cash sale, ___ is completed.
A. a debit
B. an invoice
C. a sales receipt
D. receive payments

_____ 2.20.   When you add a customer using the Set Up method, you add ___.
A. complete information for a customer
B. only a customer's name
C. the customer's name, address, and telephone number
D. the customer's name and telephone number

FILL-IN

IN THE SPACE PROVIDED, WRITE THE ANSWER THAT MOST APPROPRIATELY COMPLETES THE SENTENCE.

2.21.   The report used to view only the balances on account for each customer is the _____.

2.22.   The form prepared to show a reduction to a sale on account is a(n) _____.

2.23.   The Journal report shows all transactions in the traditional _____ format.

2.24.   QuickBooks Desktop shows icons on the _____ and on the _____ that may be clicked to open the business documents used in recording transactions.

2.25.   The _____ icon is clicked to record the receipt of a payment on account.

SHORT ESSAY

For a purchase on account and the subsequent payment for the purchase, indicate which business forms are used to record the purchase and payment.

_____

_____

_____

_____

_____

END-OF-CHAPTER PROBLEM

YOUR NAME'S POOL & GARDEN OASIS

Chapter 2 continues with the entry of both cash and credit sales, receipt of payment by credit customers, credit memos, and bank deposits. In addition, reports focusing on sales and accounts receivable are prepared.

INSTRUCTIONS

Use the company file **Oasis 2018.qbw** that you used for Chapter 1. (Remember the year for the company file used should match the year of the software.) The company name should be Your Name's Pool & Garden Oasis. (You changed the company name to include your real name in Chapter 1.) Since this company was used in Chapter 1, when you see the Open a Company screen, you may see other QuickBooks Desktop files and/or folders associated with that company. QuickBooks Desktop will create them as you use a company file. Some of these files may have extensions of QBW.ND or .QBW.TLG. Folders that say QuickBooksAutoDataRecovery, SearchIndex, or Restored are common. For the most part, you do not use or change any of these files or folders, simply click the company file and click the Open button. Sometimes, when switching from one company to the next; i.e., Tech to Oasis, QuickBooks Desktop might mark your company file as read only. If this happens, refer to Chapter 1 for steps on how to change the file Properties from Read Only.

The invoices and sales receipts are numbered consecutively. Invoice 25 is the first invoice number used in this problem. Sales Receipt 15 is the first sales receipt number used when recording cash sales in this problem. If you wish, you may hide the History for customers on the invoices and sales receipts. Each invoice recorded should be a Service Invoice and contain a message. When selecting a message, choose the one that you feel is most appropriate for the transaction. Print each invoice and sales receipt as it is completed and do <u>not</u> print lines around each field. Remember that payments received on account should be recorded as Receive Payments and not as a Sales Receipt.

When recording transactions, use the following Sales Item chart to determine the item(s) billed. If the transaction does not indicate the size of the pool or property, use LandCom 1 or LandRes 1 for standard-size landscape service or PoolCom 1 or PoolRes 1 for a standard-sized pool. Remember that SpaCom 1 and SpaRes 1 are services for spas—<u>not</u> pools. If you get a message regarding the spelling of Lg., click Ignore All.

When printing reports, always remove the Date Prepared, Time Prepared, and Report Basis from the Header/Footer unless instructed otherwise by your instructor. Adjust the column size to display the information in full.

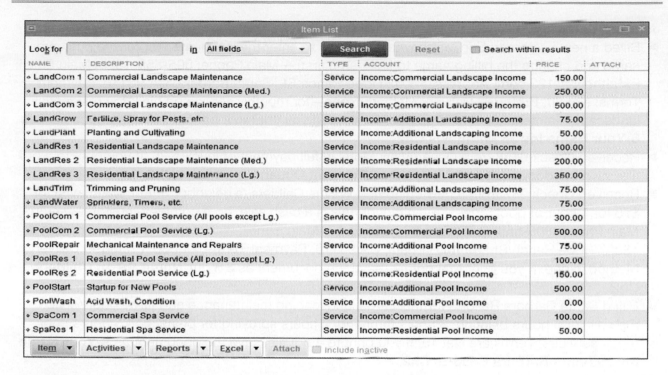

RECORD TRANSACTIONS

January 1

▶ Open the company file for **Oasis 2018** and enter the Password **QBDT2018**

▶ Billed Ocean View Motel for monthly landscape services and monthly pool maintenance services, Invoice 25. (Use a Service Invoice. Use LandCom 1 to record the monthly landscape service fee and PoolCom 1 to record the monthly pool service fee. The quantity for each item is 1.) Terms are Net 15. If you get a message regarding the spelling of Lg., click Ignore All. (Don't forget to add a Customer Message.) If you print to a pdf file, save the document as **1-Your Name Inv 25 Ocean View Motel Ch2**.

▶ Billed Jose Rios for monthly landscape and pool services at his home. Both the pool and landscaping are standard size. The terms are Net 30. (Did you use an Intuit Service Invoice?) If you print to a pdf file, save the document as **2-Your Name Inv 26 Rios Ch2**.

▶ Billed Designs for You for 2 hours shrub trimming (Item: LandTrim). Terms: Net 30. If you print to a pdf file, save the document as **3-Your Name Inv 27 Designs for You Ch2**.

▶ Change the last name for Annabelle Anderson to Annabelle Wagner for the Customer Name, Last Name, and Address Details. Then, record the receipt of Check 519 for $500 for pool startup services at her home, Sales Receipt 15. If you print to a pdf file, save the document as **4-Your Name SR 15 Wagner Ch2**.

▶ Received Check 8642 from Nancy Rhodes for $150 as payment in full on her account. (Don't forget to print the Payment Receipt.) If you print to a pdf file, save the document as **5-Your Name Rcv Pmt Rhodes Ch2**.

January 15

▶ Billed a new customer: Eric Matthews (remember to enter the last name first for the customer name and change the billing name to first name first)— Main Phone: 805-555-1875, Main Email: EMatthews@123.com, Address: 18048 Hope Ranch St., Santa Barbara, CA 93110, Payment Terms: Net 30, Preferred Delivery Method: None—for monthly service on his large residential landscape maintenance and large pool services. If you print to a pdf file, save the document as **6-Your Name Inv 28 Matthews Ch2**.

▶ Received Check 6758 from Ocean View Motel in full payment of Invoice 25. If you print to a pdf file, save the document as **7-Your Name Rcv Pmt Ocean View Motel Ch2**.

▶ Received Check 987 from a new customer: Wayne Childers (a neighbor of Eric Matthews) for $75 for 1 hour of pool repairs. Even though this is a cash sale, do a complete customer setup: Main Phone: 805-555-7175, Fax: 805-555-5717, Main E-mail: wchilders@abc.com, Address: 18087 Hope Ranch St., Santa Barbara, CA 93110, Payment Terms: Net 30. Preferred Delivery Method: None. If you print to a pdf file, save the document as **8-Your Name SR 16 Childers Ch2**.

▶ Billed Santa Barbara Resorts for their large landscaping maintenance and large pool service. Also bill for 5 hours planting, 3 hours trimming, 2 hours spraying for pests, and 3 hours pool repair services. Terms are Net 15. If you print to a pdf file, save the document as **9-Your Name Inv 29 Santa Barbara Resorts Ch2**.

January 30

▶ Received Check 1247 for $525 as payment in full from Designs for You. If you print to a pdf file, save the document as **10-Your Name Rcv Pmt Designs for You Ch2**.

▶ Received Check 8865 from Donna Vines for amount due. If you print to a pdf file, save the document as **11-Your Name Rcv Pmt Vines Ch2**.

▶ Billed Central Coast Resorts for large landscaping maintenance and large pool service. Terms are Net 15. If you print to a pdf file, save the document as **12-Your Name Inv 30 Central Coast Resorts Ch2**.

▶ Billed State Street Apartments for standard-size commercial landscape maintenance (LandCom1) and standard-size commercial pool service. Terms are Net 30. If you print to a pdf file, save the document as **13-Your Name Inv 31 State St Apts Ch2**.

▶ Deposit all cash receipts (this includes checks from both Sales Receipts and Payments on Account). Print the Deposit Summary. If you print to a pdf file, save the document as **14-Your Name Dep Sum Ch2**. (If you have difficulty printing a Deposit Summary as a pdf file, you may print the Deposit Slip and the Summary will be included.)

PRINT REPORTS AND BACKUP

▶ Customer Balance Detail Report for all transactions. Remember to remove Date Prepared and Time Prepared from all reports. Use Portrait orientation. If you print to a pdf file, save the document as **15-Your Name Cust Bal Detail Ch2**.

▶ Sales by Item Summary Report for 1/1/2018 through 1/30/2018. Portrait orientation. If you print to a pdf file, save the document as **16-Your Name Sales by Item Sum Ch2**.

▶ Journal report for 1/1/2018 through 1/30/2018. Remember to Expand the transactions in the report. Print in Landscape orientation, fit to one page wide. If you print to a pdf file, save the document as **17-Your Name Journal Ch2**.

▶ Trial Balance for 1/1/2018 through 1/30/2018. Portrait orientation. If you print to a pdf file, save the document as **18-Your Name Trial Bal Ch2**.

▶ Backup your work to **Oasis 2018 (Backup Ch. 2)**.

CHAPTER 2 CHECKLISTS

YOUR NAME'S TECH SERVICES

The checklist below shows all business forms and reports printed during training. Check each one that you printed. In the document names below, Your Name and Ch2 have been omitted, and report dates are given.

___	1-Inv 1: Garcia	___	16-SR 3: Research Corp.
___	2-Inv 2: McBride	___	17-Sales by Cust Detail, January 1-12, 2018
___	3-Inv 3 Allen	___	18-SR 1 (Corrected): Ray Morris
___	4-Inv 4: Baker and Martinez	___	19-Sales by Item Sum, January 1-14, 2018
___	5-Inv 5: Collins & Day	___	20-Rcv Pmt: Research Corp.
___	6-Inv 6: Clark, Hill, and Scott	___	21-Rcv Pmt: Johnson, Leavitt, and Moraga
___	7-Cust Bal Sum, January 5, 2018	___	22-Rcv Pmt: Taylor Illustrations
___	8-Cust Bal Detail: Baker and Martinez	___	23-Rcv Pmt: McBride, CPA
___	9-Inv 5 (Corrected): Collins & Day	___	24-Rcv Pmt: Wagner Productions
___	10-Trans List by Cust, January 1-7, 2018	___	25-Rcv Pmt: Garcia
___	11-Cust Bal Detail	___	26-Rcv Pmt: Brooks, Stark, & Thompson
___	12-CM 7: Baker and Martinez		
___	13-Inv 8: Collins	___	27-Dep Sum
___	14-SR 1: Morris	___	28-Journal, January 1-15, 2018
___	15-SR 2: Morris	___	29-Trial Balance, January 15, 2018

YOUR NAME'S POOL & GARDEN OASIS

The checklist below shows all business forms and reports printed during training. Check each one that you printed. In the document names below, Your Name and Ch2 have been omitted, and report dates are given.

___	1-Inv 25 Ocean View Motel	___	10-Rcv Pmt Designs for You
___	2-Inv 26 Rios	___	11-Rcv Pmt Vines
___	3-Inv 27 Designs for You	___	12-Inv 30 Central Coast Resorts
___	4-SR 15 Wagner	___	13-Inv 31 State Street Apartments
___	5-Rcv Pmt Rhodes	___	14-Dep Sum
___	6-Inv 28 Matthews	___	15-Cust Bal Detail, January 1-30,2018
___	7-Rcv Pmt Ocean View Motel	___	16-Sales by Item Sum, January 1-30, 2018
___	8-SR 16:Childers	___	17-Journal, January 1-30, 2018
___	9-Inv 29:Santa Barbara Resorts	___	18-Trial Bal, January 1-30, 2018

PAYABLES AND PURCHASES: SERVICE BUSINESS

3

LEARNING OBJECTIVES

At the completion of this chapter you will be able to:

3.01. Enter, edit, correct, and print bills.
3.02. Prepare and print the Transaction List by Vendor report.
3.03. Use QuickZoom in a report.
3.04. Understand Accrual Basis accounting.
3.05. Enter and edit bill in the Accounts Payable Register.
3.06. Prepare Register QuickReport.
3.07. Use Bill Tracker.
3.08. Prepare Unpaid Bills Detail report.
3.09. Delete Bill.
3.10. Add Vendor.
3.11. Enter Vendor Credit and view Accounts Payable Register.
3.12. Pay Bills and print Bill Payments Checks.
3.13. Write Checks to pay bills.
3.14. Edit, void, delete, and print checks.
3.15. Prepare Check Detail, Missing Check, and Voided/Deleted Transaction Summary reports.
3.16. Add Petty Cash Account, establish the Petty Cash Fund, and pay expenses with Petty Cash.
3.17. Purchase an asset with a company check.
3.18. Customize the report format to remove Date Prepared, Time Prepared, and Report Basis from the report header.
3.19. Prepare the Accounts Payable Aging Summary, Vendor Balance Summary, Accounts Payable Graph, Journal, and Trial Balance reports.

ACCOUNTING FOR PAYABLES AND PURCHASES

In a service business, most of the accounting for purchases and payables is simply paying bills for expenses incurred in the operation of the business. Purchases are for things used in the operation of the business. Some transactions will be in the form of cash purchases, and others will be purchases on account.

Bills can be paid when they are received or when they are due. Rather than use cumbersome journals, QuickBooks Desktop continues to focus on recording transactions based on the business document; therefore, you use the Enter Bills and Pay Bills features of the program to record the receipt and payment of bills. QuickBooks Desktop can remind you when payments are due and can calculate and apply discounts earned for paying bills early. Payments can be made by recording payments in the Pay Bills window or, if using the cash basis for accounting, by writing a check. A cash purchase can be recorded by writing a check or by using petty cash. Even though

QuickBooks Desktop focuses on recording transactions on the business forms used, all transactions are recorded behind the scenes in the Journal.

QuickBooks Desktop uses a Vendor List for all vendors with which the company has an account. QuickBooks Desktop does not refer to the Vendor List as the Accounts Payable Ledger; yet, that is exactly what it is. The total of the Vendor List/Accounts Payable Ledger will match the total of the Accounts Payable account in the Chart of Accounts/General Ledger. The Vendor List may be accessed through the Vendor Center.

As in Chapter 2, corrections can be made directly on the business form or within the account. New accounts and vendors may be added on the fly as transactions are entered. Reports illustrating vendor balances, unpaid bills, accounts payable aging, transaction history, and accounts payable registers may be viewed and printed. Graphs analyzing the amount of accounts payable by aging period provide a visual illustration of accounts payable.

TRAINING TUTORIAL AND PROCEDURES

The following tutorial will once again work with Your Name's Tech Services. As in Chapter 2, transactions will be recorded for this fictitious company. You should enter the transactions for Chapter 3 in the same company file that you used to record the Chapter 2 transactions. The tutorial for Your Name's Tech Services will continue in Chapter 4, where accounting for bank reconciliations, financial statement preparation, and closing an accounting period will be completed. To maximize training benefits, you should follow the Training Procedures given in Chapter 2.

DATES

As in the other chapters and throughout the text, the year used for the screen shots is 2018, which is the same year as the version of the program. You may want to check with your instructor to see if you should use 2018 as the year for the transactions. The year you used in Chapters 1 and 2 should be the same year that you use in Chapters 3 and 4.

PRINTING

Throughout the text, you will be instructed to print business documents and reports. Everything that is to be printed within the chapter and in the end-of-chapter problem has everything to be printed listed on a checklist on the last page of the chapter. In some instances, your instructor may direct you to change what you print. Always verify items to be printed with your instructor. The reports in the text have the Date Prepared, Time Prepared, and Report Basis removed from the header in all reports. Check with your instructor to see if you should do this.

BEGINNING THE TUTORIAL

In this chapter, you will be entering bills incurred by the company in the operation of the business. You will also be recording the payment of bills, purchases using checks, and purchases/payments using petty cash.

The Vendor List keeps information regarding the vendors with whom you do business and is the Accounts Payable Ledger. Vendor information includes the vendor names, addresses, telephone numbers, payment terms, credit limits, and account numbers. You will be using the following list for vendors with which Your Name's Tech Services has an account:

As in the previous chapters, all transactions are listed in memos. The transaction date will be the same as the memo date unless specified otherwise within the transaction. Vendor names, when necessary, will be given in the transaction. Unless other terms are provided, the terms are Net 30. Once a specific type of transaction has been entered in a step-by-step manner, additional transactions of the same or a similar type will be made without having instructions provided. Of course, you may always refer to instructions given for previous transactions for ideas or for steps used to enter those transactions. To determine the account used in the transaction, refer to the Chart of Accounts. When you are entering account information on a bill, clicking on the drop-down list arrow will show a list of the Chart of Accounts.

OPEN QUICKBOOKS DESKTOP AND COMPANY FILE

   Open QuickBooks Desktop and Your Name's Tech Services as instructed in Chapter 1 (the transactions for both Chapters 1 and 2 will be in this company file)

ENTER BILL

QuickBooks Desktop provides accounts payable tracking. Entering bills as soon as they are received is an efficient way to record your liabilities. Once bills have been entered, QuickBooks Desktop will be able to provide up-to-date cash flow reports. A bill is divided into two sections: a vendor-related section (the upper part of the bill that looks like a check and has a memo text box under it) and a detail section (the area that is divided into columns for Account, Amount, and Memo). The vendor-related section of the bill is where information for the actual bill is entered, including a memo with information about the transaction. The detail section is where the expense accounts, amounts, and transaction explanations are indicated.

> **MEMO**
> **DATE**: January 16, 2018
>
> Record the bill: Creative Advertising prepared and placed advertisements in local business publications announcing our new hardware and network installation service. Received Creative's Invoice 9875 for $260 as a bill with terms of Net 30.

 Record a bill

Click the **Enter Bills** icon in the Vendors section of the Home Page
Verify that Bill and Bill Received are marked at the top of the form
Complete the Vendor-section of the bill:
    Click the drop-down list arrow next to **VENDOR**
    Click **Creative Advertising**
- Name is entered as the vendor.

    Tab to **DATE**
- As with other business forms, when you tab to the date, it will be highlighted.
- When you type in the new date, the highlighted date will be deleted.

    Type **01/16/18** as the date
    Tab to **REF. NO.**
    Type the vendor's invoice number: **9875**
    Tab to **AMOUNT DUE**
    Type **260**
- QuickBooks Desktop will automatically insert the .00 after the amount.

    Tab to **TERMS**
    Click the drop-down list arrow next to **TERMS**
    Click **Net 15**
- QuickBooks Desktop automatically changes the Bill Due date to show 15 days from the transaction date.

    Click the drop-down list arrow for **TERMS**, and click **Net 30**
- QuickBooks Desktop automatically changes the Bill Due date to show 30 days from the transaction date.

    Tab to or click the first line in **MEMO** at the bottom of the Vendor section
    Enter the transaction explanation of **Ads for Hardware/Network Installation Services**
- The memo will appear as part of the transaction in the Accounts Payable account as well as in any report that used the individual transaction information.

Complete the Detail section of the bill using the **Expenses** tab
- Notice that the Expenses tab shows $260, the amount of the bill. QuickBooks Desktop automatically entered the amount when it was entered in the Vendor Section of the bill.

    Tab to or click in the column for **ACCOUNT**
    Click the drop-down list arrow next to **ACCOUNT**
    Click **Advertising Expense**
- Based on the accrual method of accounting, Advertising Expense is selected as the account used in this transaction because this expense should be matched against the revenue of the period.

    The **AMOUNT** column already shows **260.00**—no entry required

To Copy the memo **Ads for Hardware/Network Installation Services** from the Memo text box in the Vendor section of the bill to the Memo column in the Detail section of the bill:

- Click to the left of the letter **A** in Ads
- Highlight the memo text—**Ads for Hardware/Network Installation Services** by holding down the primary mouse button and dragging through the memo text
- Click **Edit** on the menu bar; and then, click **Copy**
  - Notice that the keyboard shortcut **Ctrl+C** is listed. This shortcut could be used rather than using the Edit menu and the Copy command.

- This copies the text and places it in a temporary storage area of Windows called the Clipboard.

Click in the **MEMO** column on the Expenses tab

Click **Edit** on the menu bar; and then, click **Paste**

- Notice the keyboard shortcut **Ctrl+V**.
- This inserts a copy of the material in the Windows Clipboard into the Memo column.
- This memo prints on all reports that include the transaction.

Click the **Save** icon at the top of the bill to save the transaction, leave it on the screen, and update the History

- If you get an Information Changed box for terms, click **No**.
- The Recent Transaction section of the Vendor History has been updated to include this bill.

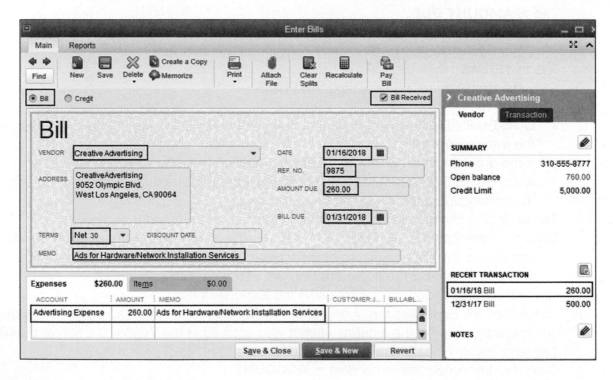

Do <u>not</u> click Save & Close

EDIT AND CORRECT ERRORS

If an error is discovered while you are entering information, it may be corrected by positioning the cursor in the field containing the error. You may do this by tabbing to move forward through each field or pressing Shift+Tab to move back to the field containing the error. If the error is highlighted, type the correction. If the error is not highlighted, you can correct it by pressing the backspace or the delete key as many times as necessary to remove the error, and then type the correction. (*Alternate method:* Point to the error, highlight it by dragging the mouse through the error, and then type the correction.)

 Practice editing and making corrections to the bill for Creative Advertising

Click the drop-down list arrow for **Vendor**
Click **California Telephone Co.**
Tab to **DATE**
To increase the date by one day, press +
- You may press shift and the = key next to the backspace key, or you may press the + key on the numerical keypad.

Press + two more times
- The date should be **01/19/18**.

To decrease the date by one day, press -
- You may type a hyphen (-) next to the number **0** or you may press the hyphen (-) key on the numerical keypad.

Press - two more times
- The date should be **01/16/18**.

Change the date by clicking on the calendar next to the date
Click **19** on the calendar for January 2018
Click the calendar again
Click **16** to change the date back to 01/16/2018
To change the amount, click between the **2** and the **6** in **AMOUNT DUE**
Press the **Delete** key two times to delete the **60**
Key in **99** and press the **Tab** key
- The Amount Due should be **299.00**. The amount of 299.00 should also be shown on the Expenses tab in the detail section of the bill.

Click the drop-down list arrow for **VENDOR**
Click **Creative Advertising**
Click to the right of the last **9** in **AMOUNT DUE**
Backspace two times to delete the **99**
Key in **60**
- The **AMOUNT DUE** should once again show **260.00**.

Refer to the original bill from Creative Advertising shown before Edit and Correct Errors to verify your entries
- Since you received the bill from the vendor, you do not print this entry unless your professor requests printing. When you print a bill, it automatically prints with lines around each field. If you print to a pdf file, save the document as **1-Your Name Bill Creative Ch3**.

Click the **Save & New** button to record the bill and go to the next bill
- If you get the Recording Transaction dialog box, click **Yes**.

PREPARE BILL WITH TWO EXPENSES

> **MEMO**
>
> **DATE**: January 18, 2018
>
> The company is trying out a 3D printer for a month to evaluate its relevancy to the company. Received a bill from Supply Spot for one month's rental of 3D printer, $25, and for supplies, which were consumed during January, $20, Invoice 1035A, Terms Net 10.

 Record a bill using two expense accounts

Complete the vendor-related section of the bill
Click the drop-down list arrow next to **VENDOR**
Click **Supply Spot**
Tab to or click **DATE**
- If you click in Date, you will have to delete the current date.
Enter **01/18/18**
Tab to or click in **REF NO**, enter the Vendor's invoice number: **1035A**
Tab to or click **AMOUNT DUE**
Enter **45**
Tab to or click on the line for **TERMS**
Type **Net 10** on the line for Terms, press the **Tab** key
You will get a **Terms Not Found** message box
Click the **Set Up** button
Complete the information required in the **New Terms** dialog box:
    Net 10 should appear as the Terms
    Standard should be selected
    Change the **Net due** from 0 to **10** days
    Discount percentage should be **0%**
    Discount if paid within **0** days

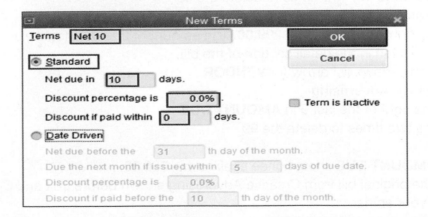

    Click **OK**
Tab to or click **MEMO** beneath the Terms
Enter **3D Printer Rental and Supplies for the Month** as the transaction description

To complete the **DETAIL SECTION** of the bill, use the Expenses tab and click the first line
for **ACCOUNT**

Click the drop-down list arrow next to **ACCOUNT**

Click **Equipment Rental**

- Because a portion of this transaction is for equipment that is being rented, Equipment
Rental is the appropriate account to use.

AMOUNT column shows **45.00**

Change this to reflect the actual amount of the Equipment Rental

Tab to **AMOUNT** to highlight

Type **25**

Tab to **MEMO**

Enter **3D Printer Rental for the Month** as the transaction explanation

Tab to **ACCOUNT**

Click the drop-down list arrow next to **ACCOUNT**

Click **Office Supplies Expense**

- The transaction information indicates that the 3D Printer supplies will be used within the
month of January. Using Office Supplies Expense account correctly charges the
supplies expense against the period.
- If the transaction indicated that the 3D Printer supplies were purchased to have on
hand, the appropriate account to use would be the asset Office Supplies.
- Remember the formula:
  - Used within the month = Expense
  - Have on hand = Asset

The **AMOUNT** column correctly shows **20.00** as the amount

Tab to or click **MEMO**

Enter **3D Printer Supplies for the Month** as the transaction explanation

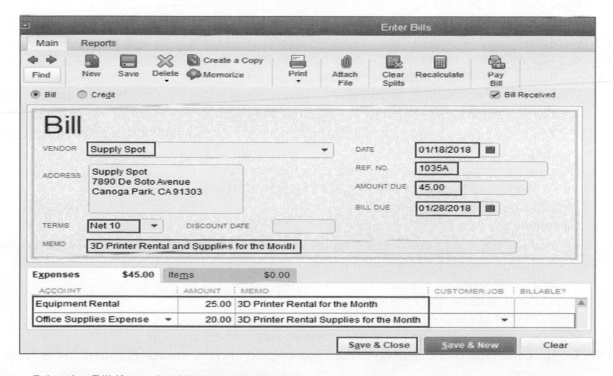

Print the Bill if required by your instructor

- If you print to a pdf file, save the document as **2-Your Name Bill Supply Spot Ch3**.

Click **Save & Close** to close the bill

- If you get an Information Changed message regarding the change of Terms for Supply Spot, click **Yes**. This will change the Terms to Net 10 for all transactions with Supply Spot.

TRANSACTION LIST BY VENDOR REPORT

To obtain information regarding individual transactions grouped by vendor, you prepare a Transaction List by Vendor Report. This allows you to view the vendors with recorded transactions. The type of transaction is identified; for example, the word *Bill* appears when you have entered the transaction as a bill. The transaction date, any invoice numbers or memos entered when recording the transaction, the accounts used, and the transaction amounts appear in the report.

 Prepare a **Transaction List by Vendor Report**

Click **Reports** on the Top Icon Bar to open the Report Center
Click **Vendors & Payables** to select the type of report
Double-click **Transaction List by Vendor** in the Vendor Balances Section
Enter the Dates From **01/01/18** To **01/18/18**, press **Tab**
Once the report is displayed, click the **Customize Report** button
Click the **Header/Footer** tab
Click **Date Prepared** and **Time Prepared** to deselect these features
Click **OK**
Resize the width of the Memo column so the memos are displayed in full:
Position the cursor on the sizing diamond between **Memo** and **Account**

- The cursor turns into a plus with arrows pointing left and right. | Memo ⊹ Account |

Hold down the primary (left) mouse button
Drag the cursor from the diamond between **Memo** and **Account** to the right until you have the memo displayed in full

- You will see a dotted vertical line while you are dragging the mouse and holding down the primary mouse button.

Look at the other columns, if any have … to represent information not shown, point to the sizing diamond and drag until the information is shown

- You may make columns smaller by pointing to the sizing diamond and dragging to the left.

Once the columns have been resized, click the **Print** button
You may choose Report or Save As PDF, click **Report**
Click **Landscape** for the orientation
Click **Preview**

- You will be able to see how the report will appear when it is printed. If the report prints two-pages wide, you may want to resize the columns until you can get it to print on one-page wide.

Click **Close** to close the **Preview**
Click **Cancel** to cancel printing
With the resized report on the screen, look at each vendor account

- Note the type of transaction in the Type column and the invoice numbers in the Num column.

- The Memos shown are the ones entered in the Vendor (upper) section of the bill.
- The **Account** column shows **Accounts Payable** as the account.
- As in any traditional accounting transaction recording a purchase on account, the Accounts Payable account is credited.
- The **Split** column shows the other accounts used in the transaction.
- If the word **-SPLIT-** appears in this column, it indicates that more than one account was used.
- The transaction for Supply Spot has -SPLIT- in the Split Column. This is because the transaction used two accounts: Equipment Rental and Office Supplies Expense for the debit portion of the transaction.

Your Name's Tech Services
Transaction List by Vendor
January 1 - 18, 2018

Type	Date	Num	Memo	Account	Clr	Split	Debit	Credit
Creative Advertising								
Bill	01/16/2018	9875	Ads for Hardware/Network Installation Services	Accounts Payable		Advertising Expense		260.00 ◀
Supply Spot								
Bill	01/18/2018	1035A	3D Printer Rental and Supplies for the Month	Accounts Payable		-SPLIT-		45.00

Print the report in Landscape orientation (11-inches wide by 8 ½ inches long) as instructed in Chapter 2, do <u>not</u> close the report
- If you print to a pdf file, save the document as **3-Your Name Trans List by Vend Ch3**.

QUICKZOOM

Sofia Sanchez wants more detailed information regarding the accounts used in the Split column of the report. Specifically, she wants to know what accounts were used for the transaction of January 18, 2018 for Supply Spot. To see the account names, Sofia will use the QuickZoom feature of QuickBooks Desktop.

➡️ Use QuickZoom

Point to the word **-SPLIT-** in the Split column
- The mouse pointer turns into .

Double-click to **Zoom** in to see the accounts used in the transaction
- This returns you to the *original bill* entered for Supply Spot for the transaction of 01/18/2018.
- The Expense accounts used are Equipment Rental and Office Supplies Expense.

Click the **Close** button on the bill to return to the Transaction List by Vendor Report
To close the report, click the **Close** button
- If you get a Memorize Report dialog box, click **No**.

Close the Report Center

EDIT VENDOR

The Vendor Center contains a list of all the vendors with whom Your Name's Tech Services has an account. As information changes or errors in the vendor information are noted, the Vendor Information may be edited.

> **MEMO**
> **DATE**: January 18, 2018
>
> In the Vendor Name, Company Name, Address, and Print Name on Check As for Greg's Garage and Auto Service, change the word **and** to the symbol **&**. Add a space between Greg'sGarage in the address.

 Open the Vendor Center and correct the address for Greg's Garage and Auto Services

Click **Vendors** on the Top Icon Bar, then click **Vendor Center**
Click **Greg's Garage and Auto Services** in the Vendor List, click the **Edit** icon
In the VENDOR NAME delete the word **and**; then, enter the symbol **&** (make sure there is a space before and after the symbol)
Repeat to change the COMPANY NAME
In the ADDRESS DETAILS BILLED FROM section, click between **Greg's** and **Garage**, press the **Space** bar
Change the word **and** in the Billed From section to the symbol **&** (make sure there is a space before and after the symbol)
Click the **Payment Settings** tab
Change the PRINT NAME ON CHECK AS to: **Greg's Garage & Auto Services**
Click **OK**
View the corrected information as shown; and, then, close the Vendor Center

ACCRUAL METHOD OF ACCOUNTING

The accrual method of accounting matches the expenses of a period against the revenue of the period. Frequently, when in training, there may be difficulty in determining whether something is recorded as an expense or as an asset (a prepaid expense). When you buy or pay for something in advance that will eventually be an expense for operating the business, it is recorded as an increase to an asset rather than an increase to an expense.

When you have an expense that is paid for in advance, such as insurance, it is called a prepaid expense. At the time the prepaid asset is used (such as using one month of the six months of insurance shown in the Prepaid Insurance account), an adjusting entry is made to account for the amount used during the period. This adjusting entry will be made in Chapter 4.

Unless otherwise instructed in a transaction, use the accrual basis of accounting when recording the following entries. (Notice the exception in the first transaction.)

PREPARE ADDITIONAL BILLS

 Enter the four transactions in the memo

3

MEMO

DATE: January 19, 2018

Received a bill from Computer Professionals Magazine for a six-month subscription. Invoice 1553, $74, Net 30 days. (Enter as a Dues and Subscriptions expense.) Memo: Six-Month Subscription.

Sofia Sanchez received office supplies from Supply Spot, Invoice 1050A, $450, terms Net 10 days. These supplies will be used over a period of several months so record the entry in the <u>asset</u> account Office Supplies. Memo: Supplies to have on hand.

While Emily Edwards was on her way to a training session at Baker & Martinez, the company car broke down. Greg's Garage & Auto Services towed and repaired the car for a total of $575, Net 30 days, Invoice 8608, Memo: Auto Repairs.

Received a bill from Valley Insurance Company for the annual auto insurance premium, $2,850, terms Net 30, Invoice 3659, Memo: Annual Auto Insurance (Note: This is a prepaid expense).

- Refer to the instructions given for the two previous transactions entered.
- Remember, the Vendor's Invoice Number is entered as the REF. NO.
- When recording bills, you will need to determine the accounts used in the transaction. Refer to the Chart of Accounts/General Ledger for account names.
- If a memo is required for a bill, enter it in the Vendor (top) section and in the Detail (lower) section of the bill.
- To go from one bill to the next, click the **Save & New** button.
- Do not change terms for any of the vendors.
- If you print to a pdf file, save the documents as **4-Your Name Bill Computer Prof Mag Ch3**, **5-Your Name Bill Supply Spot Ch3**, **6-Your Name Bill Greg's Garage Ch3**, **7-Your Name Bill Valley Ins Ch3**.
- After entering the fourth bill, click **Save & Close**.

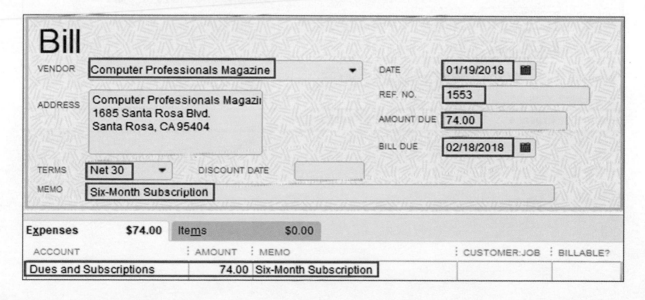

- After you enter the vendor's name on the next bill, the information from the previous bill appears on the screen. As you enter the transaction, simply delete any unnecessary information. This may be done by tabbing to the information and pressing the delete key until the information is deleted. Or you may drag through the information to highlight, then press the Delete key. After the "old" information is deleted, enter the new information. If the amount of $450 doesn't show on the Expenses tab automatically, simply enter $450 in the Amount Column. You will need to delete information on the second line of Expenses.)

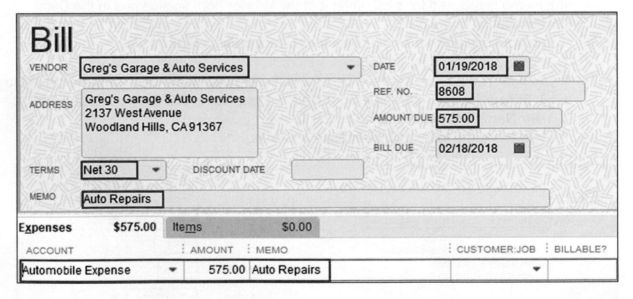

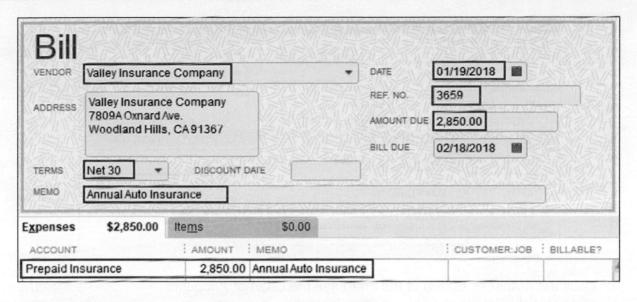

ENTER BILL IN ACCOUNTS PAYABLE REGISTER

The Accounts Payable Register maintains a record of all the transactions recorded within the Accounts Payable account. Entering a bill directly into the Accounts Payable Register can be faster than filling out all the information through Enter Bills. When entering a bill in the register, QuickBooks Desktop also completes a bill behind the scenes.

> **MEMO**
>
> **DATE**: January 19, 2018
>
> Rapid Delivery Service provides our delivery service for training manuals delivered to customers. Received the monthly bill for January deliveries from Rapid Delivery Service, $175, terms Net 10, Invoice 4688.

 Use the **Accounts Payable Register** to record the above transaction

Click the **Chart of Accounts** icon on the Home Page
   OR
Use the keyboard shortcut **Ctrl+A**
Click **Accounts Payable**

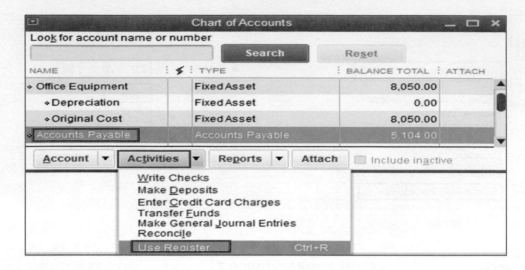

Click the **Activities** button at the bottom of the Chart of Accounts
Click **Use Register**
> **OR**

Use the keyboard shortcut **Ctrl+R**

DATE	NUMBER	VENDOR		DUE DATE	BILLED	✔	PAID	BALANCE
	TYPE	ACCOUNT	MEMO					
01/19/2018	3659	Valley Insurance Company		02/18/2018	2,850.00			4,529.00
	BILL	Prepaid Insuran	Annual Auto Insu					
01/19/2018	8608	Greg's Garage & Auto Services		02/18/2018	575.00			5,104.00
	BILL	Automobile Expe	Auto Repairs					
19/2018 📅	Number	Vendor	▼	Due Date 📅	Billed		Paid	
		Account ▼	Memo					

Splits

☐ 1-Line   ☐ Show open balance   ENDING BALANCE   **5,104.00**

Sort by   Date, Type, Number/Ref ▼   Record   Restore

The transaction date of **01/19/2018** is highlighted in the blank entry at the end of the
   Accounts Payable Register
• If it is not, click in the date column in the blank entry and key in **01/19/18**.
The word *Number* is in the next column
Tab to or click in the **NUMBER** column
• The word *Number* disappears.
Enter the Invoice Number **4688**
Tab to or click in the **VENDOR** column
Click the drop-down list arrow for **VENDOR**
Click **Rapid Delivery Service**

Tab to or click in the **DUE DATE** column

Since the transactions terms are Net 10, enter the DUE DATE of **01/29/2018**

- There is no place in the register to enter the Terms. Since Rapid Delivery normally uses 30-day terms for us, you will need to enter the Due Date for the Net 10 terms in the transaction.

Tab to or click in the **BILLED** column

Enter the amount **175**

Tab to or click **ACCOUNT**

- Note that "Bill" is inserted into the Type field.

Click the drop-down list arrow for **ACCOUNT**

Determine the appropriate account to use for the delivery expense

- Scroll through the accounts until you find the one appropriate for this entry.

Click **Postage and Delivery**

Tab to or click **Memo**

For the transaction memo, key **January Delivery Expense**

- If you view the bill that QuickBooks Desktop prepares when entering this transaction, you will see the memo in the Vendor (top) section of the bill but not in the Detail (lower) section of the bill.

Click the **Record** button to record the transaction

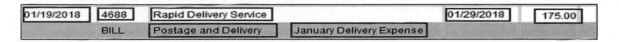

Do <u>not</u> close the register

EDIT TRANSACTION IN ACCOUNTS PAYABLE REGISTER

Because QuickBooks Desktop makes corrections extremely user friendly, a transaction can be edited or changed directly in the Accounts Payable Register as well as on the original bill. By eliminating the columns for TYPE and MEMO, it is possible to change the register to show each transaction on one line. This can make the register easier to read.

MEMO

DATE: January 20, 2018

Upon examination of the invoices and the bills entered, Sofia Sanchez discovers two errors: The actual amount of the invoice for Rapid Delivery Services was $195. The amount recorded was $175. The amount of the Invoice for *Computer Professionals Magazine* was $79, not $74. Change the transaction amounts for these transactions.

 Correct the above transactions in the Accounts Payable Register

Click the check box for **1-line** to select

- Each Accounts Payable transaction will appear on one line.

Click the transaction for *Rapid Delivery Service*

Click between the **1** and **7** in the BILLED column for the transaction

Press **Delete** to delete the 7, type **9**

- The amount should be **195.00**.

Scroll through the register until the transaction for *Computer Professionals Magazine* is visible

Click the transaction for *Computer Professionals Magazine*

The **Recording Transaction** dialog box appears on the screen

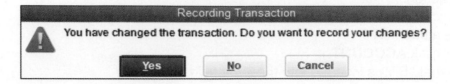

Click **Yes** to record the changes to the Rapid Delivery Service transaction

- The transaction for *Computer Professionals Magazine* will be the active transaction.

Click between the **4** and the **decimal point** in the BILLED column

Press the **Backspace** key one time to delete the 4, type **9**

- The amount for the transaction should be **79.00**.

Click the **Record** button at the bottom of the register to record the change in the transaction

Click **Yes** on the Recording Transaction Dialog Box

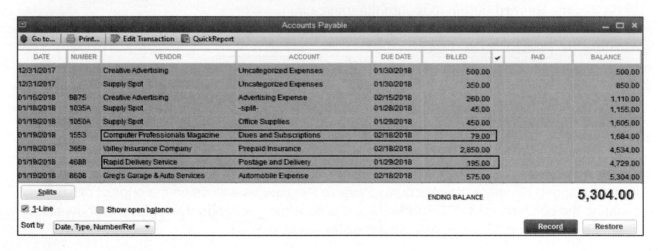

        Do <u>not</u> close the register

PREPARE REGISTER QUICKREPORT

After editing a transaction, you may want to view information about a specific vendor. This can be done quickly and efficiently by clicking the vendor's name within a transaction and then clicking the QuickReport button at the top of the Register.

MEMO

DATE: January 20, 2018

Several transactions have been entered for Supply Spot. You like to view transaction information for all vendors that have several transactions within a short period of time.

Prepare a QuickReport for Supply Spot
Click any field in any transaction for *Supply Spot*
Click the **QuickReport** button at the top of the Register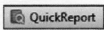
- The Register QuickReport for All Transactions for Supply Spot appears on the screen.
Remove the **Date Prepared, Time Prepared,** and **Report Basis** as previously instructed
Resize any columns that are not fully displayed and make the Amount column smaller
Click the **Print** button, click **Report**
Select **Landscape** orientation
Click **Preview** to view the report before printing

3

Your Name's Tech Services
Register QuickReport
All Transactions

Type	Date	Num	Memo	Account	Paid	Open Balance	Amount
Supply Spot							
Bill	12/31/2017		Opening balance	Accounts Payable	Unpaid	350.00	350.00
Bill	01/18/2018	1035A	3D Printer Rental and Supplies for the Month	Accounts Payable	Unpaid	45.00	45.00
Bill	01/19/2018	1050A	Supplies to have on hand	Accounts Payable	Unpaid	450.00	450.00
Total Supply Spot						845.00	845.00
TOTAL						**845.00**	**845.00**

- The report appears on the screen as a full page.
- Sometimes, a full-page report on the screen cannot be read.
To read the text in the report, click the report page shown
- If a report contains more than one page, click the **Next Page** button at the top of the report.
When finished viewing the report, click **Close**
- You will return to the **Print Reports** screen.
After resizing, the report should fit on one page; if it doesn't keep resizing or click **Fit report to one page wide** to select
Click **Print** button on the **Print Reports** screen
- If you print to a pdf file, save the document as **8-Your Name QuickReport Supply Spot Ch3**.
Close the **Register QuickReport**, the **Accounts Payable Register**, and the **Chart of Accounts**

PREPARE UNPAID BILLS DETAIL REPORT

It is possible to get information regarding unpaid bills by simply preparing a report—no more digging through tickler files, recorded invoices, ledgers, or journals. QuickBooks Desktop prepares an Unpaid Bills Report listing each unpaid bill grouped and subtotaled by vendor.

MEMO
DATE: January 25, 2018

Sofia Sanchez prepares an Unpaid Bills Report for you each week. Even though Your Name's Tech Services is a small business, you like to have a firm control over cash flow, so you can determine which bills will be paid during the week.

Prepare and print an Unpaid Bills Report

Click **Unpaid Bills Detail** in the **Vendors & Payables** list on the Reports Menu
    OR
Click **Reports** on the Top Icon Bar, click **Vendors & Payables**, and double-click **Unpaid**
    Bills Detail in the Vendor Balances section of the Report Center
Remove the Date Prepared and Time Prepared from the report header
Provide the report date by clicking in the text box for **Dates**, dragging through the date to
    highlight, and typing **01/25/18**
Tab to generate the report

Your Name's Tech Services
Unpaid Bills Detail
As of January 25, 2018

Type	Date	Num	Due Date	Aging	Open Balance
Computer Professionals Magazine					
Bill	01/19/2018	1553	02/18/2018		79.00 ◀
Total Computer Professionals Magazine					79.00
Creative Advertising					
Bill	12/31/2017		01/30/2018		500.00
Bill	01/16/2018	9875	02/15/2018		260.00
Total Creative Advertising					760.00
Greg's Garage & Auto Services					
Bill	01/19/2018	8608	02/18/2018		575.00
Total Greg's Garage & Auto Services					575.00
Rapid Delivery Service					
Bill	01/19/2018	4688	01/29/2018		195.00
Total Rapid Delivery Service					195.00
Supply Spot					
Bill	01/18/2018	1035A	01/28/2018		45.00
Bill	01/19/2018	1050A	01/29/2018		450.00
Bill	12/31/2017		01/30/2018		350.00
Total Supply Spot					845.00
Valley Insurance Company					
Bill	01/19/2018	3659	02/18/2018		2,850.00
Total Valley Insurance Company					2,850.00
TOTAL					**5,304.00**

Adjust column widths as necessary and print in **Portrait** orientation
- If you print to a pdf file, save the document as **9-Your Name Unpaid Bills Detail Ch3**.
Click **Close** to close the report
Click **No** if you get a Memorize Report dialog box
If necessary, click **Close** to close the **Report Center**

DELETE BILL

QuickBooks Desktop makes it possible to delete any bill that has been recorded. No adjusting
entries are required to do this. Simply access the bill or go to the transaction in the Accounts
Payable Register and delete the bill.

> **MEMO**
> **DATE**: January 26, 2018
>
> After reviewing the Unpaid Bills Report, Sofia realizes that the bill recorded for *Computer Professionals Magazine* should have been recorded for *Computer Technologies Magazine*.

 Delete the bill recorded for Computer Professionals Magazine

Access the Chart of Accounts in one of the following three ways:
   Click the **Chart of Accounts** icon on the Home Page
   Use the keyboard shortcut **Ctrl+A**
   Use the menu bar, click **Lists**, and click **Chart of Accounts**
With the Chart of Accounts showing on the screen, click **Accounts Payable**
Open the Accounts Payable Register using one of the three following ways:
   Use keyboard shortcut **Ctrl+R**
   Click **Activities Button**, click **Use Register**
   Double-click the Accounts Payable account
Click on the bill for *Computer Professionals Magazine*
To delete the bill, use one of the following two methods:
   Click **Edit** on the QuickBooks Desktop menu bar, click **Delete Bill**
   Use the keyboard shortcut **Ctrl+D**

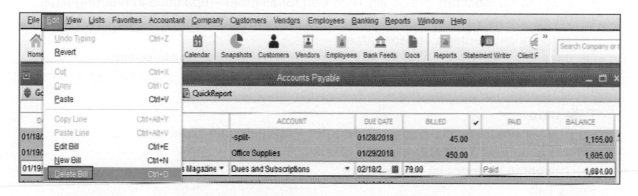

- The **Delete Transaction** dialog box appears on the screen.

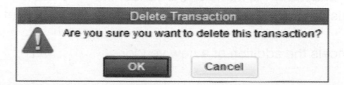

Click **OK** to delete the bill
- Notice that the transaction no longer appears in the Accounts Payable Register and that the Ending Balance of the account is 5,225.00 rather than 5,304.00.
Close the **Accounts Payable Register**
Close the **Chart of Accounts**

ADD VENDOR WHILE RECORDING BILL

When you type the first letter(s) of a vendor name on the Vendor Line, QuickBooks Desktop tries to match the name to one in the Vendor List and enter it on the Vendor line. If the vendor is not in the Vendor List, a QuickBooks Desktop dialog box for Vendor Not Found appears with choices for Quick Add—adding just the vendor name—or Set Up—adding the vendor name and all vendor account information. When the new vendor information is complete, QuickBooks Desktop fills in the blanks on the bill for the vendor, and you finish entering the rest of the transaction.

> **MEMO**
> **DATE**: January 26, 2018
>
> Record the bill for a six-month subscription to *Computer Technologies Magazine*. The transaction date is 01/19/18, amount $79, Terms Net 30, Invoice 1553. This is recorded as an expense. The address and telephone for *Computer Technologies Magazine* is 12405 Menlo Park Drive, Menlo Park, CA 94025, 510-555-3829.

   Record the transaction

Access the **Enter Bills** screen
- Step-by-step instructions will be provided only for entering a new vendor.
- Refer to transactions previously recorded for all other steps used in entering a bill.
- When you key the first few letters of a vendor name, QuickBooks Desktop will automatically enter a vendor name.

On the line for VENDOR, type the **C** for *Computer Technologies Magazine*
- The vendor name **CA Water** appears on the vendor line and is highlighted and the list of Vendor names that start with C is displayed.

Type **omp**
- The vendor name changes to **Computer Professionals Magazine**.

Finish typing **uter Technologies Magazine**
- The entire Vendor List is displayed.

Press **Tab**

The **Vendor Not Found** dialog box appears on the screen with buttons for:
- **Quick Add**—adds only the name to the vendor list.
- **Set Up**—adds the name to the vendor list and allows all account information to be entered.
- **Cancel**—cancels the addition of a new vendor.

Click **Set Up**
- Computer Technologies Magazine is shown in the VENDOR NAME text box.

If necessary, highlight the VENDOR NAME in the VENDOR NAME text box

Copy the name to the Company Name text box by using the **Ctrl+C** keyboard shortcut for copy

Click in the COMPANY NAME text box and use **Ctrl+V** to paste the name into the text box
- Since this is a new vendor, notice that there is no OPENING BALANCE to enter.

Tab to or click in the text box for **Main Phone**

Enter the telephone number **510-555-3829**

Tab to or click the first line for **BILLED FROM** in the **ADDRESS DETAILS** section
* Computer Technologies Magazine appears as the first line in the address.

Position the cursor at the end of the name, press **Enter** or click the line beneath the company name (Do not tab)

Type the address listed in the Memo

Press **Enter** at the end of each line

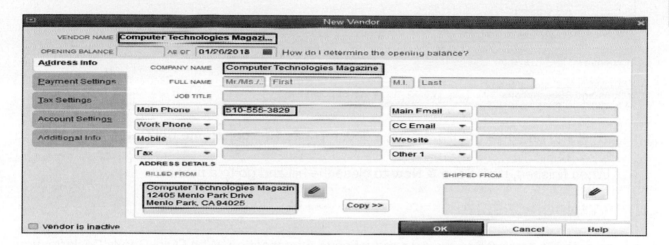

To enter the information for Terms, click the **Payment Settings** tab on the left side of the New Vendor screen

Click drop-down list arrow next to **PAYMENT TERMS**

Click **Net 30**

Make sure **PRINT NAME ON CHECK AS** shows **Computer Technologies Magazine**
* If not enter the name.

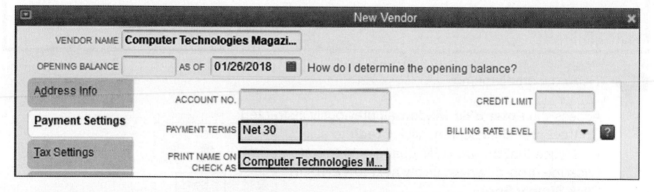

Click the **OK** button for **New Vendor** screen
* The information for Vendor, Terms, and the Dates is filled in on the Enter Bills screen.

If necessary, change the transaction date to **01/19/18**

Complete the bill using the information in the Memo and the instructions previously provided for entering bills

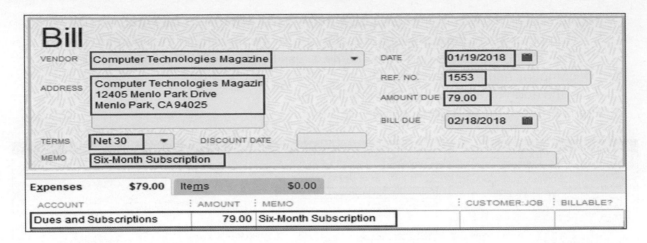

- If you print to a pdf file, save the document as **10-Your Name Bill Comp Tech Mag Ch3**.

When finished, click **Save & New** to close the bill and go to a new bill

ENTER VENDOR CREDIT

Credit memos are prepared to record a reduction to a transaction. With QuickBooks Desktop, you use the Enter Bills window to record credit memos received from vendors acknowledging a return of or an allowance for a previously recorded bill and/or payment. The amount of a credit memo is deducted from the amount owed.

MEMO

DATE: January 26, 2018

Received Credit Memo 789 for $5 from Supply Spot for a return of 3D printer supplies that were damaged.

 Record a credit memo

Access the **Enter Bills** window as previously instructed

On the **Enter Bills** screen, click **Credit** to select

- Notice that the word *Bill* changes to *Credit*.

Click the drop-down list arrow next to **VENDOR**

Click **Supply Spot**

Tab to or click the **DATE**

Type **01/26/18**

Tab to or click **REF. NO.**

Type **789**

Tab to or click **CREDIT AMOUNT**

Type **5**

Tab to or click in **MEMO** in the vendor (upper) section of the Credit

Enter **Returned Damaged 3D Printer Supplies**

Tab to or click the first line of **ACCOUNT**

Click the drop-down list arrow

Since the 3D printer supplies were to be used within the month, this was entered originally as an expense, click the account **Office Supplies Expense**
- The AMOUNT column should show **5.00**; if not, enter **5**.

Copy the Memo to the **MEMO** column in the detail (lower) section of the Credit

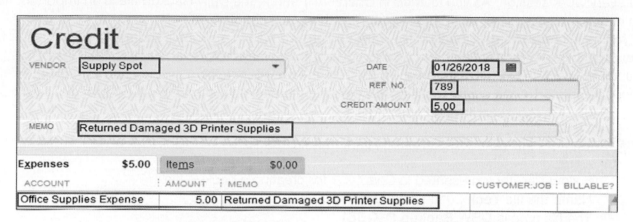

- If you print to a pdf file, save the document as **11-Your Name CM Supply Spot Ch3**. Click **Save & Close** to record the credit and exit **Enter Bills**
- QuickBooks Desktop records the credit in the Accounts Payable account and shows the transaction type as BILLCRED in the Accounts Payable Register.

VIEW CREDIT IN ACCOUNTS PAYABLE REGISTER

When recording the credit in the last transaction, QuickBooks Desktop listed the transaction type as BILLCRED in the Accounts Payable Register.

 Verify the credit from Supply Spot

Follow steps previously provided to access the Accounts Payable Register
If a check mark shows in the **1-Line** check box, remove it by clicking the check box
- This changes the display in the Accounts Payable Register from 1-Line to multiple lines.

Look at the **Number/Type** column and verify the type **BILLCRED**
- Notice the balance of 5,299.00. The balance of Accounts Payable after the bill for Computer Technologies Magazine was entered was 5,304.00. The new balance of 5,299.00 is 5.00 less, which is the amount of the credit.

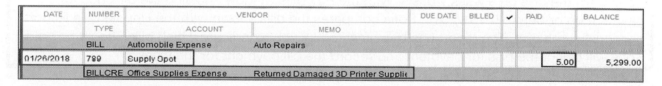

Close the **Accounts Payable Register** and the **Chart of Accounts**

PREPARE DAILY BACKUP

A backup file is prepared as a safeguard in case you make an error. After several transactions have been recorded, it is wise to prepare a backup file. In addition, a backup should be made at the end of every work session. As you learned in Chapters 1 and 2, the Daily Backup file is an important file to create for saving your work as you progress through a chapter.

If you have created a daily backup file while you are working in a chapter and make an error later in your training and cannot figure out how to correct it, you may restore the backup file. Restoring your daily backup file will restore your work from the previous training session and eliminate the work completed in the current session. By creating the backup file now, it will contain your work for Chapters 1, 2 and up through entering the Credit Memo in Chapter 3.

   Prepare the Tech 2018 (Daily Backup).qbb file

Follow the steps presented in Chapter 1 for creating a backup file
Name the file **Tech 2018 (Daily Backup)**
The file type is **QBW Backup (* .QBB)**
- This uses the same backup file that you prepared in Chapter 2.
- The daily backup file will now contain the work from Chapters 1 and 2 plus Chapter 3 up through entering the credit for a vendor.

PAY BILLS

When using QuickBooks Desktop, you should pay any bills recorded in Enter Bills directly from Pay Bills. QuickBooks Desktop will mark the bills "Paid" and will prepare the bill payment check automatically. If you have recorded a bill for a transaction and pay it by using Write Checks, the bill will not be marked Paid and will continue to show up as an amount due. If you have not entered a bill for an amount you owe, then it is paid by completing Write Checks.

Using the Pay Bills window enables you to determine which bills to pay, the method of payment—check or credit card—and the appropriate account. When determining which bills to pay, QuickBooks Desktop allows you to display the bills by due date, discount date, vendor, or amount. All bills may be shown, or bills that are due by a certain date may be displayed.

MEMO

DATE: January 26, 2018

Sofia pays the bills on a weekly basis. With the Pay Bills window showing the bills due for payment on or before 01/31/2018, Sofia compares the bills shown with the Unpaid Bills Report previously prepared. The report has been marked by you to indicate which bills should be paid. Sofia will select the bills for payment and record the bill payment for the week.

   Pay the bills for the week

Click the **Pay Bills** icon in the Vendors section of the Home Page to access the **Pay Bills** window
- The Pay Bills screen is comprised of three sections:
  - SELECT BILLS TO BE PAID
  - DISCOUNT & CREDIT INFORMATION FOR HIGHLIGHTED BILL
  - PAYMENT

Complete the SELECT BILLS TO BE PAID section:

If necessary, click **Show All Bills** to select

Click the drop-down list arrow for Filter By, click **All vendors**

Sort By should be **Due Date**

- If this is not showing, click the drop-down list arrow next to the **Sort By** text box, click **Due Date**.

Scroll through the list of bills

Click the drop-down list arrow next to the **Sort By** text box

Click **Vendor**

- This shows you how much you owe each vendor.

Again, click the drop-down list arrow next to the **Sort By** text box

Click **Amount Due**

- This shows you your bills from the highest amount owed to the lowest.

Click drop-down list arrow next to the **Sort By** text box, click **Due Date**

- The bills will be shown according to the date due.

Click **Due on or before** in the Select Bills to be Paid Section for Show Bills to select this option

Click in the text box for the date

Drag through the date to highlight, enter **01/31/18** as the date, press **Tab**

- Since you pressed Tab after making a change to **Show Bills**, you must select **Filter By** or you will get a warning message. If this happens, click **OK**.

Click the drop-down list arrow on **Filter By**. Select **All Vendors**.

Scroll through the list of bills due

Select the bills to be paid

- The bills shown on the screen are an exact match to the bills you marked to be paid when you reviewed the Unpaid Bills Report.

Click the **Select All Bills** button beneath the listing of bills

- The **Select All Bills** button changes to **Clear Selections** so bills can be unmarked and the bills to be paid may be selected again.
- If you do not want to pay all the bills shown, mark each bill to be paid by clicking on the individual bill or using the down-cursor key to select a bill and then press the space bar.

To apply the **$5** credit from **Supply Spot**, click in the **VENDOR** column for the **$45** transaction for Supply Spot with a DUE DATE of **01/28/2018**

- This will highlight the bill and leave the check in the check box for selecting the bill. If you click the check box and remove the check mark, you will need to click the check box a second time to mark the bill as being selected.
- Notice that All Vendors is removed from Filter By. It is fine to leave it blank because the bills to be paid have been selected.

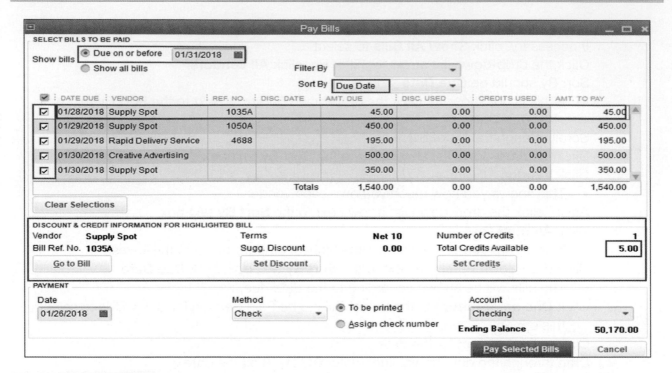

Click the **Set Credits** button

Complete the DISCOUNT & CREDIT INFORMATION FOR HIGHLIGHTED BILL section:

    The **Vendor** is **Supply Spot**

    The Number of **Credits** is **1**

    Total Credits Available is **$5.00**

Click the **Set Credits** button

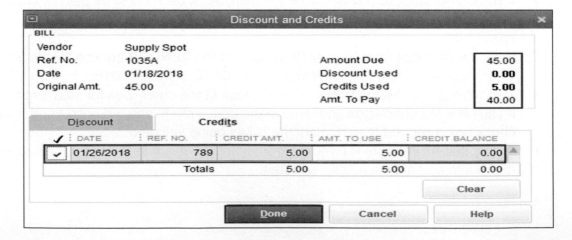

Make sure that there is a check mark √ in the √ column on the **Discounts and Credits** screen

Click **Done** on the **Discounts and Credits** screen
- Notice that the **CREDITS USED** column for the transaction displays **5.00** and the **AMT. TO PAY** for the bill is **40.00**.

	DATE DUE	VENDOR	REF. NO.	DISC. DATE	AMT. DUE	DISC. USED	CREDITS USED	AMT. TO PAY
☑	01/28/2018	Supply Spot	1035A		45.00	0.00	5.00	40.00
☑	01/29/2018	Supply Spot	1050A		450.00	0.00	0.00	450.00
☑	01/29/2018	Rapid Delivery Service	4688		195.00	0.00	0.00	195.00
☑	01/30/2018	Creative Advertising			500.00	0.00	0.00	500.00
☑	01/30/2018	Supply Spot			350.00	0.00	0.00	350.00
				Totals	1,540.00	0.00	5.00	1,535.00

- Make sure that Supply Spot is marked along with the other bills to be paid.

Complete the PAYMENT section:

Tab to or click **Date** in the **PAYMENT** section of the screen
Enter the **Date** of **01/26/18**
Check should be selected as the **Method**
Make sure **To be printed** has been selected
- If it is not selected, click in the radio button to select.
The **Account** should be **Checking**

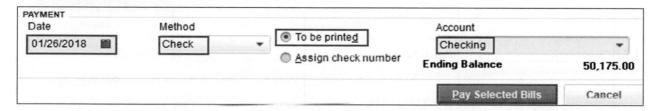

Click the **Pay Selected Bills** button to record your payments and close the **Pay Bills** window
After clicking Pay Selected Bills, you will see a Payment Summary screen

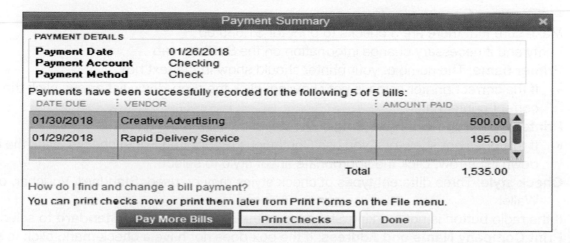

- Only two vendors are shown in the Payment Summary, scroll through the Payment Summary and review the Vendors and Amounts Paid. Notice the three amounts for Supply Spot of $40, $450, and $350.

Continue with the PRINTING CHECKS FOR BILLS section

PRINT CHECKS FOR BILLS

Once bills have been marked and recorded as paid, you may handwrite checks to vendors, or you may have QuickBooks Desktop print the checks to vendors. If there is more than one amount due for a vendor, QuickBooks Desktop totals the amounts due to the vendor and prints one check to the vendor.

 Print the checks for the bills paid

Click **Print Checks** on the Payment Summary screen
Bank Account should be **Checking**
- If this is not showing, click the drop-down list arrow, click **Checking**.
The **First Check Number** should be **1**
- If not, delete the number showing, and key **1**.
In the √ column, the checks selected to be printed are marked with a check mark

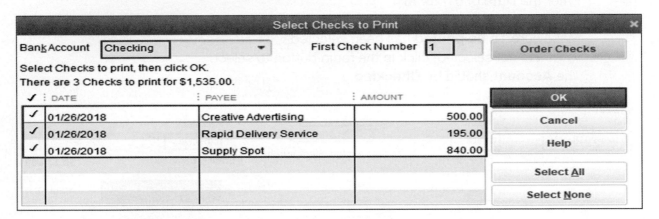

- Notice that the three bills from Supply Spot have been combined into one check for payment.
Click **OK** to print the checks
- The **Print Checks** screen appears.
Make sure that there are 3 checks to print for $1,535.00
Verify and if necessary change information on the **Settings** tab
Printer name: The name of your printer should show in the text box
- If the correct printer name is not showing, click the drop-down list arrow, click the correct printer name.
Printer type: **Page-oriented (Single sheets)** should be in the text box
- If this does not show or if you use Continuous (Perforated Edge) checks, click the drop-down list arrow, click the appropriate sheet style to select.
Check style: Three different types of check styles may be used: Standard, Voucher, or Wallet
If the radio button is not marking Standard as the check style, click **Standard** to select
Print Company Name and Address: If the box does not have a check mark, click to select
Use Logo should not be selected; if a check mark appears in the check box, click to deselect
Print Signature Image should not have a check mark
- Notice the Number of checks on first page is 3.

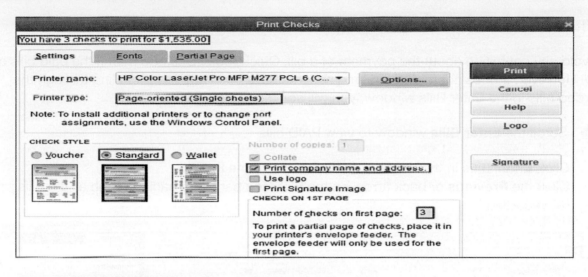

Click **Print** to print the checks
- All three checks will print on one page.
- If you print to a pdf file, save the document as **12-Your Name Cks 1-3 Ch3**.

Print Checks - Confirmation dialog box appears

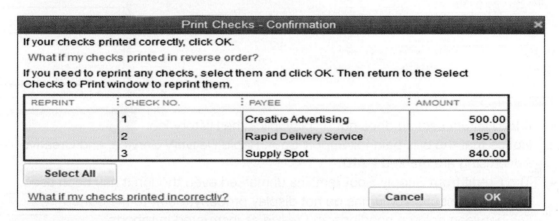

In addition to verifying the correct amount, payee, and payment date, review the checks for the following:
- The checks have the address for Your Name's Tech Services, the name and address of the company being paid, and the amount being paid.
- The actual checks will not have a check number printed because QuickBooks Desktop is set up to work with preprinted check forms containing check numbers.
- In the memo section of the check, any memo entered on the bill shows.
- If there was no memo entered for the bill, the vendor account number appears as the memo.
- If you cannot get the checks to print on one page, it is perfectly acceptable to access the checks by clicking the **Write Checks** icon in the Banking section of the Home Page and printing them one at a time. This method is also useful if you need to correct a check and reprint it.

If checks **printed** correctly, click **OK**
- If the checks did not print correctly, click the checks that need to be reprinted to select, and then click **OK**. Return to the Select Checks to print window and reprint them.
- If you get a message box regarding purchasing checks, click **No**.

REVIEW PAID BILLS

To avoid any confusion about the payment of a bill, QuickBooks Desktop marks the paid bills as PAID. However, it does not mark credit memos that have been applied. Scrolling through the recorded bills in the Enter Bills window, you will see the marked bills.

   Scroll the **Enter Bills** window to view PAID bills

Click **Enter Bills** in the Vendors section of the Home Page
Click the **Previous** or back arrow on the Bills Icon bar to go back through all the bills recorded

- If the History section does not display, click the History icon .
- Notice that the bills paid for Supply Spot, Rapid Delivery Service, and Creative Advertising are marked **PAID**.
- The Credit from Supply Spot remains unmarked even though it has been used.
- If the Detail section columns do not display properly, point to the dotted line between column headings and resize as instructed in reports.

Look at the History for Supply Spot

- Notice the Open Balance is 0.00. In the Recent Transaction section, all the bills have been marked paid, the Bill Pmt – Check and the $5 credit are shown.

Click the **Save & New** button

WRITE CHECKS TO PAY BILLS

Although it is more efficient to record all bills in the Enter Bills window and pay all bills through the Pay Bills window, QuickBooks Desktop also allows bills to be paid by writing a check to record and pay bills. This may be a more appropriate process for bills that you pay routinely every month. (Remember, though, if you record a bill in Enter Bills, you **must** use Pay Bills to write the bill payment check.) When you write a check, it is **not** entered as a bill in Enter Bills.

When writing a check to record a bill and its payment, you will note that the check window is divided into two main areas: the check face and the detail area. The check face includes information such as the date of the check, the payee's name, the check amount, the payee's address, and a line for a memo—just like a paper check. The detail area is used to indicate transaction accounts and amounts.

> **MEMO**
> **DATE**: January 30, 2018
>
> Since these transactions were not recorded as bills, write the checks to record and pay for them.
>
> Pacific Realtors, $1,500.00
> California Telephone Co., $350.00
> SCE (Electricity), $250.00
> CA Water, $35.00
> So Cal Gas Co. (Heating), $175.00

 Write checks to pay the rent, telephone, and utility bills listed above

Click the **Write Checks** icon in the Banking section of the Home Page
    OR
Use the keyboard shortcut **Ctrl+W**
The BANK ACCOUNT used for the check should be **Checking**.

- The ENDING BALANCE of the Checking account is shown. This lets you know how much money is in the account before you write the check. This will not change until the check is saved.
- NO. is where the check number will be entered.

NO. should show **To Print**, which means that the check will be printed later

- If a number is shown for the check number, click the **Print Later** checkbox on the Write Checks - Checking Icon Bar.

Tab to or click **Date**
Enter **01/30/18**
To complete the <u>check face</u>, click the drop-down list arrow next to **PAY TO THE ORDER OF**
Click **Pacific Realtors**
Tab to or click in the text box for **$**
Enter the amount of the rent, **1500**
Tab to or click **MEMO**

- If you do not provide a memo on the check, QuickBooks Desktop will enter an account number, a telephone number, an address, or a description as the memo.
- Since the address for Your Name's Tech Services is on West Avenue, leave the memo as shown.
- The memo will print on the check, not on reports.

Use the **Expenses** tab to complete the <u>detail section</u> of the check
Tab to or click the first line of **ACCOUNT**
Click the drop-down list arrow for **ACCOUNT**
Click the Expense Account **Rent**

- The total amount of the check is shown in AMOUNT column.
- If you want a transaction description to appear in reports, enter the description in the MEMO column in the detail section of the check. Because these are standard transactions, no memo is entered.

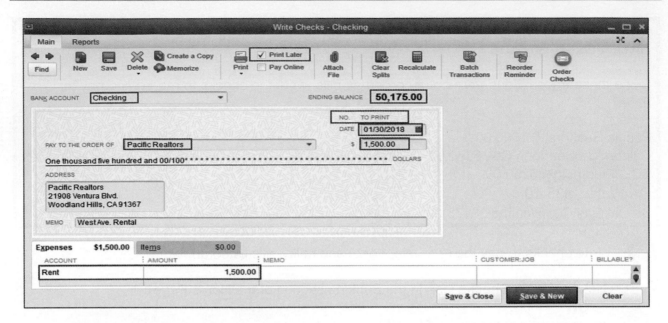

Do <u>not</u> print any of the checks being entered

Click the **Save & New** button or click **New** on the Check Icon bar to record the check and advance to the next check

Repeat the steps indicated above to record payment of the telephone bill and the utility bills for electricity, water, and heating (gas)

- While entering the bills, you may see a dialog box on the screen, indicating that QuickBooks Desktop allows you to do online banking. Online banking will not be used at this time. Click **OK** to close the dialog box.
- Since these are all routine transactions, there is no need to enter a Memo. Remember, QuickBooks Desktop will enter your account number as the Memo.

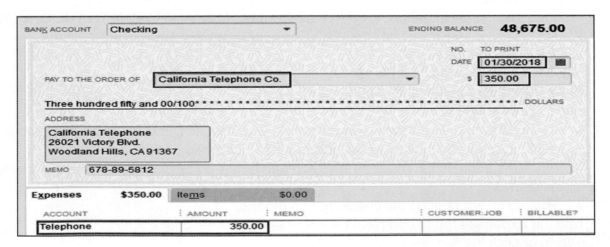

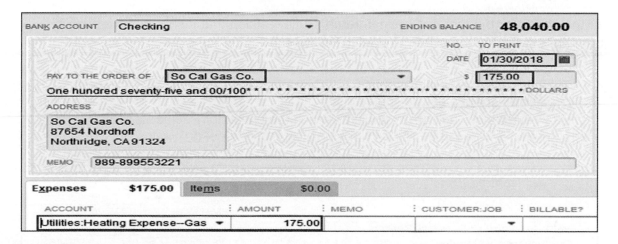

ENTER A DUPLICATE CHECK

To illustrate how easy it is to accidentally create a duplicate check, the check to SCE will be duplicated. Later in the chapter, it will be deleted.

  Click the drop-down list arrow and click **SCE**
- The first payment entered for the payment of the bill for electricity appears on the screen.
- This is helpful but can cause a duplicate entry to be made.

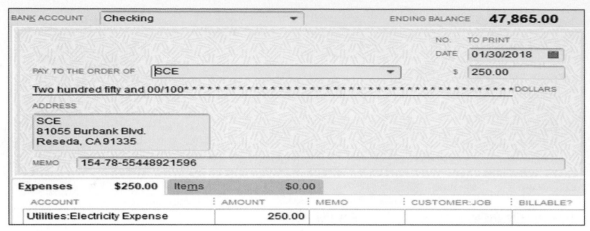

Duplicate Check

Click the **Save & Close** button to record the second payment for the electric bill and exit the **Write Checks** window

EDIT CHECKS

Mistakes can occur in business—even on a check. QuickBooks Desktop allows for checks to be edited at any time. You may use either the Check Register or the Write Checks window to edit checks.

MEMO

DATE: January 30, 2018

Once the check for the rent had been entered, Sofia realized that it should have been for $1,600.00. Edit the check written to Pacific Realtors.

 Revise the check written to pay the rent
Open **Write Checks** as previously instructed
Click **Previous** or back arrow until you reach the check for Pacific Realtors
Change the amount in the **$** text box under the DATE to **1600**, press the **Tab** key

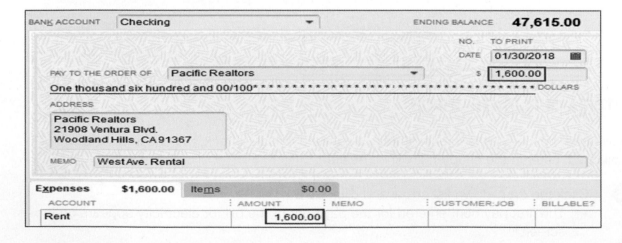

Do <u>not</u> print the check
Click **Save & Close**
Click **Yes** on the screen asking if you want to save the changed transaction

VOID CHECKS

QuickBooks Desktop allows checks to be voided. Rather than deleting the transaction, voiding a check changes the amount of the check to zero but keeps a record of the transaction. The check may be voided in the Checking account register or on the check. The following transaction will show you how to void a check in the Checking account register.

MEMO
DATE: January 30, 2018

The telephone bill should not have been paid until the first week of February. Void the check written to pay the telephone bill.

 Void the check written to pay the telephone bill

Click the **Check Register** icon in the BANKING section of the Home Page
- Make sure **Checking** is shown as the Register account.

Void the check written for the telephone expense:
Click anywhere in the check to **California Telephone Co.**
Click **Edit** on the QuickBooks Desktop menu bar at the top of the screen—<u>not</u> the Edit Transaction button
Click **Void Check**
Click the **Record** button in the Checking Register
Click **Yes** on the Recording Transaction dialog box
Click **No, just void the check** on the QuickBooks Desktop dialog box

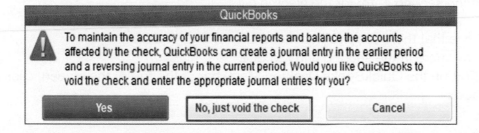

- The amount of the check is now 0.00. The memo shows VOID: Monthly Telephone Bill.
Do <u>not</u> close the register for checking

DATE	NUMBER	PAYEE		PAYMENT	✔	DEPOSIT	BALANCE
	TYPE	ACCOUNT	MEMO				
01/30/2018		California Telephone Co.		0.00	✔		50,175.00
	CHK	Telephone	VOID: 678-89-5812				
01/30/2018	To Print	Pacific Realtors		1,600.00			48,575.00
	CHK	Rent	West Ave. Rental				
01/30/2018	To Print	SCE		250.00			48,325.00
	CHK	Utilities:Electricity Expense	154-78-55448921596				
01/30/2018	To Print	CA Water		35.00			48,290.00
	CHK	Utilities:Water	6598-71212251				
01/30/2018	To Print	So Cal Gas Co.		175.00			48,115.00
	CHK	Utilities:Heating Expense--G 989-899553221					
01/30/2018	To Print	SCE		250.00			47,865.00
	CHK	Utilities:Electricity Expense	154-78-55448921596				
Splits				ENDING BALANCE			**47,865.00**

DELETE CHECKS

Deleting a check completely removes it and any transaction information for the check from QuickBooks Desktop. Make sure you want to remove the check before deleting it. Once it is deleted, a check cannot be recovered. It is often preferable to void a check than to delete it because a voided check is maintained in the company records; whereas, no record is kept in the active company records of a deleted check. However, in this instance, a duplicate check may cause confusion, so it is better to delete it.

MEMO

DATE: January 30, 2018

In reviewing the register for the checking account, Sofia discovered that two checks were written to pay the electric bill. Delete the second check.

   Delete the second entry for the electric bill

- Notice that there are two transactions showing for SCE.

Click anywhere in the second entry to SCE

Click **Edit** on the QuickBooks Desktop Menu bar at the top of the screen, click **Delete Check**

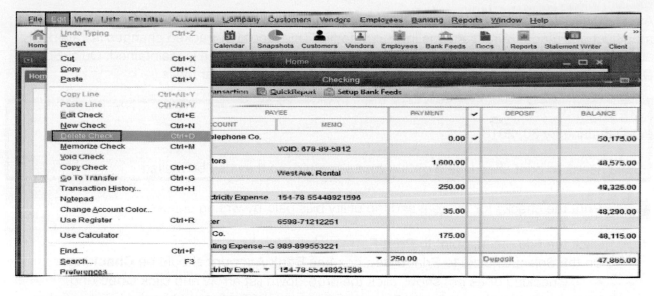

Click **OK** on the **Delete Transaction** dialog box
- After you have clicked the **OK** button, there is only one transaction in Checking for SCE.
Click **1-Line** to display the register on one line

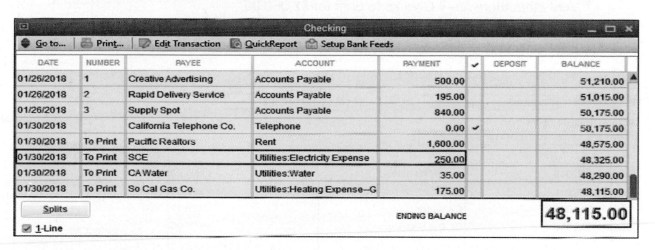

- Notice the change in the Checking account balance.
Close the **Check Register**

PRINT CHECKS

Checks may be printed as they are entered, or they may be printed later. When checks are to be printed, QuickBooks Desktop inserts the words *To Print* rather than a check number in the Check Register. The appropriate check number is indicated during printing. Because QuickBooks Desktop is so flexible, a company must institute a system for cash control. For example, if the check for rent of $1,500 had been printed, QuickBooks Desktop would allow a second check for $1,600 to be printed. To avoid any impropriety, more than one person should be designated to review checks. As a matter of practice in a small business, the owner or a person other than the one writing checks should sign the checks. Pre-numbered checks should be used, and any checks printed but not mailed should be submitted along with those for signature.

As a further safeguard, QuickBooks Desktop automatically tracks all the additions, deletions, and modifications made to transactions in your data file. This record of tracked changes is called an audit trail. The audit trail ensures that an accurate record of your data is maintained. QuickBooks Desktop Audit Trail Report should be printed and viewed on a regular basis.

MEMO
DATE: January 30, 2018

Sofia needs to print checks and obtain your signature, so they can be mailed.

 Print the checks for the rent and the utility bills paid by writing checks

Click the **File** menu, point to **Print Forms**, click **Checks**
On the Select Checks to Print dialog box, the **Bank Account** should be **Checking**
- If Checking does not show, click the drop-down list arrow and click **Checking**.
Because Check Nos. 1, 2, and 3 were printed previously, **4** should be the number in the
  First Check Number text box
- If not, delete the number showing, and key **4**.
- Verify that there are 4 Checks to print for $2,060.00.
In the √ column, the checks selected for printing are marked with a check mark
- If not, click the **Select All** button.

Select Checks to Print			
Bank Account **Checking** ▼ First Check Number **4**			**Order Checks**
Select Checks to print, then click OK.			
There are 4 Checks to print for $2,060.00.			
√ DATE	PAYEE	AMOUNT	**OK**
√ 01/30/2018	Pacific Realtors	1,600.00	Cancel
√ 01/30/2018	SCE	250.00	Help
√ 01/30/2018	CA Water	35.00	
√ 01/30/2018	So Cal Gas Co.	175.00	Select All
			Select None

Click **OK** to print the checks
- The **Print Checks** screen appears.
Verify and, if necessary, change information on the **Settings** tab to use **Standard Checks**
  as previously shown in this chapter
Click **Print** to print the checks
- The checks have the address for Your Name's Tech Services, the name and address of
  the company being paid, and the amount being paid. There is no check number printed
  on the checks because QuickBooks Desktop is set up to use pre-numbered checks.
- If you run into difficulties or find you made an error and want to correct and/or print an
  individual check, you may do so by printing directly from the check.
- If you print to a pdf file, save the document as **13-Your Name Cks 4-7 Ch3**.
Did check(s) print OK? dialog box appears
If the checks printed correctly, click **OK**

CHECK DETAIL REPORT

Once checks have been printed, it is important to review information about checks. The Check Detail Report provides detailed information regarding each check, including the checks for 0.00 amounts. Information indicates the type of transaction, the date, the check number, the payee, the account used, the original amount, and the paid amount of the check.

> **MEMO**
> **DATE**: January 30, 2018
>
> Now that the checks have been printed, Sofia prints a Check Detail Report. She will give this to you to review as you sign the printed checks.

➡ Print a Check Detail Report

Open the **Report Center**
The type of report should be **Banking**
Double-click **Check Detail** to select the report
Remove the **Date Prepared** and **Time Prepared** from the report header
The report is From **01/01/18** and To **01/30/18**
Tab to **generate** report
- Checks prepared through Pay Bills show Bill Pmt-Check.
- The checks prepared through Write Checks show Check.
Resize the columns as previously instructed

Your Name's Tech Services
Check Detail
January 1 - 30, 2018

Type	Num	Date	Name	Item	Account	Paid Amount	Original Amount
▶ Check		01/30/2018	California Telephone Co.		Checking		0.00 ◀
TOTAL						0.00	0.00
Bill Pmt -Check	1	01/26/2018	Creative Advertising		Checking		-500.00
Bill		12/31/2017			Uncategorized Expenses	-500.00	500.00
TOTAL						-500.00	500.00
Bill Pmt -Check	2	01/26/2018	Rapid Delivery Service		Checking		-195.00
Bill	4688	01/19/2018			Postage and Delivery	-195.00	195.00
TOTAL						-195.00	195.00
Bill Pmt -Check	3	01/26/2018	Supply Spot		Checking		-840.00
Bill		12/31/2017			Uncategorized Expenses	-350.00	350.00
Bill	1035A	01/18/2018			Equipment Rental	-22.22	25.00
					Office Supplies Expense	-17.78	20.00
Bill	1050A	01/19/2018			Office Supplies	-450.00	450.00
TOTAL						-840.00	845.00
Check	4	01/30/2018	Pacific Realtors		Checking		-1,600.00
					Rent	-1,600.00	1,600.00
TOTAL						-1,600.00	1,600.00

Partial Report

Print the report in **Landscape** Orientation
- If you print to a pdf file, save the document as **14-Your Name Ck Detail Ch3**.
Click **Close** to close the report
Do not close the Report Center

MISSING CHECKS REPORT

A Missing Checks Report lists the checks written for a bank account in order by check number. If there are any gaps between numbers or duplicate check numbers, this information is provided. The report indicates the type of transaction, Check or Bill Pmt-Check, check date, check number, payee name, account used for the check, the split or additional accounts used, and the amount of the check. Check means that you wrote the check and Bill Pmt-Check means the check was written when you used Pay Bills.

MEMO

DATE: January 30, 2018

To see a listing of all checks printed, view a Missing Checks Report for all dates.

 View a Missing Checks Report

Double-click **Missing Checks** in the Banking section of Reports to select the report being prepared
- If **Checking** appears for Specify Account on the **Missing Checks** dialog box, click **OK**.
- If it does not appear, click the drop-down list arrow, click **Checking**, click **OK**.

Examine the report:

Your Name's Tech Services
Missing Checks
All Transactions

Type	Date	Num	Name	Memo	Account	Split	Amount
Bill Pmt -Check	01/26/2018	1	Creative Advertising	1-2567135-54	Checking	Accounts Payable	-500.00
Bill Pmt -Check	01/26/2018	2	Rapid Delivery Service	January Delivery Expense	Checking	Accounts Payable	-195.00
Bill Pmt -Check	01/26/2018	3	Supply Spot	456-45623	Checking	Accounts Payable	-840.00
Check	01/30/2018	4	Pacific Realtors	West Ave. Rental	Checking	Rent	-1,600.00
Check	01/30/2018	5	SCE	154-78-55448921596	Checking	Electricity Expense	-250.00
Check	01/30/2018	6	CA Water	6598-71212251	Checking	Water	-35.00
Check	01/30/2018	7	So Cal Gas Co.	989-899553221	Checking	Heating Expense...	-175.00

- In a transaction that is decreasing cash, you would credit cash or checking and debit the expense or accounts payable account used in the transaction.
- The **Account** in all cases is **Checking**, which is the account credited.
- The **Split** column indicates which accounts in addition to Checking have been used in the transaction. The Split accounts are the accounts debited.

Look at the **Type** column:
- The checks written through Pay Bills indicate the transaction type as **Bill Pmt-Check** and the Split account is **Accounts Payable**.
- The bills paid by writing the checks show **Check** as the transaction type and indicates the other accounts used.

Close the report without printing, do <u>not</u> close the Report Center

VOIDED/DELETED TRANSACTION SUMMARY

QuickBooks Desktop has a report for all voided/deleted transactions. This report appears in the Accountant & Taxes section for reports. This report may be printed as a summary or in detail. It will show all the transactions that have been voided and/or deleted.

> **MEMO**
> **DATE:** January 30, 2018
>
> To be better informed about the checks that have been written, you have Sofia prepare the Voided/Deleted Transaction Summary Report for January.

 Prepare the Voided/Deleted Transaction Summary report

Click **Accountant & Taxes** in the Report Center
Double-click **Voided/Deleted Transaction Summary** in the Account Activity section
The report dates are **All**

Your Name's Tech Services
Voided/Deleted Transactions Summary
Entered/Last Modified

Num	Action	Entered/Last Modified	Date	Name	Memo	Account	Split	Amount
Transactions entered or modified by Admin								
Check								
	Voided Transaction	01/18/2018 11:22:15	01/30/2018	California Telephone Co.	VOID: 678-89-5812	Checking	Telephone	0.00
	Changed Transaction	01/18/2018 11:03:44	01/30/2018	California Telephone Co.	678-89-5812	Checking	Telephone	-350.00
	Changed Transaction	01/18/2018 11:00:04	01/30/2018	California Telephone Co.	678-89-5812	Checking	Telephone	0.00
	Added Transaction	01/18/2018 10:56:19	01/30/2018	California Telephone Co.	678-89-5812	Checking	Telephone	-350.00
Check								
	Deleted Transaction	01/18/2018 11:31:46						0.00
	Added Transaction	01/18/2018 11:14:19	01/30/2018	SCE	154-78-55448921596	Checking	Utilities:Electricity Expense	-250.00

- The Entered Last Modified column shows the actual date and time that the entry was made. The report header shows your computer's current date and time (not shown). The dates and times shown will <u>not</u> match your date and time.
- In addition, your report may not match the one illustrated if you have voided or deleted anything else during your work session.

Close the report without printing, and close the Report Center

PETTY CASH

Frequently, a business will need to pay for small expenses with cash. These might include expenses such as postage, office supplies, and miscellaneous expenses. For example, rather than write a check for postage due of 75 cents, you would use money from petty cash. QuickBooks Desktop allows you to establish and use a petty cash account to track these small expenditures. Normally, a Petty Cash Voucher or Petty Cash Ticket is prepared; and, if available, the receipt(s) for the transaction is (are) stapled to it. In QuickBooks Desktop you can scan a receipt and attach it electronically to the transaction. (This will be discussed in Appendix B.) It is important in a business to keep accurate records of the petty cash expenditures. Procedures for control of the

Petty Cash fund need to be established to prohibit access to and unauthorized use of the cash. Periodically, the petty cash expenditures are recorded so that the records of the company accurately reflect all expenses incurred in the operation of the business.

ADD PETTY CASH ACCOUNT

QuickBooks Desktop allows accounts to be added to the Chart of Accounts list at any time. Petty Cash is identified as a "Bank" account type so it will be placed at the top of the Chart of Accounts along with other checking and savings accounts.

MEMO
DATE: January 30, 2018

There are small items that should be paid for using cash. As a result, a petty cash account needs to be established. After Petty Cash has been created, it should be funded for $100.00.

 Add Petty Cash to the **Chart of Accounts**

Access **Chart of Accounts** as previously instructed
Click the **Account** button at the bottom of the Chart of Accounts, click **New** or use the keyboard shortcut **Ctrl+N**
Click **Bank** on the Add New Account: Choose Account Type screen
Click the **Continue** button
Enter **Petty Cast** in the **Account Name** text box
• Yes, it should be Cash and will be changed later. Enter Cast.
Leave the other items blank

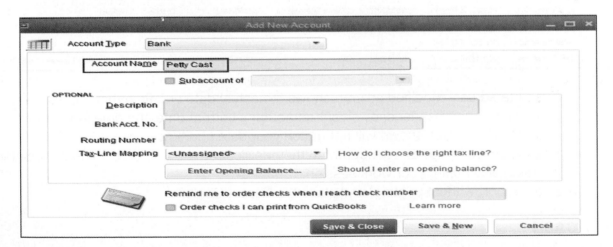

Click **Save & Close** to record the new account
• If you get a message to Set Up Bank Feed, click **No**.
Look at the Chart of Accounts and see that you misspelled the name as Petty Cast
Click **Petty Cast**
Edit the account name by using the keyboard shortcut **Ctrl+E**
Change the account name to **Petty Cash**

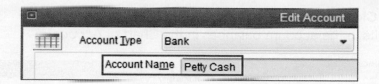

Click **Save & Close**
*   If you get a dialog box, to Set up Bank Feed, click **No**.
Do not close the **Chart of Accounts**

ESTABLISH PETTY CASH FUND

Once the account has been established, the petty cash fund must have money to pay for small expenses. Two alternate methods for obtaining the funds for Petty Cash are: make a withdrawal from the company checking account at the bank or write a check for cash and then cash it at the bank. If a check is used to obtain cash, the transaction is recorded when writing the check. If a withdrawal is made, it is either recorded directly in the Checking account register or by completing a Transfer Funds Between Accounts. Since you know how to write a check and how to record a transaction in an account register, completing the Transfer of Funds will be illustrated below.

   Record the Transfer of Funds from Checking to Petty Cash

Click the **Banking** menu
Click **Transfer Funds**
*   As discussed above, this method may be used when a withdrawal is made from the Checking account and the amount is made available for Petty Cash.
*   If the cursor is not already in the DATE text box, click in it.
*   The date should be highlighted; if it is not, drag through the date to highlight.
If the DATE shown is not 01/30/2018, enter **01/30/18**
Click the drop-down list arrow for TRANSFER FUNDS FROM
Click **Checking**
*   The **ACCOUNT BALANCE** for Checking should show **48,115.00**.
Click the drop-down list arrow for **TRANSFER FUNDS TO**
Click **Petty Cash**
*   The **ACCOUNT BALANCE** for Petty Cash should show **0.00**.
Tab to or click in the text box for **TRANSFER AMOUNT**
Enter **100**
Click after the **MEMO** that says **Funds Transfer**
Add **to Establish Petty Cash Fund**

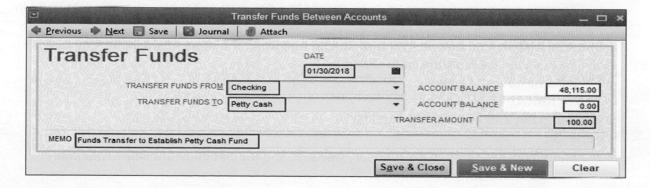

Click **Save & Close** button to record the transfer
View the results in the account balances in the Chart of Accounts

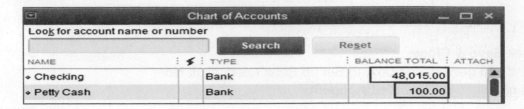

Do not close the **Chart of Accounts**

PAY EXPENSE WITH PETTY CASH

As petty cash is used to pay for small expenses in the business, these payments must be recorded. QuickBooks Desktop makes it a simple matter to record petty cash expenditures directly into the Petty Cash Register.

> **MEMO**
> **DATE**: January 30, 2018
>
> Record the petty cash expenditures made during the week: postage due, 34 cents; purchased staples and paperclips, $3.57 (this is an expense); reimbursed Emily Edwards for gasoline purchased for company car, $13.88.

   In the Petty Cash account, record a compound entry for the above expenditures

In the **Chart of Accounts,** double-click **Petty Cash** to open the **Register**
Click in the **DATE** column, highlight the date if necessary
Type **01/30/18**
Tab to Number, enter **1** for the number
- This would be the number of the Petty Cash Voucher or Petty Cash Ticket that would be filled out and have the receipts stapled to it.
- No entry is required for Payee.
Tab to or click **Payment**
Enter **17.79** (you must type the decimal point)
Tab to or click in **Account** text box
Since the total amount of the transaction will be split among three expense accounts, click the **Splits** button at the bottom of the screen
- You will get an area where you can record the different accounts and amounts used in this transaction.
In the **ACCOUNT** column showing on the screen, click the drop-down list arrow
Scroll until you see **Postage and Delivery**
Click **Postage and Delivery**
Tab to **AMOUNT** column
- Using the Tab key will highlight **17.79**.
Type **.34**
- MEMO notations are not necessary because the transactions are self-explanatory.

Tab to or click the next blank line in **ACCOUNT**

Repeat the steps listed above to record **3.57** for **Office Supplies Expense** and **13.88** for
   Automobile Expense

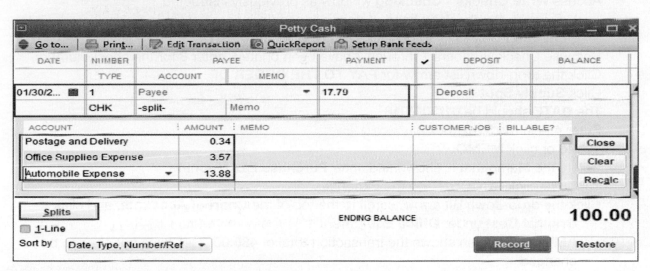

Click the **Close** button for Splits when all expenses have been recorded
Click **Record** to record the transaction

01/30/2018	1				17.79			-17.79
	CHK	-split-						
01/30/2018							100.00	82.21
	TRANSFI	Checking	Funds Transfer to Establish Petty Cash Fund					

- Since the transfer of funds and the recording of petty cash expenditures are shown on the same date, the expenditures show first.
- Notice that after the Record button has been clicked, the word "payee," the account name, and memo are removed from the transaction. Instead of showing the accounts used, **-split-** is shown.
- In the Num column, the transaction is marked as a CHK. This refers to the number of the Petty Cash Voucher or Ticket, but QuickBooks Desktop does not use an identifier of Voucher or Ticket.
- Verify the account Ending Balance of 82.21.

Close the **Petty Cash Register** and the **Chart of Accounts**

PURCHASE ASSET WITH COMPANY CHECK

Not all purchases will be transactions on account. If something is purchased and paid for with a check, a check is written, and the purchase is recorded.

MEMO

DATE: January 30, 2018

You need to purchase a fax machine and found one on sale at Supply Spot for $486. Write a company check for the purchase of the asset.

Record the check written for the purchase of a fax machine

Access **Write Checks - Checking** window as previously instructed
- You wrote the check by hand. It does not need printing. If there is a check mark. in the **Print Later** box, click to deselect. **NO.** should show as **1**.

Because Check Numbers 1 through 7 have been printed, enter **8** for the check number

Click the drop-down list arrow for **PAY TO THE ORDER OF**

Click **Supply Spot**

The **DATE** should be **01/30/2018**

Enter **486** in the **$** text box

Tab to or click **MEMO**

Delete the Memo that is shown and enter **Purchase Fax Machine**

Tab to or click **ACCOUNT** on the **Expenses** tab

Click the drop-down list arrow, scroll to the top of the **Chart of Accounts**, and click **Original Cost** under **Office Equipment**
- **AMOUNT** column shows the transaction total of **486.00**. This does not need to be changed.

Click **MEMO**, enter **Purchase Fax Machine**

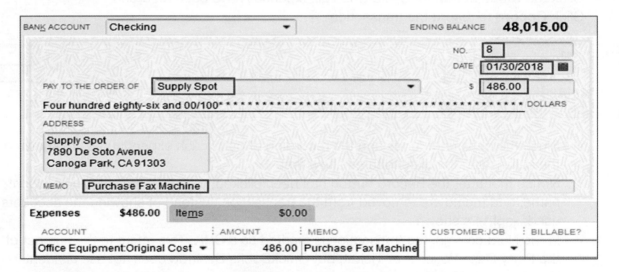

Click **Save & Close** to record the check and exit the **Write Checks - Checking** window without printing

CUSTOMIZE REPORT FORMAT (OPTIONAL)

The report format used in one company may not be appropriate for all companies that use QuickBooks Desktop. To allow program users the maximum flexibility, QuickBooks Desktop makes it very easy to customize many of the user preferences of the program. For example, you may customize menus, reminder screens, as well as reports and graphs.

 Customize the report preferences to make permanent changes to eliminate the date prepared, time prepared, and report basis from reports

Check with your instructor to see if you should complete this section
- If you do not need to change the header, simply read the information presented.

Click the QuickBooks Desktop **Edit** menu, click **Preferences**
Scroll through the items listed on the left side of the screen until you get to Reports & Graphs
Click the **Reports & Graphs**
Click the **Company Preferences** tab
Click the **Format** button

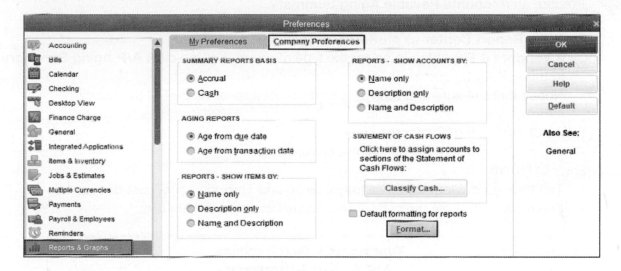

- If necessary, click the **Header/Footer** tab.

Click **Date Prepared**, **Time Prepared**, and **Report Basis** to deselect

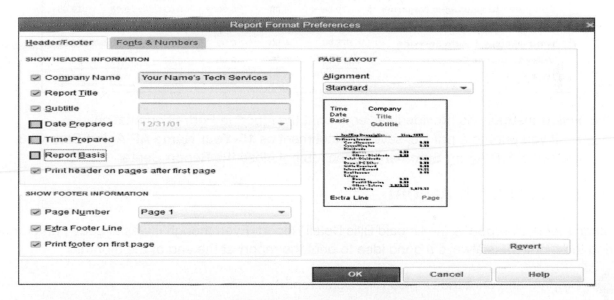

Click **OK** to save the change, click **OK** to close **Preferences**

ACCOUNTS PAYABLE AGING SUMMARY

It is important in a business to maintain a good credit rating and to make sure that payments are made on time. To avoid overlooking a payment, the Accounts Payable Aging Summary lists the vendors to which the company owes money and shows how long the money has been owed.

 Prepare an **Accounts Payable Aging Summary**

Open the **Report Center** as previously instructed
Click **Vendors & Payables** to select the type of report, double-click **A/P Aging Summary** in the **A/P Aging** section
- Notice that the date and time prepared do not appear as part of the heading information.
Tab to or click in the box for the **Date**
- If it is not highlighted, highlight the current date.
Enter **01/30/18**
- Tab through but leave Interval (days) as 30 and Through (days past due) as 90.
- The report will show the current bills as well as any past due bills.

Your Name's Tech Services
A/P Aging Summary
As of January 30, 2018

	Current	1 – 30	31 – 60	61 – 90	> 90	TOTAL
Computer Technologies Magazine ▶	79.00 ◀	0.00	0.00	0.00	0.00	79.00
Creative Advertising	260.00	0.00	0.00	0.00	0.00	260.00
Greg's Garage & Auto Services	575.00	0.00	0.00	0.00	0.00	575.00
Valley Insurance Company	2,850.00	0.00	0.00	0.00	0.00	2,850.00
TOTAL	**3,764.00**	**0.00**	**0.00**	**0.00**	**0.00**	**3,764.00**

Follow instructions provided earlier to print the report in Portrait orientation
- If you print to a pdf file, save the document as **15-Your Name AP Aging Sum Ch3**.
Close the **A/P Aging Summary** screen; do <u>not</u> close the Report Center

UNPAID BILLS DETAIL REPORT

Another important report is the Unpaid Bills Detail Report. Even though it was already printed once during the month, it is always a good idea to print the report at the end of the month.

 Prepare and print the Unpaid Bills Detail report

Follow instructions provided earlier in the chapter to prepare an **Unpaid Bills Detail Report** for **01/30/2018**

Your Name's Tech Services
Unpaid Bills Detail
As of January 30, 2018

Type	Date	Num	Due Date	Aging	Open Balance
Computer Technologies Magazine					
Bill	01/19/2018	1553	02/18/2018		79.00 ◄
Total Computer Technologies Magazine					79.00
Creative Advertising					
Bill	01/16/2018	9875	02/15/2018		260.00
Total Creative Advertising					260.00
Greg's Garage & Auto Services					
Bill	01/19/2018	8608	02/18/2018		575.00
Total Greg's Garage & Auto Services					575.00
Valley Insurance Company					
Bill	01/19/2018	3659	02/18/2018		2,850.00
Total Valley Insurance Company					2,850.00
TOTAL					**3,764.00**

Print in Portrait orientation; then, close the report
- If you print to a pdf file, save the document as **16-Your Name Unpaid Bills Detail Ch3**.
- If you get a Memorize Report dialog box, remember to always click No.

Do not close the Report Center

VENDOR BALANCE SUMMARY

There are two Vendor Balance Reports available in QuickBooks Desktop. There is a Summary Report that shows unpaid balances for vendors and a Detail Report that lists each transaction for a vendor. To see how much is owed to each vendor, prepare a Vendor Balance Summary report.

 Prepare and print a **Vendor Balance Summary Report**

Double-click **Vendor Balance Summary** in the Vendor Balances section
The report dates will say **All**
- The report should show only the totals owed to each vendor on January 30, 2018.

Your Name's Tech Services
Vendor Balance Summary
All Transactions

	Jan 30, 18
Computer Technologies Magazine ►	79.00 ◄
Creative Advertising	260.00
Greg's Garage & Auto Services	575.00
Valley Insurance Company	2,850.00
TOTAL	**3,764.00**

- If you print to a pdf file, save the document as **17-Your Name Vend Bal Sum Ch3**.

Follow steps listed previously to print the report in Portrait orientation
Close the report; do not close the **Report Center**

ACCOUNTS PAYABLE GRAPH BY AGING PERIOD

Graphs provide a visual representation of certain aspects of the business. It is sometimes easier to interpret data in a graphical format. For example, to determine if any payments are overdue for accounts payable accounts, use an Accounts Payable Graph to provide that information instantly on a bar chart. In addition, the Accounts Payable Graph feature of QuickBooks Desktop also displays a pie chart showing what percentage of the total amount payable is owed to each vendor.

    Prepare an Accounts Payable Graph

> Double-click **Accounts Payable Graph** in the Vendors & Payables section of the Report Center
> Click the **Dates** button at the top of the report
> Enter **01/30/18** for **Show Aging as of** in the **Change Graph Dates** text box
> Click **OK**

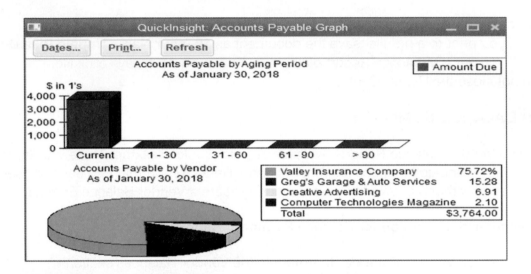

Click the **Dates** button again; enter **02/28/18** for the date
Click **OK**
- Notice that the bar moved from Current to 1-30. This means at the end of February the bills will be between 1 and 30 days overdue.

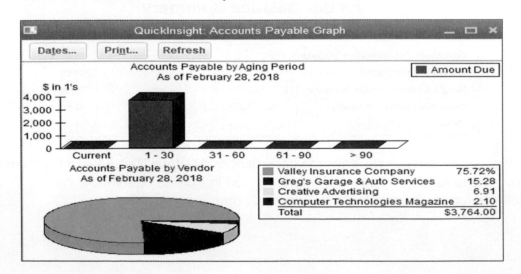

QUICKZOOM TO VIEW GRAPH DETAILS

To obtain detailed information from a graph, use the QuickZoom feature. For example, to see the overdue category of an individual account, double-click on a vendor in the pie chart or in the legend, and this information will appear in a separate bar chart.

 Use QuickZoom to see how many days overdue the Valley Insurance Company's bill will be at the end of February

Double-click the section of the pie chart for **Valley Insurance Company**
- The bar chart shows the bill will be in the 1-30-day category at the end of February.

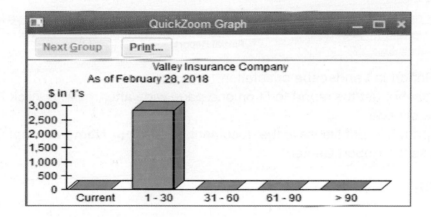

Close the QuickZoom Graph for Valley Insurance Company
Close the **QuickInsight: Accounts Payable Graph**

JOURNAL REPORT

It is always a good idea to review your transactions for appropriate amounts, accounts, and items used. In tracing errors, the Journal report is an invaluable tool. If you suspect an error, always check the transaction dates, amounts, accounts used, and items listed in the Memo column to verify the accuracy of your entry.

 Prepare the Journal report in the Accountant & Taxes section of the Report Center as previously instructed

The report dates are From **01/01/18** To **01/30/18**
Click the **Expand** button to display each transaction in full
Resize the columns as previously instructed so you can see the accounts in full and so the report may be printed on one-page in width
- Review the report and check the dates, amounts, accounts, and items used.
- Scroll through the report. You will see the transactions entered in Chapters 2 and 3.

Your Name's Tech Services
Journal
January 1 - 30, 2018

Trans #	Type	Date	Num	Adj	Name	Memo	Account	Debit	Credit
64	Transfer	01/30/2018				Funds Transfer to Establish Petty Cash Fund	Checking		100.00
						Funds Transfer to Establish Petty Cash Fund	Petty Cash	100.00	
								100.00	100.00
65	Check	01/30/2018	1				Petty Cash		17.79
							Postage and Delivery	0.34	
							Office Supplies Expense	3.57	
							Automobile Expense	13.88	
								17.79	17.79
66	Check	01/30/2018	8		Supply Spot	Purchase Fax Machine	Checking		486.00
					Supply Spot	Purchase Fax Machine	Original Cost	486.00	
								486.00	486.00
TOTAL								**45,217.79**	**45,217.79**

Partial Report

Print the Report in **Landscape** orientation
- If you cannot get the report to fit on one-page wide after resizing, click **Fit report to 1 page(s) wide**.
- If you print to a pdf file, save the document as **18-Your Name Journal Ch3**.

Do <u>not</u> close the Report Center

TRIAL BALANCE

It is always helpful to create a trial balance as of a specific date to show the balance of each account in debit and credit format. This report proves that Debits equal Credits.

Prepare a Trial Balance as previously instructed

The report dates are From **01/01/18** To **01/30/18**
Your account balances should match the following:

Your Name's Tech Services
Trial Balance
As of January 30, 2018

	Jan 30, 18	
	Debit	Credit
Checking	47,529.00	
Petty Cash	82.21	
Accounts Receivable	17,650.00	
Office Supplies	950.00	
Prepaid Insurance	2,850.00	
Undeposited Funds	0.00	
Company Cars:Original Cost	49,000.00	
Office Equipment:Original Cost	8,536.00	
Accounts Payable		3,764.00
Loan Payable	0.00	
Loan Payable:Company Cars Loan		35,000.00
Loan Payable:Office Equipment Loan		4,000.00
Owner's Equity	0.00	
Student's Name, Capital		53,135.00
Student's Name, Capital:Investments		25,000.00
Income:Cloud Services Income		150.00
Income:Installation Income		175.00
Income:Technical Support Income		750.00
Income:Training Income		7,850.00
Advertising Expense	260.00	
Automobile Expense	588.88	
Dues and Subscriptions	79.00	
Equipment Rental	25.00	
Office Supplies Expense	18.57	
Postage and Delivery	195.34	
Rent	1,600.00	
Telephone	0.00	
Utilities:Electricity Expense	250.00	
Utilities:Heating Expense—Gas	175.00	
Utilities:Water	35.00	
TOTAL	**129,824.00**	**129,824.00**

Print the report
- If you print to a pdf file, save the document as **19-Your Name Trial Bal Ch3**.
Close the Report Center

BACK UP AND CLOSE COMPANY

Whenever an important work session is complete, you should always back up your data. If your data disk or company file is damaged or an error is discovered later, the backup file (.qbb) may be restored to the same or a new company file and the information used for recording transactions. As in previous chapters, you should close the company at the end of each work session.

 Follow the instructions given in Chapters 1 and 2 to back up data for Your Name's Tech Services and to close the company. Refer to the instructions provided by your professor for making a duplicate disk

Name your back up file **Tech 2018 (Backup Ch. 3)**

SUMMARY

In this chapter, bills were recorded and paid, checks were written, and reports were prepared. The petty cash fund was established and used for payments of small expense items. Checks were voided, deleted, and corrected. Accounts were added and modified. QuickReports were accessed in various ways, and QuickZoom was used to obtain transaction detail while in various reports. Reports were prepared for Missing Checks and Check Details. Unpaid Bills and Vendor Balance Summary Reports provided information regarding bills that had not been paid. The graphing feature of QuickBooks Desktop allowed you to determine Accounts Payable by aging period and to see the percentage of Accounts Payable for each vendor.

END-OF-CHAPTER QUESTIONS

TRUE/FALSE

ANSWER THE FOLLOWING QUESTIONS IN THE SPACE PROVIDED BEFORE THE QUESTION NUMBER.

3

_____ 3.01. In a service business, most of the accounting for purchases and payables is simply paying bills for expenses incurred in the operation of the business.

_____ 3.02. Credit Memos are prepared to record a reduction to a transaction.

_____ 3.03. Report columns may not be resized, and report formats may not be customized.

_____ 3.04. When using QuickBooks Desktop, checks may not be written in a checkbook.

_____ 3.05. A Missing Check report lists any duplicate check numbers or gaps between check numbers.

_____ 3.06. The Account Type for Petty Cash is Bank.

_____ 3.07. The Accounts Payable Register keeps track of all checks written in the business.

_____ 3.08. A cash purchase can be recorded by writing a check or by using petty cash.

_____ 3.09. Once a report format has been customized as a QuickBooks Desktop preference for a company, all reports will automatically use the customized format.

_____ 3.10. When using the Write Checks feature of QuickBooks Desktop, it is possible to duplicate a check.

MULTIPLE CHOICE

WRITE THE LETTER OF THE CORRECT ANSWER IN THE SPACE PROVIDED BEFORE THE QUESTION NUMBER.

_____ 3.11. To erase an incorrect amount in a bill, you may ___, then key the correction.
A. drag through the amount to highlight
B. position the cursor in front of the amount and press the delete key until the amount has been erased
C. position the cursor after the amount and press the backspace key until the amount has been erased
D. all the above

_____ 3.12. When using QuickBooks Desktop's graphs, information regarding the percentage of accounts payable owed to each vendor is displayed as a ___.
A. pie chart
B. bar chart
C. line chart
D. both A and B

_____ 3.13.   A correction to a bill that has been recorded is made on the bill or ___.
A. on the check
B. on the Accounts Payable Graph
C. in the Accounts Payable Register
D. none of the above

_____ 3.14.   To increase the date on a bill by one day, ___.
A. press the + key
B. press the - key
C. tab
D. press the # key

_____ 3.15.   A check may be edited in the ___.
A. Write Checks window
B. Check Register
C. Pay Bills window
D. both A and B

_____ 3.16.   When you enter a bill, typing the first letter(s) of a vendor's name on the Vendor line ___.
A. enters the vendor's name on the line if the name is in the Vendor List
B. displays a list of vendor names
C. displays the Address Info tab for the vendor
D. both A and B

_____ 3.17.   If a withdrawal from the bank is used to fund Petty Cash, a ___ is recorded in QuickBooks Desktop.
A. Transfer Funds Between Accounts
B. Check
C. Credit Memo for the Cash account
D. Nothing needs to be recorded

_____ 3.18.   A Vendor Balance Summary report includes ___ .
A. balances for all vendors
B. balances for all vendors that are owed money
C. all vendors with zero balances
D. all vendors with overdue balances

_____ 3.19.   When a bill is deleted, ___.
A. the amount is changed to 0.00
B. the word "Deleted" appears as the Memo
C. it is removed without a trace
D. both A and B

_____ 3.20.   If a bill is recorded in the Enter Bills window, it is important to pay the bill by ___.
A. writing a check
B. using the Pay Bills window
C. using petty cash
D. allowing QuickBooks Desktop to generate the check automatically five days before the due date

FILL-IN

IN THE SPACE PROVIDED, WRITE THE ANSWER THAT MOST APPROPRIATELY COMPLETES THE SENTENCE.

3.21.   The keyboard shortcut to edit or modify an account in the Chart of Accounts is _____.

3.22.   The _____ section of a check is used to record the check date, payee, and amount for the actual check. The _____ area of a check is used to record the accounts used for the bill, the amount for each account used, and transaction explanations.

3.23.   Payment for expenses using petty cash are recorded in the _____.

3.24.   An Accounts Payable Graph by Aging Period shows a _____ chart detailing the amounts due by aging period and a _____ chart showing the percentage of the total amount payable owed to each vendor.

3.25.   Three different check styles may be used in QuickBooks Desktop: _____, _____, or _____.

SHORT ESSAY

When viewing a Transaction by Vendor Report that shows the entry of a bill for the purchase of office supplies and office equipment, you will see the term -**split**- displayed. Explain what the term **Split** means when used as a column heading and when used within the Split column for the bill indicated.

_____

_____

_____

_____

_____

END-OF-CHAPTER PROBLEM

YOUR NAME'S POOL & GARDEN OASIS

Chapter 3 continues with the transactions for bills, bill payments, and purchases for Your Name's Pool & Garden Oasis. Cash control measures have been implemented. As the owner, you prepare, print, and sign the checks and any related reports.

INSTRUCTIONS

Continue to use the **Oasis 2018.qbw** company file that you used in Chapters 1 and 2. Record the bills, bill payments, and purchases as instructed within the chapter. Read the transactions carefully and review the Chart of Accounts when selecting transaction accounts. Print reports and graphs as indicated. Even though not required, bills may be printed and are included on the Checklist. Check with your instructor to see if printing bills is assigned. If a bill is recorded on the Enter Bills screen, it should be paid on the Pay Bills screen—not by writing the check.

RECORD TRANSACTIONS

January 1
▶ Change the vendor information for Mike's Cooling/Heating to Ben's Cooling & Heating. You will need to change the Vendor Name, the Company Name, the Billed From Address, and on the Payment Settings tab the Print Name on Check As.
▶ Received a bill from Giacchi Communications for cellular phone service, $485, Net 10, Invoice 1109, Memo: January Cell Phone Services. If you print to a pdf file, save the document as **1-Your Name Bill Giacchi Com Ch3**.
▶ Received a bill from Office Junction for the purchase of office supplies to have on hand, $275, Net 30, Invoice 5895. (Since this is a prepaid expense an asset account is used.) No memo is necessary. If you print to a pdf file, save the document as **2-Your Name Bill Office Junction Ch3**.
▶ Received a bill from Midway Motors for truck service and repairs, $519, Net 10, Invoice 7684, Memo: Truck Service and Repairs. (Use Automobile Expense as the account for this transaction. We will change the name to something more appropriate in Chapter 4.) . If you print to a pdf file, save the document as **3-Your Name Bill Midway Motors Ch3**.
▶ Received a bill from Mission Gasoline for gasoline for the month, $375, Net 10, Invoice 853, Memo: January Gasoline. If you print to a pdf file, save the document as **4-Your Name Bill Mission Gasoline Ch3**.
▶ Received a bill from Ben's Cooling & Heating for a repair of the office heater, $150, Net 30, Invoice 87626, Memo: Heater Repair. (The heater is part of the building.) If you print to a pdf file, save the document as **5-Your Name Bill Ben's Cooling Ch3**.

January 15
▶ Add a new expense account: Disposal Expense, Description: SB County Dump Charges.
▶ Received a bill from SB County Dump for disposing of lawn, tree, and shrub trimmings, $180, Net 30, Invoice 6567, no memo necessary. If you print to a pdf file, save the document as **6-Your Name Bill SB Dump Ch3**.

▶ Received a bill from SB Water, $25, Net 10, Invoice 7098, no memo necessary. If you print to a pdf file, save the document as **7-Your Name Bill SB Water Ch3**.

▶ Change the QuickBooks Desktop Company Preferences to customize the report format so that reports refresh automatically, and that the Date Prepared, the Time Prepared, and the Report Basis do not print as part of the header. (Verify this with your instructor.)

▶ Prepare an Unpaid Bills Detail Report for January 15, 2018; resize columns as needed, print in Portrait orientation. If you print to a pdf file, save the document as **8-Your Name Unpaid Bills Ch3**.

▶ Pay all bills *due on or before January 15*, print the checks. (Use Pay Bills to pay bills that have been entered in the Enter Bills window.) Make sure the Payment Date is 01/15/2018. Use standard style for the checks. If you print to a pdf file, save the document as **9-Your Name Cks 1-4 Ch3**.

▶ Add Petty Cash to the Chart of Accounts.

▶ After obtaining $50 as a cash withdrawal from the bank, complete a Transfer Funds form to transfer $50 from Checking to Petty Cash, Memo: Funds Transfer to Establish Petty Cash Fund.

▶ Record a bill from Repairs RX. Add this new vendor as you record the transaction. Additional information needed to do a complete Set Up is: 7234 State Street, Santa Barbara, CA 93110, Main Phone: 805-555-0770, Main Email: RepairsRX@sb.com, Website: www.RepairsRX, Terms: Net 10. The bill was for the repair of the lawn mower (equipment), $75, Invoice 5126, Memo: Lawn Mower Repair. If you print to a pdf file, save the document as **10-Your Name Bill Repairs RX Ch3**.

▶ Change the telephone number for SB County Dump. The new number is 805-555-3798.

▶ Prepare, resize columns, and print the Vendor Balance Detail Report for all transactions. If you print to a pdf file, save the document as **11-Your Name Vend Bal Detail Ch3**.

January 30

▶ Received a $10 credit from Repairs RX. The repair of the lawn mower wasn't as extensive as originally estimated. (No Ref No.) Print the Credit Memo. If you print to a pdf file, save the document as **12-Your Name CM Repairs RX Ch3**.

▶ Record the use of Petty Cash to pay for postage due 64 cents, and office supplies, $1.59 (this is a current expense). Memo notations are not necessary.

▶ Write and print Check 5 to Repairs RX to buy a lawn fertilizer spreader as a cash purchase of equipment, $349, Check Memo: Purchase Fertilizer Spreader. Print the check. (If you get a dialog box indicating that you currently owe money to Repairs RX, Click **Continue Writing Check**. Remember, this is a purchase of equipment.) If you print to a pdf file, save the document as **13-Your Name Ck 5 Repairs RX Ch3**.

▶ Prepare, resize columns and print an Unpaid Bills Detail Report for January 30. If you print to a pdf file, save the document as **14-Your Name Unpaid Bills Ch3**.

▶ Pay all bills *due on or before January 30*; print the checks. (Note: There may be some bills that were due after January 15 but before January 30. Be sure to pay these bills now. If any vendor shows a credit and has a bill that is due, apply it to the bill prior to payment. You may need to click on each bill individually to determine whether there is a credit to be applied.) Print the checks using standard style. If you print to a pdf file, save the document as **15-Your Name Cks 6-7 Ch3**.

▶ Prepare an Accounts Payable Graph as of 1/30/2018. Do not print.

▶ Prepare a QuickZoom Graph for SB County Dump as of 1/30/2018. Do not print.

► Prepare the Journal report for January 1-30, 2018, expand the report, resize the columns, and then print the report in Landscape. If you print to a pdf file, save the document as **16-Your Name Journal Ch3**.

► Print a Trial Balance for January 1-30, 2018. If you print to a pdf file, save the document as **17-Your Name Trial Bal Ch3**.

► Back up your data and close the company.

CHAPTER 3 CHECKLISTS

YOUR NAME'S TECH SERVICES

The checklist below shows all the business forms and reports printed during training. Check each one that you printed. In the document names below, Your Name and Ch3 have been omitted, and report dates are given. (Note: When paying bills and printing a batch of checks, your checks may be in a different order than shown below. Do not be concerned if your check numbers are not an exact match.)

___ 1-Bill Creative Advertising (Optional)
___ 2-Bill Supply Spot (Optional)
___ 3-Trans List by Vend
___ 4-Bill Comp Prof Mag
___ 5-Bill Supply Spot
___ 6-Greg's Garage
___ 7-Bill Valley Ins
___ 8-QuickReport Supply Spot
___ 9-Unpaid Bills Detail, January 25, 2018
___ 10-Bill Comp Tech Mag
___ 11-CM Supply Spot
___ 12-Cks 1-3
    Ck 1 Creative Advertising
    Ck 2 Rapid Delivery Service
    Ck 3 Supply Spot

___ 13-Cks 4-7
    Ck 4 Pacific Realtors
    Ck 5 SCE
    Ck 6 CA Water
    Ck 7 So Cal Gas Co
___ 14-Ck Detail, January 1-30, 2018
___ 15-AP Aging Sum, January 30, 2018
___ 16-Unpaid Bills Detail, January 30, 2018
___ 17-Vend Bal Sum, January 30, 2018
___ 18-Journal, January 1-30, 2018
___ 19-Trial Bal, January 1-30, 2018

YOUR NAME'S POOL & GARDEN OASIS

The checklist below shows all the business forms and reports printed during training. Check each one that you printed. In the document names below, Your Name and Ch3 have been omitted, and report dates are given. (Note: When paying bills and printing a batch of checks, your checks may be in a different order than shown below. Do not be concerned if your check numbers are not an exact match.)

___ 1-Bill Giacchi Com (Optional)
___ 2-Bill Office Junction (Optional)
___ 3-Bill Midway Motors (Optional)
___ 4-Bill Mission Gasoline (Optional)
___ 5-Bill Ben's Cooling (Optional)
___ 6-Bill SB Dump (Optional)
___ 7-Bill SB Water (Optional)
___ 8-Unpaid Bills, January 15, 2018
___ 9-Cks 1-4
    Ck 1 Giacchi Com
    Ck 2 Midway Motors
    Ck 3 Mission Street Gasoline
    Ck 4 SB County Dump

___ 10-Bill Repairs RX (Optional)
___ 11-Vend Bal Detail
___ 12-CM Repairs RX
___ 13-Ck 5 Repairs RX
___ 14-Unpaid Bills, January 30, 2018
___ 15-Cks 6-7
    Ck 6 Repairs RX
    Ck 7 SB Water
___ 16-Journal, January 1-30, 2018
___ 17-Trial Bal, January 1-30, 2018

GENERAL ACCOUNTING AND END-OF-PERIOD PROCEDURES: SERVICE BUSINESS

4

LEARNING OBJECTIVES

At the completion of this chapter, you will be able to:

4.01.   Change account names and view the effect on subaccounts.
4.02.   Make accounts inactive and delete accounts.
4.03.   Record adjustments for accrual basis accounting, which include depreciation and prepaid expenses.
4.04.   Prepare the Journal report.
4.05.   Record owner withdrawals.
4.06.   Record cash and non-cash investments by an owner.
4.07.   Prepare a Balance Sheet (Standard) Report.
4.08.   Reconcile the bank statement, record bank service charges, automatic payments, and mark cleared transactions.
4.09.   Prepare and print a Reconciliation Detail Report.
4.10.   Use the Checking Account Register.
4.11.   Edit Cleared Transactions.
4.12.   Select Accrual-Basis Reporting Preferences.
4.13.   Prepare and print a Trial Balance.
4.14.   Understand how to export reports to Excel.
4.15.   Prepare and print Cash Flow Forecast and Statement of Cash Flows reports.
4.16.   Prepare multiple reports including: Accountant: Profit and Loss and Accountant: Balance Sheet.
4.17.   Record closing entries including the transfer of Net Income into Capital and closing Drawing.
4.18.   Create an archive company file.
4.19.   Understand how to assign passwords.
4.20.   Set period closing date and edit closed transactions.

GENERAL ACCOUNTING AND END-OF-PERIOD PROCEDURES

As previously stated, QuickBooks Desktop operates from the standpoint of a business document rather than an accounting form, journal, or ledger. While QuickBooks Desktop does incorporate all these items into the program, in many instances they operate behind the scenes. QuickBooks Desktop does not require special closing procedures at the end of a period. At the end of the fiscal year, QuickBooks Desktop transfers the net income into the Owner's Equity account and allows you to protect the data for the year by assigning a closing date to the period. All the transaction detail is maintained and viewable, but it will not be changed unless OK is clicked on a warning screen.

Even though a formal closing does not have to be performed within QuickBooks Desktop, when you use accrual-basis accounting, several transactions must be recorded to reflect all expenses and income for the period. For example, bank statements must be reconciled, and any charges or bank collections need to be recorded. During the business period, the accountant for the company will review things such as account names, adjusting entries, depreciation schedules, owner's equity adjustments, and so on. Sometimes the changes and adjustments will be made by the accountant in a separate file called the Accountant's Copy of the business files. This file is then imported into the company file that is used to record day-to-day business transactions, and all adjustments made by the accountant are added to the current company file. There are certain restrictions to the types of transactions that may be made on an Accountant's Copy of the business files.

Once necessary adjustments have been made, reports reflecting the end-of-period results of operations should be prepared. For archive purposes at the end of the fiscal year an additional backup disk is prepared and stored.

TRAINING TUTORIAL AND PROCEDURES

The following tutorial will once again work with Your Name's Tech Services. As in Chapters 2 and 3, transactions will be recorded for this fictitious company. To maximize training benefits, you should follow the steps illustrated in Chapter 2 and be sure to use the same file that you used to record transactions for Chapters 1, 2 and 3.

OPEN QUICKBOOKS DESKTOP AND COMPANY FILE

 Open QuickBooks Desktop

Open Your Name's Tech Services as previously instructed
- This file should contain all the transactions that you recorded for Chapters 2 and 3.
Check the title bar to verify that Your Name's Tech Services is the open company
Prepare a Journal report for 01/01/18 – 01/30/18
Verify that all transactions from Chapters 2 and 3 are shown
- Hint: the last transaction should be the Check 8 written to Supply Spot for the purchase of a Fax machine and the report total should be $45,217.79.
Close the Journal report without printing

DATES

As in the other chapters in the text, the year used for the screen shots is 2018, which is the same year as the version of the program. You may want to check with your instructor to see if you should use 2018 as the year for the transactions. Be sure to use the same year for all the transactions in Chapters 2, 3, and 4.

PRINTING

Throughout the text, you will be instructed when to print business documents and reports. Everything that is to be printed within the chapter is listed on the checklist at the end of the chapter. The end-of-chapter problem also has everything to be printed listed on the same checklist. As in the other chapters, check with your instructor for printing requirements.

BEGIN TUTORIAL

In this chapter, you will be recording end-of-period adjustments, reconciling bank statements, changing account names, and preparing traditional end-of-period reports. Because QuickBooks Desktop does not perform a traditional "closing" of the books, you will learn how to assign a closing date to protect transactions and data recorded during previous accounting periods.

As in the earlier chapters, all transactions are listed on memos. Unless otherwise specified, the transaction date will be the same as the memo date. Once a specific type of transaction has been entered in a step-by-step manner, additional transactions of the same or a similar type will be made without instructions being provided. Of course, you may always refer to instructions given for previous transactions for ideas or for steps used to enter those transactions. To determine the account used in the transaction, refer to the Chart of Accounts, which is also the General Ledger.

CHANGE ACCOUNT NAME

Even though transactions have been recorded during the month of January, QuickBooks Desktop makes it a simple matter to change the name of an existing account. Once the name of an account has been changed, all transactions using the "old" name are updated and show the "new" account name.

MEMO
DATE: January 31, 2018

Upon the recommendation from the company's CPA, you decided to change the names of several accounts: Student's Name, Capital to Your Name, Capital (Use your actual name); Company Cars to Business Vehicles; Company Cars Loan to Business Vehicles Loan; Automobile Expense to Business Vehicles Expense; Auto Insurance Expense to Business Vehicles Insurance; Office Equipment Loan to Office Furniture/Equipment Loan; and Office Equipment to Office Furniture/Equipment.

    Change the account names

Access the **Chart of Accounts** using the keyboard shortcut **Ctrl+A**
Scroll through accounts until you see **Student's Name, Capital**, click the account.
Click the **Account** button at the bottom of the Chart of Accounts, click **Edit Account**
   OR
Use the keyboard shortcut **Ctrl+E**
On the **Edit Account** screen, highlight **Student's Name**
Enter your name
- The name of the account should be **Your Name, Capital** (your real name!).
Click **Save & Close** to record the name change and close the **Edit Account** screen
- Notice that the name of the account appears as **Your Name, Capital** in the Chart of Accounts and that the balance of $78,135.00 shows.
- The balances of any subaccounts of Your Name, Capital will be reflected in the account total on the Chart of Accounts and in reports.
- While the subaccount names remain unchanged, the name of the account to which they are attached is changed.

Follow the steps above to change the names of:

Company Cars to **Business Vehicles**
- If the subaccount included Company Cars as part of the subaccount name, the subaccount name would need to be changed. Changing the name of the master account does not change the name of a related subaccount.
- Remember the account name was changed in Chapter 1 after the Tech 2018 (Backup Ch. 1).qbb file was created. When the backup file was restored, the account name reverted to the original name of Company Cars.

Company Cars Loan to **Business Vehicles Loan**

Automobile Expense to **Business Vehicles Expense**

Delete the Description by highlighting it and then pressing the **Delete** key

Auto Insurance Expense to **Business Vehicles Insurance** (Subaccount of Insurance Expense)

Office Equipment to **Office Furniture & Equipment**

Office Equipment Loan to **Office Furniture/Equipment Loan**
- Due to exceeding the allotted number of characters in an account name, the / was used to separate the words Furniture and Equipment.

Do not close the **Chart of Accounts**

EFFECT OF ACCOUNT NAME CHANGE ON SUBACCOUNTS

Any account (even a subaccount) that uses Company Cars (the master account) as part of the account name needs to be changed. When the account name of Company Cars was changed to Business Vehicles, the subaccounts of Company Cars automatically became subaccounts of Business Vehicles. Because the subaccount did not include "Company Cars" as part of the account name, the name did not change. If the subaccount included "Company Cars" as part of the account name, then the subaccount name would need to be changed.

 Examine the Depreciation and Original Cost accounts for Business Vehicles

Click **Depreciation** under Business Vehicles
Use the keyboard shortcut **Ctrl+E**
The text box for **Subaccount of** shows as **Business Vehicles**
- Remember you do not have to change the name of the Depreciation account. You are just verifying that Depreciation is a subaccount of Business Vehicles.

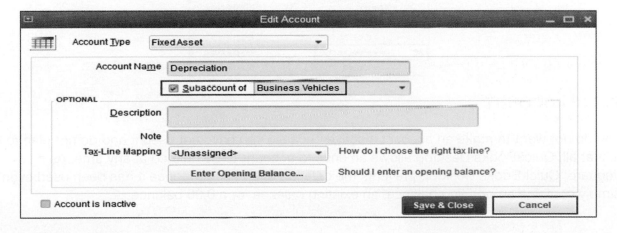

Click **Cancel**
- Repeat the above steps to examine the **Original Cost** account.
- Examine **Your Name, Capital** and **Office Furniture/Equipment** and their subaccounts.

Do not close the **Chart of Accounts**

MAKE ACCOUNT INACTIVE

If you are not using an account and do not have plans to use it in the future, the account may be made inactive. The account remains available for use, yet it does not appear on your chart of accounts unless you check the Show All check box.

MEMO

DATE: January 31, 2018

At present, the company does not plan to purchase its own building. Make **Interest Expense: Mortgage** and **Taxes: Property** inactive.

 Make the accounts listed in the memo inactive

Click **Mortgage** under Interest Expense
Click the **Account** button at the bottom of the **Chart of Accounts**
Click **Make Account Inactive**
- The account no longer appears in the Chart of Accounts.

To view all accounts including the inactive ones, click the **Include Inactive** check box next to the Attach button at the bottom of the **Chart of Accounts** and all accounts will be displayed
- Notice the icon next to Mortgage. It marks the account as inactive.

	Interest Expense	Expense
	Finance Charge	Expense
	Loan Interest	Expense
✖	Mortgage	Expense

Repeat the previous steps to make **Taxes: Property** inactive

	Taxes	Expense
	Federal	Expense
	Local	Expense
✖	Property	Expense
	State	Expense

DELETE ACCOUNT

If you do not want to make an account inactive because you have not used it and do not plan to use it at all, QuickBooks Desktop allows an unused account to be deleted at any time. As a safeguard, QuickBooks Desktop prevents the deletion of an account once it has been used even if it simply contains an opening balance, an existing balance, or a 0.00 balance.

> <u>MEMO</u>
> **DATE**: January 31, 2018
>
> In addition to previous changes to account names, you find that you do not use nor will use the expense account: Cash Discounts. Delete this account from the Chart of Accounts. In addition, delete the accounts: Inventory Asset, Cost of Goods Sold, and Dues and Subscriptions.

➡ Delete the **Cash Discounts** expense account

Scroll through accounts until you see Cash Discounts, click **Cash Discounts**
Click the **Account** button at the bottom of the Chart of Accounts, click **Delete Account OR** use the keyboard shortcut **Ctrl+D**
Click **OK** on the **Delete Account** dialog box

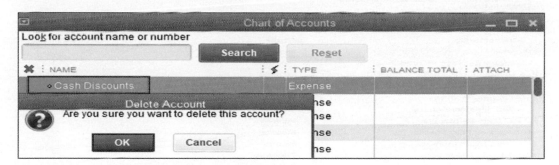

- The account has now been deleted.

Repeat the above steps for the deletion of **Inventory Asset**, **Cost of Goods Sold**, **Dues and Subscriptions**

- Since this Dues and Subscriptions account has been used, QuickBooks Desktop will not allow it to be deleted.
- As soon as you try to delete Dues and Subscriptions, a **QuickBooks Message** appears. It describes the problem (account has a balance or has been used) and offers a solution (make account inactive).

Click **Cancel**

- The account remains in the Chart of Accounts.

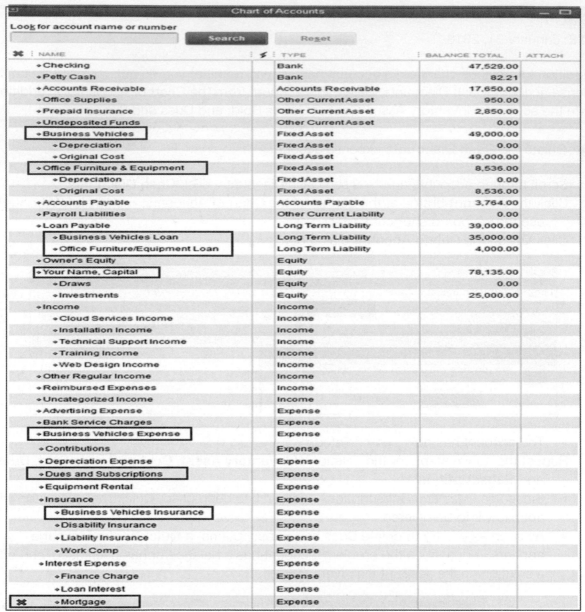

Partial Chart of Accounts

Review the changes made, and then close the **Chart of Accounts**

To print the Chart of Accounts, click **Reports** on the menu bar, point to **List**, click **Account Listing** (QuickBooks Desktop will insert the date of your computer as the report date)

Click the **Customize Report** button then click the **Header/Footer** tab

In the text box for Subtitle, enter **January 31, 2018**, click the **OK** button

Resize the columns of the reports to show the columns in full

To hide the column for **Tax Line**, drag the diamond on the right-side of **Tax Line** to the diamond on the right-side of **Description**

Repeat the procedures to hide the Description column

- Notice that the master/controlling account appears as part of the subaccount name. To see this, look at Business Vehicles: Depreciation.

Print in Portrait orientation and close the report

- If you print to a pdf file, save the document as **1-Your Name Acct List Ch4**.

ADJUSTMENTS FOR ACCRUAL-BASIS ACCOUNTING

As previously stated, the accrual-basis of accounting matches the income and the expenses of a period to arrive at an accurate figure for net income or net loss. Thus, the revenue is earned at the time the service is performed or the sale is made no matter when the actual cash is received. The cash-basis of accounting records income or revenue at the time cash is received no matter when the sale was made or the service performed. The same holds true when a business purchases items or pays bills. In accrual-basis accounting, the expense is recorded at the time the bill is received or the purchase is made regardless of the actual payment date. In cash-basis accounting, the expense is not recorded until it is paid. In QuickBooks Desktop, the Summary Report Basis for either Accrual or Cash is selected as a Report Preference. The default setting is Accrual.

For example, to record $1,000 of sales on account and one year of insurance for $600 in November: Using the accrual-basis of accounting, you would record $1,000 as income or revenue and $600 as a prepaid expense in an asset account—Prepaid Insurance. Month by month, an adjusting entry for $50 would be made to record the amount of insurance used for the month. In the accrual-basis of accounting, when the $1,000 payment on account is received, it will not affect income. It will be recorded as an increase in cash and a decrease in accounts receivable. When using the cash-basis of accounting, you would have no income and $600 worth of insurance recorded as an expense for November with nothing else recorded for insurance until the following November. The income of $1,000 would not be shown until the cash payment was received. A Statement of Profit & Loss prepared in November would show:

November	Accrual		Cash	
Income		$1,000		$ 0
Insurance Expense	($600/12) =	-50		-600
Net Profit (Loss)	Profit	$950	Loss	-$600

When you are using the accrual-basis of accounting, there are several internal transactions that must be recorded. These entries are called adjusting entries. Some items used in a business are purchased and or paid for in advance. When this occurs, they are recorded as an asset. These are called prepaid expenses. As these are used, they become expenses of the business. For example, insurance for the entire year would be used up month by month and should, therefore, be a monthly expense. Commonly, the insurance is billed and paid for six months or one year. Until the insurance is used, it is an asset. Each month, the portion of the insurance used becomes an expense for the month. (Refer to the chart above.) Another example for adjusting entries is regarding equipment. Since it does wear out and will eventually need to be replaced, rather than wait until replacement to record the use of the equipment, an adjusting entry is made to allocate the use of equipment as an expense for a period. This is called depreciation.

ADJUSTING ENTRIES—PREPAID EXPENSES

As previously stated, a prepaid expense is an item that is paid for in advance. Examples of prepaid expenses include: Insurance—policy is usually for six months or one year; Office Supplies—buy to have on hand and use as needed. (This is different from supplies that are purchased for immediate use.) A prepaid expense is an asset until it is used. As the insurance or supplies are used, the amount used becomes an expense for the period. In accrual-basis accounting, an adjusting entry is made in the General Journal at the end of the period to allocate the amount of prepaid expenses (assets) used to expenses.

The transactions for these adjustments may be recorded in the register for the account by clicking on the prepaid expense (asset) in the Chart of Accounts, or they may be made in the General Journal.

As a note: The General Journal is used when you want to record a transaction. Wherever a transaction is entered, it is recorded in the Journal. Entries recorded in the Journal are displayed in the Journal Report.

MEMO

DATE: January 31, 2018

Sofia, remember to record the monthly adjustment for Prepaid Insurance. The amount we paid for the year for business vehicles insurance was $2,850. Also, we used $350 worth of office supplies this month. Please adjust accordingly

---

 Record the adjusting entries for office supplies expense and business vehicles insurance expense in the General Journal

> To access the General Journal, click **Company** on the menu bar; and then, click **Make General Journal Entries...**
> On the screen regarding Assigning Numbers to Journal Entries, click **Do not display this message in the future** to insert a check mark; and then, click **OK**
> The General Journal Entries screen appears
> - Note the checkbox for Adjusting Entry.
> - A list of entries made Last Month is shown at the bottom of the screen.
>   - ○ If the date of your computer does not match the text, you may not have anything shown in the List of Entries.
>   - ○ If you wish, you can change the period to be displayed by clicking the drop-down list arrow for **List of Selected General Journal Entries** and selecting a period or you may hide the list by clicking the **Hide List** icon on the Make General Journal Entries icon bar.

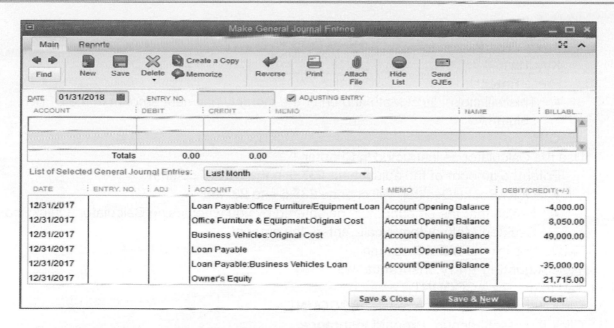

Record the adjusting entry for Prepaid Insurance

Enter **01/31/18** as the **DATE**

- QuickBooks Desktop will enter the year as 2018.
- **ENTRY NO.** is left blank unless you wish to record a specific number.
- Because all transactions entered for the month have been entered in the Journal as well as on an invoice or a bill, all transactions automatically have a Journal entry number.
- Notice the check box for **ADJUSTING ENTRY** is marked. The ADJUSTING ENTRY check box allows QuickBooks Desktop to indicate that an entry is an adjustment.
- Adjusting journal entries are entered by accountants to make after-the-fact changes to specific accounts.
- Accountants record adjustments for a variety of reasons, including depreciation, prepaid income or expenses; adjusting sales tax payable; and entering bank or credit card fees or interest.
- You can view a list of all adjusting journal entries in the Adjusting Journal Entries report.
- By default, the ADJUSTING ENTRY checkbox is selected for new transactions.

Tab to or click the **ACCOUNT** column

Click the drop-down list arrow for **ACCOUNT**; click the expense account **Business Vehicles Insurance**

Tab to or click **DEBIT**

- The $2,850 given in the memo is the amount for the year; you may calculate the amount of the adjustment for the month by using QuickBooks Desktop QuickMath or the Calculator.

Use QuickBooks Desktop QuickMath

    Enter **2850** by:

        Keying the numbers on the **10-key pad** (preferred)

- Be sure Num Lock is on. If not, press Num Lock to activate.

    OR

Typing the numbers at the top of the keyboard

Press **/** for division

Key **12**

Press **Enter**

- This will close QuickMath and enter the monthly payment amount in the DEBIT column.

OR

Use the Calculator as instructed in Chapter 1

Enter the amount of the adjustment **237.5** in the **DEBIT** column

- QuickBooks Desktop will change 237.5 into 237.50.
- Notice that the amount must be entered by you when using Calculator; QuickBooks Desktop Math automatically enters the amount.

Tab to or click the **MEMO** column

Type **Adjusting Entry, Insurance**

Tab to or click **ACCOUNT**

Click the drop-down list arrow for **ACCOUNT**

Click the asset account **Prepaid Insurance**

- The amount for the Credit column should be entered automatically. However, there are several reasons why an amount may not appear in the Credit column. If 237.50 does not appear, type it in the Credit column.
- If the memo does not appear automatically, tab to or click the **MEMO** column, and type **Adjusting Entry, Insurance**.

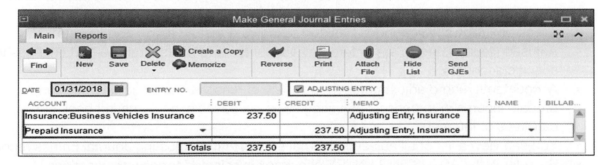

- Note the Totals for the Debit and Credit shown at the bottom of the screen.

Click **Save & New** to record the adjustment and advance to the next **Make General Journal Entries** screen

Repeat the above procedures to record the adjustment for the office supplies used

Use the Memo **Adjusting Entry, Supplies**

- The amount given in the memo is the actual amount of the supplies used in January, so you will not need to use QuickMath or the calculator.
- Remember, when supplies are purchased to have on hand, the original entry records an increase to the asset Office Supplies. Once the supplies are used, the adjustment correctly records the amount of supplies used as an expense.

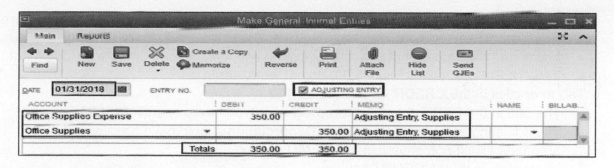

Click **Save & New**

ADJUSTING ENTRIES—DEPRECIATION

Equipment and other long-term assets lose value over their lifetime. Unlike supplies—where you can see, for example, the paper supply diminishing—it is very difficult to see how much of a computer has been "used up" during the month. To account for the fact that machines do wear out and need to be replaced, an adjustment is made for depreciation. This adjustment correctly matches the expenses of the period against the revenue of the period.

The adjusting entry for depreciation can be made in the account register for Depreciation, or it can be made in the General Journal.

MEMO

DATE: January 31, 2018

Having received the necessary depreciation schedules, Sofia records the adjusting entry for depreciation: Business Vehicles, $583 per month; Equipment, $142 per month.

 Record a compound adjusting entry for depreciation of the equipment and the business vehicles in the **General Journal**

Continue to use **Make General Journal Entries**
- The **DATE** should show as **01/31/18** and **ADJUSTING ENTRY** should have a check. If not, enter the date and click ADJUSTING ENTRY to select.

ENTRY NO. is left blank
- Normally, the debit portion of a General Journal entry is entered first. However, to use the automatic calculation feature of QuickBooks Desktop, you will enter the **credit** entries first.

Tab to or click in the **ACCOUNT** column

Click the drop-down list arrow for **ACCOUNT**, click **Depreciation** under **Business Vehicles**
- Make sure that you do <u>not</u> click the controlling account, Business Vehicles.

Tab to or click in the **CREDIT** column, enter **583**

Tab to or click in the **MEMO** column, enter **Adjusting Entry, Depreciation**

Tab to or click the **ACCOUNT** column
- The amount of the 583 credit shows in the DEBIT column temporarily.

Click the drop-down list arrow for **ACCOUNT**; click **Depreciation** under **Office Furniture & Equipment**
- Make sure that you do <u>not</u> use the controlling account, Office Furniture & Equipment.
- If the DEBIT column shows 583.00, do not worry about it.

Tab to or click in the **CREDIT** column, enter **142**
- The 583 in the DEBIT column is removed when you tab to or click **MEMO**.
- The adjusting entry **Adjusting Entry, Depreciation** should have been entered automatically. If not, enter it in the **MEMO** column.

Tab to or click in the **ACCOUNT** column
Click the drop-down list arrow for **ACCOUNT**, click **Depreciation Expense**
The **DEBIT** column should automatically show **725**
- If 725 does not appear, enter it in the DEBIT column. The MEMO **Adjusting Entry, Depreciation** should be entered automatically. If not, enter it.

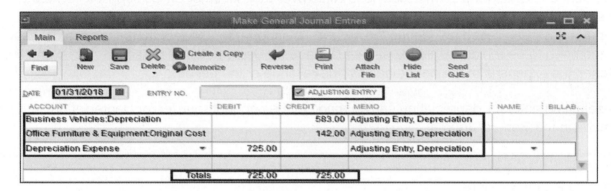

Click the **Save** icon to record the adjustment
- If you get a message regarding Tracking Fixed Assets, click **Do not display this message in the future** and click **OK**.

Click the drop-down list arrow for **List of Selected General Journal Entries** shown below the Totals
Click **This Fiscal Year**
- If your computer does not have 2018 as the year, click **Last Fiscal Year**.

View the entries recorded in 2018
- Note that only the first line/account used in a transaction appears.
- If you click on one of the transactions, it will take to you that transaction in the General Journal.

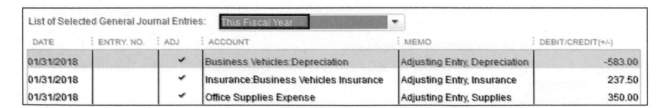

Click **Save & Close** to close **Make General Journal Entries**

JOURNAL REPORT

Once transactions have been entered in the General Journal, it is important to view them. QuickBooks Desktop refers to the General Journal as the location of transaction entry and to the

Journal as a report. Even with the special ways in which transactions are entered in QuickBooks Desktop through invoices, bills, checks, account registers, and general journal entries, the Journal represents the book of original entry. To view all the transactions recorded for the company the Journal report is prepared. The Journal report may be viewed or printed at any time.

    View the Journal report for January

Click **Reports** on the menu bar, point to **Accountant & Taxes,** and click **Journal**
If you get the Collapsing and Expanding Transactions dialog box, click the **Do not display this message in the future**; and then, click **OK**
Always **Expand** your transactions even if not specifically instructed to do so
Enter the dates from **01/01/18** to **01/31/18**
Tab to generate the report
- Notice that the transactions do not begin with the adjustments entered directly into the General Journal.
- The first transaction displayed is the entry for Invoice 1 to Juan Garcia.
- If corrections or changes are made to entries, the transaction numbers may differ from the key. Since QuickBooks Desktop assigns transaction numbers automatically, disregard any discrepancies in transaction numbers.

Scroll through the report to view all transactions recorded in the Journal report
Verify the total Debit and Credit Columns of $46,530.29
- If your totals do not match, check for errors and make appropriate corrections.
- Since the adjusting entries were marked as adjustments when entered in the General Journal, the Adj column shows checks for these entries.

Your Name's Tech Services
Journal
January 2018

Trans #	Type	Date	Num	Adj	Name	Memo	Account	Debit	Credit
67	General Journal	01/31/2018		✓		Adjusting Entry, Insurance	Business Vehicles Insurance	237.50	
				✓		Adjusting Entry, Insurance	Prepaid Insurance		237.50
								237.50	237.50
68	General Journal	01/31/2018		✓		Adjusting Entry, Supplies	Office Supplies Expense	350.00	
				✓		Adjusting Entry, Supplies	Office Supplies		350.00
								350.00	350.00
69	General Journal	01/31/2018		✓		Adjusting Entry, Depreciation	Depreciation		583.00
				✓		Adjusting Entry, Depreciation	Depreciation		142.00
				✓		Adjusting Entry, Depreciation	Depreciation Expense	725.00	
								725.00	725.00
TOTAL								**46,530.29**	**46,530.29**

Partial Report

Close the Journal report without printing

OWNER WITHDRAWALS

In a sole proprietorship an owner cannot receive a paycheck because he or she owns the business. An owner withdrawing money from a business—even to pay personal expenses—is like withdrawing money from a savings account. A withdrawal simply decreases the owner's capital. QuickBooks Desktop allows you to establish a separate account for owner withdrawals. If a separate account is not established, owner withdrawals may be subtracted directly from the owner's capital or investment account.

> **MEMO**
>
> **DATE:** January 31, 2018
>
> Even though you work in the business full time, you do not earn a paycheck. Prepare the check for your monthly withdrawal, $2,500.00.

 Write Check 9 to yourself for your $2,500 withdrawal

Open the **Write Checks - Checking** window:
Click **Banking** on the menu bar, click **Write Checks**
> **OR**

Click the **Write Checks** icon in the Banking section of the Home Page
> **OR**

Use the keyboard shortcut **Ctrl+W**
NO. should be **TO PRINT**
- If not, click the check box **Print Later** on the Write Checks - Checking icon bar.

DATE should be **01/31/18**
Enter **Your Name** (type your real name) on the **PAY TO THE ORDER OF** line
Press the **Tab** key
- Because your name was not added to any list when the company was created, the **Name Not Found** dialog box appears on the screen.

Click **Quick Add** to add your name to a list

The **Select Name Type** dialog box appears
Click **Other**

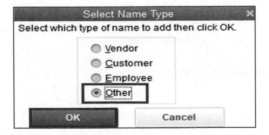

Click **OK**
- Your name is added to a list of "Other" names, which are used for owners, partners, and other miscellaneous names.

Tab to or click in the text box for **$**

- If necessary, delete any numbers showing for the amount (0.00).

Enter **2500** in the text box for **$**

Tab to or click **MEMO** on the check face and enter **Monthly Withdrawal**

Tab to or click in the **ACCOUNT** column in the detail section at the bottom of the check

Click the drop-down list arrow, click the Equity Account: **Draws**

- This account is a subaccount of Your Name, Capital.
- The amount 2,500.00 should appear in the **AMOUNT** column.
- If it does not, tab to or click in the **AMOUNT** column and enter 2500.

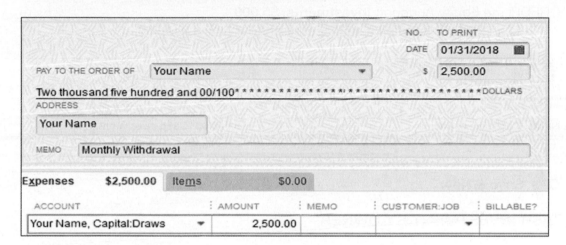

Click **Print** to print the check

The **Print Check** dialog box appears; the **Printed Check Number** should be **9**

- If necessary, change the number to 9.

Click **OK**

Print the standard style check as previously instructed

- If you print to a pdf file, save the document as **2-Your Name Ck 9 Owner Ch4**.

Once the check has printed successfully, click **OK** on the **Print Checks - Confirmation** dialog box

Click **Save & Close** to record the check, close any reminder screens that may appear

CASH INVESTMENT BY OWNER

An owner may decide to invest more of his or her personal cash in the business at any time. The new investment is entered into the owner's investment account and into cash. The investment may be recorded in the account register for checking or in the register for the owner's investment account. It may also be recorded in the General Journal.

MEMO

DATE: January 31, 2018

You received money from a certificate of deposit. Rather than reinvest in another certificate of deposit, you have decided to invest an additional $5,000 in the company.

Record the owner's additional cash investment in the General Journal

Access Make General Journal Entries as previously instructed
The **DATE** should be **01/31/18**
- Nothing is needed for ENTRY No.
This is <u>not</u> an adjusting entry, so click **ADJUSTING ENTRY** to remove the check
DEBIT **Checking, $5,000**
The MEMO for both entries should be **Cash Investment**
CREDIT the Equity Account: **Investments, $5,000**
- This account is listed as a subaccount of Your Name, Capital.

DATE 01/31/2018	ENTRY NO.			☐ ADJUSTING ENTRY		
ACCOUNT		DEBIT	CREDIT	MEMO	NAME	BILLAB.
Checking		5,000.00		Cash Investment		
Your Name, Capital:Investments			5,000.00	Cash Investment		
	Totals	5,000.00	5,000.00			

Click **Save & New**

NON-CASH INVESTMENT BY OWNER

An owner may make investments in a business at any time. The investment may be cash; but it may also be something such as reference books, equipment, tools, buildings, and so on. Additional investments by an owner(s) are added to owner's equity. In the case of a sole proprietorship, the investment is added to the Capital account for Investments.

MEMO
DATE: January 31, 2018

Originally, you planned to have an office in your home as well as in the company and purchased new office furniture for your home. Since then, you decided the business environment would appear more professional if the new furniture were in the company office rather than your home. You gave the new office furniture to the company as an additional owner investment. The value of the investment is $3,000.00.

   Record the non-cash investment in the General Journal

The **DATE** should be **01/31/18**, **ENTRY NO**. should be blank, **ADJUSTING ENTRY** should
   <u>not</u> be marked
DEBIT **Original Cost** (the subaccount of **Office Furniture/Equipment**) **$3,000**
The MEMO for both entries should be **Investment of Furniture**
CREDIT **Investments** (the subaccount of **Your Name, Capital**) **$3,000**
- When you select the account and press tab, the Memo should automatically appear. If
   it does not, copy the memo for the second entry rather than retype it, drag through the
   memo text to highlight; press Ctrl+C; position the cursor in the memo area for the
   second entry; press Ctrl+V.

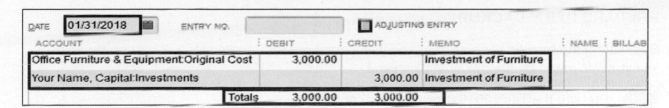

DATE	01/31/2018		ENTRY NO.			ADJUSTING ENTRY			
ACCOUNT			DEBIT	CREDIT	MEMO			NAME	BILLAB
Office Furniture & Equipment:Original Cost			3,000.00		Investment of Furniture				
Your Name, Capital:Investments				3,000.00	Investment of Furniture				
		Totals	3,000.00	3,000.00					

Click **Save & Close** to record and exit
- If you get a message regarding Tracking Fixed Assets, click **OK**.

BALANCE SHEET (STANDARD)

Prior to writing the check for the monthly withdrawal, there had been no withdrawals by the owner, and the drawing account balance was zero. Once a withdrawal is made, that amount is carried forward in the owner's drawing account. Subsequent withdrawals are added to this account. When you view the Balance Sheet, notice the balance of the Drawing account after the check for the withdrawal was written. Also notice the Net Income account that appears in the equity section of the Balance Sheet. This account is automatically added by QuickBooks Desktop to track the net income for the year.

     View a Balance Sheet (Standard)

Click **Reports** on the menu bar, point to **Company & Financial**, and click **Balance Sheet Standard**
- Unless otherwise instructed, all Balance Sheets prepared are Standard.

Tab to or click **As of**

Enter the date **01/31/18**

Tab to generate the report
- Note that the Report Basis for Accrual or Cash may be selected at the top of the report. Accrual should be selected.

Scroll through the report
- Notice the Equity section, especially Net Income.
- The ▼ next to Equity and Your Name, Capital show that the report is expanded. If you click it, you will collapse the detail and only the heading **Equity** and the total equity amount of **$88,020.71** will show. Do <u>not</u> collapse the section.

Your Name's Tech Services
Balance Sheet
As of January 31, 2018

	Jan 31, 18
▼ Equity	
▼ Your Name, Capital	
Draws	-2,500.00
Investments	33,000.00
Your Name, Capital - Other	53,135.00
Total Your Name, Capital	83,635.00
Net Income	4,385.71
Total Equity	88,020.71
TOTAL LIABILITIES & EQUITY	130,784.71

Partial Report

Close the report without printing

PREPARE DAILY BACKUP

By creating the backup file now, it will contain your work for Chapters 1, 2, 3 and up through the investments made by the owner in Chapter 4.

  Prepare the Tech 2018 (Daily Backup).qbb file

Follow the steps presented in Chapter 1 for creating a backup file
Name the file **Tech 2018 (Daily Backup)**
The file type is **QBW Backup (* .QBB)**
Click **Yes** on the Confirm Save As screen

BANK RECONCILIATION

Each month, the checking account should be reconciled with the bank statement to make sure that the balances agree. The bank statement will rarely have an ending balance that matches the balance of the checking account. This is due to several factors: outstanding checks (written by the business but not paid by the bank), deposits in transit (deposits that were made too late to be included on the bank statement), bank service charges, interest earned on checking accounts, collections made by the bank, and errors made in recording checks and/or deposits by the company or by the bank.

To have an accurate amount listed as the balance in the checking account, it is important that the differences between the bank statement and the checking account be reconciled. If something such as a service charge or a collection made by the bank appears on the bank statement, it needs to be recorded in the checking account.

Reconciling a bank statement is an appropriate time to find any errors that may have been recorded in the checking account. The reconciliation may be out of balance because a transposition was made (recording $94 rather than $49), a transaction was recorded backwards, a transaction was recorded twice, or a transaction was not recorded at all. If a transposition was made, the error may be found by dividing the difference by 9. For example, if $94 was recorded and the actual transaction amount was $49, you would subtract 49 from 94 to get 45. The number 45 can be evenly divided by 9, so your error was a transposition. If the error can be evenly divided by 2, the transaction may have been entered backwards. For example, if you were out of balance $200, look to see if you had any $100 transactions. Perhaps you recorded a $100 debit, and it should have been a credit (or vice versa).

BEGIN RECONCILIATION

To begin the reconciliation, you need to open the Reconcile - Checking window. Verify the information shown for the checking account. The Opening Balance should match the amount of the final balance on the last reconciliation, or it should match the starting account balance.

MEMO
DATE: January 31, 2018

Received the bank statement from Valley Bank. It is dated January 31, 2018. Sofia Sanchez needs to reconcile the bank statement and to print a Detail Reconciliation Report.

Reconcile the bank statement for January

Click the **Reconcile** icon in the Banking section of the Home Page to open
  the **Begin Reconciliation** window and enter preliminary information
The **Account** should be **Checking**
  If not, click the drop-down list arrow, click **Checking**
The **Statement Date** should be **01/31/2018**
- The Statement Date is entered automatically by the computer. If the date is not shown
  as 01/31/2018, change it.
Beginning Balance should be **12,870**
- This is the same amount as the checking account starting balance.

ENTER BANK STATEMENT INFORMATION

Some information appearing on the bank statement is entered into the Begin Reconciliation
window as the next step. This information includes the ending balance, bank service charges, and
interest earned.

 Use the following bank statement as you follow the written instructions to reconcile the
checking account (Do **not** try to reconcile the bank statement without following the
instructions provided.

VALLEY BANK
12345 West Burbank Avenue
Woodland Hills, CA 91377
(818-555-0330)

Your Name's Tech Services
2895 West Avenue
Woodland Hills, CA 91367
Acct. # 123-456-7890   **January, 2018**

Beginning Balance, January 1, 2018			**$12,870.00**
1/02/2018 Deposit	25,000		37,870.00
1/15/2018 Deposit	13,840.00		51,750.00
1/26/2018 Check 1		500.00	51,210.00
1/29/2018 Check 2		195.00	51,015.00
1/29/2018 Check 3		840.00	50,175.00
1/30/2018 Cash Transfer		110.00	50,065.00
1/31/2018 Business Vehicle Loan Pmt.: $467.19 Principal, $255.22 Interest		722.41	49,342.59
1/31/2018 Office Furniture/Equipment Loan Pmt.: $29.17 Principal, $53.39 Interest		82.56	49,260.03
1/31/2018 Service Charge		8.00	49,252.03
1/31/2018 Interest	66.43		49,318.46
Ending Balance, January 31, 2018			**49,318.46**

Enter the **Ending Balance** from the Bank Statement, **49,318.46**

Tab to or click **Service Charge**

Enter **8**

Tab to or click Service Charge **Date**; if necessary, change to **01/31/2018**

- Don't forget to check the date, especially the year. If you leave an incorrect date, you will have errors in your accounts and in your reports.

Click the drop-down list arrow for **Account**

- Shortcut: If you click the drop-down list arrow, you do not have to Tab to the account text box.

Click **Bank Service Charges**

Tab to or click **Interest Earned**, enter **66.43**

Tab to or click Interest Earned **Date**; if necessary, change to **01/31/2018**

Click the drop-down list arrow for **Account**

Scroll through the list of accounts, click **Interest Income**

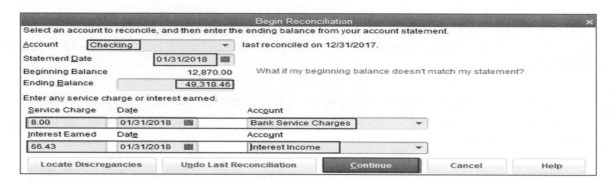

Click the **Continue** button

MARK CLEARED TRANSACTIONS

Once bank statement information for service charges and interest has been entered, compare the checks and deposits listed on the statement with the transactions for the checking account. Remember, the dates shown for the checks on the bank statement are the dates the checks were processed by the bank, not the dates the checks were written. If a deposit or a check is listed correctly on the bank statement and in the Reconcile - Checking window, it has cleared and should be marked. An item may be marked individually by positioning the cursor on a deposit or a check and clicking the primary mouse button. If all deposits and checks match, click the Mark All button. To remove all the checks, click the Unmark All button. To unmark an individual item, click the item to remove the check mark.

 Mark cleared checks and deposits

As you compare the bank statement with the **Reconcile - Checking** window, click the items that appear on both statements

- *Note*: The date next to the check or the deposit on the bank statement is the date the check or deposit cleared the bank, not the date the check was written, or the deposit was made.
- If you are unable to complete the reconciliation in one session, click the **Leave** button to leave the reconciliation and return to it later.
- Under *no* circumstances should you click **Reconcile Now** until the reconciliation is complete.

Make sure that the **Highlight Marked** checkbox in the lower-left corner is checked
- This will change the background color of everything that you mark and make it easier to view the selections in the reconciliation.

For Deposits and Other Credits, include the Voided Check for **0.00** on **01/30/2018**

Even though the transaction shows 110.00 on the Bank Statement, select the transaction for **100.00** on **01/30/2018** on the Checks and Payments side of the screen
- This was the transfer from Checking to Petty Cash.

Once you have marked the transactions that appear on the bank statement and in the Reconcile-Checking screen, look at the bottom of screen

In the section labeled "**Items you have marked cleared**" should show the following:

3 Deposits and Other Credits for 38,840.00
- This includes the voided check to California Telephone Co.

4 Checks and Payments for 1,635.00
- This includes the $100 for petty cash.

On the right-side of the lower section next to the Modify button, the screen should show:

The Service Charge is -8.00

The Interest Earned is 66.43

The Ending Balance is 49,318.46

The Cleared Balance is 50,133.43

There is a Difference of -814.97

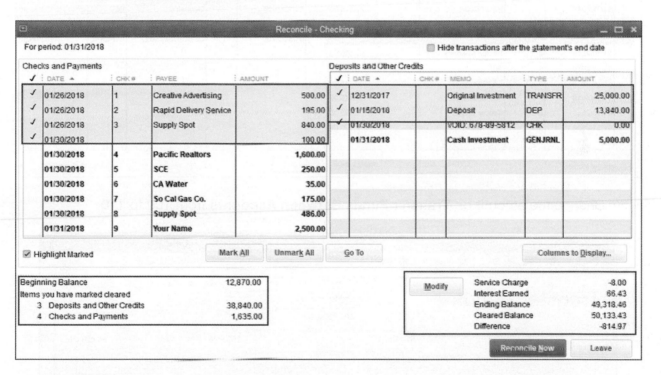

CORRECTING ENTRIES—BANK RECONCILIATION

As you complete the reconciliation, you may find errors that need to be corrected or transactions that need to be recorded. Anything entered as a service charge or interest earned will be entered automatically when the reconciliation is complete and the Reconcile Now button is clicked. To correct an error such as a transposition or an incorrect amount, click on the entry, then click the Go To button. The original entry will appear on the screen. The correction can be made and will show in the Reconcile - Checking window. If there is a transaction, such as an automatic loan payment to the bank, you need to access the register for the account used in the transaction and enter the payment.

 Correct the error on the cash transfer into Petty Cash

> In the section of the reconciliation for **Checks and Payments**, click the entry for **100.00** dated **01/30/2018**
> - This was the Cash transfer to Petty Cash from Checking.
> Click the **Go To** button

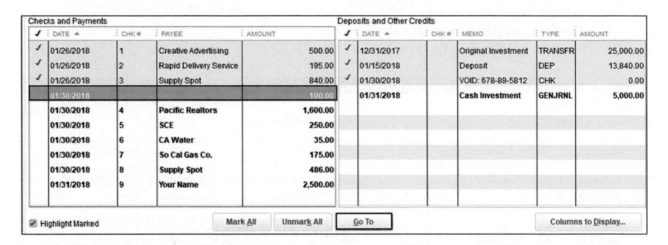

Change the amount on **Transfer Funds Between Accounts** from 100 to **110**

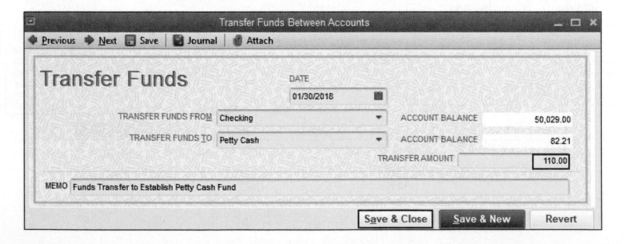

Click **Save & Close**

Click **Yes** on the **Recording Transaction** dialog box
- Notice that the amount for the Petty Cash transaction now shows 110.

Click the cash transfer to Petty Cash transaction to mark it (if not already marked)
- The amount shown at the bottom of the Reconcile window for the 4 Checks and Payments, shows 1,645.00.

ADJUSTING ENTRIES—BANK RECONCILIATION

 With the **Reconcile - Checking** window still showing, enter the automatic loan payments

To enter the automatic payments, access the Checking Account Register by using the keyboard shortcut **Ctrl+R**
- If the check box for Shown on 1-Line is marked, click to deselect.

In the blank transaction at the bottom of the Checking register enter the **Date, 01/31/18**

Tab to or click **Number**

Enter **Transfer**

Tab to or click **Payee**

Enter **Valley Bank**

Tab to or click the **Payment** column
- Because Valley Bank does not appear on any list, you will get a **Name Not Found** dialog box when you move to another field.

Click the **Quick Add** button to add the name of the bank to the Name list

Click **Other**

Click **OK**
- Once the name of the bank has been added to the Other list, the cursor will be positioned in the **PAYMENT** column.

Enter the amount of the Business Vehicles Loan payment of **722.41** in the **PAYMENT** column

Since more than one account is used, click the **Splits** button at the bottom of the register

Click the drop-down list arrow for **ACCOUNT**

Click **Loan Interest** under Interest Expense

Tab to or click **AMOUNT**, delete the amount 722.41 shown

Enter **255.22** as the amount of interest

Tab to or click **MEMO**

Enter **Business Vehicles Loan, Interest**

Tab to or click **ACCOUNT**

Click the drop-down list arrow for **ACCOUNT**

Click **Business Vehicles Loan** a subaccount of Loan Payable
- The correct amount of principal, 467.19, should be showing for the amount.

Tab to or click **MEMO**

Enter **Business Vehicles Loan, Principal**

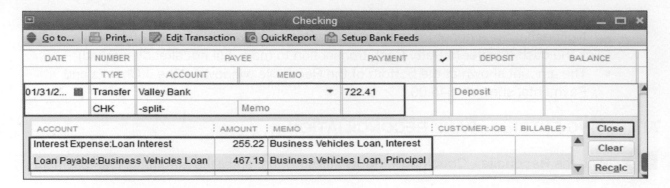

Click the **Close** button in the Splits window

- This closes the window for the information regarding the way the transaction is to be "split" between accounts.

For the **Memo** in the Checking Register, record **Loan Pmt. Business Vehicles**

Click the **Record** button to record the transaction

- Because the **Register** organizes transactions according to date and the transaction type, you will notice that the loan payment will not appear as the last transaction in the Register. You may need to scroll through the Register to see the transaction since transfers are shown before other transactions entered on the same date.

01/31/2018	Transfer	Valley Bank		722.41			46,796.59
	CHK	-split-	Loan Pmt. Business Vehicles				

Repeat the procedures to record the loan payment for office furniture and equipment

- When you enter the Payee as Valley Bank, the amount for the previous transaction (722.41) appears in Amount.

Enter the new amount, **82.56**

Click **Splits** button

Click the appropriate accounts and enter the correct amount for each item

- *Note*: The amounts for the previous loan payment automatically appear. You will need to enter the amounts for both accounts in this transaction.
- Refer to the bank statement for details regarding the amount of the payment for interest and the amount of the payment applied to principal.

ACCOUNT	AMOUNT	MEMO	CUSTOMER:JOB	BILLABLE?
Interest Expense:Loan Interest	53.39	Office Furniture/Equipment Loan, Interest		
Loan Payable:Office Furniture/Equipment Loan	29.17	Office Furniture/Equipment Loan, Principal		

Click **Close** to close the window for the information regarding the "split" between accounts

Enter the transaction Memo **Loan Pmt. Office Furniture/Equipment**

Click **Record** to record the loan payment

01/31/2018	Transfer	Valley Bank		82.56			46,714.03
	CHK	-split-	Loan Pmt Office Furniture & Equipment				

Close the **Checking** Register

- You should return to **Reconcile - Checking**.

Scroll through **Checks and Payments** until you find the two Transfers to Valley Bank for loan payments

Mark the two entries

- At this point, the **Ending Balance** and **Cleared Balance** should be equal—$49,318.46 with a difference of 0.00.

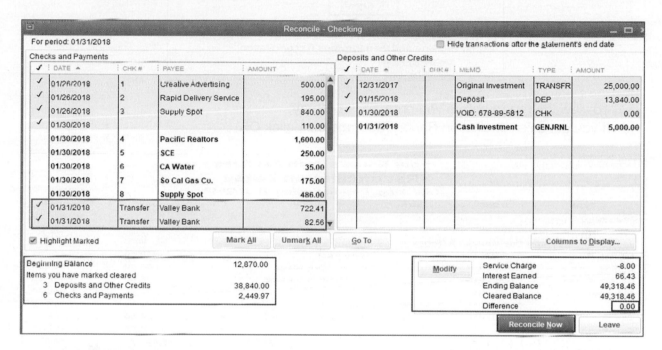

If your entries agree with the above, click **Reconcile Now** to finish the reconciliation

- If your reconciliation is not in agreement, do <u>not</u> click **Reconcile Now** until the errors are corrected.
- Once you click **Reconcile Now**, you may not return to this **Reconciliation - Checking** window.
- If you get an information screen regarding Online Banking, click **OK**.

RECONCILIATION DETAIL REPORT

As soon as the Ending Balance and the Cleared Balance are equal or when you finish marking transactions and click Reconcile Now, a screen appears allowing you to select the level of Reconciliation report you would like to print. You may select Summary and get a report that lists totals only or Detail and get all the transactions that were reconciled on the report. You may print the report at the time you have finished reconciling the account or you may print the report later by returning to the Reconciliation window. If you think you may want to print the report again in the future, print the report to a file to save it permanently.

 Print a **Reconciliation Detail Report**

On the **Select Reconciliation Report** screen, click **Detail**

Select Reconciliation Report   ✕

Congratulations! Your account is balanced. All marked items have been cleared in the account register.

Select the type of reconciliation report you'd like to see.

- ○ Summary
- ● Detail
- ○ Both

To view this report at a later time, select the Report menu, display Banking and then Previous Reconciliation.

Display   Print...   Close

To view the report before you print, click **Display**;
If you get a Reconciliation Report message box, click **OK**

Your Name's Tech Services
Reconciliation Detail
Checking, Period Ending 01/31/2018

Type	Date	Num	Name	Clr	Amount	Balance
Beginning Balance						**12,870.00**
Cleared Transactions						
Checks and Payments - 7 items						
Bill Pmt –Check	01/26/2018	3	Supply Spot	✓	–840.00	–840.00
Bill Pmt –Check	01/26/2018	1	Creative Advertising	✓	–500.00	–1,340.00
Bill Pmt –Check	01/26/2018	2	Rapid Delivery Service	✓	–195.00	–1,535.00
Transfer	01/30/2018			✓	–110.00	–1,645.00
Check	01/31/2018	Transfer	Valley Bank	✓	–722.41	–2,367.41
Check	01/31/2018	Transfer	Valley Bank	✓	–82.56	–2,449.97
Check	01/31/2018			✓	–8.00	–2,457.97
Total Checks and Payments					–2,457.97	–2,457.97
Deposits and Credits - 4 items						
Transfer	12/31/2017			✓	25,000.00	25,000.00
Deposit	01/15/2018			✓	13,840.00	38,840.00
Check	01/30/2018		California Telephone Co.	✓	0.00	38,840.00
Deposit	01/31/2018			✓	66.43	38,906.43
Total Deposits and Credits					38,906.43	38,906.43
Total Cleared Transactions					36,448.46	36,448.46
Cleared Balance					36,448.46	49,318.46
Uncleared Transactions						
Checks and Payments - 6 items						
Check	01/30/2018	4	Pacific Realtors		–1,600.00	–1,600.00
Check	01/30/2018	8	Supply Spot		–486.00	–2,086.00
Check	01/30/2018	5	SCE		–250.00	–2,336.00
Check	01/30/2018	7	So Cal Gas Co.		–175.00	–2,511.00
Check	01/30/2018	6	CA Water		–35.00	–2,546.00
Check	01/31/2018	9	Your Name		–2,500.00	–5,046.00
Total Checks and Payments					–5,046.00	–5,046.00
Deposits and Credits - 1 item						
General Journal	01/31/2018				5,000.00	5,000.00
Total Deposits and Credits					5,000.00	5,000.00
Total Uncleared Transactions					–46.00	–46.00
Register Balance as of 01/31/2018					36,402.46	49,272.46
Ending Balance					**36,402.46**	**49,272.46**

- The uncleared information may be different from the report above. This is because your computer's date may be different than January 31, 2018. If the cleared balance is $49,318.46, your report should be considered correct.

Resize the columns in report as previously instructed; and then, print the report in Portrait orientation

- If you print to a pdf file, save the document as **3-Your Name Bank Rec Ch4**.

If your report printed correctly, close the report

CHECKING ACCOUNT REGISTER

Once the bank reconciliation has been completed, it is wise to scroll through the Checking account register to view the effect of the reconciliation on the account. You will notice that the check column shows a check mark for all items that were marked as cleared during the reconciliation. If an error is discovered later, the transaction may be changed, and the correction will be reflected in the Beginning Balance on the reconciliation.

View the register for the Checking account

Open the Chart of Accounts and access the Checking account register as previously instructed
To display more of the register, click the check box for **1-Line**
Scroll through the register
- Notice that the transactions are listed in chronological order and that cleared transactions have a check mark.

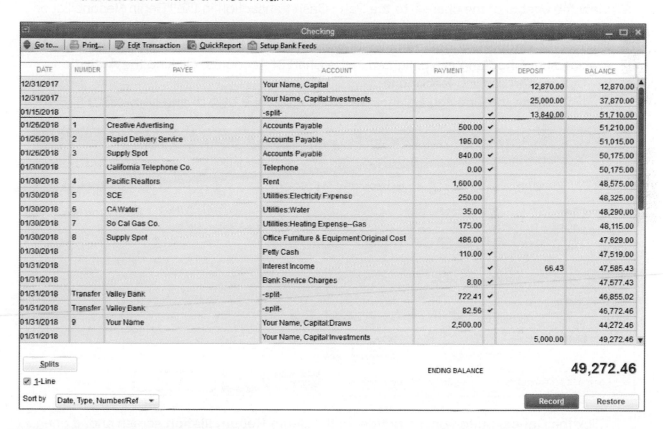

DATE	NUMBER	PAYEE	ACCOUNT	PAYMENT	✓	DEPOSIT	BALANCE
12/31/2017			Your Name, Capital		✓	12,870.00	12,870.00
12/31/2017			Your Name, Capital:Investments		✓	25,000.00	37,870.00
01/15/2018			-split-		✓	13,840.00	51,710.00
01/26/2018	1	Creative Advertising	Accounts Payable	500.00	✓		51,210.00
01/26/2018	2	Rapid Delivery Service	Accounts Payable	195.00	✓		51,015.00
01/26/2018	3	Supply Spot	Accounts Payable	840.00	✓		50,175.00
01/30/2018		California Telephone Co.	Telephone	0.00	✓		50,175.00
01/30/2018	4	Pacific Realtors	Rent	1,600.00			48,575.00
01/30/2018	5	SCE	Utilities:Electricity Expense	250.00			48,325.00
01/30/2018	6	CA Water	Utilities:Water	35.00			48,290.00
01/30/2018	7	So Cal Gas Co.	Utilities:Heating Expense—Gas	175.00			48,115.00
01/30/2018	8	Supply Spot	Office Furniture & Equipment:Original Cost	486.00			47,629.00
01/30/2018			Petty Cash	110.00	✓		47,519.00
01/31/2018			Interest Income		✓	66.43	47,585.43
01/31/2018			Bank Service Charges	8.00	✓		47,577.43
01/31/2018	Transfer	Valley Bank	-split-	722.41	✓		46,855.02
01/31/2018	Transfer	Valley Bank	-split-	82.56	✓		46,772.46
01/31/2018	9	Your Name	Your Name, Capital:Draws	2,500.00			44,272.46
01/31/2018			Your Name, Capital:Investments			5,000.00	49,272.46

Splits
☑ 1-Line

ENDING BALANCE **49,272.46**

Sort by Date, Type, Number/Ref

Record Restore

EDIT CLEARED TRANSACTIONS

Edit a transaction that was marked and cleared during the bank reconciliation:

Edit the **Petty Cash** transaction:
Click in the entry for the transfer of funds to **Petty Cash** on January 30
Change the **Payment** amount to **100**
Click the **Record** button

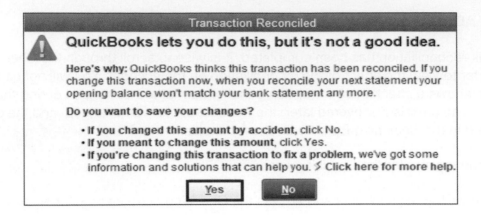

Click **Yes** on the **Transaction Reconciled** dialog box
- The transaction amount has been changed.

Close the **Checking Register**

Do <u>not</u> close the **Chart of Accounts**

View the effects of the change to the Petty Cash transaction in the "Begin Reconciliation window":

Display the **Begin Reconciliation** window by:

Making sure **Checking** is highlighted in the Chart of Accounts, clicking the **Activities** button, and clicking **Reconcile**
- Notice that the Opening Balance has been increased by $10 and shows $49,328.46.

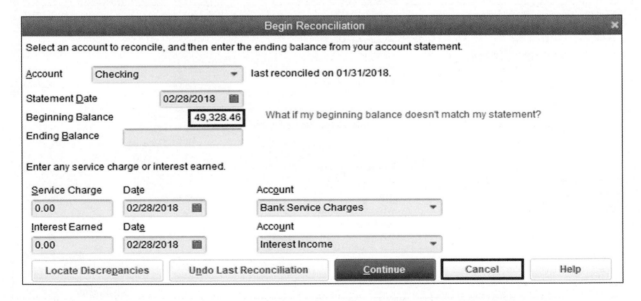

Click the **Cancel** button on the bottom of the **Begin Reconciliation** screen and, if open, return to the Chart of Accounts

Open the **Checking** account register

Change the amount for the **Petty Cash** transaction back to **110**

Click **Record** to record the change

Click **Yes** on the **Transaction Reconciled** dialog box

Reopen the **Begin Reconciliation** following the steps presented earlier
- Make sure the Beginning Balance shows **49,318.46**.

Close the **Checking Register**, and, if open, the **Chart of Accounts**

SELECT ACCRUAL-BASIS REPORTING PREFERENCE

QuickBooks Desktop allows a business to customize the program and select certain preferences for reports, displays, graphs, accounts, and so on. There are two report preferences available in QuickBooks Desktop: Cash and Accrual. You need to choose the one you prefer. If you select Cash as the report preference, income on reports will be shown as of the date payment is received and expenses will be shown as of the date you pay the bill. If Accrual is selected, QuickBooks Desktop shows the income on the report as of the invoice date and expenses as of the bill date. Prior to printing end-of-period reports, it is advisable to verify which reporting basis is selected. If cash has been selected and you are using the accrual-basis, it is imperative that you change your report basis. On many reports, you may make the selection for the report being prepared at the top of the report; however, the default report basis is selected in Preferences.

4

> ### MEMO
> **DATE**: January 31, 2018
>
> Prior to printing reports, check the report preference selected for the company. If necessary, choose Accrual.

 Select **Accrual** as the **Summary Reports Basis**

Click **Edit** on the menu bar, click **Preferences**
Scroll through the Preferences list until you see **Reports & Graphs**
Click **Reports & Graphs**, click the **Company Preferences** tab
If necessary, click **Accrual** to select the **Summary Reports Basis**

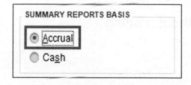

Click **OK** to close the **Preferences** window

JOURNAL REPORT

After entering several transactions, it is helpful to view the Journal report. In the Journal report, all transactions, regardless of the method of entry are shown in traditional debit/credit format. (Remember, you may have learned this report as the General Journal in your concepts course.)

 View the **Journal** report for January

Click the **Reports** icon to open the Report Center, use the view you prefer
Click **Accountant & Taxes** as the type of report, and double-click **Journal**
- If you will be preparing several reports, using the Report Center is much more efficient than using the Reports menu.
Tab to or click **From**
- If necessary, delete the existing date.
Enter **01/01/18**

Tab to or click **To**
Enter **01/31/18**
Tab to generate the report
Click the **Expand** button
Scroll through the report
Verify the total of $57,919.69
- If your total does not match, you may have an error in a date used, an amount entered, a transaction not entered, etc.

Your Name's Tech Services
Journal
January 2018

Trans #	Type	Date	Num	Adj	Name	Memo	Account	Debit	Credit
73	Check	01/31/2018	Transfer		Valley Bank	Loan Pmt. Business Vehicles	Checking		722.41
					Valley Bank	Business Vehicles Loan, Interest	Loan Interest	255.22	
					Valley Bank	Business Vehicles Loan, Principal	Business Vehicles Loan	467.19	
								722.41	722.41
74	Check	01/31/2018	Transfer		Valley Bank	Loan Pmt. Office Furniture & Equipment	Checking		82.56
					Valley Bank	Office Furniture/Equipment Loan, Interest	Loan Interest	53.39	
					Valley Bank	Office Furniture/Equipment Loan, Principal	Office Furniture/Equipment Loan	29.17	
								82.56	82.56
75	Check	01/31/2018				Service Charge	Checking		8.00
						Service Charge	Bank Service Charges	8.00	
								8.00	8.00
76	Deposit	01/31/2018				Interest	Checking	66.43	
						Interest	Interest Income		66.43
								66.43	66.43
TOTAL								**57,919.69**	**57,919.69**

Partial Report

Close the **Journal** report without printing
Do <u>not</u> close the Report Center

TRIAL BALANCE

After all adjustments have been recorded and the bank reconciliation has been completed, it is wise to prepare the Trial Balance. As in traditional accounting, the QuickBooks Desktop Trial Balance proves that debits equal credits.

<u>MEMO</u>
DATE: January 31, 2018

Because adjustments have been entered, prepare a Trial Balance.

    Prepare and print the Trial Balance

Double-click **Trial Balance** in the Accountant & Taxes section of the Report Center
Enter the dates from **01/01/18** to **01/31/18**, and Tab to generate the report
Scroll through the report and study the amounts shown
- Notice that the final totals of debits and credits are equal: $138,119.07.
- A partial report is shown on the next page.

Your Name's Tech Services
Trial Balance
As of January 31, 2018

	Jan 31, 18	
	Debit	Credit
Owner's Equity	0.00	
Your Name, Capital		53,135.00
Your Name, Capital:Draws	2,500.00	
Your Name, Capital:Investments		33,000.00
Income:Cloud Services Income		150.00
Income:Installation Income		175.00
Income:Technical Support Income		750.00
Income:Training Income		7,850.00
Advertising Expense	260.00	
Bank Service Charges	8.00	
Business Vehicles Expense	588.88	
Depreciation Expense	725.00	
Dues and Subscriptions	79.00	
Equipment Rental	25.00	
Insurance:Business Vehicles Insurance	237.50	
Interest Expense:Loan Interest	308.61	
Office Supplies Expense	368.57	
Postage and Delivery	195.34	
Rent	1,600.00	
Telephone	0.00	
Utilities:Electricity Expense	250.00	
Utilities:Heating Expense--Gas	175.00	
Utilities:Water	35.00	
Interest Income		66.43
TOTAL	**138,119.07**	**138,119.07**

Partial Report

Resize the columns and **Print** the **Trial Balance** in Portrait orientation as previously
  instructed
- If you print to a pdf file, save the document as **4-Your Name Trial Bal Ch4**.
Do not close the **Report Center** or the **Trial Balance**

EXPORT REPORTS TO EXCEL (OPTIONAL)

Many of the reports prepared in QuickBooks Desktop can be exported to Microsoft Excel. This
allows you to take advantage of the extensive filtering options available in Excel, hide detail for
some but not all groups of data, combine information from two different reports, change titles of
columns, add comments, change the order of columns, and to experiment with "what if"
scenarios. To use this feature of QuickBooks Desktop you must also have Microsoft Excel.

 Optional Exercise: Export a report from QuickBooks Desktop to Excel

With the **Trial Balance** on the screen, click the [Excel ▼] button on the Trial Balance icon
  bar
Click **Create New Worksheet**

On the Send Report to Excel message screen, make sure **Create new worksheet in a new workbook** are marked

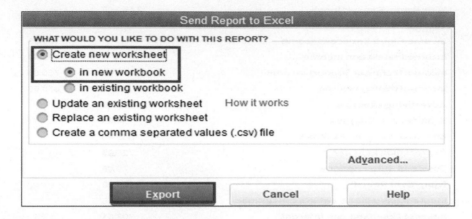

Click the **Export** button

- The **Trial Balance** will be displayed in Excel.
- The Book number may change depending on how many reports have been sent to Excel. The following example shows Book2.

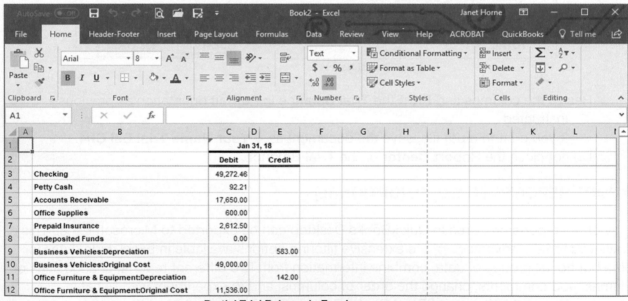

Partial Trial Balance in Excel

Double-click in Cell **C1**, change the heading by typing **JANUARY 31, 2018**
Double-click in Cell **C2**, type **DEBIT** to change Debit to all capitals
Double-click in Cell **E2**, type **CREDIT** to change Credit to all capitals

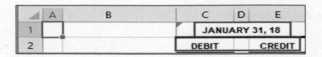

Click the **Close** button in the top right corner of the Excel title bar to close Excel
Click **Don't Save** to close Excel without saving the Trial Balance
Close the **Trial Balance**, do <u>not</u> close the **Report Center**

CASH FLOW FORECAST

In planning for the cash needs of a business, QuickBooks Desktop can prepare a Cash Flow Forecast. This report is useful when determining the expected income and disbursement of cash. It is important to know if your company will have enough cash on hand to meet its obligations. A company with too little cash on hand may have to borrow money to pay its bills, while another company with excess cash may miss out on investment, expansion, or dividend opportunities. QuickBooks Desktop Cash Flow Forecast does not analyze investments. It simply projects the amount you will be receiving if all those who owe you money pay on time and the amounts you will be spending if you pay your accounts payable on time.

MEMO
DATE: January 31, 2018

Since this is the end of January, prepare the Cash Flow Forecast for February 1-28, 2018.

 Prepare Cash Flow Forecast for February

The Report Center should still be on the screen; if it is not, open it as previously instructed
Click **Company & Financial** in the type of reports section, scroll through the list of reports, double-click **Cash Flow Forecast**
Enter the **From** date of **02/01/18** and the **To** date of **02/28/18**
- This will change **Dates** from Next 4 Weeks to **Custom**.
Tab to generate the report
- Notice that **Periods** show **Week**. Use Week, but click the drop-down list arrow to see the periods available for the report.
- If you are not using 2018 as the year, the individual amounts listed per week may be different from the report shown. If the totals are the same, consider the report as being correct.
- Analyze the report for February: The Beginning Balance for Accounts Receivable shows the amounts due from customers as of 1/31/18.
- Depending on whether or not you applied the Credit Memo to Invoice 4 in Chapter 2, you may have a $400 difference in the Accounts Receivable detail and the Projected Balance; however, the Ending Balance for Accounts Receivable and Projected Balance will still be the same.
- The amounts for Accnts Receivable and Accnts Payable for the future weeks are for the customer payments you expect to receive and the bills you expect to pay. This information is based on the due dates for invoices and bills and on the credit memos recorded.
- The Bank Accnts amount for future weeks is based on deposits made or deposits that need to be made.
- Net Inflows summarizes the amounts that should be received and the amounts that should be paid to get a net inflow of cash.
- The Proj Balance is the total in all bank accounts if all customer and bill payments are made on time.

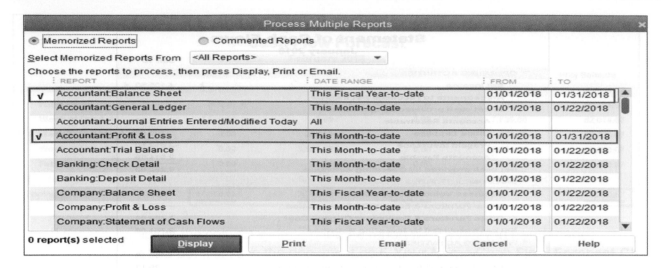

Click the **Display** button

ACCOUNTANT: PROFIT & LOSS REPORT

Because all income, expenses, and adjustments have been made for the period, a Profit & Loss Report can be prepared. This statement is also known as the Income Statement and shows the income and the expenses for the period and the net income or the net loss for the period (Income – Expenses = Net Profit or Net Loss).

The Accountant: Profit & Loss Report is prepared from Multiple Reports on the Reports Menu. It gives the same data as a Standard Profit & Loss prepared from the Company & Financial section on the Reports Menu or in the Report Center. This report summarizes income and expenses. When preparing multiple reports, changes made to customize reports in the Report Center or reports prepared from the Reports Menu are not used.

 View the **Accountant: Profit & Loss Report**

Scroll through the report prepared using the Multiple Reports feature to view the income and expenses listed
- In Chapter 3 report preferences were change so the Date Prepared, Time Prepared, and Report Basis did not appear in reports prepared in the Report Center or from the Reports Menu.
- When using Multiple Reports, the Date Prepared, Time Prepared, and Report Basis will be included in the report.

1:08 PM 01/31/18 Accrual Basis	Your Name's Tech Services **Profit & Loss** January 2018	
		Jan 18
Total Expense		4,855.90
Net Ordinary Income		4,069.10
▼ Other Income/Expense		
▼ Other Income		
Interest Income		66.43
Total Other Income		66.43
Net Other Income		66.43
Net Income		4,135.53

Partial Report

- Make note of the Net Income of $4,135.53.
Close the report without printing

ACCOUNTANT: BALANCE SHEET

The Balance Sheet proves the fundamental accounting equation: Assets = Liabilities + Owner's Equity. When all transactions and adjustments for the period have been recorded, a balance sheet should be prepared. The Accountant: Balance Sheet provides the same data as a Standard Balance Sheet and shows as of the report dates the balance in each balance sheet account with subtotals provided for assets, liabilities, and equity. As with the Accountant: Profit & Loss Report, customizations made for reports in the Report Center or on the Reports Menu will not be used when preparing multiple reports.

 View the **Accountant: Balance Sheet**

Scroll through the report prepared using the Multiple Reports feature to view the assets, liabilities, and equities listed
- As with the Accountant: Profit & Loss Report, the report customization to remove the date prepared, time prepared, and report basis is not used when preparing multiple reports.
- Notice the Net Income listed in the Equity section of the report. This is the same amount of Net Income shown on the Profit & Loss Report, $4,135.53.
- Your Name, Capital – Other is the balance of the Your Name, Capital account. The word Other is used by QuickBooks Desktop so that it is not confused with the Equity Section heading Your Name, Capital.
- Also note the Total Assets of $130,038.17. Compare that to the Total Liabilities & Equity of $130,038.17. This proves the Fundamental Accounting Equation of
Assets = Liabilities + Owner's Equity.

1:14 PM	Your Name's Tech Services	
01/31/18	**Balance Sheet**	
Accrual Basis	As of January 31, 2018	
		Jan 31, 18
TOTAL ASSETS		130,038.17
▼ LIABILITIES & EQUITY		
▶ Liabilities		42,267.64
▼ Equity		
▼ Your Name, Capital		
Draws		-2,500.00
Investments		33,000.00
Your Name, Capital - Other		53,135.00
Total Your Name, Capital		83,635.00
Net Income		4,135.53
Total Equity		87,770.53
TOTAL LIABILITIES & EQUITY		130,038.17

Partial Report

Close the report without printing

CLOSING ENTRIES

In accounting, there are four closing entries that need to be made to close the books for a period. They include closing all income and expense accounts, closing the drawing account, closing the Income Summary account, and transferring the net income or net loss to the owner's capital account.

In QuickBooks Desktop, setting a closing date will replace closing the income and expense accounts. QuickBooks Desktop does not close the owner's drawing account. This closing entry will be completed in this chapter. QuickBooks Desktop does not use an Income Summary account so net income is automatically transferred into owner's equity. While it is included on the Balance Sheet in the Equity section, QuickBooks Desktop categorizes Owner's Equity as a Retained Earnings account. Therefore, the account only contains the amount of Net Income earned and is separate from Your Name, Capital. According to GAAP, a sole proprietorship should have net income included in the owner's capital account. The following section will illustrate the transfer of Net Income into Your Name, Capital.

TRANSFER NET INCOME/OWNER'S EQUITY INTO CAPITAL

Because Your Name's Tech Services is a sole proprietorship, the amount of net income should be included in the balance of Your Name, Capital rather than set aside in a separate account— Owner's Equity—as QuickBooks Desktop does automatically. In many instances, this is the type of adjustment the CPA makes on the Accountant's Copy of the QuickBooks Desktop company files. The adjustment may be made before the closing date for the fiscal year, or it may be made after the closing has been performed. Because QuickBooks Desktop automatically transfers Net Income into the Retained Earnings account named Owner's Equity, the closing entry will transfer the net income into the Your Name, Capital account. This adjustment is made in a General Journal entry that debits Owner's Equity and credits Your Name, Capital. After you have entered the adjustment, a Standard Balance Sheet prepared before the end of the year will include an amount in Net Income and the same amount as a negative in Owner's Equity. If you view this report after the end of the year, you will not see any information regarding Owner's Equity or Net Income because the adjustment correctly transferred the amount into Your Name, Capital.

If you prefer to use the power of the program and not make the adjustment, QuickBooks Desktop simply carries the amount of Owner's Equity forward. Each year net income is added to Owner's Equity. On the Balance Sheet, Owner's Equity and/or Net Income appears as part of the equity section.

  Transfer the net income into Your Name, Capital account

> Open the General Journal by clicking **Company** on the menu bar, and clicking **Make General Journal Entries...**
> If you get a screen regarding Assigning Numbers to Journal Entries, click **Do not display this message in the future**, and then click **OK**
> Enter the date of **01/31/18**
> Since this a closing entry, if necessary, click the checkbox for ADJUSTING ENTRY to <u>remove</u> the check mark
> The first account used is **Owner's Equity**
> * Remember, Owner's Equity is a Retained Earnings account and contains all the net income earned by the business.
> Debit **Owner's Equity** the amount of Net Income **4,135.53**
> * This is the amount of Net Income shown in the Profit & Loss report.
> The Memo is **Transfer Net Income into Capital**
> The other account used is **Your Name, Capital**
> * **4,135.53** should appear as the credit amount for **Your Name, Capital**.
> * If the memo does not appear when pressing tab, enter the same Memo.

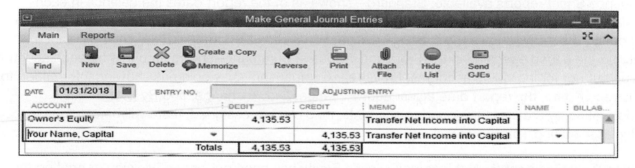

> Click **Save & New**
> If a Retained Earnings screen appears, click **OK**

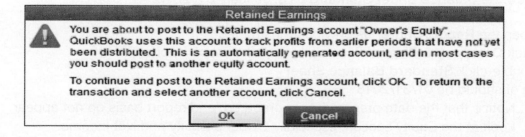

CLOSE DRAWING

The closing entry to transfer the net income into Your Name, Capital has already been made. While this is not the actual end of the fiscal year for Your Name's Tech Services, the closing entry for the Drawing account will be entered at this time so that you will have experience in recording this closing entry.

 Close Draws into Your Name, Capital

On the new **Make General Journal Entries** screen, make sure the **DATE** is **01/31/18**
Since this a closing entry, the check box for ADJUSTING ENTRY is not marked
Debit **Your Name, Capital**, for the amount in the drawing account **2,500**
The Memo for the transaction is **Close Drawing**
Credit **Draws**, for **2,500**

DATE 01/31/2018	ENTRY NO.			ADJUSTING ENTRY		
ACCOUNT		DEBIT	CREDIT	MEMO	NAME	BILLAE
Your Name, Capital		2,500.00		Close Drawing		
Your Name, Capital:Draws			2,500.00	Close Drawing		
	Totals	2,500.00	2,500.00			

Click **Save & Close**

BALANCE SHEET STANDARD

In addition to the Accountant: Balance Sheet, QuickBooks Desktop has several different types of Balance Sheet reports available: <u>Standard</u>—shows as of the report dates the balance in each balance sheet account with subtotals provided for assets, liabilities, and equity; <u>Detail</u>—for each account, the report shows the starting balance, transactions entered, and the ending balance during the period specified in the From and To dates; <u>Summary</u>—shows amounts for each account type but not for individual accounts; <u>Prev. Year Comparison</u>—has columns showing information for the report date, the report date a year ago, $ change, and % change; and <u>By Class</u>—has information by the class assigned to accounts, if no class is assigned, there will be columns for Unclassified and Total.

Once the adjustment for Net Income/Owner's Equity has been performed, viewing or printing the Balance Sheet will show you the status of the Equity.

 View the **Balance Sheet Standard** as of January 31, 2018

Open the **Report Center** as previously instructed
Click **Company & Financial**, scroll through the list of reports
Double-click **Standard Balance Sheet**
As of should be **01/31/2018**
- Notice that the date prepared, time prepared, and report basis do not appear.
- Look at the Equity section, especially Owner's Equity and Net Income.

- Remember, Your Name, Capital – Other is the balance of the Your Name, Capital account and is used by QuickBooks Desktop to avoid confusion between the actual account and the section heading.
- The amount of Net Income has been added to Your Name, Capital - Other. The Owner's Equity and Net Income amounts shown cancel out each other (notice the positive Net Income and the negative Owner's Equity).
- Draws is no longer shown on the Balance Sheet.
- Verify these two transactions by adding the net income of 4,135.53 to 53,135.00, which was shown as the balance of the Your Name, Capital - Other account on the Balance Sheet prepared before the adjusting entry was made. Then subtract 2,500.00, which is the amount of the owner withdrawals that were subtracted from Capital. The Total Your Name, Capital - Other should be 54,770.53.

Your Name's Tech Services
Balance Sheet
As of January 31, 2018

	Jan 31, 18
▼ Equity	
Owner's Equity	-4,135.53
▼ Your Name, Capital	
Investments	33,000.00
Your Name, Capital - Other	54,770.53
Total Your Name, Capital	87,770.53
Net Income	4,135.53
Total Equity	87,770.53
TOTAL LIABILITIES & EQUITY	130,038.17

Partial Report

Change the **As of** date on the Balance Sheet to **01/31/19**, press **Tab**
- Notice the Equity section. Nothing is shown for Owner's Equity or Net Income.

Your Name's Tech Services
Balance Sheet
As of January 31, 2019

	Jan 31, 19
▼ Equity	
▼ Your Name, Capital	
Investments	33,000.00
Your Name, Capital - Other	54,770.53
Total Your Name, Capital	87,770.53
Total Equity	87,770.53
TOTAL LIABILITIES & EQUITY	130,038.17

Partial Report

Close the **Balance Sheet** without printing
Close the Report Center

JOURNAL REPORT

Normally, you would prepare a Journal report before completing the end-of-period procedures so you would have a printed or "hard copy" of the data for January. At this point, we will postpone printing until all the closing procedures have been completed.

END-OF-PERIOD BACKUP

Once all end-of-period procedures have been completed, a regular backup and a second/archival backup of the company data should be made. Preferably the archive copy will be located someplace other than on the business premises. The archive copy is set aside in case of emergency or in case damage occurs to the original company file and current backup copies of the company data. Normally, a backup and an archive copy would be made before closing the period. Since we will be making changes to transactions for the closed period, the backup will be made at the end of the chapter.

 Prepare an archive copy of your company file

> For training purposes, use your USB drive
> Follow the procedures given previously to make your backup files
> Name the file **Tech 2018 (Archive 01-31-18)**
> - In actual practice, the company (.qbw) file would be on your hard drive and the backup (.qbb) file would be stored on a separate USB drive, online, or in the cloud.
> - If you get a QuickBooks Desktop screen regarding the file's location, click **Use this Location**.
> Once the archive copy has been made, click **OK** on the QuickBooks Desktop Information dialog box to acknowledge the successful backup

PASSWORDS

Not every employee of a business should have access to all the financial records for the company. In some companies, only the owner will have complete access. In others, one or two key employees will have full access while other employees are provided limited access based on the jobs and tasks they perform. Passwords are secret words used to control access to data. QuickBooks Desktop has several options available when assigning passwords.

To assign passwords, you must have an administrator. The administrator has unrestricted access to all of QuickBooks Desktop functions, sets up users and user passwords for QuickBooks Desktop and for Windows, and assigns areas of transaction access for each user. Areas of access can be limited to transaction entry for certain types of transactions or a user may have unrestricted access into all areas of QuickBooks Desktop and company data. To obtain more information regarding QuickBooks Desktop' passwords, refer to Help.

Currently, you are the QuickBooks Desktop Administrator, have full access to all areas of the program, and use the password **QBDT2018** when you open the company file. A password should always be kept secret. It should be easy for the individual to remember, yet difficult for someone else to guess. Birthdays, names, initials, and similar devices are not good passwords because the information is too readily available. Never write down your password where it can be easily found or seen by someone else. Make sure your password is something you won't forget. Otherwise, you will not be able to access your Company file. In QuickBooks Desktop passwords are case sensitive. It is wise to use a complex password. The requirements for a password to be accepted as complex are: a minimum of seven characters including at least one number and one uppercase letter. Use of special characters is also helpful. Complex passwords should be changed every 90 days. For training purposes, your password is not complex, and you will not change it unless

QuickBooks Desktop requires you to after using it for 90 days. If you change your password, use **2018QBDT** for the new one.

Since the focus of the text is in training in all aspects of QuickBooks Desktop, no passwords will be assigned. Also, if you set a password and then forget it, you will not be able to access QuickBooks Desktop; and your instructor will not be able to override your password.

SET PERIOD CLOSING DATE

Instead of closing entries for income and expense accounts, QuickBooks Desktop uses a closing date to indicate the end of a period. When a closing date is assigned, income and expenses are effectively closed. When a transaction involving income or expenses is recorded after the closing date, it is considered part of the new period and will not be used in calculating net income (or loss) for the previous period.

A closing date assigned to transactions for a period prevents changing data from the closed period without acknowledging that a transaction has been changed. This is helpful to discourage casual changes or transaction deletions to a period that has been closed. Setting the closing date is done by accessing Preferences in QuickBooks Desktop.

MEMO
DATE: January 31, 2018

Protect the company data by setting the closing date of 1/31/18.

 Assign the closing date of **01/31/18** to the transactions for the period

> Click **Edit** on the menu bar, click **Preferences**
> Click **Accounting** in the list of Preferences
> Click **Company Preferences**
>   **OR**
> Click **Accountant** on the menu bar; and then click **Set Closing Date...**
> Click the **Set Date/Password** button

> Enter **01/31/18** as the closing date.

Set Closing Date and Password ✕

To keep your financial data secure, QuickBooks recommends assigning all other users their own username and password, in Company > Set Up Users.

DATE

QuickBooks will display a warning, or require a password, when saving a transaction dated on or before the closing date.   More details...

☐ Exclude estimates, sales orders and purchase orders from closing date restrictions

Closing Date   `01/31/2018` 📅

PASSWORD

QuickBooks strongly recommends setting a password to protect transactions dated on or before the closing date.

Closing Date Password   [ ]

Confirm Password   [ ]

To see changes made on or before the closing date, view the Closing Date Exception Report in Reports > Accountant & Taxes.

OK   **Cancel**

Because you are training, do not enter anything in the text boxes for Password
- If you set a closing date password, it must be used if you edit a closed period.

Click the **OK** button

If you get a No Password Entered screen, click **Do not display this message in the future**; and then click **No**.

Click **OK** to close the period and to close Preferences

EDIT CLOSED PERIOD TRANSACTION

Even though the month of January has been "closed," transactions still appear in the account registers, the Journal report, and so on. If it is determined that an error was made in a previous period, QuickBooks Desktop does allow the correction. The edited transactions may not be changed unless you click Yes on the screen warning you that you have changed a transaction to a closed period. Changes to transactions involving income and expenses will also necessitate a change to the transfer of net income into the owner's capital account.

MEMO

DATE: January 31, 2018

After reviewing the Journal report for January, you determine that the amount of supplies used was $325, not $350. Make the correction to the adjusting entry of January 31. This will also require a change to the closing entry to transfer Net Income.

 Change Office Supplies adjusting entry to $325 from $350

Access the **Office Supplies** account register as previously instructed
Click the **DECREASE** column for the GENJRN Entry recorded to the account on 01/31/18
Change 350 to **325**
Click **Record**
Click **Yes** on the Recording Transaction dialog box
The **QuickBooks Desktop** warning dialog box regarding the closed period appears

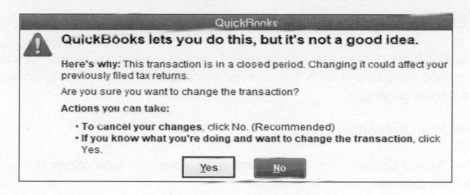

Click **Yes**

- Notice the Balance for Office Supplies now shows 625 instead of 600.

01/31/2018				325.00		625.00
	GENJRN	Office Supplies Expense	Adjusting Entry, Supplies			

Close the Register for **Office Supplies** and close the **Chart of Accounts**

- The adjusting entry used to transfer Owner's Equity/Net Income into the owner's capital account also needs to be adjusted because of the change.

Change the Adjusting Entry transferring Net Income from Owner's Equity into Your Name, Capital

Click the **Company** menu

Click **Make General Journal Entries...** on the Accountant or the Company menus

Click the back arrow on the Make General Journal Entries icon bar until you find the entry adjusting Owner's Equity

- Since the correction to Office Supplies decreased the amount of the expense by $25, there is an increase in net income of $25 (Income – Expenses = Net Income).

Change the Debit to Owner's Equity by 25.00 from 4135.53 to **4160.53**

Change the Credit to Your Name, Capital by 25.00 from 4135.53 to **4160.53**

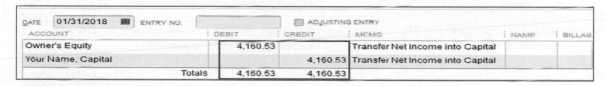

Click **Save & Close**

Click **Yes** on the Recording Transaction dialog box

Click **Yes** on the QuickBooks Desktop dialog box regarding transactions in a closed period

Click **OK** on the Retained Earnings dialog box

REDO ARCHIVE COPY OF COMPANY FILE

Since we have made changes to transactions for the closed period, the archive copy of the company file should be redone.

 Redo the archive copy of the company data

Replace the previous file **Tech 2018 (Archive 1-31-18)**

Follow the procedures given previously to make your backup files

JOURNAL REPORT

Normally, you would have printed the Journal report prior to closing the period. Since changes to the "previous" period have been made, the Journal report would need to be reprinted to replace the one printed before closing.

 Print the Journal report for January

>Open the Report Center, click **Accountant & Taxes** as the type of report
>Double-click **Journal**
>Click the **Expand** button
>Enter the dates From **01/01/18** To **01/31/18**
>- Notice that the report contains all the transactions from Chapters 2, 3, and 4.
>Click the **Expand** button
>Resize the columns to display the information in full
>Verify that the final total for debits and credits is **$64,555.22**
>- If it is not, make the necessary corrections to incorrect transactions. Frequent errors include incorrect dates, incorrect accounts used, incorrect amounts, and incorrect sales items.

Your Name's Tech Services
Journal
January 2018

Trans #	Type	Date	Num	Adj	Name	Memo	Account	Debit	Credit
75	Check	01/31/2018				Service Charge	Checking		8.00
						Service Charge	Bank Service Charges	8.00	
								8.00	8.00
76	Deposit	01/31/2018				Interest	Checking	66.43	
						Interest	Interest Income		66.43
								66.43	66.43
77	General Journal	01/31/2018				Transfer Net Income into Capital	Owner's Equity	4,160.53	
						Transfer Net Income into Capital	Your Name, Capital		4,160.53
								4,160.53	4,160.53
78	General Journal	01/31/2018				Close Drawing	Your Name, Capital	2,500.00	
						Close Drawing	Draws		2,500.00
								2,500.00	2,500.00
TOTAL								**64,555.22**	**64,555.22**

Partial Report

>Adjust column widths to display information in full, print in **Landscape** orientation after selecting **Fit report to one page wide**
>- If you print to a pdf file, save the document as **7-Your Name Journal Ch4**.
>Close the **Journal report** do <u>not</u> close the **Report Center**

TRIAL BALANCE

After the adjustments have been recorded and the "closing" has been completed, it is helpful to print reports. A Trial Balance is printed to prove that debits still equal credits. Post-closing reports are typically prepared as of the last day of the fiscal year after all closing entries for the year have been recorded. Since our closing was simply for a period, this means that income and expenses will be shown in the Trial Balance and in the Profit & Loss reports for January.

Print a Trial Balance to prove that debits equal credits

Click **Accountant & Taxes** in the **Report Center**, double-click **Trial Balance**
Enter the Dates: From **01/01/18** and To **01/31/18**, tab to generate the report
Scroll through the report and study the amounts shown
- Notice that the final totals of debits and credits are equal.
- Notice that Office Supplies has a balance of $625.00 and Office Supplies Expense is $343.57, which is the 25.00 change you made in the register after the period was closed.

4

Your Name's Tech Services
Trial Balance
As of January 31, 2018

	Jan 31, 18 Debit	Credit
Your Name, Capital		54,795.53
Your Name, Capital:Draws	0.00	
Your Name, Capital:Investments		33,000.00
Income:Cloud Services Income		150.00
Income:Installation Income		175.00
Income:Technical Support Income		750.00
Income:Training Income		7,850.00
Advertising Expense	260.00	
Bank Service Charges	8.00	
Business Vehicles Expense	588.88	
Depreciation Expense	725.00	
Dues and Subscriptions	79.00	
Equipment Rental	25.00	
Insurance:Business Vehicles Insurance	237.50	
Interest Expense:Loan Interest	308.61	
Office Supplies Expense	343.57	
Postage and Delivery	195.34	
Rent	1,600.00	
Telephone	0.00	
Utilities:Electricity Expense	250.00	
Utilities:Heating Expense--Gas	175.00	
Utilities:Water	35.00	
Interest Income		66.43
TOTAL	**139,779.60**	**139,779.60**

Partial Report

Print the report in **Portrait** orientation
- If you print to a pdf file, save the document as **8-Your Name Trial Bal Ch4**.

QUICKZOOM

QuickZoom is a QuickBooks Desktop feature that allows you to make a closer observation of transactions, amounts, and other entries. With QuickZoom you may zoom in on an item when the mouse pointer turns into a magnifying glass with a Z inside. If you point to an item, such as Interest Expense, and you do not get a magnifying glass with a Z inside, you cannot zoom in on the item. This means that you can see transaction details for Interest Expense.

Use QuickZoom to view the details of Office Supplies Expense

Scroll through the Trial Balance until you see Office Supplies Expense
Position the mouse pointer over the amount of Office Supplies Expense, **343.57**
- Notice that the mouse pointer changes to .
Double-click the primary mouse button
- A Transactions by Account report appears on the screen showing the transactions for Office Supplies Expense for 01/01/18 to 01/31/2018.
If necessary, enter the From date **010118** and the To date **013118**
- QuickBooks Desktop will enter the / in a date and convert the year to four digits.
Tab to generate the report; then scroll through the report
- Notice the adjusting entry for $325. It is marked by a check in the Adj column.

Your Name's Tech Services
Transactions by Account
As of January 31, 2018

Type	Date	Num	Adj	Name	Memo	Clr	Split	Debit	Credit	Balance
Office Supplies Expense										
Bill	01/18/2018	1035A		Supply Spot	3D Printer Rental Supplies for the Month		Accounts Payable	20.00		20.00
Credit	01/26/2018	789		Supply Spot	Returned Damaged 3D Printer Supplies		Accounts Payable		5.00	15.00
Check	01/30/2018	1					Petty Cash	3.57		18.57
General Journal	01/31/2018		✓		Adjusting Entry, Supplies		Office Supplies	325.00		343.57
Total Office Supplies Expense								348.57	5.00	343.57
TOTAL								348.57	5.00	343.57

Close the Transactions by Account report without printing; close the **Trial Balance**

PROFIT & LOSS (STANDARD)

In addition to the Standard Profit & Loss, which summarizes income and expenses, QuickBooks Desktop has several different types of Profit & Loss reports available: Detail—shows the year-to-date transactions for each income and expense account. The other Profit & Loss reports are like the Standard Profit & Loss but have additional information displayed as indicated in the following: YTD Comparison—summarizes your income and expenses for this month and compares them to your income and expenses for the current fiscal year; Prev Year Comparison—summarizes your income and expenses for both this month and this month last year; By Job—has columns for each customer and job and amounts for this year to date; By Class—has columns for each class and sub-class with the amounts for this year to date, and Unclassified—shows how much you are making or losing within segments of your business that are not assigned to a QuickBooks Desktop class.

Since the closing was done as of January 31, 2018, the Profit & Loss Report for January 31, 2018 will give the same data as a Profit & Loss Report prepared manually on January 31. To verify the closing of income and expense accounts for January, you would prepare a Profit & Loss Report for February 1. Since no income had been earned or expenses incurred in the new period, February, the Net Income will show $0.00.

➡ Print a Profit & Loss Standard report for January and view the report for February

Click **Company & Financial** in the **Report Center**, double-click **Profit & Loss Standard**
The **Dates** are From **01/01/18** To **01/31/18**

- Note the Net Income of **4,160.53**.
- The following report is shown in a collapsed format. Rather than seeing each income account or each expense account, you will simply see the totals for Income and Expenses.

Your Name's Tech Services
Profit & Loss
January 2018

	Jan 18
▼ **Ordinary Income/Expense**	
▼ Income	
▶ Income	8,925.00
Total Income	8,925.00
▶ Expense	4,830.90
Net Ordinary Income	4,094.10
▼ Other Income/Expense	
▼ Other Income	
Interest Income	66.43
Total Other Income	66.43
Net Other Income	66.43
Net Income	**4,160.53**

Print the report in **Portrait** orientation
- If you print to a pdf file, save the document as **9-Your Name P & L Ch4**.

 To view the effect of closing the period, prepare the Profit & Loss report for February

Change the dates From **02/01/18** to **02/01/18**
Tab to generate the report

Your Name's Tech Services
Profit & Loss
February 2018

	Feb 18
Net Income ▶	0.00 ◀

- Note the Net Income of **0.00**.
Close the **Profit & Loss Report**

BALANCE SHEET (STANDARD)

Proof that assets are equal to liabilities and owner's equity needs to be displayed in a Balance Sheet. Because this report is for January, the adjustment to Owner's Equity and Net Income will result in both accounts being included on the Balance Sheet. If, however, this report was prepared for the year, neither account would appear.

Prepare and print a **Balance Sheet Standard** report for January 31, 2018, and view the report as of January 31, 2019

Prepare a **Balance Sheet Standard** as previously instructed
Tab to or click **As of**, enter **01/31/18**
Tab to generate the report
Scroll through the report to view the assets, liabilities, and equities listed

- Because this report is for January, both Owner's Equity and Net Income are included on this report.
- Also notice that the amount of Owner's Equity shows -4,160.53 and Net Income shows 4,160.53. This is the amount of the adjusting entry after the $25.00 change in supplies.

Your Name's Tech Services
Balance Sheet
As of January 31, 2018

	Jan 31, 18
▼ **ASSETS**	
▼ **Current Assets**	
▶ Checking/Savings	49,364.67
▶ Accounts Receivable	17,650.00
▶ Other Current Assets	3,237.50
Total Current Assets	70,252.17
▶ **Fixed Assets**	59,811.00
TOTAL ASSETS	**130,063.17**
▼ **LIABILITIES & EQUITY**	
▶ Liabilities	42,267.64
▼ **Equity**	
Owner's Equity	-4,160.53
▼ Your Name, Capital	
Investments	33,000.00
Your Name, Capital - Other	54,795.53
Total Your Name, Capital	87,795.53
Net Income	4,160.53
Total Equity	87,795.53
TOTAL LIABILITIES & EQUITY	**130,063.17**

Partially Collapsed Report

Print the report in **Portrait** orientation
- If you print to a pdf file, save the document as **10-Your Name Bal Sheet Ch4**.
Change the date to **01/31/19**, tab to generate the report
Scroll through the report to view the assets, liabilities, and equities listed
- Because this report is prepared after the end of the fiscal year, neither Owner's Equity nor Net Income is included on this report.

Your Name's Tech Services
Balance Sheet
As of January 31, 2019

	Jan 31, 19
▼ASSETS	
▶ Current Assets	70,252.17
▶ Fixed Assets	59,811.00
TOTAL ASSETS	130,063.17
▼LIABILITIES & EQUITY	
▶ Liabilities	42,267.64
▼ Equity	
▼ Your Name, Capital	
Investments	33,000.00
Your Name, Capital - Other	54,795.53
Total Your Name, Capital	87,795.53
Total Equity	87,795.53
TOTAL LIABILITIES & EQUITY	130,063.17

Partially Collapsed Report

Close the **Balance Sheet** for **January 2019** without printing
Close the **Report Center**

END-OF-CHAPTER BACKUP AND CLOSE COMPANY

As in previous chapters, you should back up your company and then close the company. This backup file will contain all your work for Chapters 1-4.

Follow instructions previously provided to back up company files, close the company, and make a duplicate disk

Name the backup **Tech 2018 (Backup Ch. 4)**

SUMMARY

In this chapter, end-of-period adjustments were made, a bank reconciliation was performed, backup and archive copies were prepared, and a period was closed. The use of Net Income and Owner's Equity accounts was explored and interpreted for a sole proprietorship. Account name changes were made, and the effect on subaccounts was examined. Even though QuickBooks Desktop focuses on entering transactions on business forms, a Journal recording each transaction is kept by QuickBooks Desktop. This chapter presented transaction entry directly into the General Journal in Debit/Credit format, which were then displayed in the Journal report. The differences between accrual-basis and cash-basis accounting were discussed. Company preferences were established for reporting preferences. Owner withdrawals and additional owner investments were made. Many of the different report options available in QuickBooks Desktop were examined, and the exporting of reports to Excel was explored. A variety of reports were printed. Correction of errors was explored, and changes to transactions in "closed" periods were made. The fact that QuickBooks Desktop does not require an actual closing entry at the end of the period was examined.

END-OF-CHAPTER QUESTIONS

TRUE/FALSE

ANSWER THE FOLLOWING QUESTIONS IN THE SPACE PROVIDED BEFORE THE QUESTION NUMBER.

_____ 4.01.   Additional investments made by an owner may be cash or noncash items.

_____ 4.02.   Accrual-basis accounting matches the income from the period and the expenses for the period to determine the net income or net loss for the period.

_____ 4.03.   Reconciliation Report may be printed as a summary or detailed report.

_____ 4.04.   In a sole proprietorship, an owner's name is added to the Vendor List for recording withdrawals.

_____ 4.05.   Once an account has been used in a transaction, no changes may be made to the account name.

_____ 4.06.   In QuickBooks Desktop, the Journal report is called the book of final entry.

_____ 4.07.   Adjusting entries are recorded when cash-basis accounting is used.

_____ 4.08.   QuickBooks Desktop shows every transaction, no matter where it was entered, in the Journal report.

_____ 4.09.   When completing a bank reconciliation, anything entered as a service charge or as interest earned will be entered in the Journal automatically when the reconciliation is complete.

_____ 4.10.   A Balance Sheet is prepared to prove the equality of debits and credits.

MULTIPLE CHOICE

WRITE THE LETTER OF THE CORRECT ANSWER IN THE SPACE PROVIDED BEFORE THE QUESTION NUMBER.

_____ 4.11.   To close a period, you must ___.
    A. have a closing password
    B. enter a closing date in the Company Preferences for Accounting
    C. enter a closing date in the Company Preferences for Company
    D. enter the traditional closing entries for income and expenses in debit/credit format in the General Journal

_____ 4.12. A QuickBooks Desktop backup file ___ .
   A. is a condensed file containing company data
   B. is prepared in case of emergencies or errors
   C. must be restored before information can be used
   D. all the above

_____ 4.13. When a master account name such as "cars" is changed to "automobiles," the subaccount "depreciation" ___.
   A. needs to be changed to a subaccount of automobiles
   B. automatically becomes a subaccount of automobiles
   C. cannot be changed
   D. must be deleted and re-entered

_____ 4.14. A bank statement may ___.
   A. show service charges or interest not yet recorded
   B. be missing deposits in transit or outstanding checks
   C. show automatic payments
   D. all the above

_____ 4.15. The report that proves Assets = Liabilities + Owner's Equity is the ___.
   A. Trial Balance
   B. Income Statement
   C. Profit & Loss Report
   D. Balance Sheet

_____ 4.16. An error known as a transposition can be found by ___.
   A. dividing the amount out of balance by 9
   B. dividing the amount out of balance by 2
   C. multiplying the difference by 9, then dividing by 2
   D. dividing the amount out of balance by 5

_____ 4.17. The type of Profit & Loss report showing year-to-date transactions instead of totals for each income and expense account is a ___ Profit & Loss Report.
   A. Standard
   B. YTD Comparison
   C. Prev Year Comparison
   D. Detailed

_____ 4.18. To permanently remove the Date Prepared, Time Prepared, and Report Basis from the heading of all reports, ___.
   A. change the Report Preferences
   B. modify the Header on the individual report
   C. it cannot be removed
   D. once you remove it from a report header, it never shows up again

_____ 4.19.   If the adjusting entry to transfer Net Income/Owner's Equity into the owner's capital account is made prior to the end of the year, the Balance Sheet shows ___.

     A.   Owner's Equity

     B.   Net Income

     C.   both Net Income and Owner's Equity

     D.   none of the above because the income/earnings has been transferred into capital

_____ 4.20.   The type of Balance Sheet Report showing information for today and a year ago is a ___ Balance Sheet.

     A.   Standard

     B.   Summary

     C.   Comparison

     D.   Detailed

FILL-IN

IN THE SPACE PROVIDED, WRITE THE ANSWER THAT MOST APPROPRIATELY COMPLETES THE SENTENCE.

4.21.   Report Preferences are selected to set the report default as _____ -basis or _____-basis.

4.22.   Bank reconciliations should be performed on a(n) _____ basis.

4.23.   In a sole proprietorship, an owner's paycheck is considered a(n) _____.

4.24.   Exporting report data from QuickBooks Desktop to _____ can be made to perform "what if" scenarios.

4.25.   The Cash Flow Forecast Projected Balance column shows the total in all bank accounts if all _____ and _____ payments are made on time.

SHORT ESSAY

Describe the steps used to record an automatic loan payment that appears on a bank statement.

_____

_____

_____

_____

_____

_____

_____

END-OF-CHAPTER PROBLEM

YOUR NAME'S POOL & GARDEN OASIS

Chapter 4 continues with the end-of-period adjustments, bank reconciliation, archive copies, and closing the period for Your Name's Pool & Garden Oasis. The company does use a certified public accountant for guidance and assistance with appropriate accounting procedures. The CPA has provided information for use in recording adjusting entries and so on.

INSTRUCTIONS

Continue to use the company file **Oasis 2018.qbw** that you used for Chapters 1, 2, and 3. Record the adjustments and other transactions as you were instructed in the chapter. Always read the transaction carefully and review the Chart of Accounts when selecting transaction accounts. Expand reports, adjust columns so they display in full, and print the reports and journals as indicated.

RECORD TRANSACTIONS

January 31
► Change the names of the following accounts:
  ○ **Student's Name, Capital** to **Your Name, Capital**
    ▪ Remember to use your actual name.
  ○ **Business Trucks** to **Business Vehicles** (Notice that the names of the subaccounts were not affected by this name change.)
  ○ **Business Trucks Loan** to **Business Vehicles Loan**
  ○ **Automobile Expense** to **Business Vehicles Expense** (Delete the description)
  ○ **Auto Insurance Expense** to **Business Vehicles Insurance**
  ○ Capitalize the i in income for the account **Residential Landscape income**
► Make the following accounts inactive:
  ○ **Recruiting**
  ○ **Travel & Ent** (Notice that the subaccounts are also made inactive.)
► Delete the following accounts:
  ○ **Sales**
  ○ **Services**
  ○ **Amortization Expense**
  ○ **Interest Expense: Mortgage**
  ○ **Taxes: Property**
► Print the Chart of Accounts by clicking **Reports** on the menu bar, pointing to **List**, clicking **Account Listing.** Adjust the column widths so that all information is displayed, hide the Tax Line and Description columns. Use Portrait orientation. If you print to a pdf file, save the document as **1-Your Name Acct List Ch4**.

January 31

▶ Enter adjusting entries in the General Journal for:
  ○ Office Supplies Used, $185. Memo: January Supplies Used
  ○ Business vehicles insurance expense for the month, $250. Memo: January Insurance Expense
  ○ Depreciation for the month (Use a compound entry), Memo: January Depreciation
    ▪ Business Vehicles, $950
    ▪ Equipment, $206.25
▶ Enter transactions for Owner's Equity (These General Journal entries are not adjusting entries):
  ○ Additional cash investment by you, $2,000. Memo: Investment: Cash
  ○ Additional noncash investment by owner, $1,500 of lawn equipment. Memo: Investment: Equipment (Note: The value of the lawn equipment is the original cost of the asset.)
  ○ Write the Check 8 for the owner withdrawal of $1,000. Memo: January Withdrawal (Use your real name and add it as "Other," include the memo on the check face and in the Memo column in the detail section of the check.) Print the check. If you print to a pdf file, save the document as **2-Your Name Ck 8 Owner Ch4**.
▶ Prepare Bank Reconciliation and Enter Adjustments for the Reconciliation for January 31, 2018. (Be sure to enter automatic payments, service charges, and interest. Pay close attention to the dates—especially for service charges and interest earned.)

PARADISE BANK
1234 Coast Highway
Santa Barbara, CA 93100   (805) 555-9310

Your Name's Pool & Garden Oasis
18527 State Street
Santa Barbara, CA 993103

Acct. # 987-352-9152			January 31, 2018
Beginning Balance January 1, 2018			**$23,850.00**
1/18/2018 Check 1		485.00	23,365.00
1/18/2018 Check 2		669.00	23,185.00
1/18/2018 Check 3		375.00	22,810.00
1/18/2018 Check 4		180.00	22,141.00
1/31/2018 Service Charge		10.00	22,131.00
1/31/2018 Business Vehicles Loan Pmt.: Interest, 795.54; Principal, 160.64		956.18	21,174.82
1/31/2018 Interest	59.63		21,234.45
Ending Balance January 31, 2018			**$21,234.45**

▶ Print a Detailed Reconciliation Report in Portrait orientation. If you print to a pdf file, save the document as **3-Your Name Bank Rec Ch4**.
▶ Change or Verify Reports & Graphs Preferences: Summary Reports Basis to Accrual.
▶ Transfer Net Income/Owner's Equity into Capital Account (Did you prepare a Profit & Loss report for January to find out the amount of Net Income?) Use the Memo: Transfer Net Income into Capital. (This is not an adjusting entry.)
▶ Close the Draws account. Use the Memo: Close Drawing. (This is not an adjusting entry.)

► Prepare the archive backup file: **Oasis 2018 (Archive 01-31-18)**.
► Close the period. The closing date is **01/31/18**. (Do <u>not</u> use a password.)
► Edit a Transaction from a closed period: Discovered an error in the amount of office supplies used. The amount used should be **$175**, not $185. (Don't forget to adjust Owner's Equity and Capital.)
► Replace the archive backup file: **Oasis (Archive 01-31-18)**.

January 31

Use the dates given for each report, expand, resize columns, and print the following in Portrait orientation unless specified as Landscape:

► Cash Flow Forecast for February 1-28, 2018 (Landscape orientation). If you print to a pdf file, save the document as **4-Your Name Cash Flow Forecast Ch4**.
► Statement of Cash Flows, January 1-31, 2018. If you print to a pdf file, save the document as **5-Your Name Stmt of Cash Flows Ch4**.
► Journal report for January 1-31, 2018. (Expand the report. Use Landscape orientation, and Fit report to one page wide) If you print to a pdf file, save the document as **6-Your Name Journal Ch4**.
► Trial Balance, January 31, 2018. If you print to a pdf file, save the document as **7-Your Name Trial Bal Ch4**.
► Profit & Loss Report (Standard), January 31, 2018. If you print to a pdf file, save the document as **8-Your Name P & L Ch4**.
► Balance Sheet (Standard), January 31, 2018. If you print to a pdf file, save the document as **9-Your Name Bal Sheet Ch4**.
► Backup your work to **Oasis 2018 (Backup Ch. 4)**.

CHAPTER 4 CHECKLISTS

YOUR NAME'S TECH SERVICES

The checklist below shows all the business forms and reports printed during training. Check each one that you printed. In the document names below, Your Name and Ch4 have been omitted, and report dates are given.

___ 1-Acc List	___ 6-Stmt of Cash Flows, January 1-31, 2018
___ 2-Ck 9 Owner	___ 7-Journal, January 1-31, 2018
___ 3-Bank Rec	___ 8-Trial Bal, January 1-31, 2018
___ 4-Trial Bal, January 1-31, 2018	___ 9-P & L, January 1-31, 2018
___ 5-Cash Flow Forecast, February 1-28, 2018	___ 10-Bal Sheet, January 1-31, 2018

YOUR NAME'S POOL & GARDEN OASIS

The checklist below shows all the business forms and reports printed during training. Check each one that you printed. In the document names below, Your Name and Ch4 have been omitted, and report dates are given.

___ 1-Acc List

___ 2-Ck 8 Owner

___ 3-Bank Rec

___ 4-Cash Flow Forecast, February 1-28, 2018

___ 5-Stmt of Cash Flows, January 1-31, 2018

___ 6-Journal, January 1-31, 2018

___ 7-Trial Bal, January 1-31, 2018

___ 8-P & L, January 1-31, 2018

___ 9-Bal Sheet, January 1-31, 2018

PRACTICE SET 1
SERVICE BUSINESS

YOUR NAME'S CONCIERGE
FOR YOU

Sources: Tashh1601/123RF.com
Redlinevector/123RF.com,
Realwebicons/123RF.com,
Maxx-Studio/Shutterstock

The following is a comprehensive practice set combining all the elements of QuickBooks Desktop studied in Chapters 1-4. In this practice set, you will keep the books for a company for one month. Entries will be made to record invoices, receipt of payments on invoices, cash sales, bills and bill payments, and credit memos for invoices and bills. Account names will be added, changed, deleted, and made inactive. Customer, vendor, owner names, and items will be added to the appropriate lists. Adjusting entries for depreciation, supplies used, and insurance expense will be recorded. A bank reconciliation will be prepared. Reports will be prepared to analyze sales, bills, and receipts. Formal reports including the Trial Balance, Profit and Loss Statement, and Balance Sheet will be prepared.

YOUR NAME'S CONCIERGE FOR YOU

Located in Beverly Hills, California, Your Name's Concierge for You is a service business that helps with errands, shopping, home repairs, and simple household chores. The company is going to start supplying transportation for children and others who do not drive. Rates are on a per-hour basis and differ according to the service performed.

Your Name's Concierge for You is a sole proprietorship owned and operated by you. You have one assistant, Ellen Ross, helping you with errands, scheduling of duties, and doing the bookkeeping for Your Name's Concierge for You. In addition, a part-time employee, Alex Power, works weekends for Your Name's Concierge for You.

INSTRUCTIONS

Use the company file **Concierge 2018.qbw**. If you get a message to update the file, follow the steps listed in QuickBooks Desktop.

The following lists are used for all sales items, customers, and vendors. You will be adding additional customers and vendors as the company is in operation. When entering transactions, you are responsible for any memos or customer messages you wish to include in transactions. Unless otherwise specified, the terms for each sale or bill will be the terms specified in the Customer or Vendor List. (View the terms for the individual customers or vendors in the Customer and Vendor Centers.)

Customers:

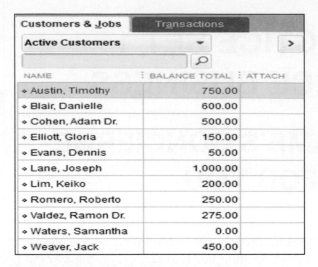

Vendors:

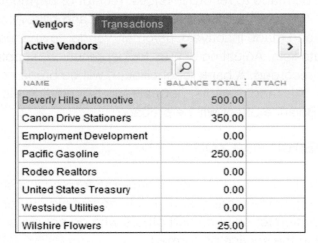

Sales Items:

Each Item is priced per hour. Unless otherwise specified within the transactions, a minimum of one hour is charged for any service provided. As you can see, there is no difference in amount between the first hour of a service and any additional hours of service.

RECORD TRANSACTIONS

Enter the transactions for Your Name's Concierge for You and print as indicated. When preparing invoices, use an Intuit Service Invoice form, a message of your choosing, and do not e-mail invoices or accept online payments. Start numbering the Invoices with number 35 and Sales Receipts with the number 22. Unless the transaction indicates something different, use the standard terms provided by QuickBooks Desktop. Print invoices and sales receipts without lines. Provide transaction memos when needed for clarification. Print invoices, sales receipts, credit memos, and checks as they are entered. Unless instructed to do so by your professor, do not print Payment Receipts and Bills (even if not printed, they are included on the transmittal sheet). Always resize the columns in reports to display information in full.

Week 1: January 1-6, 2018:
- ► Change the company name and legal name from Your Name's Concierge for You to **Your Name's Concierge for You**. (**Type your actual name!** For example, Robin Rosen would enter Robin Rosen's Concierge for you).
- ► Check with your instructor to see if you should change Report Preferences so that the Report Header/ Footer should not include the Date Prepared, Time Prepared, or the Report Basis. If so, make the changes.
- ► Add a new Item: Type: **Service**, Name: **Transport**, Description: **Transportation**; Rate: **35.00**, Account: **Services**.
- ► Change the Capital account Student's Name, Capital to **Your Name, Capital**. (Use your own name.)
- ► Find all accounts with the name **Automobile** as part of the account name. Change every occurrence of Automobile to **Business Vehicles**. Delete any unwanted descriptions.
- ► Find all accounts with the name **Office Equipment** as part of the account name. Change every occurrence of Office Equipment to **Office Furniture/Equipment**. Delete any unwanted descriptions.
- ► Make the following inactive: **Interest Expense: Mortgage**; **Taxes: Property**; **Travel & Ent**.
- ► Delete the following accounts: **Reimbursed Expenses**, **Sales**, **Amortization Expense**, **Professional Development**, and **Recruiting**.
- ► Add **Petty Cash** to the Chart of Accounts. Transfer **$100** from Checking to Petty Cash to fund the account. Use January 1, 2018 as the transaction date.
- ► Print an Account Listing in Portrait orientation. Customize the Report on the Header/Footer tab, change the Subtitle to show the date: **January 1, 2018**. Hide the columns for Description and Tax Line and resize any columns that are not displayed in full. If you print to a pdf file, save the document as **1-Your Name Acct List PS1**.
- ► Prior to recording any transactions, print a Trial Balance as of January 1, 2018. If you print to a pdf file, save the document as **2-Your Name Trial Bal PS1**.

1/1/18
- ► Change the name of the vendor Canon Drive Stationers to **Canon Stationers**.
- ► Change the description for the sales item Pets from Pet Sitting to **Pet Care**.
- ► We were out of paper, toner cartridges for the laser printer, and various other office supplies that we need to have on hand. Received a bill—Invoice 8106—from Canon Stationers for $450 for the office supplies we received today. (Even though the Bills are listed on the transmittal sheet, check with your instructor to see if you should print them. If you do print Bills, print without lines around each field.) If you print to a pdf file, save the document as **3-Your Name Bill Canon Stationers PS1**.

▶ Dr. Adam Cohen has arranged for you to take his dogs to the vet for shots and to feed and walk his dogs 1 hour per day every day. Bill Dr. Cohen for 3 hours transport and Pet Care for one hour a day for 14 days, terms Net 30. (Refer to the Item List for the appropriate sales items and put this all on Invoice 35. Remember to use an <u>Intuit Service Invoice</u> as the business form.) Use an appropriate customer message and print the invoice without lines. On the Name Information Changed dialog box, click "No" so you do not change the terms for Dr. Cohen from Net 15 to Net 30. If you print to a pdf file, save the document as **4-Your Name Inv 35 Cohen PS1**.

▶ Samantha Waters is having a party in two weeks. Bill Samantha Waters for 12 hours of party planning. Invoice 36, terms Net 30. If you print to a pdf file, save the document as **5-Your Name Inv 36 Waters PS1**.

1/2/18

▶ Mr. Weaver's mother has several doctor appointments. He has asked Your Name's Concierge for You to take her to these appointments. Bill Jack Weaver for 8 hours of transportation. (Because of the current date of your computer and terms of net 10, you will find that this and many of the invoices you prepare will be marked Past Due. Disregard this message.) If you print to a pdf file, save the document as **6-Your Name Inv 37 Weaver PS1**.

1/3/18

▶ Gloria Elliott needed to have her shelves relined. You did part of the house this week and will return next week to continue the work. Bill her for 12 hours of household chores for this week. If you print to a pdf file, save the document as **7-Your Name Inv 38 Elliott PS1**.

1/4/18

▶ Record the bill from Western Insurance, (7654 Western Avenue, Hollywood, CA 90721, Main Phone 310-555-1598, Main Email: **WesternIns@abc.com**, Fax 310-555-8951, terms Net 30) for Business Vehicles Insurance for the year, $2,400, Invoice 2287. If you print to a pdf file, save the document as **8-Your Name Bill Western Ins PS1**.

▶ Received checks for Customer Payments on account for balances dated 12/31/2017 from the following customers: Dr. Ramon Valdez, $275, Check 713; Roberto Romero, $250, Check 36381; Jack Weaver, $450, Check 6179; Joseph Lane, $1,000, Check 38142. (Even though the Payment Receipts are listed on the checklist, check with your instructor to see if you should print them.) If you print to a pdf file, save the document as **9-Your Name Rcv Pmt Valdez PS1, 10-Your Name Rcv Pmt Romero PS1, 11-Your Name Rcv Pmt Weaver PS1, 12-Your Name Rcv Pmt Lane PS1**.

1/5/18

▶ Prepare Sales Receipt 22 to record a cash sale. Received Check 2894 for 2 hours of errands and 1 hour of household chores for a new customer: Fatema Nasseri, 18062 Beverly Drive, Beverly Hills, CA 90210, Main Phone: 310-555-7206, Fax: 310-555-6027, Main E-mail: **FNasseri@abc.com**, Payment Terms: Net 10, Preferred Delivery Method: None. (*Note:* Remember to key the last name first for the customer name.) Print the sales receipt. If you print to a pdf file, save the document as **13-Your Name SR 22 Nasseri PS1**.

1/6/18

▶ Prepare Unpaid Bills Detail Report for January 6, 2018. Print the report. If you print to a pdf file, save the document as **14-Your Name Unpaid Bills PS1**.

▶ Pay bills for the amount owed to Wilshire Flowers and Pacific Gasoline on December 31. (Refer to the Vendor List shown on the second page of the practice set or to the Unpaid Bills Detail Report to determine the amounts for the checks. Remember that the due dates will not be 12/31/17 they will be 01/10/18.) Print the checks using a Standard check style—they may be printed on one page or individually. If you print to a pdf file, save the document as **15-Your Name Cks 1-2 PS1**.

▶ Make the bank deposit for the week. Deposit date is 1/6/18. Print a Deposit Summary. If you print to a pdf file, save the document as **16-Your Name Dep Sum PS1**.

▶ Print Trial Balance from 01/01/18 to 01/06/18. If you print to a pdf file, save the document as **17-Your Name Trial Bal PS1**.

▶ Back up your work for the week. Use **Concierge 2018 (Backup Week 1)** as the file name.

PS
1

Week 2: January 7-13, 2018
1/9/18

▶ Received checks for payment on accounts from the following customers:
Dr. Cohen, $500, No. 7891; Ms. Lim, $200, No. 97452; Ms. Blair, $600, No. 925; Mr. Evans, $50, No. 178; and Mr. Austin, $750, No. 3916. If you print to a pdf file, save the document as **18-Your Name Rcv Pmt Cohen PS1**, **19-Rcv Pmt Lim PS1**, **20-Rcv Pmt Blair PS1**, **21-Rcv Pmt Evans PS1**, **22-Rcv Pmt Austin PS1**.

▶ Received a bill—Invoice 81085—from Pacific Gasoline, $325 for the bi-weekly gasoline charge. If you print to a pdf file, save the document as **23-Your Name Bill Pacific Gasoline PS1**.

▶ Every week we put fresh flowers in the office to provide a welcoming environment for any customers who happen to come into the office. Received a bill—Invoice 9287—from Wilshire Flowers for $60 for office flowers for two weeks. (Miscellaneous Expense) If you print to a pdf file, save the document as **24-Your Name Bill Wilshire Flowers PS1**.

1/10/18

▶ Danielle Blair really likes the floral arrangements in the office of Your Name's Concierge for You. She has asked that flowers be brought to her home and arranged throughout the house. When you complete the placement of the flowers in the house, Danielle gives you Check 387 for $180 for 3 hours of errands and 3 hours of household chores. This is payment in full for three weeks of floral arrangements. Prepare the Sales Receipt. If you print to a pdf file, save the document as **25-Your Name SR 23 Blair PS1**.

▶ Joseph Lane has arranged for Your Name's Concierge for You to supervise and coordinate the installation of new tile in his master bathroom. Bill Mr. Lane for 5 hours of repair service for hiring the subcontractor, scheduling the installation for 1/14, 1/15 and 1/16, and contract preparation. If you print to a pdf file, save the document as **26-Your Name Inv 39 Lane PS1**.

1/11/18

▶ Returned faulty printer cartridge that we had purchased in December to have on hand. Received Credit Memo 5 from Canon Stationers, $95. (Did you use the asset account?) If you print to a pdf file, save the document as **27-Your Name CM Canon Stationers PS1**.

1/13/18

▶ Pay all bills for the amounts due on or before January 13. (*Hint:* Are there any credits to apply?) There should be two checks. Print the checks–all on one page or individually. If you print to a pdf file, save the document as **28-Your Name Cks 3-4 PS1**.

▶ Correct Invoice 38 issued to Gloria Elliott on 1/03/18. The number of hours billed should be 14 instead of 12. Print the corrected invoice. (Do not change the date.) If you print to a pdf file, save the document as **29-Your Name Inv 38 Elliott Corrected PS1**.

▶ Make the bank deposit for the week. Deposit date is 1/13/18. Print a Deposit Summary. If you print to a pdf file, save the document as **30-Your Name Dep Sum PS1**.

▶ Print Trial Balance from 01/01/18 to 01/13/18. If you print to a pdf file, save the document as **31-Your Name Trial Bal PS1**.

▶ Back up your work for the week. Use **Concierge 2018 (Backup Week 2)** as the file name.

Week 3: January 14-20, 2018

1/15/18

▶ Pay postage due 64 cents. Use Petty Cash. Number is 1 for Petty Cash.

▶ Print Petty Cash Account QuickReport by clicking the Report button at the bottom of the Chart of Accounts. Print in Landscape orientation. If you print to a pdf file, save the document as **32-Your Name Petty Cash QuickReport PS1**.

1/17/18

▶ Mr. Lane's bathroom tile was installed on 1/14, 1/15 and 1/16. The installation was completed to his satisfaction. Bill him for 24 hours of repair service. If you print to a pdf file, save the document as **33-Your Name Inv 40 Lane PS1**.

1/18/18

▶ Danielle Blair's neighbor, Alex Levin, really liked the flowers in Danielle's house and asked you to bring flowers to his home and office. This week he gave you Check 90-163 for 1 hour of errands and 1 hour of household chores. Add him to the customer list: Alex Levin, Main Phone: 310-555-0918, 236 West Camden Drive, Beverly Hills, CA 90210, Payment Terms: Net 10, Preferred Delivery Method: None. If you print to a pdf file, save the document as **34-Your Name SR 24 Levin PS1**.

1/19/18

▶ Tonight is Samantha's big party. She has arranged for both you and Alex to supervise the party from 3 p.m. until 1 a.m. Bill Samantha Waters for 20 hours of party planning and supervision. If you print to a pdf file, save the document as **35-Your Name Inv 41 Waters PS1**.

▶ Print a Customer Balance Summary Report for all transactions. If you print to a pdf file, save the document as **36-Your Name Cust Bal Sum PS1**.

1/20/18

▶ Record the checks received from customers for the week: Mr. Weaver, $280, No. 9165, Ms. Elliott, $150, No. 7-303, Dr. Cohen, $455, No. 89162, and Mr. Lane, $325, No. 38197. If you print to a pdf file, save the document as **37-Your Name Rcv Pmt Weaver PS1**, **38-Your Name Rcv Pmt Elliott PS1**, **39-Your Name Rcv Pmt Cohen PS1**, **40-Your Name Rcv Pmt Lane PS1**.

▶ Make the bank deposit for the week. Deposit date is 1/20/18. Print a Deposit Summary. If you print to a pdf file, save the document as **41-Your Name Dep Sum PS1**.

▶ Print Trial Balance from 01/01/18 to 01/20/18. If you print to a pdf file, save the document as **42-Your Name Trial Bal PS1**.

▶ Back up your work for the week. Use **Concierge 2018 (Backup Week 3)** as the file name.

Week 4: January 21-27, 2018
1/23/18

▶ Samantha's party went so smoothly on the 19th that you went home at 11 p.m. rather than 1 a.m. (Alex stayed until 1 a.m.) Issue Credit Memo 42 to Samantha Waters for 2 hours of party planning and supervision. Apply the credit to Invoice 41 dated January 19, 2018. If you print to a pdf file, save the document as **43-Your Name CM 42 Waters PS1**.

▶ Dennis Evans arranged to have his pets cared for by Your Name's Concierge for You during the past 7 days. Bill him for 1 hour of pet care each day. Dennis wants to add a doggie door and a fenced area for his dog. Bill him 24 hours of repair service for the planning and overseeing of the project. If you print to a pdf file, save the document as **44-Your Name Inv 43 Evans PS1**.

▶ Use Petty Cash to pay for a box of file folders to be used immediately in reorganizing some of the files in the office, $14.84. (This is an expense and is Check 2 for Petty Cash.)

▶ Print a Petty Cash Account QuickReport in Landscape. Fit the report to one page wide. If you print to a pdf file, save the document as **45-Your Name Petty Cash QuickReport PS1**.

1/24/18

▶ You arranged for theater tickets, dinner reservations, and an after-theater surprise party for Dr. Valdez to celebrate his wife's birthday. Bill him for 4 hours of errands, 3 hours shopping for the gift, and 8 hours of party planning. If you print to a pdf file, save the document as **46-Your Name Inv 44 Valdez PS1**.

▶ Received a bill—Invoice 9802—from Wilshire Flowers for $60 for office flowers for two weeks. If you print to a pdf file, save the document as **47-Your Name Bill Wilshire Flowers PS1**.

▶ Received a bill—Invoice 81116—from Pacific Gasoline, $355 for the bi-weekly gasoline charge. If you print to a pdf file, save the document as **48-Your Name Bill Pacific Gasoline PS1**.

▶ Write a check to Canon Stationers for the purchase of a new printer for the office, $500. (*Note:* If you get a warning to use Pay Bills because we owe the company money, click Continue Writing Check.) Print the check using standard-style checks. If you print to a pdf file, save the document as **49-Your Name Ck 5 Canon Stationers PS1**.

PS
1

1/27/18

▶ Dr. Cohen has arranged for Your Name's Concierge for You to feed and walk his dogs every day. Bill him for Pet Care, 1 hour per day for the past two weeks. In addition, Dr. Cohen is going to have a party and wants Your Name's Concierge for You to plan it for him. Bill him for 20 hours party planning. When the dogs were puppies they did some damage to the interior of the house. To prepare for the party several areas in the house need to be reorganized and repaired. Bill him for 18 hours of household chores and 20 hours of repairs. If you print to a pdf file, save the document as **50-Your Name Inv 45 Cohen PS1**.

▶ Write checks to pay for telephone, rent, and utilities. The telephone company will need to be added to the Vendor List. Vendor information is provided in each transaction. Print the checks using standard-style checks. They may be printed as a batch or individually. If you print to a pdf file, save the document as **51-Your Name Cks 6-8 PS1**.
   ○ Monthly telephone bill: $150, Bel Air Telephone. Add the vendor: Bel Air Telephone, Main Phone 310-555-4972, 2015 Beverly Boulevard, Bel Air, CA 90047, Payment Terms Net 30.
   ○ Monthly rent for office space: $1,500, Rodeo Realtors.
   ○ Monthly utility bill for $424.00 from Westside Utilities is for: Water $195 and Gas and Electric $229.

▶ Prepare and print in Portrait orientation an Unpaid Bills Detail Report for January 27. If you print to a pdf file, save the document as **52-Your Name Unpaid Bills PS1**.

▶ Pay bills for all amounts due on or before January 27. Print check(s). If you print to a pdf file, save the document as **53-Your Name Ck 9 Wilshire Flowers PS1**.

▶ Prepare a Check Detail Report from 1/1/18 to 1/27/18. Use Landscape orientation and fit report to one page wide. If you print to a pdf file, save the document as **54-Your Name Ck Detail PS1**.

▶ Record payments received from customers: Ms. Waters, $600, No. 4692; Dr. Cohen, $1,550, No. 7942; Mr. Evans, $735, No. 235; Dr. Valdez, $645, No. 601; Ms. Elliott, $140, No. 923-10. (If any of the payments are not payments in full, leave as an underpayment. Include the Memo: Partial Payment.) If you print to a pdf file, save the document as **55-Your Name Rcv Pmt Waters PS1**, **56-Your Name Rcv Pmt Cohen PS1**, **57-Your Name Rcv Pmt Evans PS1**, **58-Your Name Rcv Pmt Valdez PS1**, **59-Your Name Rcv Pmt Elliott PS1**.

▶ Make the bank deposit for the week. Deposit date is 1/27/18. If you print to a pdf file, save the document as **60-Your Name Dep Sum PS1**.

▶ Print Customer Balance Detail Report in Portrait orientation for All Transactions. If you print to a pdf file, save the document as **61-Your Name Cust Bal Detail PS1**.

▶ Print Trial Balance from 01/01/18 to 01/27/18. If you print to a pdf file, save the document as **62-Your Name Trial Bal PS1**.

▶ Back up your work for the week. Use **Concierge 2018 (Backup Week 4)** as the file name.

Week 5: January 28-30, 2018
1/30/18

▶ Write a check for your monthly withdrawal, $1,200. If you print to a pdf file, save the document as **63-Your Name Ck 10 Owner PS1**.

▶ Since a fax machine is a business necessity, you decided to give your new fax machine to Your Name's Concierge for You. Record this $350 investment of equipment by you.

► Because they are remodeling the offices, Rodeo Realtors decreased the amount of rent to $1,000 per month. Correct and reprint Check 7 for rent payment. If you print to a pdf file, save the document as **64-Your Name Ck 7 Rodeo Realtors Corrected PS1**.

► Record adjusting entries for:
  o Business Vehicles Insurance, $200.
  o Office Supplies Used, $150.
  o Depreciation: Business Vehicles, $500 and Office Furniture/Equipment, $92.

► Print Trial Balance from 01/01/18 to 01/30/18. If you print to a pdf file, save the document as **65-Your Name Trial Bal PS1**.

► Back up your work for the week. Use **Concierge 2018 (Backup Week 5)** as the file name.

End of the Month: January 31, 2018
► Prepare the bank reconciliation using the following bank statement. Record any adjustments necessary because of the bank statement.

PS
1

Golden Bank 1234 Rodeo Drive Beverly Hills, CA 90210			
Your Name's Concierge for You 2789 Robertson Boulevard Beverly Hills, CA 90210			
Beginning Balance, January 1, 2018			$25,350.00
1/1/2018, Transfer		100.00	25,250.00
1/6/2018, Deposit	2,070.00		27,320.00
1/7/2018, Check 1		250.00	27,070.00
1/7/2018, Check 2		25.00	27,045.00
1/13/2018, Deposit	2,280.00		29,325.00
1/15/2018, Check 3		500.00	28,825.00
1/16/2018, Check 4		255.00	28,570.00
1/20/2018, Deposit	1,270.00		29,840.00
1/28/2018, Check 5		500.00	29,340.00
1/29/2018, Check 7		1,000.00	28,340.00
1/31/2018, Payment: Business Vehicles Loan: Interest $551.87; Principal $177.57		729.44	27,610.56
1/31/2018, Payment: Office Furniture/ Equipment Loan: Interest $59.45; Principal $15.44		74.89	27,535.67
1/31/2018, Service Charge		25.00	27,510.67
1/31/2018, Interest	53.00		27,563.67
Ending Balance, January 31, 2018			$27,563.67

▶ Print a Reconciliation Detail Report. If you print to a pdf file, save the document as **66-Your Name Bank Rec PS1**.

▶ Print the following reports as of 1/31/18:
  ○ Trial Balance from 1/1/18 through 1/31/18 in Portrait. If you print to a pdf file, save the document as **67-Your Name Trial Bal PS1**.
  ○ Cash Flow Forecast from 2/1/18 through 2/28/18 in Landscape. If you print to a pdf file, save the document as **68-Your Name Cash Flow Forecast PS1**.
  ○ Statement of Cash Flows from 1/1/18 through 1/31/18 in Portrait. If you print to a pdf file, save the document as **69-Your Name Stmt of Cash Flows PS1**.
  ○ Profit & Loss (Standard) from 1/1/18 through 1/31/18 in Portrait. If you print to a pdf file, save the document as **70-Your Name P & L PS1**.

▶ Transfer the Net Income/Owner's Equity to owner's Capital account.

▶ Close the Drawing account.

▶ Close the period as of 01/31/18. Do not use any passwords.

▶ Prepare a Balance Sheet (Standard) as of 1/31/18. Print in Portrait. If you print to a pdf file, save the document as **71-Your Name Bal Sheet PS1**.

▶ Prepare the Journal from 1/1/18 through 1/31/18, expand the report, print in Landscape orientation, and Fit to 1 page wide. If you print to a pdf file, save the document as **72-Your Name Journal PS1**.

▶ Create an Archive Backup named **Concierge 2018 (Archive 01-31-18)**.

▶ Back up your work for the week. Use **Concierge 2018 (Backup Complete)** as the file name.

PRACTICE SET 1 CHECKLIST

YOUR NAME'S CONCIERGE FOR YOU

Mark the items in the following checklist as you complete and/or print them; then attach the documents and reports in the order listed when you submit them to your instructor. Printing is optional for Payment Receipts and Bills (unless your instructor requires them to be printed); however, they are included in the checklist, so they can be marked as they are completed.

(Note: When paying bills and printing a batch of checks, your checks may be in a different order than shown below. If you print the checks to the correct company and have the correct amounts, do not be concerned if your check numbers are not an exact match.)

Week 1
___ 1-Acct List
___ 2-Trial Bal, January 1, 2018
___ 3-Bill Canon Stationers
___ 4-Inv 35 Cohen
___ 5-Inv 36 Waters
___ 6-Inv 37 Weaver
___ 7-Inv 38 Elliott
___ 8-Bill Western Ins
___ 9-Rcv Pmt Valdez
___ 10-Rcv Pmt Romero
___ 11-Rcv Pmt Weaver
___ 12-Rcv Pmt Lane
___ 13-SR 22 Nasseri
___ 14-Unpaid Bills, January 6, 2018
___ 15-Cks 1-2
    Check 1 Pacific Gasoline
    Check 2 Wilshire Flowers
___ 16-Dep Sum, January 6, 2018
___ 17-Trial Balance, January 1-6, 2018

Week 2
___ 18-Rcv Pmt Cohen
___ 19-Rcv Pmt Lim
___ 20-Rcv Pmt Blair
___ 21-Rcv Pmt Evans
___ 22-Rcv Pmt Austin
___ 23-Bill Pacific Gasoline
___ 24-Bill Wilshire Flowers
___ 25-SR 23 Blair
___ 26-Inv 39 Lane
___ 27-CM Canon Stationers
___ 28-Cks 3-4
    Ck 3 Beverly Hills Automotive
    Ck 4 Canon Stationers

___ 29-Inv 38 (Corrected): Elliott
___ 30-Dep Sum, January 13, 2018
___ 31-Trial Bal, January 1-13, 2018

Week 3
___ 32-Petty Cash QuickReport, January 1-
    15, 2018
___ 33-Inv 40 Lane
___ 34-SR 24 Levin
___ 35-Inv 41 Waters
___ 36-Cust Bal Sum, January 1-19, 2018
___ 37-Rcv Pmt Weaver
___ 38-Rcv Pmt Elliott
___ 39-Rcv Pmt Cohen
___ 40-Rcv Pmt Lane
___ 41-Dep Sum, January 20, 2018
___ 42-Trial Bal, January 1-20, 2018

Week 4
___ 43-CM 42 Waters
___ 44-Inv 43 Evans
___ 45-Petty Cash QuickReport,
    January 1-23, 2018
___ 46-Inv 44 Valdez
___ 47-Bill Wilshire Flowers
___ 48-Bill Pacific Gasoline
___ 49-Ck 5 Canon Stationers
___ 50-Inv 45 Cohen
___ 51-Cks 6-8
    Ck 6 Bel Air Telephone
    Ck 7 Rodeo Realtors
    Ck 8 Westside Utilities
___ 52-Unpaid Bills, January 27, 2018
___ 53-Ck 9 Wilshire Flowers
___ 54-Ck Detail, January 1-27, 2018

Week 4 Continued

___ 55-Rcv Pmt Waters

___ 56-Rcv Pmt Cohen

___ 57-Rcv Pmt Evans

___ 58-Rcv Pmt Valdez

___ 59-Rcv Pmt Elliott

___ 60-Dep Sum, January 27, 2018

___ 61-Cust Bal Detail, January 1-27, 2018

___ 62-Trial Bal, January 1-27, 2018

Week 5

___ 63-Ck 10 Owner

___ 64-Ck 7 Rodeo Realtors Corrected

___ 65-Trial Bal, January 1-30, 2018

End of the Month

___ 66-Bank Rec

___ 67-Trial Bal, January 1-31, 2018

___ 68-Cash Flow Forecast, February 1-28, 2018

___ 69-Stmt of Cash Flows, January 2018

___ 70-P & L, January 1-31, 2018

___ 71-Bal Sheet, January 31, 2018

___ 72-Journal, January 1-31, 2018

SALES AND RECEIVABLES: MERCHANDISING BUSINESS

5

LEARNING OBJECTIVES

At the completion of this chapter, you will be able to:

5.01. Enter sales transactions for a retail business.
5.02. Understand the use of and requirements for complex passwords.
5.03. Use account numbers.
5.04. Use lists including the Customer & Jobs, Item, and Payment Method lists.
5.05. Customize Report Preferences and business forms.
5.06. Sell inventory items.
5.07. Analyze an invoice in the Journal, view the accounts used when selling inventory items, understand what is recorded behind the scenes.
5.08. Understand the use of the Inventory Asset, Cost of Goods Sold, and Sales Tax Liability accounts.
5.09. Understand the use of More Secure Web Mail and the bulk clear feature for the send queue.
5.10. Enter Sales Orders and then create Sales Order Invoices.
5.11. Add a word to the QuickBooks Desktop dictionary.
5.12. Prepare, analyze, and print the Customer Balance Detail report.
5.13. Understand and use Sales Discounts.
5.14. Add new sales items and accounts.
5.15. Add a new customer with a shipping address and modify existing customer records.
5.16. Void and delete sales forms, understand how to batch void/delete business forms, and prepare a Voided/Deleted Transactions Summary report.
5.17. Prepare a Credit Memo and apply it to an Invoice.
5.18. Record cash sales with sales tax.
5.19. Enter Debit and Credit Card sales.
5.20. Understand the requirements for customer credit card protection.
5.21. Prepare and print a Sales by Item Summary report.
5.22. Correct business forms.
5.23. Analyze a QuickReport for Cash Customer.
5.24. View the Sales Tax Liability register.
5.25. Use the Customer Center.
5.26. Add a credit card to a customer's account.
5.27. Select the Collections Center preferences and view the Collections Center.
5.28. View Income Tracker.
5.29. Record customer payments on account, record credit card payments, use applied credits, and apply sales discounts.
5.30. Record late payments with discounts and credits.
5.31. Prepare the Customer Balance Summary and the Transactions List by Customer.
5.32. Make deposits.

5.33.   Record a non-sufficient funds (NSF) check.

5.34.   Issue a Credit Memo and refund check.

5.35.   Prepare and print the Journal, Trial Balance, and Inventory Valuation Detail reports.

5.36.   Memorize reports and use them.

5.37.   Print Profit & Loss report.

ACCOUNTING FOR SALES AND RECEIVABLES

Rather than using a traditional Sales Journal to record transactions using debits and credits and special columns, QuickBooks Desktop uses an Invoice to record sales on account. Because cash sales do not involve accounts receivable, a Sales Receipt is prepared, and the money is placed into the Undeposited Funds account until a deposit is made. When customers pay the amount due on their invoices, the payment is entered using Receive Payments. All transactions, regardless where they are recorded are placed in the Journal. A new account, sales item, or customer can be added as transactions are entered. Customer information may be changed in the Customer List. The Customer List is the same as the Accounts Receivable Subsidiary Ledger.

For a retail business, QuickBooks Desktop tracks inventory, maintains information on reorder limits, tracks the quantity of merchandise on hand, maintains information on the value of the inventory, computes the cost of goods sold using the average cost basis, and informs you of the percentage of sales for each inventory item. Early-payment discounts as well as discounts to certain types of customers can be given. Different price levels may be created for sales items and/or customers.

A multitude of reports are available when using QuickBooks Desktop. Accounts receivable reports include Customer Balance Summary and Customer Balance Detail reports. Sales reports provide information regarding the amount of sales by item. Transaction Reports by Customer are available as well as the traditional accounting reports such as Trial Balance, Profit and Loss, and Balance Sheet. QuickBooks Desktop also has graphing capabilities so that you can see and evaluate your accounts receivable and sales. Reports created in QuickBooks Desktop may be exported to Microsoft Excel.

DOWNLOAD COMPANY FILES

Refer to Chapter 1 procedures for downloading company files for Chapters 5-8.

   Download **Company Files** for **Casual_2018**, **Desert_2018**, **Sierra_2018**, **Swim_2018**, and **Total_2018**; also download the **Logo Files** for **Books Logo**, **Canine Logo**, and **Coffee Logo**

- Follow the steps provided in Chapter 1 to download the company files and to make sure the company files are not marked as "Read Only" or "Archive."
- In addition to the five company files there are three logo files that will be used in Chapter 9 and the final practice set that should be downloaded following the same steps that are used to download a company file.

TRAINING TUTORIAL

The following tutorial is a step-by-step guide to recording sales (both cash and credit) for a fictitious company. This company is called Your Name's Sierra Sports. In addition to recording transactions using QuickBooks Desktop, you will prepare several reports and graphs for the company. The tutorial for Your Name's Sierra Sports will continue in Chapters 6 and 7, when accounting for payables, bank reconciliations, financial statement preparation, and closing an accounting period for a merchandising business will be completed.

Since the company used in training is fictitious, there are transactions that will be entered for illustration but will not be able to be entered in a way that will take full advantage of QuickBooks Desktop. For example, in an actual business when a credit card is accepted for payment, the payment would be processed. If there are supplemental or subscription enhancements to QuickBooks Desktop, they may be noted but will not be utilized.

PROGRAM NAME AND DATES

Beginning in Chapter 5, the program name of QuickBooks Accountant Desktop may be referred to as QuickBooks DT rather than QuickBooks Desktop. These names may be used interchangeably. As in Chapters 1-4, the year used for the screen shots is 2018, which is the same year as the version of the program. Verify the year you are to use with your instructor. The year you use in Chapter 5 should be the year you use in Chapters 6 and 7. Because your computer date will not be for 2018, invoices may be marked Past Due. Disregard this notice. The text will not show Past Due on invoices.

PRINTING

As in Chapters 1-4, you will be instructed when to print business documents and reports. Everything that may be printed within the chapter and for the end-of-chapter problem are listed on a checklist at the end of the chapter. As you print, check off the document on the checklist. Always verify items to be printed with your instructor.

BASIC INSTRUCTIONS

In this chapter you will be entering both accounts receivable and cash sale transactions for a retail company that sells merchandise and charges its customers sales tax. As in previous chapters, all transactions are listed on memos. The transaction date will be the same date as the memo date unless otherwise specified within the transaction. Customer names, when necessary, will be given in the transaction. Unless otherwise specified, all terms for customers on account are Net 30 days.

Even when instructions for a transaction are given step-by-step, always refer to the memo for transaction details. Once a specific type of transaction has been entered in a step-by-step manner, additional transactions will be made without having instructions provided. Of course, you may always refer to previous instructions.

COMPANY PROFILE

Your Name's Sierra Sports is a sporting goods store located in Mammoth Lakes, California. Currently, the company is open only during the winter. As a result, the company specializes in equipment, clothing, and accessories for skiing and snowboarding. The company is a partnership between you and Larry Muir. Each partner has a 50 percent share of the business, and both of you devote all your efforts to Your Name's Sierra Sports. You have several part-time employees who work during ski season. There is a full-time bookkeeper and manager, Ruth Morgan, who oversees purchases, maintains the inventory, and keeps the books for the company.

OPEN A COMPANY

Use the Sierra 2018.qbw file to complete the training in Chapters 5, 6, and 7.

  Open **QuickBooks DT**, and open **Sierra_2018.qbw**

- Use the **Sierra 2018.qbw** file that you downloaded.
- The file name may show as **Sierra_2018** or **Sierra 2018**. Either way it is shown, the file is the same.
- If QuickBooks DT has received an update from Intuit, you may get a screen to Update Company. If so, click **Yes**.
- If you see the "What's New" icon on the right-side of the Home Page, click the 🗙 to close it.
- If you get a message that says, "Set Closing Date Password?" click **Do not display this message in the future**, and then click **No**.

COMPLEX PASSWORD REQUIREMENTS

QuickBooks requires the use of a complex password. A complex password contains at least 7 characters, including one number and one uppercase letter. You have been using the password QBDT2018 for each company in the text. The password should be changed every 90 days. If you get a Sensitive Data Protection Setup requirement screen or a notice that you must change your password, use **2018QBDT** for the new password.

If you need to provide an answer to a Challenge Question, I would choose "Name of your first manager?" and use your professor's name for the answer.

ADD YOUR NAME TO THE COMPANY NAME

As in earlier chapters, each student in the course will be working with the same company and printing the same documents. Personalizing the company name to include your name will help identify many of the documents you print during your training.

  Add your name to the company name

Click **Company** on the menu bar, click **My Company,** click the **Edit** icon 🖉
In the Company Name text box, drag through the words **Your Name's** to highlight
Type **Your Real Name's**

- Type your real name, *not* the words *Your Real Name*. For example, Pamela Preston would type—**Pamela Preston's**.

Repeat for the Legal Name on the Legal Information tab
Click **OK**

- The title bar now shows Your Name's Sierra Sports.

Your Name's Sierra Sports - QuickBooks Accountant Desktop 2018

Close the My Company screen

ACCOUNT NUMBERS

QuickBooks DT has a choice to use or not use account numbers for the accounts in the Chart of Accounts. In this section of the text, account numbers will be used.

The account numbering may be four or five digits. The structure is:

ACCOUNT NUMBER	TYPE OF ACCOUNT
1000-1999	Assets
2000-2999	Liabilities
3000-3999	Capital
4000-4999	Income or Revenue
5000-5999	Cost of Goods Sold
6000-6999	Expenses
7000-7999	Other Income
8000-8999	Other Expenses

LISTS

As you learned in Chapters 1-4, much of the organization of QuickBooks DT is dependent on lists. The primary types of lists you will use in the chapter are a Customer List and a Sales Item List. There are also lists for templates, payment methods, terms, customer messages, and so on.

Customers & Jobs List

The names, addresses, telephone numbers, credit terms, credit limits, balances, and tax terms for all established credit customers are contained in the Customers & Jobs List. The Customers & Jobs List is also the Accounts Receivable Ledger. You will be using the following Customers & Jobs List for established credit customers:

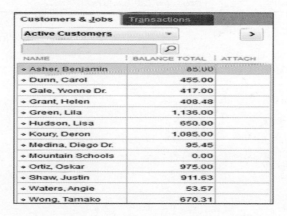

Item List

Sales are often made up of various types of income. In Your Name's Sierra Sports there are several income accounts. To classify income regarding the type of sale, the sales account may have subaccounts. When recording a transaction for a sale, QuickBooks DT requires that a Sales Item be used. When the sales item is created, a sales account is required. When the sales item is used in a transaction, the income is credited to the appropriate sales/income account. For example, Ski Boots is a sales item and uses Equipment Income, a subaccount of Sales, when a transaction is recorded.

QuickBooks DT uses lists to organize sales items. Using lists for sales items allows for flexibility in billing and a more accurate representation of the way in which income is earned. If the company charges a standard price for an item, the price of the item will be included on the list. Your Name's Sierra Sports sells all items at different prices, so the price given for each item is listed at 0.00.

In a retail business with an inventory, the number of units on hand can be tracked; and, when the amount on hand gets to a predetermined limit, an order can be placed. By giving an item a Maximum, the quantity to order can be calculated easily. The following Item List for the various types of merchandise and sales categories will be used for Your Name's Sierra Sports:

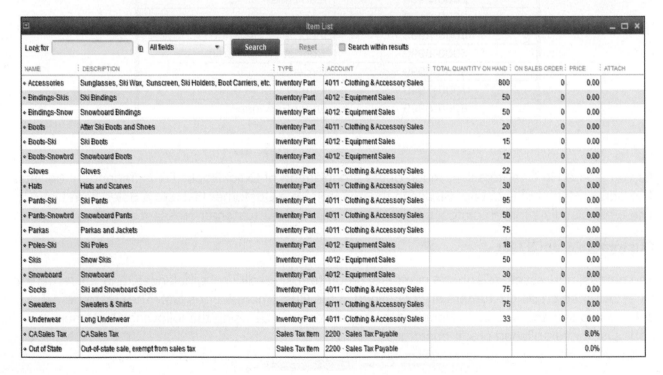

NAME	DESCRIPTION	TYPE	ACCOUNT	TOTAL QUANTITY ON HAND	ON SALES ORDER	PRICE	ATTACH
Accessories	Sunglasses, Ski Wax, Sunscreen, Ski Holders, Boot Carriers, etc.	Inventory Part	4011 · Clothing & Accessory Sales	800	0	0.00	
Bindings-Skis	Ski Bindings	Inventory Part	4012 · Equipment Sales	50	0	0.00	
Bindings-Snow	Snowboard Bindings	Inventory Part	4012 · Equipment Sales	50	0	0.00	
Boots	After Ski Boots and Shoes	Inventory Part	4011 · Clothing & Accessory Sales	20	0	0.00	
Boots-Ski	Ski Boots	Inventory Part	4012 · Equipment Sales	15	0	0.00	
Boots-Snowbrd	Snowboard Boots	Inventory Part	4012 · Equipment Sales	12	0	0.00	
Gloves	Gloves	Inventory Part	4011 · Clothing & Accessory Sales	22	0	0.00	
Hats	Hats and Scarves	Inventory Part	4011 · Clothing & Accessory Sales	30	0	0.00	
Pants-Ski	Ski Pants	Inventory Part	4011 · Clothing & Accessory Sales	95	0	0.00	
Pants-Snowbrd	Snowboard Pants	Inventory Part	4011 · Clothing & Accessory Sales	50	0	0.00	
Parkas	Parkas and Jackets	Inventory Part	4011 · Clothing & Accessory Sales	75	0	0.00	
Poles-Ski	Ski Poles	Inventory Part	4012 · Equipment Sales	18	0	0.00	
Skis	Snow Skis	Inventory Part	4012 · Equipment Sales	50	0	0.00	
Snowboard	Snowboard	Inventory Part	4012 · Equipment Sales	30	0	0.00	
Socks	Ski and Snowboard Socks	Inventory Part	4011 · Clothing & Accessory Sales	75	0	0.00	
Sweaters	Sweaters & Shirts	Inventory Part	4011 · Clothing & Accessory Sales	75	0	0.00	
Underwear	Long Underwear	Inventory Part	4011 · Clothing & Accessory Sales	33	0	0.00	
CA Sales Tax	CA Sales Tax	Sales Tax Item	2200 · Sales Tax Payable			8.0%	
Out of State	Out-of-state sale, exempt from sales tax	Sales Tax Item	2200 · Sales Tax Payable			0.0%	

CUSTOMIZE THE PAYMENT METHOD LIST

QuickBooks DT does not automatically include all methods of payment in the list. It allows the list to be customized for an individual company. There is no need to have a list of payment methods that you do not use. By customizing the list, you will avoid errors by listing the methods of payment you accept.

> **MEMO**
> **DATE:** January 1, 2018
>
> After viewing the Payment Method List, you realize that you need to add MasterCard and delete Discover Card as payment methods.

 Add MasterCard and delete Discover from the Payment Method list

Click **Lists** on the menu bar, point to **Customer & Vendor Profile Lists**
Click **Payment Method List**
Click the **Payment Method** button, click **New**
Enter **MasterCard** in the Payment Method text box
Click the drop-down list arrow for **Payment Type**, click **MasterCard**, click **OK**
Click **Discover** in the list, use **Ctrl+D** to delete
Click **OK** on the Delete Payment Method message box

Close the Payment Method List

CUSTOMIZE REPORT PREFERENCES

The report format used in one company may not be appropriate for all companies that use QuickBooks DT. The preferences selected in QuickBooks DT are only for the current company. In Chapters 2-4, report preferences were changed for Your Name's Tech Services, but those changes have no effect on Your Name's Sierra Sports. The header/footer for reports in Your Name's Sierra Sports must be customized to eliminate the printing of the date prepared, time prepared, and report basis as part of a report heading. (As in earlier chapters, check with your instructor to see if you should do this.)

> **MEMO**
> **DATE:** January 1, 2018
>
> Before recording any transactions or preparing any reports, customize the report format by removing the date prepared, time prepared, and report basis from report headings.

 Customize the preferences as indicated in the memo

> Click **Edit**, click **Preferences**, click **Reports and Graphs**
> Click the **Company Preferences** tab, click the **Format** button
> Click the **Header/Footer** tab
> Click **Date Prepared**, **Time Prepared**, and **Report Basis** to deselect

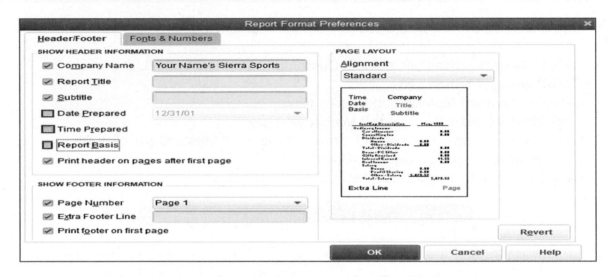

> Click **OK** to save the change; click **OK** to close **Preferences**

CUSTOMIZE BUSINESS FORMS

In QuickBooks DT it is possible to customize the business forms used in recording transactions. Forms that may be customized include Credit Memo, Estimate, Invoice, Purchase Order, Sales Order, Sales Receipt, Statement, and Donation. In addition to customizing the forms within QuickBooks DT, Intuit allows users to download templates of forms without charge by accessing the Forms/Intuit Community. To do this, click the Lists menu, click Templates, click the Templates button, and click Download Templates.

In earlier chapters some student names included as part of the company name may not have printed on the same line as the company name. To provide more room for the company title, QuickBooks DT's Layout Designer must be used. Some business forms may be changed directly within the form, while others need to have the form duplicated. When you access an invoice, for example, QuickBooks DT uses a ready-made form. This is called a *template*. To make changes to an invoice, you must first duplicate the template and then make changes to it.

> **MEMO**
> **DATE:** January 1, 2018
>
> Customize the forms for Sales Receipt, Credit Memo, Custom Sales Order, and the template used for Product Invoices.

 Customize the forms listed in the Memo

Click the **Create Sales Receipts** icon to open a sales receipt
Click the **Formatting** tab in the Sales Receipt Icon bar

Click the **Customize Data Layout** icon
- Look at the tabs for Header, Columns, Footer, and Print. Each tab has selections that you may select to indicate what is shown on the form when it is displayed on the screen or when it is printed.

Click in the Default Title text box for Sales Receipt, highlight and delete the words Sales Receipt, key in **SALES RECEIPT**
Click the **Layout Designer** button at the bottom of the Additional Customization screen
- If you get a Layout Designer Message regarding overlapping fields, click **Do not display this message in the future**, and then click **OK**.

Click the **Layout Designer** button at the bottom of the Additional Customization screen
Point to one of the black squares (sizing handles) on the left border of the frame around the words SALES RECEIPT
When the cursor turns into a double arrow, hold the primary (left) mouse button and drag until the size of the frame begins at **5 ½** on the ruler bar

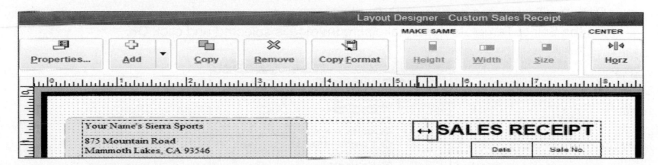

Click in the text box for **Your Name's Sierra Sports**
Drag the right border of the frame until it is a **5 ¼** on the ruler bar

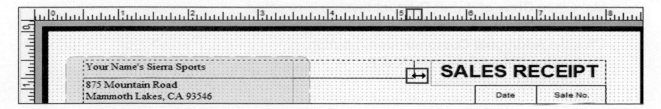

Click **OK** on Layout Designer; click **OK** on the Additional Customization screen
Close the **Enter Sales Receipts** screen
Repeat the steps to customize the **Credit Memo**

- The Default Title should be in all capital letters, and the company name and form names should be resized.

Click **Lists** on the menu bar, click **Templates**

- A template is a predesigned form and defines what is shown, determines the structure, and contains the visual elements on the form.
- *Note:* As you scroll through the Template list, you will see that the Custom Credit Memo, Custom Sales Receipt, and Custom Sales Order are on the list.

Click **Custom Sales Order**, click the **Templates** button, click **Edit template**

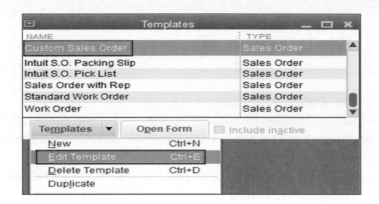

Click the **Additional Customization...** button
Change the title to **SALES ORDER**
Click **Layout Designer** and resize the text boxes for Your Name's Sierra Sports and SALES
    ORDER as instructed for the SALES RECEIPT
Scroll through the Template List, click **Intuit Product Invoice** on the Templates List

- The Intuit Product Invoice is designed for Intuit preprinted forms. To customize the invoice, a duplicate copy of the Intuit Product Invoice must be made. The original template may <u>not</u> be customized.

Click the **Templates** button, click **Duplicate**
On the Select Template Type make sure **Invoice** is selected and click **OK**

Make sure **Copy of: Intuit Product Invoice** is selected
Click the **Templates** button, click **Edit Template**
Click the **Additional Customization...** button
Change the Default Title to **INVOICE**
Click the tab for **Columns**

- Even though you made a copy of the Product Invoice, QuickBooks DT sometimes changes the order of the columns on the Copy of: Intuit Product Invoice.

If necessary, type the correct number into the Order column to make sure that the order matches the following:

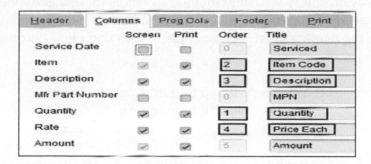

Click the **Basic Customization** button

- Since the current date of your computer will not match the text, all your invoices will be marked Past Due. You can remove this from your printed Invoice but not from the screen.
- Note: this can only be done on the duplicate of the Invoice. The original Invoice template, cannot be customized.

Click **Print Past Due Stamp**

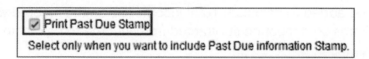

- When the invoice is on the screen, you will be able to turn the PAST DUE stamp on or off for printing by clicking either Turn On or Turn Off.

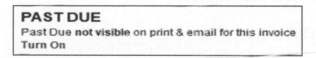

Click the **Layout Designer** button

- If you get the Layout Designer message, click **OK**; and, then, click the Layout Designer button again.

Change the layout as instructed for SALES RECEIPTS

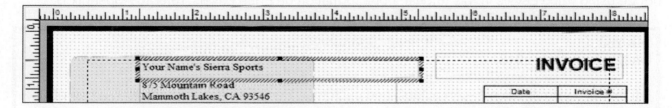

Click **OK** until you return to the Template List

- If you go back to the Additional Customization and then the Basic Customization screens, click **OK** on each screen.

Close the Template List

INVENTORY

When your company sells inventory items, QuickBooks DT keeps track of each inventory item, the number of items on hand, and the value of the items. Unless you use the Enterprise version of QuickBooks DT, the only inventory valuation method available for use is Average Cost. Average Cost adds the cost of all the inventory items together, divides by the total number of items on hand, and the result is the average cost. For example, if your company purchased and sold widgets:

<blockquote>

50 widgets cost $ 5 to purchase   = $250

50 widgets cost $10 to purchase   = $500

Total value   = $750

$750 total value / 100 widgets = $7.50 average cost

</blockquote>

When inventory items are purchased to have on hand for resale, QuickBooks DT shows the average cost of the item in the Inventory Asset account. When the item is sold, the average cost of the item is removed behind the scenes from Inventory Asset by a credit and transferred to Cost of Goods Sold by a debit.

When an item is sold, income is earned. The amount of income earned will be different from the average cost of the item. On the Profit & Loss Statement all the income earned from different revenue accounts will be added to calculate Total Income. Since the income was earned by selling items, the cost of the items sold must be subtracted from income to calculate gross profit.

On the Profit & Loss report, the total of Cost of Goods Sold is calculated as: Cost of Goods Sold – Merchandise Purchases Discounts = Net Cost of Goods Sold. The Net Cost of Goods Sold is subtracted from Total Income to determine the Gross Profit. Expenses are subtracted from Gross Profit to determine the Net Income or Net Loss.

ENTER SALE ON ACCOUNT

Because QuickBooks DT operates on a business form premise, a sale on account is entered via an invoice. When you sell merchandise on account, you prepare an invoice including sales tax and payment terms and QuickBooks DT records the transaction in the Journal and updates the customer's account automatically. QuickBooks DT allows you to set up different price levels for customers. Since our small company has not established sales prices for each item it sells, we will not be using Price Levels in this tutorial. For information on Price Levels, refer to Appendix B.

<blockquote>

MEMO

DATE: January 2, 2018

Bill the following: Invoice 1—An established customer, Benjamin Asher, purchased a pair of after-ski boots for $75.00 on account. Terms are Net 15.

</blockquote>

  Record the sale on account shown in the transaction above.

Access a blank invoice as previously instructed in Chapter 2

To remove the customer's history on the invoice, click the **Hide history** tab
- If you hide the history and the invoice becomes wider, resize by pointing to the right edge of the invoice until you get a double arrow, and then hold down the primary mouse button and drag to the left.

Click the drop-down list arrow next to **CUSTOMER:JOB**, click **Asher, Benjamin**

TEMPLATE is **Copy of: Intuit Product Invoice**
- QuickBooks DT does not allow you to permanently change the default invoice. It should remember to use the same invoice if you enter several invoices at a time, but it may revert back to the default invoice the next time you enter an invoice.
- Notice the change in the format when using a product invoice rather than a service invoice.
- The PAST DUE stamp is not shown in the screen shots.

Tab to **Date** and enter the date of **01/02/2018**

Invoice **1** should be showing in the **Invoice #** box

There is no PO Number to record, **Terms** should be indicated as **Net 15**

Tab to or click **QUANTITY**, type **1**
- The quantity is 1 because you are billing for one pair of after-ski boots.

Click the drop-down list arrow next to **ITEM CODE**
- Refer to the memo above and the Item list for appropriate billing information.

Click **Boots** to bill for one pair of after-ski boots
- The Description **After Ski Boots and Shoes** is automatically inserted.

Once the ITEM CODE has been entered (Boots), an icon appears in the Quantity column

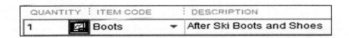

Click on the icon to see the current availability of Boots in stock

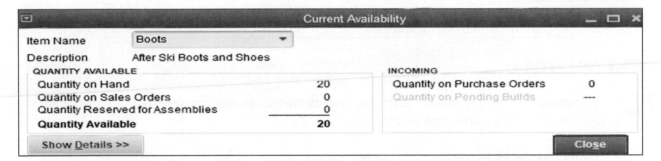

Click **Close** on the Current Availability screen

Tab to or click **PRICE EACH**

Type in the amount of the after-ski boots **75**
- Because the price on ski boots differs with each style, QuickBooks DT a sales price has not been entered for the item. It must be inserted during the invoice preparation. If you chose to set up separate sales items for each type of ski boot, sales prices could be and should be assigned. In addition, different price levels could be designated for the item.

Click in the drop-down list arrow for **CUSTOMER MESSAGE**
- If you get a dialog box regarding Price Levels, click **Do not display this message in the future**, and click **OK**. (Information about Price Levels is in Appendix B.)

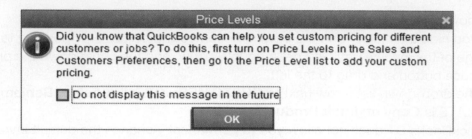

- QuickBooks DT will automatically calculate the total in the **AMOUNT** column.
- Because this is a taxable item, QuickBooks DT inserts the word **Tax** in the **TAX** column. Click the message **Thank you for your business.**
- Notice that QuickBooks DT automatically calculates the tax for the invoice and adds it to the invoice total.

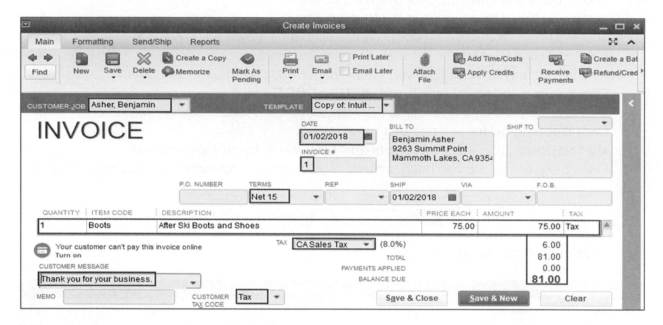

PRINT AN INVOICE

 With Invoice 1 on the screen, print the invoice with lines around each field immediately after entering the corrected information

Follow the instructions given previously for printing invoices

- If you get a message regarding printing Shipping Labels, click the **Do not display this message in the future** checkbox, click **OK**. As a note, the printing labels feature allows you to print a sheet of labels on a standard printer. It also allows you to print a single label when using a Zebra-compatible continuous feed printer. A Zebra printer is a small desktop printer that is designed for label, wristband, receipt, or ticket printing.
- When you click print, the invoice is saved. Because the date of your computer is not January 2, 2018, you may find that your invoice is marked PAST DUE. Disregard this notice. It will not be shown in the text.

Make sure that the check box for **Do not print lines around each field** does **not** have a check mark; if it does, click the box to remove the check mark. This will print lines around data in the invoice.

☐ Do not print lines around each field.

- If you print to a pdf file, save the document as **1-Your Name Inv 1 Asher Ch5**. When finished printing, click **Save & Close**

ANALYZE INVOICE IN JOURNAL

As learned previously, QuickBooks DT records all transactions in the Journal. When recording sales in a merchandising business, QuickBooks DT will not only debit Accounts Receivable and credit Sales, it will also debit Cost of Goods Sold, credit Inventory Asset, debit Sales Discounts (if a discount was used), and credit Sales Tax Payable. This is important because it allows QuickBooks DT to keep an accurate record of inventory on hand, to calculate the Cost of Goods Sold, keep track of sales discounts used, and record the liability for sales taxes.

 Prepare the Journal for January 1-2, 2018 as previously instructed and analyze the entry for Invoice 1

Click the **Do not display this message in the future** on the Collapsing and Expanding Transactions dialog box, then click **OK**
Click the **Expand** button
Enter the dates **From 01/01/18** and **To 01/02/18**, press **Tab**

Your Name's Sierra Sports
Journal
January 1 - 2, 2018

Trans #	Type	Date	Num	Adj	Name	Memo	Account	Debit	Credit
48	Invoice	01/02/2018	1		Asher, Benjamin		1200 - Accounts Receivable	81.00	
					Asher, Benjamin	After Ski Boots and Shoes	4011 - Clothing & Accessory Sales		75.00
					Asher, Benjamin	After Ski Boots and Shoes	1120 - Inventory Asset		30.00
					Asher, Benjamin	After Ski Boots and Shoes	5000 - Cost of Goods Sold	30.00	
					State Board of Equ...	CA Sales Tax	2200 - Sales Tax Payable		6.00
								111.00	111.00
TOTAL								**111.00**	**111.00**

- Note the $81.00 debit to Accounts Receivable is for the total amount of the invoice. This amount is matched with corresponding credits to Clothing & Accessory Sales for $75.00 (the amount of the sale) and to Sales Tax Payable for $6.00 (the sales tax collected).
- There is also a debit to Cost of Goods Sold for $30.00 (the average cost of the item) and credits to Inventory Asset for $30.00 (the average cost of the item). Since you no longer have the item available for sale, this removes it from the inventory on hand and places the value into the cost of goods sold.
- Because QuickBooks DT removes the average cost of the asset from Inventory Assets and puts it into Cost of Goods Sold, the Total of the transaction recorded for Invoice 1 includes this and becomes $111.00 not $81.00.
Close the Journal without printing
- If you get a Memorize Report dialog box, click **Do not display this message in the future**; and then, click **No**.

INVENTORY ASSETS, COST OF GOODS SOLD, SALES TAX LIABILITY

The following illustrates the types of accounts and calculations used in the Journal for an invoice entered for the sale of a pair of after ski boots:

Sales: The amount for which an inventory item is sold is entered into the revenue account. The pair of after ski boots was sold for $75 and is recorded as a credit to increase income.

Inventory Assets: When a merchandise item is on hand it is an asset. QuickBooks DT uses Inventory Asset as the account. To reduce an asset, you credit the account for the value of the item. QuickBooks DT uses the Average Cost method of inventory valuation. As previously illustrated, the average cost of an item is calculated by dividing the total value of the item by the number of items. If, for example, there are 20 pairs of after ski boots in stock, the Average Cost is calculated:

$$10 \text{ pair cost } \$40 \text{ to purchase} = \$400$$
$$10 \text{ pair cost } \$20 \text{ to purchase} = \underline{\$200}$$
$$\text{Total value} = \qquad\qquad \$600$$

$$\$600 \text{ total value} / 20 \text{ pairs of boots} = \$30 \text{ average cost per pair}$$

Cost of Goods Sold: Is used to keep track of the amount the merchandise cost the company. This amount is deducted from sales to determine the amount of gross profit earned when the merchandise sold. If the pair of after ski boots is sold for $75 and it cost the company $30, the amount of gross profit is $45. (Sales - Cost of Goods Sold = Gross Profit). Since the cost of goods sold will ultimately decrease the revenue, you debit the account.

Sales Tax: When sales tax is collected, it is a liability that is owed to the government. To record the liability, you credit the liability account—Sales Tax Payable.

ENTER TRANSACTIONS WITH MORE THAN ONE SALES ITEM

Frequently, sales to customers will be for more than one item. For example, new bindings are usually purchased along with a new pair of skis or a snowboard. Invoices can be prepared to bill a customer for several items at once.

MEMO
DATE: January 3, 2018

Bill the following: Invoice 2—Every year Dr. Diego Medina gets new ski equipment. Bill him for his equipment purchase for this year: skis, $425; ski bindings, $175; ski boots, $250; and ski poles, $75.

 Record a transaction on account for a sale involving several taxable sales items:

Create an invoice for **Medina, Diego Dr.** as previously instructed
Verify the TEMPLATE as **Copy of: Intuit Product Invoice**
- Since QuickBooks DT does not let you select a specific invoice as the default, you will need to verify that you are using the Copy of: Intuit Product Invoice.
DATE is **01/03/18**; **INVOICE #** is **2**

There is no PO NUMBER; **TERMS** should be indicated as **2% 10 Net 30**
- The terms mean that if Dr. Medina's payment is received within ten days, he will get a two percent discount. Otherwise, the full amount is due in 30 days.

QUANTITY, type **1**

Click the drop-down list arrow for **ITEM CODE**, click **Skis**

Tab to or click **PRICE EACH,** enter **425**, press **Tab**
- Because Dr. Medina is a taxable customer and Skis are a taxable item, sales tax is indicated by **Tax** in the **TAX** column.

Tab to or click the second line for **QUANTITY**, type **1**

Click the drop-down list arrow next to **ITEM CODE**, click **Bindings-Skis**

Tab to or click **PRICE EACH**, enter **175**
- Notice that sales tax is indicated by **Tax** in the **TAX** column.

Repeat the above steps to enter the information for the ski boots and the ski poles and use a quantity of 1 for each item

Click the drop-down list arrow next to **CUSTOMER MESSAGE**

Click **Thank you for your business.**
- QuickBooks DT automatically calculated the tax for the invoice and added it to the invoice total.

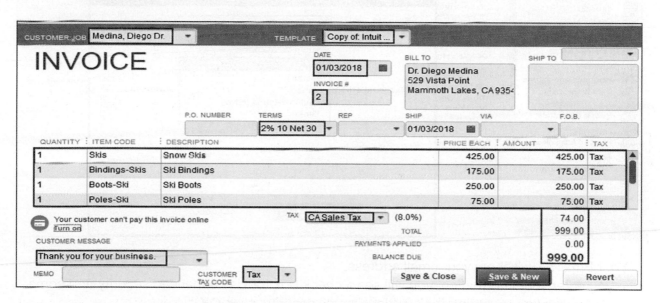

Print the invoice, and the click **Save** icon on the Invoice Main icon bar
- If you print to a pdf file, save the document as **2-Your Name Inv 2 Medina Ch5**.

EMAIL INVOICES (INFORMATION ONLY)

In addition to printing and mailing invoices, QuickBooks DT allows invoices to be sent to customers via email. While this text will not actually require sending invoices by email, it is important to be aware of this time-saving feature. To use the email feature of QuickBooks DT, you must subscribe to one of QuickBooks DT other services. However, QuickBooks DT now supports different Web Mail providers and can be used without charge or any required QuickBooks DT subscriptions. Web mail providers include: Gmail, Hotmail, Yahoo Mail, Outlook, Outlook Express, Windows Mail, or your own SMTP email provider.

You may send each invoice when it is completed, or you may click Email Later and then send the invoices in a batch later. You would enter the Email address information as illustrated in the following steps.

Information only: To email an invoice, you must activate email by clicking **Edit** on the menu bar, clicking **Preferences**, and clicking **Send Forms**
- If you have an active subscription for QuickBooks Connect, Intuit Data Protect, QuickBooks Attached Documents, Intuit Commissions Manager, or QuickBooks Time and Billing Manager, you may use QuickBooks Email.

Since Your Name's Sierra Sports does not have any subscriptions, click **Web Mail**
- If you select Outlook to send email, you do not have to provide more information.

Click the **Add** button to create your Email Id

On the Add Email Info dialog box, enter your Email ID

Click the drop-down list arrow for Email Provider, click the one you use

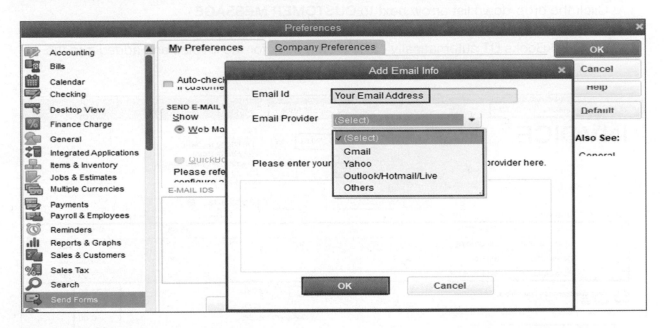

- Your Email ID will show your email address.

Once you enter your information, you will see a check box for Use enhanced security and some other information regarding the additional email security, click **OK**

You will now be prompted to sign in to your Intuit Account

Enter your Intuit Account Email or user ID and Password, click **Sign In**

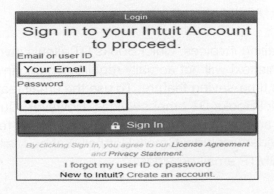

If you want Internet Explorer to remember your password, click **Yes** on the AutoComplete Passwords message

Select an option for verification of your account, then click **Continue**

Enter the six-digit code you received in in your email, click **Continue**

You may add your current mobile number to the new screen and click Continue, or you may click Skip for now

On the Webmail Authorization screen, verify your email address or telephone number, click **Next**

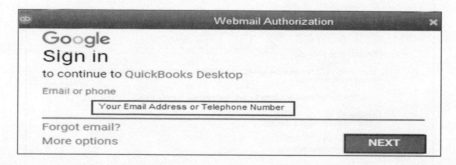

On the Welcome screen, enter your **Password**, then click **Next**

When you have successfully completed the Webmail Authorization, you click **Allow** to let QuickBooks DT read, send, delete, and manage your email

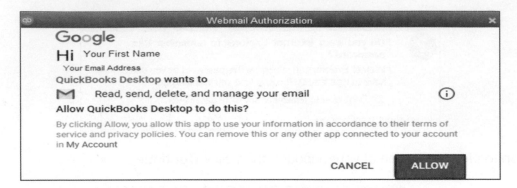

Click **OK** to close the Preferences screen

With the invoice for Dr. Medina showing on the Create Invoices screen, click the **Email** icon

Since Dr. Medina does not have an email address, enter your Email address, click **OK**

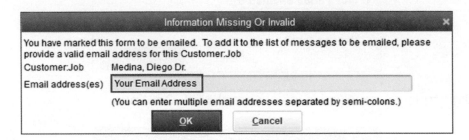

A Send Invoice screen will appear containing information for:

    FROM: Your Email address.

    TO: The email address of your customer. (Your email is used in the example.)

    ATTACH: Shows that Inv. 2 will be attached to the message as a PDF file.

    TEMPLATE: Basic Invoice

    SUBJECT: Invoice 2 from Your Name's Sierra Sports.

    The Email Text is prewritten but may be changed.

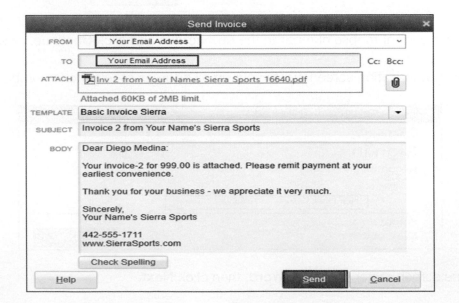

Click **Send**

When the email has been sent, you will get a QuickBooks DT Information box, click **OK**

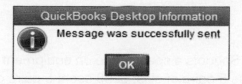

Using Gmail, this is what your email will look like

* Note the attachment for the invoice.

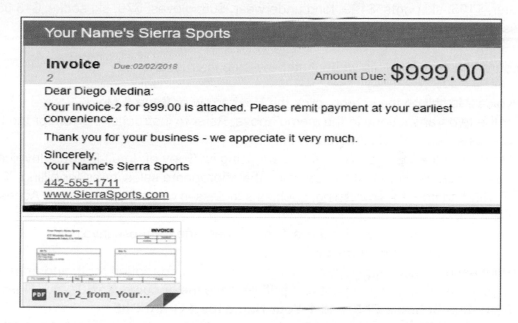

If you did not send each invoice individually, you may send a batch

To send a batch, you would click the **File** menu, click **Send** Forms

Each invoice should be marked automatically

* If you want to remove an invoice, click the marked check box to deselect the invoice. Then, click the invoice you want to remove to select it. Click the **Remove** button.

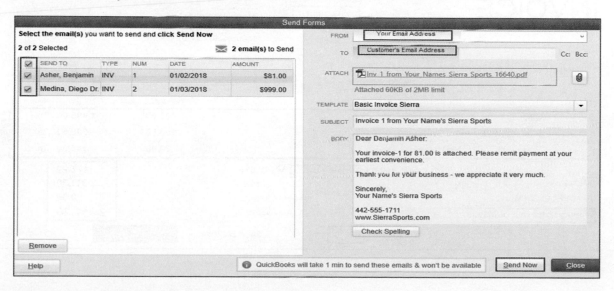

When ready to send the invoices, click **Send Now**

PREPARE INVOICES WITHOUT INSTRUCTIONS

> **MEMO**
>
> **DATE:** January 3, 2018
>
> Invoice 3—We give Mountain Schools a special rate on equipment and clothing for the ski team. This year the school purchases 5 pairs of skis, $299 each; 5 pairs of ski bindings, $100 each; and 5 sets of ski poles, $29 each. Terms 2/10 Net 30.
>
> Invoice 4—Helen Grant purchased a new ski outfit. Quantity is 1 for all items: parka, $249; hat, $25; sweater, $125; ski pants, $129; long underwear, $68; gloves, $79; ski socks, $15.95; sunglasses, $89.95; and boot carrier, $2.95. Terms are Net 15.

 Prepare and print invoices without step-by-step instructions.

If Invoice 2 is still on the screen, click the **Next** arrow or **Save & New**
Enter the two transactions in the memo above. Refer to instructions given for the two previous transactions entered.

- Make sure the TEMPLATE that you are using is: Copy of: Intuit Product Invoice.
- Always use the Item List to determine the appropriate sales items for billing. If you do not find an item for something, such as sunglasses or boot carriers, use Accessories for the item.
- Use *"Thank you for your business."* as the message for these invoices.
- If you make an error, correct it.
- Print each invoice immediately after you enter the information for it, and print lines around each field. If you print to a pdf file, save the document as **3-Your Name Inv 3 Mountain Schools Ch5**, and **4-Your Name Inv 4 Grant Ch5**.
- If you get a Check Spelling on Form message for Snowboard, click **Ignore All**.
- Click **Save & Close** after Invoice 4 has been entered and printed.

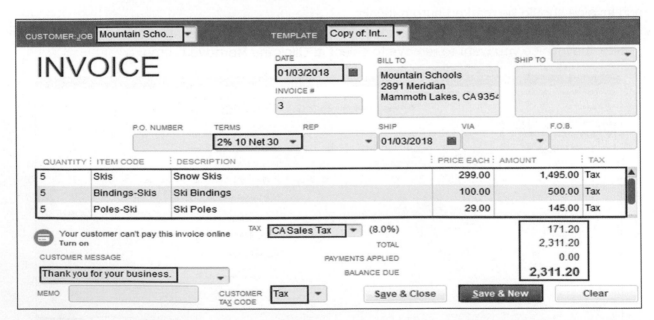

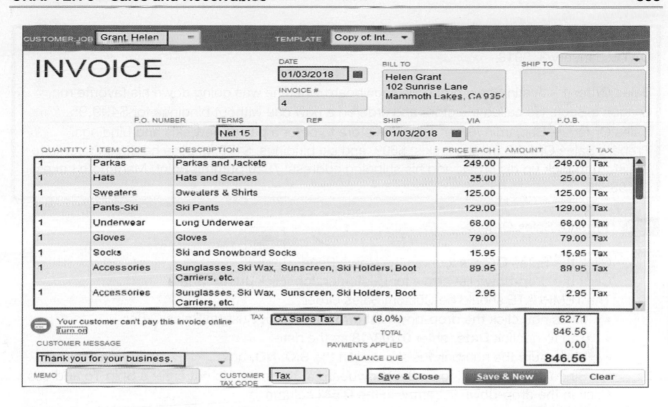

ENTER SALES ORDERS

Sales orders help you manage the sale of the products your customers order. Using sales orders is optional and must be selected as a Preference. Typically, when a customer places an order, a sales order is filled out with the customer information and the items ordered. The sales order is fulfilled when you get the products to your customer. Once the sales order is fulfilled, you create an invoice based on your sales order.

When you create and fill out a sales order, you have not recorded the sale—you've only recorded the information you need to fulfill the order. The sale is recorded only after you create an invoice. For example, items you sell are not deducted from inventory until you create an invoice based on the sales order.

When Your Name's Sierra Sports receives a telephone order, a sales order is prepared. When the customer comes to the store to pick up the merchandise or when the merchandise is shipped, an invoice is created from the Sales Order.

When a customer is added to the Customer List and a complete setup is performed, you click on the Payment Settings tab and enter the credit limit amount in the Credit Limit field. If a transaction is entered that exceeds the credit limit, a dialog box appears with information regarding the transaction amount and the credit limit for a customer. To override the credit limit, click OK on the dialog box. This does not change the credit limit for the customer.

MEMO

DATE: January 3, 2018

Sales Order 1—Justin Shaw broke his snowboard when he was going down his favorite run, Dragon's Back. He called the store and ordered a new one without bindings for $499.95.

Sales Order 2—Benjamin Asher called the store to order a pair of new skis and bindings. Prepare Sales Order 2 for snow skis, $599, and ski bindings, $179. In case he doesn't come to the store to pick up his order, add his shipping address: 7620 Summit Point, Mammoth Lakes, CA 93546.

    Prepare Sales Orders

Click the **Sales Orders** icon on the Home Page
Click the drop-down list arrow for Customer:Job, click **Justin Shaw**
The TEMPLATE should be Custom Sales Order

- If it is not, click the drop-down list arrow and click Custom Sales Order.
- Tab to or click **Date**, enter **01/03/18** as the date.
- Make sure the number **1** is showing in the **S.O. NO.** box.
- Since Justin is picking up the snowboard at the store, do not enter a Ship To address.

Click in the drop-down list arrow in the **ITEM** column
Click **Snowboard**, press Tab until you get to the **ORDERED** column
Enter **1** for **ORDERED**, press Tab; enter the **RATE** of **499.95**, press Tab

- If you get a message regarding Price Levels, click **Do not display this message in the future**, then click **OK**.

Click the drop-down list arrow for **CUSTOMER MESSAGE**, click **Thank you for your business.**

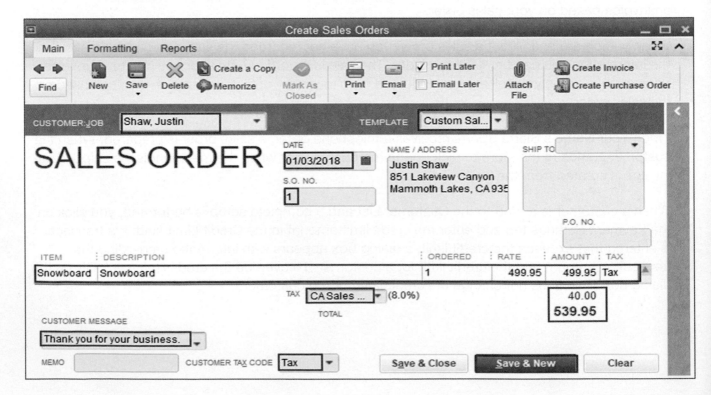

Click **Print** and print the Sales Order
- Verify that the check box for Do <u>not</u> print lines is not marked. You will now get lines to print on the Sales Orders.
- If you print to a pdf file, save the document as **5-Your Name SO 1 Shaw Ch5**.
- If you get a Check Spelling on Form message for Snowboard, always click **Ignore All**.
- If you get a message regarding Shipping Labels, click **Do not display this message in the future** and then, click **OK**.
- After printing the Sales Order, notice the addition of the Invoiced and Clsd columns.

Click **Save & New**
- If you get a Recording Transaction message, click **Yes**.

Prepare Sales Order 2 for Benjamin Asher as previously instructed
Add the Ship To address
Click the drop-down list arrow for **Ship To**
Click <**Add New**>
The Address Name **Ship To 1** should appear automatically
Tab to **Address**
Key **Benjamin Asher**, press **Enter**; key **7620 Summit Point**, press **Tab**
City is **Mammoth Lakes**, press **Tab**; State is **CA**, press **Tab**; Zip Code is **93546**
- You do not need to include information for Country/Region or Note.
- Leave the check marks in **Show this window again when address is incomplete or unclear** and in **Default shipping address**.

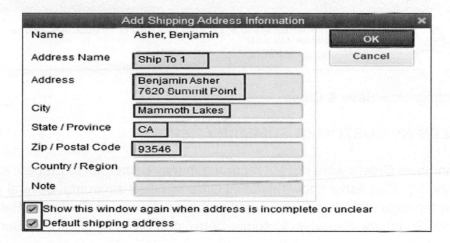

Click **OK**
Complete Sales Order 2 as previously instructed

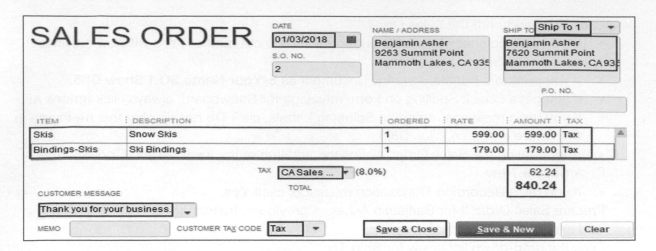

Print the Sales Order

- If you print to a pdf file, save the document as **6-Your Name SO 2 Asher Ch5**.

Since this transaction puts Benjamin over his established credit limit, a Recording Transaction message appears

- If you click **No**, you are returned to the sales order to make changes.
- If you click **Yes**, the sales order will be printed.

Click **Yes** to exceed the credit limit go to the Print One Sales Order screen

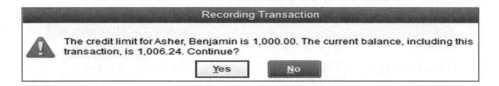

After printing, click **Save & Close**

PREPARE SALES BY CUSTOMER SUMMARY REPORT

To prove that the Sales Orders were not yet recorded, it may be helpful to prepare a report to see if either Justin Shaw or Ben Asher show the Sales Orders in their accounts. Several reports would prove this. Using the date of 01/03/18, you could prepare a Journal, a Customer Balance Detail, a Customer Balance Summary, Sales by Customer Detail, or a Sales by Customer Summary, among others.

 Prepare a Sales by Customer Summary report

Click **Reports** on the Menu bar, point to **Sales**, click **Sales by Customer Summary**
Enter the dates From: **01/03/18** and To: **01/03/18**, and press Tab to generate the report

Your Name's Sierra Sports
Sales by Customer Summary
January 3, 2018

		Jan 3, 18
Grant, Helen	▶	783.85 ◀
Medina, Diego Dr.		925.00
Mountain Schools		2,140.00
TOTAL		**3,848.85**

- Because the Sales Orders were not recorded as a sale, you will not see Justin Shaw or Ben Asher in the report.
Close the report without printing

PREPARE OPEN SALES ORDERS BY CUSTOMER REPORT

To see open sales orders, it is helpful to prepare the Open Sales Orders by Customer report. This report will show the customer's name. It will also show the date, num, amount, and open balance of the sales order. Once an Invoice is prepared for the Sales Order, it will no longer be shown in this report.

 Prepare an Open Sales Orders by Customer report

Click **Reports** on the Menu bar, point to **Sales**, click **Open Sales Order by Customer Summary**
Make sure the Dates are for **All**, press Tab to generate the report

Your Name's Sierra Sports
Open Sales Orders by Customer
All Transactions

Type	Date	Num	Memo	Amount	Open Balance
Asher, Benjamin					
Sales Order	01/03/2018	2		840.24	840.24 ◀
Total Asher, Benjamin				840.24	840.24
Shaw, Justin					
Sales Order	01/03/2018	1		539.95	539.95
Total Shaw, Justin				539.95	539.95
TOTAL				**1,380.19**	**1,380.19**

Print the report in Portrait orientation following instructions previously provided
- If you print to a pdf file, save the document as **7-Your Name Open SO by Cust Ch5**.
Close the report after printing

CREATE INVOICES FOR SALES ORDERS

When a sales order is filled, shipped, or picked up at the store, an invoice is created. Creating an invoice enters the sale in the Journal, decreases inventory on hand, and increases accounts receivable and sales.

<u>MEMO</u>

DATE: January 4, 2018

Create the following invoices from Sales Orders 1 and 2:

Invoice 5—Justin Shaw picked up his new snowboard: Terms 1% 10 Net 30.

Invoice 6—Benjamin Asher came into the store to pick up his new skis and bindings. He added a ski carrier for $10.99 to his purchase. Payment Terms 1% 10 Net 30. (Include the additional purchase on Invoice.)

 Create Invoices from Sales Orders 1 and 2

> Click the **Sales Orders** icon and click **Previous** until the Sales Order 1 is shown
> Click **Create Invoice** on the Create Sales Orders Icon bar

> Make sure **Create invoice for all of the sales order(s).** is selected, click **OK**

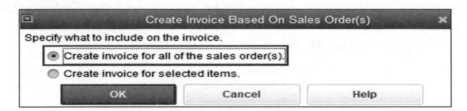

- Invoice 5 appears on the screen. The template used is Custom S. O. Invoice.

Customize the form to allow room for your name and to print the default title as **INVOICE**:
> Click **Formatting** on the Create Invoices Icon bar
> Click **Customize Data Layout**
> Key in **INVOICE** for the Default Title
> Click the **Basic Customization** button
> Click **Print Past Due Stamp** to mark
>> - This will allow you to turn off the printing of PAST DUE on Sales Order Invoices.
> Click **Layout Designer**
>> - If you get the message regarding Layout Designer, click **OK**; click Layout Designer again; and then resize.

Resize INVOICE to begin at **5 ½"** and Your Name's Sierra Sports to end at **5 ¼"**

Click **OK** to close Layout Designer, and then click **OK** on Additional Customization

- Notice the columns for Ordered, Prev. Invoiced, Backordered, and Invoiced.
- The Terms of 1% 10 Net 30 automatically appear because they are the standard terms for Justin Shaw.

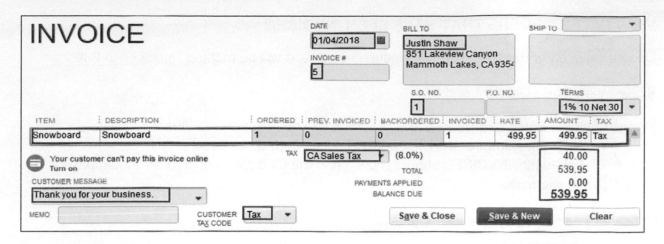

Print the invoice
- If you print to a pdf file, save the document as **8-Your Name SO Inv 5 Shaw Ch5**.

Click **Ignore All** on the Check Spelling on Form for Snowboard

Close Create Invoices

Repeat the steps listed previously to create the Invoice for Benjamin Asher

When Invoice 6 appears on the screen, add the additional item:

> Click the drop-down list arrow for ITEM, select **Accessories**, and enter **1** in the INVOICED COLUMN, and **10.99** in the RATE column

- If you get a message box for Custom Pricing, click **No**.

Make sure you use **Terms** of **1% 10 Net 30**

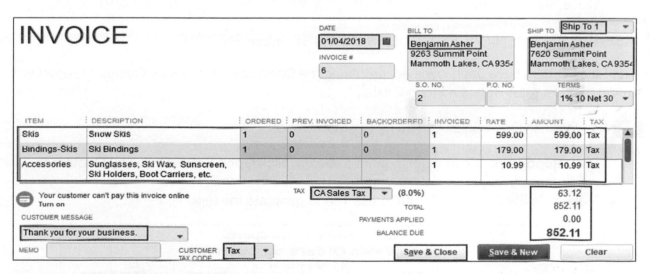

Print the invoice
- If you print to a pdf file, save the document as **9-Your Name SO Inv 6 Asher Ch5**.

Click **Yes** on the Recording Transaction message to exceed the credit limit

- If you get a Recording Transaction message about the sales order being linked to the invoice, click **Yes**.

Click **No** on the Information Changed message to change the Terms for Benjamin

Close Create Invoices

VIEW SALES ORDERS THAT HAVE BEEN INVOICED

Once a sales order has been used to create an invoice, it will be marked "Invoiced in Full"

     View Sales Orders 1 and 2

Click the **Sales Orders** icon and **Previous** to view Sales Orders 1 and 2
- Note the stamped "INVOICED IN FULL" on both Sales Orders.
- For Justin, INVOICED should show 1 and the Clsd (Closed) column should have a check mark.

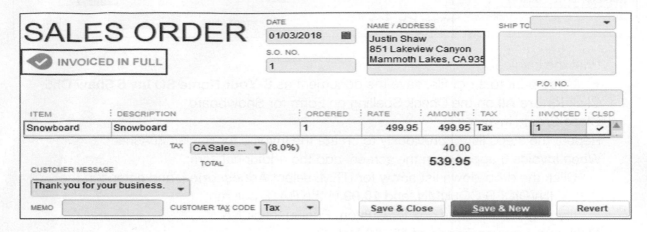

Close Sales Orders

PREPARE AN OPEN SALES ORDERS BY CUSTOMER REPORT

Once Sales Orders have been invoiced, preparing the Open Sales Orders by Customer report will confirm that the sales orders no longer exist.

     Prepare an Open Sales Orders by Customer report

Click **Reports** on the Menu bar, point to **Sales**, click **Open Sales Order by Customer Summary**
Make sure the Dates are for **All**, press Tab to generate the report

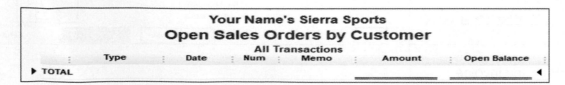

No sales orders are shown
Close the report without printing

ENTER TRANSACTION AND ADD A WORD TO THE DICTIONARY

As was experienced in the last set of transactions, QuickBooks DT has spell check. When the previous invoices were printed, QuickBooks DT's Spell Check identified snowboard as being misspelled. In fact, the word is spelled correctly. It just needs to be added to the QuickBooks DT dictionary. This is done by clicking the Add button when the word is highlighted in spell check.

MEMO
DATE: January 4, 2018

Invoice 7—Angie Waters decided to get a new snowboard, $489.95; snowboard bindings, $159.99; snowboard boots, $249; and a special case to carry her boots, $49.95. Terms are Net 30.

➡️ Prepare Invoice 7 as instructed previously

Make sure to use **Copy of: Intuit Product Invoice** for the Template

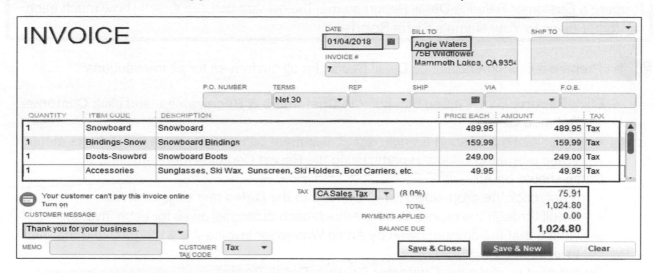

Print the invoice
- If you print to a pdf file, save the document as **10-Your Name Inv 7 Waters Ch5**.

When the **Check Spelling on Form** appears, and the word **Snowboard** is highlighted, click the **Add** button

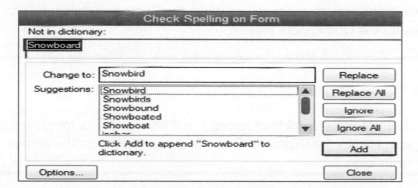

A Recording Transaction message box appears; click **Yes** to exceed the credit limit
After Invoice 7 has been entered and printed click **Save & Close**

ACCOUNTS RECEIVABLE REPORTS

A variety of reports are available regarding accounts receivable. Data regarding customers may be displayed based on account aging, open invoices, collections, customer balances; or they may be itemized according to the sales by customer. Many reports may be printed in a summarized form while other reports provide detailed information.

PREPARE CUSTOMER BALANCE DETAIL REPORT

The Customer Balance Detail Report lists information regarding each customer. The information provided includes the customer name, all invoices with a balance, the date of the invoice, the invoice number, the account used to record the invoice, the amount of each invoice, the balance after each invoice, and the total balance due from each customer.

> **MEMO**
> **DATE:** January 5, 2018
>
> Prepare a Customer Balance Detail Report so that the owners can see exactly how much each customer owes to Your Name's Sierra Sports.

 Prepare a Customer Balance Detail Report for all customers for all transactions:

Click **Reports** on the menu bar, point to **Customers & Receivables**, and click **Customer Balance Detail**
- *Note:* When preparing a single report, it is more convenient to use the Reports menu. When preparing several reports, using the Report Center is more efficient.

Dates should be **All**
- If not, click the drop-down list arrow next to the **Dates** text box, click **All**.
- Scroll through the report. See how much each customer owes for each invoice.
- Notice that the amount owed by Angie Waters for Invoice 7 is $1,024.80 and that her total balance is $1,078.37.

Do not print or close the **Customer Balance Detail Report**

USE QUICKZOOM

QuickZoom is a feature of QuickBooks DT that allows you to view additional information within a report. For example, an invoice may be viewed when the Customer Balance Detail Report is on the screen simply by using the QuickZoom feature.

> **MEMO**
> **DATE:** January 5, 2018
>
> The bookkeeper, Ruth Morgan, could not remember if Invoice 7 was for ski equipment or snowboard equipment. With the Customer Balance Detail Report on the screen, use QuickZoom to view Invoice 7.

 Use QuickZoom in the Customer Balance Detail Report to view Invoice 7

Position the cursor over any part of the information about Invoice 7
- The cursor will turn into a magnifying glass with a letter **Z** inside.

Double-click
- Invoice 7 appears on the screen.
- Check to make sure the four items on the invoice are: Snowboard, Bindings-Snow, Boots-Snowbrd, and Accessories.

With Invoice 7 on the screen, proceed to the next section.

CORRECT AND PRINT INVOICE

QuickBooks DT allows corrections and revisions to an invoice even if the invoice has been printed. The invoice may be corrected by going directly to the original invoice or by accessing the original invoice via the Accounts Receivable Register.

MEMO

DATE: January 5, 2018

While viewing Invoice 7 for Angie Waters in QuickZoom, the bookkeeper, Ruth Morgan, realizes that the snowboard should be $499.95, not the $489.95 that is on the original invoice. Make the correction and reprint the invoice.

 Correct Invoice 7

Click in the **PRICE EACH** column
Change the amount for the snowboard to **499.95**
Press Tab to change the **AMOUNT** calculated for the Snowboard
Print the corrected Invoice 7
- If you print to a pdf file, save the document as **11-Your Name Inv 7 Waters Corrected Ch5**.
Click **Yes** on the Recording Transaction dialog box to record the change to the transaction
A **Recording Transaction** message box appears on the screen regarding the credit limit of $500 for Angie Waters
Click **Yes** to accept the current balance of $1,089.17
When the invoice has been printed, click **Save & Close**
- This closes the invoice and returns you to the Customer Balance Detail Report.

PRINT CUSTOMER BALANCE DETAIL REPORT

When you return to a report after using QuickZoom, any corrections or changes should show in the report.

 Review the correction for Invoice 7, then resize columns, and print the report

- The correction for Invoice 7 should be shown in the report. If it does not show, click the **Refresh** button.
- Notice that the total amount for Invoice 7 is $1,035.60 and that Angie Waters' total balance is $1,089.17.
- As you can see, the Account column does not fully display the account names.
Resize the columns as instructed in Chapter 2 to display the Account names in full as shown below

Your Name's Sierra Sports
Customer Balance Detail
All Transactions

Type	Date	Num	Account	Amount	Balance
Waters, Angie					
Invoice	12/31/2017		1200 · Accounts Receivable	53.57	53.57
Invoice	01/04/2018	7	1200 · Accounts Receivable	1,035.60	1,089.17
Total Waters, Angie				1,089.17	1,089.17

After the columns have been resized, click **Print**

- Verify that **Fit report to one page wide** is not selected.
- If it is selected, click the check box to remove the check mark.

Click **Preview**

- The report will fit on one page wide and the account names will be shown in full.

Click **Close** to close the **Preview**, then click **Print**

- If you print to a pdf file, save the document as **12-Your Name Cust Bal Detail Ch5**.

Your Name's Sierra Sports
Customer Balance Detail
All Transactions

Type	Date	Num	Account	Amount	Balance
Wong, Tamako					
Invoice	12/31/2017		1200 · Accounts Receivable	670.31	670.31
Total Wong, Tamako				670.31	670.31
TOTAL				13,607.86	13,607.86

Partial Report

After the report is printed, close the **Customer Balance Detail Report**

- If you get a Memorize Report dialog box, click **Do not display this message in the future**, and then click **No**.

DISCOUNTS

There are three types of discounts used in QuickBooks DT: Sales Discount, Purchase Discount, and Merchandise Discount. In Chapter 5, Sales Discounts will be used for customer payments. A Sales Discount is used when you give customers a discount for early payment with terms of 2% 10 Net 30 or 1% 10 Net 30. The Sales Discount account is categorized as an Income account. Using a sales discount results in a decrease in income because the company will receive less money for a sale. However, receiving a payment early is a good reason to offer a sales discount.

ADD NEW ITEMS AND ACCOUNTS

To accommodate the changing needs of a business, all QuickBooks DT lists allow you to make changes at any time. New items and accounts may be added in the Item List or Chart of Accounts. They may also be added *"on the fly"* while entering invoice information. The Item List stores information about the items the company sells.

Your Name's Sierra Sports does not use price levels, so it is appropriate to have an item allowing for sales discounts. Sales discounts decrease income and function as a contra account to income (like accumulated depreciation decreasing the value of an asset). Having a discount item allows discounts to be recorded on the sales form. A discount can be a fixed amount or a percentage. A discount is calculated only on the amount shown in the line above it. To allow the entire amount of the invoice to receive the discount, an item for a subtotal will need to be added. When you complete the sales form, the subtotal item will appear before the discount item.

MEMO
DATE: January 5, 2018

Add items for Sales Discounts and Subtotal. Add a new income account, 4050 Sales Discount, to the Chart of Accounts. The description for the account should be Discount on Sales.

 Add new items and accounts

Click the **Items & Services** icon on the QuickBooks DT Home Page
Use the keyboard shortcut **Ctrl + N** to add a new item
Item **TYPE** is **Discount**
Tab to or click **Item Name/Number**, type **Nonprofit Discount**
Tab to or click **Description**, type **10% Discount to Nonprofit Agencies**
Tab to or click **Amount or %**, key in **10%**
- The % sign must be included to differentiate between a $10 discount and a 10% discount.
Click the drop-down list arrow for **Account**
Scroll to the top of the list, and then, click **<Add New>**
Complete the information for a New Account:
Account Type should be **Income**
- If <u>not</u>, click the drop-down list arrow next to the text box for Type. Click **Income**.
- Giving a sales discount to a customer means that your profit for selling an inventory item is less. This will mean that revenue decreases, and this will ultimately decrease the amount of Net Income.
Tab to or click in the **Number** text box, enter the Account Number **4050**
- Your Name's Sierra Sports uses account numbers for all accounts.
- Numbers in the 4000 category are income.
Tab to or click **Account Name**, enter **Sales Discounts**
Tab to or click **Description**, enter **Discount on Sales**

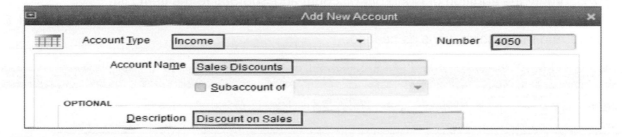

Click **Save & Close** to add the **Sales Discounts** account

Click **OK** to close the **New Account** dialog box, and return to the New Item screen
- At the bottom of the screen you should see the Tax Code as **Tax** and the statement **Discount is applied before sales tax** should be displayed.

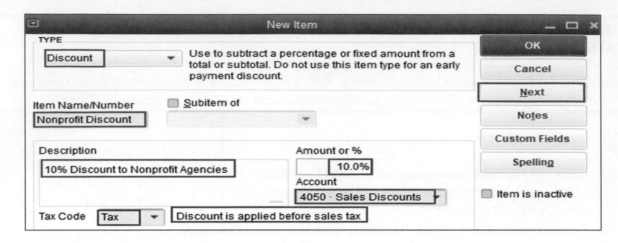

Click **Next** on the **New Item** dialog box

- A discount is calculated only on the line above it on the sales form. To allow the entire amount of the invoice to receive the discount, the subtotal needs to be calculated. Because of this, an item for a subtotal must be added.

Repeat the steps for adding a New Item to add **Subtotal**

TYPE is **Subtotal**, **Item Name/Number** is **Subtotal**, and **Description** is **Subtotal**

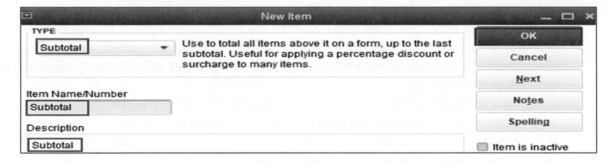

Click **OK** to add the new item and to close the **New Item** screen

- Verify the addition of Nonprofit Discount and Subtotal to the Item List.
- If you find an error, click on the item with the error, use the keyboard shortcut **Ctrl + E**, and make corrections as needed.

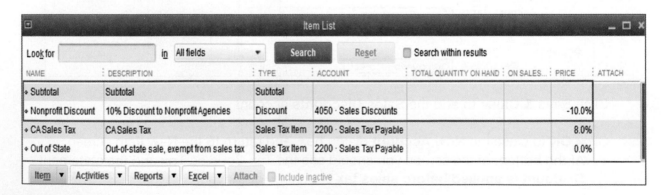

Close the **Item List**

CORRECT INVOICE TO INCLUDE SALES DISCOUNT

Once a new item has been created, it may be used on previously recorded sales forms.

> **MEMO**
> **DATE:** January 6, 2018
>
> Now that the appropriate accounts for sales discounts have been created, use the Accounts Receivable Register to correct Invoice 3 for Mountain Schools to give the schools a 10% discount as a nonprofit organization.

 Correct the invoice to Mountain Schools in the Accounts Receivable Register

Use the keyboard shortcut, **Ctrl + A** to open the Chart of Accounts
In the Chart of Accounts, double-click **Accounts Receivable**
- Double-clicking opens the register.

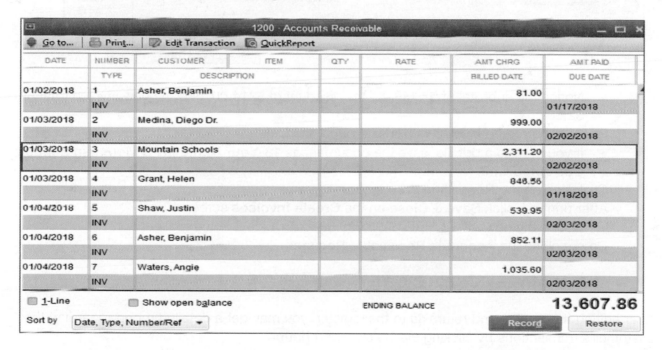

If necessary, scroll through the register until the transaction for **Invoice 3** is on the screen
- **Look** at the **NUMBER/TYPE** column to identify the number of the invoice and the type of transaction.
- On the **NUMBER** line you will see a <u>check number</u> or an <u>invoice number</u>.
- Currently, our Accounts Receivable Register only contains invoices. On the **TYPE** line you will see **INV**. If a payment had been received on account, you would see **PMT** on the Type line.

Click anywhere in the transaction for Invoice 3 to Mountain Schools
Click the **Edit Transaction** button at the top of the register or use the shortcut **Ctrl+E**
- Invoice 3 appears on the screen.

Click in **ITEM CODE** beneath the last item, Poles-Ski
Click the drop-down list arrow for **ITEM CODE**, click **Subtotal**
- You may need to scroll through the Item List until you find Subtotal.

- Remember, to calculate a discount for everything on the invoice, QuickBooks DT must calculate the subtotal for the items on the invoice.

Tab to or click the next blank line in **ITEM CODE**

Click **Nonprofit Discount**

- You may need to scroll through the Item List until you find Nonprofit Discount.

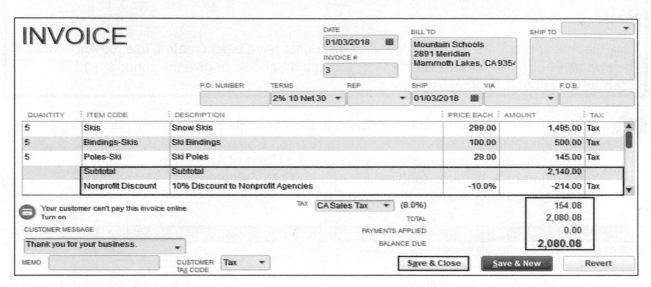

- Notice the subtotal of $2,140.00, the discount of $214.00, and the new invoice total of $2,080.08.

Print the corrected invoice with lines around each field

- If you print to a pdf file, save the document as **13-Your Name Inv 3 Mountain Schools Corrected Ch5**.

Click **Yes** on the **Recording Transaction** screen

After printing, click **Save & Close** on the **Create Invoices** screen

- Notice the new AMT CHRG of $2,080.08 for Invoice 3 in the register.

Do not close the **Accounts Receivable Register**

VIEW AND ANALYZE QUICKREPORT

After editing the invoice and returning to the register, you may get a detailed report regarding the customer's transactions by clicking the QuickReport button.

 Prepare a QuickReport for Invoice 3

With the cursor in Invoice 3, click the **QuickReport** button at the top of the Accounts Receivable register to view the **Mountain Schools** account

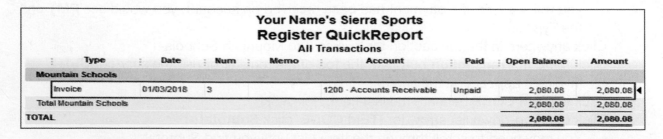

- Notice that the total of Invoice 3 is $2,080.08

Close the **QuickReport** without printing, the **Accounts Receivable Register**, and the **Chart of Accounts**

ADD NEW CUSTOMER WITH SHIPPING ADDRESS

QuickBooks DT allows customers to be added at any time. They may be added to the company records through the Customer List, through Add/Edit Multiple List entries, or they may be added *on the fly* as you create an invoice or sales receipt. When adding *on the fly*, you may choose between Quick Add (used to add only a customer's name) and Set Up (used to add complete information for a customer).

MEMO
DATE: January 8, 2018

Add a new customer: Rec Center, Main Phone: 442-555-5151, Main Email: RecCenter@abc.com, Fax: 442-555-1515, Address Details: 985 Old Mammoth Road, Mammoth Lakes, CA 93546, Credit Limit: 5,000, Terms: 1%10 Net 30, Preferred Delivery Method: None, Tax Code: Tax, Tax Item: CA Sales Tax, there is no opening balance.

 Add a new customer in the Customer Center

Click the **Customers** icon on the icon bar or the **Customers** button in the Customers section of the Home Page

Use the keyboard shortcut **Ctrl + N** to create a new customer

In the **Customer** text box, enter **Rec Center**

- QuickBooks DT will show the current date of your computer as the As of Date even though there is no Opening Balance.

Tab to or click **COMPANY NAME**

Enter **Rec Center** or copy the Customer Name as previously instructed

Tab to or click in the text box for **Main Phone**, enter the telephone number

Tab to or click in the text box for **Main Email**, enter the email address

Tab to or click in the text box for **Fax**, enter the fax number

In the INVOICE/BILL TO section for ADDRESS DETAILS, click at the end of Rec Center, press **Enter**

Key in the address

Click the **Copy>>** button to copy the address to SHIP TO

Verify that the same company address information appears on the Add Shipping Address Information screen, and click **OK**

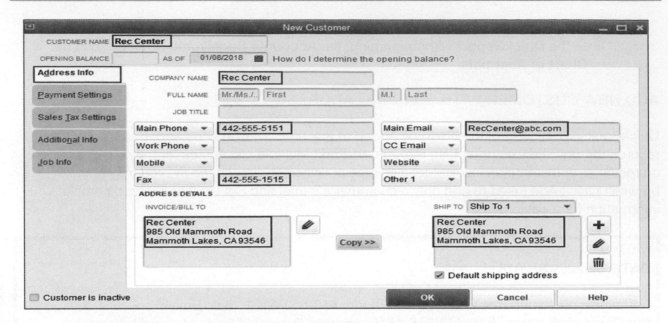

Click the **Payment Settings** tab

Tab to or click in the text box for **CREDIT LIMIT**, enter **5,000**

Click the drop-down list arrow for **PAYMENT TERMS**, click **1% 10 Net 30**

Click the drop-down list arrow for **PREFERRED DELIVERY METHOD**, click **None**

- Note: You may also add An ACCOUNT NUMBER, a PREFERRED PAYMENT METHOD, and CREDIT CARD INFORMATION on this screen. This will be done later in the chapter.

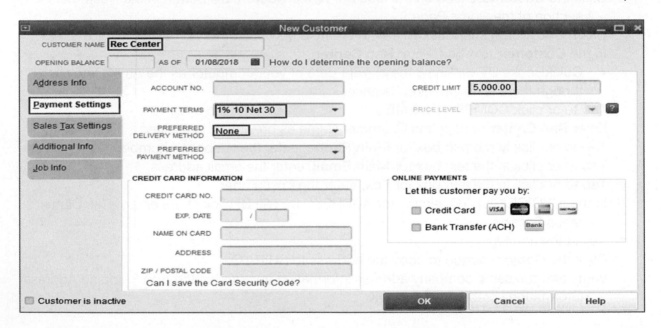

Click the **Sales Tax Settings** tab

Verify that the **TAX CODE** is **Tax** and that the **TAX ITEM** is **CA Sales Tax**

- If not, click the drop-down arrows for each and click on the proper selection.

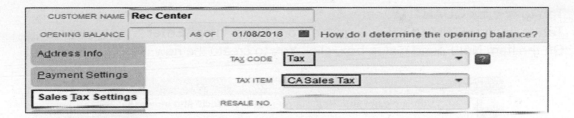

- The Additional Info tab allows you to include information regarding the customer type and sales rep info. In addition, Custom Fields may be created.
- If you itemize customers based on contracted jobs, Job Info will allow you to include information about the jobs being performed.

Click **OK** to complete the addition of Rec Center as a customer

- Verify the addition of Rec Center to the Customer:Job List.

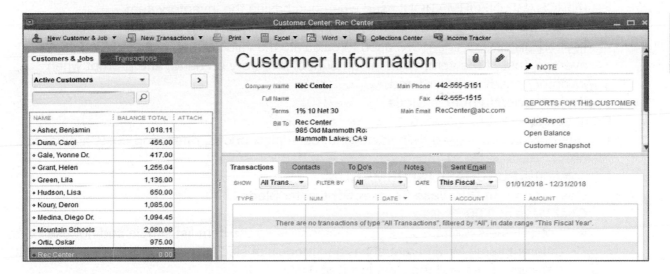

Close the **Customer Center**

RECORD SALE OF NEW ITEM

Once a customer has been added, sales may be recorded for a customer.

> **MEMO**
> **DATE:** January 8, 2018
>
> Record a sale of 5 sleds at $119.99 each, 5 toboggans at $229.95, and 5 helmets at $69.95 each to Rec Center. Because the sale is to a nonprofit organization, include a nonprofit discount.

 Record the sale on account and add three new sales items as indicated in the Memo

Access a blank invoice by using the keyboard shortcut **Ctrl + I**
Enter invoice information for **Rec Center** on the customized invoice copy as previously instructed
Date of the invoice is **01/08/2018**
INVOICE # is **8**

Tab to or click **QUANTITY**, enter **5**

Tab to or click **ITEM CODE**, key in the word **Sleds**, press **Enter**

On the Item Not Found dialog box, click **Yes** to create the new item.

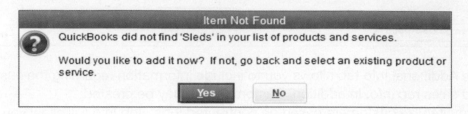

On the **New Item** screen, click **Inventory Part** for **TYPE**

- If necessary, click the drop-down list menu to get a list of choices for **TYPE**.

The Inventory Item is divided into three parts:

- <u>PURCHASE INFORMATION</u>: used when purchasing the inventory item.
- <u>SALES INFORMATION</u>: used when selling the merchandise.
- <u>INVENTORY INFORMATION</u>: used to calculate the value of the item, calculate the average cost of the item, track the amount of inventory on hand, and prompt when inventory needs to be ordered.

The **Item Name/Number** is **Sleds**

Do <u>not</u> enable Unit of Measure

- Unit of Measure is used to indicate what quantities, prices, rates, and costs are based on.

Complete the **PURCHASE INFORMATION**:

Description on Purchase Transactions enter **Sleds**

Cost leave at **0.00**

- Your Name's Sierra Sports has elected to keep the item list simple and not use different items for different styles and models of sleds. Thus, sleds are purchased at different prices and the Cost is left at 0.00.

COGS Account is **5000 - Cost of Goods Sold**

- If 5000 – Cost of Goods Sold is not shown, click the drop-down list arrow and click the account to select it.

Preferred Vendor: leave blank because we do not use the same vendor for this item every time we order it

Complete the **SALES INFORMATION**:

Description on Sales Transactions is **Sleds**

- If Sleds was not inserted at the same time as the Purchase Information Description, enter **Sleds** for the description.

Sales Price leave at **0.00**

- As with the Purchase Information, the Sales Price remains as 0.00.

Tax Code is **Tax** because sales tax is collected on this item

Click the drop-down list arrow for **Income Account**, click **4012 Equipment Sales**

Complete the **INVENTORY INFORMATION**:

Asset Account should be **1120 Inventory Asset**

- If this account is not in the **Asset Account** text box, click the drop-down list arrow, click **1120 Inventory Asset**. This asset account keeps track of the value of the inventory we have on hand.

Tab to **Reorder Point (Min)**, enter **5**

Tab to **Max**, enter **7**

Tab to **On hand**, enter **10**

Tab to or click **Total Value**

- IMPORTANT: QuickBooks DT uses this amount and date to calculate the average cost.
- To calculate the average cost, multiply the number of sleds by their purchase price; and then, add the value of all sleds together. For example, five of the ten sleds were purchased by Your Name's Sierra Sports for $75 each (Total $375). The other five sleds were purchased for $60 each (Total $300) Total value: $375 + $300 = $675.

Total Value of the sleds is **$675**

Tab to **As of**

- The date is very important! A common error in training is to use the computer date—not the date in the text. An incorrect date may cause a change in the value of your inventory, and it is very difficult to correct the date later.

Enter the As of date **01/08/18**

Check your entry with the following screen shot:

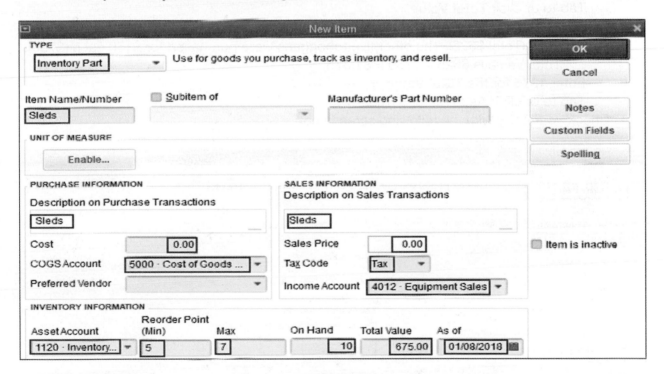

Click **OK** to add Sleds as a sales item and return to Invoice 8

On the invoice, tab to or click **PRICE EACH**, enter **119.99**

Tab to or click the second line in **QUANTITY**, enter **5**

Tab to or click **ITEM CODE**

Click the drop-down list arrow for **ITEM CODE**

- There is no item listed for Toboggans.

Click **<Add New>** at the top of the **Item List**

On the **New Item** screen, click **Inventory Part** for **TYPE**

Tab to or click **Item Name/Number**, enter **Toboggans**

Do not enable Unit of Measure

Complete **PURCHASE INFORMATION**:

    Tab to or click **Description on Purchase Transactions** enter **Toboggans**

    Cost is **0.00**

    COGS Account is **5000 Cost of Goods Sold**

- If 5000 – Cost of Goods Sold is not shown, click the drop-down list arrow and click **5000 Cost of Goods Sold** to select the account.

    Preferred Vendor leave blank

Complete **SALES INFORMATION**:

    Description on Sales Transactions should be **Toboggans**

    Sales Price leave at **0.00**

    Tax Code should be **Tax**

    Click the drop-down list arrow for **Income Account**

    Click **4012 Equipment Sales**

Complete the **INVENTORY INFORMATION**:

    Asset Account should be **1120 Inventory Asset**

    Tab to or click **Reorder Point (Min)**, enter **5**, tab to or click **Max**, enter **7**

    Tab to or click **On Hand**, enter **10**

    Tab to or click **Total Value**

- Five of the ten toboggans were purchased by Your Name's Sierra Sports for $125 each (Total $625). The other five toboggans were purchased for $150 each ($750). Total Value is $625 + $750 = $1,375.

    Enter **1375** for the **Total Value**

    Tab to or click **As of**, enter **01/08/18**

Check your entry with the following screen shot:

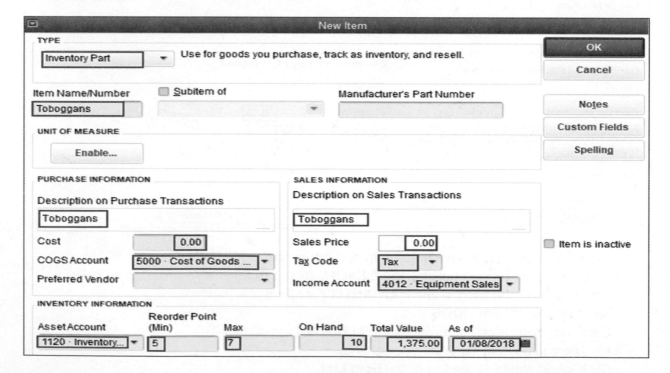

Click **OK** to add Toboggans as a sales item and return to Invoice 8
Enter the Price for the Toboggans of **229.95**
Repeat the steps shown above to add **Helmets** as a sales item
Name, Purchase Description, and Sales Description: **Helmets**
Cost and Sales Price are **0.00**
COGS account is **5000 Cost of Goods Sold**
Income Account is **4011 Clothing & Accessory Sales**
Asset Account is **1120 Inventory Asset**
Enter the **Reorder Point (Min)** of 5, **Max of 30**, and **On Hand 25**
Calculate the Total Value: purchased 10 helmets @ $25 each, purchased 15 helmets @ $30
    each, enter the amount of **Total Value** as of **01/08/2018**

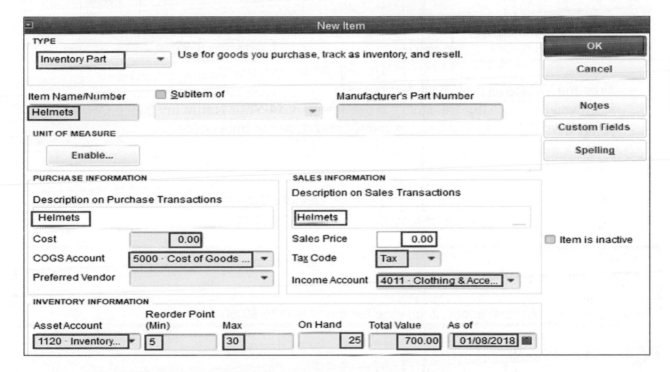

Click **OK**, then, use the information in the Memo to complete the invoice
- Remember that Rec Center is a nonprofit organization and is entitled to a Nonprofit Discount.

The **CUSTOMER MESSAGE** is **Thank you for your business.**

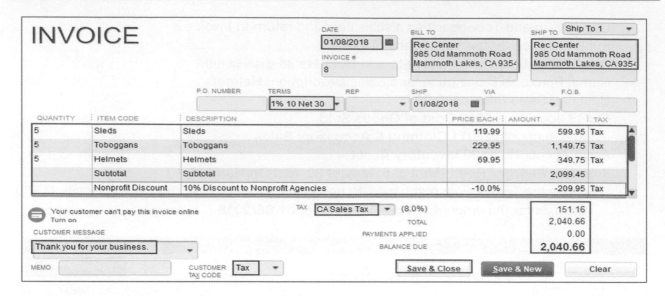

Print the invoice as previously instructed
- If you print to a pdf file, save the document as **14-Your Name Inv 8 Rec Center Ch5**.

Click **Save & Close** to record the invoice and close the transaction

MODIFY CUSTOMER RECORDS

Occasionally information regarding a customer will change. QuickBooks DT allows customer accounts to be modified at any time by editing the Customer List.

MEMO

DATE: January 8, 2018

To update Angie Waters' account, change her credit limit to $2,500.00.

 Edit an account

Use **Ctrl + J** to access the **Customer List**
Double-click **Waters, Angie** on the Customer:Job List.
Click the **Payment Settings** tab
Tab to or click **CREDIT LIMIT**, enter **2500** for the amount
Click **OK** to record the change and exit the information for Angie Waters
Close the **Customer Center**

VOID AND DELETE SALES FORMS

Deleting an invoice or sales receipt completely removes it and any transaction information for it from QuickBooks DT. Make sure you want to remove the invoice before deleting it. Once it is deleted, an invoice cannot be recovered. If you want to correct financial records for an invoice that is no longer viable, it is more appropriate to void the invoice. When an invoice is voided, it remains in the QuickBooks DT system, but QuickBooks DT does not count it. Voiding an invoice should be used only if there have been no payments made on the invoice. If any payment has been received, a Credit Memo would be prepared to record a return.

BATCH DELETE/VOID TRANSACTIONS—READ ONLY

The following demonstration is to be <u>read</u> to gain an understanding of how to perform batch delete/void for transactions. Do **not** do this at part of your work. Your work will continue with the section for **Delete Invoice and Sales Order**.

While QuickBooks DT contains several batch processes, including e-mail, invoice, print, and commented reports. Batch delete/void is a powerful and timesaving feature for QuickBooks DT.

To illustrate the procedures, this section will demonstrate the batch/void transactions for Invoice 5—Justin Shaw and Invoice 6—Benjamin Asher.

Click **Accountant** on the Menu bar
Click **Batch Delete/Void Transactions**

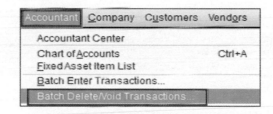

On the Batch Delete/Void Transactions screen, change the following:
    TRANSACTION TYPE: **Invoices**
        Make sure **Show linked transactions** and **Show voided transactions** are marked with a
          check
    CUSTOMER:JOB: **All**
    SHOW TRANSACTIONS BY: **Transaction Date**
    FOR: **Custom**
    FROM: **01/01/2018**
    TO: **01/31/2018**

You will see a listing of Invoices and Linked transactions
Click the transaction for **1/4/2018** for **Shaw, Justin**
- Notice the Transactions linked to the highlighted invoice at the bottom of the screen. It shows Sales Order 1.
- Note the comment: **If you delete or void this invoice, QuickBooks DT will unlink these transactions from it but won't delete or void them.**
- This means that once you void or delete the marked invoice (or other transactions), you must go back and manually void or delete the linked transaction.

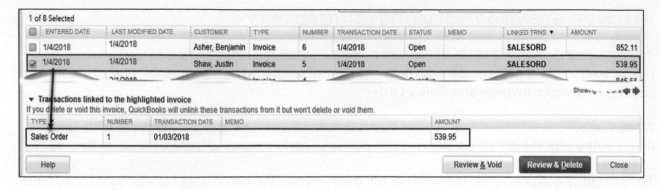

Click the transaction for **1/3/2018** for **Asher, Benjamin**
- Even though the invoices for both Justin Shaw and Benjamin Asher are selected, the Transactions linked to the highlighted invoice at the bottom of the screen changes to show Sales Order 2 for Benjamin Asher because his invoice was the most recently selected.

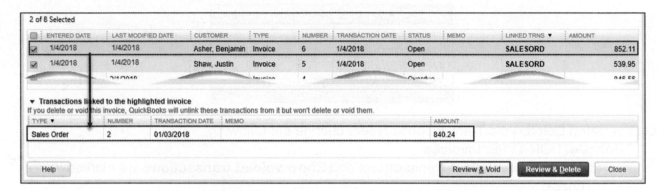

At the bottom of the screen, click the **Review & Void** button

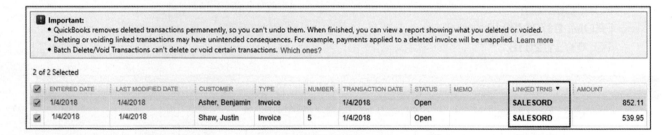

- Notice the column for LINKED TRNS shows SALESORD for both selected invoices.

Click the button for Backup and Void

Click **Yes** on the Void Transaction screen

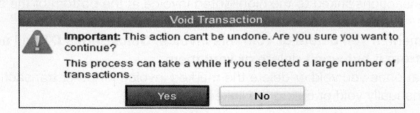

On the Create Backup screen, prepare a Local backup following the same backup procedures you have been using.

- If you decide you have voided an incorrect document, you may restore this backup.

Click the **View Voided Transactions Summary** on the Void Transaction dialog box

- The Voided/Deleted Transactions Summary will be shown on the screen.

Your Name's Sierra Sports

Voided/Deleted Transactions Summary

Entered/Last Modified Current Date

Num	Action	Entered/Last Modified	Date	Name	Memo	Account	Split	Amount
Transactions voided in current session								
Invoice 5								
5	Voided Transaction	Current Date and Time	01/04/2018	Shaw, Justin	VOID:	1200 · Accounts Receivable	-SPLIT-	0.00 ◀
5	Added Transaction	Current Date and Time	01/04/2018	Shaw, Justin		1200 · Accounts Receivable	-SPLIT-	539.95
Invoice 6								
6	Voided Transaction	Current Date and Time	01/04/2018	Asher, Benjamin	VOID:	1200 · Accounts Receivable	-SPLIT-	0.00
6	Added Transaction	Current Date and Time	01/04/2018	Asher, Benjamin		1200 · Accounts Receivable	-SPLIT-	852.11

The same procedures for Batch Void would be used to Batch Delete Invoices, Bills, and Checks except that you would click Delete rather than Void

DELETE INVOICE AND SALES ORDER

RESUME WORK now that you have read the BATCH DELETE/VOID TRANSACTIONS section.

Since Sales Orders may not be voided or deleted in a batch, to finalize the batch void or delete, the Linked Transactions (Sales Orders) for Justin Shaw should be voided or deleted individually. Since you did not batch delete the invoices, you must delete it individually.

> ### MEMO
> **DATE:** January 8, 2018
>
> Justin Shaw lost his part-time job. He decided to repair his old snowboard and return the new one he purchased from Your Name's Sierra Sports. Delete Invoice 5. Since the invoice was made from Sales Order 1, delete the sales order.

 Delete Invoice 5 and Sales Order 1

Open Create Invoices
Access Invoice 5 using **Find** on the Main icon bar for Create Invoices
Click the **Find** button   Find
On the Find Invoices screen, enter **5** for Invoice #
- You may enter any or all the information items shown.

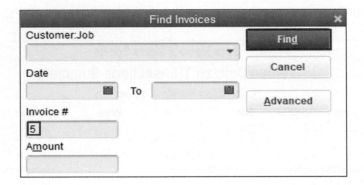

Click the **Find** button
- Invoice 5 is now on the screen.

Click the **Delete** icon on the Create Invoices Main icon bar
Click **OK** in the **Delete Transaction** dialog box
- The cursor is now positioned on Invoice 6.
Click **Previous** or **Back** arrow   ◀
- Now the cursor is positioned on Invoice 4.
Click **Save & Close** on the **Create Invoices** screen to close the invoice
- When you delete an invoice that was prepared from a sales order, the sales order must be deleted as well.
Access Sale Order 1 as previously instructed
- Notice that the Sales Order is no longer marked INVOICED IN FULL.
Delete the Sales Order following the same procedures used when deleting an invoice
Click **OK** when asked if you want to delete the transaction
Close **Create Sales Orders**

VOID INVOICE

You would follow the same procedures to void an invoice and its accompanying sales order. If you did not prepare an invoice from a sales order, it is voided as presented in previous chapters.

> <u>MEMO</u>
> **DATE:** January 8, 2018
>
> Ben Asher did not like the after-ski boots and returned them to Your Name's Sierra Sports. Since this is the only item on the invoice, you decided to void the invoice rather than create a credit memo. Void Invoice 1.

 Void Invoice 1

Display Invoice 1 on the screen
Click the drop-down arrow below the Delete icon on the Create Invoices Main Icon Bar
Click **Void**
- The amount of the invoice is now 0.00 and the Memo says VOID:

Print the voided invoice
- If you print to a pdf file, save the document as **15-Your Name Inv 1 Asher Void Ch5**.

Click **Save & Close**
Click **Yes** on the Recording Transaction dialog box
- If you get a Cash Basis Reports Affected dialog box, click **Do not display this message in the future**, then click **OK**.

VIEW CUSTOMER BALANCE DETAIL REPORT

 View the **Customer Balance Detail Report**

Prepare the report from the Report Center
Scroll through the report
- Look at Justin Shaw's account. Notice that Invoice 5 does not show up in the account listing. When an invoice is deleted, there is no record of it anywhere in the report. Nothing is shown for the Sales Order because a sales order is not recorded in accounts or journals.
- Look at Benjamin Asher's account. The amount for Invoice 1 shows as **0.00**.

5

Your Name's Sierra Sports
Customer Balance Detail
All Transactions

Type	Date	Num	Account	Amount	Balance
Asher, Benjamin					
Invoice	12/31/2017		1200 · Accounts Receivable	85.00	85.00 ◀
Invoice	01/02/2018	1	1200 · Accounts Receivable	0.00	85.00
Invoice	01/04/2018	6	1200 · Accounts Receivable	852.11	937.11
Total Asher, Benjamin				937.11	937.11
Shaw, Justin					
Invoice	12/31/2017		1200 · Accounts Receivable	911.63	911.63
Total Shaw, Justin				911.63	911.63
TOTAL				**14,796.45**	**14,796.45**

Partial Report

Close the report without printing, do <u>not</u> close the Report Center

PREPARE VOIDED/DELETED TRANSACTIONS SUMMARY

The report that lists the information regarding voided and deleted transactions is the Voided/Deleted Transaction Detail Report.

 View the Voided/Deleted Transactions Detail Report

Click **Accountant & Taxes** in the Report Center
Double-click **Voided/Deleted Transactions Summary**
Use **All** as the date selection.
- The Entered Last Modified column shows the actual date and time that the entry was made.
- In addition, your report may not match the one illustrated if you have voided or deleted anything else during your work session.
Scroll through the report to see the transactions
- Notice the entries for Invoice 1 include both the original and the voided entries.
- The entries for Invoice 5 show the original entry and the deleted entry.
- Sales Order 1 shows both the original and deleted transactions.

Your Name's Sierra Sports
Voided/Deleted Transactions Summary
Entered/Last Modified

Num	Action	Entered/Last Modified	Date	Name	Memo	Account	Split	Amount
Transactions entered or modified by Admin								
Invoice 1								
1	Voided Transaction	01/08/2018 11:05:07	01/02/2018	Asher, Benjamin	VOID:	1200 · Accounts Receivable	-SPLIT-	0.00 ◄
1	Added Transaction	01/02/2018 16:50:04	01/02/2018	Asher, Benjamin		1200 · Accounts Receivable	-SPLIT-	81.00
Invoice 5								
5	Deleted Transaction	01/08/2018 10:44:54						0.00
5	Added Transaction	01/04/2018 12:27:54	01/04/2018	Shaw, Justin		1200 · Accounts Receivable	-SPLIT-	539.95
Sales Order 1								
1	Deleted Transaction	01/08/2018 10:45:24						0.00
1	Added Transaction	01/03/2018 08:38:23	01/03/2018	Shaw, Justin		90200 · Sales Orders	-SPLIT-	539.95

Close the report without printing, and close the Report Center

PREPARE CREDIT MEMOS

A credit memo is prepared to show a reduction to a transaction and to notify a customer that a change has been made to a transaction. If the invoice has already been sent to the customer, it is more appropriate and less confusing to make a change to a transaction by issuing a credit memo rather than voiding an invoice.

When applying a credit to an invoice, QuickBooks DT marks either the oldest invoice or the invoice that matches the amount of the credit.

MEMO
DATE: January 10, 2018

Credit Memo 9—Angie Waters returned the boot carrying case purchased for $49.95 on Invoice 7.

Credit Memo 10—Benjamin Asher returned the ski carrier purchased for $10.99 on Invoice 6.

Prepare the Credit Memos in the Memo above

Click the **Refunds and Credits** icon on the Home Page
CUSTOMER:JOB is **Waters, Angie**
Use the **Custom Credit Memo** Template
The **Date** of the Credit Memo is **01/10/18**
The **Credit No.** field should show the number **9**
- Because Credit Memos are included in the numbering sequence for invoices, this number matches the number of the next blank invoice.

There is no PO No.
Click the drop-down list arrow next to **ITEM**, click **Accessories**
Tab to or click in **QTY**, type in **1**
Tab to or click **RATE**, enter **49.95**
Press tab to enter 49.95 in the **AMOUNT** column
Click the drop-down list arrow for CUSTOMER MESSAGE, click **<Add New>**
Key in **We have processed your return.** as the Message, click **OK**

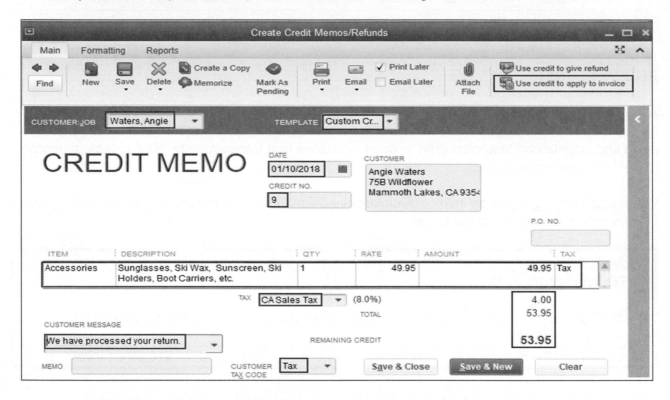

Since the return was for an item purchased on Invoice 7, it is appropriate to apply the credit to Invoice 7
Click the **Use Credit to apply to an invoice** on the Create Credit Memos/Refunds icon bar
Click **Yes** if you get a Recording Transaction message box
The Apply Credit to Invoices screen will appear.

- Unless an exact match in the Amt. Due occurs, QuickBooks DT applies the credit to the oldest item.
- You will see a checkmark in the column next to the date of 12/31/2017, which is the Opening Balance and the oldest transaction. You will also see a check mark for the Date 01/04/2018. This is because the oldest transaction is selected by QuickBooks DT and because the amount of the credit is for more than the opening balance.

Since the credit is for a return to the boot carrier purchased on Invoice 7, click the **Clear Selections** button

Click in the check column to mark Invoice 7 on 01/04/2018

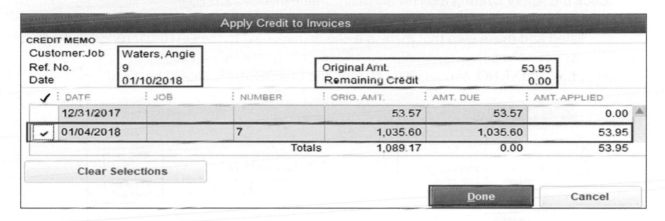

Click **Done**

Print the credit memo <u>with</u> lines around each field as previously instructed

- If you print to a pdf file, save the document as **16-Your Name CM 9 Waters Ch5**.

Click **Save & New**

Repeat the procedures given to record Credit Memo 10 for Benjamin Asher

- Do <u>not</u> apply the credit to Invoice 6.

Print the credit memo

- If you print to a pdf file, save the document as **17-Your Name CM 10 Asher Ch5**.

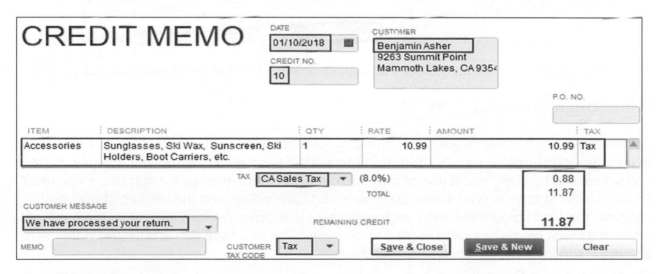

Click **Save & Close**

Click **OK** on the Available Credit screen to **Retain as an available credit**

APPLY CREDIT TO INVOICE

When a Credit Memo is recorded, it may be applied to an invoice at the time the credit is recorded. If that is not done, it is possible to go to the invoice and apply the credit directly to it.

 Apply Credit Memo 10 to Invoice 6

> Click the **Create Invoices** icon on the Home Page
> Click the Previous button until you get to Invoice 6 for Benjamin Asher
> Click the **Apply Credits** icon on the Main Create Invoices icon bar
> - In the Available Credits section of the Apply Credits screen, look at the information listed and make sure that there is a check mark next to the DATE 01/10/2018, if not click to select.
> - The CREDIT NO. should show 10, and the CREDIT AMT. should be 11.87.

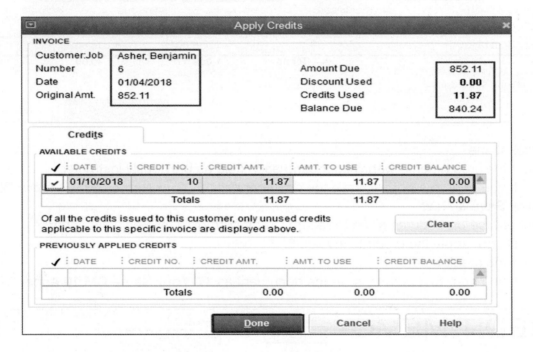

> Click **Done** on the Apply Credits screen, click **Save & Close** on Create Invoices

PRINT OPEN INVOICES REPORT

To determine which invoices are still open—they have not been paid—QuickBooks DT allows you to print an Open Invoices report. This report lists unpaid invoices and statement charges grouped and subtotaled by customer. It also shows the transaction date, the Invoice number, a Purchase Order number (if there is one), terms of the sale, due date, aging, and the amount of the open balance. The total amount due from each customer for all open invoices less credit memos is also listed. If a credit memo has been applied to an invoice, the new total due is reflected in this report and the credit memo is not shown separately.

MEMO

DATE: January 10, 2018

Ruth needs to prepare and print an Open Invoices Report to give to Larry and you, so you can see which invoices are open. When preparing the report, adjust the width of the columns. The report should be one page wide without selecting the print option *Fit report to one page wide.*

　　Prepare, resize, and print an Open Invoices Report

> Click **Reports** on the Menu bar, point to **Customers & Receivables**, and click **Open Invoices**
> Enter the date **011018**
> - QuickBooks DT will insert the / between the items in the date.
> Press the **Tab** key to generate the report
> - Notice the amount due for Invoice 7. It now shows $981.65 as the total rather than $1,035.60. This verifies that the credit memo was applied to Invoice 7.
> - The amount due for Invoice 6 to Benjamin Asher now shows $840.24 as the total rather than $852.11.
> - The total of the report is $14,730.63.
> Resize the columns as previously instructed, print the report
> Click **Print**, use Portrait orientation
> - If you print to a pdf file, save the document as **18-Your Name Open Inv Ch5**.
> Close the **Open Invoices Report**
> - If you get a Memorize Report dialog box, click **Do not display this message in the future**; and then, click **No**.

PREPARE DAILY BACKUP

As previously discussed, a backup file is prepared in case you make an error. After several transactions have been recorded, it is wise to prepare a backup file. In addition, a backup should be made at the end of every work session. The Daily Backup file is an appropriate file to create for saving your work as you progress through a chapter. By creating the backup file now, it will contain your work for Chapter 5 up through the preparation of the credit memos.

　　Prepare the Sierra 2018 (Daily Backup).qbb file

> Follow the steps presented in Chapter 1 for creating a backup file
> Name the file **Sierra 2018 (Daily Backup)**
> The file type is **QBW Backup (* .QBB)**

RECORD CASH SALES WITH SALES TAX

As you learned in previous chapters, not all sales in a business are on account. In many instances, payment is made at the time the merchandise is purchased. This is entered as a cash sale and will include sales tax, if any. Sales with cash, debit cards, credit cards, or checks as the payment method are entered as cash sales. When entering a cash sale, you prepare a Sales Receipt rather than an Invoice. QuickBooks DT records the transaction in the Journal and places the amount of cash received in an account called *Undeposited Funds*. The funds received remain in Undeposited

Funds until you record a deposit to your bank account. The amount of sales tax collected is entered as a Sales Tax Liability because you owe the amount of sales tax you collected to the government.

MEMO

DATE: January 11, 2018

Record Sales Receipt 1—Received <u>cash</u> from a customer who purchased a pair of sunglasses, $29.95; a boot carrier, $2.99; and some lip balm, $1.19. Use the message *Thank you for your business.*

 Enter the above transaction as a cash sale to a cash customer

Click the **Create Sales Receipts** icon on the Home Page
- Depending on the size of your computer screen, the History can take up more room than you wish. You may want to hide the history panel.

If any of the columns in the Sales Receipt are not shown in full, resize them by pointing between the column headings and dragging the double arrow until the column is shown in full

Enter **Cash Customer** in the **CUSTOMER:JOB** text box, press Tab

Because Your Name's Sierra Sports does not have a customer named Cash Customer, a **Customer:Job Not Found** dialog box appears on the screen.

Click **Quick Add** to add the customer name Cash Customer to the Customer List
- Details regarding Cash Customer are not required, so Quick Add is the appropriate method to use to add the name to the list.
- Now that Cash Customer has been added to the Customer:Job List, the cursor moves to the **Template** field.

Template should be **Custom Sales Receipt**
- If not, click the drop-down list arrow and click Custom Sales Receipt.

Tab to or click **Date**, type **01/11/18**
- As shown in earlier chapters, the date may be entered 01/11/2018; 01/11/18; or 011118; or by clicking on the calendar, clicking the forward or back arrows until you get to the correct month, and then clicking on the date.

Sale No. should be **1**

Click the **Cash** icon on the Sales Receipt
- QuickBooks DT will allow you to accept cash, checks, credit cards, debit cards, and e-checks.
- Your business may subscribe to the optional QuickBooks Payments, to allow credit card, debit card, and e-payment processing to be completed without additional software or hardware.

- If you do not subscribe to QuickBooks Merchant Accounts, you can still accept the different methods of payment by using your merchant account processor (bank for example).

Use **Accessories** as the **ITEM** for each of the items sold and complete the Sales Receipt as instructed in Chapter 2

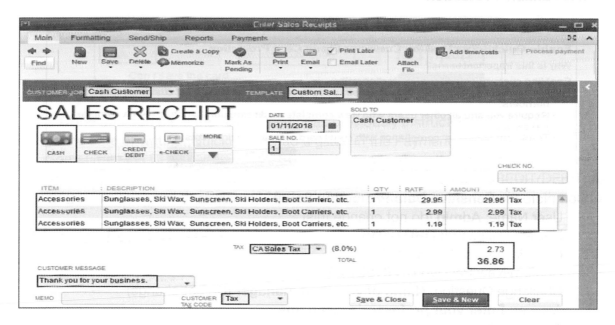

Print the Sales Receipt <u>with</u> lines around each field as previously instructed
- If you print to a pdf file, save the document as **19-Your Name SR 1 Cash Cust Ch5**.
Because QuickBooks DT saves automatically before printing, you may get a Recording Transaction dialog box after printing; if so, always click **Yes**
Click **Save & New**

DEBIT CARDS AND CREDIT CARDS

In QuickBooks DT, Debit and Credit cards sales are treated the same as a cash sale. When you prepare the Sales Receipt, the payment method is selected by clicking on the Credit/Debit button and the amount of the sale is placed into the Undeposited Funds account. When the actual bank deposit is made, the amount is deposited into the checking or bank account. The bank fees for the cards are deducted directly from the bank account. When a company accepts debit and/or credit cards as payment methods, payments may be processed through the company's merchant account processor or QuickBooks Payments (may be called QuickBooks Merchant Services).

ENABLE CUSTOMER CREDIT CARD PROTECTION

QuickBooks DT users who store, process, or transmit customer debit card and/or credit card information in QuickBooks DT are required to protect that information by complying with the Payment Card Industry Data Security Standard (PCI DSS). To enable QuickBooks DT Customer Credit Card Protection, you must create a complex password for you and all others who view complete credit card numbers. The password must be changed every 90 days, and the three-digit number near the signature panel on the back of the credit card or the four-digit number above the credit card number on the front of the credit card must not be stored. If you do not provide protection, your business may be liable for fines and other damages.

SALE NO. should be **3**
Click the **CHECK** button on the Sales Receipt
Tab to or click **CHECK NO.**, type **5589**
Complete and print Sales Receipt 3 as previously instructed
- If you print to a pdf file, save the document as **21-Your Name SR 3 Cash Cust Ch5**.

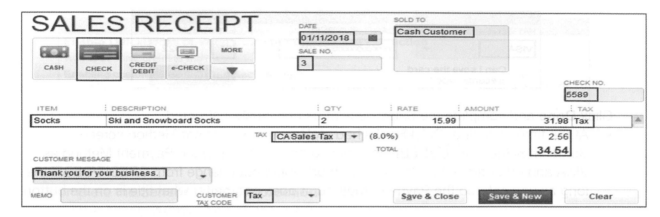

Click **Save & New**

ENTER SALE PAID BY DEBIT CARD

As previously mentioned, when customers use a debit card as payment, it is processed just like a credit card sale.

<u>**MEMO**</u>

DATE: January 11, 2018

Record Sales Receipt 4 for the sale of a sweater, $89.95, to a Cash Customer using a Debit card. The number is 5308 4007 1892 4657 with an expiration date of 02/2023. The message for the Sales Receipt is *Thank you for your business.*

 Record the Debit Card purchase by Cash Customer

CUSTOMER:JOB is **Cash Customer**, **DATE** is **01/11/2018**, **SALE NO.** is **4**
Click the button that shows either **CREDIT/DEBIT** or **VISA**
- Sometimes, the previous payment method; such as, VISA, may show on the Payment button other times it stays as CREDIT/DEBIT.
To Complete the Enter Card Information:
  For **PAYMENT** click the drop-down list arrow, click **Debit Card**, press Tab
  CARD NUMBER is **5308 4007 1892 4657**, press Tab
  EXP DATE is **02** for the month, tab to the year and enter **2023**

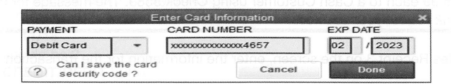

Click **Done**

Record the transaction and print Sales Receipt 4 as previously instructed

- Make sure a check number wasn't entered automatically. If it was, remove it.
- If you print to a pdf file, save the document as **22-Your Name SR 4 Cash Cust Ch5**.

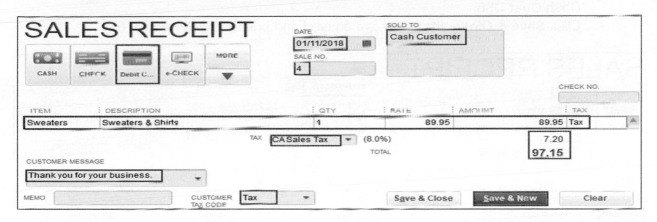

Click **Save & New**

ENTER ADDITIONAL CASH SALES TRANSACTIONS

MEMO

DATE: January 12, 2018

After a record snowfall, the store is very busy. Use Cash Customer as the customer name. Record the following cash, check, credit card, and debit card sales:

Sales Receipt 5—Cash Customer used Check 196 to purchase a parka, $249.95, and ski pants, $129.95.

Sales Receipt 6—Cash Customer used a Debit card number 5320 7971 4542 2526 with an expiration date of 03/2024 to purchase a snowboard, $389.95, and snowboard bindings, $189.95.

Sales Receipt 7—Cash Customer purchased a pair of gloves for $89.95 and paid cash.

Sales Receipt 8—Cash Customer purchased a pair of snowboard boots for $229.95 using Master Card number 5293 5159 7847 4924 with an expiration date of 04/2020.

 Repeat the procedures used previously to record the transactions listed above

- Use the date 01/12/2018 (or the year you have used previously).
- For Sales Receipt 8, click the Payment Method button that says either CREDIT/DEBIT or DEBIT Card, click the button, then click the drop-down list arrow and click MasterCard, enter the card number, and expiration date. Notice that the button next to e-CHECK changes to MasterC...
- Always use the Item List to determine the appropriate sales items for billing.
- Use **Thank you for your business.** as the CUSTOMER MESSAGE for these sales receipts.

- Print each Sales Receipt immediately after entering the information for it. If you print to a pdf file, save the document as **23-Your Name SR 5 Cash Cust Ch5**, **24-Your Name SR 6 Cash Cust Ch5**, **25-Your Name SR 7 Cash Cust Ch5**, **26-Your Name SR 8 Cash Cust Ch5**.
- Click **Save & Close** after you have entered and printed Sales Receipt 8.

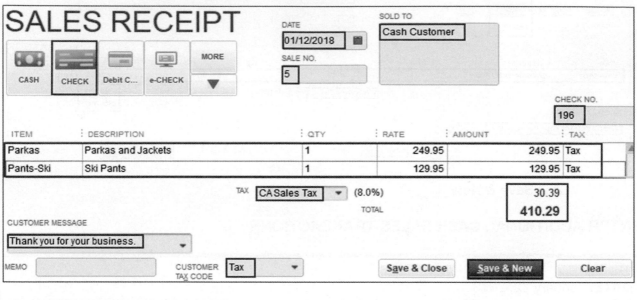

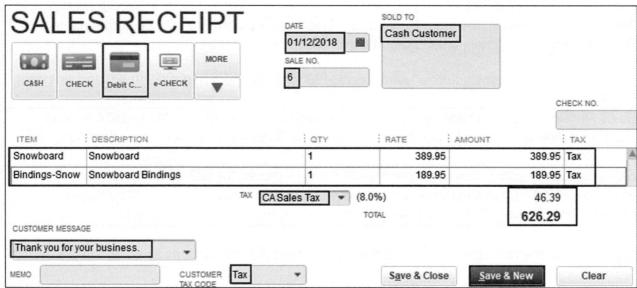

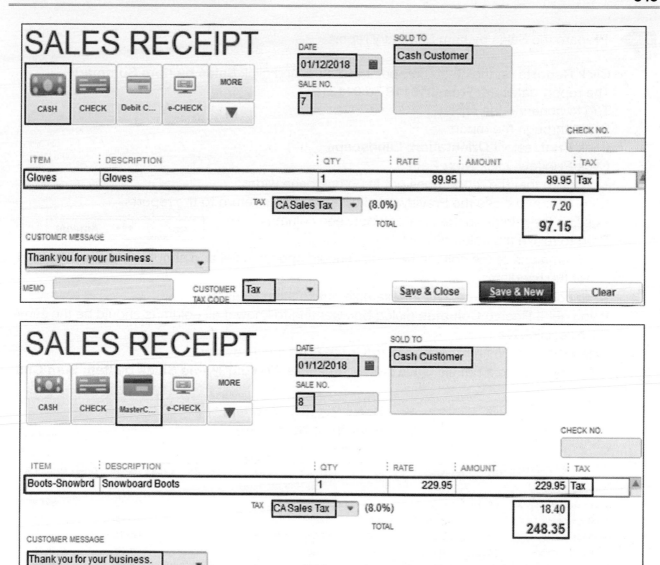

PRINT SALES BY ITEM SUMMARY REPORT

The Sales by Item Summary Report gives the amount or value of the merchandise. For each item, it analyzes the quantity of merchandise on hand, gives the percentage of the total sales, and calculates the: average price, cost of goods sold, average cost of goods sold, gross margin, and percentage of gross margin. By totaling each column, information is also provided regarding the total inventory.

MEMO

DATE: January 13, 2018

Near the middle of the month, Ruth prepares a Sales by Item Summary Report to obtain information about sales, inventory, and merchandise costs. Prepare this report in landscape orientation for 1/1/2018-1/13/2018. Adjust the widths of the columns so the report prints on one page without selecting the print option *Fit report to one page wide*.

Prepare the Sales by Item Summary report

Click **Reports** on the menu bar, point to **Sales**, and click **Sales by Item Summary**
The report dates are From **010118** To **011318**
Tab to generate the report
Scroll through the report
Click **Print**, select **Orientation: Landscape**
Click **Preview**, click **Next Page**
- Notice that the report does not fit on one page wide.

Click **Close** to close the Preview, and click **Cancel** to return to the report
Position the cursor on the diamond between columns
Drag to resize the columns

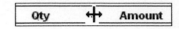

- The names of the column headings should appear in full and should not have **...** as part of the heading.
- If columns are large, Qty for example, make them smaller.

If you get a **Resize Columns** dialog box wanting to know if all columns should be the same size, click **No**
When the columns have been resized, click **Print** and **Preview**
- If you print to a pdf file, save the document as **27-Your Name Sales by Item Sum Ch5**.

Your Name Mountain Sports
Sales by Item Summary
January 1 - 13, 2015
Jan 1 - 13, 15

	Qty	Amount	% of Sales	Avg Price	COGS	Avg COGS	Gross Margin	Gross Margin %
▼ Inventory								
Accessories ▶	5 ◀	127.03	1.4%	25.41	18.30	3.66	108.73	85.6%
Bindings-Skis	7	854.00	9.7%	122.00	525.00	75.00	329.00	38.5%
Bindings-Snow	2	349.94	4%	174.97	150.00	75.00	199.94	57.1%
Boots	0	0.00	0.0%	0.00	0.00	0.00	0.00	0.0%
Boots-Ski	1	250.00	2.8%	250.00	75.00	75.00	175.00	70.0%
Boots-Snowbrd	2	478.95	5.4%	239.48	150.00	75.00	328.95	68.7%
Gloves	2	168.95	1.9%	84.48	30.00	15.00	138.95	82.2%
Hats	1	25.00	0.3%	25.00	8.00	8.00	17.00	68.0%
Helmets	5	349.75	4%	69.95	140.00	28.00	209.75	60%
Pants-Ski	2	258.95	2.9%	129.48	60.00	30.00	198.95	76.8%
Parkas	2	498.95	5.6%	249.48	116.66	58.33	382.29	76.6%
Poles-Ski	6	220.00	2.5%	36.67	180.00	30.00	40.00	18.2%
Skis	7	2,519.00	28.5%	359.86	700.00	100.00	1,819.00	72.2%
Sleds	6	799.90	9%	133.32	405.00	67.50	394.90	49.4%
Snowboard	2	889.90	10.1%	444.95	200.00	100.00	689.90	77.5%
Socks	3	47.93	0.5%	15.98	9.00	3.00	38.93	81.2%
Sweaters	2	214.95	2.4%	107.48	50.00	25.00	164.95	76.7%
Toboggans	5	1,149.75	13%	229.95	687.50	137.50	462.25	40.2%
Underwear	1	68.00	0.8%	68.00	8.00	8.00	60.00	88.2%
Total Inventory	61.00	9,270.95	104.8%	151.98	3,512.46	57.58	5,758.49	62.1%
▼ Discounts								
Nonprofit Discount		-423.95	-4.8%					
Total Discounts		-423.95	-4.8%					
TOTAL	61	8,847.00	100.0%	145.03		57.58		

When the report fits on one page wide, print and close the report

CORRECT AND PRINT SALES RECEIPT

QuickBooks DT makes correcting errors user friendly. When an error is discovered in a transaction such as a cash sale, you can simply return to the form where the transaction was recorded and correct the error. Thus, to correct a sales receipt, you could click Customers on the menu bar, click Enter Sales Receipts, click the Previous or Back arrow until you found the appropriate sales receipt, and then correct the error. Since cash or checks received for cash sales are held in the Undeposited Funds account until the bank deposit is made, a sales receipt can be accessed through the Undeposited Funds account in the Chart of Accounts. Accessing the receipt in this manner allows you to see all the transactions entered in the account for Undeposited Funds.

When a correction for a sale is made, QuickBooks DT not only changes the form, it also changes all Journal and account entries for the transaction to reflect the correction. QuickBooks DT then allows a corrected sales receipt to be printed.

> **MEMO**
>
> **DATE:** January 13, 2018
>
> After reviewing transaction information, you realize that the date for Sales Receipt 1 was entered incorrectly. Change the date to 1/8/2018.

5

 Use the Undeposited Funds account register to correct the error in the memo above, and print a corrected Sales Receipt

Open the **Chart of Accounts**, use the keyboard shortcut **Ctrl+A**
Double-click **Undeposited Funds**
- The register maintains a record of all the transactions recorded within the Undeposited Funds account.

Click anywhere in the transaction for **RCPT 1**
- Look at the **REF/TYPE** column to see the type of transaction.
- The number in the REF column indicates the number of the sales receipt or the customer's check number.
- Type shows **RCPT** for a sales receipt.

12000 · Undeposited Funds

Go to... Print... Edit Transaction QuickReport

DATE	REF	PAYEE		DECREASE	✔	INCREASE	BALANCE
	TYPE	ACCOUNT	MEMO				
01/11/2018	1	Cash Customer				36.86	36.86
	RCPT	-split-					
01/11/2018	2	Cash Customer				215.95	252.81
	RCPT	-split-					
01/11/2018	3	Cash Customer				34.54	287.35
	RCPT	-split-					
01/11/2018	4	Cash Customer				97.15	384.50
	RCPT	-split-					
01/12/2018	5	Cash Customer				410.29	794.79
	RCPT	-split-					
01/12/2018	6	Cash Customer				626.29	1,421.08
	RCPT	-split-					
01/12/2018	7	Cash Customer				97.15	1,518.23
	RCPT	-split-					
01/12/2018	8	Cash Customer				248.35	1,766.58
	RCPT	-split-					

☐ 1-Line

Sort by Date, Type, Number/Ref ▼

ENDING BALANCE **1,766.58**

Click **Edit Transaction** or double-click the transaction
- The sales receipt appears on the screen.

Tab to or click **DATE** field, and change the Date to **01/08/18**

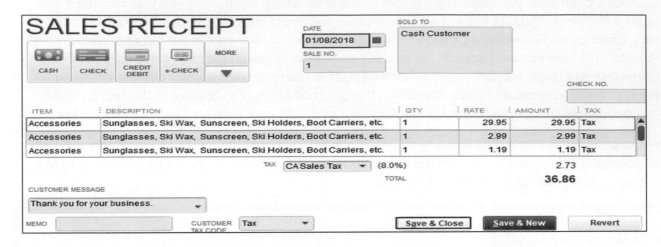

Print the corrected sales receipt as previously instructed
- If you print to a pdf file, save the document as **28-Your Name SR 1 Cash Cust Corrected Ch5**.

Click **Yes** on the **Recording Transactions** dialog box, click **Save & Close**

Return to the **Register for Undeposited Funds** do <u>not</u> close the register

VIEW AND ANALYZE CASH CUSTOMER QUICKREPORT

After editing the sales receipt and returning to the register, you may get a detailed report regarding the customer's transactions by clicking the QuickReport button. If you use Cash Customer for all cash sales, a QuickReport will be for all the transactions of Cash Customer.

 Prepare a QuickReport for Cash Customer

Sales Receipt 1 is still selected

Click the **QuickReport** button to display the Register QuickReport for Cash Customer
- All transactions for Cash Customer appear in the report.

Because there are no entries in the Memo and Clr columns, drag the diamond between
  columns to eliminate the columns for **Memo** and **Clr**

Widen the **Account** column so **Undeposited Funds** appears in full

Your Name Mountain Sports
Register QuickReport
All Transactions

Type	Date	Num	Account	Split	Amount
Cash Customer					
Sales Receipt	01/08/2015	1	12000 · Undeposited Funds	-SPLIT-	36.86
Sales Receipt	01/11/2015	2	12000 · Undeposited Funds	-SPLIT-	215.95
Sales Receipt	01/11/2015	3	12000 · Undeposited Funds	-SPLIT-	34.54
Sales Receipt	01/11/2015	4	12000 · Undeposited Funds	-SPLIT-	97.15
Sales Receipt	01/12/2015	5	12000 · Undeposited Funds	-SPLIT-	410.29
Sales Receipt	01/12/2015	6	12000 · Undeposited Funds	-SPLIT-	626.29
Sales Receipt	01/12/2015	7	12000 · Undeposited Funds	-SPLIT-	97.15
Sales Receipt	01/12/2015	8	12000 · Undeposited Funds	-SPLIT-	248.35
Total Cash Customer					1,766.58
TOTAL					**1,766.58**

- Notice the following:
  - Date for Sales Receipt 1 has been changed to **01/08/2018**.
  - Account used is Undeposited Funds.
  - Split column contains the other accounts used in the transactions.
  - For all the transactions you see the word -**SPLIT**- rather than an account name.
    - Split means that more than one account was used for the transaction.
    - In addition to sales items, sales tax was charged, so each transaction will show -**SPLIT**-.
  - Verify that Sales Receipt 2 had one sales item by using QuickZoom to view the actual sales receipt.

Use QuickZoom by double-clicking anywhere on the information for Sales Receipt 2
- The item sold is Sleds. Also note the CA Sales Tax.

Close **Sales Receipt 2**

Close the report without printing, and close the register for **Undeposited Funds**

Do not close the **Chart of Accounts**

VIEW SALES TAX PAYABLE REGISTER

The Sales Tax Payable Register shows a detailed listing of all transactions with sales tax. The option of 1-Line may be selected to view each transaction on one line rather than the standard two lines. The account register provides information regarding the vendor and the account used for the transaction.

View the register for the Sales Tax Payable account

Double-click **2200-Sales Tax Payable** in the Chart of Accounts
Once the register is displayed, click **1-Line** to view the transactions
- The amount of sales tax for each sale, whether cash or credit, in which sales tax was collected is displayed.

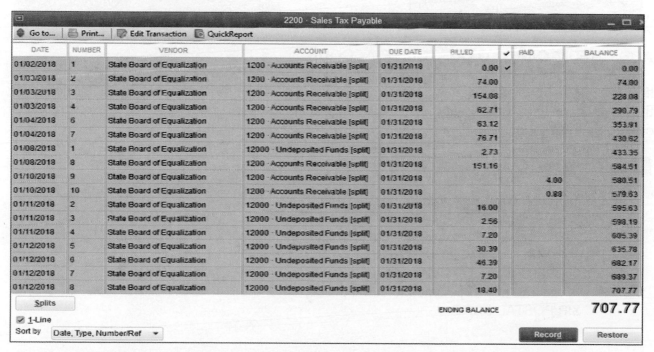

DATE	NUMBER	VENDOR	ACCOUNT	DUE DATE	BILLED	✔	PAID	BALANCE
01/02/2018	1	State Board of Equalization	1200 · Accounts Receivable [split]	01/31/2018	0.00	✔		0.00
01/03/2018	2	State Board of Equalization	1200 · Accounts Receivable [split]	01/31/2018	74.00			74.00
01/03/2018	3	State Board of Equalization	1200 · Accounts Receivable [split]	01/31/2018	154.08			228.08
01/03/2018	4	State Board of Equalization	1200 · Accounts Receivable [split]	01/31/2018	62.71			290.79
01/04/2018	6	State Board of Equalization	1200 · Accounts Receivable [split]	01/31/2018	63.12			353.91
01/04/2018	7	State Board of Equalization	1200 · Accounts Receivable [split]	01/31/2018	76.71			430.62
01/08/2018	1	State Board of Equalization	12000 · Undeposited Funds [split]	01/31/2018	2.73			433.35
01/08/2018	8	State Board of Equalization	1200 · Accounts Receivable [split]	01/31/2018	151.16			584.51
01/10/2018	9	State Board of Equalization	1200 · Accounts Receivable [split]	01/31/2018			4.00	580.51
01/10/2018	10	State Board of Equalization	1200 · Accounts Receivable [split]	01/31/2018			0.88	579.63
01/11/2018	2	State Board of Equalization	12000 · Undeposited Funds [split]	01/31/2018	16.00			595.63
01/11/2018	3	State Board of Equalization	12000 · Undeposited Funds [split]	01/31/2018	2.56			598.19
01/11/2018	4	State Board of Equalization	12000 · Undeposited Funds [split]	01/31/2018	7.20			605.39
01/12/2018	5	State Board of Equalization	12000 · Undeposited Funds [split]	01/31/2018	30.39			635.78
01/12/2018	6	State Board of Equalization	12000 · Undeposited Funds [split]	01/31/2018	46.39			682.17
01/12/2018	7	State Board of Equalization	12000 · Undeposited Funds [split]	01/31/2018	7.20			689.37
01/12/2018	8	State Board of Equalization	12000 · Undeposited Funds [split]	01/31/2018	18.40			707.77

ENDING BALANCE **707.77**

Splits

☑ 1-Line

Sort by Date, Type, Number/Ref

Close the register for **Sales Tax Payable**, and the **Chart of Accounts**

CUSTOMER CENTER

The Customer Center provides information about individual customers. The customer list shows all your customers and their Balance Total. As you click each customer, you will see the customer information and transaction details for the individual customer. You may also view transaction details for specific types of transactions by clicking the drop-down list arrow.

  View the Customer Center and the information for Cash Customer

> Click the **Customers** icon to open the Customer Center; then click **Cash Customer**
> Click the drop-down list arrow next to **Show** to see the list of the types of transactions that may be displayed

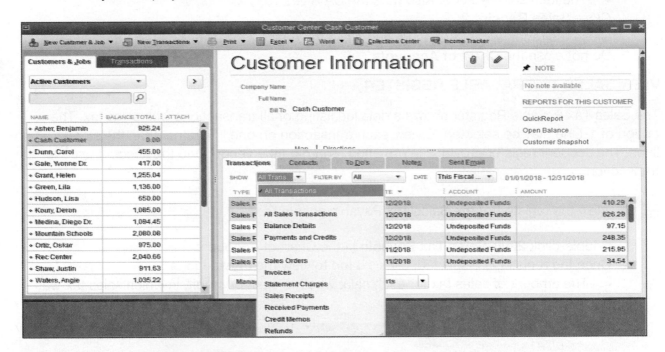

ADD CREDIT CARD TO CUSTOMER ACCOUNT

If your customer prefers to pay you with a credit card, you may keep the credit card information in the Payment Settings section of the customer record. In addition, you may also mark the credit card to be used for online payments (not available for use in training).

  Add Credit Card information for Angie Waters

> Double-click **Waters, Angie** in the Customer Center
> Click the **Payment Settings** tab
> Since you are entering Angie's credit card information, click the drop-down list arrow for **PREFERRED PAYMENT METHOD**, and click **MasterCard**
> Enter CREDIT CARD NO. **5443 0376 3134 0342**, the EXP. DATE of **06/2024**
> Press the **Tab** key three times to automatically enter the NAME ON CARD, ADDRESS, and ZIP/POSTAL CODE

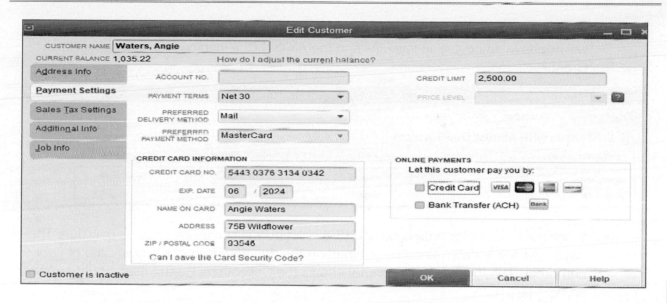

- For security reasons, the Card Security Code (CSC) may not be saved.
- Note the Online Payments section. If you subscribe to QuickBooks Payments, you may accept credit card and bank transfers (ACH) payments from online customers. You are charged a fee for each payment collected online. This is not available for use in training.

Click **OK** to save the credit card information for Angie

Do <u>not</u> close the Customer Center

SELECT COLLECTIONS CENTER PREFERENCES

QuickBooks DT has a Collection Center that will display Overdue and Almost Due invoices.

 Set the Preferences to use the Collection Center

Click **Edit** on the Menu Bar, click **Preferences**, click **Sales & Customers**, click the **Company Preferences** tab

- On the Company Preferences tab, look at the section for COLLECTIONS CENTER; if it is not marked, click **Enable Collections Center** to select the feature. If it is marked, do <u>not</u> click it.

> COLLECTIONS CENTER
> ☑ Enable Collections Center

Click **OK** on the Preferences

- If you get a Warning screen to close all its open windows, click **OK**.
- If you got a warning screen, click the **Home** icon to redisplay the Home Page, and click the **Customers** icon to reopen the Customer Center.

VIEW COLLECTIONS CENTER

To use the Collection Center, you must go to the Customer Center and click the Collections Center icon. The Collections Center is date driven based on the date of your computer and the due date of the transactions. Since your computer date will not match the text, you will see all the invoices as overdue.

 Open the Collections Center to view Overdue Invoices

Click the **Collections Center** icon at the top of the Customer Center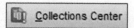

- When the computer date matches the text date of 01/13/2018, your Collections Center will not have any overdue invoices and the Almost Due invoices tab will show Helen Grant.

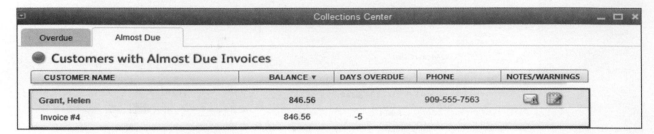

- Since your computer date is not 01/13/2018, you will see all invoices as overdue. The days overdue is determined by subtracting the due date from the actual date of your computer. The following screen shot shows the Collections Center as it would appear on 02/14/2018.

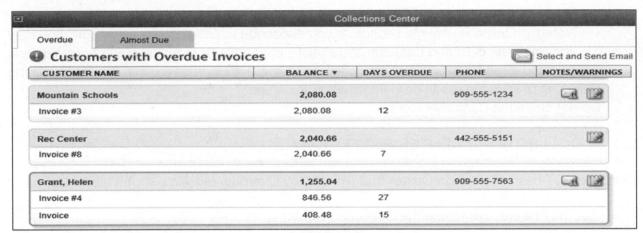

Partial Report

- Note the Invoice for Helen Grant.

  Close the **Collections Center**, do <u>not</u> close the Customer Center

VIEW INCOME TRACKER

QuickBooks DT has an Income Tracker that provides information about all forms of income. The Income Tracker uses the date of your computer to determine whether an invoice is Open or Overdue. The amounts for Unbilled Sales Orders, Unpaid Invoices, Overdue receipts, and Paid amounts for the past 30 days are displayed in colored blocks at the top of the Income Tracker. You may get information on all Customers or a single customer. You may display all types of income transactions or select an individual type. You may display all income transactions or just the ones that are open, paid, or overdue. You may also select a date range of transactions to display.

For each transaction, information is provided regarding the customer name, type of transaction, the business document number, the transaction date, the due date, the amount, the open balance, the date that you last sent an email, the status of the transaction, and an action column where you can print or email the row of information regarding a transaction.

 View the Income Tracker

Click the **Income Tracker** icon at the top of the Customer Center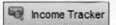
- May need to adjust column widths to display information in full.
- Look at the transaction for Helen Grant and note that it is due on January 18, 2018.
- The screen shot was taken with a computer date of 01/13/2018. Since your computer date is not the same, your Income Tracker will show all invoices as Overdue.

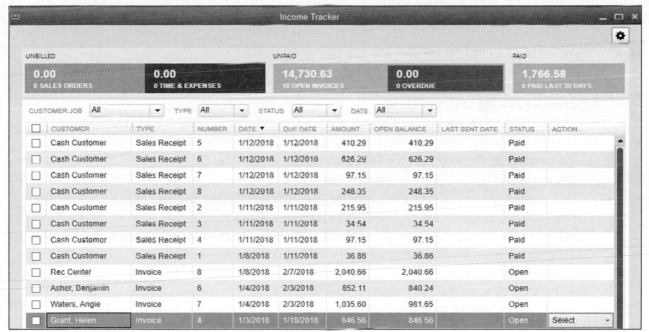

Partial List

Close the Income Tracker and the Customer Center

CUSTOMER PAYMENTS ON ACCOUNT

As previously noted, whenever money is received, whether it is for a cash sale or when customers pay the amount they owe on account, QuickBooks DT uses the account called *Undeposited Funds* to record the receipt of funds. The money stays in the account until a bank deposit is made. The amount is then transferred into Checking. When you start to record a payment on account, you see the customer's balance, any credits or discounts, and a complete list of unpaid invoices. QuickBooks DT automatically applies the payment received to a matching amount or to the oldest invoice.

If a customer owes you money for a purchase made "on account" (an invoice) you record the payment in Receive Payments. If a customer paid you at the time the purchase was made, a sales receipt was prepared, and the amount received was recorded at that time.

RECORD CUSTOMER PAYMENT ON ACCOUNT

> **MEMO**
> **DATE:** January 13, 2018
>
> Record the following receipt of Check 765 for $975 from Oskar Ortiz as payment in full on his account.

 Record the payment on account detailed in the Memo

Click the **Receive Payments** icon on the QuickBooks DT Home Page
RECEIVED FRO<u>M</u> is **Ortiz, Oskar**
- Notice that the total amount owed appears as the CUSTOMER BALANCE.

Tab to or click in the text box for **PAYMENT AMOUNT**, enter **975**
Tab to or click in the text box for **DATE**
- Notice when the cursor moves into the **DATE** text box, the invoice is checked, and in the lower-right portion of the form the AMOUNT FOR SELECTED INVOICES section shows the payment amount as APPLIED.
- When recording a payment on account, QuickBooks DT places a check mark in the √ column to indicate the invoice for which the payment is received.

Type **01/13/18** for the DATE
Click the **Check** icon for the Payment Method
Tab to or click **CHECK #**, enter **765**

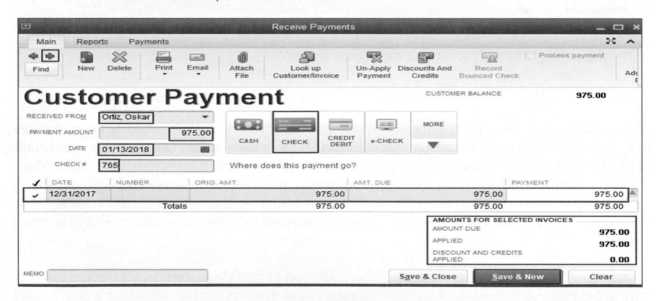

Click the **Print** icon and print the Payment Receipt
- If you print to a pdf file, save the document as **29-Your Name Rcv Pmt Ortiz Ch5**.

Click the **Next** arrow or **Save & New** to record this payment and advance to the next
   Receive Payments screen

RECORD CREDIT CARD PAYMENT AND USE APPLIED CREDIT

If there are any existing credits (such as a Credit Memo) on an account that have not been applied to the account, they may be applied to a customer's account when a payment is made. If a credit was recorded and applied to an invoice, the total amount due on the invoice will reflect the credit.

> **MEMO**
> **DATE:** January 13, 2018
>
> Angie Waters used her MasterCard for $1,035.22 to pay her account in full. Apply unused credits when recording her payment on account.

 Record the credit card payment by Angie Waters and apply her unused credits

RECEIVED FROM is **Waters, Angie**
- Notice the Customer Balance shows the total amount owed by the customer.
- In the center portion of the **Receive Payments** screen, notice the list of unpaid invoices for Angie Waters.
- Angie has her MasterCard recorded in her account. Notice that the Credit/Debit button automatically changed to show MasterC...

Tab to or click **AMOUNT**, enter **1035.22**
Tab to or click **DATE**, type the date **01/13/18**
Click the **MasterC...** icon for the Payment Method
- Note that the information for Angie's MasterCard was automatically inserted.

Click **Done**
- Notice the ORIG. AMT. of the two transactions, the AMT. DUE, and the PAYMENT amounts. The AMT. DUE for Invoice 7 shows 981.65 this reflects the application of the Credit Memo 9 for $53.95 that was previously recorded.

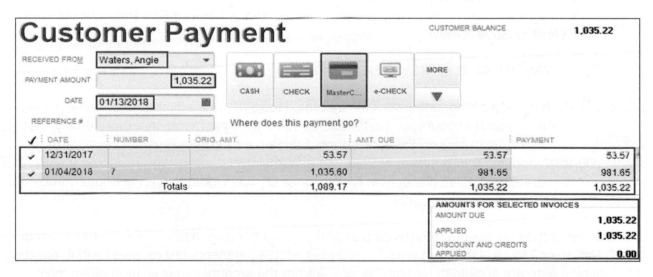

To view Angie's credits, click the line for Invoice 7
Click the **Discounts And Credits** icon on the Receive Payments Icon bar
- The Discounts and Credits screen is shown on the screen.
Click the **Credits** tab

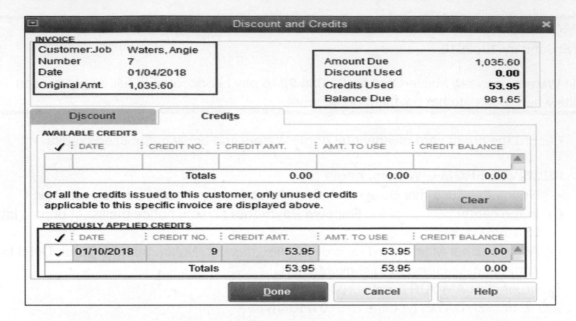

- If you did not apply a credit directly to an invoice, the Available Credits will show the information for CREDIT NO. 9. You may apply the credit now by clicking in the √ column in the AVAILABLE CREDITS section.

Click the **Done** button

Print the Payment Receipt
- If you print to a pdf file, save the document as **30-Your Name Rcv Pmt Waters Ch5**.

Click **Next** or **Save & New**

RECORD PAYMENT AND APPLY DISCOUNT

Giving a customer a sales discount lowers the income. However, one advantage of making a sales discount available is that it encourages customers to make their payments in a more timely manner and brings in cash to the business. Sales discounts function as a contra revenue account by decreasing total income. This is similar in theory to accumulated depreciation reducing the value of an asset. When creating a sales discount in QuickBooks DT you would use an account number in the 4000 category for income accounts.

Each customer may be assigned terms as part of the customer information. When terms such as 1% 10 Net 30 or 2% 10 Net 30 are given, customers whose payments are received within ten days of the invoice date are eligible to deduct 1% or 2% from the amount owed when making their payments.

QuickBooks DT will automatically calculate the amount of discount that is being applied to a payment. In certain circumstances, you should override QuickBooks DT calculations. For example, if a payment is postmarked after the due date, QuickBooks DT will not show a discount. You may change this by clicking the Discounts And Credits icon and entering the discount amount yourself. To do this, use QuickMath: key in the total amount owed in the Amount of Discount text box, press * to multiply, key in .02 (the discount percentage), and press Enter. The Balance Due is automatically calculated by QuickBooks DT.

Another instance in which an override is essential is if a customer has made a return. QuickBooks DT always calculates the amount of the discount on the original Amount Due. To override this, subtract the amount of the return from the original amount due to determine the actual amount owed. Then, calculate the discount amount by multiplying the corrected amount due by the discount percentage. For example: Using a transaction with an Amount Due of $500, a Credit Used of $50, and Discount Terms of 2%, calculating the 2% discount can have different results. If you allow QuickBooks DT to calculate the discount, (2% of $500 = $10) The Balance Due would be: $500 - $50 (return) - $10 (discount) = $440 Balance Due. More accurately, the amount due of $500 less a return of $50 equals a corrected amount due of $450. A 2% discount on $450 is $9, which leaves a Balance Due of $441.

MEMO

DATE: January 13, 2018

Received Check 9813 for $2,020.25 from Rec Center as full payment for Invoice 8. Record the payment and the 1% discount for early payment under the invoice terms of 1% 10 Net 30.

5

 Record the receipt of the check and apply the discount to the above transaction

RECEIVED FROM is **Rec Center**
- The total amount owed, $2,040.66, appears as the CUSTOMER BALANCE.

Enter the **PAYMENT AMOUNT** of **2020.25**
- Notice that this amount is different from the balance of $2,040.66.
- The PAYMENT AMOUNT is entered in the **PAYMENT** column for Invoice 8.
- You will get a message in the UNDERPAYMENT section, which is in the lower-left portion of Receive Payments.

DATE is **011318**
Click the **CHECK** icon for the Payment Method
Tab to or click **CHECK #**, enter **9813**
Click in the text box for **MEMO** below the UNDERPAYMENT section
Key in **Includes Early Payment Discount**
- Since the column for DISC. DATE is displayed, you will see that the Invoice is being paid within the discount date and is eligible to receive a discount.
Click the **Discounts And Credits** icon on the Receive Payments Icon bar
- Make sure the Discount tab is selected. If not, click the tab.
- QuickBooks DT displays the 1% discount amount, which was calculated on the total amount due. If your computer does not display this discount amount, enter 20.41 in the Amount of Discount text box.
Click the drop-down list arrow for **Discount Account**, click **4050 Sales Discounts**

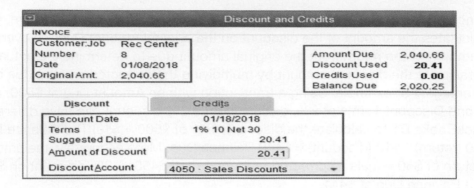

Click the **Done** button at the bottom of the Discounts and Credits screen to apply the discount of $20.41

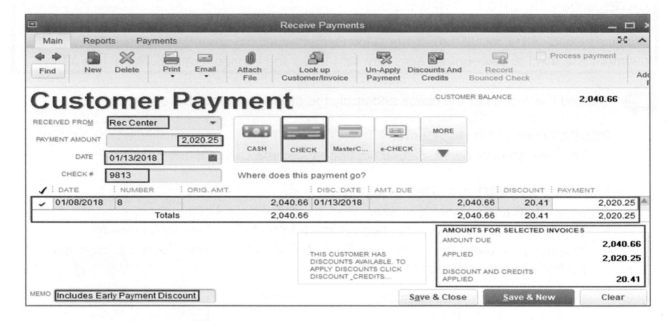

- Notice that ORIG. AMT. stays the same, $2,040.66; the AMT. DUE for Invoice Number 8 shows $2,040.66; the discount date of 01/13/2018 is the date the discount was applied to the payment, the discount amount of $20.41 shows in the DISCOUNT column, and the PAYMENT shows $2,020.25.
- In the area for AMOUNTS FOR SELECTED INVOICES, you will see the AMOUNT DUE, 2,040.66; APPLIED, 2,020.25; and DISCOUNTS AND CREDITS APPLIED, 20.41.
- The Underpayment section no longer appears.
- You may or may not have a message "This Customer has Discounts Available. To Apply Discounts, click Discount_Credits..." Once you save the Customer Payment, the message should disappear.

Print the Payment Receipt
- If you print to a pdf file, save the document as **31-Your Name Rcv Pmt Rec Ctr Ch5**.

Click the **Next** arrow or **Save & New**

RECORD LATE PAYMENT WITH DISCOUNT

As learned previously, QuickBooks DT will automatically calculate discounts. If you receive a payment after the due date, QuickBooks DT will not calculate a discount. The discount must be entered on the Discounts and Credit screen.

MEMO
DATE: January 14, 2018

Received Debit Card Payment dated January 10 and postmarked January 11 for $2,038.48 from Mountain Schools. Date the payment receipt 01/14/18. Debit Card Number 5299 7935 6678 7338, Expiration 09/2025.

Record the receipt of the payment and apply the appropriate discounts to the above transactions

Click the **Look up Customer/Invoice** icon on the Receive Payments Icon bar
Click the drop-down list arrow for **Search by** on the Find a Customer/Invoice screen
Click **Customer Name:Job**
Tab to or click in the **Customer** text box, enter **Mountain Schools**
Click the **Search** button
Click the line for **Invoice 3**

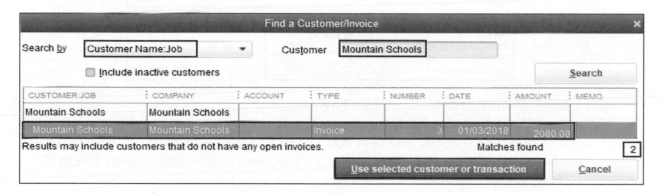

Click the **Use selected customer or transaction** button
- Notice that **Mountain Schools** is shown in RECEIVED FROM and that the PAYMENT AMOUNT shows 2,080.08.

Change the PAYMENT AMOUNT TO **2038.48**
Use the DATE **01/14/2018**
Click the **MasterC...** icon
- The last credit or debit payment received was a MasterCard, so QuickBooks DT shows that on the button.

Click the drop-down list arrow for **PAYMENT**, the click **Debit Card**

Enter the **CARD NUMBER** of **5299 7935 6678 7338**, and the **EXP DATE** of **09/2025**
Click **Done**
- Notice that the MasterC… button now shows Debit C…
- Note the UNDERPAYMENT of $41.60.

Click the **Discounts And Credits** icon on the Receive Payments icon bar
Make sure the **Discount** tab is selected
- Note that the Amount Due and the Balance Due are both 2,080.08. The Discount Date shows as 01/13/2018 with Terms of 2% 10 Net 30 and a Suggested Discount is shown as 0.00.
- Even though we are recording the payment after the discount date, the check was postmarked within the discount period. We will apply the discount for early payment to this transaction.
- Since the payment is being recorded after the discount date, you need to calculate and enter the amount of the 2% discount.

Click in the **Amount of Discount** text box, and enter **2080.08,** then press the * (asterisk)
- This opens QuickMath.

Enter **.02**, press **Enter**, press **Tab**
- QuickMath calculates the 2% discount of $41.60, enters it into the text box, and shows the amount as Discount Used at the top of the Discounts and Credits screen.
- Once the Discount Used is applied, the Balance Due shows 2,038.48.

The Discount Account is **4050 Sales Discounts**

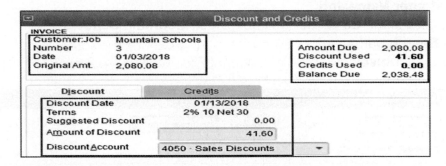

Click **Done** and return to the Customer Payment
Enter the MEMO: **Includes Early Payment Discount**
- Notice that the Customer Payment now shows a DISC. DATE of 01/14/2018 and that the AMOUNTS FOR SELECTED INVOICES includes the DISCOUNT AND CREDITS APPLIED of $41.60.

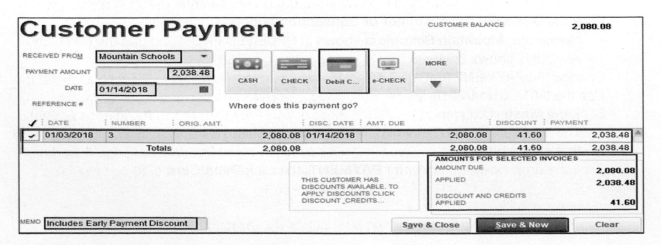

Print the Customer Payment and then click **Save & Close**
- If you print to a pdf file, save the document as **32-Your Name Rcv Pmt Mountain Schools Ch5**.

RECORD LATE PAYMENT WITH CREDIT AND DISCOUNT

Sometimes, QuickBooks DT automatic calculation of a discount is not correct. For example, when a payment is received and a return has been made, QuickBooks DT will apply the discount to the original amount owed, which gives a discount on returned merchandise. In this instance, the discount must be calculated on the amount owed after the credit has been applied.

MEMO
DATE: January 14, 2018

On January 13, we received but did not record Check 152 dated January 11 and postmarked 1/12 from Benjamin Asher for $916.84 to pay his account in full. Date the payment receipt 01/13/18.

5

➡ Record the payment described above

Click the Create Invoices icon on the Home Page; click Previous until you get to Invoice 6 for Benjamin Asher

Click the **Receive Payments** icon on the Create Invoices Main icon bar

- A Receive Payments screen opens for recording the transaction.
- Since we accessed the Receive Payments screen from an invoice, the amount of the invoice was inserted as the PAYMENT AMOUNT.
- Also note that Invoice 6 has a check mark in the check column.

Change the PAYMENT AMOUNT to **916.84** for **Benjamin Asher**, press Tab
- Now both transactions have been marked.

Use the date the check was received **01/13/18** as the DATE

Click **CHECK** for the Payment method, and enter CHECK # **152**
- Once all the transaction information is entered, notice the UNDERPAYMENT of $8.40.
- Since the payment was received within the discount period, the discount needs to be applied.

Click the line for Number 6 on the Receive Payments window and then click the **Discounts And Credits** icon, make sure the **Discount** tab is selected and that Number is 6 is shown
- Analyze the information displayed:
  - 852.11 shows as the Original Amt. and the Amount Due for Invoice 6.
  - 8.52 is the Discount Used, which is the amount QuickBooks DT calculates for the discount on the original Amount Due rather than the Balance Due.
  - 11.87 is the Credits Used (The credit of 11.87 was applied to the invoice when the return was recorded.)
  - 831.72 is the Balance Due (This is incorrect because the discount should not be calculated before the Credit Used is subtracted. It should be calculated 852.11 – 11.87 = 840.24 Balance Due.)

The terms are **1% 10 Net 30**

Click in the **Amount of Discount** text box, delete the discount of **8.52**

Use QuickMath to calculate the discount amount:
Amount Due **852.11** – Credits Used **11.87** * **.01** (discount percentage) = a discount of **8.40**, press **Enter** to enter the discount, press **Tab** to update Discount Used

- Note that QuickBooks DT shows the Suggested Discount of 8.52, which is the discount for the Amount Due before subtracting the Credits Used. The Discount Used is 8.40, the amount calculated by QuickMath.

Use the Discount Account **4050 Sales Discounts**

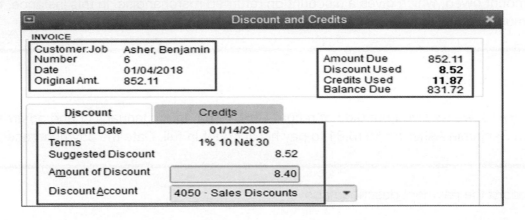

Click **Done**

Enter the MEMO: **Includes Early Payment Discount**

- Notice that AVAILABLE CREDITS shows 0.00 but says "THIS CUSTOMER HAS DISCOUNTS AVAILABLE… This is because QuickBooks DT calculated that a discount of 8.52 was available. Disregard this message.

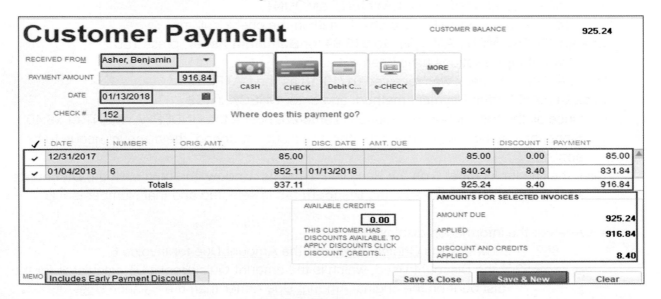

Print the Customer Payment, click **Save & New**

- If you print to a pdf file, save the document as **33-Your Name Rcv Pmt Asher Ch5**.

RECORD ADDITIONAL PAYMENTS ON ACCOUNT

> ### MEMO
> **DATE:** January 14, 2018
>
> Received Check 3951 from Dr. Diego Medina for $1,094.45.
>
> Received Debit Card payment for $500 from Lila Green in partial payment of account. Debit Card Number 4556 6464 7132 2396, Expiration 05/2021. Leave this as an Underpayment. Enter the memo: Partial Payment.
>
> Received Visa payment from Helen Grant for $408.48 in payment of the 12/31/2017 balance. Visa Card Number 4716 2206 4431 2259, Expiration 06/2024.
>
> Received Check 819 from Justin Shaw for $100 in partial payment of his account. Leave this as an underpayment.

 Refer to the previous steps listed to enter the above payments:

- Any partial payments should be noted as a Memo.
- A partial payment should have *LEAVE THIS AS AN UNDERPAYMENT* marked. Refer to Chapter 2 if you do not remember how to record an underpayment.
- Be sure to apply any discounts.

Print a Payment Receipt for each payment recorded

- If you print to a pdf file, save the documents as **34-Your Name Rcv Pmt Medina Ch5**, **35-Your Name Rcv Pmt Green Ch5**, **36-Your Name Rcv Pmt Grant Ch5**, **37-Your Name Rcv Pmt Shaw Ch5.**

Click the **Save & Close** button after all payments received have been recorded

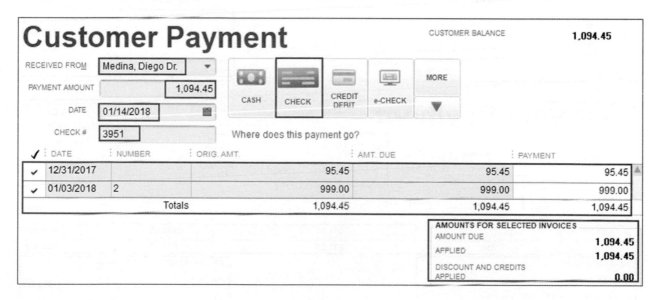

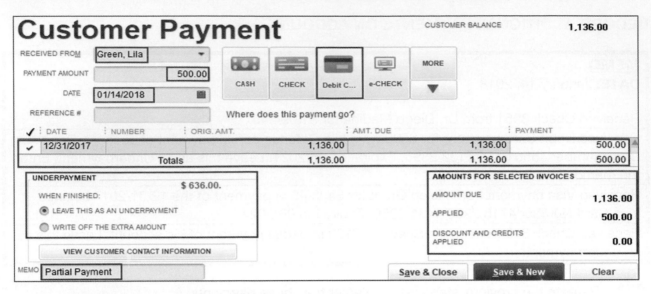

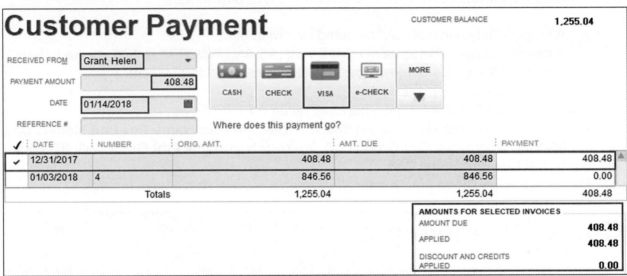

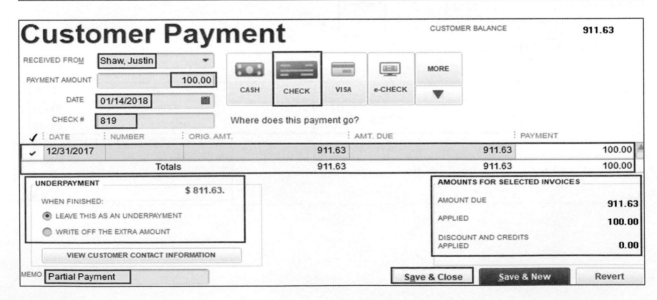

PRINT CUSTOMER BALANCE SUMMARY

A report that will show you the balance owed by each customer is the Customer Balance Summary. The report presents the total balance owed by each customer as of a certain date.

MEMO

DATE: January 14, 2018

Larry and you want to see how much each customer owes to Your Name's Sierra Sports. Print a Customer Balance Summary Report for All Transactions.

 Prepare and print a **Customer Balance Summary** following the steps given previously for printing the report in Portrait orientation

Your Name's Sierra Sports
Customer Balance Summary
All Transactions

	Jan 14, 18
Dunn, Carol ▶	455.00 ◀
Gale, Yvonne Dr.	417.00
Grant, Helen	846.56
Green, Lila	636.00
Hudson, Lisa	650.00
Koury, Deron	1,085.00
Shaw, Justin	811.63
Wong, Tamako	670.31
TOTAL	**5,571.50**

Print the report as instructed then close the report
- If you print to a pdf file, save the document as **38-Your Name Cust Bal Sum Ch5**.

VIEW TRANSACTION LIST BY CUSTOMER

To see the transactions for customers, you need to prepare a report called Transaction List by Customer. This report shows all sales, credits, and payments for each customer on account and for the customer named Cash Customer. The report does not show the balance remaining on account for the individual customers.

 View the Transaction List by Customer

Click the **Reports** icon to open the **Report Center**, click **Customers & Receivables**
Double-click **Transaction List by Customer**
Enter the dates from **01/01/18** to **01/14/18**
Tab to generate the report and scroll through the report

Your Name's Sierra Sports
Transaction List by Customer
January 1 - 14, 2018

Type	Date	Num	Memo	Account	Clr	Split	Debit	Credit
Asher, Benjamin								
Invoice	01/02/2018	1	VOID:	1200 · Accounts Receivable	✓	-SPLIT-	0.00	◄
Sales Order	01/03/2018	2		90200 · Sales Orders		-SPLIT-	840.24	
Invoice	01/04/2018	6		1200 · Accounts Receivable		-SPLIT-	852.11	
Credit Memo	01/10/2018	10		1200 · Accounts Receivable		-SPLIT-		11.87
Payment	01/13/2018	152	Includes Early Payment Discount	12000 · Undeposited Funds		1200 · Accounts Receivable	916.84	
Cash Customer								
Sales Receipt	01/08/2018	1		12000 · Undeposited Funds		-SPLIT-	36.86	
Sales Receipt	01/11/2018	2		12000 · Undeposited Funds		-SPLIT-	215.95	
Sales Receipt	01/11/2018	3		12000 · Undeposited Funds		-SPLIT-	34.54	
Sales Receipt	01/11/2018	4		12000 · Undeposited Funds		-SPLIT-	97.15	
Sales Receipt	01/12/2018	5		12000 · Undeposited Funds		-SPLIT-	410.29	
Sales Receipt	01/12/2018	6		12000 · Undeposited Funds		-SPLIT-	626.29	
Sales Receipt	01/12/2018	7		12000 · Undeposited Funds		-SPLIT-	97.15	
Sales Receipt	01/12/2018	8		12000 · Undeposited Funds		-SPLIT-	248.35	
Grant, Helen								
Invoice	01/03/2018	4		1200 · Accounts Receivable		-SPLIT-	846.56	
Payment	01/14/2018			12000 · Undeposited Funds		1200 · Accounts Receivable	408.48	
Green, Lila								
Payment	01/14/2018		Partial Payment	12000 · Undeposited Funds		1200 · Accounts Receivable	500.00	
Medina, Diego Dr.								
Invoice	01/03/2018	2		1200 · Accounts Receivable		-SPLIT-	999.00	
Payment	01/14/2018	3951		12000 · Undeposited Funds		1200 · Accounts Receivable	1,094.45	
Mountain Schools								
Invoice	01/03/2018	3		1200 · Accounts Receivable		-SPLIT-	2,080.08	
Payment	01/14/2018		Includes Early Payment Discount	12000 · Undeposited Funds		1200 · Accounts Receivable	2,038.48	
Ortiz, Oskar								
Payment	01/13/2018	765		12000 · Undeposited Funds		1200 · Accounts Receivable	975.00	
Rec Center								
Invoice	01/08/2018	8		1200 · Accounts Receivable		-SPLIT-	2,040.66	
Payment	01/13/2018	9813	Includes Early Payment Discount	12000 · Undeposited Funds		1200 · Accounts Receivable	2,020.25	
Shaw, Justin								
Payment	01/14/2018	819	Partial Payment	12000 · Undeposited Funds		1200 · Accounts Receivable	100.00	
Waters, Angie								
Invoice	01/04/2018	7		1200 · Accounts Receivable		-SPLIT-	1,035.60	
Credit Memo	01/10/2018	9		1200 · Accounts Receivable		-SPLIT-		53.95
Payment	01/13/2018			12000 · Undeposited Funds		1200 · Accounts Receivable	1,035.22	

- Information is shown for the Invoices, Sales Receipts, Credit Memos, and Payments made on the accounts and the Num column shows the Invoice numbers, Sales Receipt numbers, Credit Memo numbers, or Check numbers. Nothing is shown for beginning balances or for Debit and Credit card numbers.

Close the report <u>without</u> printing and close the Report Center

MAKE DEPOSITS

When cash sales are made and payments on accounts are received, QuickBooks DT places the money received in the *Undeposited Funds* account. Once the deposit is recorded, the funds are transferred from *Undeposited Funds* to the account selected when preparing the deposit, usually Cash or Checking.

> **MEMO**
> **DATE:** January 14, 2018
>
> Deposit all cash, checks, debit card, and credit card receipts for cash sales and payments on account into the Checking account.

 Deposit cash, checks, debit card, and credit card receipts

Click the **Record Deposits** icon on the QuickBooks DT Home Page
The View payment method type should be **All types**
- The **Payments to Deposit** window shows all amounts received for cash sales (including bank credit cards) and payments on account that have not been deposited in the bank organized by payment method—Cash, Check, VISA, Debit Card, and MasterCard.

Sort is by **Payment Method**
- Notice that the **check** column to the left of the Date column is empty.

Click the **Select All** button
- Notice the check marks in the check column.

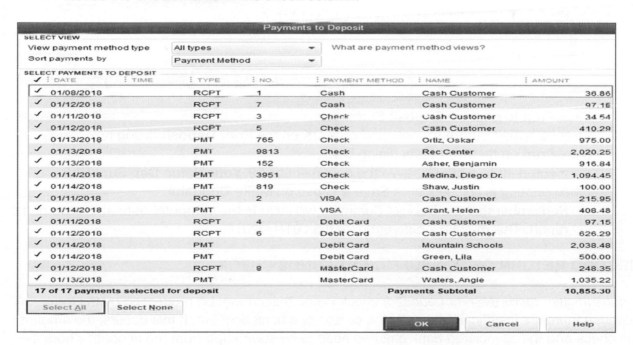

✓	DATE	TIME	TYPE	NO.	PAYMENT METHOD	NAME	AMOUNT
✓	01/08/2018		RCPT	1	Cash	Cash Customer	36.86
✓	01/12/2018		RCPT	7	Cash	Cash Customer	97.16
✓	01/11/2018		RCPT	3	Check	Cash Customer	34.54
✓	01/12/2018		RCPT	5	Check	Cash Customer	410.29
✓	01/13/2018		PMT	765	Check	Ortiz, Oskar	975.00
✓	01/13/2018		PMT	9813	Check	Rec Center	2,020.25
✓	01/13/2018		PMT	152	Check	Asher, Benjamin	916.84
✓	01/14/2018		PMT	3951	Check	Medina, Diego Dr.	1,094.45
✓	01/14/2018		PMT	819	Check	Shaw, Justin	100.00
✓	01/11/2018		RCPT	2	VISA	Cash Customer	215.95
✓	01/14/2018		PMT		VISA	Grant, Helen	408.48
✓	01/11/2018		RCPT	4	Debit Card	Cash Customer	97.15
✓	01/12/2018		RCPT	6	Debit Card	Cash Customer	626.29
✓	01/14/2018		PMT		Debit Card	Mountain Schools	2,038.48
✓	01/14/2018		PMT		Debit Card	Green, Lila	500.00
✓	01/12/2018		RCPT	8	MasterCard	Cash Customer	248.35
✓	01/13/2018		PMT		MasterCard	Waters, Angie	1,035.22

17 of 17 payments selected for deposit   **Payments Subtotal**   **10,855.30**

Select All   Select None

OK   Cancel   Help

5

Click **OK** to close the **Payments to Deposit** screen and go to the **Make Deposits** screen
On the **Make Deposits** screen, **Deposit To** should be **1100 Checking**
Date should be **01/14/2018**
- Tab to date and change if not correct.

Your Make Deposits screen should look like the following:

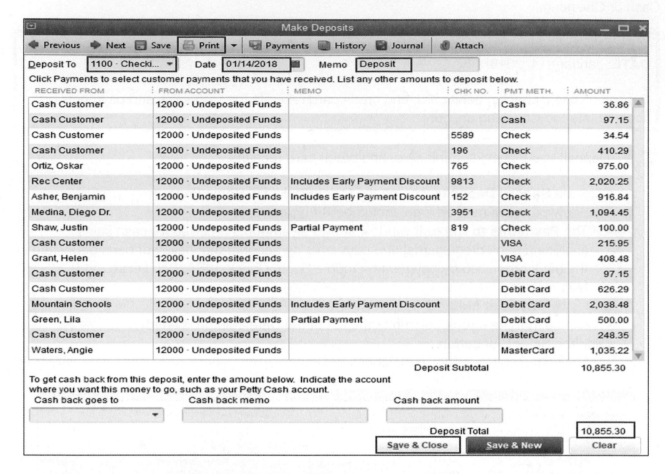

RECEIVED FROM	FROM ACCOUNT	MEMO	CHK NO.	PMT METH.	AMOUNT
Cash Customer	12000 · Undeposited Funds			Cash	36.86
Cash Customer	12000 · Undeposited Funds			Cash	97.15
Cash Customer	12000 · Undeposited Funds		5589	Check	34.54
Cash Customer	12000 · Undeposited Funds		196	Check	410.29
Ortiz, Oskar	12000 · Undeposited Funds		765	Check	975.00
Rec Center	12000 · Undeposited Funds	Includes Early Payment Discount	9813	Check	2,020.25
Asher, Benjamin	12000 · Undeposited Funds	Includes Early Payment Discount	152	Check	916.84
Medina, Diego Dr.	12000 · Undeposited Funds		3951	Check	1,094.45
Shaw, Justin	12000 · Undeposited Funds	Partial Payment	819	Check	100.00
Cash Customer	12000 · Undeposited Funds			VISA	215.95
Grant, Helen	12000 · Undeposited Funds			VISA	408.48
Cash Customer	12000 · Undeposited Funds			Debit Card	97.15
Cash Customer	12000 · Undeposited Funds			Debit Card	626.29
Mountain Schools	12000 · Undeposited Funds	Includes Early Payment Discount		Debit Card	2,038.48
Green, Lila	12000 · Undeposited Funds	Partial Payment		Debit Card	500.00
Cash Customer	12000 · Undeposited Funds			MasterCard	248.35
Waters, Angie	12000 · Undeposited Funds			MasterCard	1,035.22

Deposit Subtotal: 10,855.30

To get cash back from this deposit, enter the amount below. Indicate the account where you want this money to go, such as your Petty Cash account.

Cash back goes to | Cash back memo | Cash back amount

Deposit Total: 10,855.30

Click **Print** to print the **Deposit Summary**
Select **Deposit summary only** and click **OK** on the **Print Deposit** dialog box
Click **Print** on the **Print Lists** dialog box
- If you print to a pdf file, save the document as **39-Your Name Dep Sum Ch5**.

When printing is finished, click **Save & Close** on **Make Deposits**
- Remember that the Deposit Summary will include the computer date at the top of the report. This may be a different date than 01/14/2018.

RECORD RETURN OF NONSUFFICIENT FUNDS CHECK

A *nonsufficient funds* (*NSF* or *bounced*) check is one that cannot be processed by the bank because there are insufficient funds in the customer's bank account. If this occurs, the amount of the check and the associated bank charges need to be subtracted from the account where the check was deposited. Also, the Accounts Receivable account needs to be updated to show the amount the customer owes you for the check that "bounced." To track the amount of a bad check and to charge a customer for the bank charges and any penalties you impose, Other Charge items may need to be created and an invoice for the total amount due must be prepared.

Money received for the bad check charges from the bank and for Your Name's Sierra Sports is recorded as income. When the bank account is reconciled, the amount of bank charges will be an expense that offsets the income recorded on the invoice for the NSF check.

MEMO

DATE: January 15, 2018

The bank returned Oskar Ortiz's Check 765 marked NSF. The bank imposed a $10 service charge for the NSF check. Your Name's Sierra Sports charges a $25 fee for NSF checks. Record the NSF (Bounced) Check.

Record the NSF (Bounced) Check from Oskar Ortiz and all the related charges

Go to the Receive Payments screen where Oskar's $975 check was recorded
- If not already selected, click the 12/31/2017 Invoice for the Opening balance of 975.00 to select.
- Notice the Customer Payment shows the ORIG. AMT., AMT. DUE, and PAYMENT as 975.00.

Click the **Record Bounced Check** icon on the Receive Payments icon bar

On the Manage Bounced Check screen, enter:

> BANK FEE of **10.00**, the DATE is **01/15/2018**, the EXPENSE ACCOUNT is **6120 Bank Service Charges**

Enter **25.00** for the CUSTOMER FEE
- When the amount of the Bank Fee of $10 is subtracted from the $25 Customer Fee charged by Your Name's Sierra Sports, the net result of the Customer Fee will result in $15 for other income.

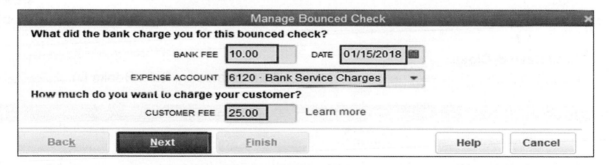

Click **Next**

Read the Bounced Check Summary

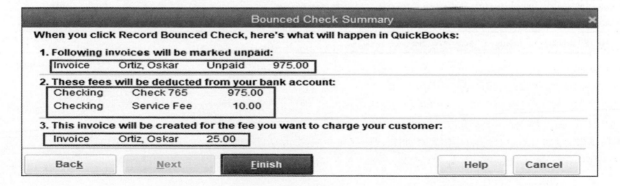

- The Invoice for the Opening Balance will now be marked as unpaid, Check 765 for $975 will be deducted from our checking account, the $10 bank fee will be deducted from the checking account and shown as an expense, and an Invoice will be created for the $25 Customer Fee charged by Your Name's Sierra Sports.

Click **Finish** and view the Customer Payment information

- Notice the CUSTOMER BALANCE of 1,000.00. This is the $975 due from the bounced check and the $25 Customer Fee collected by Your Name's Sierra Sports. The transaction for 12/31/2017 now shows as PAYMENT 0.00, the payment made on 01/15/2018 basically cancels out the Payment recorded earlier for the 12/31/2017 balance. Invoice 11 was created for the additional $25 owed for the bad check fee.
- If the date for Invoice 11 shows as 01/14/18 (the last transaction date used), you may leave it as that date.

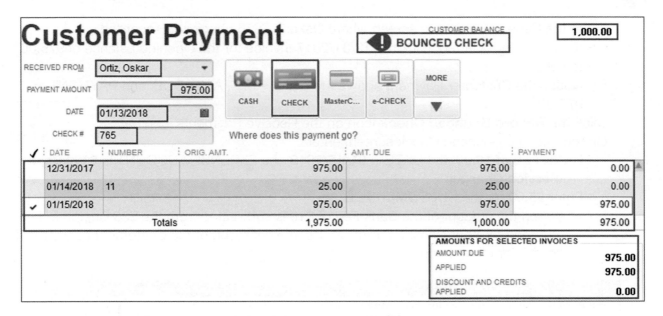

Click **Save & Close**

Open the Item List to see the Bounced Check Item created by QuickBooks DT

- Note that the NAME is Bounce Check Charge and the ACCOUNT is 5009 Returned Check Charges.
- Notice that the other income accounts are in the 4000 category for Income. While 5009 Returned Check was assigned a 5000 category for Cost of Goods Sold.

Open the Chart of Accounts, scroll through until you see Account 5009 Returned Check Charges

Click on the account and use the keyboard shortcut **Ctrl+E** to edit the account

Change the Account Number to **4090** so that it is in the same number category as the other income accounts

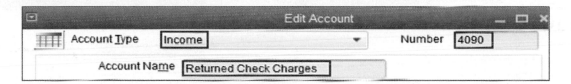

Click **Save & Close** to change the account number

Look at the Income accounts and note how they are organized

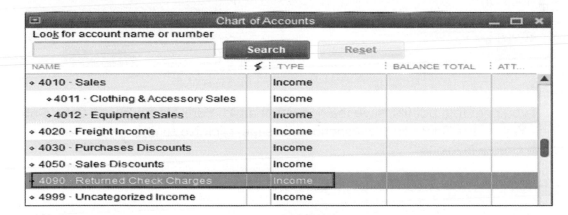

Close the Chart of Accounts, open **Create Invoices**

Go to the Opening balance invoice for Oskar Ortiz and notice that it shows a Balance Due of 975.00

Change the TEMPLATE to Copy of: Intuit Produce Invoice

Click the drop-down list arrow for TERMS, click **Due on receipt**

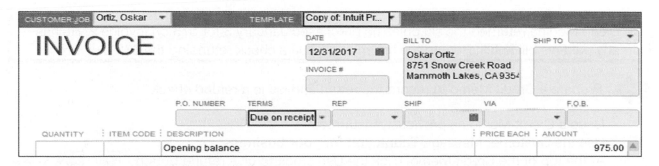

Print the Revised Invoice for the Opening balance, click **Yes** to record the transaction, click **Yes** to change an entry for a closed period, click **No** on the Information Changed dialog box to change the Terms

- If you print to a pdf file, save the document as **40-Your Name Inv Ortiz Revised Ch5**.
Go to **Invoice 11**, review the invoice
Change TEMPLATE to **Copy of: Intuit Product Invoice**
Make sure that **01/15/2018** is shown for DATE and SHIP; if not, change it
Click the drop-down list arrow for TERMS, click **Due on Receipt**
Insert the CUSTOMER MESSAGE **Please remit to above address.**
- QuickBooks DT should enter the MEMO for Bounced Check# 765 automatically; if not, enter it.

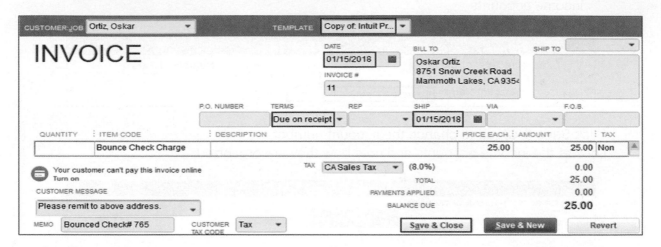

Print Invoice 11
- If you print to a pdf file, save the document as **41-Your Name Inv 11 Ortiz Ch5**.
Click **Yes** on the Recording Transaction message, click **No** to change the Terms
Close Create Invoices

ISSUE CREDIT MEMO AND REFUND CHECK

If merchandise is returned and the invoice has been paid in full or the sale was for cash, a refund check may be issued at the same time the credit memo is prepared. Simply clicking the "Use credit to give refund" icon instructs QuickBooks DT to prepare a refund check for you.

MEMO

DATE: January 15, 2018

Dr. Diego Medina returned the ski poles he purchased January 3 for $75 on Invoice 2. He has already paid his bill in full. Record the return and issue a check refunding the $75 plus tax.

     Prepare a Credit Memo to record the return and issue a refund check

Issue a Credit Memo as previously instructed
Use the Customer Message **Thank you for your business.**
At the top of the Credit Memo, click the Use credit to give refund button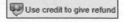
The Issue a Refund dialog box appears.

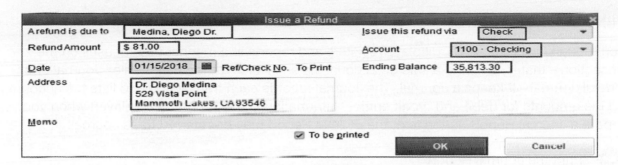

Verify the information and click **OK**.

The Credit Memo will be stamped "REFUNDED."

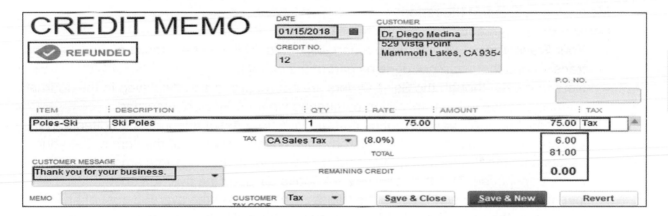

Print the Credit Memo with lines around each field

- If you print to a pdf file, save the document as **42-Your Name CM 12 Medina Ch5**.

Click **Save & Close** to record the **Credit Memo** and exit

Click the **Write Checks** icon on the Home Page, click the **Previous** or back arrow until you get to the check for Dr. Medina

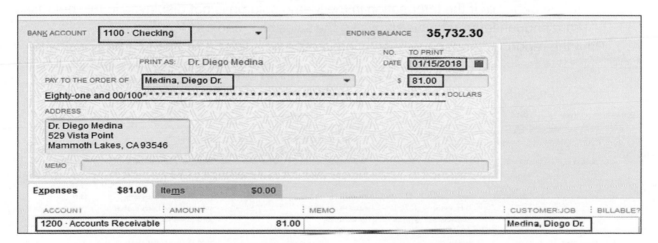

- Note that Medina, Diego Dr. appears in the CUSTOMER:JOB column on the Expenses tab. This indicates that the refund check is linked to the customer.

Print Check 1 in <u>Standard</u> format as previously instructed

- If you print to a pdf file, save the document as **43-Your Name Ck 1 Medina Ch5**.

Click **OK** on the Print Checks – Confirmation screen

Click **Save & Close** on the **Write Checks** screen

PRINT JOURNAL REPORT

Even though QuickBooks DT displays registers and reports in a manner that focuses on the transaction—that is, entering a sale on account via an invoice rather than a Sales Journal or a General Journal—it keeps a Journal. The Journal records each transaction and lists the accounts and the amounts for debit and credit entries. Information in the Journal is displayed when you prepare a Journal Report. In the text, the Journal Report may be referred to as Journal.

 Print the Journal Report

> Open the **Report Center** and prepare the **Journal** as previously instructed
> The report date is from **01/01/18** to **01/15/18**
> Make sure to **Expand** the report
> Scroll through the report to view the transactions
> - Your Trans # may not match the report illustrated. This can be a result of your deleting transactions that were not done as part of the chapter.
> - Note that even though the Sales Orders are not recorded and displayed in the Journal, there is a space in the transaction numbering where they were recorded.
> - For each item sold, you will notice that the Inventory Asset account is credited and the Cost of Goods Sold account is debited. This moves the value of the item out of your assets and into the cost of goods sold. The amount is not the same amount as the one in the transaction. This is because QuickBooks DT uses the average cost method of inventory valuation and records the transaction based on the average cost of an item rather than the specific cost of an item. The Memo column contains the Sales Item used in the transaction.
> Resize the columns by positioning the cursor on the diamond and dragging so that the report columns do not have a lot of blank space
> Since it has not been used, eliminate the **Adj** column from the report
> - Make sure that the account names are displayed in full.
> - It is acceptable if the Information in the Memo column is not displayed in full, but make sure enough information is shown so the sales item can be identified.
> Print the report in **Landscape** orientation; if need be, click **Fit report to 1 pages(s) wide**

Your Name's Sierra Sports
Journal
January 1 - 15, 2018

Trans #	Type	Date	Num	Name	Memo	Account	Debit	Credit
81	General Journal	01/15/2018		Ortiz, Oskar	Bounced Check# 765	1200 - Accounts Receivable	975.00	
				Ortiz, Oskar	Bounced Check# 765	1100 - Checking		975.00
							975.00	975.00
82	General Journal	01/15/2018			Bank service charges for bounced check# 765	6120 - Bank Service Charges	10.00	
				Ortiz, Oskar	Bank service charges for bounced check# 765	1100 - Checking		10.00
							10.00	10.00
83	Invoice	01/15/2018	11	Ortiz, Oskar	Bounced Check# 765	1200 - Accounts Receivable	25.00	
				Ortiz, Oskar	Bounced Check# 765	4090 - Returned Check Charges		25.00
				State Board of Equalization	CA Sales Tax	2200 - Sales Tax Payable	0.00	
							25.00	25.00
84	Credit Memo	01/15/2018	12	Medina, Diego Dr.		1200 - Accounts Receivable		81.00
				Medina, Diego Dr.	Ski Poles	4012 - Equipment Sales	75.00	
				Medina, Diego Dr.	Ski Poles	1120 - Inventory Asset	30.00	
				Medina, Diego Dr.	Ski Poles	5000 - Cost of Goods Sold		30.00
				State Board of Equalization	CA Sales Tax	2200 - Sales Tax Payable	6.00	
							111.00	111.00
85	Check	01/15/2018	1	Medina, Diego Dr.		1100 - Checking		81.00
				Medina, Diego Dr.		1200 - Accounts Receivable	81.00	
							81.00	81.00
TOTAL							37,603.89	37,603.89

Partial Report

When the report is printed, close it.
* If you print to a pdf file, save the document as **44-Your Name Journal Ch5**.
Do not close the Report Center

PRINT TRIAL BALANCE

When all sales transactions have been entered, it is important to print the trial balance and verify that the total debits equal the total credits.

 Prepare and print the Trial Balance

Prepare the report from the Report Center as previously instructed
The report dates are from **01/01/2018** to **01/15/2018**

Your Name's Sierra Sports
Trial Balance
As of January 15, 2018

	Jan 15, 18	
	Debit	Credit
1100 · Checking	35,732.30	
1200 · Accounts Receivable	6,571.50	
1120 · Inventory Asset	32,766.54	
12000 · Undeposited Funds	0.00	
1311 · Office Supplies	850.00	
1312 · Sales Supplies	575.00	
1340 · Prepaid Insurance	250.00	
1511 · Original Cost	5,000.00	
1521 · Original Cost	4,500.00	
2000 · Accounts Payable		8,500.00
2100 · Visa		150.00
2200 · Sales Tax Payable		701.77
2510 · Office Equipment Loan		3,000.00
2520 · Store Fixtures Loan		2,500.00
3000 · Owners' Equity	0.00	
3010 · Your Name & Muir Capital		26,159.44
3011 · Your Name, Investment		20,000.00
3012 · Larry Muir, Investment		20,000.00
4011 · Clothing & Accessory Sales		1,759.51
4012 · Equipment Sales		7,436.44
4050 · Sales Discounts	494.36	
4090 · Returned Check Charges		25.00
5000 · Cost of Goods Sold	3,482.46	
6120 · Bank Service Charges	10.00	
TOTAL	90,232.16	90,232.16

Print the Trial Balance in **Portrait** orientation
* If you print to a pdf file, save the document as **45-Your Name Trial Bal Ch5**.
Do not close the Report Center

PREPARE INVENTORY VALUATION DETAIL REPORT

To obtain information regarding the inventory, you may prepare an Inventory Valuation Summary or an Inventory Valuation Detail report. Both reports give you information regarding sales items, the number on hand, the average cost, and asset value. The detail report includes information for transactions that affected the value of your inventory during an accounting period.

The detail report includes the type of transaction, date of transaction, customer name, number, quantity, and cost. If an inventory item was not used within the report dates, it will not be included in the detail report. Preparing the Inventory Valuation Detail will allow you to verify the inventory items used, the average cost for each transaction, and the number of items on hand.

Prepare and print an Inventory Valuation Detail report in Landscape orientation for January 1-15, 2018

Click **Inventory** in the Report Center
Double-click **Inventory Valuation Detail**
Enter the dates From **01/01/18** To **01/15/18**
Resize the columns to display the information in full
Use Landscape orientation

Your Name's Sierra Sports
Inventory Valuation Detail
January 1 - 15, 2018

Type	Date	Name	Num	Qty	Cost	On Hand	Avg Cost	Asset Value
Sweaters								
Invoice	01/03/2018	Grant, Helen	4	-1		74	25.00	1,850.00
Sales Receipt	01/11/2018	Cash Customer	4	-1		73	25.00	1,825.00
Total Sweaters						73		1,825.00
Toboggans								
Inventory Adjust	01/08/2018			10		10	137.50	1,375.00
Invoice	01/08/2018	Rec Center	8	-5		5	137.50	687.50
Total Toboggans						5		687.50
Underwear								
Invoice	01/03/2018	Grant, Helen	4	-1		32	8.00	256.00
Total Underwear						32		256.00
Total Inventory						1,435		31,016.54
TOTAL						1,435		31,016.54

Partial Report

Print the report, do <u>not</u> close the Report Center
- If you print to a pdf file, save the document as **46-Your Name Inventory Val Detail Ch5**.

PREPARE AND MEMORIZE INVENTORY VALUATION SUMMARY

Preparing the Inventory Valuation Summary will allow you to verify the number on hand, average cost, asset value, percentage of Total Assets, sales price, retail value, and percentage of Total Retail value for each inventory item whether or not it was used during the report period.

Once a report has been prepared and customized, it may be memorized for future use. Any changes to the report will be saved and will be used automatically the next time the report is prepared.

Prepare the Inventory Valuation Summary report and then memorize it

Double-click **Inventory Valuation Summary** in the Report Center
The date should be **01/15/18**, press **Tab**
Since no information is shown for **Sales Price**, **Retail Value**, **% of Tot Retail**, remove the columns from the report as instructed previously

Click the **Memorize** button
Click **OK** on the Memorize Report dialog box

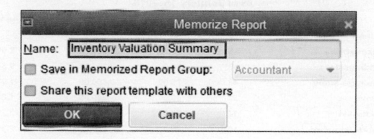

Close the report and the Report Center

PREPARE MEMORIZED REPORT

To illustrate the use of a memorized report, the previous report was closed after it was memorized. It may be used to prepare the report in its memorized format.

 Prepare the Memorized Report, Inventory Valuation Summary

Click **Reports** on the Menu bar, point to **Memorized Reports**, and click **Inventory Valuation Summary**

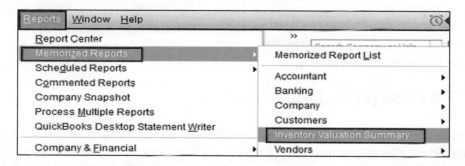

Enter the date As of **01/15/2018**

- The Inventory Valuation Summary is shown without columns for Sales Price, Retail Value, % of Tot Retail.

Your Name's Sierra Sports
Inventory Valuation Summary
As of January 15, 2018

	On Hand	Avg Cost	Asset Value	% of Tot Asset
Inventory				
Accessories ▶	795	3.66	2,906.70	8.9% ◀
Bindings-Skis	43	75.00	3,225.00	9.8%
Bindings-Snow	48	75.00	3,600.00	11.0%
Boots	20	30.00	600.00	1.8%
Boots-Ski	14	75.00	1,050.00	3.2%
Boots-Snowbrd	10	75.00	750.00	2.3%
Gloves	20	15.00	300.00	0.9%
Hats	29	8.00	232.00	0.7%
Helmets	20	28.00	560.00	1.7%
Pants-Ski	93	30.00	2,790.00	8.5%
Pants-Snowbrd	50	35.00	1,750.00	5.3%
Parkas	73	58.33	4,258.34	13.0%
Poles-Ski	13	30.00	390.00	1.2%
Skis	43	100.00	4,300.00	13.1%
Sleds	4	67.50	270.00	0.8%
Snowboard	28	100.00	2,800.00	8.5%
Socks	72	3.00	216.00	0.7%
Sweaters	73	25.00	1,825.00	5.6%
Toboggans	5	137.50	687.50	2.1%
Underwear	32	8.00	256.00	0.8%
Total Inventory	1,485		32,766.54	100.0%
TOTAL	**1,485**		**32,766.54**	**100.0%**

Close the report without printing

PRINT PROFIT & LOSS (STANDARD)

Chapter 5 focuses on receivables. To see the income earned for the month, you prepare a Profit & Loss (Standard) report. On this statement, you will see the income earned for each sales account. Sales Discounts will be subtracted from Sales and the Returned Check Charges will be added to Sales to calculate the Total Income. The Cost of Goods Sold section will include the total of the average cost for all the items sold. Cost of Goods Sold is subtracted from Total Income to get the Gross Profit. Finally, the Expenses are listed and subtracted from Gross Profit to get the Net Income.

Prepare and print the Profit & Loss (Standard) report for January 1-15, 2018

Follow previous instructions to prepare the report for January 1-15, 2018
- Unless instructed otherwise, all Profit & Loss reports will be Standard.
Analyze the Profit & Loss report
- Note: Total Sales is calculated by adding account 4011 and 4012 together.
- 4050 Sales Discounts are subtracted, and 4090 Returned Check Charges are added to 4010 Sales to calculate Total Income.
- 5000 Cost of Goods Sold is the total of the average cost of all items sold.
- The Total COGS is subtracted from Total Income to get the Gross Profit.
- The Expenses are listed and totaled and then subtracted from Gross Profit to get the Net Income.

Your Name's Sierra Sports
Profit & Loss
January 1 - 15, 2018

	Jan 1 - 15, 18
▼ Ordinary Income/Expense	
▼ Income	
▼ 4010 · Sales	
4011 · Clothing & Accessory Sales ►	1,759.51 ◄
4012 · Equipment Sales	7,436.44
Total 4010 · Sales	9,195.95
4050 · Sales Discounts	-494.36
4090 · Returned Check Charges	25.00
Total Income	8,726.59
▼ Cost of Goods Sold	
5000 · Cost of Goods Sold	3,482.46
Total COGS	3,482.46
Gross Profit	5,244.13
▼ Expense	
6120 · Bank Service Charges	10.00
Total Expense	10.00
Net Ordinary Income	5,234.13
Net Income	5,234.13

Print the report

- If you print to a pdf file, save the document as **47-Your Name P & L Ch5**.

BACK UP YOUR NAME'S SIERRA SPORTS

Whenever an important work session is complete, you should always back up your data. If your data or storage media is damaged or an error is discovered later, the backup can be restored, and the information can be used for recording transactions. The backup being made will contain all the transactions entered in Chapter 5. In addition, it is always wise to make a duplicate of your data on a separate storage media or a different location just in case the original is damaged.

 Back up data for Your Name's Sierra Sports to **Sierra 2018 (Backup Ch 5).qbb**

SUMMARY

In this chapter, cash, bank charge card, and credit sales were prepared for Your Name's Sierra Sports, a retail business, using sales receipts, sales orders, and invoices. Credit memos and refund checks were issued, and customer accounts were added and revised. Invoices and sales receipts were edited, deleted, and voided. Invoices were created from Sales Orders. Cash payments were received, and bank deposits were made. Methods of payment included cash, checks, credit cards, and debit cards. Nonsufficient funds payments were recorded, and penalty charges were made. New accounts were added to the Chart of Accounts, and new items were added to the Item List while entering transactions. Inventory items were added and sold. Sales tax was recorded for each inventory item sold.

All the transactions entered reinforced the QuickBooks DT concept of using the business form to record transactions rather than entering information in journals. The Journal report was accessed, analyzed, and printed. The importance of reports for information and decision-making was illustrated. Sales reports emphasized both cash and credit sales according to the customer or according to the sales item generating the revenue. Accounts receivable reports focused on amounts owed by credit customers. The traditional trial balance emphasizing the equality of debits and credits was prepared. A report was memorized. A memorized report was used to prepare a report.

END-OF-CHAPTER QUESTIONS

TRUE/FALSE

ANSWER THE FOLLOWING QUESTIONS IN THE SPACE PROVIDED BEFORE THE QUESTION NUMBER.

_____ 5.01.   Sales tax must be calculated manually and added to sales receipts.

_____ 5.02.   If a return is made after an invoice has been paid in full, a refund check is issued along with a credit memo.

_____ 5.03.   The Discounts And Credits icon on the Receive Payments window allows discounts to be applied to invoices being paid by clicking Cancel.

_____ 5.04.   Reports prepared using the Report Center may not be customized and memorized.

_____ 5.05.   QuickBooks DT automatically applies a payment received to the most current invoice.

_____ 5.06.   Items on a Sales Order are immediately removed from inventory.

_____ 5.07.   All business forms must be duplicated before they can be customized.

_____ 5.08.   Cash sales are recorded in the Receive Payments window and marked paid.

_____ 5.09.   If a customer issues a check that is returned marked NSF, you may charge the customer the amount of the bank charges and any penalty charges you impose.

_____ 5.10.   A customer may use a credit card to pay for an invoice with an applied credit.

MULTIPLE CHOICE

WRITE THE LETTER OF THE CORRECT ANSWER IN THE SPACE PROVIDED BEFORE THE QUESTION NUMBER.

_____ 5.11.   A credit card sale is treated exactly like a ___.
       A. cash sale
       B. sale on account until reimbursement is received from a bank
       C. sale on account
       D. bank deposit

_____ 5.12.   Information regarding details of a customer's balance may be obtained by viewing the ___.
       A. Trial Balance
       B. Customer Balance Summary Report
       C. Customer Balance Detail Report
       D. Check Detail report

_____ 5.13.   If the word -Split- appears in the Split column of a report rather than an account name, it means that the transaction is split between two or more ___.
   A. accounts or items
   B. customers
   C. journals
   D. reports

_____ 5.14.   Even though transactions are entered via business documents such as invoices and sales receipts, QuickBooks DT keeps track of all transactions ___.
   A. in a chart
   B. in the master account register
   C. on a graph
   D. in the Journal

_____ 5.15.   If a transaction is ___, it will not show up in the Customer Balance Detail Report.
   A. voided
   B. deleted
   C. corrected
   D. canceled

_____ 5.16.   A report prepared to obtain information about sales, inventory, and merchandise costs is a ___.
   A. Stock Report
   B. Income Statement
   C. Sales by Vendor Summary Report
   D. Sales by Item Summary Report

_____ 5.17.   If a customer has a balance for an amount owed and a return is made, a credit memo is prepared and ___.
   A. a refund check is issued
   B. the amount of the return is applied to an invoice
   C. the customer determines whether to apply the amount to an invoice or to get a refund check
   D. any of the above

_____ 5.18.   When adding a customer *on the fly*, you may choose to add just the customer's name by selecting ___.
   A. Quick Add
   B. Set Up
   C. Condensed
   D. none of the above—a customer cannot be added *on the fly*

_____ 5.19. The Item List stores information about ___.
A. each item that is out of stock
B. each item in stock
C. each customer with an account
D. each item a company sells

_____ 5.20. Purchase information regarding an item sold by the company is entered ___.
A. in the Invoice Register
B. when adding a sales item
C. only when creating the company
D. when the last item in stock is sold

FILL-IN

IN THE SPACE PROVIDED, WRITE THE ANSWER THAT MOST APPROPRIATELY COMPLETES THE SENTENCE.

5.21. A report showing all sales, credits, payments, and remaining balance for each customer on account is the _____ _____ report.

5.22. If the Quantity and Price Each are entered on an invoice, pressing the _____ key will cause QuickBooks DT to calculate and enter the correct information in the Amount column of the invoice.

5.23. When you receive payments from customers, QuickBooks DT places the amount received in an account called _____ .

5.24. When a customer with a balance due on an account makes a payment, it is recorded in _____ .

5.25. QuickBooks DT allows you to view additional information within a report by using the _____ feature.

SHORT ESSAY

Explain why you would use Find to locate an invoice. Based on chapter information, what is used to instruct Find to limit its search?

_____
_____
_____
_____
_____

END-OF-CHAPTER PROBLEM

YOUR NAME'S CALIFORNIA CASUAL

Your Name's California Casual is a men's and women's clothing store located in San Luis Obispo, California, that specializes in resort wear. The store is owned and operated by you and your partner Elizabeth Jones. Elizabeth keeps the books and runs the office for the store, and you are responsible for buying merchandise and managing the store. Both partners sell merchandise in the store, and they have some college students working part time during the evenings and on the weekends.

INSTRUCTIONS

As in previous chapters, use a copy of **Casual_2018.qbw** that you downloaded following the directions presented in Chapter 1. (They file may also be shown as Casual 2018.qbw. Either way is fine.) If QuickBooks DT wants to update the program, click Yes. Open the company, and record the following transactions using Invoices, Sales Receipts, and Receive Payments. Your Name's California Casual accepts cash, checks, debit cards, and credit cards for *cash* sales. Make bank deposits as instructed. Print the reports as indicated. Add new accounts, items, and customers where appropriate. Pay attention to the dates and note that the year is **2018**. Verify the year to use with your instructor and use it for Casual in Chapters 5, 6, and 7. The password for the company is **QBDT2018**.

When recording transactions, use the Item List to determine the item(s) sold. All transactions are taxable unless otherwise indicated. Terms for sales on account are the standard terms assigned to each customer individually. If a customer exceeds his or her credit limit, accept the transaction. When receiving payment for sales on account, always check to see if a discount should be given. A customer's beginning balance is not eligible for a discount. The date of the sale begins the discount period. A check should be received or postmarked within ten days of the invoice to qualify for a discount. If the customer has any credits to the account because of a return, apply the credits to the appropriate invoice. If the customer makes a return and does not have a balance on account, prepare a refund check for the customer.

Invoices begin with number 15, are numbered consecutively, and have lines printed around each field. Sales Receipts begin with number 25, are also numbered consecutively, and have lines printed around each field. Sales Orders are accepted for orders made by telephone, begin with the number 1, and have lines printed around each field. Each invoice, sales order and sales receipt should contain a message. Use the one you feel is most appropriate. If you write any checks, keep track of the check numbers used. QuickBooks DT does not always display the check number you are expecting to see. Remember that QuickBooks DT does not print check numbers on checks because most businesses use prenumbered checks.

If a transaction can be printed, print the transaction when it is entered unless your instructor specifies the transactions to print.

LISTS

The Item List and Customers & Jobs List are displayed for your use in determining which sales item and customer to use in a transaction.

Item List

Customer & Jobs List

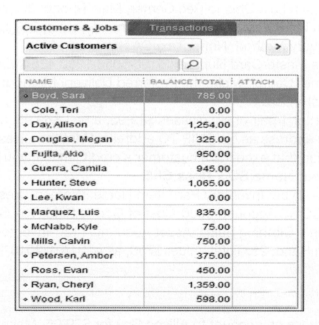

RECORD TRANSACTIONS

January 1, 2018:

▶ Add your name to the Company Name and the Legal Name. The name will be **Your Name's California Casual** (Type your actual name, *not* the words *Your Name*. For example, the company for John Pierce would be John Pierce's California Casual.)

▶ Check with your instructor to see if you should change the company preferences so that the date prepared, time prepared, and report basis do not print as part of the heading on reports. If so, change the preferences. Have the reports refresh automatically.

▶ Enable Customer Credit Card Protection. Change the Password from QBDT2018 to **2018QBDT**. Use your professor's last name to answer the question for your first manager.

▶ Customize the **Product Invoice**, **Sales Receipt**, **Sales Order**, and **Credit Memo** so that there is enough room to display your name in full on the same line as the company name. Also, change the Default Titles to all capital letters. (Invoice should be INVOICE).

▶ Customize the **Payment Method List** by adding MasterCard and deleting Discover Card.

▶ Use your Copy of: Intuit Product Invoice to prepare Invoice 15 to record the sale on account for 1 belt $29.95, 1 pair of men's shorts $39.95, and a man's shirt $39.95 to Kwan Lee. Add a Customer Message. (If you get dialog boxes regarding Price Levels or Printing Shipping Labels, click "Do not display this message in the future," and click OK.) Print the invoice. If you print to a pdf file, save the document as **1-Your Name Inv 15 Lee Ch5**.

▶ Received Check 3305 from Megan Douglas for $325 in payment of her account in full. Print the payment receipt. If you print to a pdf file, save the document as **2-Your Name Rcv Pmt Douglas Ch5**.

▶ Add a new customer: San Luis Obispo Rec Center, Main Phone: 805-555-2241, Address: 451 Marsh Street, San Luis Obispo, CA 93407, Payment Terms: 2% 10 Net 30, Credit Limit: $1,000, Preferred Delivery Method: None, Tax: CA Sales Tax.

▶ Add Amber Petersen's MasterCard Number: 5195 5658 1280 4264, Expiration 02/2023 to account in the Customer Center. Make the Preferred Delivery Method: None, and the Preferred Payment Method: MasterCard.

▶ Prepare a Sales Order for 1 pair of sunglasses $89.95, a belt $69.95, and a tie $39.95 to Evan Ross. Add his mailing address as his SHIP TO address. Print the Sales Order. (Remember to approve any transaction that exceeds a customer's credit limit.) If you print to a pdf file, save the document as **3-Your Name SO 1 Ross Ch5**.

▶ Add a new sales item—Type: Inventory Part, Item Name: Women-Dress, Description: Women's Dresses, Cost: 0.00, COGS Account: 5000-Cost of Goods Sold, Tax Code: Tax, Income Account: 4011 Women's Clothing Sales, Asset Account: 1120-Inventory Asset; Reorder Point: (Min) 20, Max 100, On Hand: 25, Total Value: $750, as of 01/01/2018—be sure to use the correct date.

January 3, 2018:

▶ Record the sale of 1 dress on account to Allison Day for $79.95. Make sure you are using the Copy of the Product Invoice. If you print to a pdf file, save the document as **4-Your Name Inv 16 Day Ch5**.

▶ San Luis Obispo Rec Center purchased 5 men's shirts on account $29.95 each, 5 pair of men's shorts $29.95 each. Because San Luis Obispo Rec Center is a nonprofit organization, include a subtotal for the sale and apply a 10% sales discount for a nonprofit organization. (Create any new sales items necessary by following the instructions given in the chapter. If you need to add an income account for Sales Discounts to the Chart of Accounts, assign account number 4050.

The nonprofit discount is marked Taxable, so the discount is applied before adding sales tax.) If you print to a pdf file, save the document as **5-Your Name Inv 17 SLO Rec Ch5**.

▶ Sold 1 woman's blouse $59.95 to a cash customer using Check 378 for the full amount including tax. Record the sale to Cash Customer on Sales Receipt 25. (If necessary, refer to steps provided within the chapter for instructions on creating a cash customer.) If you print to a pdf file, save the document as **6-Your Name SR 25 Cash Cust Ch5**.

▶ Received a belt returned by Luis Marquez. The original price of the belt was $49.95. Prepare a Credit Memo. Add the new message **Your return has been processed.** to the Credit Memo. Apply the credit to his Opening Balance, then print the Credit Memo. If you print to a pdf file, save the document as **7-Your Name CM 18 Marquez Ch5**.

▶ Sold a dress to a customer for $99.95. The customer paid with her Visa Number 4024 0071 1712 7497, Expiration Date 05/2025. Record the sale. If there is a number in CHECK NO., delete it. If you print to a pdf file, save the document as **8-Your Name SR 26 Cash Cust Ch5**.

▶ Sold a scarf $19.95 plus tax for cash. Record the sale. (Hint: Look at the description for the Access-Ties item.) If you print to a pdf file, save the document as **9-Your Name SR 27 Cash Cust Ch5**.

▶ Received payments on account from the following customers:
  ○ Karl Wood, $598.00, Check 145. If you print to a pdf file, save the document as **10-Your Name Rcv Pmt Wood Ch5**.
  ○ Amber Petersen, $375, paid with MasterCard on file. If you print to a pdf file, save the document as **11-Your Name Rcv Pmt Petersen Ch5**.
  ○ Calvin Mills, $750, Check 81502. If you print to a pdf file, save the document as **12-Your Name Rcv Pmt Mills Ch5**.
  ○ Luis Marquez, $781.05, Debit Card 4304 9616 6746 9164, Expiration 03/2023. If you print to a pdf file, save the document as **13-Your Name Rcv Pmt Marquez Ch5**.

January 5, 2018:

▶ Evan Ross came into the store to pick up his items on order. Create an invoice from the sales order. (Use the date 01/05/18, approve any transaction that exceeds a customer's credit limit, and customize the Sales Order Invoice so that the Default Title is INVOICE. Click the Basic Customization button and select Print Past Due Stamp. As you did for other templates earlier, use Layout to resize your name and the default title so they do not overlap.) Print the invoice. If you print to a pdf file, save the document as **14-Your Name Inv 19 Ross Ch5**.

▶ Deposit all cash, checks, debit card, and credit card receipts. Print a Deposit Summary. If you print to a pdf file, save the document as **15-Your Name Dep Sum Ch5**.

January 7, 2018:

▶ Evan Ross returned the tie he purchased on 01/05/18 for $39.95. (Did you apply this to Invoice 19?) If you print to a pdf file, save the document as **16-Your Name CM 20 Ross Ch5**.

January 15, 2018:

▶ Received an NSF notice from the bank for the check for $325 from Megan Douglas. Enter the necessary transaction for this nonsufficient funds (bounced) check to be paid on receipt. The bank's charges are $15, and Your Name's California Casual charges $30 for all NSF checks. (If necessary, refer to steps provided within the chapter for instructions on changing the QuickBooks DT Account 5009 Returned Check Charges to Account Number 4090.) Access Invoice 21. Make sure the Invoice DATE is 01/15/2018. Make the following changes:

TEMPLATE Copy of: Intuit Product Invoice, TERMS "Due on receipt" and CUSTOMER MESSAGE Please remit to above address. Print Invoice 21. If you print to a pdf file, save the documents as **17-Your Name Inv 21 Douglas Ch5**. Edit Megan's Opening Balance invoice to show terms of Due on receipt. Use the template "Copy of Intuit Product Invoice." Save the invoice without printing. Accept any messages regarding previous periods. Do not change her Terms permanently.

▶ Calvin Mills returned a shirt he had purchased for $54.99 plus tax. Record the return. Check the balance of his account. If there is no balance, issue a refund check. Print the Credit Memo and Check 1. If you print to a pdf file, save the document as **18-Your Name CM 22 Mills Ch5** and **19-Your Name Ck 1 Mills Ch5**.

▶ Sold 3 men's shirts to a cash customer, $39.95 each plus tax. He used his MasterCard 5521 8901 8809 6229, Expiration 07/2021 for payment. If you print to a pdf file, save the document as **20-Your Name SR 28 Cash Cust Ch5**.

▶ Sold on account 1 dress $99.99, 1 pair of women's sandals $79.95, and a belt $39.95 to Sara Boyd. If you print to a pdf file, save the document as **21-Your Name Inv 23 Boyd Ch5**.

▶ Sold 1 pair of women's shorts $34.95 to a cash customer. Paid with Check 8160. If you print to a pdf file, save the document as **22-Your Name SR 29 Cash Cust Ch5**.

▶ Received payments on account from the following customers:
   o Partial payment from Steve Hunter, $250, Debit Card Number 4024 0071 2771 5075, Expiration 11/2021. Leave as an underpayment. If you print to a pdf file, save the document as **23-Your Name Rcv Pmt Hunter Ch5**.
   o Payment in full from Kyle McNabb, Visa Number 4929 5768 2116 6401, Expiration 12/2024. If you print to a pdf file, save the document as **24-Your Name Rcv Pmt McNabb Ch5**.
   o Received $1,338.62 from Allison Day as payment in full on account, Check 2311. The payment was postmarked 1/11/2018. (Apply the discount to Invoice 16, click the line for Invoice 16; click the Discounts And Credits icon; use QuickMath to calculate the 2 percent discount and enter the amount on the Discounts And Credits screen, select the appropriate account for the sales discount, click Done to apply the discount. If you print to a pdf file, save the document as **25-Your Name Rcv Pmt Day Ch5**.
   o Received Check 2805 for $619.24 as payment in full from Evan Ross. (If eligible for a discount on Invoice 19, apply it to the actual amount that is owed after the return rather than accept QuickBooks DT's discount on the original invoice amount.) If you print to a pdf file, save the document as **26-Your Name Rcv Pmt Ross Ch5**.

▶ Sold on account to Camila Guerra: 3 pairs of men's pants $75.00 each, 3 men's shirts $50.00 each, 3 belts $39.99 each, 2 pairs of men's shoes $90.00 each, 2 ties $55.00 each, and 1 pair of sunglasses $75.00. (If the amount of the sale exceeds Camila's credit limit, accept the sale anyway.) If you print to a pdf file, save the document as **27-Your Name Inv 24 Guerra Ch5**.

▶ Change the Sales Item Access-Shades to Access-Sunglasses.

▶ Sold on account 1 pair of sunglasses $95.00, 2 dresses $99.95 each, and 2 pairs of women's shoes $65.00 each to Amber Petersen. If you print to a pdf file, save the document as **28-Your Name Inv 25 Petersen Ch5**.

▶ Print Customer Balance Detail Report for All Transactions in Portrait orientation. Adjust column widths so the account names are shown in full and the report is one page wide without selecting Fit report to one page wide. The report length may be longer than one page. If you print to a pdf file, save the document as **29-Your Name Cust Bal Detail Ch5**.

▶ Print a Sales by Item Summary for 01/01/2018 to 01/15/2018 in Landscape orientation. Adjust column widths so the report fits on one page wide. Do not select Fit report to one page wide. If you print to a pdf file, save the document as **30-Your Name Sales by Item Sum Ch5**.

▶ Deposit <u>all</u> payments, checks, and charges received from customers. Print the Deposit Summary. If you print to a pdf file, save the document as **31-Your Name Dep Sum Ch5**.

▶ Print a Journal for 01/01/2018 to 01/15/2018 in Landscape orientation. (Remember to <u>Expand</u> the report, adjust the column widths, and remove any unused columns from display. To print the report on one page wide, the information in the memo column may not be shown in full.) If you print to a pdf file, save the document as **32-Your Name Journal Ch5**.

▶ Print the Trial Balance for 01/01/2018 to 01/15/2018. If you print to a pdf file, save the document as **33-Your Name Trial Bal Ch5**.

▶ Print an Inventory Valuation Summary for 01/15/2018. (Remove the columns for Sales Price, Retail Value, and % of Tot Retail). Memorize the report. If you print to a pdf file, save the document as **34-Your Name Inventory Val Sum Ch5**.

▶ Print Profit & Loss (Standard) for 01/01/2018 to 01/15/2018 If you print to a pdf file, save the document as **35-Your Name P & L Ch5**.

▶ Backup your work to Casual 2018 (Backup Ch. 5).

5

CHAPTER 5 CHECKLISTS

YOUR NAME'S SIERRA SPORTS

The checklist below shows all the business forms and reports printed during training. Check each one that you printed. In the document names below, Your Name and Ch5 have been omitted, and report dates are given.

___ 1-Inv 15 Asher	___ 25-SR 7 Cash Cust
___ 2-Inv 2 Medina	___ 26-SR 8 Cash Cust
___ 3-Inv 3 Mountain Schools	___ 27-Sales by Item Sum
___ 4-Inv 4 Grant	___ 28-SR 1 Cash Cust (Corrected)
___ 5-SO 1 Shaw	___ 29-Rcv Pmt Ortiz
___ 6-SO 2 Asher	___ 30-Rcv Pmt Waters
___ 7-Open SO by Cust	___ 31-Rcv Pmt Rec Center
___ 8-SO Inv 5 Shaw	___ 32-Rcv Pmt Mountain Schools
___ 9-SO Inv 6 Asher	___ 33-Rcv Pmt Asher
___ 10-Inv 7 Waters	___ 34-Rcv Pmt Medina
___ 11-Inv 7 Waters (Corrected)	___ 35-Rcv Pmt Green
___ 12-Cust Bal Detail	___ 36-Rcv Pmt Grant
___ 13-Inv 3 Mountain Schools (Corrected)	___ 37-Rcv Pmt Shaw
___ 14-Inv 8 Rec Center	___ 38-Cust Bal Sum
___ 15-Inv 1 Asher (Voided)	___ 39-Dep Sum
___ 16-CM 9 Waters	___ 40-Inv Ortiz (Revised)
___ 17-CM 10 Asher	___ 41-Inv 11 Ortiz
___ 18-Open Inv	___ 42-CM 12 Medina
___ 19-SR 1 Cash Cust	___ 43-Ck 1 Medina
___ 20-SR 2 Cash Cust	___ 44-Journal, January 1-15, 2018
___ 21-SR 3 Cash Cust	___ 45-Trial Bal, January 1-15, 2018
___ 22-SR 4 Cash Cust	___ 46-Inventory Val Detail, January 1-15, 2018
___ 23-SR 5 Cash Cust	___ 47-P & L, January 1-15, 2018
___ 24-SR 6 Cash Cust	

YOUR NAME'S CALIFORNIA CASUAL

The checklist below shows all the business forms and reports printed during training. Check each one that you printed. In the document names below, Your Name and Ch5 have been omitted, and report dates are given.

___ 1-Inv 15 Lee	___ 19-Ck 1 Mills
___ 2-Rcv Pmt Douglas	___ 20-SR28 Cash Cust
___ 3-SO 1 Ross	___ 21-Inv 23 Boyd
___ 4-Inv 16 Day	___ 22-SR 29 Cash Cust
___ 5-Inv 17 SLO Rec Center	___ 23-Rcv Pmt Hunter
___ 6-SR 25 Cash Cust	___ 24-Rcv Pmt McNabb
___ 7-CM 18 Marquez	___ 25-Rcv Pmt Day
___ 8-SR 26 Cash Cust	___ 26-Rcv Pmt Ross
___ 9-SR 27 Cash Cust	___ 27-Rcv Pmt Guerra
___ 10-Rcv Pmt Wood	___ 28-Inv 25 Peterson
___ 11-Rcv Pmt Petersen	___ 29-Cust Bal Detail
___ 12-Rcv Pmt Mills	___ 30-Sales by Item Sum, January 1-15, 2018
___ 13-Rcv Pmt Marquez	___ 31-Dep Sum
___ 14-Inv 19 Ross	___ 32-Journal, January 1-15, 2018
___ 15-Dep sum	___ 33-Trial Bal, January 1-15, 2018
___ 16-CM 20 Ross	___ 34-Inventory Val Sum, January 1-15, 2018
___ 17-Inv 21 Douglas	___ 35-P & L, January 1-15, 2018
___ 18-CM 22 Mills	

PAYABLES AND PURCHASES: MERCHANDISING BUSINESS

LEARNING OBJECTIVES

At the completion of this chapter you will be able to:

6.01. Understand the concepts for computerized accounting for payables in a merchandising business.
6.02. Use Reminders.
6.03. Prepare Inventory Stock Status Report by Item.
6.04. Customize, prepare, and print Purchase Orders.
6.05. Add a new vendor.
6.06. Merge vendors.
6.07. Assign preferred vendor and a cost to inventory items.
6.08. Prepare Purchase Order QuickReport.
6.09. Change reorder limits and view the effect on Reminders.
6.10. Use the Inventory Center.
6.11. Prepare an inventory report in the Inventory Center.
6.12. Record Items received with and without a bill.
6.13. Change Search Preferences.
6.14. Understand the different Search features available in QuickBooks DT.
6.15. Prepare a report from Search.
6.16. Enter a bill for items received.
6.17. Record a partial receipt of merchandise ordered.
6.18. Close Purchase Order manually.
6.19. Enter a bill credit from a vendor.
6.20. Use Bill Tracker.
6.21. Record purchase with a company credit card.
6.22. Pay for inventory using a company credit card.
6.23. Add/edit multiple list entries.
6.24. Enter Bills.
6.25. Assign terms and accounts to vendors.
6.26. Create and use memorized transactions.
6.27. Enter a bill and edit transactions in the Accounts Payable register.
6.28. Prepare a register QuickReport.
6.29. Understand the different types of discounts available in QuickBooks DT.
6.30. Prepare an Unpaid Bill report.
6.31. Customize, memorize, and add comments to reports.
6.32. Pay bills with and without discounts and credits.
6.33. Print checks to pay bills.
6.34. Pay bills with a company credit card.
6.35. Prepare a Sales Tax Liability report.

6.36. Pay Sales Tax.

6.37. Prepare and print Vendor Balance Detail, Trial Balance, and Journal reports.

6.38. Prepare and print a memorized report.

ACCOUNTING FOR PAYABLES AND PURCHASES

In a merchandising business, much of the accounting for purchases and payables consists of ordering merchandise for resale and paying bills for expenses incurred in the operation of the business. Purchases are for things used in the operation of the business. Some transactions will be in the form of cash purchases; others will be purchases on account. Bills can be paid when they are received or when they are due. Merchandise received must be checked against purchase orders. Completed purchase orders must be closed. Rather than use journals, QuickBooks DT continues to focus on recording transactions based on the business document; therefore, you use the Enter Bills and Pay Bills features of the program to record the receipt and payment of bills. While QuickBooks DT does not refer to it as such, the Vendor List is the same as the Accounts Payable Subsidiary Ledger.

QuickBooks DT can remind you when inventory needs to be ordered and when payments are due. Purchase orders are prepared when ordering merchandise and sent to a vendor who will process the order and send the merchandise to the company. When the merchandise is received, the quantity received is recorded. The program automatically tracks inventory and uses the average cost method to value the inventory.

If the bill accompanies the merchandise, both the bill and the merchandise receipt are recorded together on a bill. If the merchandise is received without a bill, the receipt of items is recorded; and, when the bill arrives, it is recorded separately. When the inventory receipt is recorded, the purchase order is closed automatically.

QuickBooks DT can calculate and apply discounts earned for paying bills early. Payments can be made by recording payments in the Pay Bills window; or, if using the cash basis for accounting, by writing a check. Merchandise purchased may be paid for at the same time the items and the bill are received, or it may be paid for later. A cash purchase can be recorded by writing a check, using a credit or debit card, or using petty cash. Even though QuickBooks DT focuses on recording transactions on the business forms used, all transactions are recorded behind the scenes in the Journal.

As in previous chapters, corrections can be made directly on the bill or within the account register. New accounts and vendors may be added *on the fly* as transactions are entered. Purchase orders, bills, or checks may be voided or deleted. Reports illustrating vendor balances, unpaid bills, accounts payable aging, sales tax liability, transaction history, accounts payable registers, and inventory may be viewed and printed. Once a report is prepared, you may add a comment to it and print and/or save the commented report. A commented report may <u>not</u> be exported to Excel.

TRAINING TUTORIAL AND PROCEDURES

The following tutorial will once again work with the fictitious company, Your Name's Sierra Sports. Use the company file for Your Name's Sierra Sports that contains the transactions you entered for Chapter 5. Continue using the same year that you used in Chapter 5. The text uses the year 2018.

INVENTORY STOCK STATUS BY ITEM REPORT

In addition to the Inventory Valuation Detail Report prepared in Chapter 5, several Inventory Reports are available for viewing and/or printing. One report is the Inventory Stock Status by Item report. This report provides information regarding the stock on hand, the stock on order, and the stock that needs to be reordered.

MEMO
DATE: January 16, 2018

More detailed information regarding inventory stock on hand, ordered, and needing to be ordered needs to be provided. View the report for Inventory Stock Status by Item.

 View the **Inventory Stock Status by Item Report**

Click **Reports** on the Menu bar, point to **Inventory,** click **Inventory Stock Status by Item**
The dates are From **01/01/18** and To **01/16/18**
Tab to generate the report
View the report:

Your Name's Sierra Sports
Inventory Stock Status by Item
January 1 - 16, 2018

	Pref Vendor	Reorder Pt (Min)	Max	On Hand	Available	Order	On PO	Reorder Qty	Sales/Week
Inventory									
Accessories	▶ Sports Accessories	100	850	795	795		0	0	2.2 ◀
Bindings-Skis	Boots & Bindings	10	65	43	43		0	0	3.1
Bindings-Snow	Boots & Bindings	5	65	48	48		0	0	0.9
Boots	Snow Shoes & More	10	35	20	20		0	0	0
Boots-Ski	Footwear Galore	10	35	14	14		0	0	0.4
Boots-Snowbrd	Footwear Galore	10	35	10	10	✓	0	25	0.9
Gloves	Sports Clothes, Inc.	20	45	20	20	✓	0	25	0.9
Hats	Sports Accessories	20	40	29	29		0	0	0.4
Helmets		5	30	20	20		0	0	2.2
Pants-Ski	Sports Clothes, Inc.	10	100	93	93		0	0	0.9
Pants-Snowbrd	Sports Clothes, Inc.	10	100	50	50		0	0	0
Parkas	Sports Clothes, Inc.	25	100	73	73		0	0	0.9
Poles-Ski	Snow Sports, Inc.	15	28	13	13	✓	0	15	2.2
Skis	Snow Sports, Inc.	15	60	43	43		0	0	3.1
Sleds		5	7	4	4	✓	0	3	2.6
Snowboard	Snow Sports, Inc.	15	60	28	28		0	0	0.9
Socks	Footwear Galore	25	100	72	72		0	0	1.3
Sweaters	Sports Clothes, Inc.	25	100	73	73		0	0	0.9
Toboggans		5	7	5	5	✓	0	2	2.2
Underwear	Sports Clothes, Inc.	30	50	32	32		0	0	0.4

- Since the columns for On Sales Order, For Assemblies, and Next Delivery contain no information, they have been removed for better clarity.
- Notice the items marked in the Order column. This tells you that you need to prepare and send purchase orders.
- If the items on hand are equal to or less than the number of items indicated in the Reorder Pt (Min), QuickBooks DT marks the Order column.
- The marked items are the same items that were shown in Reminders.
- To enable you to determine the quantity to order, QuickBooks DT shows you the Max column, so you can see the maximum number to have in stock.
- The column for Reorder Qty calculates the amount to reorder. This is based on the difference between the maximum and the number on hand.

Make note of the items and quantities that need to be ordered, and close the report

PURCHASE ORDERS

Using the QuickBooks DT Purchase Order feature helps you track your inventory. Information regarding the items on order or the items received may be obtained at any time. Once merchandise has been received, QuickBooks DT marks the purchase order *Received in full,* which closes the purchase order automatically. The Purchase Order feature must be selected as a Preference when setting up the company, or it may be selected prior to processing your first purchase order. QuickBooks DT will automatically set up an account called Purchase Orders in the Chart of Accounts. The account does not affect the balance sheet or the profit and loss statement of the company. As with other business forms, QuickBooks DT allows you to customize your purchase orders to fit the needs of your individual company or to use the purchase order format that comes with the program. In addition, for customer sales orders with Ship To addresses, a purchase order can be prepared directly from the sales order and shipped to the customer.

VERIFY PURCHASE ORDERS PREFERENCE

Verify that Purchase Orders are active by checking the Company Preferences for inventory.

MEMO
DATE: January 16, 2018

Prior to completing the first purchase order, verify that Purchase Orders are active.

 Verify that Purchase Orders are active

Click **Edit** menu, click **Preferences**
Click **Items & Inventory**, click the **Company Preferences** tab
- Make sure there is a check mark in the check box for **Inventory and purchase orders are active**. If not, click the check box to select.

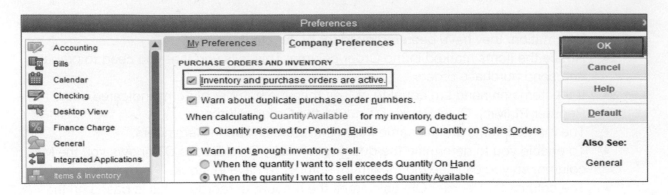

Click **OK** to accept and close the Preferences screen

CUSTOMIZE PURCHASE ORDERS

As instructed in Chapter 5, business forms may be customized. Prior to recording your first purchase order, it should be customized.

  Customize a Purchase Order

Click the **Purchase Orders** icon in the **Vendors** section of the Home Page

Click the **Formatting** tab on the Create Purchase Orders Icon bar, click **Customize Data Layout**

Change the Default Title in the Additional Customization screen to **PURCHASE ORDER**

On the Additional Customization screen, click the **Layout Designer...** button

- If you get a message regarding overlapping fields, click **Do not display this message in the future**, click **OK**, and then click **Layout Designer**.

Follow the procedures in Chapter 5 to change the size for **PURCHASE ORDER** to begin at **5**

Expand the area for **Your Name's Sierra Sports** to 4 ¾

Click **OK** to close the Layout Designer

Click **OK** to close the Additional Customization screen

Do <u>not</u> close the Purchase Order

PREPARE PURCHASE ORDER

Once Purchase Orders are active, they may be prepared. Typically, Purchase orders are prepared to order merchandise; but they may also be used to order non-inventory items like supplies or services. The same purchase order may not be sent to several vendors. Each vendor should receive a separate purchase order. A purchase order may have more than one item listed. To determine the quantity to order, you may order any quantity, or you may order the amount suggested in the Reorder Qty column on the Inventory Stock Status by Item report.

> **MEMO**
> **DATE:** January 16, 2018
>
> With only 10 pairs of snowboard boots in stock in the middle of January an additional 25 pairs of boots in assorted sizes need to be ordered from Footwear Galore for $75 per pair. Prepare Purchase Order 1.

 Prepare Purchase Order 1 for 25 pairs of snowboard boots

Purchase Order 1 should be on the screen
- If not, click the **Purchases Order** icon on the Home Page.

If you wish to save space on the screen, click the Hide History button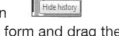

To resize the purchase order so it is smaller, point to the edge of the form and drag the sizing handle

Click the drop-down list arrow for **Vendor**, click **Footwear Galore**

The Template should be Custom Purchase Order, select if necessary

Tab to or click **Date**, enter **01/16/2018**
- P.O. No. should be 1. If not, enter 1 as the P.O. No.

Tab to or click **Item**, click **Boots-Snowbrd**

Tab to or click **Qty**, enter **25**
- The cost of the item was entered when Boots-Snowbrd was created. The Rate should appear automatically as **75.00**.

Tab to generate Amount

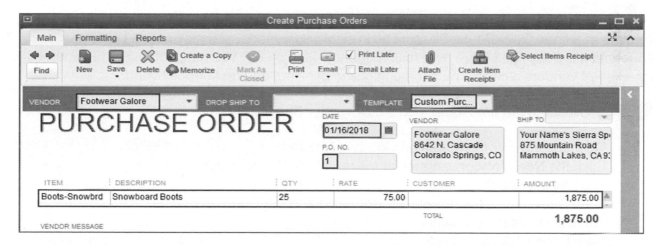

On the Create Purchase Orders **Main** Icon bar, click **Print** to print the **Purchase Order**

Check printer settings
- Be sure to print lines around each field.

Click **Print**
- If you print to a pdf file, save the document as **1-Your Name PO 1 Footwear Galore Ch6**.

Click **Save & Close**
- Sometimes, after printing, you will get a Recording Transaction message, if you have made no changes, click **Yes**.

ADD NEW VENDOR

> ### MEMO
> **DATE:** January 16, 2018
>
> Add a new vendor: Snow Stuff, Main Phone: 303-555-7765, Fax: 303-555-5677, Main E-mail: **SnowStuff@ski.com**, 7105 Camino del Rio, Durango, CO 81302, Terms: 2% 10 Net 30, Credit Limit: $2,000.

    Add a new vendor

Open the **Vendor Center** as previously instructed
Click the **New Vendor...** button at the top of the Vendor Center
Click **New Vendor**
Enter **Snow Stuff** for the **Vendor** name and the **Company** name
There is no Opening Balance
Use the information in the Memo to complete the Address Info tab as previously instructed
Click the **Payment Settings** tab, click the drop-down list arrow for **PAYMENT TERMS**,
and click **2% 10 Net 30**
Tab to or click **CREDIT LIMIT**, enter **2000**
Click **OK** to add the new vendor, do <u>not</u> close the Vendor Center

MERGE DUPLICATE VENDORS

On occasion, you may have duplicates of vendors. If this happens, you may merge up to four vendors at a time. QuickBooks DT must be in single-user mode, you may not be using an Accountant's Copy File (.QBA), and multi-currency must be off. You may not merge tax authorities, tax exempt vendors, vendors paid through online banking, or direct deposit vendors.

    To illustrate the procedure, add a new vendor **Snow Stuff, Inc.**

Open the **Vendor Center** as previously instructed
Click the **New Vendor...** button at the top of the Vendor Center
Click **New Vendor**
Enter **Snow Stuff, Inc.** for the **Vendor** name and the **Company** name
There is no Opening Balance
Main Phone: **303-555-7765**
Fax: **303-555-5677**
Main Email: **SnowStuff@ski.com**
Address info: **7105 Camino del Rio, Durango, CO 81302**
Click the **Payment Settings** tab, click the drop-down list arrow for **PAYMENT TERMS**,
and click **2% 10 Net 30**
Tab to or click **CREDIT LIMIT**, enter **2000**
Click **OK** to add Vendor
• Notice that the Vendor Center shows both Snow Stuff and Snow Stuff, Inc. as vendors.
Close the Vendor Center

Click the **Accountant** menu
Point to **Client Data Review** then click **Merge Vendors**

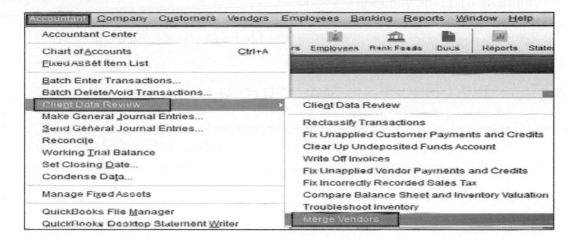

Click in the check boxes for Snow Stuff and Snow Stuff, Inc. to select the vendors

Click **Snow Stuff** to select the Master Vendor
- The information for Snow Stuff, Inc. will be merged into Snow Stuff.

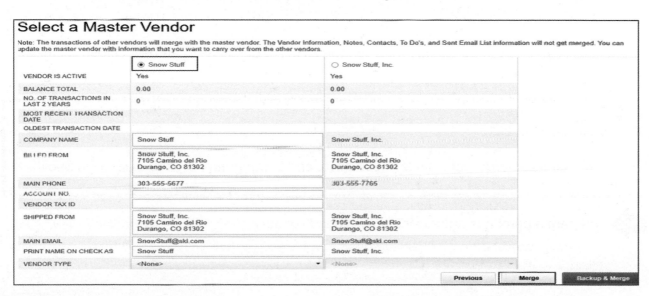

Click **Merge**

- If you click **Backup & Merge** QuickBooks DT will make a backup of your company file before merging the vendors.

Click **Yes** on the Confirmation message

When the merge is complete, click **OK** on the Merge Complete message

Close the Merge Vendors screen

ASSIGN PREFERRED VENDOR AND COST TO ITEM

Most of the items in the Item List have a Preferred Vendor and a Cost entered as Purchase Information. This enables you to prepare a purchase order and have QuickBooks DT insert the Vendor Name and cost automatically when an Item Code is entered on a Purchase Order.

 Assign Snow Stuff as the Preferred Vendor for Sleds and Toboggans. Also assign a Cost of $50 to Sleds and $110 to Toboggans

Open the **Item List** as previously instructed

Double-click **Sleds**

Click in the text box for **Cost**, enter **50**, press **Tab** twice

Click the drop-down list arrow for **Preferred Vendor**

Click **Snow Stuff**, click **OK**

Repeat for Toboggans using **$110** for Cost and **Snow Stuff** as the Preferred Vendor

Close the Item List

PREPARE PURCHASE ORDER FOR MULTIPLE ITEMS

If more than one item is purchased from a vendor, all items purchased can be included on the same purchase order.

MEMO

DATE: January 16, 2018

Prepare a purchase order for 3 sleds @ $50 each, and 2 toboggans @ $110 each from Snow Stuff.

 Prepare a purchase order using an assigned vendor

Click the **Purchase Orders** icon on the Home Page
- The **Date** should be **01/16/2018**.
- P.O. No. should be **2**. If it is not, enter **2**.

Tab to or click the first line in the column for **Item**

Click the drop-down list arrow for **Item**, click **Sleds**
- Vendor information for Snow Stuff is automatically completed.

Tab to or click **Qty**, enter **3**
- The quantities ordered for sleds and toboggans are the same quantities listed in the Reorder Qty column of the Inventory Stock Status by Item report.
- The purchase cost of $50 is automatically entered.

Tab to generate the total for **Amount**

Repeat steps necessary to enter the information to order 2 toboggans

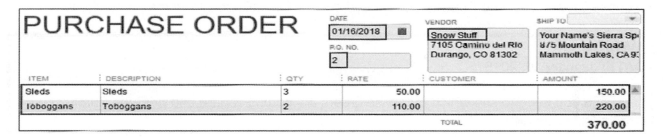

Print **Purchase Order 2**
- If you print to a pdf file, save the document as **2-Your Name PO 2 Snow Stuff Ch6**.

Click **Save & New** to save **Purchase Order 2** and go to the next purchase order
- If you get a Recording Transaction message, click **Yes**.

ENTER ADDITIONAL PURCHASE ORDERS

MEMO

DATE: January 16, 2018

After referring to the Inventory Stock Status by Item report, prepare purchase orders:

    25 pairs of gloves @ 15.00 each from Preferred Vendor: Sports Clothes, Inc.

    12 sets of ski poles @ 30.00 each from Preferred Vendor: Snow Sports, Inc.

 Prepare and print the purchase orders indicated above.

Compare your completed purchase orders with the ones following:
- If you print to a pdf file, save the documents as **3-Your Name PO 3 Sports Clothes Ch6**, and **4-Your Name PO 4 Snow Sports Ch6**.

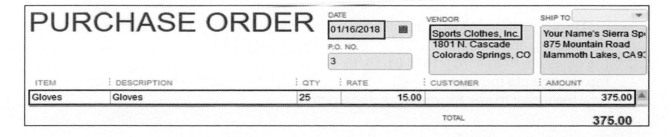

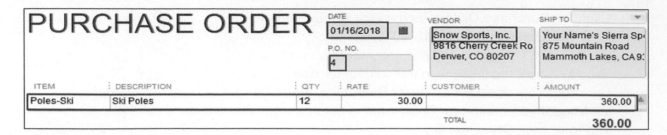

Save and Close after entering and printing Purchase Order 4

PURCHASE ORDERS QUICKREPORT

To see a list of purchase orders that have been prepared, open the Chart of Accounts, select Purchase Orders, click the Reports button, and choose QuickReport from the menu shown.

> **MEMO**
> **DATE:** January 16, 2018
>
> Larry and you need to see which purchase orders are open. Prepare and print the Purchase Orders QuickReport.

 View the open purchase orders for Your Name's Sierra Sports

Click the **Chart of Accounts** icon on the Home Page
Scroll through the accounts until you get to the end of the accounts
Your will see **2 Purchase Orders** in the Name column and **Non-Posting** in the Type column
- Non-posting means that the information on the Purchase Order will not be posted to any accounts.

Click **2 Purchase Orders**
Click the **Reports** button
Click **QuickReport: 2 Purchase Orders**

- The list shows all open purchase orders and the purchase order date, number, vendor, account, and amount.

The dates are from **01/01/18** to **01/16/18**
Tab to generate the report
View the report to see the open purchase orders

Your Name's Sierra Sports
Account QuickReport
As of January 16, 2018

Type	Date	Num	Name	Memo	Split	Amount
2 · Purchase Orders						
Purchase Order	01/16/2018	1	Footwear Galore		1120 - Inventory Asset	-1,875.00
Purchase Order	01/16/2018	2	Snow Stuff		-SPLIT-	-370.00
Purchase Order	01/16/2018	3	Sports Clothes, Inc.		1120 - Inventory Asset	-375.00
Purchase Order	01/16/2018	4	Snow Sports, Inc.		1120 - Inventory Asset	-360.00
Total 2 · Purchase Orders						-2,980.00
TOTAL						**-2,980.00**

Close the **Purchase Order QuickReport** without printing and close the **Chart of Accounts**

CREATE PURCHASE ORDER FROM A SALES ORDER WITH DROP SHIP INSTRUCTIONS—INFORMATION ONLY

Once a Sales Order for merchandise has been created, it may be used to create a Purchase Order. If the Sales Order has a Ship To address and the Create Purchase Order Based on the Sales Transaction dialog box is marked Drop ship to customer, the order can be sent directly to the customer.

Click **Sales Orders** on the Home screen, complete the Sales Order as instructed in Chapter 5
- The Sales Order completed for Benjamin Asher in Chapter 5 is shown in this example.
Click **Create Purchase Order** icon on the Main Tab bar for Create Sales Orders

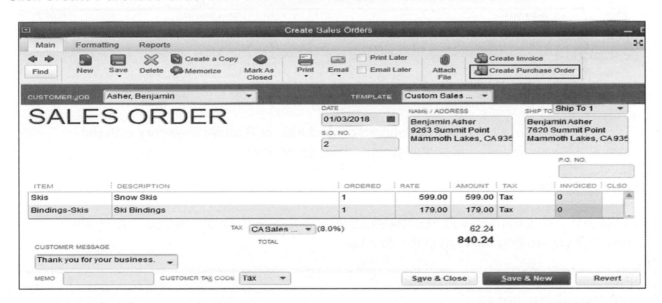

On the Create Purchase Order Based on the Sales Transaction dialog box, make sure **Create purchase order for all allowed items.** is marked
Click **Drop ship to customer** to select

Click **OK**

- The Create Purchase Orders screen will be shown.

Click the drop-down list arrow for VENDOR

Click the vendor name (Snow Sports, Inc. in the example)

- Notice that SHIP TO is for **Benjamin Asher**.
- The snow skis and ski bindings will be shipped directly to Benjamin Asher.
- The MEMO is Sales Order 2:

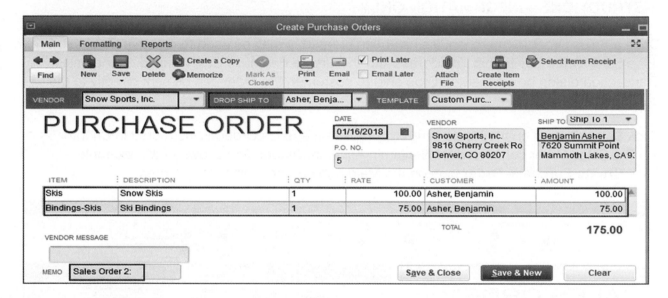

When you receive the bill, follow the standard procedures for Receive Inventory with Bill
Return to the Sales Order and Create Invoice for Benjamin Asher.

CHANGE REORDER LIMITS

Any time that you determine your reorder limits are too low or too high, you can change the
Reorder Point by editing the Item in the Item List.

MEMO

DATE: January 16, 2018

View the Item List to see the amount on hand for each item. In viewing the list, Larry and you
determine that there should be a minimum of 35 sets of long underwear on hand. Currently,
there are 32 sets of long underwear in stock. Change the Reorder Point (Min) for long
underwear to 35.

View the **Item List** as previously instructed

Scroll through Item List, double-click **Underwear**
Click in **Reorder Point (Min)**
Change 30 to **35**

- Notice the Average Cost. For example, 32 on hand * $8 average cost = $256 total value. If 16 pair cost $10 each, the value would be $160. If the other 16 pair cost $6 each, the value would be $96. The total value for all 16 would be $160 + $96 = $256. Remember $256 / 32 = $8 average cost.

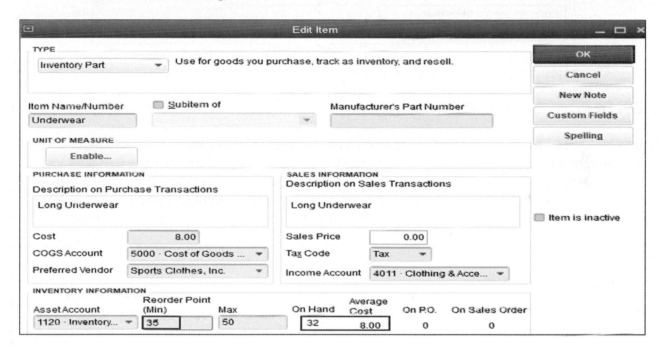

Click **OK** to save and exit, close the **Item List**

VIEW EFFECT OF REORDER POINT ON REMINDERS

Once the reorder point has been changed and the quantity on hand is equal to or falls below the new minimum, the item will be added to Reminders, so you will be reminded to order it.

MEMO
DATE: January 16, 2018

Look at Reminders to see what items need to be ordered.

 View **Reminders**

Open **Reminders** using the Company Menu and expand Inventory to Reorder as previously instructed

- The items shown previously on the Reminders List as Inventory to Reorder (Snowboard Boots, Gloves, Ski Poles, Sleds, and Toboggans) are no longer present because they have been ordered. Underwear appears because the reorder point has been changed.
- If your computer date is not January 16, 2018 your Reminders screen will be different.

Reminders

Today, Tuesday 16, January 2018	Upcoming
▶ BILLS TO PAY (5)	-8,500.00
▶ OVERDUE INVOICES (1)	975.00
▼ INVENTORY TO REORDER (1)	
Underwear - Long Underwear	

Close **Reminders**

VIEW REPORT IN INVENTORY CENTER

QuickBooks DT has an Inventory Center that gives information about each inventory item. Changes may be made to inventory items in the Center as well as on the Items & Services List. Several Inventory Reports are available for viewing and/or printing when you are in the Inventory Center. One report is the Inventory Stock Status by Item report. This report provides information regarding the stock on hand, the stock on order, and the stock that needs to be reordered.

> **MEMO**
> **DATE:** January 16, 2018
>
> More detailed information regarding the stock on hand, stock ordered, and stock needing to be ordered needs to be provided. Open the Inventory Center and prepare the report for Inventory Stock Status by Item.

 Open the Inventory Center and view the **Inventory Stock Status by Item Report**

Click the **Vendors** menu, point to **Inventory Activities,** click **Inventory Center**
Click **Underwear**
- Note the Reorder Point of 35 that was changed earlier in the chapter and the Quantity on Hand.
- At the bottom of Inventory Information, you will see that Underwear was sold on Invoice 4.

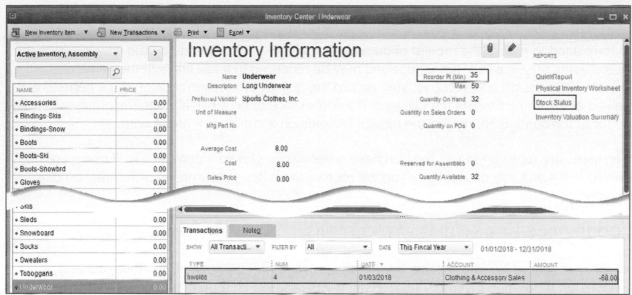

Partial Listing

In the Reports area on the right side of Inventory Information, click **Stock Status**
The dates are From **01/01/18** to **01/16/18**
Tab to generate the report (Columns with zero are removed from the following)

Your Name's Sierra Sports
Inventory Stock Status by Item
January 1 - 16, 2018

	Pref Vendor	Reorder Pt (Min)	Max	On Hand	Available	Order	On PO	Reorder Qty	Next Deliv	Sales/Week
Inventory										
Accessories	Sports Accessories	100	850	795	795		0	0		2.2
Bindings-Skis	Boots & Bindings	10	65	43	43		0	0		3.1
Bindings-Snow	Boots & Bindings	5	65	48	48		0	0		0.9
Boots	Snow Shoes & More	10	35	20	20		0	0		0
Boots-Ski	Footwear Galore	10	35	14	14		0	0		0.4
Boots-Snowbrd	Footwear Galore	10	35	10	10		25	0	01/16/2018	0.9
Gloves	Sports Clothes, Inc.	20	45	20	20		25	0	01/16/2018	0.9
Hats	Sports Accessories	20	40	29	29		0	0		0.4
Helmets		5	30	20	20		0	0		2.2
Pants-Ski	Sports Clothes, Inc.	10	100	93	93		0	0		0.9
Pants-Snowbrd	Sports Clothes, Inc.	10	100	50	50		0	0		0
Parkas	Sports Clothes, Inc.	25	100	73	73		0	0		0.9
Poles-Ski	Snow Sports, Inc.	15	28	13	13		12	0	01/16/2018	2.2
Skis	Snow Sports, Inc.	15	60	43	43		0	0		3.1
Sleds	Snow Stuff	5	7	4	4		3	0	01/16/2018	2.6
Snowboard	Snow Sports, Inc.	15	60	28	28		0	0		0.9
Socks	Footwear Galore	25	100	72	72		0	0		1.3
Sweaters	Sports Clothes, Inc.	25	100	73	73		0	0		0.9
Toboggans	Snow Stuff	5	7	5	5		2	0	01/16/2018	2.2
Underwear	Sports Clothes, Inc.	35	50	32	32	✓	0	18		0.4

Scroll through the report
- Notice the Items in stock and the reorder point for items.
- Find the items marked as needing to be ordered. They are marked with a √.
- Notice the Next Deliv dates of the items that have been ordered.

Close the report without printing, and close the Inventory Center

RECEIVING ITEMS ORDERED

The form used to record the receipt of items in QuickBooks DT depends on the way in which the ordered items are received. Items received may be recorded in three ways. If the items are received without a bill and you pay later, record the receipt on an item receipt. If the items are received at the same time as the bill, record the item receipt on a bill. If the items are received and paid for at the same time, record the receipt of items on a check or a credit card.

When items are received in full, the purchase order will be closed automatically. If items are not received in full and you do not think you will receive them later, a purchase order may be closed manually.

RECORD RECEIPT OF ITEMS WITHOUT BILL

The ability to record inventory items prior to the arrival of the bill keeps quantities on hand, quantities on order, and inventory up to date. Items ordered on a purchase order that arrive without a bill are recorded on an item receipt. When the bill arrives, it is recorded separately.

> <u>**MEMO**</u>
> **DATE:** January 18, 2018
>
> The sleds and toboggans ordered from Snow Stuff arrive without a bill. Record the receipt of the 3 sleds and 2 toboggans.

 Record the receipt of the items above

    Click the **Receive Inventory** icon on the Home Page
    Click **Receive Inventory without Bill**
    Click **Hide History** and **resize** the Item Receipt as previously discussed
    On the Item Receipt, click the drop-down list arrow for **Vendor**, click **Snow Stuff**
    Click **Yes** on the **Open POs Exist** message box

- An **Open Purchase Orders** dialog box appears showing all open purchase orders for the vendor, Snow Stuff.

    Point to any part of the line for P.O. NO. 2
    Click to select **Purchase Order 2**

- This will place a check mark in the check mark column.

Click **OK**

Change the date to **01/18/2018**.

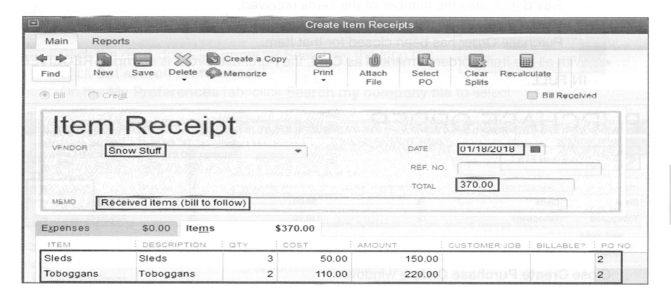

- REF. NO. is blank.
- Notice that the **Items** tab displays the Total of $370.
- In the columns, information for sleds and toboggans is completed.
- Notice the **Memo** of *Received items (bill to follow)*.
- The Item Receipt may be printed but is not required. Check with your instructor to see if you should print this document. If you print to a pdf file, save the document as **5-Your Name Item Rct Ch6**.

Click **Save & Close**

VERIFY PURCHASE ORDER RECEIVED IN FULL

As each line on a Purchase Order is received in full, QuickBooks DT marks it as *Clsd*. When all the items on the Purchase Order are marked *Clsd*, QuickBooks DT automatically stamps the P.O. as *Received in Full* and closes the purchase order.

On the Create Purchase Orders Main Icon bar, you may use Find to locate a specific Purchase Order.

MEMO

DATE: January 18, 2018

View the original Purchase Order 2 to verify that it has been stamped "Received in Full" and each item received is marked "Clsd."

To make sure all current information is shown, click **Update search information** (on the lower-left side of the Search screen)

- If you get a Search Update message, click **OK**.
- Search will find the purchase orders that have been prepared, list the Purchase Orders account, and, give you a list of Menu Items that may be used to prepare reports.

Scroll through the Search results until you get to **Menu Item**

Point to the Menu Item **Open Purchase Orders** on the Search screen

- Action items of Locate Menu, Launch, and Add to Favorites should appear.

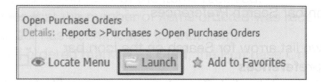

Click the **Launch** icon and the report will be shown on the screen

Your Name's Sierra Sports
Open Purchase Orders
All Transactions

Type	Date	Name	Num	Deliv Date	Amount	Open Balance
Purchase Order	01/16/2018	Footwear Galore	1	01/16/2018	1,875.00	1,875.00
Purchase Order	01/16/2018	Sports Clothes, Inc.	3	01/16/2018	375.00	375.00
Purchase Order	01/16/2018	Snow Sports, Inc.	4	01/16/2018	360.00	360.00
Total					**2,610.00**	**2,610.00**

- Since the Item Receipt for Purchase Order 2 has been recorded, it no longer shows as an Open Purchase Order.

Close the report without printing and close Search

ENTER BILL FOR ITEMS RECEIVED

For items that are received prior to the bill, the receipt of items is recorded as soon as the items arrive. This keeps the inventory up to date. When the bill is received, it must be recorded. To do this, indicate that the bill is entered against Inventory. When completing a bill for items already received, QuickBooks DT fills in all essential information on the bill.

A bill is divided into two sections: a <u>vendor-related</u> section (the upper part of the bill that looks like a check and has a memo text box under it) and a <u>detail</u> section (the area that has two tabs marked Items and Expenses). The vendor-related section of the bill is where information for the actual bill is entered, including a memo with information about the transaction. The detail section is where the information regarding the items ordered, the quantity ordered and received, and the amounts due for the items received is recorded.

MEMO

DATE: January 19, 2018

Record the bill for the sleds and toboggans already received from Snow Stuff, Vendor's Invoice 97 dated 01/18/2018, Terms 2% 10 Net 30.

Record the above bill for items already received

Click the **Enter Bills Against Inventory** icon on the Home Page

On the **Select Item Receipt** screen, click the drop-down list arrow for **Vendor**, click **Snow Stuff**

Click anywhere on the line **01/18/2018 Received items (bill to follow)** to select the Item Receipt

- The line for the item receipt will be highlighted.
- Unlike many of the other screens, there is no check column, so click the line to highlighted and select the Item Receipt.

Click **OK**

- QuickBooks DT displays the **Enter Bills** screen and the completed bill for Snow Stuff.
- The date shown is the date of the Vendor's bill **01/18/2018**. If not, change it.

Tab to or click **Ref No.**, type the vendor's invoice number **97**

- Notice that the **Amount Due** of 370 has been inserted.
- TERMS of **2% 10 Net 30** and dates for DISCOUNT DATE and BILL DUE are shown.

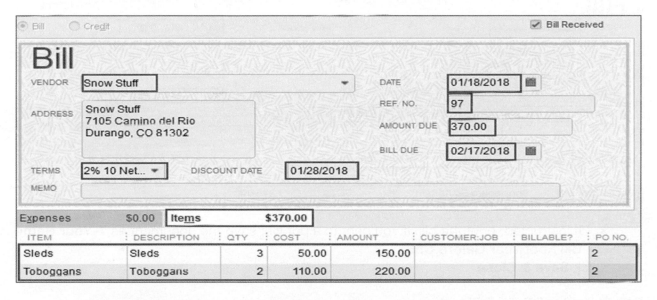

- If instructed to do so by your instructor, print the Bill. If you print to a pdf file, save the document as **6-Your Name Bill Snow Stuff Ch6**.

Click **Save & Close**

- If you get a Recording Transaction message box regarding the fact that the transaction has been changed, always click **Yes**.

RECORD RECEIPT OF ITEMS AND BILL

When ordered items are received and accompanied by a bill, the receipt of the items is recorded while entering the bill.

MEMO

DATE: January 19, 2018

Received 25 pairs of snowboard boots and a bill from Footwear Galore. Record the bill dated 01/18/2018 and the receipt of the items.

 Record the receipt of the items and the bill

Click **Receive Inventory** icon on the QuickBooks DT Home Page
Click **Receive Inventory with Bill**
Click the drop-down list for **Vendor**, click **Footwear Galore**
Click **Yes** on the **Open POs Exist** message box
On the Open Purchase Orders screen, click anywhere in the line for PO 1 to select and insert a check mark in the √ column
Click **OK**

- The bill appears on the screen and is complete.
- Make sure the date is **01/19/2018**. If not, change the date.
- Because no invoice number was given, leave the **REF. NO.** blank.

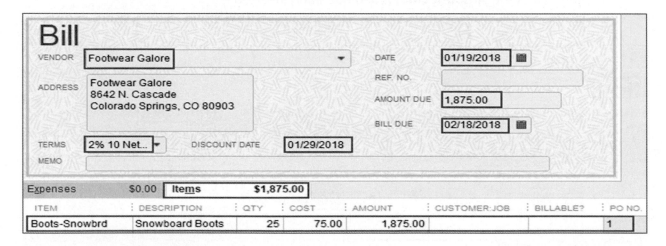

- If instructed, print the bill. If you print to a pdf file, save the document as **7-Your Name Bill Footwear Galore Ch6**.
- Click **Save & Close**

EDIT PURCHASE ORDER

As with any other form, purchase orders may be edited once they have been prepared. Click on the Purchase Order icon on the QuickBooks DT Home Page.

> **MEMO**
>
> **DATE:** January 19, 2018
>
> Ruth realized that Purchase Order 4 should be for 15 pairs of ski poles. Change the purchase order and reprint.

 Change Purchase Order 4

Access Purchase Order 4 as previously instructed
- Even though QuickBooks DT suggested a Reorder Qty of 12, you may choose to order any quantity you wish.

Click in **Qty**; change the number from 12 to **15**

Tab to recalculate the amount due for the purchase order

- Notice the columns for Rcv'd and Clsd. Those are included on the Purchase Order when it was saved originally.

Print the **Purchase Order** as previously instructed
- If you print to a pdf file, save the document as **8-Your Name PO 4 Snow Sports Revised Ch6**.

Click **Save & Close** to record the changes and exit

Click **Yes** on the **Recording Transaction** dialog box to save the changes

RECORD PARTIAL MERCHANDISE RECEIPT

Sometimes when items on order are received, they are not received in full. The remaining items may be delivered as back-ordered items. This will usually occur if an item is out of stock, and you must wait for delivery until more items are manufactured and/or received by the vendor. With QuickBooks DT you record the number of items you receive, and the bill is recorded for that amount.

> **MEMO**
>
> **DATE:** January 19, 2018
>
> Record the bill and the receipt of 20 pairs of gloves ordered on Purchase Order 3. On the purchase order, 25 pairs of gloves were ordered. Sports Clothes, Inc. will no longer be carrying these gloves, so the remaining 5 pairs of gloves on order will not be shipped. Manually close the purchase order. The date of the bill is 01/18/2018.

Record the receipt of and the bill for 20 pairs of gloves from Sports Clothes, Inc.

Access **Receive Inventory with Bill** as previously instructed
If necessary, change the **Date** of the bill to **01/18/2018**
Click the drop-down list arrow for **Vendor**, click **Sports Clothes, Inc.**
Click **Yes** on **Open POs Exist** dialog box
Click anywhere in the line for **P.O. 3** on **Open Purchase Orders** dialog box
Click **OK**
Click the **Qty** column on the Items tab in the Enter Bills window
Change the quantity to **20**
Tab to change **Amount** to **300**
- Notice the **Amount Due** on the bill also changes.
Print if instructed to do so
- If you print to a pdf file, save the document as **9-Your Name Bill Sports Clothes Ch6**.
Click **Save & Close** to record the items received and the bill

CLOSE PURCHASE ORDER MANUALLY

If you have issued a purchase order and it is determined that you will not be receiving the remaining items on order, the purchase order should be closed manually.

 Close Purchase Order 3 using **Advanced Find** to locate Purchase Order 3

Use the keyboard shortcut **Ctrl+F**; and then, click the **Advanced** tab
Scroll through CHOOSE FILTER, click **Transaction Type**
- A filter helps to narrow the search for locating something.
Click the drop-down list arrow for **Transaction Type**, click **Purchase Order**
Click **Find**
- A list of all purchase orders is shown on the screen.
- The information shown includes the date of the Purchase Order, type (PURCHORD), purchase order number, vendor name, accounts used, the item(s) ordered, and the amount of the purchase order.
- Unlike Search Company File, no reports are shown.
Click **Purchase Order 3** for **Sports Clothes, Inc.**, then click **Go To**

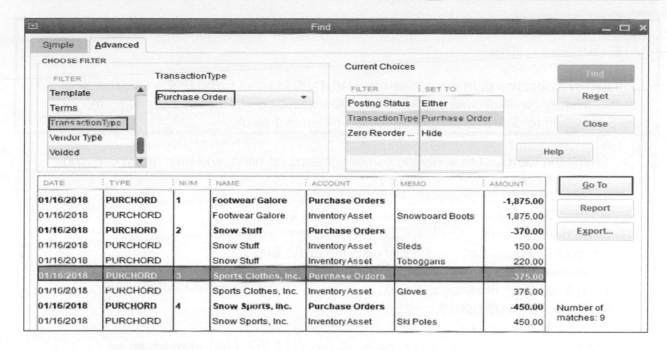

- P.O. 3 will show on the screen.
- Notice that the ordered **Qty** is 25, **Backordered** is 5, and **Rcv'd** is 20.

Click the **Clsd** column for Gloves to mark and close the purchase order

- Notice the check mark in the Clsd column. Backordered is now 0.
- Below the form title PURCHASE ORDER, you will see a check mark and the word CLOSED.

Print the Closed Purchase Order, click **Yes** on Recording Transactions

- If you print to a pdf file, save the document as **10-Your Name PO 1 Sports Clothes Closed Ch6**.

Click **Save & Close**, close **Find**

ENTER CREDIT FROM VENDOR

Credit memos are prepared to record a reduction to a transaction. With QuickBooks DT you use the Enter Bills window to record credit memos received from vendors acknowledging a return of items purchased or an allowance for a previously recorded bill and/or payment. The amount of a credit memo can be applied to the amount owed to a vendor when paying bills. Sometimes, a credit for a bill is called Bill Credit to distinguish it from a customer's credit memo.

MEMO

DATE: January 21, 2018

Upon further inspection of merchandise received, Ruth Morgan found that one of the sleds received from Snow Stuff, was cracked. The sled was returned. Received Credit Memo 9915 from Snow Stuff for $50 (the full amount on the return of 1 sled).

 Check the **Item List** to verify the number of sleds on hand, and then return one sled

> Access **Item List** as previously instructed
> - Look at Sleds to verify that there are 7 sleds in stock.
> Close the **Item List**
> To record the return of one sled, access the **Enter Bills**
> On the **Enter Bills** screen, click **Credit** to select
> - The word *Bill* changes to *Credit*.
> Enter the date **01/21/2018**
> Click the **Items** tab
> Tab to or click the first line in the **Item** column, click the drop-down list arrow
> Click **Sleds**
> - The Vendor **Snow Stuff**, the Amount Due **50**, and the Cost **50** are entered automatically.
> Tab to or click **Qty**, enter **1**
> Click in the text box for **Date**; enter **01/21/18**
> Tab to or click **Ref. No.**, type **9915**
> **Memo**, enter **Returned 1 Damaged Sled**

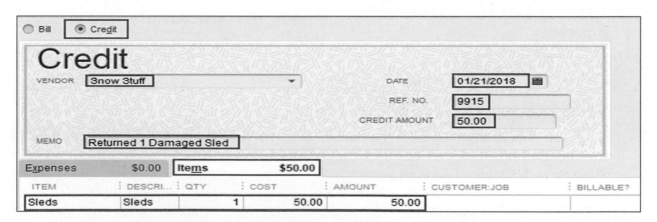

> Print the Credit Memo if instructed to do so
> - If you print to a pdf file, save the document as **11-Your Name CM Snow Stuff Ch6**.
> Click **Save & Close** to record the credit and exit the **Enter Bills** window
> - QuickBooks DT decreases the quantity of sleds on hand and creates a credit with the vendor that can be applied when paying the bill. The Credit Memo also appears in the Accounts Payable account in the **Paid** column, which decreases the amount owed and shows the transaction type as BILLCRED in the Accounts Payable register.

 Verify that there are 6 sleds in stock after the return.

Access the **Item List**
Verify the number of sleds and then close the list

 View the return in the Accounts Payable register

Access the **Chart of Accounts** as previously instructed
Double-click **Accounts Payable** to open the Register
Scroll through the register until you see the BILLCRED for Snow Stuff

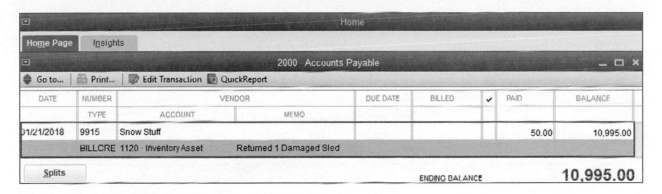

Close the **Accounts Payable Register** and the **Chart of Accounts**

BILL TRACKER—INFORMATION ONLY

Bill Tracker is like the Income Tracker in Chapter 5. Bill Tracker summarizes and simplifies the information needed to manage bills in one screen. This information is presented with a "dashboard" layout. Bill tracker includes information regarding purchase orders, unbilled purchase orders, open/unpaid bills, overdue bills, bill payments, and unreceived item receipts.

Different filters may be applied to Bill Tracker for data management of bills. Filters include: Vendor (may select all vendors or a single vendor), Type (select the transaction type such as Bills, Purchase Orders, Item Receipts, and others), Status (choose All, Open, Overdue, or Paid transactions for display), Dates (select a range of dates to display) Group By (may select to group transactions by Vendor. This enables you to select an individual vendor, expand or collapse the list for the vendor, and get a subtotal by vendor).

Action is used perform an action on a selected transaction. For bills actions include pay, copy, or print. For purchase orders actions include print, close, email, copy, or convert to a bill. At the bottom of the screen is a drop-down list arrow for Manage Transactions. This is a shortcut to create new purchase orders, bills, credit card charges, checks, or edit the highlighted row. In addition, Batch Actions are available and allow several transactions to be processed at the same time. These include batch print purchase orders, batch pay bills, and batch close purchase orders.

For each transaction, information is provided regarding the Vendor name, Type of transaction, the business document number, the transaction date, the due date, the status, the amount due, and the action to take for this transaction.

 View Bill Tracker

Click the **Bill Tracker** icon on the Icon bar or at the top of the Vendor Center

- May need to adjust column widths to display information in full.
- The following screen shot was taken with a computer date of 01/21/2018. Since your computer date is not the same, your Bill Tracker will show all bills as Overdue.
- January transactions show due dates that are based on the terms for the vendor and the invoice date.
- Look at the bill for 12/31/17 Boots & Bindings (this was the opening balance). It is due on January 10, 2018 and is marked Overdue.
- To pay this bill, you would go to the Action column and click Pay Bill.

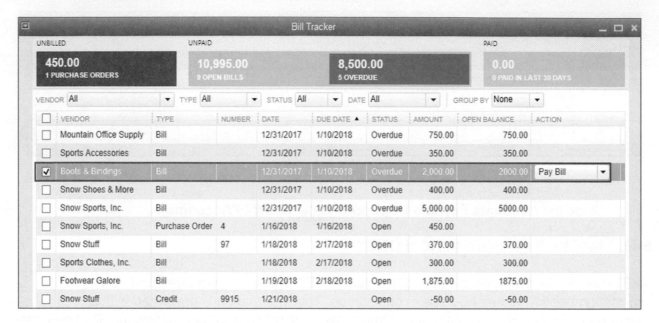

- If you click the action Pay Bills, you will be taken to the Pay Bills screen.
- If you click and select several transactions, you can click the Batch Actions button and then select the desired process (Pay Bills in this example).

- When you see the Pay Bills screen, all the transactions will appear. Clicking the Pay Selected Bills button will process checks for the bills marked with a check.

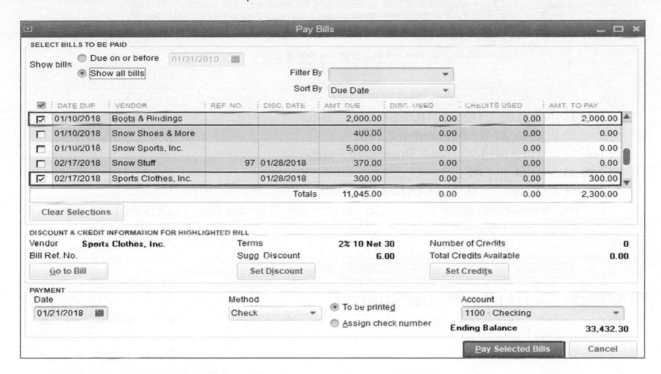

Click Cancel on Pay Bills, close Bill Tracker; and, if open, close the Vendor Center

RECORD CREDIT CARD PURCHASE

Some businesses use credit cards as an integral part of their finances. Many companies have a credit card that is used primarily for gasoline purchases for company vehicles. Other companies use credit cards as a means of paying for expenses or purchasing merchandise or other necessary items for use in the business.

MEMO
DATE: January 21, 2018

Ruth discovered that she was out of paper. She purchased a box of paper to have on hand from Mountain Office Supply for $21.98. Rather than add to the existing balance owed to the company, Ruth used the company's Visa credit card.

 Purchase the above office supplies using the company's Visa credit card

Click the **Enter Credit Card Charges** icon in the **Banking** section of the Home Page

Credit Card should indicate **2100 Visa**
- The radio button for Purchase/Charge should be selected; if not, click to mark.

Click the drop-down list arrow for **Purchased From**, click **Mountain Office Supply**
Click **OK** on the **Warning** screen

DATE should be **01/21/2018, REF NO.** is blank

Tab to or click **AMOUNT**, enter **21.98**

Tab to or click **MEMO**, enter **Purchase Paper**

Tab to or click the **ACCOUNT** column on the **Expenses** tab, click the drop-down list arrow for **Account**, click **1311 Office Supplies**

- This transaction is for supplies to have on hand, so the Asset Account 1311 Office Supplies is used.

- When entering a Credit Card transaction using Enter Credit Card Charges, QuickBooks DT does <u>not</u> enable you to print a copy of the transaction.

Click **Save & New** to record the charge and go to the next credit card entry

PAY FOR INVENTORY ITEMS WITH CREDIT CARD

It is possible to pay for inventory items using a credit card. The payment may be made using the Pay Bills window, or it may be made by recording an entry for Credit Card Charges. If you are purchasing something that is on order, you may record the receipt of merchandise on order first, or you may record the receipt of merchandise and the credit card payment at the same time.

MEMO

DATE: January 21, 2018

Note from You: Ruth, record the receipt of 10 ski poles from Snow Sports, Inc. Pay for the ski poles using the company's Visa credit card.

 Pay for the ski poles received using the company's Visa credit card

Click the drop-down list for **Purchased From** click **Snow Sports, Inc.**

Click the **Yes** button on the **Open POs Exist** message box

Click the line containing PO NO. 4 on the **Open Purchase Orders** dialog box
Click **OK**

- If you get a warning screen regarding outstanding bills, click **OK**.

Click the **Clear Qtys** button on the bottom of the screen to clear 15 from Qty column
Tab to or click **Qty**, enter **10**
Tab to change the Amount to 300

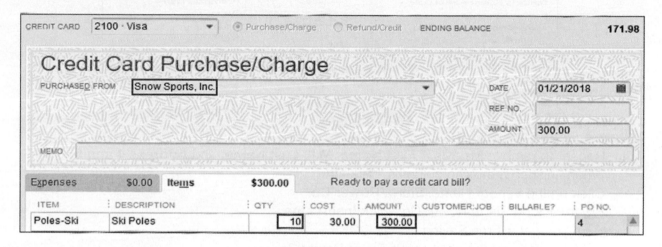

Click **Save & Close** to record and close the transaction

CONFIRM RECEIPT OF SKI POLES

Access Purchase Order 4 as previously instructed

- The **Rcv'd** column should show **10** and **Backordered** should show **5**.
- Notice that the **Qty** column shows **15** and **Clsd** is <u>not</u> marked. This indicates that 5 sets of ski poles are still on order.

Close Purchase Order 4 without changing or printing

ADD/EDIT MULTIPLE LIST ENTRIES

Vendors, customers, and list items may be added through the add/edit multiple list entries on the list menu. This feature is especially useful when importing data from Excel spreadsheets into QuickBooks DT. In addition, it may be used to quickly add one or more records to a list.

MEMO
DATE: January 23, 2018

Add a new vendor, *Mammoth News*, 1450 Main Street, Mammoth Lakes, CA 93546, Main Phone: 909-555-2525, Fax: 909-555-5252, E-mail: mammothnews@ski.com.

Add the new vendor using Add/Edit Multiple List Entries

Click the **Lists** menu
Click **Add/Edit Multiple List Entries**
Click the drop-down list arrow for **List**, click **Vendors**

Click the **Customize Columns** button and remove unwanted columns
Click **Alt. Phone** in the Chosen Columns
Click **Remove**

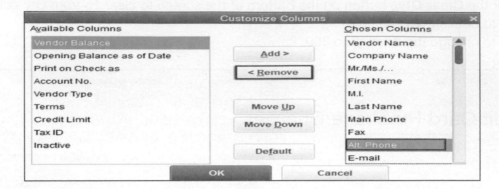

Repeat to remove **Mr./Ms./**, **First Name**, **M.I.**, **Last Name**, and **Address 4 and 5**
When finished removing columns, click **OK**
Click on the Vendor Name, **Sierra Power Co.**
<u>Right</u>-click on Sierra Power Co., click **Insert Line**
- If you get a Time Saving tip, click **OK**.
- A blank line is inserted above Sierra Power Co.

In the Vendor Name column on the blank line, enter **Mammoth News**
Press, **Tab**
Enter the Company Name **Mammoth News**
Tab to or click in the column for **Main Phone**, enter **909-555-2525**
Tab to or click **FAX**, enter **909-555-5252**
Tab to or click **E-mail**, enter **mammothnews@ski.com**
Tab to or click **Address 1**, enter **Mammoth News**
Tab to or click **Address 2**, enter **1450 Main Street**
Tab to or click **Address 3**, enter **Mammoth Lakes, CA 93546**

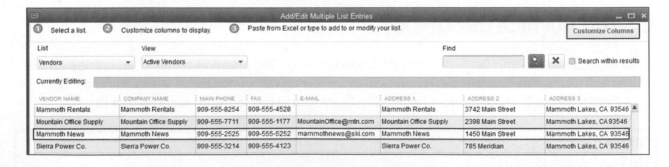

Click **Save Changes**
Click **OK** on the Record(s) Saved dialog box. click **Close**

PREPARE DAILY BACKUP

As previously discussed, a backup file is prepared as a precaution in case you make an error. By creating the backup file now, it will contain your work for Chapters 5 and 6 up through adding the new vendor Mammoth News.

Prepare Sierra (Daily Backup).qbb file

> Follow the steps presented in Chapter 1 for creating a backup file
> Name the file **Sierra 2018 (Daily Backup)**
> The file type is **QBW Backup (* .QBB)**

ENTER BILLS

Whether the bill is to pay for expenses incurred in the operation of a business or to pay for merchandise to sell in the business, QuickBooks DT provides accounts payable tracking for all vendors owed. Entering bills as soon as they are received is an efficient way to record your liabilities. Once bills have been entered, QuickBooks DT will be able to provide up-to-date cash flow reports and will remind you when it's time to pay your bills.

As previously stated, a bill is divided into two sections: a vendor-related section and a detail section. The vendor-related section of the bill is where information for the actual bill is entered. If the bill is for paying an expense, the Expenses tab is used for the detail section. Using this tab allows you to indicate the expense accounts for the transaction, to enter the amounts for the various expense accounts, and to provide transaction explanations. If the bill is for merchandise, the Items tab will be used to record the receipt of the items ordered.

If you use the Document Center, you may scan the bill you receive, store it in the Doc Center, and attach it to the bill electronically. (Refer to Appendix B for more detailed information and examples of using the Document Center and Attaching a document electronically.)

MEMO
DATE: January 23, 2018

Placed an ad in *Mammoth News* announcing our February sale. Record the receipt of the bill from *Mammoth News* for $95.00, Terms Net 30, Invoice 3822.

 Enter the bill

> Click the **Enter Bills** icon on the Home Page
> Complete the **Vendor Section** of the bill:
>> VENDOR: **Mammoth News**
>> DATE: **01/23/18**
>> REF NO.: **3822** (the vendor's invoice number)
>> AMOUNT DUE: **95**
>> TERMS: **Net 30**
>> - QuickBooks DT automatically changes the Bill Due date to show 30 days from the transaction date.
>> - Since the terms are Net 30, there is no Discount Date.
>> - At this time no change will be made to the Bill Due date, and nothing will be inserted as a memo.
> Complete the **Detail Section** of the bill:
>> - If necessary, click the **Expenses** tab.
>> Click the drop-down list arrow for ACCOUNT, click **<Add New>**

- **Type** of account should show **Expense**. If not, click **Expense**.

Click **Continue**

Enter **6140** as the account number in Number

Account Name: enter **Advertising Expense**

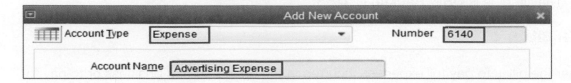

Click **Save & Close**

6140 Advertising Expense shows as the ACCOUNT

- Based on the accrual method of accounting, Advertising Expense is selected as the account for this transaction because this expense should be matched against the revenue of the period.
- The Amount column already shows 95.00—no entry required.
- Tab to or click the first line in the column for **Memo**.

Enter the transaction explanation of **Ad for February Sale**

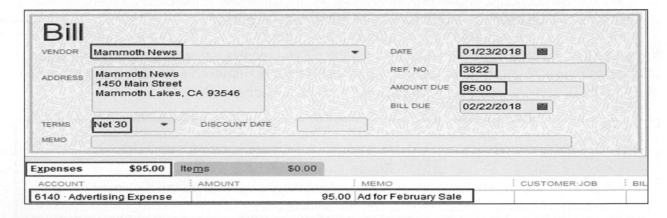

Print if instructed to do so

- If you print to a pdf file, save the document as **12-Your Name Bill Mammoth News Ch6**.
  - Since no terms were assigned when the company was added to the Vendor List, click **Yes** on the **Name Information Changed** dialog box

Click **Save & Close**

ASSIGN TERMS AND ACCOUNTS TO VENDORS

Once a vendor has been established, changes can be made to the vendor's account information. The changes will take effect immediately and will be reflected in recorded transactions for the vendor.

> **MEMO**
> **DATE:** January 23, 2018
>
> Add payment terms and assign expense accounts for the following vendors:
>   Sierra Power Company: Payment Terms of Net 30, 6391 Gas and Electric
>   Sierra Telephone Co.: Payment Terms of Net 30, 6340 Telephone
>   Sierra Water Company: Payment Terms of Net 30, 6392 Water
>   Mammoth News: 6140 Advertising Expense

 Change the terms and assign expense accounts as indicated in the Memo above

Access the **Vendor List** in the Vendor Center as previously instructed
Double-click on **Sierra Power Co.**
Click **Payment Settings** tab
Click the drop-down list arrow for PAYMENT TERMS, click **Net 30**
Click the **Account Settings** tab
Click the drop-down list arrow, click the expense account **6391 Gas and Electric**
Click **OK**
Repeat for the other vendors indicated in the memo above
When you enter the information for Mammoth News, verify that the terms are Net 30
If the Print Name on Check As is blank, enter **Mammoth News**
Add the expense account **6140 Advertising Expense**
Close the **Vendor Center** when all changes have been made

CREATE MEMORIZED TRANSACTION

Transactions that are entered on a regular basis may be memorized for use. QuickBooks DT can automatically create the transactions for you. After entering the standard information on a bill to Sierra Power Co., you can have QuickBooks DT memorize the transaction. Then, next month you select the transaction in the Memorized Transaction List and QuickBooks DT prepares the bill.

 Memorize the bill for Sierra Power Co.

Access **Enter Bills** as previously instructed
VENDOR: is **Sierra Power Company**
*   Notice that the terms and account are entered automatically.

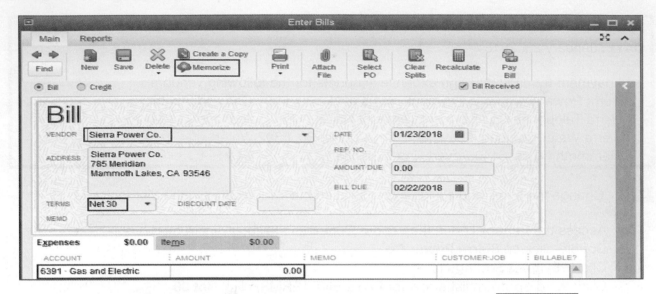

With the bill to Sierra Power Co. showing on the screen, click the  icon on the Enter Bills Main Icon bar

- On the Memorize Transaction screen, note the Name **Sierra Power Co.**

The Transaction is marked to **Add to my Reminders List**, do <u>not</u> change this

- You have the option to Automate Transaction Entry, so QuickBooks DT can automatically prepare the bill on the frequency you select.
- You may also tell QuickBooks DT the number of payments remaining. This is great if you are using the transaction to pay a loan.
- If you selected Automate Transaction Entry, you may tell QuickBooks DT how many Days in Advance to Enter the transaction.

Click the drop-down list arrow for **How Often**

Click **Monthly**

Click the Calendar icon for Next Date, click **01/25/2018**

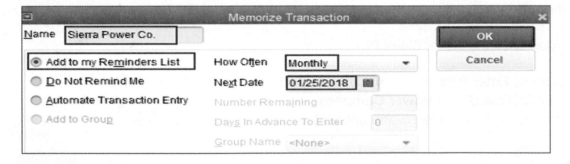

Click **OK**

Close the Enter Bills screen <u>without</u> saving the bill for Sierra Power Co.

Click the **Lists** menu on the Menu bar, click **Memorized Transaction List**

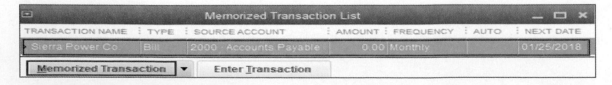

Click the **Memorized Transaction** button, click **Print List**

Click **OK** on the List Reports message, click **Print**
- If you print to a pdf file, save the document as **13-Your Name Memorized Trans List Ch6**.

After printing the list, click the transaction to Sierra Power Co. to select

USE MEMORIZED TRANSACTION

Once a transaction has been memorized, it may be used to record a bill. This removes a lot of the repetitive work and streamlines the process for recurring bills.

> MEMO
>
> **DATE:** January 25, 2018
>
> Record the bill to Sierra Power Company electrical power for January: Invoice 3510-1023, $359.00.

 Use the Memorized Transaction List to record a bill

With Sierra Power Co. highlighted, click the **Enter Transaction** button on the Memorized Transaction List
The prepared Bill to Sierra Power Co. appears on the screen
Make sure the DATE is **01/25/2018**
Enter the REF. NO. **3510-1023**
Enter the AMOUNT DUE **359.00**

Print if instructed to do so; and then click **Save & New**
- If you print to a pdf file, save the document as **14-Your Name Bill Sierra Power Ch6**.

PREPARE ADDITIONAL BILLS

It is more efficient to record bills in a group or batch than it is to record them one at a time. If an error is made while preparing the bill, correct it. Your Name's Sierra Sports uses the accrual basis of accounting. In the accrual method of accounting the expenses of a period are matched against the revenue of the period. Unless otherwise instructed, use the accrual basis of accounting when recording entries.

MEMO

DATE: January 25, 2018

Record the following bills:

Sierra Telephone Co. telephone service for January: Invoice 7815, $156.40.

Sierra Water Co. water for January: Invoice 3105, $35.00.

 Enter the two transactions in the memo above.

- Refer to the instructions given for previous transactions.
- These are standard transactions, so no Memo is required.
- Print if instructed to do so. If you print to a pdf file, save the documents as **15-Your Name Bill Sierra Telephone Ch6**, and **16-Your Name Bill Sierra Water Co**.
  When finished, click **Save & Close** and close the **Memorize Transaction List**

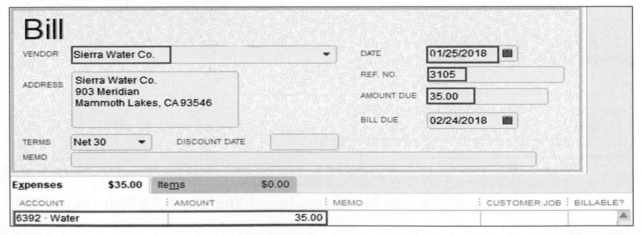

ENTER BILL IN ACCOUNTS PAYABLE REGISTER

The Accounts Payable Register maintains a record of all the transactions recorded within the Accounts Payable account. Not only is it possible to view all the account activities through the account's register, it is also possible to enter a bill directly into the Accounts Payable register. This can be faster than filling out all the information through Enter Bills.

MEMO

DATE: January 25, 2018

Received a bill for the rent from Mammoth Rentals. Use the Accounts Payable Register and record the bill for rent of $950, Invoice 7164, due February 4, 2018.

 Use the Accounts Payable Register to record the above transaction:

Use the keyboard shortcut, **Ctrl+A** to access the Chart of Accounts
Double-click **2000 Accounts Payable** to open the Accounts Payable register
The date is highlighted in the blank entry, key in **01/25/18** for the transaction date
The word *Number* is in the next column
Tab to or click **Number**
- The word *Number* disappears.

Enter the Vendor's Invoice Number **7164**
Click the drop-down list arrow for the VENDOR, click **Mammoth Rentals**
- When there is a drop-down list arrow, you do not need to tab or click in the field.

Tab to or click **DUE DATE**; and, if necessary, enter the due date **02/04/18**
Tab to or click **BILLED**, enter the amount **950**
Click the drop-down list arrow for **Account**
Determine the appropriate account to use for rent
- If all the accounts do not appear in the drop-down list, scroll through the accounts until you find the one that is appropriate for this entry.

Click **6300 Rent**
Click **Record** to record the transaction
- If the bill for Rent shows before Telephone that is fine. Since they have the same transaction date, QuickBooks DT alphabetized the Vendor names.

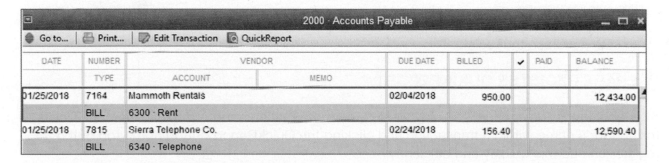

DATE	NUMBER	VENDOR		DUE DATE	BILLED	✔	PAID	BALANCE
	TYPE	ACCOUNT	MEMO					
01/25/2018	7164	Mammoth Rentals		02/04/2018	950.00			12,434.00
	BILL	6300 · Rent						
01/25/2018	7815	Sierra Telephone Co.		02/24/2018	156.40			12,590.40
	BILL	6340 · Telephone						

Do <u>not</u> close the register

EDIT TRANSACTION IN ACCOUNTS PAYABLE REGISTER

Because QuickBooks DT makes corrections extremely user friendly, a transaction can be edited or changed directly in the Accounts Payable Register as well as on the original bill. By eliminating the columns for Type and Memo, it is possible to change the register to show each transaction on one line. This can make the register easier to read.

> **MEMO**
>
> **DATE:** January 25, 2018
>
> Upon examination of the invoices and the bills entered, Ruth discovers an error: The actual amount of the bill from the water company was **$85**, not $35. Change the transaction amount for this bill.

 Correct the above transaction in the Accounts Payable Register

Click the check box for **1-line** to select
- Each Accounts Payable transaction will appear on one line.

Click the transaction for Sierra Water Co.
Change the amount of the transaction from $35.00 to **$85.00**
Click the **Record** button at the bottom of the register
Click **Yes** on the Record Transaction dialog box

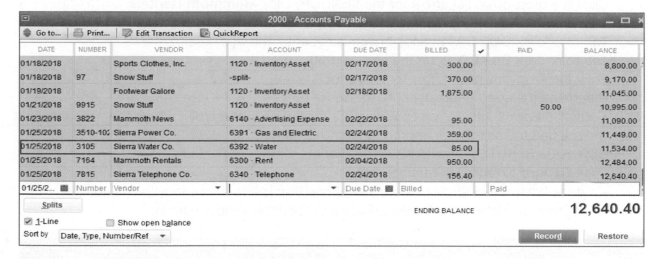

Do <u>not</u> close the register

PREPARE REGISTER QUICKREPORT

After editing the transaction, you may want to view information about a specific vendor. Clicking the vendor's name within a transaction and clicking the QuickReport button at the top of the register can do this quickly and efficiently.

> **MEMO**
> **DATE:** January 25, 2018
>
> More than one transaction has been entered for Snow Stuff. Both Larry and you like to view transaction information for vendors that have several transactions within a short period.

 Prepare a QuickReport for Snow Stuff

Click any field in any transaction for Snow Stuff
Click the **QuickReport** button at the top of the Register
- The Register QuickReport for All Transactions for Snow Stuff appears on the screen.
Resize the columns and print in Portrait orientation
- If you print to a pdf file, save the document as **17-Your Name QuickReport Snow Stuff Ch6.**

Your Name's Sierra Sports
Register QuickReport
All Transactions

Type	Date	Num	Memo	Account	Paid	Open Balance	Amount
Snow Stuff							
Bill	01/18/2018	97		2000 · Accounts Payable	Unpaid	370.00	370.00
Credit	01/21/2018	9915	Returned 1 Damaged Sled	2000 · Accounts Payable	Unpaid	-50.00	-50.00
Total Snow Stuff						320.00	320.00
TOTAL						**320.00**	**320.00**

Click the **Close** button to close the report
Close the Accounts Payable register and the Chart of Accounts

 If you have been instructed to print bills, print the bills prepared and edited in the Accounts Payable register

Open **Enter Bills**; click **Previous** until you get to the bill for **Mammoth Rentals**
Print as previously instructed
- If you print to a pdf file, save the document as **18-Your Name Bill Mammoth Rentals Ch6.**
Repeat to print the corrected bill for **Sierra Telephone Co.**
- If you print to a pdf file, save the document as **19-Your Name Bill Sierra Telephone Corrected Ch6.**

DISCOUNTS

There are three types of discounts used in QuickBooks DT: Sales Discount, Purchase Discount, and Merchandise Discount.

A Sales Discount is used when you give customers a discount for early payment with terms of 2% 10 Net 30 or 1% 10 Net 30. Sales Discount is categorized as an Income account. Using a sales discount results in a decrease in income because the company will receive less money for a sale. In Chapter 5, Sales Discounts were used for customer payments.

A Purchase Discount is a discount for early payment for purchases made to run the business. Example, a discount on office supplies purchased. A purchase discount is categorized as an Income account because it results in an increase in income since it costs you less to run the business.

A Merchandise Discount is a discount on sales items purchased for resale This is categorized as a Cost of Goods Sold account because the use of this discount results in a decrease in the amount you pay for the goods (merchandise) you sell. This is used in this chapter for payments for sales items purchased.

PREPARE UNPAID BILLS DETAIL REPORT

It is possible to get information regarding unpaid bills by simply preparing a report. No more digging through tickler files, recorded invoices, ledgers, or journals. QuickBooks DT prepares an Unpaid Bills Detail Report listing each unpaid bill grouped and subtotaled by vendor.

Comments may be added to lines in a report. On an Unpaid Bills report, it could be helpful to add comments to the bills that should be paid.

MEMO

DATE: January 25, 2018

Ruth Morgan prepares an Unpaid Bills Report each week. Because Your Name's Sierra Sports is a small business, you like to have a firm control over cash flow, so you can determine which bills will be paid during the week. Add the comment "Pay this Bill" to each bill eligible for a discount.

 Prepare an **Unpaid Bills Detail Report**

Click **Reports** on the menu bar, point to **Vendors & Payables**, click **Unpaid Bills Detail**
Enter the date of **01/25/18** as the report date
Tab to generate report
Adjust column size as necessary to display all data in the columns in full
- Notice the Due Dates for the bills. Bills from the end of the previous year are due on January 10.
- The days shown for Aging will be different from the report shown because the aging is based on the date of your computer.
- Note: The Unpaid Bills report does not give you information regarding discount eligibility. If a column showing Terms was in the report, you could determine which bills would be eligible for a discount.

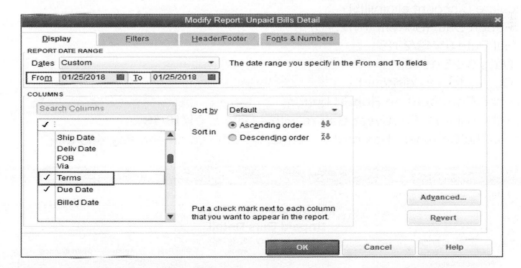

Your Name's Sierra Sports
Unpaid Bills Detail
As of January 25, 2018

Type	Date	Num	Due Date	Aging	Open Balance
Snow Stuff					
Credit	01/21/2018	9915			–50.00
Bill	01/18/2018	97	02/17/2018		370.00
Total Snow Stuff					320.00
Sports Accessories					
Bill	12/31/2017		01/10/2018	15	350.00
Total Sports Accessories					350.00
Sports Clothes, Inc.					
Bill	01/18/2018		02/17/2018		300.00
Total Sports Clothes, Inc.					300.00
TOTAL					**12,640.40**

Partial Report

CUSTOMIZE AND MEMORIZE REPORT

While many reports come with QuickBooks DT, sometimes you do not have all the information that you want displayed in the report. Just as you can customize the header/footer for a report, you can also customize the information shown within a report.

 Customize the Unpaid Bills Detail report to show Terms

With the Unpaid Bills report showing on the screen, click the **Customize Report** button
The REPORT DATE RANGE should be From **01/25/2018** and To **01/25/2018**
Scroll through the COLUMNS until you see the word **Terms**, and click to mark

Click **OK**, Terms are now displayed in the report
Adjust the column widths to displayed everything in full; yet, print one-page wide
Click the **Memorize** button
The Name of the report is: **Unpaid Bills Detail with Terms**

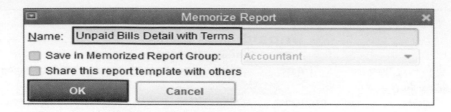

Click **OK**

Close the Unpaid Bills Report

USE MEMORIZED REPORT

To use the report in the future, click Reports on the Menu Bar, click Memorized Reports, and click Unpaid Bills Detail with Terms

Use the Memorized Report Unpaid Bills with Terms

Click **Reports** on the Menu bar, click **Memorized Reports**, and click **Unpaid Bills with Terms**

Make sure the date is **01/25/2018**, press **Tab**.

ADD COMMENTS TO REPORT

With the Unpaid Bills with Terms for 01/25/2018 on the screen, comment on the report

- Look at the vendors who show Terms of 2% 10 Net 30. If any of the bills qualify for a discount or use a credit, enter a comment.

Calculate Discount eligibility:

    Report Date (Current) 01/25/2018

    Bill Date 01/19/2018

    Days 6 (25-19=6)

    Qualify for 2% discount

Click the **Comment on Report** button

Click the bill from **Footwear Galore** with a Date of **01/18/18**

Click in the Comment Box next to Terms, type the comment: **Pay this Bill**

Click **Save** on the Comments
Repeat for Sports Clothes, Inc.
For **Snow Stuff** you need to make two comments:
> On the Credit, click in the box next to Credit, enter comment **Use this credit**
> For the bill, comment **Pay this Bill** as you did for Footwear Galore and Sports Clothes, Inc.

Print in Portrait orientation
- If you print to a pdf file, save the document as **20-Your Name Commented Unpaid Bills Ch6**.
- The Commented report can also be saved and/or be emailed with the comments. However, it cannot be exported to Excel.

Close the report without saving, click **No** on Save Your Commented Report?
Close the Unpaid Bills Detail with Terms

PAY BILLS

When using QuickBooks DT, you may choose to pay your bills directly from the Pay Bills command and let QuickBooks DT write your checks for you, or you may choose to write the checks yourself. If you recorded a bill, you should use the Pay Bills feature of QuickBooks DT to pay the bill. If no bill was recorded, you should pay the bill by writing a check in QuickBooks DT. Using the Pay Bills window enables you to determine which bills to pay, the method of payment—check or credit card—and the appropriate account. When you are determining which bills to pay, QuickBooks DT allows you to display the bills by due date, discount date, vendor, or amount. All bills may be displayed, or only those bills that are due by a certain date may be displayed.

In addition, when a bill has been recorded and is paid using the Pay Bills feature of QuickBooks DT, the bill will be marked *Paid in Full* and the amount paid will no longer be shown as a liability. If you record a bill and pay it by writing a check and *not* using the Pay Bills feature of QuickBooks DT, the bill won't be marked as paid and it will continue to be shown as a liability.

MEMO
DATE: January 25, 2018

Whenever possible, Ruth Morgan pays the bills on a weekly basis. Show all the bills in the Pay Bills window. As indicated in the comments on the Unpaid Bills report, select the bills for Footwear Galore and Sports Clothes, Inc. with discounts dates of 1/28/2018.

 Pay the bills that are eligible for a discount

Click **Pay Bills** on the QuickBooks DT Home Page
Click **Show All Bills** to select
Filter By **All vendors**
Sort By **Due Date**
In the PAYMENT section at the bottom of the **Pay Bills** window, verify and/or select the following items:
> **Date** is **01/25/18**
> **Method** is **Check**

To be printed should be selected
Account is **1100 Checking**

Scroll through the list of bills

- The bills will be shown according to the date due.

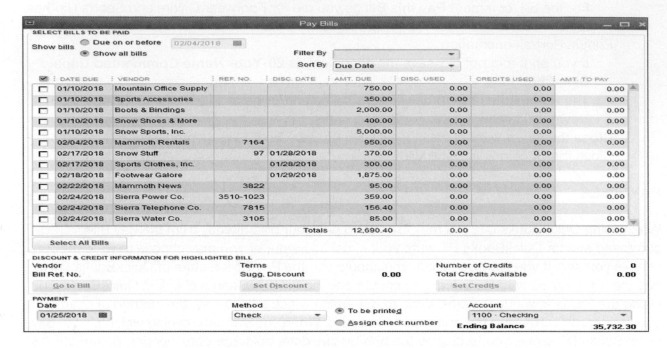

Select the bills to be paid and apply the discounts:

Click in the check mark column for the transaction for **Footwear Galore** with a DUE DATE of 2/18/2018 and a DISC Date of 01/29/2018

Click the **Set Discount** button

- Verify the Suggested Discount of **37.50**.

Click the drop-down list arrow for the Discount Account

- Scroll through the list of accounts.
- There is account 4030 Purchases Discounts, but it is not appropriate for this transaction. This income account is used for purchases of things used by the business <u>not</u> for merchandise sold by the business.
- There is 4050 Sales Discounts. This income account is used when we give discounts to customers.
- The bill payment is for merchandise purchased to sell in the business. A cost of goods sold discount account needs to be created for merchandise discounts.

Click **<Add New>**

Click the drop-down list arrow for **Account Type**, click **Cost of Goods Sold**

- Remember the Cost of Goods sold is the average cost you pay for an item you sell and is calculated on the Profit & Loss Statement using the formula: Total Income – Cost of Goods Sold = Gross Profit; Gross Profit – Expenses = Net Profit.
- Using Merchandise Discounts for early payment will decrease the overall Cost of Goods Sold and increase Profit or Net Income. Example: Cost of Goods Sold – Merchandise Discounts = Net Cost of Goods Sold.
- If Cost of Goods Sold is $1,000 and you subtract Merchandise Discounts of $100 the Net Cost of Goods Sold is $900. Without the discount, Cost of Goods Sold is $1,000.

Enter **5200** as the account number
Enter the account name **Merchandise Discounts**
Click **Subaccount** and select **5000 Cost of Goods Sold** as the account

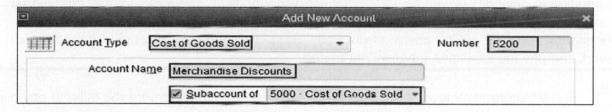

Click **Save & Close** to return to the Discount and Credits screen

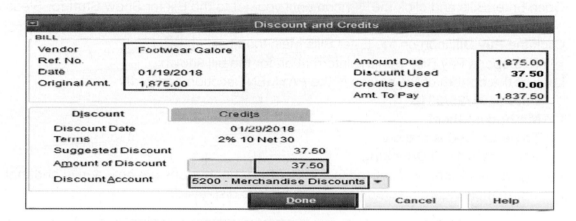

Click **Done** to record the discount
Repeat the steps for the bill from Sports Clothes, Inc. that is eligible for a discount

	DATE DUE	VENDOR	REF. NO.	DISC. DATE	AMT. DUE	DISC. USED	CREDITS USED	AMT. TO PAY
☑	02/17/2018	Sports Clothes, Inc.		01/28/2018	300.00	6.00	0.00	294.00
☑	02/18/2018	Footwear Galore		01/29/2018	1,875.00	37.50	0.00	1,837.50
				Totals	12,690.40	43.50	0.00	2,131.50

- Once you click **Done** to accept the discount, the DISC. USED and AMT. TO PAY amounts change to reflect the amount of the discount taken.
- Notice the totals provided indicating the DISC. USED and the AMT. TO PAY for the two selected bills.

Click the **Pay Selected Bills** button,

- Notice the two payments shown.

Click the **Done** button on the **Payment Summary** screen

PAY BILL WITH CREDIT AND DISCOUNT

When paying bills, it is a good idea to apply credits received for returned or damaged merchandise to the accounts as payment is made. If you want to pay a specific bill, you may access it in Enter Bills and then click the Pay Bills icon. Information for the bill will show in the Pay Bills window.

MEMO

DATE: January 25, 2018

In addition to paying bills with an early-payment discount, Ruth also looks for any credits that may be applied to the bill as part of the payment. As indicated in the Unpaid Bills report comments, apply the credit received from Snow Stuff, then apply the discount on the amount owed, and pay the bill within the discount period.

 Apply the credit received from Snow Stuff, as part of the payment for the bill and pay bill within the discount period

Open Enter Bills and click the ← icon until you get to the <u>Bill</u> for Snow Stuff for Sleds and Toboggans

Click the **Pay Bill** icon on the Enter Bills Main Icon bar 🖨 Pay Bill

- This opens Pay Bills with the information for the bill shown.

Look at the bottom of the screen in the PAYMENT section and verify:

Date of **01/25/2018**
Method is **Check**
To be printed is marked
Account is **1100 Checking**

- Notice that both the Set Credits and Set Discount buttons are now active and that information regarding credits and discounts is displayed.

Click the **Set Credits** button
Make sure there is a check in the Check Mark column for the credit amount of **50.00**
Click the **Discount** tab

- On the Discounts and Credits screen, verify the Amount Due of **370**, the Discount Used of **7.40**, and the Credits Used of **50.00**, leaving an Amt. To Pay of **312.60**.

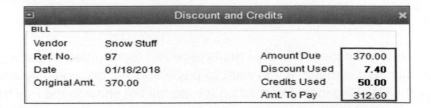

- QuickBooks DT calculates the discount on the original amount of the invoice rather than the amount due after subtracting the credit. You need to recalculate the discount on the amount due after the credit.

Click in the Amount of Discount column and use QuickMath to calculate the correct discount:

Remove the 7.40 shown

Enter the Amount Due **370** – Credits Used **50** * Discount Percentage **.02**

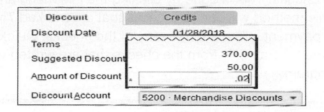

Press **Enter** to enter the discount amount of **6.40**, press **Tab** to update Discount Used

Make sure the Discount Account is **5200 Merchandise Discounts**

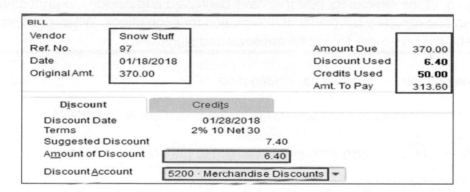

Click the **Done** button

Review the information for DISC USED **6.40** and AMT. TO PAY **313.60**

	DATE DUE	VENDOR	REF. NO.	DISC. DATE	AMT. DUE	DISC. USED	CREDITS USED	AMT. TO PAY
☑	02/17/2018	Snow Stuff	97	01/28/2018	370.00	6.40	50.00	313.60
				Totals	370.00	6.40	50.00	313.60

Click **Pay Selected Bills**, click **Done** on the Payment Summary

- Note that the bill for Snow Stuff appears and is marked PAID.

VERIFY BILLS MARKED PAID

 View Paid Bills

Click **Previous** (Back arrow icon) and view all the bills for Sports Clothes, Inc. and Footwear Galore that were paid in Pay Bills to verify that they are marked as paid

- Notice that the Credit for Snow Stuff is *not* marked in any way to indicate that it has been used.

Close the Enter Bills screen

PRINT CHECKS TO PAY BILLS

Once bills have been selected for payment and any discounts taken or credits applied, the checks should be printed, signed, and mailed. QuickBooks DT has three methods that may be used to print checks. Checks may be printed immediately after a bill has been paid, which is the most efficient method. Secondly, checks may be accessed and printed one at a time using the Write Checks window. This allows you to view the Bill Payment Information for each check. The third way is to print a batch of checks. This is done by clicking the File menu and selecting checks from the Print Forms menu. This method will print all checks that are marked *To be printed* but will not allow you to view the bill payment information for any of the checks. QuickBooks DT does not separate the checks it writes in Pay Bills from the checks that are written when using the Write Checks feature of the program.

MEMO

DATE: January 25, 2018

Ruth needs to print the checks for bills that have been paid and decides to print checks individually, so she can view bill payment information for each check. When she finishes with the checks, she will give them to you for approval and signature.

    Print the checks for bills that have been paid

Access the Write Checks window using the keyboard shortcut **Ctrl+W**
- A blank check will show on the screen.

Click **Previous** (Back arrow icon) until you get to the check for **Footwear Galore**

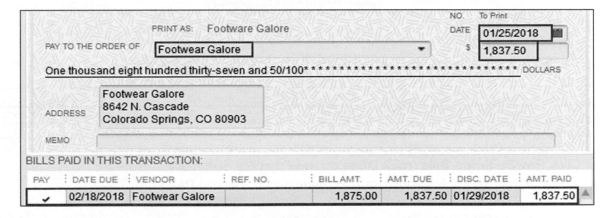

Click **Print** at the top of the window to print the check

Click **OK** on the Print Check screen to select Check 2
- Check 1 was issued in Chapter 5 to Dr. Diego Medina for a return. If Check 2 is not on the Print Check screen, change the check number to 2.

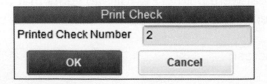

- On the **Print Checks** screen, verify the printer name, printer type. Select **Standard** check style.
Print Company Name and Address should be selected
- If is not marked with a check, click the check box to select.
Click **Print** to print the check
- If you print to a pdf file, save the document as **21-Your Name Ck 2 Footwear Galore Ch6**.
Click **OK** on the **Print Checks – Confirmation** screen
Click **Previous** or **Next** arrow icons and repeat the steps to print Check 3 for Sports Clothes, Inc., and Check 4 for Snow Stuff
- If you print to a pdf file, save the documents as **22-Your Name Ck 3 Sports Clothes Ch6**, **23-Your Name Ck 4 Snow Stuff Ch6**.

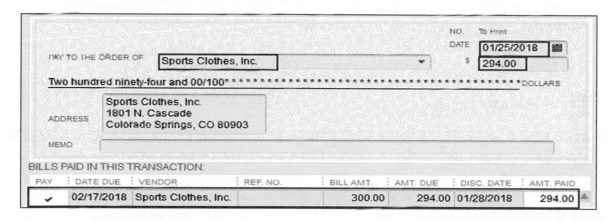

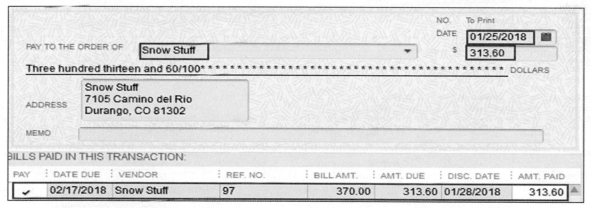

- Notice that the amount of the check to Snow Stuff is $313.60. This allows for the original bill of $370 less the return of $50 and the discount of $6.40.
Close the **Write Checks** window

PAY BILLS USING CREDIT CARD

A credit card may be used to pay a bill rather than a check. Use the Pay Bills feature but select Pay By Credit Card rather than Pay By Check.

MEMO

DATE: January 25, 2018

In viewing the bills due, you direct Ruth to pay the bills to Sports Accessories and Snow Shoes & More using the Visa credit card.

 Pay the above bills with a credit card

Access **Pay Bills** as previously instructed
Select **Show all bills**
Filter By **All vendors** and Sort By **Vendor**
Scroll through the list of bills and select **Snow Shoes & More** and **Sports Accessories** by clicking in the check mark column
Make the following selections in the **PAYMENT** section:
Date should be **01/25/2018**
For **Method** click the drop-down list arrow, click **Credit Card** to select
• Account should show 2100 Visa. If it does not, click the drop-down list arrow and click **2100 Visa**.

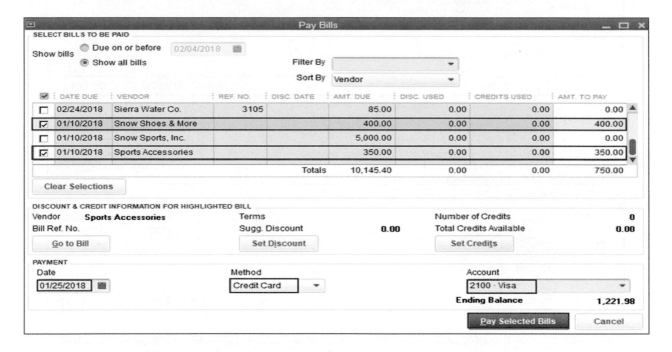

Click **Pay Selected Bills** to record the payment

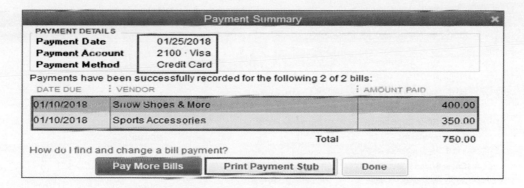

To have a printed record of your payment, click **Print Payment Stub**
- If necessary, change the date range to **12/25/2017**.
- Using a credit card in Pay Bills is the only place you can print a Payment Stub for a credit card transaction. You must be logged in to QuickBooks DT as an administrator or assigned permission to do this.

Click **OK**, click **Print** on the Print Bill Payment Stubs
- If you print to a pdf file, save the document as **24-Your Name Visa Pmt Stub Ch6**.

VERIFY CREDIT CARD PAYMENT OF BILLS

Paying bills with a credit card in Pay Bills automatically creates a Credit Card transaction in QuickBooks DT. This can be verified through the Visa account register in the Chart of Accounts and through Enter Credit Card Charges. The entry into QuickBooks DT does not actually charge the credit card. It only records the transaction.

MEMO
DATE: January 25, 2018

Verify the credit card charges for Sports Accessories and Snow Shoes & More.

Verify the credit card charges by viewing the Visa Account Register and the Bill Payments (Credit Card) - Visa

Access the **Visa Account Register** in the **Chart of Accounts**
Scroll through the register view the charges

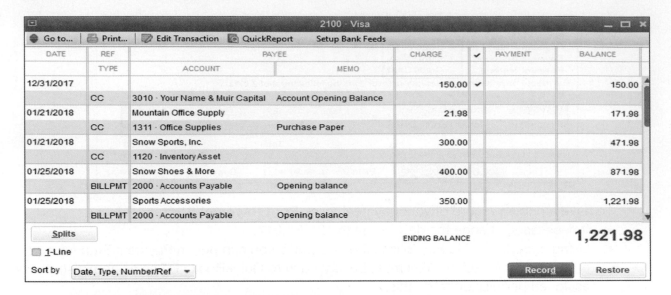

Close the **Visa Account Register** and the **Chart of Accounts**

Click the **Enter Credit Card Charges** icon

Click **Previous** arrow on the Enter Credit Card Charges – Visa screen until you see the payments to Sports Accessories and Snow Shoes & More

- Notice that the form title changes to Bill Payments (Credit Card) – Visa.

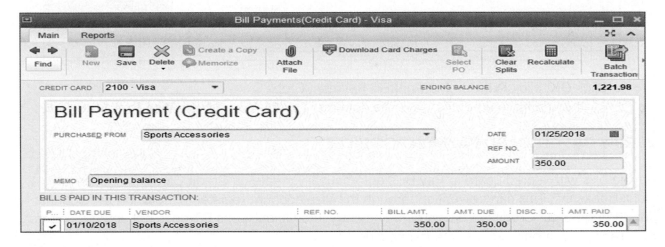

Close Bill Payments

SALES TAX

When a company is set up in QuickBooks DT, a Sales Tax Payable liability account is automatically created if the company charges sales tax. The Sales Tax Payable account keeps track of as many tax agencies as the company needs. As invoices are written, QuickBooks DT records the tax liability in the Sales Tax Payable account. To determine the sales tax owed, a Sales Tax Liability Report is prepared.

SALES TAX LIABILITY REPORT

The Sales Tax Liability Report shows your total taxable sales, the total nontaxable sales, and the amount of sales tax owed to each tax agency.

> **MEMO**
> **DATE:** January 25, 2018
>
> Prior to paying the sales tax, Ruth prepares the Sales Tax Liability Report.

 Prepare the Sales Tax Liability Report

Click the **Manage Sales Tax** icon in the Vendors section of the Home Page
Click the **Sales Tax Liability** report

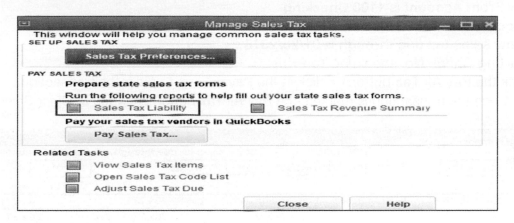

The Report Dates are From **01/01/2018** To **01/25/2018**
- If necessary, adjust the column widths so the report will fit on one page.
- If you get a message box asking if all columns should be the same size as the one being adjusted, click **No**.

	Total Sales	Non-Taxable Sales	Taxable Sales	Tax Rate	Tax Collected	Sales Tax Payable As of Jan 25, 18
State Board of Equalization						
CA Sales Tax	8,797.00	25.00	8,772.00	8.0%	701.77	701.77
Total State Board of Equalization	8,797.00	25.00	8,772.00		701.77	701.77
TOTAL	**8,797.00**	**25.00**	**8,772.00**		**701.77**	**701.77**

Your Name's Sierra Sports
Sales Tax Liability
January 1 - 25, 2018

Print in Landscape orientation and close the report after printing
- If you print to a pdf file, save the document as **25-Your Name Sales Tax Liability Ch6**.

PAY SALES TAX

Use the Manage Sales Tax window to determine how much sales tax you owe and to write a check to the tax agency. QuickBooks DT will update the sales tax account with payment information.

MEMO

DATE: January 25, 2018

Note from Larry: Ruth, pay the sales taxes owed.

   Pay the sales taxes owed

The Manage Sales Tax screen should be showing
Click the **Pay Sales Tax** button
Pay From Account is **1100 Checking**
Check Date is **01/25/2018**
Show sales tax due through is **01/25/2018**
Starting Check No. should be **To Print**
Click the **Pay All Tax** button or click in the Pay column to mark the transaction
- Once the transaction is marked, the Pay All Tax button changes to Clear Selections.

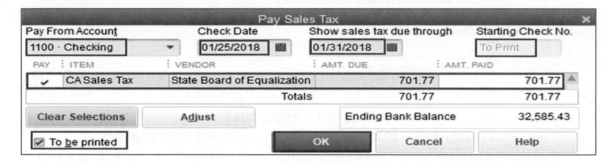

- Once **Pay All Tax** has been clicked and the Sales Tax item is selected, the **Ending Bank Balance** changes to reflect the amount in checking.

Click **OK**, and then click **Close** on the Manage Sales Tax screen

   Use Print Forms to print Check 5 for the payment of the Sales Tax

Click **File** on the Menu bar, point to **Print Forms**, click **Checks**
- Verify the Bank Account 1100 Checking, the First Check Number 5, and the check mark in front of State Board of Equalization. If your screen does not match the following, make the appropriate changes.

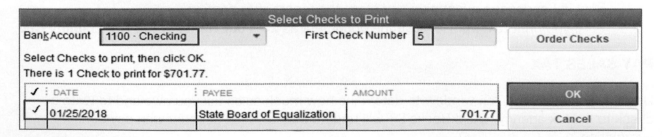

Click **OK**, click **Print**, Check Style is **Standard**, click **OK** on the **Print Checks – Confirmation** screen
  • If you print to a pdf file, save the document as **26-Your Name Ck 5 State Board of Equalization Ch6**.

VIEW TAX PAYMENT CHECK IN CHECK REGISTER

Whenever a check is prepared, it will show in the Register for the Checking account.

 View the payment made for sales tax

Click the **Check Register** icon on the Banking section of the Home Page
  • The register for 1100-Checking is shown.
Scroll through the register to view the information for Check 5, and then close it

VENDOR BALANCE DETAIL

When dealing with payables, it is important to be able to see the details of all the transactions made with each vendor during the period.

 Prepare and print the Vendor Balance Detail

Open the **Report Center** as previously instructed
Select **Vendors & Payables** section, double-click **Vendor Balance Detail**
Report is prepared for All Transactions

Your Name's Sierra Sports
Vendor Balance Detail
All Transactions

Type	Date	Num	Account	Amount	Balance
Snow Stuff					
Bill	01/18/2018	97	2000 · Accounts Payable	370.00	370.00
Credit	01/21/2018	9915	2000 · Accounts Payable	-50.00	320.00
Bill Pmt -Check	01/25/2018	4	2000 · Accounts Payable	-313.60	6.40
Discount	01/25/2018	4	2000 · Accounts Payable	-6.40	0.00
Total Snow Stuff				0.00	0.00
Sports Accessories					
Bill	12/31/2017		2000 · Accounts Payable	350.00	350.00
Bill Pmt -CCard	01/25/2018		2000 · Accounts Payable	-350.00	0.00
Total Sports Accessories				0.00	0.00
Sports Clothes, Inc.					
Bill	01/18/2018		2000 · Accounts Payable	300.00	300.00
Bill Pmt -Check	01/25/2018	3	2000 · Accounts Payable	-294.00	6.00
Discount	01/25/2018	3	2000 · Accounts Payable	-6.00	0.00
Total Sports Clothes, Inc.				0.00	0.00
TOTAL				9,395.40	9,395.40

Partial Report

Print the report in Portrait orientation
  • If you print to a pdf file, save the document as **27-Your Name Vendor Bal Detail Ch6**.

PREPARE MEMORIZED REPORT

To obtain information regarding the inventory, you may prepare an Inventory Valuation Summary or an Inventory Valuation Detail report. Both reports give you information regarding an item, the number on hand, the average cost, and asset value. The summary report also gives information regarding an item's percentage of total assets, sales price, retail value, and percentage of total retail. The detail report includes information for transactions using inventory items. In addition to the information shown in both reports, the detail report includes type of transaction, date of transaction, customer name, number, quantity, and cost.

Preparing the Inventory Valuation Summary will allow you to verify the number on hand, average cost, asset value, percentage of Total Assets, sales price, retail value, and percentage of Total Retail value for each inventory item.

 Prepare and print an Inventory Valuation Summary report in Landscape orientation as of January 25, 2018

> To use the Memorized Report, click **Reports** on the Menu bar, point to Memorized Reports, click **Inventory Valuation Summary**

> Enter the date **01/25/18**, press **Tab**
> - Because we customized the report in Chapter 5 and then memorized it, all the changes we made were saved as part of the memorized report. This means that the columns we removed are not shown.
> - If you prepare the report from the Reports menu or Report Center, the columns for Sales Price, Retail Value, % of Tot Retail will be shown.

Your Name's Sierra Sports
Inventory Valuation Summary
As of January 25, 2018

	On Hand	Avg Cost	Asset Value	% of Tot Asset
Inventory				
Accessories	795	3.66	2,906.70	8.2%
Bindings-Skis	43	75.00	3,225.00	9.1%
Bindings-Snow	48	75.00	3,600.00	10.1%
Boots	20	30.00	600.00	1.7%
Boots-Ski	14	75.00	1,050.00	3.0%
Bouts-Snowbrd	35	75.00	2,625.00	7.4%
Gloves	40	15.00	600.00	1.7%
Hats	29	8.00	232.00	0.7%
Helmets	20	28.00	560.00	1.6%
Pants-Ski	93	30.00	2,790.00	7.8%
Pants-Snowbrd	50	35.00	1,750.00	4.9%
Parkas	73	58.33	4,258.34	12.0%
Poles-Ski	23	30.00	690.00	1.9%
Skis	43	100.00	4,300.00	12.1%
Sleds	6	60.00	360.00	1.0%
Snowboard	28	100.00	2,800.00	7.9%
Socks	72	3.00	216.00	0.6%
Sweaters	73	25.00	1,825.00	5.1%
Toboggans	7	129.64	907.50	2.6%
Underwear	32	8.00	256.00	0.7%
Total Inventory	**1,544**		**35,551.54**	**100.0%**
TOTAL	**1,544**		**35,551.54**	**100.0%**

Print in Landscape orientation, and then close the report
- If you print to a pdf file, save the document as **30-Your Name Inventory Val Sum Ch6**.

BACK UP COMPANY

 Follow the instructions given in previous chapters to back up data for Your Name's Sierra Sports, use the file name **Sierra 2018 (Backup Ch. 6)**.

SUMMARY

In this chapter, purchase orders were completed, inventory items were received, and bills were recorded. Payments for purchases and bills were made by cash and by credit card, credit memos were recorded, and early payment discounts were applied. Sales taxes were paid. Vendors, inventory items, and accounts were added while transactions were being recorded. Accounts were assigned to vendors and preferred vendors were added to sales items. Various reports were prepared to determine unpaid bills, account and vendor QuickReports, and sales tax liability. Reports were customized, contained comments, and memorized.

END-OF-CHAPTER QUESTIONS

TRUE/FALSE

ANSWER THE FOLLOWING QUESTIONS IN THE SPACE PROVIDED BEFORE THE QUESTION NUMBER.

_____ 6.01. Receipt of purchase order items is never recorded before the bill arrives.

_____ 6.02. A bill can be paid by check or credit card.

_____ 6.03. The Cost of Goods Sold Account Merchandise Discounts is used to record discounts to customers.

_____ 6.04. The Vendor Center displays the vendor list and information about individual vendors.

_____ 6.05. When you prepare a Commented Report, it may be printed, saved, emailed, and exported to Excel.

_____ 6.06. A Sales Tax account is automatically created if a company indicates that it charges sales tax on sales.

_____ 6.07. Since purchase discounts are a cost of doing business, they are categorized as an expense.

_____ 6.08. When a credit is received from a vendor for the return of merchandise, it may be applied to a payment to the same vendor.

_____ 6.09. You may use a credit card to pay for inventory items.

_____ 6.10. A purchase order is closed automatically when a partial receipt of merchandise is recorded.

MULTIPLE CHOICE

WRITE THE LETTER OF THE CORRECT ANSWER IN THE SPACE PROVIDED BEFORE THE QUESTION NUMBER.

_____ 6.11. If an order is received with a bill but is incomplete, QuickBooks DT will ___.
   A. record the bill for the full amount ordered
   B. record the bill only for the amount received
   C. not allow the bill to be prepared until all the merchandise is received
   D. close the purchase order

_____ 6.12. The Purchase Order feature must be selected as a preference ___.
   A. when setting up the company
   B. prior to recording the first purchase order
   C. is automatically set when the first purchase order is prepared
   D. either A or B

_____ 6.13. A faster method of entering bills can be entering the bills ___.
   A. while writing the checks for payment
   B. in the Pay Bills window
   C. in the Accounts Payable Register
   D. none of the above

_____ 6.14. A discount received for a purchase of an inventory item is recorded in the ___ account.
   A. Income account: Purchases Discounts
   B. Expense account: Sales Discounts
   C. Cost of Goods Sold account: Merchandise Discounts
   D. Asset account: Inventory Asset

_____ 6.15. A Preferred Vendor is selected for an existing Item ___.
   A. in the Vendor Center
   B. on the Edit Item screen
   C. on the Purchase Order
   D. when entering the Bill

_____ 6.16. Sales tax is paid by using the ___ window.
   A. Pay Bills
   B. Manage Sales Tax
   C. Write Check
   D. Credit Card

_____ 6.17. When recording a bill, you can ___ so the same transaction is entered when recording the bill next month.
   A. customize My Preferences for Bills
   B. memorize a report
   C. memorize a transaction
   D. None of the above

_____ 6.18. To Comment on a report, you must ___.
   A. write your comments on a printed report
   B. create a custom report that includes a column for Comments
   C. add comments by clicking the Comment on Report button in a report
   D. prepare a report from the Comments section in the Report Center

6

_____ 6.19. When items ordered are received with a bill, you record the receipt ___.
  A. on an item receipt form
  B. on the bill
  C. on the original purchase order
  D. in the Journal

_____ 6.20. A memorized report is prepared from ___.
  A. the Reports Menu
  B. the Report Center
  C. a QuickReport
  D. All the above

FILL-IN

IN THE SPACE PROVIDED, WRITE THE ANSWER THAT MOST APPROPRIATELY COMPLETES THE SENTENCE.

6.21. In the Vendor Center, expense accounts for vendors are assigned using the _____ tab when editing or adding a vendor.

6.22. The _____ Report shows the total taxable sales and the amount of sales tax owed.

6.23. You may use QuickBooks's pay bills feature to pay bills using a _____ or a _____ for payment.

6.24. A purchase order can be closed _____ or_____.

6.25. To add a new column to a report, you click the _____ button.

SHORT ESSAY

Describe the cycle of obtaining merchandise. Include the process from ordering the merchandise through paying for it. Include information regarding the QuickBooks DT forms prepared for each phase of the cycle, the possible ways in which an item may be received, and the ways in which payment may be made.

_____

_____

_____

_____

_____

_____

END-OF-CHAPTER PROBLEM

YOUR NAME'S CALIFORNIA CASUAL

Chapter 6 continues with the transactions for purchase orders, merchandise receipts, bills, bill payments, and sales tax payments. Your partner, Elizabeth Jones, prints the checks, purchase orders, and related reports; you sign the checks. This procedure establishes cash control procedures and lets both owners know about the checks being processed.

INSTRUCTIONS

Continue to use the copy of Your Name's California Casual you used in Chapter 5. Open the company—the file used is **Casual 2018.qbw**. Record the purchase orders, bills, payments, and other transactions as instructed within the chapter. Always read the transactions carefully and review the Chart of Accounts when selecting transaction accounts. Add new vendors and minimum quantities where indicated. Verify with your instructor the required printing and whether to print Bills. Otherwise, print all purchase orders, bills, and checks. Print reports as indicated making sure to resize columns so all information is displayed in full. The first purchase order used is Purchase Order 1. When paying bills, always check for credits that may be applied to the bill, and always check for discounts.

In addition to the Item List and the Chart of Accounts, you will need to use the Vendor List when ordering merchandise and paying bills.

Active Vendors	▼	>

NAME	BALANCE TOTAL	ATTACH
Accessories Galore	0.00	
Amazing Shoes	450.00	
Cavalier Clothes	2,598.00	
Off-the-Cuff	3,053.00	
State Board of Equalization	188.31	
SunSpecs, Inc.	500.00	

RECORD TRANSACTIONS

January 5, 2018:
► Customize a Purchase Order template so the Default Title is **PURCHASE ORDER**, Company Name is expanded to **4 ¾**, and PURCHASE ORDER begins at **5**.
► Hide the History and resize the Purchase Order to make it smaller on the screen.
► Change Reorder Point (Min) for Women-Dress from 20 to 25 and Max from 100 to 40.
► Change Reorder Point (Min) for Women-Pants from 25 to 30 and Max from 39 to 40.
► Assign the vendor Off-the-Cuff for Women's Dresses.
► Prepare and print an Inventory Stock Status by Item Report for January 1-5, 2018 in Landscape orientation. Remove the unused columns for On Sales Order, On PO, and Next Deliv. Manually adjust column widths so vendors' names are shown in full. (Note: In Chapter 5, transactions were entered through January 15. If you prepare the report based on January 15,

it will be different from this one.) If you print to a pdf file, save the document as **1-Your Name Stock Status by Item Ch6**.

▶ Prepare Purchase Orders for all items marked Order on the Stock Status by Item Inventory Report. When preparing a Purchase Order that uses an assigned vendor, VENDOR information will be completed when the Item is entered. The quantity for each item ordered is 10. The rate is $35 for dresses and $20 for pants. Print purchase orders with lines around each field. If you print to a pdf file, save the documents as **2-Your Name PO 1 Off-the-Cuff Ch6**, and **3-Your Name PO 2 Cavalier Clothes Ch 6**.

  ○ If you get an Item's Cost Changed dialog box asking if you want to update the item with the new cost, click **Do not display this message in the future**, and click **No**.

▶ Change the Vendor Name Cavalier Clothes to Trendy Clothing, Inc. Make sure to change Vendor Name, Company Name, and Billed From as well. Change the Main Email to **TrendyClothing@abc.com**. Finally, on the Payment Settings tab change the Print Name on Check As.

▶ Reprint Purchase Order 2. If you print to a pdf file, save the document **4-Your Name PO 2 Trendy Clothing Revised Ch 6**.

▶ Add a new vendor: Contempo Clothing, Main Phone: 805-555-5512, Main Email: **Contempo@slo.com**, Fax: 805-555-2155, 9382 Grand Avenue, San Luis Obispo, CA 93407, Payment Terms: 2% 10 Net 30, Credit Limit: $2000.

▶ Assign Contempo Clothing as the Preferred Vendor for dresses.

▶ Order an additional 10 dresses from Contempo Clothing. The rate for the dresses is $25. Print the Purchase Order. If you print to a pdf file, save the document as **5-Your Name PO 3 Contempo Clothing Ch6**.

▶ Prepare and print a Purchase Order QuickReport for January 1-5, 2018. If you print to a pdf file, save the document as **6-Your Name PO QuickReport Ch6.**

January 8, 2018:

▶ Received pants that were ordered on Purchase Order 2 from Trendy Clothing, Inc. without the bill. Enter the receipt of merchandise. The transaction date is 01/08/2018. Print the Item Receipt if instructed to do so. If you print to a pdf file, save the document as **7-Your Name Item Rct Trendy Clothing Ch6.**

▶ Received dresses and the bill for items ordered on Purchase Order 1 from Off-the-Cuff. Use date of 01/08/2018. Enter the receipt of the merchandise and the bill. Print the Bill. If you print to a pdf file, save the document as **8-Your Name Bill Off-the-Cuff Ch6.**

▶ Received 8 dresses and the bill from Contempo Clothing ordered on Purchase Order 3. Enter the receipt of the merchandise and the bill. Print the bill. If you print to a pdf file, save the document as **9-Your Name Bill Contempo Clothing Ch6.** This dress style has been discontinued so close the Purchase Order manually and print it. If you print to a pdf file, save the document as **10-Your Name PO 3 Contempo Clothing Closed Ch6.**

▶ After recording the receipt of merchandise, view the three purchase orders. Notice which ones are marked *Received in Full* and *Closed*.

January 9, 2018:

▶ Received the bill from Trendy Clothing, Inc. for the pants received on 01/08/18. The bill was dated 01/08/2018 (use this date for the bill). Print the bill if instructed to do so. If you print to a pdf file, save the document as **11-Your Name Bill Trendy Clothing Ch6.**

January 10, 2018:

▶ Discovered unstitched seams in two pairs of women's pants ordered on PO 2. Return the pants for credit. Use 2340 as the Reference number. Print the Credit. If you print to a pdf file, save the document as **12-Your Name CM Trendy Clothing Ch6**.

January 12, 2018:

▶ Pay for the dresses from Contempo Clothing with the company's Visa credit card. (Take a purchase discount if the transaction qualifies for one. Use the Cost of Goods Sold Subaccount 5200 Merchandise Discounts for the discount. Create any necessary accounts.) Print the Bill Payment Stub. Make sure the Select Bill Payment Stubs to Print shows the dates of 01/01/18 thru 01/12/18. If you print to a pdf file, save the document as **13-Your Name Bill Pmt Stub Contempo Clothing Ch6**.

January 15, 2018:

▶ Add new vendors:
  ○ SLO Rental Co., Main Phone: 805-555-4100, Fax: 805-555-0014, 301 Marsh Street, San Luis Obispo, CA 93407, Payment Terms: Net 30. Assign Account: 6280 Rent.
  ○ SLO Telephone, Main Phone: 805-555-1029, 8851 Hwy. 58, San Luis Obispo, CA 93407. Payment Terms: Net 30. Assign Account: 6340 Telephone.
▶ Create a Memorized Transaction for rent. How Often: Monthly, Next Date: 01/15/2018. When you finish the transaction for rent, clear the Bill without saving.
▶ Create a Memorized Transaction for telephone. How Often: Monthly, Next Date: 01/15/2018. Clear the Bill. Close Bills. Print the Memorize Transaction List. If you print to a pdf file, save the document as **14-Your Name Memorized Transaction List Ch6**.
▶ Use the Memorized Transaction List to record and print the bills for rent of $1,150.00 and telephone service of $79.85. Use the date 01/15/18. If you print to a pdf file, save the documents as **15-Your Name Bill SLO Rental Ch6** and **16-Your Name Bill SLO Telephone**.

January 18, 2018:

▶ Prepare an Unpaid Bills Detail report. Customize the report by adding a column for Terms. Memorize the report. Name is Unpaid Bills Detail with Terms. If there are any bills that qualify for a discount or have a credit, add the comment "Pay this Bill" or "Use This Credit." Print the Commented Report. Do not save the Commented Report. If you print to a pdf file, save the document as **17-Your Name Unpaid Bills with Terms Ch6**.
▶ Pay the bills indicated in the Commented Unpaid Bills Detail report. Take any discounts for which you are eligible. If there are any credits, apply the credit and calculate the appropriate discount (if eligible) prior to paying the bill. Pay the bill(s) by check.
▶ Print Check Nos. 2 and 3 for the bills that were paid. If you print to a pdf file, save the documents as **18-Your Name Ck 2 Off-the-Cuff Ch6** and **19-Your Name Ck 3 Trendy Clothing Ch6**.

January 25, 2018:

▶ Purchase office supplies to have on hand for $250 with the company's Visa credit card from a new vendor (Office Masters, Main Phone: 805-555-9915, Main Email: **OfficeMasters@slo.com**, Fax: 805-555-5199, 8330 Grand Avenue, Arroyo Grande, CA 93420, Payment Terms: Net 30, Credit Limit: $500).

▶ Pay bills for rent and telephone. Print the checks prepared for these bills. (They may be printed individually or as a batch.) If you print to a pdf file, save the document as **20-Your Name Cks 4-5 Ch6**.

January 30, 2018:

▶ Prepare Sales Tax Liability Report from 01/01/2018 to 01/30/2018. Print the report in Landscape orientation. Change columns widths, if necessary. If you print to a pdf file, save the document as **21-Your Name Sales Tax Liability Ch6**.

▶ Pay Sales Tax for the amount due through 01/30/18 and print the check. If you print to a pdf file, save the document as **22-Your Name Ck 6 State Board of Equalization Ch6**.

▶ Prepare a Vendor Balance Detail Report for All Transactions. Print in Portrait orientation. If you print to a pdf file, save the document as **23-Your Name Vendor Bal Detail Ch6**.

▶ Print a Trial Balance for 01/01/2018 to 01/30/2018. If you print to a pdf file, save the document as **24-Your Name Trial Bal Ch6**.

▶ Print the Journal for 01/01/2018 to 01/30/2018 (Size columns to display all information.) If you print to a pdf file, save the document as **25-Your Name Journal Ch6**.

▶ Use the memorized report to prepare an Inventory Valuation Summary Report for 01/30/2018. Print in Portrait. If you print to a pdf file, save the document as **26-Your Name Inventory Valuation Sum Ch6**.

▶ Back up data to **Casual 2018 (Backup Ch. 6)**.

CHAPTER 6 CHECKLISTS

YOUR NAME'S SIERRA SPORTS

The checklist below shows all the business forms printed during training. Check each one that you printed. In the document names below, Your Name and Ch6 have been omitted, and report dates are given. (Note: When paying bills and printing a batch of checks, your checks may be in a different order than shown below. Do not be concerned if your check numbers are not an exact match.)

___ 1-PO 1 Footwear Galore	___ 16-Bill Sierra Water
___ 2-PO 2 Snow Stuff	___ 17-QuickReport Snow Stuff
___ 3-PO 3 Sports Clothes	___ 18-Bill Mammoth Rentals
___ 4-PO 4 Snow Sports	___ 19-Bill Sierra Telephone Corrected
___ 5-Item Rct Snow Stuff	___ 20-Commented Unpaid Bills, January 25, 2018
___ 6-Bill Snow Stuff	___ 21-Ck 2 Footwear Galore
___ 7-Bill Footwear Galore	___ 22-Ck 3 Sports Clothes
___ 8-PO 4 Snow Sports Revised	___ 23-Ck 4 Snow Stuff
___ 9-Bill Sports Clothes	___ 24-Visa Pmt Stub
___ 10-PO 3 Sports Clothes Closed	___ 25-Sales Tax Liability, January 1-25, 2018
___ 11-CM Snow Stuff	___ 26-Ck 5 State Board of Equalization
___ 12-Bill Mammoth News	___ 27-Vendor Bal Detail
___ 13-Memorized Transaction List	___ 28-Trial Bal, January 1-25, 2018
___ 14-Bill Sierra Power	___ 39-Journal, January 18-25, 2018
___ 15-Bill Sierra Telephone	___ 30-Inventory Val Sum, January 25, 2018

6

YOUR NAME'S CALIFORNIA CASUAL

The checklist below shows all the business forms printed during training. Check each one that you printed. In the document names below, Your Name and Ch6 have been omitted, and report dates are given. (Note: When paying bills and printing a batch of checks, your checks may be in a different order than shown below. Do not be concerned if your check numbers are not an exact match.)

___ 1-Stock Status by Item, January 1-5, 2018	___ 15-Bill SLO Rental
___ 2-PO 1 Off-the-Cuff	___ 16-Bill SLO Telephone
___ 3-PO 2 Cavalier Clothes	___ 17-Unpaid Bills Detail with Terms,
___ 4-PO 2 Trendy Clothing Revised	January 1-18, 2018
___ 5-PO 3 Contempo Clothing	___ 18-Ck 2 Off-the-Cuff
___ 6-PO QuickReport, January 1-5, 2018	___ 19-Ck 3 Trendy Clothing
___ 7-Item Rct Trendy Clothing	___ 20-Cks 4-5
___ 8-Bill Off-the-Cuff	___ 21-Sales Tax Liability, January 1-30, 2018
___ 9-Bill Contempo Clothing	___ 22-Ck 6 State Board of Equalization
___ 10-PO 3 Contempo Clothing Closed	___ 23-Vendor Bal Detail
___ 11-Bill Trendy Clothing	___ 24-Trial Bal, January 1-30, 2018
___ 12-CM Trendy Clothing	___ 25-Journal, January 1-30, 2018
___ 13-Bill Pmt Stub Contempo Clothing	___ 26-Inventory Val Sum, January 1-30, 2018
___ 14-Memorized Transaction List	

GENERAL ACCOUNTING AND END-OF-PERIOD PROCEDURES: MERCHANDISING BUSINESS

LEARNING OBJECTIVES

At the completion of this chapter, you will be able to:

7.01. Change account and subaccount names.

7.02. Make accounts inactive.

7.03. Delete existing accounts.

7.04. Create individual capital accounts and subaccounts.

7.05. Understand information about fixed assets and using the Fixed Asset Manager.

7.06. Create and use a Fixed Asset Item list.

7.07. Record adjusting entries for prepaid expenses and depreciation.

7.08. Prepare Journal and Trial Balance reports.

7.09. Understand the definition of a partnership.

7.10. Record owner withdrawals.

7.11. Perform bank and credit card reconciliations.

7.12. Make an adjustment to and redo a credit card reconciliation.

7.13. Review credit card transaction after completing the reconciliation.

7.14. Prepare reports for Adjusted Trial Balance, Profit & Loss, and Balance Sheet.

7.15. Use QuickZoom in the Balance Sheet to view the capital account.

7.16. Distribute Capital to each owner.

7.17. Know what closing entries need to be recorded.

7.18. Record the transfer of Net Income into Owners' Capital Accounts.

7.19. Close Drawing accounts for both owners.

7.20. Prepare Journal Entries Entered/Modified Today report.

7.21. Understand how to export QuickBooks DT reports to Excel.

7.22. Understand how to import information from Excel into QuickBooks DT.

7.23. Close a period.

7.24. Enter a correction to a transaction in a closed period.

7.25. Record inventory adjustments.

7.26. Adjust Net Income/Owners' Equity Journal entry.

7.27. Understand how to use scheduled reports.

7.28. Prepare and print multiple reports.

GENERAL ACCOUNTING AND END-OF-PERIOD PROCEDURES

As stated in previous chapters, QuickBooks DT operates from the standpoint of the business document rather than an accounting form, journal, or ledger. While QuickBooks DT does incorporate all these items into the program, in many instances they operate behind the scenes. Instead of performing a traditional closing at the end of the fiscal year, QuickBooks DT transfers the net income into the Owners' Equity account and allows you to protect the data for the year by assigning a closing date to the period. All the transaction detail is maintained and viewable, but it will not be changed unless approved.

Even though a formal closing does not have to be performed within QuickBooks DT, when using accrual-basis accounting, several transactions must be recorded to reflect all expenses and income for the period accurately. For example, bank statements and credit cards must be reconciled; and any charges or bank collections need to be recorded. Adjusting entries such as depreciation, office supplies used, and so on will also need to be made. These adjustments may be recorded by the CPA or by the company's accounting personnel. At the end of the year, net income for the year and the owner withdrawals for the year should be transferred to the owners' capital accounts.

As in a service business, the CPA for the company will review things such as account names, adjusting entries, depreciation schedules, owners' equity adjustments, and so on. If the CPA makes the changes and adjustments, they may be made on the Accountant's Copy of the business files. An Accountant's Copy is a version of your company file that your accountant can use to make changes. You record the day-to-day business transactions; and, at the same time, your accountant works using the Accountant's Copy. The changes made by the CPA are imported into your company file. There are certain restrictions to the types of transactions that may be made on an Accountant's Copy of the company file. There are also restrictions regarding the types of entries that may be made in the company file that you are using.

Once necessary adjustments have been made, reports reflecting the end-of-period results of operations should be prepared. For archive purposes, at the end of the fiscal year, an additional backup is prepared and stored.

OPEN QUICKBOOKS DESKTOP AND COMPANY

 Open **QuickBooks DT** and **Your Name's Sierra Sports** as previously instructed

BEGIN TUTORIAL

The following tutorial will once again work with Your Name's Sierra Sports. Continue to use the same year that you used in Chapters 5 and 6. While everything that may be printed is listed on the checklist at the end of the chapter, verify the exact printing assignments and instructions with your instructor.

CHANGE ACCOUNT NAME

Even though transactions have been recorded during the month of January, QuickBooks DT makes it a simple matter to change the name of an existing account. Once the name of an account has been changed, all transactions using the old name are updated to show the new account name.

> **MEMO**
>
> **DATE:** January 31, 2018
>
> On the recommendation of the company's CPA, change the account named Freight Income to Delivery Income.

 Change the account name of Freight Income

Access the Chart of Accounts using the keyboard shortcut **Ctrl+A**
Select account **4020 Freight Income**, use the keyboard shortcut **Ctrl+E**
On the **Edit Account** screen, enter the new name **Delivery Income**
Since the account name is self-explanatory, delete the description
Click **Save & Close** on the **Edit Account** screen
• Notice that the name of the account appears as Delivery Income.

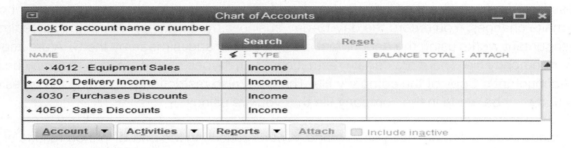

Do <u>not</u> close the **Chart of Accounts**

MAKE ACCOUNTS INACTIVE

If you are not using an account and do not have plans to do so in the future, the account may be made inactive. The account remains available for use, yet it does not appear on your Chart of Accounts unless you check the Show All check box.

> **MEMO**
>
> **DATE:** January 31, 2018
>
> Currently, Your Name's Sierra Sports does not plan to obtain any licenses or permits and does not incur Filing Fees. Make: 6230 – Licenses and Permits and 6270 - Filing Fees inactive.

 Make the accounts listed above inactive

Click **6230 – Licenses and Permits**
Click the **Account** button at the bottom of the Chart of Accounts, click **Make Account Inactive**
• The account no longer appears in the Chart of Accounts.
To view all accounts, including the inactive ones, click the **Include Inactive** check box at the bottom of the Chart of Accounts
Click account **6270 – Filing Fees**, use **Ctrl+E** to edit the account
On the Edit Account screen, click the **Account is inactive** check box in the lower-left portion of the screen

Click **Save & Close**
* Notice the icons that mark Licenses and Permits and Filing Fees as inactive accounts.

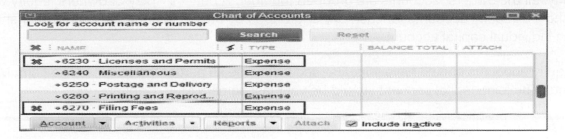

Do <u>not</u> close the **Chart of Accounts**

DELETE EXISTING ACCOUNTS

If you do not want to make an account inactive because you have not used it and do not plan to use it at all, QuickBooks DT allows the account to be deleted at any time. However, as a safeguard, QuickBooks DT does prevent the deletion of an account once it has been used at any time or contains an opening or an existing balance.

> **MEMO**
> **DATE:** January 31, 2018
>
> You do not, have not, and will not use: Account 6213 Interest Expense: Mortgage, Account 6290 Franchise Fees, Account 6523 Taxes: Property, and Account 6350 Travel & Ent. and its subaccounts. Delete these accounts from the Chart of Accounts.

 Delete the accounts listed in the memo

Select **6213 - Mortgage**, a subaccount of 6210 Interest Expense
Click the **Account** button at the bottom of the Chart of Accounts, click **Delete Account**, and click **OK** on the **Delete Account** dialog box
* The account has now been deleted.
Click, **6290 – Franchise Fees** to select the account
Use the keyboard shortcut **Ctrl+D** to delete and then click **OK** on the **Delete Account** dialog box
Follow the same procedures to delete the subaccounts of 6350 Travel & Ent.:
    6351 - Entertainment, **6352 - Meals**, and **6353 - Travel**
* *Note:* Whenever an account has subaccounts, the subaccounts must be deleted before the main account can be deleted.
When the subaccounts have been deleted; delete **6350 - Travel & Ent.**
Delete **6523 – Property,** a subaccount of 6520 Taxes
Do <u>not</u> close the Chart of Accounts

CREATE INDIVIDUAL CAPITAL ACCOUNTS

Currently, all the owners' accounts are grouped together. A better display of owners' equity would be to show all equity accounts for each owner grouped by owner. In addition, each owner should have an individual capital account.

Your equity accounts should have your first and last name as part of the title, just like Larry Muir's accounts. The joint capital account should be your last name & Muir, Capital.

MEMO

DATE: January 31, 2018

Edit Your Name & Muir, Capital to change the account number to 3100 and add your Last Name to the account name. Create separate Capital accounts for (Your) First and Last Name and Larry Muir. Name the accounts 3110 First and Last Name, Capital, and 3120 Larry Muir, Capital. In addition, change your Investment account to 3111 First and Last Name, Investment and your Drawing account to 3112 First and Last Name, Drawing. Make these subaccounts of 3110 First and Last Name, Capital. Do the same for Larry's accounts: 3121 Investment and 3122 Drawing.

 Create separate Capital accounts and change subaccounts for existing owners' equity accounts

> Click **3010 - Your Name & Muir, Capital**
> - In the controlling account 3010 you will just use your <u>last</u> name. However, in the individual capital accounts, such as, Your Name, Investment, you will use both your <u>first</u> and <u>last</u> names.
>
> Click **Account** at the bottom of the **Chart of Accounts**, click **Edit Account**
> Change the account number to **3100**
> Tab to or click **Account Name**
> Highlight the words Your Name and replace them with your <u>last</u> name; <u>add</u> a comma between Muir and Capital
> - In the textbook **3100 - Your Last Name & Muir, Capital** is shown as the account name, but your work will show your own last name. For example, the author's account name would be 3100 Horne & Muir, Capital.
>
> Click **Save & Close**
> Click **Account** at the bottom of the **Chart of Accounts**, click **New**
> Click **Equity** as the account type, click **Continue**
> Tab to or click **Number**, enter **3120**
> Tab to or click **Account Name**, enter **Larry Muir, Capital**
> Click the checkbox for **Subaccount of**; click the drop-down list arrow next to **Subaccount of**, click **3100 - Your Last Name & Muir, Capital**
> Click **Save & Close**
> Edit the account **3012 - Larry Muir, Investment** to change the Account number to **3121**. It is a **Subaccount of: 3120**
> Edit **3014 - Larry Muir, Drawing**, Account number is **3122**, **Subaccount of: 3120**

Use the keyboard shortcut **Ctrl+N** to create a new account
Click **Equity** as the account type, click **Continue**
Tab to or click **Number**, enter **3110**
Tab to or click **Account Name**, enter **First and Last Name, Capital**

- Remember to use your real <u>first</u> and <u>last</u> name.
- In the textbook **3110 - First and Last Name, Capital** is shown as the account name, but your work will show your own name. For example, the author's account name would be 3110 - Janet Horne, Capital.
- In QuickBooks DT, there is not enough room for the words "Your First and Last Name, Capital" so the account name is First and Last Name, Capital, which is used to indicate that the account name contains your actual first and last names.

Click the checkbox for **Subaccount of**; click the drop-down list arrow next to **Subaccount of**, click **3100 - Your Last Name & Muir, Capital**
Click **Save & Close**
Edit the account **3011 - Your Name, Investment** to change the **Number** to **3111**
Change the **Account Name** to **First and Last Name, Investment**

- Remember to use your actual first and last names. For example, the author's account name would be Janet Horne, Investment.

Make this a **Subaccount of: 3110 - First and Last Name, Capital**
Click **Save & Close** when the changes have been made
Edit **3013 Your Name, Drawing** to change the Number to **3112**; Account Name is **First and Last Name, Drawing**; the account is a **Subaccount of: 3110**

- Remember to use your actual first and last names.

The capital accounts appear as follows:

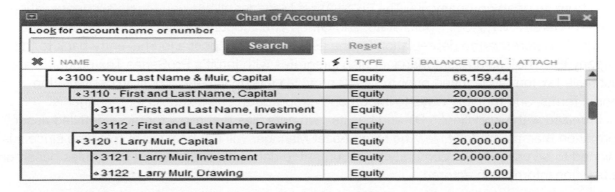

Close the **Chart of Accounts**
Use the **Reports** menu, **List** category to print the **Account Listing** in Portrait orientation
Use the date **01/31/18** for the report

- Since the report is prepared using the date of your computer, it will need to be changed to 01/31/18.

Click the **Customize Report** button at the top of the report, and then click the **Header/Footer** tab

Change **Subtitle** from the current date to **January 31, 2018**, and then, click **OK**

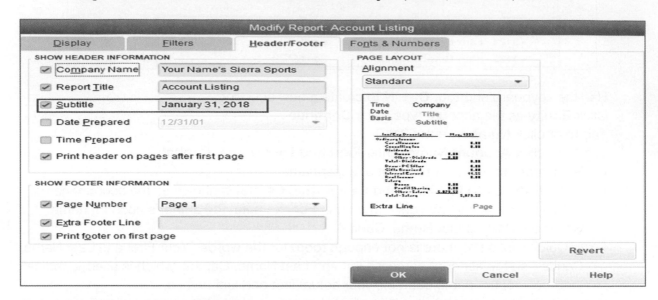

Resize the columns to display the Account Names in full—including subaccounts

Hide the columns for **Description**, **Accnt. #**, and **Tax Line**

Print in **Portrait** orientation; then close the Report

- If you print to a pdf file, save the document as **1-Your Name Acct List Ch7**.

FIXED ASSETS AND FIXED ASSET MANAGER

Fixed assets are the long-term assets that are used in in the business for longer than one year. If the company owns fixed assets, it is helpful to create a fixed asset item list.

In addition to allowing you to keep a list of fixed asset items, QuickBooks Accountant Desktop and QuickBooks Enterprise versions include a Fixed Asset Manager that is more comprehensive than the list of fixed assets. When used, the Fixed Asset Manager pulls information about the fixed assets from an open company file. The Fixed Asset Manager allows you to use six depreciation bases—Federal, AMT, ACE, Book, State, and Other. The accountant can use the Fixed Asset Manager to determine the depreciation for the assets and then post a journal entry back to the company file. The Fixed Asset Manager also integrates with Intuit's ProSeries Tax products and must have tax forms identified prior to use. It provides a wide variety of built-in depreciation reports, forms, and multiple ways to import and export data. The Fixed Asset Manager is synchronized with QuickBooks DT and has its own data files that allow for more detailed asset information than a company file. The Fixed Asset Manager will not be used at this time since it is designed to be used by the company's accountant to calculate depreciation schedules based on the taxation information entered.

FIXED ASSET ITEM LIST

As with other QuickBooks DT lists, you may keep a record of your company's fixed assets in the Fixed Asset Item List. A fixed asset is an item that a company owns and uses in its operations. A

Fixed asset is not something that the company sells, such as, inventory. Fixed assets are not going to be consumed or converted into cash within a year.

In the Fixed Asset list, you record information about your company's fixed assets including the purchase date and cost, whether the item was new or used when purchased, and the sales price if the item is sold. Note that Depreciation and Book Value are not calculated or stored in the Fixed Asset Item List and the company's Fixed Asset Item List is not using the Fixed Asset Manager.

The Fixed Asset List provides a way to keep important information about your assets in one place. This is useful to do even if your accountant uses the Fixed Asset Manager. You can create an item to track a fixed asset at several points during the asset's life cycle; however, it is recommended that you create the item when you buy the asset or create the company. You can create a fixed asset item from the Fixed Asset List or a Transaction.

MEMO
DATE: January 31, 2018

When Your Name's Sierra Sports was setup in QuickBooks DT, the Fixed Item Asset List was not created. Create the Fixed Asset Item List:

Store Fixtures: Asset Name/Number, Purchase Description, and Asset Description: Store Fixtures; Item is New; Date: 12/31/17; Cost: $4,500; Asset Account: 1520.

Office Equipment: Asset Name/Number, Purchase Description, and Asset Description: Office Equipment; Item is New; Date: 12/31/17; Cost: $5,000; Asset Account: 1510.

7

 Create a Fixed Asset Item List

Click **Lists** on the menu bar; click **Fixed Asset Item List**
Use the keyboard shortcut **Ctrl+N** to create a new item
Complete the information for the new item:
The **Asset Name/Number** is **Store Fixtures**
The **Asset Account** is **1520**
Complete the PURCHASE INFORMATION:
>   The Item is **new**
>   The **Purchase Description** should be **Store Fixtures**
>   The **Date** is **12/31/17**
>   The **Cost** is **4500**
- There is no SALES INFORMATION to record.
To complete the ASSET INFORMATION, enter **Store Fixtures** as the **Asset Description**
- Look at the bottom of the screen. Fields are provided to add information for the location, PO Number, Serial Number, and Warranty. There is also room to add Notes about the item.

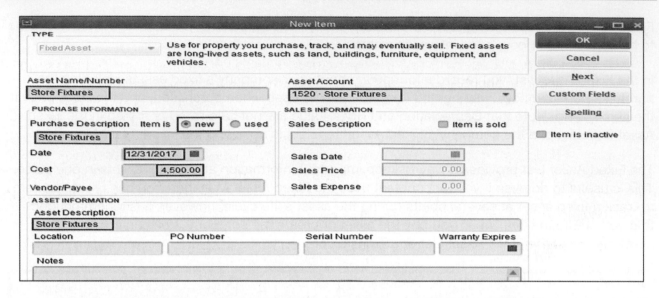

When the information is entered for Store Fixtures, click **Next**

Repeat to add the Asset: **Office Equipment**, Asset Account **1510 – Office Equipment**, Item is **new**, Date **12/31/17**, and Cost **$5,000.00** to the list

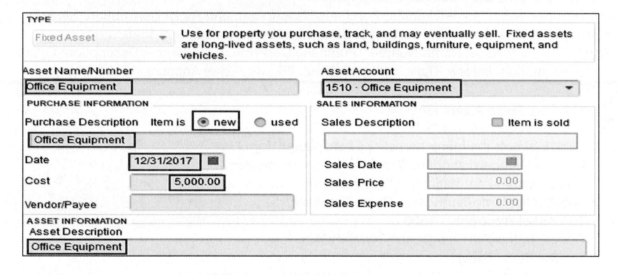

Click **OK**

To print a Fixed Asset List, click the **Reports** button at the bottom of the Fixed Asset List, click **Fixed Asset Listing**, customize the report to use the report date of **January 31, 2018**

- If you print to a pdf file, save the document as **2-Your Name Fixed Asset List Ch7**.

Close the Fixed Asset Item List

ADJUSTMENTS FOR ACCRUAL-BASIS ACCOUNTING

As previously stated, accrual-basis accounting matches the income and the expenses of a period to arrive at an accurate figure for net income or net loss. Thus, the revenue is earned at the time the service is performed or the sale is made no matter when the actual cash is received. Also, in accrual-basis accounting, the expense is recorded at the time the bill is received or the purchase is made regardless of the actual payment date. The cash basis of accounting records income or revenue at the time cash is received no matter when the sale was made, or the service was performed. Also, in cash-basis accounting, the expense is not recorded until it is paid. In QuickBooks DT, the Summary Report Basis for either Accrual or Cash is selected as a Report Preference. The default setting is Accrual.

To illustrate the different results when using accrual-basis or cash-basis accounting follows: If $1,000 sales on account and one year of insurance for $600 were recorded in November: Accrual basis would record $1,000 as income or revenue and $600 as a prepaid expense in an asset account—Prepaid Insurance. Month by month, an adjusting entry for $50 would be made to record the amount of insurance used for the month. Using the same figures, Cash basis would have no income and $600 worth of insurance recorded as an expense for November and nothing the rest of the year or during the early portion of the next year for insurance. A Profit & Loss report prepared in November would show: Accrual method—income of $1,000 and insurance expense of $50. Profit of $950. Cash method—no income and insurance expense of $600. Loss of $600.

There are several internal transactions that must be recorded when using accrual-basis accounting. These entries are called adjusting entries. Typically, adjusting entries are entered in the General Journal by accountants to make after-the-fact changes to specific accounts. For example, equipment does wear out and will eventually need to be replaced. Rather than waiting until replacement to record the usage of equipment, an adjusting entry is made to allocate the use of equipment as an expense for a period. This is called *depreciation*. Certain items that will eventually become expenses for the business may be purchased or paid for in advance. When things such as insurance or supplies are purchased or paid for, they are recorded as an asset, and are referred to as prepaid expenses. As these are used, they become expenses of the business.

ADJUSTING ENTRIES—PREPAID EXPENSES

As you learned in Chapter 4, a prepaid expense is an item that is paid for in advance. Examples of prepaid expenses include: Insurance—policy is usually for six months or one year; Office Supplies—buy to have on hand and use as needed. (This is different from supplies that are purchased for immediate use.) A prepaid expense is an asset until it is used. As the insurance or supplies are used, the amount used becomes an expense for the period. In accrual basis accounting, an adjusting entry is made in the General Journal at the end of the period to allocate the amount of prepaid expenses (assets) used to expenses.

The transactions for these adjustments may be recorded in the asset account register or they may be entered in the General Journal.

MEMO

DATE: January 31, 2018

The monthly adjustments need to be recorded. The $250 in Prepaid Insurance is the amount for two months of liability insurance. Also, we have a balance of $521.98 in office supplies and a balance of $400 in sales supplies. Adjust accordingly.

 Record the adjusting entries for insurance expense, office supplies expense, and sales supplies expense in the General Journal

Access the **General Journal** and record the adjusting entry for Prepaid Insurance
- If you get a screen regarding Assigning Numbers to Journal Entries, click **Do not display this message in the future**; and then, click **OK**.

The General Journal Entries screen appears
- Note the checkbox for Adjusting Entry and the List of Selected General Journal Entries for Last Month.
  - If the date of your computer does not match the text, you may not have anything showing in the List of Selected General Journal Entries.

To remove the list of entries, click the **Hide List** icon on the Make General Journal Entries Icon bar

Enter **01/31/18** as the **Date**
- **Entry No.** is left blank unless you wish to record a specific number.
- Because all transactions entered for the month have been entered in the Journal as well as on an invoice or a bill, they automatically have a Journal entry number. When the Journal report is printed, your transaction number may be different from the answer key. Disregard the transaction number because it can change based on how many times you delete transactions, etc.

Notice the checkbox for **Adjusting Entry** is marked
- Frequently, adjusting entries are entered by accountants in the General Journal to make after-the-fact changes to specific accounts. Common adjustments include, depreciation; prepaid income or expenses; adjusting sales tax payable; and entering bank or credit card fees or interest.
- If checked, the Adjusting Entry checkbox indicates that an entry is an adjustment.
- By default, this checkbox is selected for General Journal entries in the Accountant version of QuickBooks DT.
- A report showing all adjustments is the Adjusting Journal Entries report in the Accountant section of reports.

Tab to or click the **Account** column, click the drop-down list arrow for **Account**, click **6181 Liability Insurance**

Tab to or click **Debit**
- The $250 given in the memo is the amount for two months.

Use the QuickBooks DT Calculator to determine the amount of the entry:

    Enter **250** in the Debit column

    Press **/** for division

    Key **2**, and press **Enter**

                                               250.00

                                                /   2
- The calculation is performed, and the amount is entered in the Debit column.

Tab to or click the **Memo** column, type **Adjusting Entry, Insurance**

Tab to or click **Account**, click the drop-down list arrow for Account, click **1340 Prepaid Insurance**

- The amount for the **Credit** column should have been entered automatically; if not, enter **125**.

The Memo should have been entered automatically

- If not, enter the Memo information by using the copy command: Click the **Memo** column for the Debit entry, drag through the memo **Adjusting Entry, Insurance**, when the memo is highlighted, use the keyboard command **Ctrl+C** to copy the memo. Click in the **Memo** column for the Credit entry and use the keyboard command **Ctrl+V** to paste the memo into the column.

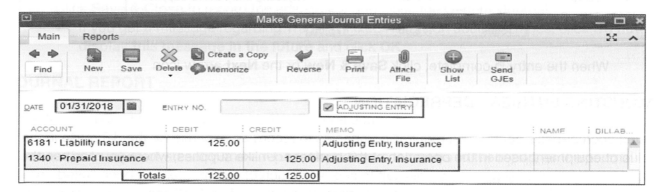

Click **Save & New** or **NEXT** (forward arrow icon)

Record the adjustment for the office supplies used

The DATE is **01/31/2018**

Click the drop-down list arrow for ACCOUNT, and then click the expense account **6472 - Office**, a subaccount of 6470 Supplies Expense

- The amount given in the memo is the balance of the account after the supplies have been used.
- The actual amount of the supplies used in January must be calculated.

Tab to the **DEBIT** column

Determine the current balance of asset account 1311 Office Supplies by using the keyboard shortcut **Ctrl+A** to access the Chart of Accounts

Make note of the balance and then close the Chart of Accounts

Use QuickMath to determine the amount:

    In the Debit column, enter the balance of the asset account, press -, enter the amount of supplies on hand listed the in memo

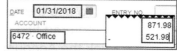

Press **Enter** for QuickBooks DT to enter the amount of the adjustment

Enter an appropriate description and complete the adjustment for office supplies

Click the drop-down list arrow for ACCOUNT on the next line, and click **1311 Office Supplies** as the account to be credited

ACCOUNT	DEBIT	CREDIT	MEMO	NAME	BILLAB...
6472 · Office	350.00		Adjusting Entry, Office Supplies		
1311 · Office Supplies		350.00	Adjusting Entry, Office Supplies		
Totals	350.00	350.00			

DATE **01/31/2018**   ENTRY NO.   ☑ ADJUSTING ENTRY

Your Name's Sierra Sports
Journal
January 2018

Trans #	Type	Date	Num	Adj	Name	Memo	Account	Debit	Credit
107	General Journal	01/31/2018		✓		Adjusting Entry, Insurance	6181 · Liability Insurance	125.00	
				✓		Adjusting Entry, Insurance	1340 · Prepaid Insurance		125.00
								125.00	125.00
108	General Journal	01/31/2018		✓		Adjusting Entry, Office Supplies	6472 · Office	350.00	
				✓		Adjusting Entry, Office Supplies	1311 · Office Supplies		350.00
								350.00	350.00
109	General Journal	01/31/2018		✓		Adjusting Entry, Sales Supplies	6471 · Sales	175.00	
				✓		Adjusting Entry, Sales Supplies	1312 · Sales Supplies		175.00
								175.00	175.00
110	General Journal	01/31/2018		✓		Adjusting Entry, Depreciation	1512 · Depreciation		85.00
				✓		Adjusting Entry, Depreciation	1522 · Depreciation		75.00
				✓		Adjusting Entry, Depreciation	6150 · Depreciation Expense	160.00	
								160.00	160.00
TOTAL								**46,933.04**	**46,933.04**

Partial Report

Close the report without printing

WORKING TRIAL BALANCE

A Working Trial Balance is a window that gathers information in one place. It is available from the Accountant's Menu. In this window, an accountant may see the net income, review and edit transactions, enter adjusting journal entries, and obtain a variety of informational reports using QuickZoom.

 Prepare a Working Trial Balance from the Accountant menu

Click **Accountant** on the Menu bar, click **Working Trial Balance**
Use the dates **From 01/01/2018** and **To 01/31/2018**, press Tab
- To analyze the report, look at Office Supplies Beginning Balance of **850** add the Transactions of **21.98**, then subtract the Adjustments of **350** to arrive at the Ending Balance of **521.98**.
- To obtain further details about Office Supplies, you could point to the Ending Balance column and use QuickZoom to prepare a Transactions by Account report (not shown).

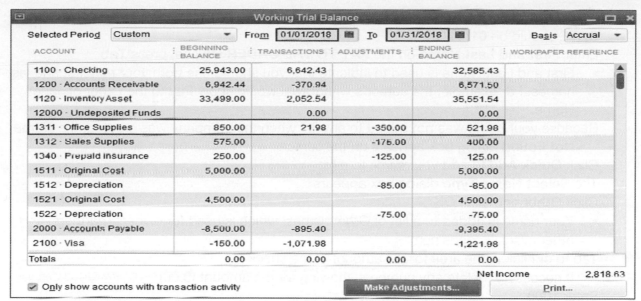

ACCOUNT	BEGINNING BALANCE	TRANSACTIONS	ADJUSTMENTS	ENDING BALANCE	WORKPAPER REFERENCE
1100 · Checking	25,943.00	6,642.43		32,585.43	
1200 · Accounts Receivable	6,942.44	-370.94		6,571.50	
1120 · Inventory Asset	33,499.00	2,052.54		35,551.54	
12000 · Undeposited Funds		0.00		0.00	
1311 · Office Supplies	850.00	21.98	-350.00	521.98	
1312 · Sales Supplies	575.00		-175.00	400.00	
1340 · Prepaid Insurance	250.00		-125.00	125.00	
1511 · Original Cost	5,000.00			5,000.00	
1512 · Depreciation			-85.00	-85.00	
1521 · Original Cost	4,500.00			4,500.00	
1522 · Depreciation			-75.00	-75.00	
2000 · Accounts Payable	-8,500.00	-895.40		-9,395.40	
2100 · Visa	-150.00	-1,071.98		-1,221.98	
Totals	0.00	0.00	0.00	0.00	

Net Income   2,818.63

☑ Only show accounts with transaction activity   Make Adjustments...   Print...

Partial Report

Close the Working Trial Balance without printing

DEFINITION OF A PARTNERSHIP

A partnership is a business owned by two or more individuals. Because it is unincorporated, each partner owns a share of all the assets and liabilities based on the percentage of his or her investment in the business or according to any partnership agreement drawn up at the time the business was created. In addition, each partner receives a portion of the profits or losses of the business. Because the business is owned by the partners, they do not receive a salary. Any funds obtained by the partners are in the form of withdrawals against their share of the profits.

OWNER WITHDRAWALS

In a partnership, owners cannot receive a paycheck because they own the business. An owner withdrawing money from a business—even to pay personal expenses—is like an individual withdrawing money from a savings account. A withdrawal simply decreases the owners' capital. QuickBooks DT allows you to establish a separate account for owner withdrawals for each owner. If a separate account is not established, owner withdrawals may be subtracted directly from each owner's capital or investment account.

MEMO
DATE: January 31, 2018

Because both partners work in the business, they do not earn a paycheck. Prepare separate checks for monthly withdrawals of $1,000 for both Larry and you.

 Write the checks for the owner withdrawals

Use the keyboard shortcut **Ctrl+W** to open the **Write Checks - Checking** window
- Make sure there is a check in the check box **Print Later**, and the NO. shows **TO PRINT**. If it is not checked, click **Print Later**.

BANK ACCOUNT should be **1100 – Checking**, if not click the drop-down arrow and select

DATE should be **01/31/18**

Enter **First and Last Name** on the **PAY TO THE ORDER OF** line, press **Tab**

- First and Last Name is used to indicate that you should use both your real <u>first</u> and <u>last</u> names. For example, the author's withdrawal would show Pay to the Order of Janet Horne.

Because your name was not added to any list when the company was created, the **Name Not Found** dialog box appears on the screen

Click **Quick Add** to add your name to a list

The **Select Name Type** dialog box appears

Click **Other** and click **OK**

- Your name is added to a list of *Other* names, which is used for owners, partners, and other miscellaneous names.

Tab to or click in the area for the amount of the check

- If necessary, delete any numbers showing for the amount (0.00).

Enter **1000**

Tab to or click **Memo**, enter **Owner Withdrawal, January**

Use the **Expenses** tab at the bottom of the check

Tab to or click in the Account column, click the drop-down list arrow, click the Equity account **3112 - First and Last Name, Drawing**

- The amount 1,000.00 should appear in the Amount column.
- If it does not, tab to or click in the Amount column and enter 1000.

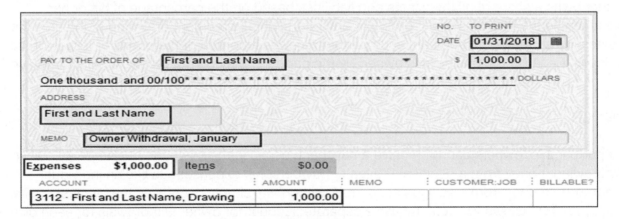

Click the **Next** arrow icon or **Save & New** and repeat the above procedures to prepare the check to Larry Muir for his $1,000 withdrawal

- Use his drawing account **3122 – Larry Muir, Drawing**.

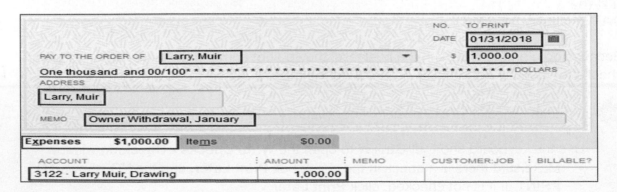

Click the **Next** arrow icon or **Save & New**

On the blank check, click the drop-down list arrow for **Print**, click **Batch**

The **Select Checks to Print** dialog box appears

Bank Account is **1100- Checking**, the **First Check Number** should be **6**

- If necessary, change the number to **6**.

If both checks have a check mark, click **OK**, if not, click **Select All** and then click **OK**

Select Checks to Print			
Ban**k** Account	1100 · Checking ▼	First Check Number	6

Select Checks to print, then click OK.
There are 2 Checks to print for $2,000.00.

✓	DATE	PAYEE	AMOUNT
✓	01/31/2018	First and Last Name	1,000.00
✓	01/31/2018	Larry, Muir	1,000.00

The Check style should be Standard

Once the check has printed successfully, click **OK** on the **Print Checks – Confirmation** dialog box

- If you print to a pdf file, save the document as **3-Your Name Cks 6-7 Ch7**.

Close **Write Checks - Checking**

PREPARE DAILY BACKUP

A backup file is prepared as a safeguard in case you make an error. By creating the backup file now, it will contain your work for Chapters 5, 6, and up through the owners' withdrawals in Chapter 7.

 Prepare the Sierra 2018 (Daily Backup).qbb file as instructed previously

BANK RECONCILIATION

Each month the Checking account should be reconciled with the bank statement to make sure both balances agree. The bank statement will rarely have an ending balance that matches the balance of the Checking account. This is due to several factors: outstanding checks, deposits in transit, bank service charges, interest earned on checking accounts, collections made by the bank, errors made in recording checks and/or deposits by the company or by the bank, etc.

To have an accurate amount listed as the balance in the Checking account, it is important that the differences between the bank statement and the Checking account be reconciled. If something such as a service charge or a collection made by the bank appears on the bank statement, it needs to be recorded in the Checking account.

Reconciling a bank statement is an appropriate time to find any errors that may have been recorded in the Checking account. The reconciliation may be out of balance because a transposition was made, a transaction was recorded backwards, a transaction was recorded twice, or a transaction was not recorded at all.

BEGIN BANK RECONCILIATION

The Begin Reconciliation screen initiates the account reconciliation. On this screen, information regarding the ending balance, service charges, and interest earned is entered.

MEMO

DATE: January 31, 2018

Received the bank statement from Old Mammoth Bank dated January 31, 2018. Reconcile the bank statement and print a Reconciliation Report.

 Reconcile the bank statement for January

Use the bank statement to complete the reconciliation

OLD MAMMOTH BANK
12345 Old Mammoth Road
Mammoth Lakes, CA 93546
(909) 555-3880

Your Name's Sierra Sports
875 Mountain Road
Mammoth Lakes, CA 93546

Acct. # 123-456-7890			January, 2018
Beginning Balance, January 1, 2018			**$25,943.00**
1/18/2018 Deposit	10,855.30		36,798.30
1/20/2018 NSF Returned Check Oskar Ortiz		975.00	35,823.30
1/20/2018 NSF Bank Charge		10.00	35,813.30
1/20/2018 Check 1		81.00	35,732.30
1/25/2018 Check 2		1,837.50	33,894.80
1/25/2018 Check 3		294.00	33,600.80
1/25/2018 Check 4		313.60	33,287.20
1/25/2018 Check 5		701.77	32,585.43
1/31/2018 Office Equip. Loan Pmt.: $10.33 Principal, $53.42 Interest		63.75	32,521.68
1/31/2018 Store Fixtures Loan Pmt.: $8.61 Principal, $44.51 Interest		53.12	32,468.56
1/31/2018 Service Charge		8.00	32,460.56
1/31/2018 Interest	54.05		32,514.61
Ending Balance, January 31, 2018			**32,514.61**

Click the **Reconcile** icon on the QuickBooks DT Home Page

Enter preliminary information on the **Begin Reconciliation** screen

- *Note:* If you need to exit the Begin Reconciliation screen before it is complete, click **Cancel**.

The **Account To Reconcile** should be **1100 Checking**

- If not, click the drop-down list arrow, click **Checking**.

- The **Statement Date** should be **01/31/18**.
- **Beginning Balance** should be **25,943.00**. This is the same amount as the Checking account starting balance and is shown on the bank statement.

Enter the **Ending Balance** from the bank statement, **32,514.61**

Tab to or click **Service Charge**, enter the **Service Charge, 8.00**

Tab to or click Service Charge **Date**, the date should be **01/31/18**

- Since the date of your computer may appear, double-check the date to avoid errors.

Click the drop-down list arrow for **Account**, click **6120 Bank Service Charges**

Tab to or click **Interest Earned**, enter **54.05**

Date is **01/31/18**

The **Account** is **7010** for **Interest Income**

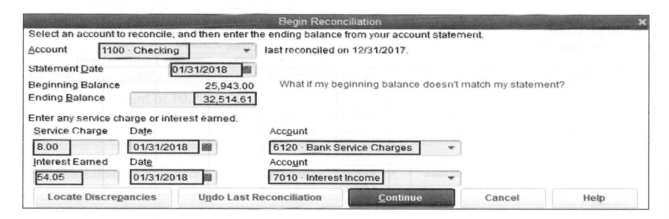

Click **Continue**

MARK CLEARED TRANSACTIONS

Once bank statement information for the ending balance, service charges, and interest earned has been entered, compare the checks and deposits listed on the statement with the transactions for the Checking account. If a deposit or a check is listed correctly on the bank statement and in the Reconcile - Checking window, it has cleared and should be marked. An item may be marked individually by positioning the cursor on the deposit or the check and clicking the primary mouse button. If all deposits and checks match, click the Mark All button to mark all the deposits and checks at once. To remove all the checks, click the Unmark All button. To unmark an individual item, click the item.

 Mark cleared checks and deposits

- *Note:* If you need to exit the Reconcile - Checking screen before it is complete, click **Leave**. If you click **Reconcile Now**, you must Undo the reconciliation and start over.
- If you need to return to the Begin Reconciliation window, click the **Modify** button.
- Notice that the **Highlight Marked** is selected. When an item has been selected or marked, the background color changes.

Compare the bank statement with the **Reconcile - Checking** window

- On the bank statement, dates may not be the same as the actual check or deposit dates.

Click the appropriate accounts and enter the correct amount for each item
- The accounts and amounts for the office equipment loan payment may appear. Click the drop-down list arrow and select the appropriate accounts for the store fixture loan payment. Be sure to use the information for Store Fixtures not the information for Office Equipment.
- Refer to the bank statement for details regarding the amount of the payment for interest and the amount of the payment applied to principal.

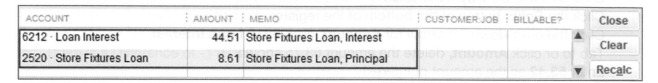

ACCOUNT	AMOUNT	MEMO	CUSTOMER:JOB	BILLABLE?	
6212 · Loan Interest	44.51	Store Fixtures Loan, Interest			Close
2520 · Store Fixtures Loan	8.61	Store Fixtures Loan, Principal			Clear
					Recalc

Click **Close** to close the window for the information regarding the "split" between accounts
Enter the transaction **Memo**: **Store Fixtures Loan, Payment**
Click **Record** to record the loan payment

		1100 · Checking					
DATE	NUMBER	PAYEE		PAYMENT	✓	DEPOSIT	BALANCE
	TYPE	ACCOUNT	MEMO				
01/31/2018	Transfer	Old Mammoth Bank		53.12			32,468.56
	CHK	-split-	Store Fixtures Loan, Payment				

Close the **Checking Register**
- You should return to the **Reconcile – Checking** screen.
Scroll to the bottom of **Checks and Payments**
- Notice the two entries for the loan payments in Checks and Payments.
Mark the two entries
- At this point the Ending Balance and Cleared Balance should be equal—$32,514.61 with a difference of 0.00.

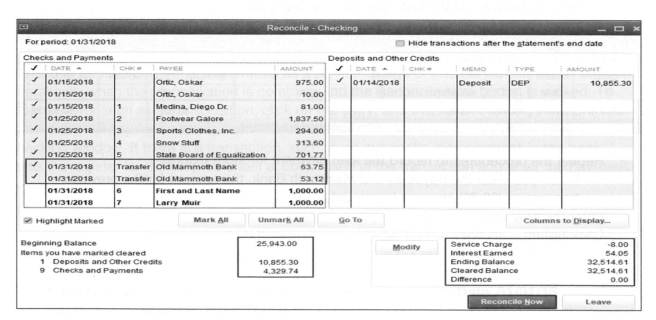

			Reconcile - Checking							

For period: 01/31/2018   ☐ Hide transactions after the statement's end date

Checks and Payments

✓	DATE ▲	CHK #	PAYEE	AMOUNT
✓	01/15/2018		Ortiz, Oskar	975.00
✓	01/15/2018		Ortiz, Oskar	10.00
✓	01/15/2018	1	Medina, Diego Dr.	81.00
✓	01/25/2018	2	Footwear Galore	1,837.50
✓	01/25/2018	3	Sports Clothes, Inc.	294.00
✓	01/25/2018	4	Snow Stuff	313.60
✓	01/25/2018	5	State Board of Equalization	701.77
✓	01/31/2018	Transfer	Old Mammoth Bank	63.75
✓	01/31/2018	Transfer	Old Mammoth Bank	53.12
	01/31/2018	6	First and Last Name	1,000.00
	01/31/2018	7	Larry Muir	1,000.00

Deposits and Other Credits

✓	DATE ▲	CHK #	MEMO	TYPE	AMOUNT
✓	01/14/2018		Deposit	DEP	10,855.30

☑ Highlight Marked   Mark All   Unmark All   Go To   Columns to Display...

Beginning Balance	25,943.00		Service Charge	-8.00
Items you have marked cleared		Modify	Interest Earned	54.05
1 Deposits and Other Credits	10,855.30		Ending Balance	32,514.61
9 Checks and Payments	4,329.74		Cleared Balance	32,514.61
			Difference	0.00

Reconcile Now   Leave

If your entries agree with the above, click **Reconcile Now** to finish the reconciliation
- If your reconciliation is not in agreement, do not click **Reconcile Now** until the errors are corrected.
- Once you click **Reconcile Now**, you may not return to this **Reconcile - Checking** window. You would have to Undo the reconciliation and start over.

PRINT RECONCILIATION REPORT

As soon as the Ending Balance and the Cleared Balance are equal or when you finish marking transactions and click Reconcile Now, a screen appears allowing you to select the level of Reconciliation Report you would like to print. You may select Summary and get a report that lists totals only or Detail and get all the transactions that were reconciled on the report. You may print the report at the time you have finished reconciling the account or you may print the report later by clicking the Reports menu, clicking Banking, and then clicking Previous Reconciliation. If you think you may want to print the report again in the future, print the report to a file to save it permanently.

 Print a Detail Reconciliation report

On the **Reconciliation Complete** screen, click **Detail**, click **Display**
- If you get a Reconciliation Report message, click **Do not display this message in the future**, and click **OK**.
Adjust the column widths so the report will print on one page and all information is displayed in full

Your Name's Sierra Sports
Reconciliation Detail
1100 · Checking, Period Ending 01/31/2018

Type	Date	Num	Name	Clr	Amount	Balance
Beginning Balance						25,943.00
Cleared Transactions						
Checks and Payments - 10 items						
General Journal	01/15/2018		Ortiz, Oskar	✓	-975.00	-975.00
Check	01/15/2018	1	Medina, Diego Dr.	✓	-81.00	-1,056.00
General Journal	01/15/2018		Ortiz, Oskar	✓	-10.00	-1,066.00
Bill Pmt -Check	01/25/2018	2	Footwear Galore	✓	-1,837.50	-2,903.50
Sales Tax Payment	01/25/2018	5	State Board of Equalization	✓	-701.77	-3,605.27
Bill Pmt -Check	01/25/2018	4	Snow Stuff	✓	-313.60	-3,918.87
Bill Pmt -Check	01/25/2018	3	Sports Clothes, Inc.	✓	-294.00	-4,212.87
Check	01/31/2018	Transfer	Old Mammoth Bank	✓	-63.75	-4,276.62
Check	01/31/2018	Transfer	Old Mammoth Bank	✓	-53.12	-4,329.74
Check	01/31/2018			✓	-8.00	-4,337.74
Total Checks and Payments					-4,337.74	-4,337.74
Deposits and Credits - 2 items						
Deposit	01/14/2018			✓	10,855.30	10,855.30
Deposit	01/31/2018			✓	54.05	10,909.35
Total Deposits and Credits					10,909.35	10,909.35
Total Cleared Transactions					6,571.61	6,571.61
Cleared Balance					6,571.61	32,514.61
Uncleared Transactions						
Checks and Payments - 2 items						
Check	01/31/2018	7	Larry Muir		-1,000.00	-1,000.00
Check	01/31/2018	6	First and Last Name		-1,000.00	-2,000.00
Total Checks and Payments					-2,000.00	-2,000.00
Total Uncleared Transactions					-2,000.00	-2,000.00
Register Balance as of 01/31/2018					4,571.61	30,514.61
Ending Balance					4,571.61	30,514.61

Print as previously instructed in Portrait orientation then close the report
- If you print to a pdf file, save the document as **4-Your Name Bank Rec Ch7**.

VIEW CHECK REGISTER

Once the bank reconciliation has been completed, it is wise to scroll through the Check Register to view the effect of the reconciliation on the Checking account. You will notice that the check column shows a check mark for all items that were marked as cleared during the reconciliation. If an error is discovered after completing the reconciliation, the transaction may be changed, and the correction will be reflected in the Beginning Balance on the next reconciliation.

 View the register for the Checking account

Click the **Check Register** icon in the Banking section of the Home Page
To display more of the register, click the check box for **1-Line**
Scroll through the register
- Notice that the transactions are listed in chronological order and that each item marked in the Bank Reconciliation now has a check mark in the check column.
- The interest earned and bank service charges appear in the register.
- Even though the bank reconciliation transactions for loan payments were recorded after the checks written on January 31 for the owner withdrawals, the bank reconciliation transactions appear before the checks because they were recorded as a Transfer.

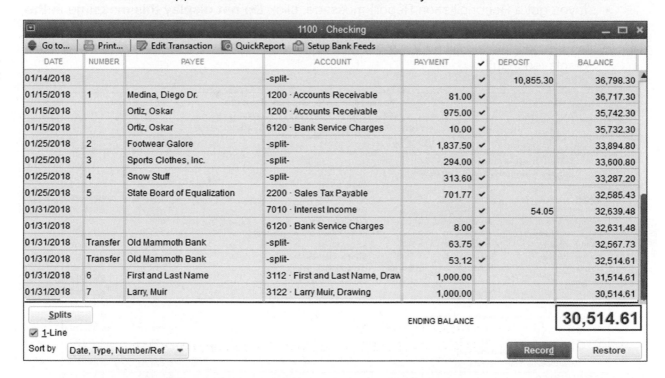

DATE	NUMBER	PAYEE	ACCOUNT	PAYMENT	✔	DEPOSIT	BALANCE
01/14/2018			-split-		✔	10,855.30	36,798.30
01/15/2018	1	Medina, Diego Dr.	1200 · Accounts Receivable	81.00	✔		36,717.30
01/15/2018		Ortiz, Oskar	1200 · Accounts Receivable	975.00	✔		35,742.30
01/15/2018		Ortiz, Oskar	6120 · Bank Service Charges	10.00	✔		35,732.30
01/25/2018	2	Footwear Galore	-split-	1,837.50	✔		33,894.80
01/25/2018	3	Sports Clothes, Inc.	-split-	294.00	✔		33,600.80
01/25/2018	4	Snow Stuff	-split-	313.60	✔		33,287.20
01/25/2018	5	State Board of Equalization	2200 · Sales Tax Payable	701.77	✔		32,585.43
01/31/2018			7010 · Interest Income		✔	54.05	32,639.48
01/31/2018			6120 · Bank Service Charges	8.00	✔		32,631.48
01/31/2018	Transfer	Old Mammoth Bank	-split-	63.75	✔		32,567.73
01/31/2018	Transfer	Old Mammoth Bank	-split-	53.12	✔		32,514.61
01/31/2018	6	First and Last Name	3112 · First and Last Name, Draw	1,000.00			31,514.61
01/31/2018	7	Larry, Muir	3122 · Larry Muir, Drawing	1,000.00			30,514.61

ENDING BALANCE **30,514.61**

Splits | ☑ 1-Line | Sort by Date, Type, Number/Ref | Record | Restore

- Notice that the final balance of the account is $30,514.61.
Close the register

CREDIT CARD RECONCILIATION

Any balance sheet account used in QuickBooks DT may be reconciled. These include assets, liabilities, and owner's equity accounts. Accounts in the Income, Expense, and Cost of Goods Sold categories are not balance sheet accounts and may not be reconciled.

As with a checking account, it is a good practice to reconcile the Credit Card account each month. When the credit card statement is received, the transactions entered in QuickBooks DT should agree with the transactions shown on the credit card statement. A reconciliation of the credit card should be completed monthly.

MEMO

DATE: January 31, 2018

The monthly bill for the Visa has arrived and is to be paid. Prior to paying the monthly credit card bill, reconcile the Credit Card account.

 Reconcile and pay the credit card bill

Click the **Reconcile** icon on the Home Page
Click the drop-down list arrow for Account
Click **2100 Visa** to select the account
Use the following credit card statement to complete the reconciliation of the Visa credit card

OLD MAMMOTH BANK			
VISA			
12345 Old Mammoth Road			
Mammoth Lakes, CA 93546			
Your Name's Sierra Sports			
875 Mountain Road			
Mammoth Lakes, CA 93546			**Acct. # 098-776-4321**
Beginning Balance, January 1, 2018		150.00	$ 150.00
1/23/2018 Mountain Office Supply		21.98	171.98
1/23/2018 Snow Sports, Inc.		300.00	471.98
1/25/2018 Sports Accessories		350.00	821.98
1/25/2018 Snow Shoes & More		400.00	1,221.98
Ending Balance, January 31, 2018			$1,221.98
Minimum Payment Due: $50.00		**Payment Due Date: February 15, 2018**	

Enter the **Statement Date** of **01/31/18**
Enter the **Ending Balance** of **1,221.98** in the **Begin Reconciliation** window

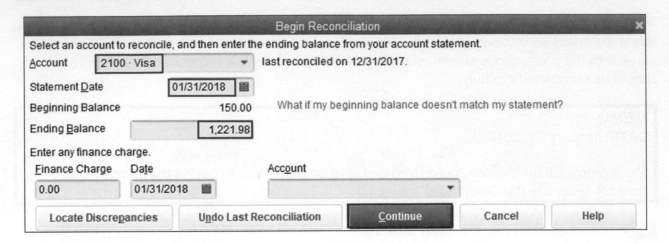

Click the **Continue** button

Mark each item that appears on both the statement and in the reconciliation **EXCEPT** for the **$400** transaction for Snow Shoes & More

ADJUSTMENT—CREDIT CARD RECONCILIATION

In QuickBooks DT, adjustments to reconciliations may be made during the reconciliation process.

 Verify that all items are marked **EXCEPT** the charge for **$400** for Snow Shoes & More

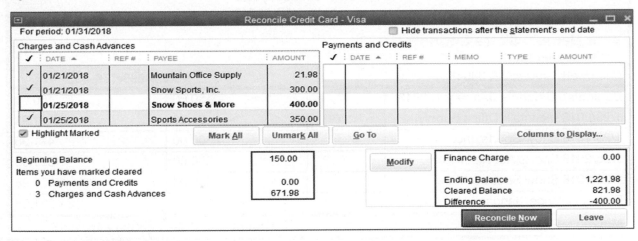

Click **Reconcile Now**

- The Reconcile Adjustment screen appears because there was a $400 Difference shown at the bottom of the reconciliation.
- Even though the error on the demonstration reconciliation is known, an adjustment will be entered and then deleted later.

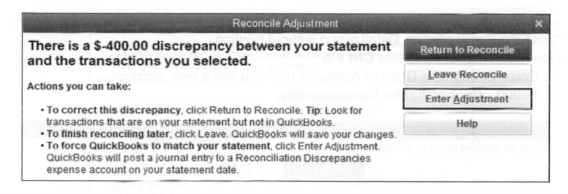

Click **Enter Adjustment**
Click **Cancel** on the Make Payment screen

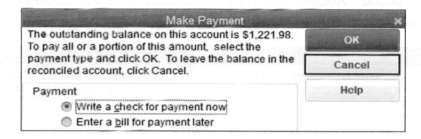

- The Reconciliation report is generated.

Click **Detail** and then click **Display**

Your Name's Sierra Sports
Reconciliation Detail
2100 · Visa, Period Ending 01/31/2018

Type	Date	Num	Name	Clr	Amount	Balance
Beginning Balance						**150.00**
Cleared Transactions						
Charges and Cash Advances - 4 items						
Credit Card Charge	01/21/2018		Snow Sports, Inc.	✔	-300.00	-300.00
Credit Card Charge	01/21/2018		Mountain Office Supply	✔	-21.98	-321.98
Bill Pmt -CCard	01/25/2018		Sports Accessories	✔	-350.00	-671.98
General Journal	01/31/2018			✔	-400.00	-1,071.98
Total Charges and Cash Advances					-1,071.98	-1,071.98
Total Cleared Transactions					-1,071.98	-1,071.98
Cleared Balance					1,071.98	1,221.98
Uncleared Transactions						
Charges and Cash Advances - 1 item						
Bill Pmt -CCard	01/25/2018		Snow Shoes & More		-400.00	-400.00
Total Charges and Cash Advances					-400.00	-400.00
Total Uncleared Transactions					-400.00	-400.00
Register Balance as of 01/31/2018					1,471.98	1,621.98
Ending Balance					**1,471.98**	**1,621.98**

- Because the date of your computer may be different from the date used in the text, there may be some differences in the appearance of the Reconciliation Detail report. If the appropriate transactions have been marked, disregard any discrepancies.
- Notice that there is a General Journal entry for -$400 in the Cleared Transactions section of the report. This is the Adjustment made by QuickBooks DT.

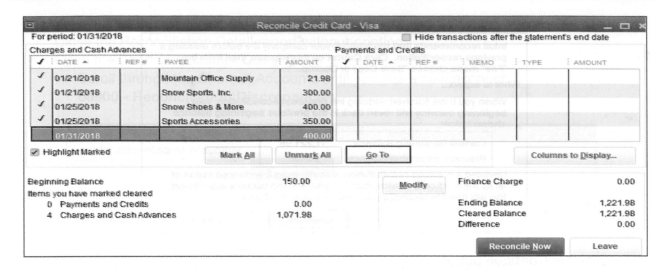

Click **Go To**
- You will go to the Make General Journal Entries screen.

Use the keyboard shortcut **Ctrl+D** to delete the entry

Click **OK** on the **Delete Transaction** screen

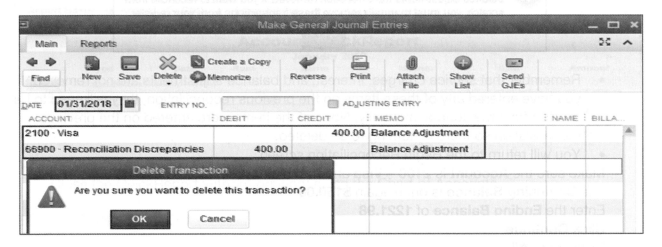

Close the **Make General Journal Entries** screen

Verify that the adjusting entry has been deleted and that the **Ending** and **Cleared Balances** are **1,221.98** and the **Difference** is **0.00**

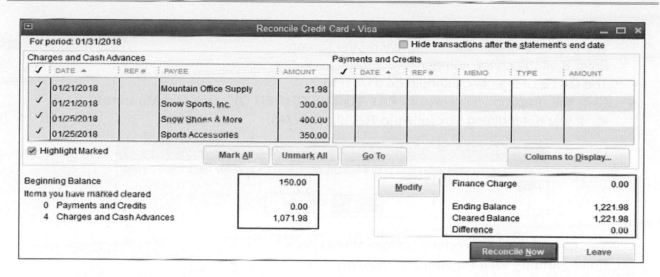

Click **Reconcile Now**

When the **Make Payment** dialog box appears on the screen

Make sure **Write a check for payment now** is selected, click **OK**

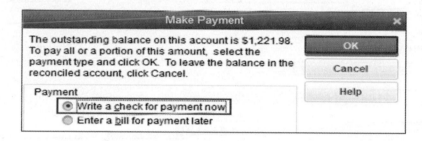

Display and print a **Reconciliation Detail Report** following the procedures given for the Bank Reconciliation Report

- If you print to a pdf file, save the document as **5-Your Name CC Rec Ch7**.

Your Name's Sierra Sports
Reconciliation Detail
2100 · Visa, Period Ending 01/31/2018

Type	Date	Num	Name	Clr	Amount	Balance
Beginning Balance						150.00
Cleared Transactions						
Charges and Cash Advances - 4 items						
Credit Card Charge	01/21/2018		Snow Sports, Inc.	✓	-300.00	-300.00
Credit Card Charge	01/21/2018		Mountain Office Supply	✓	-21.98	-321.98
Bill Pmt -CCard	01/25/2018		Snow Shoes & More	✓	-400.00	-721.98
Bill Pmt -CCard	01/25/2018		Sports Accessories	✓	-350.00	-1,071.98
Total Charges and Cash Advances					-1,071.98	-1,071.98
Total Cleared Transactions					-1,071.98	-1,071.98
Cleared Balance					1,071.98	1,221.98
Register Balance as of 01/31/2018					1,071.98	1,221.98
Ending Balance					1,071.98	1,221.98

Close the Reconciliation Detail report

The payment check should appear on the screen

Enter **8** as the check number

The **DATE** of the check should be **01/31/18**

Click the drop-down list next to **PAY TO THE ORDER OF**, click **Old Mammoth Bank**

- If you get a dialog box for **Auto Recall**, click **No**.

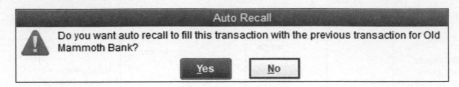

Tab to or click **Memo** on the bottom of the check

Enter **January Visa Payment** as the memo

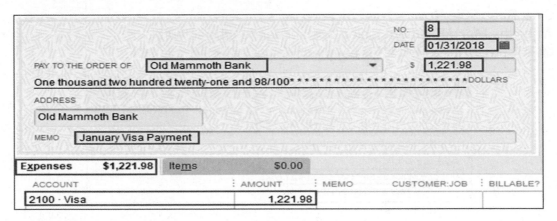

Print the standard-style check, then click **OK** on the Print Checks – Confirmation

- If you print to a pdf file, save the document as **6-Your Name Ck 8 Old Mammoth Bank Ch7**.

Click **Save & Close** to record, and exit **Write Checks**

REVIEW CREDIT CARD TRANSACTION

When a credit card charge has been reconciled, Cleared is stamped on the Credit Card Purchase/Charge transaction.

 View the paid Credit Card Purchase/Charge transaction for Snow Sports, Inc.

Click **Enter Credit Card Charges** on the Home Page

Click **Find**

Enter **Snow Sports, Inc.** in the text box for Purchased From

Click **Find**

- You will be taken to the Credit Card Purchase/Charge for $300.00.

Note that it has been marked **Cleared**

Close Enter Credit Card Charges - Visa

VIEW JOURNAL REPORT

After entering several transactions, it is helpful to view the Journal Report. In the Journal all transactions regardless of the method of entry are shown in traditional debit/credit format. Remember, Journal and Journal Report may be used synonymously.

 View the Journal Report for January

Since you will be preparing several reports, open the Report Center
Click **Accountant & Taxes** as the type of report, double-click **Journal**
The dates are from **01/31/18** to **01/31/18**, press **Tab**
Expand the Journal
Scroll through the report and view all the transactions that have been made

Your Name's Sierra Sports

Journal

January 2018

Trans #	Type	Date	Num	Adj	Name	Memo	Account	Debit	Credit
113	Check	01/31/2018	Transfer		Old Mammoth Bank	Office Equipment Loan, Payment	1100 · Checking		63.75
					Old Mammoth Bank	Office Equipment Loan, Interest	6212 · Loan Interest	53.42	
					Old Mammoth Bank	Office Equipment Loan, Principal	2510 · Office Equipment Loan	10.33	
								63.75	63.75
114	Check	01/31/2018	Transfer		Old Mammoth Bank	Store Fixtures Loan, Payment	1100 · Checking		53.12
					Old Mammoth Bank	Store Fixtures Loan, Interest	6212 · Loan Interest	44.51	
					Old Mammoth Bank	Store Fixtures Loan, Principal	2520 · Store Fixtures Loan	8.61	
								53.12	53.12
115	Check	01/31/2018				Service Charge	1100 · Checking		8.00
						Service Charge	6120 · Bank Service Charges	8.00	
								8.00	8.00
116	Deposit	01/31/2018				Interest	1100 · Checking	54.05	
						Interest	7010 · Interest Income		54.05
								54.05	54.05
118	Check	01/31/2018	8		Old Mammoth Bank	January Visa Payment	1100 · Checking		1,221.98
					Old Mammoth Bank	January Visa Payment	2100 · Visa	1,221.98	
								1,221.98	1,221.98
TOTAL								**50,333.94**	**50,333.94**

Partial Report

Close the **Journal** <u>without</u> printing
The **Report Center** should remain on the screen

PREPARE ADJUSTED TRIAL BALANCE

After all adjustments have been recorded and the bank reconciliation has been completed, it is wise to prepare an Adjusted Trial Balance. This report has columns for Unadjusted Balance, Adjustments, and Adjusted Balance. If adjusting entries have been made, the amount in the Adjustments column is subtracted from Unadjusted Balance to obtain the Adjusted Balance. The Adjusted Trial Balance proves that debits equal credits.

MEMO

DATE: January 31, 2018

Because adjustments have been entered, prepare an Adjusted Trial Balance.

 Use Accountant & Taxes in Report Center to prepare an adjusted trial balance

Report Dates are From **01/01/18** To **01/31/18**
- Scroll through the report and study the amounts shown.

Your Name's Sierra Sports
Adjusted Trial Balance
January 2018

	Unadjusted Balance		Adjustments		Adjusted Balance	
	Debit	Credit	Debit	Credit	Debit	Credit
1100 · Checking	29,292.63				29,292.63	
1200 · Accounts Receivable	6,571.50				6,571.50	
1120 · Inventory Asset	35,551.54				35,551.54	
12000 · Undeposited Funds	0.00				0.00	
1311 · Office Supplies	871.98			350.00	521.98	
1312 · Sales Supplies	575.00			175.00	400.00	
1340 · Prepaid Insurance	250.00			125.00	125.00	
1511 · Original Cost	5,000.00				5,000.00	
1512 · Depreciation				85.00		85.00
1521 · Original Cost	4,500.00				4,500.00	
1522 · Depreciation				75.00		75.00
2000 · Accounts Payable		9,395.40				9,395.40
2100 · Visa	0.00				0.00	
2200 · Sales Tax Payable	0.00				0.00	
2510 · Office Equipment Loan		2,989.67				2,989.67
2520 · Store Fixtures Loan		2,491.39				2,491.39
3000 · Owners' Equity	0.00				0.00	
3100 · Your Last Name & Muir, Capital		26,159.44				26,159.44
3111 · First and Last Name, Investment		20,000.00				20,000.00
3112 · First and Last Name, Drawing	1,000.00				1,000.00	
3121 · Larry Muir, Investment		20,000.00				20,000.00
3122 · Larry Muir, Drawing	1,000.00				1,000.00	
4011 · Clothing & Accessory Sales		1,759.51				1,759.51
4012 · Equipment Sales		7,436.44				7,436.44
4050 · Sales Discounts	494.36				494.36	
4090 · Returned Check Charges		25.00				25.00
5000 · Cost of Goods Sold	3,492.46				3,492.46	
5200 · Merchandise Discounts		49.90				49.90
6120 · Bank Service Charges	18.00				18.00	
6140 · Advertising Expense	95.00				95.00	
6150 · Depreciation Expense			160.00		160.00	
6181 · Liability Insurance			125.00		125.00	
6212 · Loan Interest	97.93				97.93	
6300 · Rent	950.00				950.00	
6340 · Telephone	156.40				156.40	
6391 · Gas and Electric	359.00				359.00	
6392 · Water	85.00				85.00	
6471 · Sales			175.00		175.00	
6472 · Office			350.00		350.00	
7010 · Interest Income		54.05				54.05
TOTAL	**90,360.80**	**90,360.80**	**810.00**	**810.00**	**90,520.80**	**90,520.80**

- If you look at the Unadjusted Balance and add or subtract the Adjustments, you will obtain the Adjusted Balance.
- Notice that the final totals of debits and credits of the Adjusted Balance columns are equal: $90,520.80.

Do not close the report

USE QUICKZOOM

Use QuickZoom to view the details of Office Supplies:

Scroll through the Trial Balance until you see **1311 Office Supplies**
Position the mouse pointer over the amount of Office Supplies, **521.98**
- Notice that the mouse pointer changes to a magnifying glass with a Z.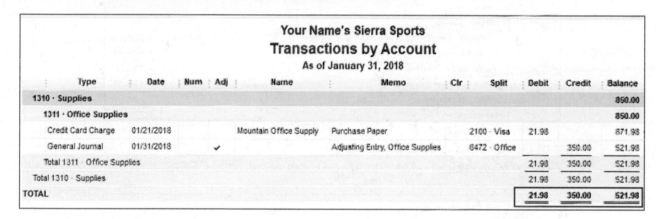
Double-click the primary mouse button
- A **Transactions by Account Report** appears on the screen showing the two transactions entered for office supplies.

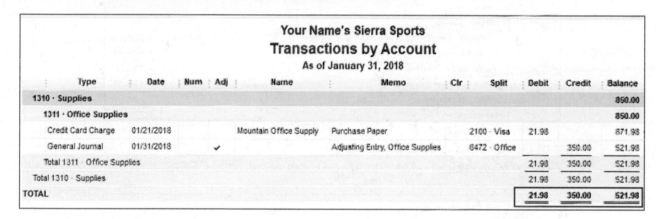

Type	Date	Num	Adj	Name	Memo	Clr	Split	Debit	Credit	Balance
1310 · Supplies										850.00
1311 · Office Supplies										850.00
Credit Card Charge	01/21/2018			Mountain Office Supply	Purchase Paper		2100 · Visa	21.98		871.98
General Journal	01/31/2018		✓		Adjusting Entry, Office Supplies		6472 · Office		350.00	521.98
Total 1311 · Office Supplies								21.98	350.00	521.98
Total 1310 · Supplies								21.98	350.00	521.98
TOTAL								21.98	350.00	521.98

Your Name's Sierra Sports
Transactions by Account
As of January 31, 2018

Close Transactions by Account and Adjusted Trial Balance reports <u>without</u> printing

PROFIT & LOSS (STANDARD)

Because all income, expenses, and adjustments have been made for the period, a Profit & Loss Report can be prepared. This report is also known as the Income Statement and shows the income, expenses, and net income or net loss for the period (Income – Expenses = Net Profit or Net Loss).

QuickBooks DT has several different types of Profit & Loss Reports available: <u>Standard</u>—summarizes income and expenses; <u>Detail</u>—shows the year-to-date transactions for each income and expense account. The other Profit & Loss reports are like the Profit & Loss Standard but have additional information displayed as indicated in the following: <u>YTD Comparison</u>—summarizes your income and expenses for this month and compares them to your income and expenses for the current fiscal year; <u>Prev Year Comparison</u>—summarizes your income and expenses for both this month and this month last year; <u>By Job</u>—has columns for each customer and job and amounts for this year to date; <u>By Class</u>—has columns for each class and sub-class with the amounts for this year to date, and <u>Unclassified</u>—shows how much you are making or losing within segments of your business that are not assigned to a QuickBooks DT class.

View a **Profit & Loss (Standard) Report**

Use the Company & Financial section of the Report Center and prepare the report
- Unless instructed otherwise, all Profit & Loss reports prepared will be Standard.
If necessary, enter the dates **From 01/01/18** and **To 01/31/18**
Scroll through the report to view the income and expenses listed

- Remember, accrual basis accounting calculates the net income based on income earned at the time the service was performed or the sale was made, and the expenses incurred at the time the bill was received or the expense was incurred. It does not matter whether the money for income has been received or the bills and expenses have been paid.
- The calculations shown below may not have all the subtotals shown in the report; but the example is given to help with understanding the calculations made.
- Total Income is calculated:
  o Total Sales – Sales Discounts + Returned Check Charges = Total Income

- Cost of Goods Sold is calculated:
  o Cost of Goods Sold – Merchandise Discounts = Total COGS.

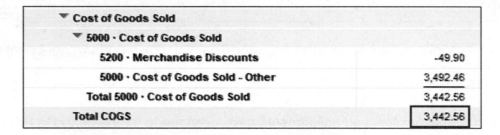

- Note the calculation to obtain the Net Income:
  o Total Income - Cost of Goods Sold = Gross Profit.
  o Gross Profit – Total Expenses = Net Ordinary Income.
  o Net Ordinary Income + Other Income – Other Expenses = Net Income

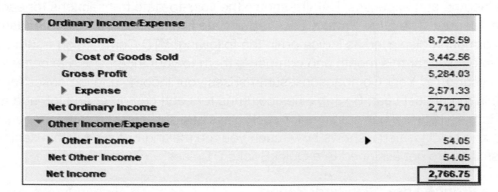

Close the **Profit & Loss Report**, do <u>not</u> close the Report Center

BALANCE SHEET (STANDARD)

The Balance Sheet proves the fundamental accounting equation: Assets = Liabilities + Owner's Equity. When all transactions and adjustments for the period have been recorded, a balance sheet should be prepared. QuickBooks DT has several different types of Balance Sheet reports available: Standard—shows as of the report dates the balance in each balance sheet account with subtotals provided for assets, liabilities, and equity; Detail—for each account the report shows the starting balance, transactions entered, and the ending balance during the period specified in the From and To dates; Summary—shows amounts for each account type but not for individual accounts; Prev. Year Comparison—has columns for the report date, the report date a year ago, $ change, and % change; and By Class—shows the value of your company or organization by class.

Since Your Name's Sierra Sports is a partnership, separate equity accounts for each partner were established earlier in the chapter. You may explore the owner information in the Balance Sheet.

 View a **Standard Balance Sheet Report**

Double-click **Balance Sheet Standard**
- Unless instructed otherwise, all Balance Sheets prepared will be Standard.

Tab to or click **As of,** enter **01/31/18**, tab to generate the report

Scroll through the report to view the assets, liabilities, and equities listed
- Notice the Equity section, especially the Investment and Drawing accounts for each owner.
- You will see that your investment and drawing accounts are separate from Larry's.
- Total 3100 Your Last Name & Muir, Capital shows a total of the capital for both owners.
- Notice that there is an amount shown for 3100 - Your Last Name & Muir, Capital – Other of $26,159.44. This balance shows how much "other" capital the owners share. Other capital can include things such as opening balances that represent value belonging to the owners. Originally, the capital for both owners was combined into one account. The report does not indicate how much of the "other" capital is for each owner.
- Notice the Net Income account listed in the **Equity** section of the report. This is the same amount of Net Income shown on the Profit & Loss Report.

Your Name's Sierra Sports
Balance Sheet
As of January 31, 2018

	Jan 31, 18
▼ **ASSETS**	
▶ Current Assets	72,462.65
▶ Fixed Assets	9,340.00
TOTAL ASSETS	81,802.65
▼ **LIABILITIES & EQUITY**	
▶ Liabilities	14,876.46
▼ Equity	
▼ 3100 · Your Last Name & Muir, Capital	
▼ 3110 · First and Last Name, Capital	
3111 · First and Last Name, Investment	20,000.00
3112 · First and Last Name, Drawing	-1,000.00
Total 3110 · First and Last Name, Capital	19,000.00
▼ 3120 · Larry Muir, Capital	
3121 · Larry Muir, Investment	20,000.00
3122 · Larry Muir, Drawing	-1,000.00
Total 3120 · Larry Muir, Capital	19,000.00
3100 · Your Last Name & Muir, Capital - Other	26,159.44
Total 3100 · Your Last Name & Muir, Capital	64,159.44
Net Income	2,766.75
Total Equity	66,926.19
TOTAL LIABILITIES & EQUITY	81,802.65

Partial Report

Do <u>not</u> close the report

QUICKZOOM TO VIEW CAPITAL – OTHER ACCOUNT

As you learned earlier, QuickZoom is a QuickBooks DT feature that allows you to make a closer observation of transactions, amounts, etc. With QuickZoom, you may zoom in on an item when the mouse pointer turns into a magnifying glass with a Z inside. If you point to an item and you do not get a magnifying glass with a Z inside, you cannot zoom in on it.

As you view the Balance Sheet, you will notice that the balance for 3100 - Your Last Name & Muir, Capital - Other is $26,159.44. To determine why there is an amount in Capital-Other, use QuickZoom to see the Transactions by Account report. You will see that the amounts for the beginning balances of the assets, liabilities, and the owners' equity have been entered in this account. Thus, the value of the Other Capital account proves the fundamental accounting equation of Assets = Liabilities + Owner's Equity.

 Use QuickZoom to view the Your Last Name & Muir, Capital – Other account

Point to the amount 26,159.44, and double-click the primary mouse button
Change the report dates **From** is **12/31/17** and **To** is **01/31/18**, press Tab to generate the report

Your Name's Sierra Sports
Transactions by Account
As of January 31, 2018

Type	Date	Num	Adj	Name	Memo	Clr	Split	Debit	Credit	Balance
Inventory Adjust	12/31/2017				Sweaters Opening balance	✓	1120 · Inventory Asset		1,875.00	33,235.00
Inventory Adjust	12/31/2017				Underwear Opening balance	✓	1120 · Inventory Asset		264.00	33,499.00
Credit Card Charge	12/31/2017				Account Opening Balance		2100 · Visa	150.00		33,349.00
General Journal	12/31/2017				Account Opening Balance		2510 · Office Equipment Loan	3,000.00		30,349.00
General Journal	12/31/2017				Account Opening Balance		2520 · Store Fixtures Loan	2,500.00		27,849.00
Deposit	12/31/2017				Account Opening Balance		1100 · Checking		25,943.00	53,792.00
Deposit	12/31/2017				Account Opening Balance		1311 · Office Supplies		850.00	54,642.00
General Journal	12/31/2017				Account Opening Balance		1511 · Original Cost		5,000.00	59,642.00
General Journal	12/31/2017				Account Opening Balance		1521 · Original Cost		4,500.00	64,142.00
Deposit	12/31/2017				Account Opening Balance		1340 · Prepaid Insurance		250.00	64,392.00
General Journal	12/31/2017				Account Opening Balance		3111 · First and Last Name, Investment	20,000.00		44,392.00
General Journal	12/31/2017				Account Opening Balance		3121 · Larry Muir, Investment	20,000.00		24,392.00
Deposit	12/31/2017				Account Opening Balance		1312 · Sales Supplies		575.00	24,967.00
General Journal	12/31/2017						4999 · Uncategorized Income		6,942.44	31,909.44
General Journal	12/31/2017						6999 · Uncategorized Expenses	8,500.00		23,409.44
Inventory Adjust	01/08/2018				Sleds Opening balance	✓	1120 · Inventory Asset		675.00	24,084.44
Inventory Adjust	01/08/2018				Toboggans Opening balance	✓	1120 · Inventory Asset		1,375.00	25,459.44
Inventory Adjust	01/08/2018				Helmets Opening balance	✓	1120 · Inventory Asset		700.00	26,159.44
Total 3100 · Your Last Name & Muir, Capital								54,150.00	80,309.44	26,159.44
TOTAL								**54,150.00**	**80,309.44**	**26,159.44**

Partial Report

- Notice that the amounts shown include the amounts for the opening balances of all the assets including each inventory item, all the liabilities, the original investment amounts (equity), and uncategorized income and expenses.
- Uncategorized Income and Expenses reflect the income earned and expenses incurred prior to the current period. This prevents previous income/expenses being included in the calculation for the net income or loss for the current period.

Close the Transactions by Account report without printing

Do <u>not</u> close the Balance Sheet

DISTRIBUTE CAPITAL TO EACH OWNER

The Balance Sheet does not indicate how much of the Capital-Other should be distributed to each partner because 3100 - Your Last Name & Muir, Capital, is a combined Capital account. To clarify this section of the report, the capital should be distributed between the two owners. Since each owner has contributed an equal amount as an investment in the business, Capital-Other should be divided equally.

 Make an adjusting entry to distribute Capital-Other between the two owners

Access the **Make General Journal Entries** screen as previously instructed
The **Date** is **01/31/18**
This is not an adjusting entry, so remove the check mark
Transfer the amount in the account **3100 - Your Last Name & Muir, Capital –Other** to the owners' individual capital accounts by debiting Account **3100** for **26159.44**
Memo for all entries in the transaction is **Transfer Capital to Partners**

Transfer one-half of the amount entered in the DEBIT column to **3110 – First and Last Name, Capital**, by crediting this account

- To determine one-half of the amount, use QuickMath as follows: Click after the credit amount, press **/**, enter **2,** and press **Enter.**

Credit **3120 - Larry Muir, Capital**, for the other half of the amount

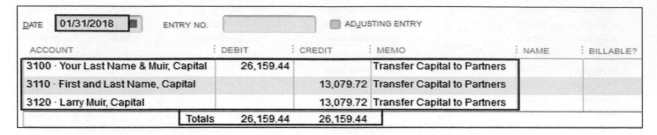

Click **Save & Close** to record and return to the Balance Sheet

- If the report does not automatically refresh, click **Refresh**.
- Notice the change in the Equity section of the Balance Sheet.
- The total of 3100 - Your Last Name & Muir, Capital, is still $64,159.44. There is no longer a 3100 - Your Last Name & Muir, Capital – Other account. Now, each owner has a Capital-Other account that shows 13,079.72.
- Look closely at the following balance sheet's equity section. Verify that your account setup matches the one shown in the text. Keep in mind that 3100 – Your Last Name & Muir, Capital, will show your actual last name. For example, the author's account would be Horne & Muir, Capital.
- Accounts 3110, 3111, 3112, and 3110 – Other should all have your actual <u>first</u> and <u>last</u> name rather than the words First and Last Name. For the author, Accounts 3110, 3111, 3112, and 3110 – Other would all have Janet Horne rather than First and Last Name.

Your Name's Sierra Sports
Balance Sheet
As of January 31, 2018

	Jan 31, 18
▼ **ASSETS**	
▶ **Current Assets**	72,462.65
▶ **Fixed Assets**	9,340.00
TOTAL ASSETS	**81,802.65**
▼ **LIABILITIES & EQUITY**	
▶ **Liabilities**	14,876.46
▼ **Equity**	
▼ **3100 · Your Last Name & Muir, Capital**	
▼ **3110 · First and Last Name, Capital**	
3111 · First and Last Name, Investment	20,000.00
3112 · First and Last Name, Drawing	-1,000.00
3110 · First and Last Name, Capital – Other	13,079.72
Total 3110 · First and Last Name, Capital	32,079.72
▼ **3120 · Larry Muir, Capital**	
3121 · Larry Muir, Investment	20,000.00
3122 · Larry Muir, Drawing	-1,000.00
3120 · Larry Muir, Capital – Other	13,079.72
Total 3120 · Larry Muir, Capital	32,079.72
Total 3100 · Your Last Name & Muir, Capital	64,159.44
Net Income	2,766.75
Total Equity	**66,926.19**
TOTAL LIABILITIES & EQUITY	**81,802.65**

Partial Report

Do <u>not</u> close the report

CLOSING ENTRIES

In traditional accrual-basis accounting, there are four entries that need to be made at the end of a fiscal year. These entries close income, expenses, and the drawing accounts and transfer the net income (or loss) into owners' equity.

Income and Expense accounts are closed when QuickBooks DT is given a closing date. This will occur later in this chapter. Once the closing date has been entered, reports prepared during the next fiscal year will not show any amounts in the income and expense accounts for the previous year.

However, QuickBooks DT does not close the owners' drawing accounts, nor does it transfer the net income into the owners' Capital accounts. If you prefer to use the power of the program and omit the last two closing entries, QuickBooks DT will keep a running account of the owner withdrawals, and it will put net Income into an Owners' Equity account. However, transferring the net income and drawing into the owners' Capital accounts provides a clearer picture of the value of the owners' equity.

ADJUSTMENT TO TRANSFER NET INCOME

Because Your Name's Sierra Sports is a partnership, the amount of net income should appear as part of each owner's capital account rather than appear as Owners' Equity. In many instances, this is the type of adjustment the CPA makes on the Accountant's Copy of the QuickBooks DT company files. The adjustment may be made before the closing date for the fiscal year, or it may be made after the closing has been performed. Because QuickBooks DT automatically transfers Net Income into Owner's Equity, which is categorized as a Retained Earnings Account type, the closing entry will transfer the net income into Owners' Equity and into each owner's capital account. This transfer is made by debiting Owners' Equity and crediting the owners' individual capital accounts. When you view a report before the end of the year, you will see an amount in Net Income and the same amount as a negative in Owners' Equity. If you view a report after the end of the year, you will not see any information regarding Owners' Equity or Net Income because the entry correctly transferred the amount to the owners' capital accounts.

On the Balance Sheet, Owners' Equity and/or Net Income appear as part of the equity section. The owners' Drawing and Investment accounts are kept separate from Owners' Equity.

 Evenly divide and transfer the net income into the 3110 - First and Last Name, Capital and 3120 - Larry Muir, Capital accounts

Select **Make General Journal Entries** as previously instructed
- Leave Adjusting Entry unmarked.

The **Date** is **01/31/18**

The first account used is **3000 Owners' Equity**

Debit **3000 Owners' Equity**, the amount of Net Income **2,766.75**
- Remember, Owner's Equity is a Retained Earnings type of account and contains all the net income earned by the business.

For the Memo record **Transfer Net Income into Capital**

Click the drop-down list arrow on the second line and select **3110 - First and Last Name, Capital** as the account

Use QuickMath to divide the 2,766.75 in half

Click after the 2,766.75 in the credit column, type /, type **2**, press **Enter**

- A credit amount of **1,383.38** should be entered for **3110 - First and Last Name, Capital**.

Click the drop-down list arrow and select **3120 Larry Muir, Capital** as the account, press Tab

- QuickBooks DT enters **1,383.37** as the credit amount for the next line.
- Because QuickBooks DT accepts only two numbers after a decimal point, the cents must be rounded. Thus, there is a 1¢ difference in the distribution between the two owners. If there is an uneven amount in the future, Larry will receive one cent more.

The Memo should be the same for all three lines

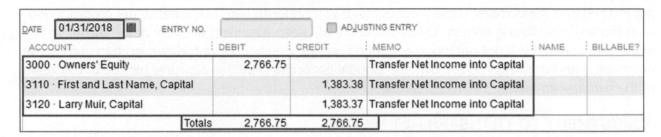

DATE 01/31/2018		ENTRY NO.		☐ ADJUSTING ENTRY			
ACCOUNT	DEBIT	CREDIT	MEMO			NAME	BILLABLE?
3000 · Owners' Equity	2,766.75		Transfer Net Income into Capital				
3110 · First and Last Name, Capital		1,383.38	Transfer Net Income into Capital				
3120 · Larry Muir, Capital		1,383.37	Transfer Net Income into Capital				
	Totals	2,766.75	2,766.75				

- Not all companies have a profit each month. If your business has a negative amount for net income, in other words, a loss, the appropriate adjustment would be to debit each owner's individual capital account and to credit Owners' Equity. For example, if Net Income (Loss) was -500.00, you would record the following: 3110 - First and Last Name, Capital—debit 250; 3120 - Larry Muir, Capital—debit 250; and 3000 Owners' Equity—credit 500.

Click **Save & Close** to record and close the **General Journal**

- If you get a Retained Earnings dialog box regarding posting a transaction to the Retained Earnings account "Owners' Equity," click **OK**.

VIEW BALANCE SHEET

Once the adjustment for Net Income/Owners' Equity has been performed, viewing or printing the Balance Sheet will show you the status of the Owners' Equity. If you keep the year as 2018, both Owners' Equity and Net Income are shown in the report. However, a Balance Sheet prepared for 2019 will show nothing for Owners' Equity or Net Income.

 Observe the effect of the adjustment to the owners' equity

Since you did not close the report, the Balance Sheet should still be on the screen

Your Name's Sierra Sports
Balance Sheet
As of January 31, 2018

	Jan 31, 18
▼ASSETS	
▶ Current Assets	72,462.65
▶ Fixed Assets	9,340.00
TOTAL ASSETS	81,802.65
▼LIABILITIES & EQUITY	
▶ Liabilities	14,876.46
▼ Equity	
3000 · Owners' Equity	-2,766.75
▼ 3100 · Your Last Name & Muir, Capital	
▼ 3110 · First and Last Name, Capital	
3111 · First and Last Name, Investment	20,000.00
3112 · First and Last Name, Drawing	-1,000.00
3110 · First and Last Name, Capital - Other	14,463.10
Total 3110 · First and Last Name, Capital	33,463.10
▼ 3120 · Larry Muir, Capital	
3121 · Larry Muir, Investment	20,000.00
3122 · Larry Muir, Drawing	-1,000.00
3120 · Larry Muir, Capital - Other	14,463.09
Total 3120 · Larry Muir, Capital	33,463.09
Total 3100 · Your Last Name & Muir, Capital	66,926.19
Net Income	2,766.75
Total Equity	66,926.19
TOTAL LIABILITIES & EQUITY	81,802.65

Partial Report

- Notice the change in the **Equity** section of the Balance Sheet. Both Net Income and Owners' Equity are shown and the amount in each owner's capital account has increased.

View a **Balance Sheet** for **January 2019**

Change the **As of** date to **01/31/2019**, press **Tab**

- Notice the Equity section. Nothing is shown for Owners' Equity or Net Income.

7

JOURNAL ENTRIES ENTERED/MODIFIED TODAY REPORT

When you record several entries into the General Journal during a given day, it can be helpful to see what has been recorded. The report is prepared in the Accountant Center. No matter what the transaction or computer dates are, the report will only include transactions that were entered today.

  Prepare Journal Entries Entered/Modified Today report in the Accountant Center

Point to **Accountant** on the Menu bar; click **Accountant Center**
In the **Memorized Reports** section, click **Journal Entries Entered/Modified Today**

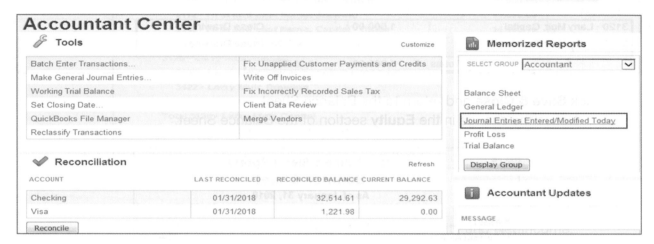

Since the date of your computer will not be 01/31/2018, enter the dates **From 01/31/18** and **To 01/31/18**, press Tab
Remove the Date Prepared and Time Prepared from the header
- This is a Memorized Report so does not use our header preferences.
- Your report may include your adjusting entries.
- Regardless of the transaction date, this report must be prepared the same day that you entered the transaction(s) in the General Journal.

Your Name's Sierra Sports
Journal Entries Entered/Modified Today
January 31, 2018

Trans #	Type	Entered/Last Modified	Date	Num	Name	Memo	Account	Debit	Credit
119	General Journal	01/31/2018 12:15:32	01/31/2018			Transfer Capital to Partners	3100 · Your Last Name & Muir, Capital	26,159.44	
						Transfer Capital to Partners	3110 · First and Last Name, Capital		13,079.72
						Transfer Capital to Partners	3120 · Larry Muir, Capital		13,079.72
								26,159.44	26,159.44
120	General Journal	01/31/2018 12:29:29	01/31/2018			Transfer Net Income into Capital	3000 · Owners' Equity	2,766.75	
						Transfer Net Income into Capital	3110 · First and Last Name, Capital		1,383.38
						Transfer Net Income into Capital	3120 · Larry Muir, Capital		1,383.37
								2,766.75	2,766.75
121	General Journal	01/31/2018 12:48:23	01/31/2018			Close Drawing	3110 · First and Last Name, Capital	1,000.00	
						Close Drawing	3112 · First and Last Name, Drawing		1,000.00
								1,000.00	1,000.00
122	General Journal	01/31/2018 12:50:36	01/31/2018			Close Drawing	3120 · Larry Muir, Capital	1,000.00	
						Close Drawing	3122 · Larry Muir, Drawing		1,000.00
								1,000.00	1,000.00
TOTAL								**30,926.19**	**30,926.19**

Do <u>not</u> print the report; close the report unless you are completing the following exercise

EXPORTING REPORTS TO EXCEL (OPTIONAL)

Many of the reports prepared in QuickBooks DT can be exported to Microsoft Excel. This allows you to take advantage of extensive filtering options available in Excel, hide detail for some but not all groups of data, combine information from two different reports, change titles of columns, add comments, change the order of columns, and experiment with "what if" scenarios. To use this feature of QuickBooks DT you must also have Microsoft Excel available for use on your computer.

 Optional Exercise: Export a report from QuickBooks DT to Excel

With the **Journal Entries Entered/Modified Today** report showing on the screen, click the **Excel** button, click **Create New Worksheet**
On the Send Report to Excel message, make sure **Create New Worksheet** and **in a new workbook** are selected or click to select

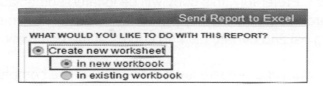

Click **Export**
- The report will be displayed in Excel.

Scroll through the report and click in Cell A18
Type **JOURNAL ENTRIES ENTERED/MODIFIED TODAY EXPORTED TO EXCEL**

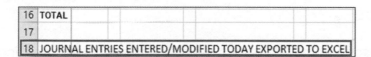

Click the **Close** button in the upper right corner of the Excel title bar to close **Excel**
Click **Don't Save** to close without saving
- You will see a Book number on the screen. The Book number changes depending on how many times you export reports to Excel.

Return to QuickBooks DT and close the report and the Accountant Center

IMPORTING DATA FROM EXCEL

There are several ways to import data into QuickBooks DT: You may use Intuit Interchange Format (.IIF) files to import lists, transactions, and data. You may also import an existing Excel or CSV file; you can enter data into a specially formatted spreadsheet and then add it to QuickBooks DT; or you can copy and paste data from Excel into QuickBooks DT by using the Add/Edit Multiple List Entries. An import file must conform to a specific structure for QuickBooks DT to interpret the data in the file correctly. QuickBooks DT has a built in Reference Guide for Importing Files that may be accessed and printed through Help. (Refer to Appendix B for more detailed information.)

JOURNAL FOR JANUARY

It is always wise to have a printed or hard copy of the data on disk. After all entries and adjustments for the month have been made, the Journal report for January should be printed. This copy should be kept on file as an additional backup to the data stored on your disk. If something happens to your disk to damage it, you will still have the paper copy of your transactions available for re-entry into the system. Normally, the Journal report would be printed before closing the period; however, we will print the Journal report at the end of the chapter so that all entries are included.

END-OF-PERIOD BACKUP

Once all end-of-period procedures have been completed, in addition to a regular backup copy of company data and a duplicate disk, a second duplicate disk of the company data should be made and filed as an archive disk. Preferably, this copy will be located someplace other than on the business premises. The archive disk or file copy is set aside in case of emergency or in case damage occurs to the original and current backup copies of the company data.

 Back up company data and prepare an archive copy of the company data

Prepare a Back Up as previously instructed
- In the **File Name** text box enter **Sierra 2018 (Archive 1-31-18)** as the name for the backup.
Also prepare a duplicate disk as instructed by your professor

CLOSE THE PERIOD

A closing date assigned to transactions for a period helps to prevent changing data from the closed period. To change a transaction after closing, you must acknowledge the entry in a dialog box before the change will be recorded. This is helpful to discourage casual changes or transaction deletions in a previous period. Setting the closing date is done by accessing Accounting Preferences in QuickBooks DT. Setting a closing date also closes the income and expenses for the period.

MEMO
DATE: January 31, 2018

Now that the closing entries for drawing and net income have been made, you want to protect the data and close income and expenses for the period. Set a closing date of 1/31/18.

 Assign the closing date of **01/31/18** to the transactions for the period ending 1/31/18

Click **Edit** on the menu bar, click **Preferences**
Click **Accounting**, click the **Company Preferences** tab
Click the **Set Date/Password** button
Enter **01/31/18** as the closing date in the Closing Date section of the Company Preferences for Accounting
Do <u>not</u> set any passwords at this time

Set Closing Date and Password

To keep your financial data secure, QuickBooks recommends assigning all other users their own username and password, in Company > Set Up Users.

DATE

QuickBooks will display a warning, or require a password, when saving a transaction dated on or before the closing date.   More details...

☐ Exclude estimates, sales orders and purchase orders from closing date restrictions

Closing Date   01/31/2018   📅

PASSWORD

QuickBooks strongly recommends setting a password to protect transactions dated on or before the closing date.

Closing Date Password

Confirm Password

To see changes made on or before the closing date, view the Closing Date Exception Report in Reports > Accountant & Taxes.

[OK]   [Cancel]

Click **OK**
- If you get a dialog box for No Password Entered, click **No**.

Click **OK** to close Preferences

ENTER CORRECTION TO CLOSED PERIOD

If it is determined that an error was made in a previous period, a correction is allowed. Before it will record any changes for previous periods, QuickBooks DT requires answering Yes on a dialog box warning of a change to a transaction that is prior to the closing date.

MEMO

DATE: January 31, 2018

After entering the closing date, Ruth reviews the Journal and reports printed at the end of January. She finds that $25 of the amount of Office Supplies should have been recorded as Sales Supplies. Transfer $25 from Office Supplies to Sales Supplies.

 Transfer $25 from Office Supplies to Sales Supplies

Access the **General Journal** as previously instructed
ADJUSTING ENTRY should be marked
Enter the DATE of **01/31/18**
The **ACCOUNT** is **1312 - Sales Supplies**
Enter the DEBIT of **25.00**
Enter the MEMO **Correcting Entry**
Use **ACCOUNT 1311 – Office Supplies** for the CREDIT
- The account 1311-Office Supplies will be shown.
- A credit amount of 25.00 should already be in the CREDIT column. If not, enter the amount.
- The MEMO **Correcting Entry** should appear.

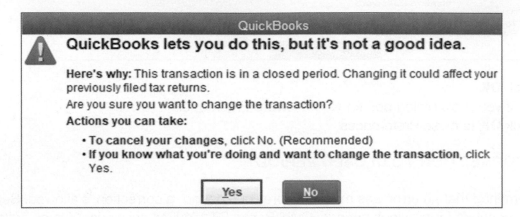

DATE 01/31/2018 🔲 ENTRY NO. ☑ ADJUSTING ENTRY					
ACCOUNT	DEBIT	CREDIT	MEMO	NAME	BILLABLE?
1312 · Sales Supplies	25.00		Correcting Entry		
1311 · Office Supplies ▾		25.00	Correcting Entry		
Totals	25.00	25.00			

Click **Save & Close**

Click **Yes** on the **QuickBooks DT** dialog box

QuickBooks

⚠ **QuickBooks lets you do this, but it's not a good idea.**

Here's why: This transaction is in a closed period. Changing it could affect your previously filed tax returns.

Are you sure you want to change the transaction?

Actions you can take:

- **To cancel your changes,** click No. (Recommended)
- **If you know what you're doing and want to change the transaction,** click Yes.

[Yes]   [No]

VERIFY CORRECTION TO OFFICE AND SALES SUPPLIES

Once the correction has been made, it is important to view the change in the accounts. The transfer of an amount of one asset into another will have no direct effect on the total assets in your reports. The account balances for Office Supplies and Sales Supplies will be changed. To view the change in the account, open the Chart of Accounts and look at the balance of each account. You may also use the account register to view the correcting entry as it was recorded in each account.

MEMO

DATE: January 31, 2018

Access the Chart of Accounts and view the change in the account balances and the correcting entry in each account's register.

 View the correcting entry in each account

Open the **Chart of Accounts** as previously instructed
- The balance for Office Supplies has been changed from 521.98 to 496.98.
- The balance for Sales Supplies has been changed from 400.00 to 425.00.

Double-click **Office Supplies** to open the account register
- Verify that the correcting entry was recorded for Office Supplies.

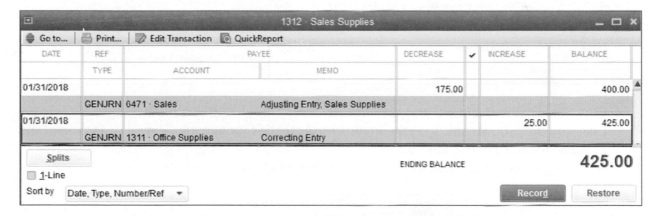

Close the **Office Supplies Register**

Repeat the steps to view the correcting entry in Sales Supplies

Close the **Sales Supplies Register** and the **Chart of Accounts**

INVENTORY ADJUSTMENTS

In a business that has inventory, it is possible that after a physical inventory is taken the number of items on hand is different from the quantity shown in QuickBooks DT. This can be caused by a variety of items: loss due to theft, fire, or flood; damage to an item in the stockroom; an error in a previous physical inventory. Even though QuickBooks DT uses the average cost method of inventory valuation, the value of an item can be changed as well. For example, assume that several pairs of after-ski boots are discounted and sold for a lesser value during the summer months. QuickBooks DT allows the quantity and value of inventory to be adjusted.

<u>MEMO</u>
DATE: January 31, 2018

After taking a physical inventory, you discover two hats that were placed next to the cleaning supplies and are discolored because bleach was spilled on them. These hats must be discarded. Record this as an adjustment to the quantity of inventory. Use the Expense account 6190 Merchandise Adjustments to record this adjustment.

 Adjust the quantity of hats

QuickBooks DT values inventory using the Average Cost Method
Open the Item List as previously instructed, double-click **Hats**
* Note the Avg. Cost of 8.00 for Hats.

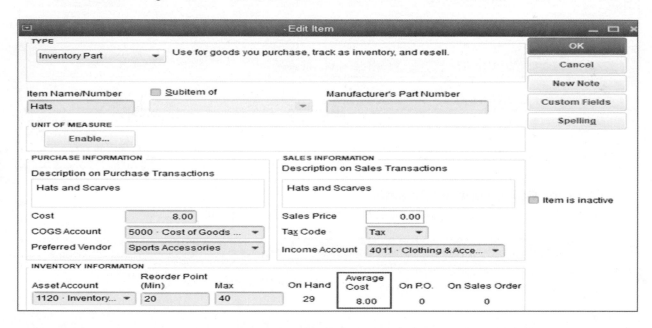

Close the Edit Item screen and the Item List
Click the drop-down arrow on the **Inventory Activities** icon in the Company section of the QuickBooks DT Home Page
Click **Adjust Quantity/Value On Hand...** in the list shown

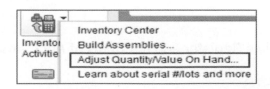

Enter the adjustment date of **013118**
Click the drop-down list arrow next to **Adjustment Account**
Click **<Add New>**
Enter the new account information:
  Type is **Expense**; Number is **6190**; Name is **Merchandise Adjustments**
  Click **Save & Close** to add the account

Click in the **ITEM** column, click the drop-down list arrow, and click **Hats**
Click in the **NEW QUANTITY** column for Hats
Enter **27**
Press **Tab** to enter the change

- Notice that the Total Value of the Adjustment is -16.00, which is -8.00 for each hat. The number of Item Adjustments is one. The Quantity on Hand is 27, Avg. Cost per Item is 8.00, and the Value is 216.00.

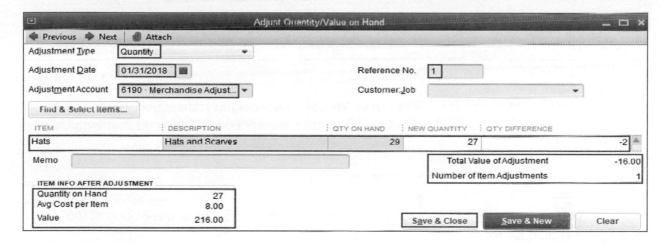

Click **Save & Close**
Click **Yes** on the **QuickBooks DT** dialog box regarding changing a transaction for a closed period

ADJUST NET INCOME/OWNERS' EQUITY JOURNAL ENTRY

The adjustment to inventory reduced the value of the inventory asset by $16.00 and increased the expenses of the business by $16.00. The change decreased the net income by $16.00; thus, the entry for Net Income/Owners' Equity made previously needs to be changed.

 Adjust the net income

Access **Make General Journal Entries**
Click **Previous** (back arrow icon) until you get to the entry debiting Owners' Equity for 2,766.75
To reduce the amount by $16.00, click after the **5**, press **–**, key in **16**, press **Enter** to change the debit to Owners' Equity to **2,750.75**
Change the credit to 3110 – First and Last Name, Capital by half of the amount of the adjustment (16 / 2 = 8) thus, 1383.38 – 8 = **1,375.38**
Change the credit to 3120 - Larry Muir, Capital by half the amount to **1,375.37**

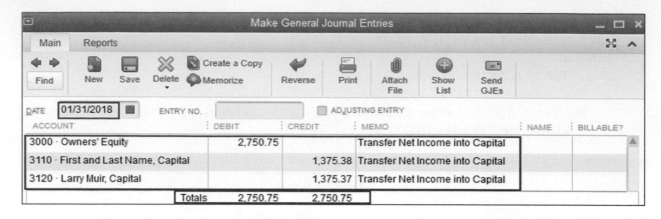

Click **Save & Close**

Click **Yes** or **OK** on all the dialog boxes for saving a changed transaction, recording a transaction in a closed period, and posting a transaction to Retained Earnings/Owners' Equity

REDO ARCHIVE COPY OF COMPANY FILE

Since we have made changes to transactions for the closed period, the archive copy of the company file should be redone.

   Create an archive copy of the company data

Replace the previous file **Sierra 2018 (Backup Archive 1-31-18)**
Follow the procedures given previously to make your backup files

REPORT FILTERS

When preparing a report, clicking the Customize Report tab and the Filters tab enables the selection of multiple items as a filter for reports. For example, you may select Account as a report filter, and then select "multiple accounts." Rather than select each account individually, a search screen appears where you can enter a value that can filter the list. In addition, there are Select All and Clear All buttons that may be used rather than having to select or deselect each item individually.

When preparing reports, there is now a Show/Hide option for report filters. The filters may be shown, hidden, edited, or deleted during report preparation. When the Show option is selected, the list of applied filters will be shown on the screen and printed on the last page of the report.

SCHEDULED REPORTS

You may set up a schedule for reports to be prepared automatically and then sent as a password protected PDF attachment to an email. The company file must be in Single-User Mode. (If in multi-user mode, the file may be switched to Single-user in the File menu.) Scheduled Reports is accessed through the Reports menu. The first step is to create the Schedule Setup by selecting the memorized reports to be prepared. The second step is to enter the scheduled time and frequency. The third and final step is to enter the details (including a password) for the email that will be sent to the selected recipients. To view scheduled reports, the Schedule Report Center is accessed. Because we are not sending password protected pdf reports, we will not be creating scheduled reports.

PREPARE REPORTS

After closing entries have been entered, it is important to print post-closing reports. Normally, those reports are dated as of the last day of or for the period. The only exception to the reports is the Profit & Loss Statement. To see that the income and expenses have been closed, the report is prepared as of the first day of the next period.

MEMO

DATE: January 31, 2018

Prepare and print the following reports for Your Name's Sierra Sports as of or for 01/31/18:
Journal, Trial Balance, Profit & Loss Report, and Balance Sheet.

JOURNAL REPORT

Since the Journal was not printed before closing the period, it should be printed at this time. This will give a printed copy of all the transactions made in Chapters 5, 6, and 7.

  Print the **Journal** for January

> Access the Journal as previously instructed
> **Expand** the report
> The dates are from **01/01/18** to **01/31/18**; Tab to generate the report
> Resize the columns so all names and accounts are shown in full and the report prints on one-page wide
> - Names, Memos, and Accounts may not necessarily be shown in full; however, make sure enough of the information shows so you can identify the names, sales items, and accounts used in transactions.

Your Name's Sierra Sports
Journal
January 2018

Trans #	Type	Date	Num	Adj	Name	Memo	Account	Debit	Credit
119	General Journal	01/31/2018				Transfer Capital to Partners	3100 · Your Last Name & Muir, Capital	26,159.44	
						Transfer Capital to Partners	3110 · First and Last Name, Capital		13,079.72
						Transfer Capital to Partners	3120 · Larry Muir, Capital		13,079.72
								26,159.44	26,159.44
120	General Journal	01/31/2018				Transfer Net Income into Capital	3000 · Owners' Equity	2,750.75	
						Transfer Net Income into Capital	3110 · First and Last Name, Capital		1,375.38
						Transfer Net Income into Capital	3120 · Larry Muir, Capital		1,375.37
								2,750.75	2,750.75
121	General Journal	01/31/2018				Close Drawing	3110 · First and Last Name, Capital	1,000.00	
						Close Drawing	3112 · First and Last Name, Drawing		1,000.00
								1,000.00	1,000.00
122	General Journal	01/31/2018				Close Drawing	3120 · Larry Muir, Capital	1,000.00	
						Close Drawing	3122 · Larry Muir, Drawing		1,000.00
								1,000.00	1,000.00
123	General Journal	01/31/2018		✓		Correcting Entry	1312 · Sales Supplies	25.00	
				✓		Correcting Entry	1311 · Office Supplies		25.00
								25.00	25.00
124	Inventory Adjust	01/31/2018	1				6190 · Merchandise Adjustments	16.00	
						Hats Inventory Adjustment	1120 · Inventory Asset		16.00
								16.00	16.00
TOTAL								**81,285.13**	**81,285.13**

Partial Report

Print the report in **Landscape** orientation
- If you print to a pdf file, save the document as **7-Your Name Journal Ch7**.

Close the **Journal**

PREPARE MULTIPLE REPORTS

When you are preparing a lot of reports at the same time, you have the option of telling QuickBooks DT to prepare multiple reports. While not every available report may be selected, frequently prepared reports are available. If you have customized report preferences, they will not be applied to multiple reports.

 Prepare and print the Trial Balance, the Profit & Loss Report, and the Balance Sheet using Multiple Reports

Reports	Window	Help
Report Center		
Memorized Reports		
Scheduled Reports		
Commented Reports		
Company Snapshot		
Process Multiple Reports		

Click **Reports** on the Menu Bar
Click **Process Multiple Reports**
On the Process Multiple Reports screen, select <All Reports>
Click **Accountant: Balance Sheet**, enter the report dates From
     01/01/18 To **01/31/18**
Repeat for Accountant: Profit & Loss, and Accountant: Trial Balance
- You can print reports directly from this screen or you can display the reports and then print from the actual reports.

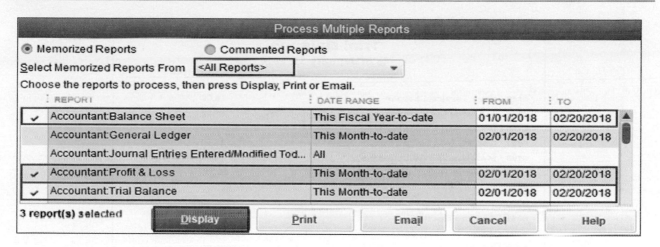

Click the **Display** button

With the reports on the screen, complete the following sections

TRIAL BALANCE

After closing the period has been completed, it is helpful to print a Trial Balance. This proves that debits still equal credits.

 Print a **Trial Balance** to prove debits still equal credits

Scroll through the report and study the amounts shown
- Notice that the final totals of debits and credits are equal.
- In Chapter 5, the header information for the report was customized so that it did not show the Date Prepared, Time Prepared, or Report Basis. That would apply to reports prepared from the Report Center or Reports menu not to Multiple Reports.

If your instructor had you customize your reports in Chapter 5, customize the Report so the Date Prepared, Time Prepared, and Report Basis are not displayed

Make sure the columns are displayed in full

To save this format in the Multiple Report list, click the **Memorize** button

Click **Replace** on the Memorize Report message box

Close the Trial Balance

Prepare the report again by clicking **Reports** on the Menu bar, and clicking **Multiple Reports**

Click **Accountant: Trial Balance** on the Process Multiple Reports screen, make sure the dates are **01/01/18** to **01/31/18**, click the **Display** button
- The report is displayed using the customized format.

Your Name's Sierra Sports
Trial Balance
As of January 31, 2018

	Jan 31, 18	
	Debit	Credit
6120 · Bank Service Charges	18.00	
6140 · Advertising Expense	95.00	
6150 · Depreciation Expense	160.00	
6181 · Liability Insurance	125.00	
6190 · Merchandise Adjustments	16.00	
6212 · Loan Interest	97.93	
6300 · Rent	950.00	
6340 · Telephone	156.40	
6391 · Gas and Electric	359.00	
6392 · Water	85.00	
6471 · Sales	175.00	
6472 · Office	350.00	
7010 · Interest Income		54.05
TOTAL	91,271.55	91,271.55

Partial Report

Print in **Portrait** orientation, then close the report

- If you print to a pdf file, save the document as **8-Your Name Trial Bal Ch7**.

PROFIT & LOSS REPORT

Since the closing was done as of January 31, 2018, the Profit & Loss Report for January 31, 2018 will give the same data as a Profit & Loss Report prepared manually on January 31, 2018. To verify the closing of income and expense accounts for January, you would prepare a Profit & Loss Report for February 1. Since no income had been earned or expenses incurred in the new period, February, the Net Income will show $0.00.

   Print a Profit & Loss report for January and view the report for February

The report should be showing on the screen
Check with your instructor to see if you should remove the Date Prepared, Time Prepared, and Report Basis as previously instructed

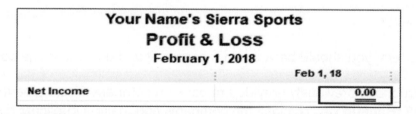

Your Name's Sierra Sports
Profit & Loss
January 2018

	Jan 18
▼ Ordinary Income/Expense	
▼ Income	
▶ 4010 · Sales	9,195.95
4050 · Sales Discounts	-494.36
4090 · Returned Check Charges	25.00
Total Income	8,726.59
▼ Cost of Goods Sold	
▶ 5000 · Cost of Goods Sold	3,442.56
Total COGS	3,442.56
Gross Profit	5,284.03
▶ Expense	2,587.33
Net Ordinary Income	2,696.70
▼ Other Income/Expense	
▶ Other Income	54.05
Net Other Income	54.05
Net Income	2,750.75

Partial Report

- Report shown above is partially collapsed. It shows section totals but not individual account totals.
- Note the Net Income of $2,750.75.

Print the January report in **Portrait** orientation

- If you print to a pdf file, save the document as **9-Your Name P & L Ch7**.

To view the effect of closing the period, prepare the Profit & Loss report for February

Change the dates From **02/01/18** to **02/01/18**, tab to generate the report

Your Name's Sierra Sports
Profit & Loss
February 1, 2018

	Feb 1, 18
Net Income	0.00

- Note the Net Income of **0.00**.

Close the **February Profit & Loss Report** without printing

BALANCE SHEET

The proof that assets equal liabilities and owners' equity after the closing entries have been made needs to be displayed in a Balance Sheet. Because this report is for a month, the adjustment to Owners' Equity and Net Income will result in both accounts being included on the Balance Sheet. If, however, this report was prepared for the following year, neither account would appear.

  Print a Balance Sheet report for January 31, 2018

The report should be showing on the screen

Check with your instructor to see if you should customize the header to remove the Date Prepared, Time Prepared, and Report Basis

Scroll through the report to view the assets, liabilities, and equities listed
- Because this report is for a one-month period, both Owners' Equity and Net Income are included on this report.

Your Name Mountain Sports **Balance Sheet** As of January 31, 2015	Jan 31, 15
▶ **ASSETS**	81,786.65
▼ **LIABILITIES & EQUITY**	
▶ **Liabilities** ▶	14,876.46 ◀
▼ **Equity**	
3000 · Owners' Equity	-2,750.75
▼ 3100 · Your Last Name & Muir, Capital	
▼ 3110 · First and Last Name, Capital	
3111 · First and Last Name, Investment	20,000.00
3110 · First and Last Name, Capital - Other	13,455.10
Total 3110 · First and Last Name, Capital	33,455.10
▼ 3120 · Larry Muir, Capital	
3121 · Larry Muir, Investment	20,000.00
3120 · Larry Muir, Capital - Other	13,455.09
Total 3120 · Larry Muir, Capital	33,455.09
Total 3100 · Your Last Name & Muir, Capital	66,910.19
Net Income	2,750.75
Total Equity	66,910.19
TOTAL LIABILITIES & EQUITY	81,786.65

Partial Report

Print the report, orientation is **Portrait**, then close the **Balance Sheet**
- If you print to a pdf file, save the document as **10-Your Name Bal Sheet Ch7**.

BACKUP COMPANY

As in previous chapters, you should back up your company and then close the company.

 Follow instructions previously provided to back up company files, name the backup **Sierra 2018 (Backup Ch. 7)**, close the company, and make a duplicate disk

SUMMARY

In this chapter, end-of-period adjustments were made, bank and credit card reconciliations were performed, backup (duplicate) and archive disks were prepared, and adjusting entries were made. A credit card reconciliation was "undone" and then completed correctly. The use of Drawing, Net Income, and Owners' Equity accounts were explored and interpreted for a partnership. The closing date for a period was assigned. Account names were changed, and new accounts were created. Even though QuickBooks DT focuses on entering transactions on business forms, a Journal recording each transaction is kept by QuickBooks DT. This chapter presented transaction entry directly into the General Journal. The difference between accrual-basis and cash-basis accounting was discussed. Owner withdrawals and distribution of capital to partners were examined. Many of the different report options and preparation procedures available in QuickBooks DT were explored, and a report was exported to Microsoft Excel. A variety of reports were printed after closing the period. Correction of errors was analyzed, corrections were made after the period was closed, and adjustments were made to inventory. The fact that QuickBooks DT does not require an actual closing entry at the end of the period was addressed.

END-OF-CHAPTER QUESTIONS

TRUE/FALSE

ANSWER THE FOLLOWING QUESTIONS IN THE SPACE PROVIDED BEFORE THE QUESTION NUMBER.

_____ 7.01. The owner's drawing account should be transferred to capital each week.

_____ 7.02. Fixed assets are used in a business within one year.

_____ 7.03. Frequent transactions may be memorized.

_____ 7.04. If Show All is selected, inactive accounts will not appear in the Chart of Accounts.

_____ 7.05. When you reconcile a bank statement, anything entered as a service charge will automatically be entered as a transaction when the reconciliation is complete.

_____ 7.06. Once the reconciliation of an account is completed, it may not be undone.

_____ 7.07. An account that is not needed may be voided.

_____ 7.08. At the end of the year, QuickBooks DT transfers the net income into Owner's Equity.

_____ 7.09. A withdrawal by an owner in a partnership reduces the owner's capital.

_____ 7.10. Inventory adjustments due to damage or loss of inventory items results in income.

MULTIPLE CHOICE

WRITE THE LETTER OF THE CORRECT ANSWER IN THE SPACE PROVIDED BEFORE THE QUESTION NUMBER.

_____ 7.11. The Fixed Asset Item list includes the name of the asset, the date of purchase, and the ___.
A. cost of the asset
B. asset account to use
C. description of the asset
D. All of the above

_____ 7.12. Adjustments for accrual basis accounting generally include adjustments to ___.
A. petty cash
B. office supplies
C. sales discounts
D. accounts payable

7

_____ 7.13. If reports are prepared for the month of January in the current year, net income will appear in the___.
A. Profit & Loss Statement
B. Balance Sheet
C. both A and B
D. neither A nor B

_____ 7.14. In QuickBooks DT, you export reports to Microsoft Excel to___.
A. print the report
B. explore "what if" scenarios with data from QuickBooks DT
C. prepare checks
D. all the above

_____ 7.15. QuickBooks DT uses the ___ method of inventory valuation.
A. LIFO
B. Average Cost
C. FIFO
D. Actual Cost

_____ 7.16. If a transaction is recorded in the General Journal, it may be viewed ___.
A. in the Journal
B. in the register for each balance sheet account used in the transaction
C. by preparing an analysis graph
D. in both A and B

_____ 7.17. Entries for bank collections of automatic payments ___.
A. are automatically recorded at the completion of the bank reconciliation
B. must be recorded after the bank reconciliation is complete
C. should be recorded when reconciling the bank statement
D. should be recorded on the first of the month

_____ 7.18. The account(s) that may be reconciled is (are) ___.
A. Balance Sheet accounts
B. Profit & Loss accounts
C. the Customer list account
D. Trial Balance accounts

_____ 7.19.   The closing entry for a drawing account transfers the balance of an owner's drawing account into the ___ account.
A. Retained Earnings
B. Net Income
C. Owner's Capital
D. Investment

_____ 7.20.   When using the accrual basis of accounting for the month of November, sales on account were $1,000.00 and the purchase of one year of insurance for $600.00 would result in the Profit & Loss report showing a ___.
A. $400.00 Profit
B. $950.00 Profit
C. $600.00 Loss
D. $1,000.00 Profit

FILL-IN

IN THE SPACE PROVIDED, WRITE THE ANSWER THAT MOST APPROPRIATELY COMPLETES THE SENTENCE.

7.21.   No matter where transactions are recorded, they all appear in the _____.

7.22.   _____ -basis accounting matches income and expenses against a period, and _____ -basis accounting records income when the money is received and expenses when the purchase is made, or the bill is paid.

7.23.   In a partnership, each owner has a share of all the _____ , _____ , and Net Income based on the percentage of his or her investment in the business or according to any partnership agreements.

7.24.   A report that you have customized by sizing, adding, and/or removing columns may be _____ so the custom format is used each time it is prepared.

7.25.   The reduction of an inventory item due to loss or damage will result in a(n) _____ to the amount of the adjusting entry to transfer Net Income into Capital.

SHORT ESSAY

Describe the entry that is made to transfer net income into the owner's capital account. Include the reason this entry should be made and how income will be listed if transfer is not recorded.

_____
_____
_____
_____
_____
_____

END-OF-CHAPTER PROBLEM

YOUR NAME'S CALIFORNIA CASUAL

Chapter 7 continues with the end-of-period adjustments, bank and credit card reconciliations, archive disks, and closing the period for Your Name's California Casual. The company does use a certified public accountant for guidance and assistance with appropriate accounting procedures. The CPA has provided information for Elizabeth to use for adjusting entries, etc.

INSTRUCTIONS

Continue to use the copy of Your Name's California Casual you used in the previous chapters. Open the company—the file used is **Casual 2018.qbw**. Record the adjustments and other transactions as you were instructed in the chapter. Always read the transaction carefully and review the Chart of Accounts when selecting transaction accounts. Print the reports and journals as indicated and resize columns for a full display of information.

RECORD TRANSACTIONS

January 31, 2018:
► Change the names and/or the account numbers and delete the descriptions of the following accounts:
  - **6260 - Printing and Reproduction** to **6260 Printing and Duplication**
  - **6350 - Travel & Ent** to **6350 - Travel Expenses**
  - **3010 - Your Last Name & Jones, Capital** to **3100 - Your Last Name & Jones, Capital**
    - Remember to use your **actual** <u>last</u> name.
► Add the following accounts:
  - Equity account **3110 - First and Last Name, Capital** (subaccount of **3100**)
    - Remember to use both your real first and last name.
  - Equity account **3120 - Elizabeth Jones, Capital** (subaccount of **3100**)
► Change the following accounts:
  - **3011 – Your First&LastName, Investment** to **3111 - First and Last Name, Investment** (subaccount of **3110**)
    - Remember to use both your real first and last name.
    - The original name of Your First&LastName, Investment did not have room for any spacing. Be sure to space between your actual first name and last name.
  - **3013 – Your First & Last Name, Drawing** to **3112 - First and Last Name, Drawing** (subaccount of **3110**)
    - Remember to use both your real first and last name.
  - **3012 - Elizabeth Jones, Investment** to **3121 - Elizabeth Jones, Investment** (subaccount of **3120**)
  - **3014 - Elizabeth Jones, Drawing** to **3122 Elizabeth Jones, - Drawing** (subaccount of **3120**)
  - **6422 – Office** to **6422 – Office Supplies** (subaccount of **6420 - Supplies Expense**)

▶ Make the following accounts inactive:
  - **6291 - Building Repairs**
  - **6351 - Entertainment**
▶ Delete the following accounts:
  - **6182 - Disability Insurance**
  - **6213 - Mortgage**
  - **6823 - Property**
▶ Print an Account Listing in Landscape orientation.
  - Do *not* show inactive accounts (If necessary, click Include inactive to remove the check mark).
  - Click the Reports button at the bottom of the Chart of Accounts and click Account Listing to display the report.
  - Resize the columns to display the Account Names in full and to hide the columns for Description, Accnt. #, and Tax Line.
  - Change the Header/Footer so the report date is January 31, 2018.
  - Print the report and if you print to a pdf file, save the document as **1-Your Name Acct List Ch7**.
▶ Create a Fixed Asset Item List for:
  - Asset Name/Number: **Office Equipment**, Item is: **New**, Purchase and Asset Description: **Office Equipment**, Date: **12/31/17**, Cost: **$8,000**, Asset Account: **1510**
  - Asset Name/Number: **Store Fixtures**, Item is: **New**, Purchase and Asset Description: **Store Fixtures**, Date: **12/31/17**, Cost: **$9,500**, Asset Account: **1520**
  - Prepare the Fixed Asset Listing by clicking **Reports** at the bottom of the Fixed Asset List, change the report date to **January 31, 2018**, print the report .
    - If you print to a pdf file, save the document as **2-Your Name Fixed Asset List Ch7**.
▶ Enter adjusting entries in the General Journal and use the memo Adjusting Entry for the following:
  - Office Supplies Used, the amount used is $35.
  - Sales Supplies Used, account balance (on hand) at the end of the month is $1,400.
  - Record a compound entry for depreciation for the month: Office Equipment, $66.67 and Store Fixtures, $79.17.
  - The amount of insurance remaining in the Prepaid Insurance account is for six months of liability insurance. Record the liability insurance expense for the month.
▶ Prepare a Working Trial Balance. For each account, use the amount in the Beginning Balance column, add or subtract the amounts in Transactions column and/or Adjustments column to verify the totals in the Ending Balance column. Do *not* print the report.
▶ Each owner withdrew $500. (Memo: January Withdrawal) Print Check Nos. 7 and 8 for the owners' withdrawals. If you print to a pdf file, save the document as **3-Your Name Cks 7-8 Ch7**.
▶ Prepare Bank Reconciliation and Enter Adjustments for the Reconciliation. (Refer to the chapter for appropriate Memo notations).

CENTRAL COAST BANK
1234 Coast Highway
San Luis Obispo, CA 93407
805-555-9300

Your Name's California Casual
2716 Marsh Street
San Luis Obispo, CA 93407

Acct. 987-352-9152   January 31, 2018

Beginning Balance, January 1, 2018			**32,589.00**
1/15/18, Deposit	3,023.30		35,612.30
1/15/18, Deposit	2,450.05		38,062.35
1/15/18, NSF Returned Check Kristie Carson		325.00	37,737.35
1/15/18, NSF Charges, Kristie Carson		15.00	37,722.35
1/15/18, Check 1		59.39	37,662.96
1/18/18, Check 2		343.00	37,319.96
1/18/18, Check 3		156.80	37,163.16
1/25/18, Check 4		1,150.00	36,013.16
1/25/18, Check 5		79.85	35,933.31
1/31/18, Service Charge		10.00	35,923.31
1/31/18, Office Equipment Loan Pmt.: $44.51 Interest, $8.61 Principal		53.12	35,870.19
1/31/18, Store Fixtures Loan Pmt.: $53.42 Interest, $10.33 Principal		63.75	35,806.44
1/31/18, Interest	73.30		35,879.74
Ending Balance, January 31, 2018			**$35,879.74**

▶ Print a Detailed Reconciliation Report in Portrait. Adjust column widths so the report fits on one page. If you print to a pdf file, save the document as **4-Your Name Bank Rec Detail Ch7**.

▶ Reconcile the Visa account using the following statement.

CENTRAL COAST BANK
1234 Coast Highway
San Luis Obispo, CA 93407
805-555-9300

Your Name's California Casual
2716 Marsh Street
San Luis Obispo, CA 93407

VISA Acct. #4187-5234-9153-235   January 31, 2018

Beginning Balance, January 1, 2018			0.00
1/9/2018 Contempo Clothing		196.00	196.00
1/18/2018, Office Masters		250.00	446.00
Minimum Payment Due: $50.00		**Payment Due Date: February 5, 2018**	

▶ Print a Detailed Reconciliation Report in Portrait. Pay Central Coast Bank for the Visa bill using Check 9. Print Check 9. If you print to a pdf file, save the documents as **5-Your Name CC Rec Ch7**, and **6-Your Name Ck 9 Ch7**.

▶ Prepare an Adjusted Trial Balance for 01/01/18 to 01/31/18. Verify the Adjusted Balance by adding or subtracting the Adjustments from the Unadjusted Balance. Size the columns to display information in full. Print the report. If you print to a pdf file, save the document as **7-Your Name Adj Trial Bal Ch7**. (Is your adjusted balance $76,553.07?)

▶ Distribute capital to each owner: divide the balance of 3100 - Your Last Name & Jones, Capital - Other equally between the two partners. (View a Balance Sheet (Standard) to see the balance of the Capital – Other account.) Record an entry to transfer each owner's portion of the Capital - Other to the individual capital accounts. (Memo: Transfer Capital to Partners) Remember, this is not an adjusting entry.

▶ Divide in half and transfer Net Income/Owners' Equity into owners' individual Capital accounts. Remember, this is not an adjusting entry.

▶ Close Drawing accounts into owner's individual Capital accounts.

▶ Prepare an archive copy of the company file.

▶ Close the period as of January 31, 2018 (Do not assign passwords).

▶ After closing the period on 01/31/18, discovered an error in the amount of Office Supplies and Sales Supplies: Transfer $40 from Office Supplies to Sales Supplies.

▶ After closing the period on 01/31/18, found one damaged tie. Adjust the quantity of ties on 01/31/18 using the Expense account 6190 Merchandise Adjustments.

▶ Change the net income/Owners' Equity adjustment to reflect the merchandise adjustment for the ties.

▶ Backup the company and redo the archive copy of the company file as well.

▶ Print the Journal for January, 2018 (Landscape orientation, Fit to one page wide). If you print to a pdf file, save the document as **8-Your Name Journal Ch7**.

▶ Print the following reports:

- Trial Balance, January 1-31, 2018. If you print to a pdf file, save the document as **9-Your Name Trial Bal Ch7**.
- Profit & Loss Report, January 31, 2018. If you print to a pdf file, save the document as **10-Your Name P & L Ch7**.
- Balance Sheet, January 31, 2018. If you print to a pdf file, save the document as **11-Your Name Bal Sheet Ch7**.

7

CHAPTER 7 CHECKLISTS

YOUR NAME'S SIERRA SPORTS

The checklist below shows all the business forms and reports printed during training. Check each one that you printed. In the document names below, Your Name and Ch7 have been omitted, and report dates are given.

___ 1-Acc List
___ 2-Fixed Asset List
___ 3-Cks 6-7
   Ck 6 Your First and Last Name
   Ck 7 Larry Muir
___ 4-Bank Rec, January 1-31, 2018

___ 5-Visa Rec, January 1-31, 2018
___ 6-Ck 8 Old Mammoth Bank
___ 7-Journal, January 1-31, 2018
___ 8-Trial Bal, January 1-31, 2018
___ 9-P & L, January 1-31, 2018
___ 10-Bal Sheet, January 1-31, 2018

YOUR NAME'S CALIFORNIA CASUAL

The checklist below shows all the business forms and reports printed during training. Check each one that you printed. In the document names below, Your Name and Ch7 have been omitted, and report dates are given.

___ 1-Acc List
___ 2-Fixed Asset List
___ 3-Cks 7-8
   Ck 7 Your First and Last Name
   Ck 8 Elizabeth Jones
___ 4-Bank Rec, January 1-31, 2018
___ 5-Visa Rec, January 1-31, 2018

___ 6-Ck 9 Central Coast Bank
___ 7-Adj Trial Bal, January 1-31, 2018
___ 8-Journal, January 1-31, 2018
___ 9-Trial Bal, January 1-31, 2018
___ 10-P & L, January 1-31, 2018
___ 11-Bal Sheet, January 1-31, 2018

PRACTICE SET 2
MERCHANDISING BUSINESS

YOUR NAME'S DESERT GOLF

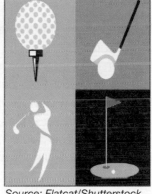

Source: Flatcat/Shutterstock

The following is a comprehensive practice set combining all the elements of QuickBooks DT studied in Chapters 5-7 of the text. Since the version of QuickBooks DT is 2018, the text shows the year as 2018. In this practice set, you will record transactions for the month of January, 2018. Check with your instructor to find out what year you should use when recording transactions. Entries will be made to record invoices, sales orders, receipt of payments on invoices, cash sales, credit card sales, debit card sales, receipt and payment of bills, purchase orders and receipts of merchandise, credit memos for invoices and bills, sales tax payments, and credit card payments. Account names will be added, changed, deleted, and made inactive. Customers, vendors, owners, and fixed assets will be added to the appropriate lists. Reports will be prepared, customized, memorized, and commented on to analyze sales, bills, receipts, and items ordered. Formal reports including the Trial Balance, Profit and Loss Statement, and Balance Sheet will be prepared. Adjusting entries for depreciation, supplies used, insurance expense, and automatic payments will be recorded. Both bank and credit card reconciliations will be prepared. Entries to display partnership equity for each partner will be made. The end of period closing will be completed.

PS
2

YOUR NAME'S DESERT GOLF

Located in La Quinta, California, Your Name's Desert Golf is a full-service golf shop that sells golf equipment and clothing. Even though Anne's name is not part of the company name, Your Name's Desert Golf is a partnership owned and operated by Anne Wells and you. Each partner contributed an equal amount to the partnership. You buy the clothing and accessory items and keep the books for the company. Anne buys the equipment and manages the store. There are several part-time employees working for the company selling merchandise.

INSTRUCTIONS

Use the file **Desert_2018.qbw**.

Remember, if the file name shows as Desert 2018.qbw that is fine, too.

When entering transactions, you are responsible for entering any memos. Unless otherwise specified, the terms for each sale or bill will be the terms on the Customer List or Vendor List. The Customer Message is usually *Thank you for your business*. However, any other appropriate message may be used. If a customer's order exceeds the established credit limit, accept the order and process it.

If the terms allow a discount for a customer, make sure to apply the discount if payment is made within the discount period. Use the Income account 4050 Sales Discounts as the discount account. On occasion, a payment may be made within the discount period but not received or recorded within it. Information within the transaction will indicate whether the payment is equivalent to a full payment. For example, if you received $98 for an invoice for $100 shortly after the discount period and the transaction indicated payment in full, apply the discount. If a customer has a credit and has a balance on the account, apply the credit to the appropriate invoice for the customer. If a customer pays a bill within the discount period and has a credit, make sure to calculate the discount on the payment amount <u>after</u> subtracting the credit. If there is no balance for a customer and a return is made, issue a credit memo and a refund check.

Always pay bills in time to take advantage of purchase discounts. Use the Cost of Goods Sold Account 5200 Merchandise Discounts for the discount account. Remember that the discount due date will be ten days from the date of the bill.

Invoices, sales orders, purchase orders, and other business forms should be printed as they are entered. To save time, printing Payment Receipts or Bills is optional. Check with your professor regarding what you should print. (All required and optional printouts are listed on the checklist.)

You may memorize transactions and reports at your discretion. If you wish to use the Prepare Multiple Reports feature, make sure to remove the Date Prepared, Time Prepared, and Report Basis from the heading unless your instructor specified that you include them on your reports.

Print business forms with lines around each field. Determine the orientation of the document for printing. Whenever possible, adjust the column widths so that account names, amounts, and item names are displayed in full and so that reports fit on one page wide. If necessary, select Fit report to one page wide. If you print your documents to a pdf file, save the documents using the same naming format that you used in the chapter. For example, 1-Your Name Report Name PS2 or 1-Your Name Business Form and Last Name PS2.

Back up your work at the end of each week.

The following lists are used for all vendors, customers, and sales items. You will be adding additional customers and vendors as the company is in operation.

Vendors:

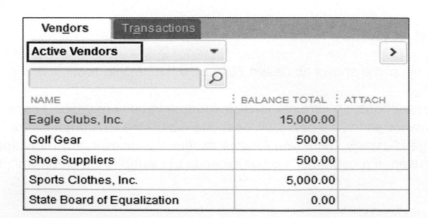

NAME	BALANCE TOTAL	ATTACH
Eagle Clubs, Inc.	15,000.00	
Golf Gear	500.00	
Shoe Suppliers	500.00	
Sports Clothes, Inc.	5,000.00	
State Board of Equalization	0.00	

Customers:

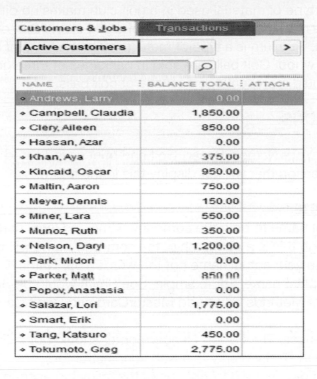

Sales Items:

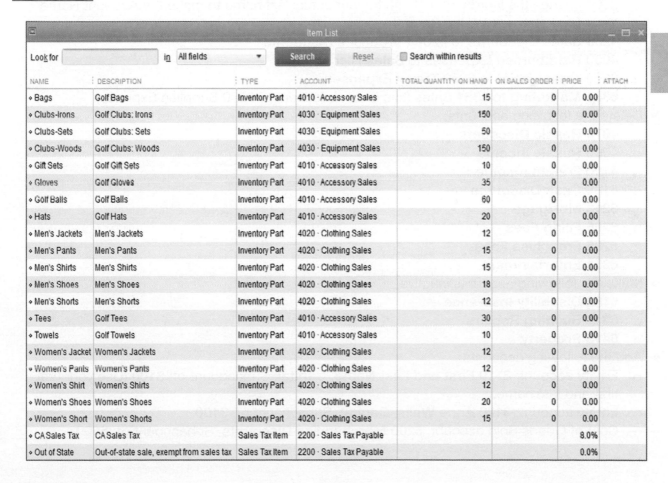

Note: Individual golf clubs are categorized as irons or woods. A complete set of clubs would be categorized as a set. The type of material used in a golf club makes no difference in a sales item. For example, graphite is a material used in the shaft of a golf club. A set of graphite clubs would refer to a set of golf clubs. Titanium is a type of metal used in the head of a golf club. A titanium wood would be sold as a wood. Golf balls are sold in packages of three golf balls called sleeves; thus, a quantity of one would represent one package of golf balls.

RECORD TRANSACTIONS:

Enter the transactions for Your Name's Desert Golf and print as indicated. If you get messages you do not want, click the selection that will <u>not</u> display this in the future.

Week 1—January 2-8, 2018:
► Add your First and Last name to both the company name and legal name for Your Name's Desert Golf. Even though this is a partnership, the company name will be **Your Name's Desert Golf**. (Remember to use your actual name *not* the words Your Name. Don't forget the apostrophe s after your last name. For example, Sue Smith would be Sue Smith's Desert Golf.)
► Customize the Payment Methods list to add MasterCard and Debit Card. Remove Discover Card.
► Change Report Preferences: The Report Header/Footer should *not* include the Date Prepared, Time Prepared, or Report Basis. (Verify this with your instructor.)
► Change the names and delete the descriptions of the following accounts:
   o **3100** change the words Your Name to your actual last name to make the Account Name **Your Last Name & Wells, Capital**
   o **4200 Sales Discounts** to **4200 Purchases Discounts**
   o **4050 Reimbursed Expenses** to **Sales Discounts**
   o **6350 Travel & Ent** to **6350 Travel Expenses**
   o **6381 Marketing** to **6381 Sales** (this is a subaccount of 6380 Supplies Expense)
► Delete the following accounts:
   o **4070 Resale Discounts**
   o **4090 Resale Income**
   o **4100 Freight Income**
   o **6130 Cash Discounts**
   o **6213 Mortgage**
   o **6265 Filing Fees**
   o **6285 Franchise Fees**
   o **6351 Entertainment**
► Make the following accounts inactive:
   o **6182 Disability Insurance**
   o **6311 Building Repairs**
   o **6413 Property**
► Add the following accounts:
   o Equity account: **3110 First and Last Name, Capital**, Subaccount of: **3100** (Use your real first and last name.)
   o Equity account: **3120 Anne Wells, Capital**, Subaccount of: **3100**
   o Cost of Goods Sold account: **5200 Merchandise Discounts**, Subaccount of: **5000**

▶ Change the following accounts:
- o **3500 Your First&LastName, Investment** to **3111 First and Last Name, Investment**; Subaccount of: **3110**. Use your <u>real</u> first and last name. Note: due to exceeding the allowed number of characters, there are no spaces between First&LastName.
- o **3400 Your First & Last Name, Drawing** to **3112 First and Last Name, Drawing**; Subaccount of: **3110**. Use your <u>real</u> first and last name.
- o **3300 Anne Wells, Investment** to **3121**, Subaccount of: **3120**
- o **3200 Anne Wells, Drawing** to **3122**, Subaccount of: **3120**

▶ Use the Reports Menu to access the List reports. Resize the columns so the Account Names, Type, and Balance Total show in full. Do <u>not</u> show the Description, Accnt. #, or Tax Line columns. Click the Customize Report button; on the Header/Footer tab change the report date to **January 2, 2018**. Print the **Account Listing** in portrait orientation. If you print to a pdf file, save the document as **1-Your Name Acct List PS2**.

▶ Create Fixed Asset Item List:
- o Asset Name: **Office Equipment**, Item is: **New**, Purchase and Asset Description: **Office Equipment**, Date: **12/31/17**, Cost: **5,000.00**, Asset Account: **1510 Office Equipment**.
- o Asset Name: **Store Fixtures**, Item is: **New**, Purchase and Asset Description: **Store Fixtures**, Date: **12/31/17**, Cost: **6,000.00**, Asset Account: **1520 Store Fixtures**.

▶ Prepare the Fixed Asset Item List Report. Resize the columns so all column information shows in full. Click the Customize Report button; on the Header/Footer tab change the report date to **January 2, 2018**. Print the Fixed Asset Item List. If you print to a pdf file, save the document as **2-Your Name Fixed Asset List PS2**.

▶ Customize **Sales Receipts**, **Purchase Orders**, **Sales Orders**, **Credit Memos**, and **Intuit Product Invoices** so that the Default Title is in all capital letters and your name will print in full on the same line as the company name.
- o Don't forget to use Basic Customization on the Copy of the Product Invoice and select **Print Past Due Stamp**.

▶ Add the Vendor: **Palm Springs Rentals**; Main Phone: **760-555-8368**; Fax **760-555-8638**; Address: **11-2951 Palm Canyon Drive, Palm Springs, CA 92262**; Payment Terms: **Net 30**. Account Settings: **6280 Rent**.

▶ Prepare a bill for Palm Springs Rentals enter the amount $2800; then Memorize the Transaction. Select **Add to my Reminders List**, How Often **Monthly**, Next Date **01/25/18**, click **OK** to memorize. Do <u>not</u> save the bill, click the **Clear** button and then close Enter Bills.

▶ Add the credit card information to Greg Tokumoto's account. Preferred Payment Method: **Visa**, Credit Card Number: **4532 5828 0103 1424**, Expiration: **03/21**. Remember to tab to fill in the name, address, and zip code.

▶ Once you complete adding Greg Tokumoto's Visa to his account, go to the Company menu, select, **Customer Credit Card Protection**. Click **Enable Protection**, complete the **Sensitive Data Protection Setup**: User Name: **Admin**, Current Password: **QBDT2018**, New and Confirmation Password: **2018QBDT**, Challenge Question: **Name of your first manager**? Answer: **Enter your professor's last name**.

▶ Print invoices, checks, sales orders, and other items as they are entered in the transactions. Check with your instructor to see if you should print Bills and Payment Receipts. They are listed on the Checklist just in case you print them.

PS
2

1/2/2018

▶ Sold 2 pairs of women's shorts @ $64.99 each, 2 women's shirts @ $59.99 each, 1 women's jacket @ $129.99, and 1 pair of women's shoes @ $179.99 to Anastasia Popov on account. (Remember: Use <u>Copy of: Intuit Product Invoice</u>. The symbol @ means at.) Print Invoice 1. If you print to a pdf file, save the document as **3-Your Name Inv 1 Popov PS2**. (Don't forget to include the name of the business form used if you print to a pdf file.)

▶ Having achieved her goal of a handicap under 30, Claudia Campbell treated herself to the new clubs she had been wanting. Sold on account 1 set of graphite clubs @ $750, 1 golf bag @ $129.95, and 5 sleeves (packages) of golf balls @ $6.95 each. (Remember to accept sales that are over the credit limit.) If you print to a pdf file, save the document as **4-Your Name Inv 2 Campbell PS2**.

▶ Change the terms for Erik Smart to Net 10. (Add a new Payment Term for Net 10.)

▶ Change Claudia Campbell's credit limit to $3,000.00.

▶ Change Azar Hassan's credit limit to $2,500.00.

▶ Azar heard that titanium would give him extra yardage with each shot. Sold 4 titanium woods (Clubs-Woods) on account to Azar Hassan @ $459.00 each. If you print to a pdf file, save the document as **5-Your Name Inv 3 Hassan PS2**.

▶ Sold 5 golf bags @ $59.99 each and 5 sets of starter clubs @ $159.99 each to Palm Springs Schools on account for the high school golf team. Palm Springs Schools, Main Phone: 760-555-4455, Main Email: **PSSchools@ps.edu**, Address: 99-4058 South Palm Canyon Drive, Palm Springs, CA 92262, Payment Terms: Net 30, Preferred Delivery Method: Mail, Credit Limit: $1,500. Even though Palm Springs Schools is a nonprofit organization, it is required pay California Sales Tax on all purchases. Include a subtotal for the sale and apply a 10% sales discount for a nonprofit organization. (Create any new sales items necessary.) If you print to a pdf file, save the document as **6-Your Name Inv 4 Palm Springs Schools PS2**.

▶ Received a telephone sales order from Dennis Meyer for 2 pairs of men's shorts @ $49.95 each, 2 men's shirts @ $59.99 each, 1 pair of men's golf shoes @ $119.99, a starter set of golf clubs for his son @ $250.00, and a new titanium driver for himself @ $549.95 (a driver is a Golf Club: Woods). If you print to a pdf file, save the document as **7-Your Name SO 1 Meyer PS2**.

▶ Correct and reprint Invoice 2 to Claudia Campbell. The golf bag price should be $179.95. If you print to a pdf file, save the document as **8-Your Name Inv 2 Campbell Corrected PS2**.

▶ Received from Greg Tokumoto, $2,175, in partial payment of his account. He made his payment using the Visa Credit Card on file. (Did you leave this as an underpayment?) If you print to a pdf file, save the document as **9-Your Name Rcv Pmt Tokumoto PS2**.

1/3/2018

▶ Sold 3 gift sets @ $14.99 each, 3 sleeves (packages) of golf balls @ $8.95 each, and 5 Golf Hats @ $25.99 to Dr. Lori Salazar on account to be given away as door prizes at an upcoming ladies' tournament. If you print to a pdf file, save the document as **10-Your Name Inv 5 Salazar PS2**.

▶ Dennis Meyer came into the store to pick up the merchandise on Sales Order 1. Create an invoice for all items from the sales order. (Use the date January 3, 2018.) Since a Sales Order Invoice is different from a regular Product Invoice, customize the Sales Order Invoice so the Default Title is INVOICE; use Basic Customization and click Print Past Due Stamp to select; resize the title INVOICE and Your Name's Desert Golf so there is room for your name on the same line. Print the invoice. (Go to Sales Order 1 and verify that each item is CLSD and that it is marked "Invoiced in Full.") If you print to a pdf file, save the document as **11-Your Name Inv 6 Meyer PS2**.

▶ Received Check 1023 for payment in full from Matt Parker for $850. If you print to a pdf file, save the document as **12-Your Name Rcv Pmt Parker PS2**.

▶ Sold a golf bag @ $99.95 and 2 golf towels @ $9.95 each to a cash customer using Visa Card Number: 4024 0071 8138 6862, Expiration: 07/23. (Remember to print Sales Receipt 1.) Did you use QuickAdd to add the Cash Customer? If you print to a pdf file, save the document as **13-Your Name SR 1 Cash Cust PS2**.

▶ Took a telephone sales order from a new customer Laura Hansen for 1 pair of women's golf shoes @ $149.95 and a set of golf clubs @ $895.00. New Customer info: Laura Hansen (Remember, last name first in the Customer List), Main Phone: 760-555-3322, Address: 45-2215 PGA Drive, Rancho Mirage, CA 92270, Copy the Address to Ship To 1, Payment Terms: 1% 10 Net 30, Preferred Delivery Method: Mail, Credit Limit: $1,500, taxable customer for California Sales Tax. If you print to a pdf file, save the document as **14-Your Name SO 2 Hansen PS2**.

▶ Received Debit Card Number: 5526 3374 5019 0624, Expiration: 06/24 for $950 from Daryl Nelson in partial payment of his account. If you print to a pdf file, save the document as **15-Your Name Rcv Pmt Nelson PS2**.

1/5/2018

▶ Laura Hansen came into the store to pick up merchandise ordered on Sales Order 2. Create the invoice from the sales order. Use the sales order date (January 3, 2018). If you print to a pdf file, save the document as **16-Your Name Inv 7 Hansen PS2**.

▶ In the Item List, change the Item Name/Number from Hats to Men's Hats. The purchase and sales descriptions should be Men's Golf Hats. Change the Reorder Point (Min) from 15 to 12 and Max from 25 to 20.

▶ Prepare and print an Inventory Stock Status by Item Report for January 1-5, 2018. Resize the columns, use Landscape orientation, and select Fit Report to 1 page wide. If you print to a pdf file, save the document as **17-Your Name Inventory Stock Status PS2**.

▶ Prepare Purchase Orders for all items marked Order on the Inventory Stock Status by Item Report. Place all orders with the preferred vendors. Prepare only one purchase order per vendor. For all items, order the number shown in the Reorder Quantity column of the Inventory Stock Status by Item report. The cost of golf bags is $40 each, gift sets are $3 each, men's shorts are $20 each, towels are $2 each, and women's shirts are $20 each. (Remember to print the purchase orders. If you get a message to change the cost for the item, click No.) If you print to a pdf file, save the documents as **18-Your Name PO 1 Golf Gear PS2** and **19-Your Name PO 2 Sports Clothes PS2**.

▶ Add a new inventory sales item: Women's Hats. The purchase and sales descriptions are Women's Golf Hats. Leave the cost and sales price at 0.00. The COGS account is 5000. Head Gear, Inc. is the preferred vendor (Add the new vendor: Head Gear, Inc., Main Phone: 310-555-8787, Main Email: **HeadGear@la.com**, Fax: 310-555-7878, Address: 45980 West Los Angeles Street, Los Angeles, CA 90025, Credit Limit: $500, Payment Terms: 2% 10 Net 30). The hats are taxable. The Income account is 4010-Accessory Sales. The Asset account is 1120-Inventory Asset. The Reorder Point (Min) is 10 and the Max is 20. Quantity on Hand is 0 as of 01/05/2018.

▶ Order 5 women's hats @ $10.00 each from Head Gear, Inc. Print the Purchase Order. If you print to a pdf file, save the document as **20-Your Name PO 3 Head Gear PS2**.

▶ Print a Purchase Order QuickReport in Landscape orientation for January 1-5, 2018. If you print to a pdf file, save the document as **21-Your Name PO QuickReport PS2**.

PS
2

1/8/2018

▶ Received Check 1822 for a cash sale of 2 men's golf hats @ $49.95 each. If you print to a pdf file, save the document as **22-Your Name SR 2 Cash Cust PS2**.

▶ Deposit all receipts (cash, checks, debit cards, and credit cards) for the week. Print the Deposit Summary. If you print to a pdf file, save the document as **23-Your Name Dep Sum PS2**.

▶ Backup your work for Week 1. Name your backup file **Desert (Backup Week 1)**.

Week 2—January 9-15:
1/10/2018

▶ Received the order from Head Gear, Inc. without the bill. If you print to a pdf file, save the document as **24-Your Name Item Rct Head Gear PS2**.

▶ Use 01/10/2018 for the bill date for both of the following transactions. Received the merchandise ordered and the bill from Golf Gear. All items were received in full except the golf bags. Of the 12 bags ordered, only 8 were received. The remaining golf bags are on backorder. Also received all the merchandise ordered and the bill from Sports Clothes, Inc. If you print to a pdf file, save the documents as **25-Your Name Bill Golf Gear PS2** and **26-Your Name Bill Sports Clothes PS2**.

▶ Dr. Lori Salazar returned 1 of the gift sets purchased on January 3. Issue a credit memo and apply it to Invoice 5. Create a new customer message to use on credit memos: **Your return has been processed.** If you print to a pdf file, save the document as **27-Your Name CM 8 Salazar PS2**.

▶ Matt Parker returned 1 pair of men's golf shorts that had been purchased for $59.95. (The shorts had been purchased previously and were part of his $850 opening balance.) Since his balance was paid in full, issue and print a refund check. Did you use the new credit memo message? If you print to a pdf file, save the documents as **28-Your Name CM 9 Parker PS2** and **29-Your Name Ck 1 Parker PS2**.

▶ Received a telephone order for 1 complete set of golf clubs from Greg Tokumoto for $1,600. If you print to a pdf file, save the document as **30-Your Name SO 3 Tokumoto PS2**.

▶ Sold two irons—a graphite sand wedge and a graphite gap wedge—@ $119.95 each to a cash customer using Debit Card Number: 5526 3374 5019 0624, Expiration Date: 02/2021. (Both clubs are classified as irons.) If you print to a pdf file, save the document as **31-Your Name SR 3 Cash Cust PS2**.

1/12/2018

▶ Greg Tokumoto came to the store and picked up the merchandise from Sales Order 3. Create the invoice from the sales order and use the sales order date for the invoice. If you print to a pdf file, save the document as **32-Your Name Inv 10 Tokumoto PS2**.

▶ Received the telephone bill for the month, $85.15 from Desert Telephone Co., Main Phone: 760-555-9285, Address: 11-092 Highway 111, Palm Springs, CA 92262, Payment Terms: Net 30, Account Settings: 6340 Telephone. If you print to a pdf file, save the document as **33-Your Name Bill Desert Telephone PS2**.

▶ Use the company Visa card to purchase $175 of office supplies to have on hand from Indio Office Supply, Main Phone: 760-555-1535, Fax: 760-555-5351, Main Email: **IOS@office.com** Address: 3950 46th Avenue, Indio, CA 92201. (Credit card charges may not be printed.)

1/14/2018

▶ The bill for the items received from Head Gear, Inc. on 1/10 arrived. Use 01/14/2018 for the bill date. If you print to a pdf file, save the document as **34-Your Name Bill Head Gear PS2**.

► Received Check 3801 for $1,963.05 from Azar Hassan in full payment of his bill. (The transaction date is 01/14/18. The payment appropriately includes the discount since the check was dated 01/10/18.) If you print to a pdf file, save the document as **35-Your Name Rcv Pmt Hassan PS2**.

► Received Check 783 for $598.69 from Anastasia Popov in full payment of her bill (The payment includes the discount since the check was dated 01/11/18.) If you print to a pdf file, save the document as **36-Your Name Rcv Pmt Popov PS2**.

► Deposit all receipts (checks, debit and credit cards, and/or cash) for the week. Print the Deposit Summary. If you print to a pdf file, save the document as **37-Your Name Dep Sum PS2**.

► Back up your work for Week 2. Name the file **Desert (Backup Week 2)**.

Week 3—January 16-22:
1/17/2018

► Oscar Kincaid purchased 1 set of golf clubs @ $1,200, 1 golf bag @ $250, 1 pair of men's shoes @ $195, and 1 putter (iron) @ $195 on account. If you print to a pdf file, save the document as **38-Your Name Inv 11 Kincaid PS2**.

► Received Check 6708 for $1,976.72 from Dr. Lori Salazar in full payment of her account. (Note: The Payment amount for Invoice 5 includes the credit for the gift set.) If you print to a pdf file, save the document as **39-Your Name Rcv Pmt Salazar PS2**.

► Received the remaining 4 golf bags and the bill from Golf Gear on an earlier purchase order. The date of the bill is 01/16/2018. If you print to a pdf file, save the document as **40-Your Name Bill Golf Gear PS2**.

1/18/2018

► Prepare an Unpaid Bills Detail report. Add a column for Terms. Memorize the Report and name it Unpaid Bills with Terms Detail. Using the date of the bill and the 10-day discount period, calculate which bills are eligible to receive a discount if paid between January 18 and 22. Write the comment Pay this Bill on each bill to be paid. (If you can take a discount for a bill paid after January 22, do not include it on this report.) Print the commented report. (Remember, if you have been instructed to export reports to Excel, you cannot export a commented report.) If you print to a pdf file, save the document as **41-Your Name Comment Unpaid Bills with Terms PS2**.

► Pay all bills marked in the Commented Unpaid Bills Report. Use Account 5200 Merchandise Discounts as the Discount Account. (Print the checks: you may use Print Forms to print a batch, or you may print them individually.) Did you pay two bills? If you print to a pdf file, save the document as **42-Your Name Cks 2-3 PS2**.

► Sold 1 golf bag @ $199.95, 1 set of graphite golf clubs @ $1,200.00, 1 putter @ $129.95 (record the putter as Golf Clubs: Irons), and 3 sleeves of golf balls @ $9.95 each on account to Dr. Lori Salazar. If you print to a pdf file, save the document as **43-Your Name Inv 12 Salazar PS2**.

► Returned 2 men's shirts that had poorly stitched seams at a cost of $20 each to Sports Clothes, Inc. Received Credit Memo 1045 from the company. If you print to a pdf file, save the document as **44-Your Name Bill Credit Sports Clothes PS2**.

1/20/2018

► Dr. Oscar Kincaid returned the putter (iron) he purchased on January 17. Issue a Credit Memo and apply it to Invoice 11. Did you use the credit memo customer message? If you print to a pdf file, save the document as **45-Your Name CM 13 Kincaid PS2**.

PS
2

- ► Sold 1 men's golf hat @ $49.95, 1 men's jacket @ $89.95, 1 towel @ $9.95, 2 packages of golf tees @ $1.95 each, and 16 sleeves of golf balls @ $5.95 each to a Cash Customer using MasterCard Number: 5413 7118 9363 2804, Expiration: 04/23. If you print to a pdf file, save the document as **46-Your Name SR 4 Cash Cust PS2**.
- ► A businessman in town with his wife bought them each a set of golf clubs @ $1,495.00 per set and a new golf bag for each of them @ $249.95 per bag. He purchased 1 men's jacket @ $179.95. His wife purchased 1 pair of golf shoes @ $189.99 and 1 women's jacket @ $149.99. He paid for the purchases using his Visa Card Number: 4024 0071 8138 6862, Expiration: 05/24. If you print to a pdf file, save the document as **47-Your Name SR 5 Cash Cust PS2**.
- ► Prepare and print an Inventory Stock Status by Item Report for January 1-20. If you print to a pdf file, save the document as **48-Your Name Inventory Stock Status PS2**.
- ► Edit the Item Golf Balls insert a space in the Purchase Description between Golf and Balls.
- ► Prepare Purchase Orders to order any inventory items indicated on the report. As with earlier orders, use the preferred vendor and issue only one purchase order per vendor. For all items except Men's Hats, order the number shown in the Reorder Quantity column of the Inventory Stock Status by Item report. For Men's Hats, we get a better price if we order at least 10 hats, so order a quantity of 10. (Golf balls cost $3.50 per sleeve, men's and women's jackets cost $20 each, and men's and women's hats cost $10 each.) If you print to a pdf file, save the documents as **49-Your Name PO 4 Golf Gear PS2**, **50-Your Name PO 5 Sports Clothes PS2**, and **51-Your Name PO 6 Head Gear PS2**.
- ► Deposit all receipts (checks, credit cards, and/or cash) for the week. Print the Deposit Summary. If you print to a pdf file, save the document as **52-Your Name Dep Sum PS2**.
- ► Back up your work for Week 3. Name the file **Desert (Backup Week 3)**.

Week 4 and End of Period—January 23-31:
1/23/2018

- ► Prepare the memorized report Unpaid Bills with Terms Detail. Using the date of the bill and the 10-day discount period, calculate which bills are eligible to receive a discount if paid between January 23 and 30. Write the comment Pay this Bill on each bill to be paid. Print the commented report. (Remember, if you have been instructed to export reports to Excel, you cannot export a comment report.) If you print to a pdf file, save the document as **53-Your Name Comment Unpaid Bills with Terms PS2**.
- ► Pay all bills indicated in the Commented Unpaid Bills with Terms Detail report. Did you pay two bills? If you print to a pdf file, save the document as **54-Your Name Cks 4-5 PS2**.
- ► Dr. Lori Salazar was declared Club Champion and won a prize of $500. She brought in the $500 cash as a partial payment to be applied to the amount she owes on her account. If you print to a pdf file, save the document as **55-Your Name Rcv Pmt Salazar PS2**.

1/24/2018

- ► Received the bill and all the items ordered from Sports Clothes, Inc. and Golf Gear. The bills are dated 01/23/2018. If you print to a pdf file, save the documents as **56-Your Name Bill Sports Clothes PS2** and **57-Your Name Bill Golf Gear PS2**.
- ► Received Check 1205 from Claudia Campbell as payment in full on her account. (No discounts applicable.) If you print to a pdf file, save the document as **58-Your Name Rcv Pmt Campbell PS2**.

1/25/2018

▶ Received Check 305 for $1,741.07 as payment in full for Invoice 11 from Dr. Oscar Kincaid. Since a Credit Memo was issued for Invoice 11, recalculate the discount to determine the appropriate amount. Since he is not paying his opening balance of $950.00, include a memo of Partial Payment. If you print to a pdf file, save the document as **59-Your Name Rcv Pmt Kincaid PS2**.

▶ Received the bill and all the hats ordered from Head Gear, Inc. The date of the bill is 01/23/2018. If you print to a pdf file, save the document as **60-Your Name Bill Head Gear PS2**.

▶ Purchased sales supplies to have on hand for $150 from Indio Office Supply. Used the company Visa for the purchase.

▶ Prepare an Unpaid Bills with Terms Detail Report for January 25, 2018. Add comments to indicate payment and amounts for all bills dated 12/31/17: Eagle Clubs, Inc. pay $5,000. (Your comment should say **Pay $5,000**), Golf Gear pay $500, and Shoe Suppliers pay $500.00. Sports Clothes, Inc. pay $1,000 (Also, add a comment for the Credit Use this Credit.). Print the commented report. (Remember, if you have been instructed to export reports to Excel, you cannot export a commented report.) If you print to a pdf file, save the document as **61-Your Name Comment Unpaid Bills with Terms PS2**.

▶ Pay the following bills for the amounts indicated in the Commented Report and print checks as a batch. Due Date for all bills will show as 01/10/2018.
  ○ Pay $5,000 to Eagle Clubs, Inc. toward the amount owed on 12/31/2017. (Change the payment amount in the Amt. To Pay column from 15,000 to 5,000.)
  ○ Pay $500 to Golf Gear to pay the amount owed on 12/31/2017.
  ○ Pay $500 to Shoe Suppliers to pay the amount owed on 12/31/2017.
  ○ Pay $1,000 to Sports Clothes, Inc., for the amount owed on 12/31/2017. (NOTE: Select the bill you want to pay. Apply the credit you have from Sports Clothes, Inc., because of returned merchandise. You want to pay $1,000 plus use the $40 credit and reduce the amount owed by $1,040, *not* $960. Once the credit is applied, you will see the Amount To Pay as $4,960. Since you are not paying the full amount owed, click in Amt. To Pay column and enter the amount you are paying. In this case, enter 1,000. When the payment is processed, $1,000 will be deducted from cash to pay for this bill and the $40 credit will be applied.)
  ○ If you print to a pdf file, save the document as **62-Your Name Cks 6-9 PS2**.

▶ Received the bill dated 01/25/18 for $2,800 rent from Palm Springs Rentals. Use Memorized Transaction List to Enter Transaction and record the bill. If you print to a pdf file, save the document as **63-Your Name Bill Palm Springs Rentals PS2**.

1/26/2018

▶ Use the Reports menu, Vendors & Payables section to prepare an Unpaid Bills Detail Report for January 26, 2018. (*Note:* check Sports Clothes, Inc., the total amount owed should be $4,360. If your report does not show this, check to see how you applied the credit when you paid bills. If necessary, QuickBooks DT does allow you to delete the previous bill payment and redo it. If this is the case, be sure to apply the credit, and record $1,000 as the payment amount.) Print the Report. If you print to a pdf file, save the document as **64-Your Name Unpaid Bills PS2**.

▶ Greg Tokumoto used his Visa card on file to pay $1,600 as a partial payment. (The opening balance has $600 applied and Invoice 10 has $1,000 applied automatically by QuickBooks DT. Accept these amounts.) If you print to a pdf file, save the document as **65-Your Name Rcv Pmt Tokumoto PS2**.

PS
2

1/29/2018

▶ Deposit all receipts for the week. If you print to a pdf file, save the document as **66-Your Name Dep Sum PS2**.

1/30/2018

▶ Use Pay Bills and pay the Rent. Print the check. If you print to a pdf file, save the document as **67-Your Name Ck 10 Palm Springs Rentals PS2**.

▶ Received the NSF (Bounced) Check 1205 Check from Claudia Campbell back from the bank. This check was for $2,891.88. Charge her the bank charge of $15 plus Your Name's Desert Golf's own NSF charge of $30. In the Chart of Accounts, change the Account Number for Returned Check Charges to 4090. Change the Terms to "Due on Receipt" for the Opening Balance Invoice, for Invoice 2, and for Invoice 14 that was automatically prepared for the Bounced Check Charge. For Invoice 14, make sure the date is 01/30/18 and use the Copy of: Intuit Product Invoice. Print all three invoices. (The Opening Balance Invoice was prepared before customizing invoices. Use it as is.) If you print to a pdf file, save the documents as **68-Your Name Opening Bal Inv Campbell Revised PS2**, **69-Your Name Inv 2 Campbell Revised PS2**, and **70-Your Name Inv 14 Campbell PS2**.

▶ Prepare Sales Tax Liability Report from January 1-30, 2018. Adjust the column widths and print the report in Landscape orientation. The report should fit on one page. If you print to a pdf file, save the document as **71-Your Name Sales Tax Liab PS2**.

▶ Pay sales tax due as of January 30, 2018 and print Check 11. If you print to a pdf file, save the document as **72-Your Name Ck 11 State Board of Equal PS2**.

▶ Print a Sales by Item Summary Report for January 1-30. Use Landscape orientation and, if necessary, adjust column widths so the report fits on one page wide. If you print to a pdf file, save the document as **73-Your Name Sales by Item Sum PS2**.

▶ Enter the following adjusting entries:
  ○ Office Supplies Used for the month is $125.
  ○ The balance of the Sales Supplies is $600 on January 30.
  ○ The amount of Prepaid Insurance represents the liability insurance for 12 months. Record the adjusting entry for the month of January.
  ○ Depreciation for the month is: Office Equipment, $83.33, Store Fixtures, $100.

▶ Record the transactions for owner's equity:
  ○ Each owner's withdrawal for the month of January is $2,000. Print the checks. If you print to a pdf file, save the document as **74-Your Name Cks 12-13 PS2**.
  ○ Divide the amount in account 3100-Your Your Last Name & Wells, Capital - Other, and transfer one-half the amount into each owner's individual Capital account. (You may view a Standard Balance Sheet for January 30 to determine the amount to divide.)

▶ Prepare and print an Adjusted Trial Balance for January. If you print to a pdf file, save the document as 75-Your Name Adj Trial Bal PS2.

▶ Back up your work for Week 4. Name the file **Desert (Backup Week 4)**.

01/31/2018

▶ Use the following bank statement to prepare a bank reconciliation. Enter adjustments.

DESERT BANK 1234-110 Highway 111 Palm Springs, CA 92270 **Your Name's Desert Golf** 55-100 PGA Boulevard Palm Springs, CA 92270 Acct. # 9857-32-922		(760) 555-3300 January 2018
Beginning Balance, January 1, 2018			$35,275.14
1/8/2018, Deposit	4,212.33		39,487.47
1/10/2018, Check 1		64.75	39,422.72
1/14/2018, Deposit	2,820.83		42,243.55
1/18/2018, Check 2		365.54	41,878.01
1/25/2018, Check 3		392.00	41,486.01
1/23/2018, Check 4		156.80	41,329.21
1/23/2018, Check 5		49.00	41,280.21
1/25/2018, Deposit	6,576.21		47,856.42
1/25/2018, Check 6		5,000.00	42,856.42
1/25/2018, Check 7		500.00	42,356.42
1/25/2018, Check 8		500.00	41,856.42
1/25/2018, Check 9		1,000.00	40,856.42
1/25/2018, Check 10		2,800.00	38,056.42
1/30/2018, NSF Returned Check Claudia Crostini		2,891.88	35,164.54
1/30/2018, NSF Bank Charge		15.00	35,149.54
1/31/2018, Service Charge, $15		15.00	35,134.54
1/31/2018, Store Fixtures Loan Pmt.: Interest, $89.03; Principal, $17.21		106.24	35,028.30
1/31/2018, Office Equipment Loan Pmt: Interest, $53.42; Principal, $10.33		63.75	34,964.55
1/31/2018, Interest	76.73		35,041.28
Ending Balance, January 31, 2018			**35,041.28**

▶ Print a Detailed Reconciliation Report. If you print to a pdf file, save the document as **76-Your Name Bank Rec PS2**.

▶ Received the Visa bill. Prepare a Credit Card Reconciliation.

DESERT BANK
VISA DEPARTMENT
1234-110 Highway 111
Palm Springs, CA 92270   (760) 555-3300

Your Name's Desert Golf

55-100 PGA Boulevard
Palm Springs, CA 92270
VISA Acct. # 9287-52-952   January 2018

Beginning Balance, January 1, 2018			0.00
1/12/2018, Indio Office Supply		175.00	175.00
1/25/2018, Indio Office Supply		150.00	325.00
Ending Balance, 1/25/2018			325.00

Minimum Payment Due, $50.00   **Payment Due Date: February 7, 2018**

▶ Print Check 14 for the credit card payment to Desert Bank and print a Reconciliation Summary Report. If you print to a pdf file, save the documents as **77-Your Name Visa Rec PS2** and **78-Your Name Ck 14 Desert Bank PS2**.

▶ View a Profit & Loss (Standard) report for 01/01/18 to 01/31/18 to get the information needed to divide the net income in half. Close the report without printing.

▶ Divide the Net Income/Owners' Equity in half and transfer one-half into each owner's individual capital account. (This is not an adjusting entry.)

▶ Close the drawing account for each owner into the owner's individual capital account. (This is not an adjusting entry.)

▶ Close the period using the closing date of 01/31/2018. Do not use a password.

▶ Edit a transaction from the closed period: Discovered an error in the Supplies accounts. Transfer $50 from 1320-Sales Supplies to 1310-Office Supplies.

▶ Adjust the number of tees on hand to 24. Use the expense account 6190 for Merchandise Adjustments. Be sure to correct the adjustment for net income/ retained earnings.

▶ Prepare an Archive Backup named **Desert (Archive 01-31-18)**.

Print Reports and Back Up

▶ Print the following:
  o Journal (Landscape orientation, Fit on one page wide) for January, 2018. If you print to a pdf file, save the document as **79-Your Name Journal PS2**.
  o Trial Balance, January 31, 2018 (Portrait orientation). If you print to a pdf file, save the document as **80-Your Name Trial Bal PS2**.
  o Standard Profit and Loss Statement, January 1-31, 2018. If you print to a pdf file, save the document as **81-Your Name P & L PS2**.
  o Standard Balance Sheet, January 31, 2018. If you print to a pdf file, save the document as **82-Your Name Bal Sheet PS2**.

▶ Back up your work to **Desert (Backup Complete)**.

PRACTICE SET 2 CHECKLIST

YOUR NAME'S DESERT GOLF

Check the items below as you complete and/or print them; then attach the documents and reports in the order listed when you submit them to your instructor. Printing is optional for Payment Receipts and Bills (unless your instructor requires them to be printed); however, they are included on the checklist, so they can be checked as they are completed. When paying bills and printing a batch of checks, your checks may be in a different order than shown below. If the checks are printed to the correct company or person and have the correct amounts, do not be concerned if your check numbers are not an exact match.

Week 1
- ___ 1-Acct List
- ___ 2-Fixed Asset List
- ___ 3-Inv 1 Popov
- ___ 4-Inv 2 Campbell
- ___ 5-Inv 3 Hassan
- ___ 6-Inv 4 Palm Springs Schools
- ___ 7-SO 1 Meyer
- ___ 8-Inv 2 Campbell Corrected
- ___ 9-Rcv Pmt Tokumoto
- ___ 10-Inv 5 Salazar
- ___ 11-Inv 6 Meyer
- ___ 12-Rcv Pmt Parker
- ___ 13-SR 1 Cash Cust
- ___ 14-SO 2 Hansen
- ___ 15-Rcv Pmt Nelson
- ___ 16-Inv 7 Hansen
- ___ 17-Inventory Stock Status, January 1-5, 2018
- ___ 18-PO 1 Golf Gear
- ___ 19-PO 2 Sports Clothes
- ___ 20-PO 3 Head Gear
- ___ 21-PO QuickReport
- ___ 22-SR 2 Cash Cust
- ___ 23-Dep Sum, January 8, 2018

Week 2
- ___ 24-Item Rct Head Gear
- ___ 25-Bill Golf Gear
- ___ 26-Bill Sports Clothes
- ___ 27-CM 8 Salazar
- ___ 28-CM 9 Parker
- ___ 29-Ck 1 Parker
- ___ 30-SO 3 Tokumoto
- ___ 31-SR 3 Cash Cust
- ___ 32-Inv 10 Tokumoto
- ___ 33-Bill Desert Telephone
- ___ 34-Bill Head Gear
- ___ 35-Rcv Pmt Hassan
- ___ 36-Rcv Pmt Popov
- ___ 37-Dep Sum, January 14, 2018

Week 3
- ___ 38-Inv 11 Kincaid
- ___ 39-Rcv Pmt Salazar
- ___ 40-Bill Golf Gear
- ___ 41-Comment Unpaid Bills with Terms, January 18, 2018
- ___ 42-Cks 2-3
- ___ 43-Inv 12 Salazar
- ___ 44-Bill Credit Sports Clothes
- ___ 45-CM 13 Kincaid
- ___ 46-SR 4 Cash Cust
- ___ 47-SR 5 Cash Cust
- ___ 48-Inventory Stock Status, January 1-20, 2018
- ___ 49-PO 4 Golf Gear
- ___ 50-PO 5 Sports Clothes
- ___ 51-PO 6 Head Gear
- ___ 52-Dep Sum, January 20, 2018

Week 4 and End of Period
- ___ 53-Comment Unpaid Bills with Terms, January 23, 2018
- ___ 54-Cks 4-5
- ___ 55-Rcv Pmt Salazar
- ___ 56-Bill Sports Clothes
- ___ 57-Bill Golf Gear
- ___ 58-Rcv Pmt Campbell
- ___ 59-Rcv Pmt Kincaid
- ___ 60-Bill Head Gear
- ___ 61-Comment Unpaid Bills with Terms, January 25, 2018
- ___ 62-Cks 6-9
- ___ 63-Bill Palm Springs Rentals
- ___ 64-Unpaid Bills, January 26, 2018
- ___ 65-Rcv Pmt Tokumoto
- ___ 66-Dep Sum, January 29, 2018
- ___ 67-Ck 10 Palm Springs Rentals
- ___ 68-Opening Bal Inv Campbell Revised
- ___ 69-Inv 2 Campbell Revised
- ___ 70-Inv 14 Campbell

PS
2

Week 4 and End of Period Continued

___ 71-Sales Tax Liab, January 1-30, 2018

___ 72-Ck 11 St Board of Equal

___ 73-Sales by Item Sum, January 1-30, 2018

___ 74-Cks 12-13

___ 75-Adj Trial Bal, January 30, 2018

___ 76-Bank Rec, January 1-31, 2018

___ 77-Vis Rec, January 1-31, 2018

___ 78-Ck 14 Desert Bank

___ 79-Journal, January 1-31, 2018

___ 80-Trial Bal, January 31, 2018

___ 81-P & L, January 1-31, 2018

___ 82-Bal Sheet, January 31, 2018

PAYROLL

8

LEARNING OBJECTIVES

At the completion of this chapter, you will be able to:

8.01. Understand the payroll options in QuickBooks Desktop.
8.02. Select Manual Payroll Option.
8.03. Understand Payroll Schedules.
8.04. Change employee information.
8.05. Add new employee.
8.06. View Payroll Item List.
8.07. Create, preview, and print paychecks.
8.08. Edit employee information.
8.09. Correct Pay Check Detail.
8.10. Void and delete paychecks.
8.11. Print Payroll Reports including: Missing Check Report, Payroll Summary Report, Earnings Summary Report, and Payroll Liability Balances Report.
8.12. Pay Taxes and Other Liabilities.
8.13. Know that payroll tax forms can be exported to Excel to summarize and customize tax form information.
8.14. Print a Journal report.

PAYROLL

8

Many times, a company begins the process of computerizing its accounting system simply to be able to do the payroll using the computer. It is much faster and easier to let QuickBooks Desktop look at the tax tables and determine how much withholding should be deducted for each employee than to have an individual perform this task. Because tax tables change frequently, QuickBooks Desktop requires its users to enroll in a payroll service plan to obtain updates. To enroll in a payroll service plan, you must have a company tax identification number. Intuit has a variety of payroll service plans that are available for an additional charge. If you do not subscribe to a payroll plan, you must calculate and enter the payroll taxes manually.

Intuit's payroll plans are changed and updated frequently; however, at the time of this writing, Intuit has the following Payroll Plans available on a subscription basis:

Payroll Basic: Essentially, this version only processes paychecks (From $20.00 to $25.00 per month plus $2.00 per month per employee). Subscribing to this plan enables you to download up-to-date tax tables into QuickBooks DT. If you use this, you enter your employee information once. Then, each pay period you will enter the hours and QuickBooks DT will use this information to automatically calculate deductions and prepare paychecks for your employees. Direct deposit is available for no additional fee. Since no tax forms are included, you will work with your accountant; or use QuickBooks DT reports to generate the data you need to fill in state and federal tax forms by hand. The service is completely integrated with QuickBooks DT.

Payroll Enhanced: Primarily used to prepare paychecks and pay taxes (From $31.20 to $39.00 per month plus $2.00 per employee). This is a more comprehensive do-it-yourself payroll solution used to calculate deductions, earnings, and payroll taxes. Enter hours and get instant paychecks. Enhanced payroll includes federal and most state tax forms, tools for tracking payroll expenses and workers compensation. Direct deposit is available for no additional fee. Enhanced payroll automatically fills in your data on quarterly federal and state tax forms. Just print, sign & mail your tax filings or use E-File to file and pay payroll taxes electronically. Year-end W-2s are included. The program is integrated with QuickBooks DT.

Full Service Payroll: Service will complete setup, run payroll, calculate payroll taxes, file payroll taxes. ($79.20 to $99.00 per month plus $2 per employee). Receive guidance when submitting employee hours online. Unlimited payrolls each month may be prepared, free direct deposit, free new hire reporting, free W-2 and 1099 printing and processing. Manage vacation, deductions, garnishments, and more for you. Guarantee error-free paychecks and payroll taxes. Free live US-based support from Intuit's experts. Payroll taxes are filed, and tax payments are made for you. The service is completely integrated with QuickBooks DT.

Online Payroll: Different levels available: Basic and Enhanced. (Basic is available for $20.00 to $25.00 per month, Enhanced is $31.20 to $39.00 per month. Both versions charge an additional $2.00 per month for each employee). Subscribing to either of these plans enables you to pay your employees. You may even use your iPhone or Android. Basic is used to pay employees. Enhanced is used to pay employees and 1099 contractors. Enhanced calculates, files, and pays federal and state taxes; and processes W-2s. Free direct deposit is included. Intuit Online Payroll is a standalone program that is integrated with QuickBooks software.

Payroll for Accounting Professionals: Intuit offers two payroll plans for accountants:

Intuit Online Payroll for Accounting Professionals: online version of QuickBooks that includes payroll. Clients enter hours, then payroll taxes and deductions are automatically calculated. Paychecks may then be approved and printed. Direct deposit is free. Accountants review the clients' payroll taxes. Quarterly and year-end payroll taxes are calculated within QuickBooks. Guaranteed to be accurate on tax calculations. (At the time of this writing the monthly rate ranged from $9.99 to $35.00 per month and from $0.50 to $2.00 per employee. This is calculated based on the number of clients.) Direct deposit, electronic payments and filings, and the ability to share data with clients are included. This integrates with QuickBooks Desktop.

Intuit Enhanced Payroll for Accountants: is a simplified after-the-fact payroll that is used to automatically copy paycheck data, get automatic tax calculations, and process federal and state tax forms. There are pre-configured reports that are included with the program that detail payroll activity by employee, payroll expense analysis, payroll tax reports, and 941/940/state liabilities reports. (At the time of this writing, the program is priced from $57.50 per month.)

DIRECT DEPOSIT

Enables payment to employees by depositing their pay directly into their checking accounts. Direct Deposit is included with subscription payroll plans.

MANUAL PAYROLL

The ability to process the payroll manually is part of the QuickBooks DT program and does not require a subscription or cost additional fees. However, if you use manual payroll for your business, it is your responsibility to obtain up-to-date payroll tax tables and tax forms.

Since all the businesses in this text are fictitious and we do not have a FEIN (Federal Employer's Identification Number) for any of them, we will not be subscribing to any of the QuickBooks Payroll Services. As a result, we will be entering all tax information for paychecks manually based on data provided in the text. Calculations will be made for vacation pay, sick pay, medical and dental insurance deductions, and so on. Paychecks will be created, printed, corrected, and voided. Tax reports, tax payments, and tax forms will be explored.

Payroll is an area of accounting that has frequent changes; for example, tax tables are frequently updated, changes in withholding or tax limits are made, etc. As a result, QuickBooks DT is modified via updates to implement changes to payroll. As a word of caution, the materials presented in this chapter are current at the time of this writing. It may be that as Intuit updates QuickBooks DT some of the things displayed in the chapter may change. If this happens, please read the information and ask your professor how to proceed.

TRAINING TUTORIAL AND PROCEDURES

The tutorial will work with the sole proprietorship, Your Name's Total Fitness, which has a gym with memberships, personal training, exercise classes, and a small boutique with fitness clothing, accessories, and equipment. Use the company file **Total 2018**. (You may also see the file as Total_2018.) Once you open your copy of the company file, transactions will be recorded for the fictitious company. To maximize training benefits, you should follow the procedures previously provided.

You have four employees Raymond Baker, who provides the management and supervision of the gym; Rafael Cruz, who is a personal trainer; Kenisha Brown, who manages the boutique shop and is the bookkeeper; and Vivian Kamaka, the Pilates instructor.

Raymond Baker and Kenisha Brown are salaried employees. Rafael Cruz and Vivian Kamaka are paid on an hourly basis. Any hours over 160 for the pay period will be paid as overtime. Paychecks for all employees are issued monthly.

PROGRAM NAME, DATES, AND REPORT PREFERENCES

Earlier in the text QuickBooks Accountant Desktop was referred to as QuickBooks Desktop or QuickBooks DT. In Chapters 8 and 9 the program will now be abbreviated to QBDT. Throughout the text, the year used for the screen shots is 2018, which is the same year as the version of the program. You may want to check with your instructor to see if you should use 2018 as the year. As in earlier chapters, verify the printing assignment with your instructor. The text will continue to include all printable items on the checklist.

 In Reports & Graphs Company Preferences, turn off the Date Prepared, Time Prepared, and Report Basis in the Header/Footer.

ADD YOUR NAME TO THE COMPANY NAME

As with previous companies, each student in the course will be working with the same company and printing the same documents. Personalizing the company name to include your name will help identify many of the documents you print during your training.

 Add your first and last name to the Company Name and Legal Name as previously instructed; make sure to add **'s** at the end of your last name

- Example: Sue Smith's Total Fitness.

CHANGE NAME OF CAPITAL ACCOUNTS

Since the owner's equity accounts have the words Student's Name as part of the account name, replace *Student's Name* with your actual name.

 Change the owner equity account names as previously instructed. Change the following:

- Remember to use your real name. If you run out of room for your name and the rest of the title, use your first initial and your last name.

Student's Name, Capital to **First & Last Name, Capital**
Student's Name, Investment to **First & Last Name, Investment**
Student's Name, Withdrawals to **First & Last Name, Withdrawals**

SELECT PAYROLL OPTION

Before entering any payroll transactions, QBDT must be informed of the type of payroll service you are selecting. Once QBDT knows what type of payroll process has been selected for the company, you will be able to create paychecks. To create paychecks manually, you must go select a Manual payroll option.

 Select a **Manual** payroll option

Open the **Employee Center**
Press **F1**
Click **Show More Answers** in the middle of the Help screen
Click **Process Payroll Manually (without a subscription to QuickBooks Payroll)**
On the Have a Question? screen, which shows the Answers in Help, click **Process payroll manually (without a subscription to QuickBooks Payroll)**

On the next screen, click the words <u>manual payroll calculations</u>
- If you get your information in a Help Article, click the same words.

> **Process payroll manually (without a subscription to QuickBooks Desktop Payroll)**
>
> **What we recommend**
>
> We strongly recommend that you sign up for QuickBooks Desktop Payroll to make sure that you have the most current tax tables available. In addition to providing current tax tables, QuickBooks Desktop Payroll provides additional features that take the worry out of doing your payroll.
>
> **If you prefer to process your payroll manually**
>
> 1. Set your company file to use the manual payroll calculations setting.
>
>   Important: When your company file is set up for manual payroll calculations, **QuickBooks inserts a "zero" amount** for each payroll item associated with a tax.

Read the information for "Are you sure you want to set your company file to use manual calculations", and then click **Set my company file to use manual calculations**

> **If you are sure you want to manually calculate your payroll taxes in QuickBooks,** click here: Set my company file to use manual calculations

The manual calculations setting is applied immediately, and you will get a QuickBooks Desktop Information screen

Close Help

- Sometimes the Help screen will be in front of the QuickBooks Desktop Information screen.

Read the message, click **OK**

PAYROLL SCHEDULES

If you subscribe to a payroll plan, you will have the option to set up Payroll schedules for processing the payroll. To set up a new payroll schedule, you will give the schedule a name, indicate how often you pay your employees on the schedule, provide the pay period end date, and specify the date that should appear on paychecks for this pay period.

Once a payroll schedule is created, employees are assigned to it based on the frequency of payment. For example, you assign the employees paid monthly to one schedule and the employees paid weekly to a different schedule. When it is time to process the payroll, you access the Payroll Center (not available without a subscription), click the Pay Employees tab, select the payroll schedule you want to run, and then click Start Scheduled Payroll. After that, you verify the hours worked and the amounts for each employee listed on the schedule, review the paycheck summary, and, finally, create paychecks.

Since we are processing payroll manually, we cannot use Payroll Schedules in the text.

CHANGE EMPLOYEE INFORMATION

Whenever a change occurs for an employee, it may be entered at any time.

> **MEMO**
>
> **DATE:** January 30, 2018
>
> Effective today, Raymond Baker will receive a pay raise to $30,000 annually. In addition, all employees will be paid monthly.

   Change the salary and pay period for Raymond Baker

> Click the **Employees** icon to open the Employee Center
> Double-click **Baker, Raymond** in the Employee list
> On the Edit Employee screen, click the **Payroll Info** Tab
> On the **Payroll Info** tab, click the drop-down list arrow for PAY FREQUENCY, click **Monthly**
> Click in the text box for the **HOURLY/ANNUAL RATE** and change the amount to **30,000**

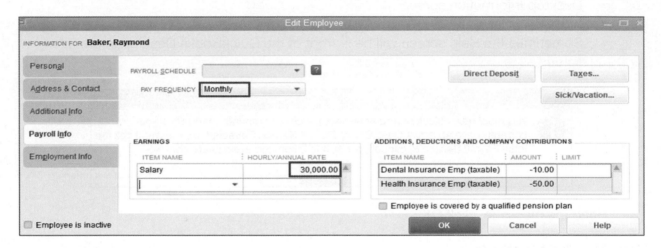

> Click **OK**
> Do <u>not</u> close the **Employee Center**
> Change the other three employees to a monthly Pay Frequency following the steps listed above

ADD NEW EMPLOYEE

As new employees are hired, they should be added.

> **MEMO**
>
> **DATE:** January 1, 2018
>
> Effective 01/30/18 hired a part-time employee to teach yoga classes. Ms. Cheryl Crown, Social Security. No.: 100-55-6936, Female, Birth date: 02/14/80, Marital Status: Single, U.S. Citizen: Yes, Ethnicity: White, Disability: No, Address: 1329 Bayshore Drive, Venice, CA 90405, Main Phone: 310-555-8529. Pay frequency: Monthly. Paid an hourly rate of $15.00 and an overtime rate of $22.50. Federal and state withholding: Single, 0 Allowances. No local taxes, dental insurance, medical insurance, sick time, or vacation time.

Add the new employee, Cheryl Crown

Click the **New Employee** button at the top of the Employee Center

On the **Personal** tab, click in the text box for **LEGAL NAME**, enter **Ms.**
Using the information provided in the memo, tab to or click in each field and enter the
    information for the **Personal** tab

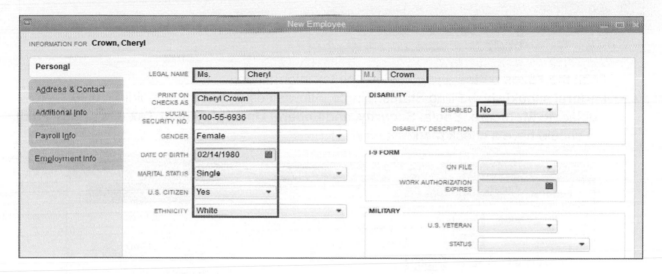

Click the **Address & Contact** tab; enter the information provided in the memo

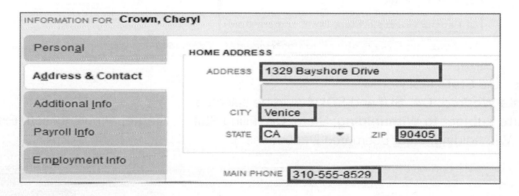

Click the **Payroll Info** tab
Select a **Monthly** pay frequency
Click in the **ITEM NAME** column under **EARNINGS**, click the drop-down list arrow that
    appears, and click **Hourly Rate**
Tab to or click in the text box for **HOURLY/ANNUAL RATE**, enter **15.00** for the hourly rate
Click in the **ITEM NAME** column under **Hourly Rate**, click the drop-down list arrow that
    appears, click **Overtime Rate**
  • QBDT enters the rate of 22.50.

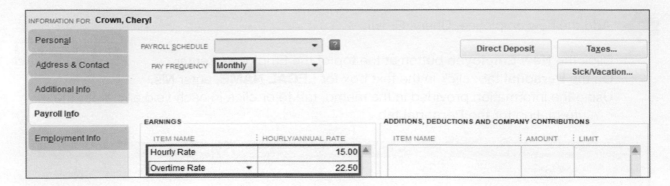

Click the **Taxes** button and complete the tax information:

Federal should show Filing Status: **Single,** Allowances: **0,** Extra Withholding: **0.00**

Subject to **Medicare**, **Social Security**, and **Federal Unemployment Tax (Company Paid)** should have a check mark

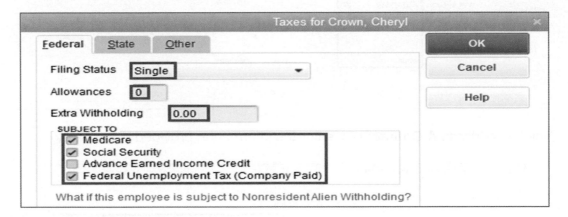

Click the **State** tab:

State Worked: **CA**, **SUI** and **SDI** should be selected

State Subject to Withholding: State: **CA**, Filing Status: **Single**, Allowances: **0**, Extra Withholding: **0.00**; Estimated Deductions: **0**

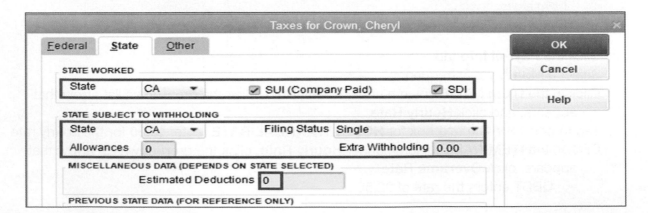

Click the **Other** tab

CA – Employment Training Tax and Medicare Employee Addl Tax should be shown

- If not, click the drop-down list arrow for **ITEM NAME**, and click **CA-Employment Training Tax**. Repeat if Medicare Employee Addl Tax is not shown.

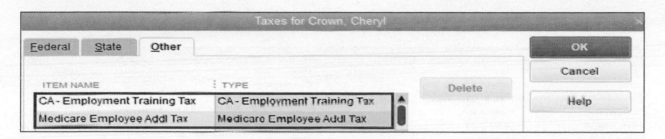

Click **OK** to complete the tax information

Click **Employment Info**

The **HIRE DATE** is **01/30/18** and in the **EMPLOYMENT DETAILS** section the **EMPLOYMENT TYPE** is **Regular**

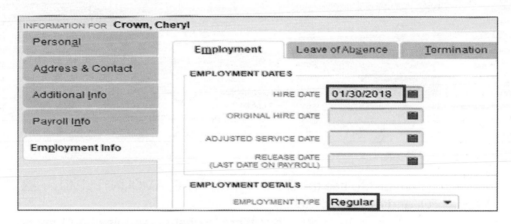

Click **OK** to complete the addition of the new employee

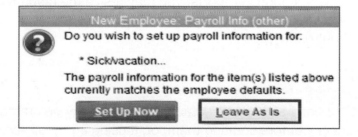

Since Cheryl does not have any sick/vacation hours, click **Leave As Is** on the New Employee: Payroll Info (other), close the Employee Center

VIEW PAYROLL ITEM LIST

The Payroll Item list contains a listing of all payroll items, and information regarding the item type, amount of deduction, annual limit for deductions (if applicable), tax tracking, vendor for payment, and the account ID.

View the Payroll Item List

Click **Employees** on the Menu bar

Click **Manage Payroll Items**, click **View/Edit Payroll Item List**

- If you get a message box regarding subscribing to a payroll service, click No anytime you see the message.

The Payroll Item List is displayed

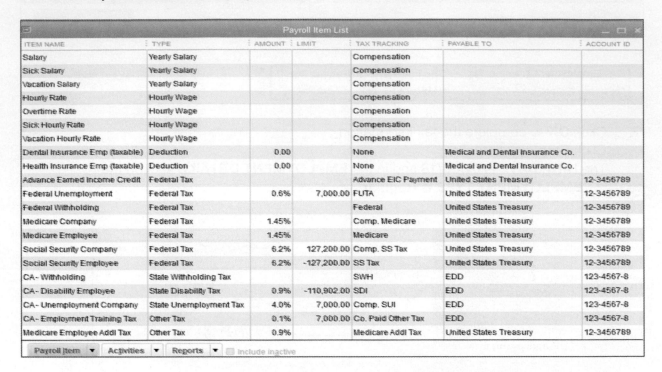

ITEM NAME	TYPE	AMOUNT	LIMIT	TAX TRACKING	PAYABLE TO	ACCOUNT ID
Salary	Yearly Salary			Compensation		
Sick Salary	Yearly Salary			Compensation		
Vacation Salary	Yearly Salary			Compensation		
Hourly Rate	Hourly Wage			Compensation		
Overtime Rate	Hourly Wage			Compensation		
Sick Hourly Rate	Hourly Wage			Compensation		
Vacation Hourly Rate	Hourly Wage			Compensation		
Dental Insurance Emp (taxable)	Deduction	0.00		None	Medical and Dental Insurance Co.	
Health Insurance Emp (taxable)	Deduction	0.00		None	Medical and Dental Insurance Co.	
Advance Earned Income Credit	Federal Tax			Advance EIC Payment	United States Treasury	12-3456789
Federal Unemployment	Federal Tax	0.6%	7,000.00	FUTA	United States Treasury	12-3456789
Federal Withholding	Federal Tax			Federal	United States Treasury	12-3456789
Medicare Company	Federal Tax	1.45%		Comp. Medicare	United States Treasury	12-3456789
Medicare Employee	Federal Tax	1.45%		Medicare	United States Treasury	12-3456789
Social Security Company	Federal Tax	6.2%	127,200.00	Comp. SS Tax	United States Treasury	12-3456789
Social Security Employee	Federal Tax	6.2%	-127,200.00	SS Tax	United States Treasury	12-3456789
CA- Withholding	State Withholding Tax			SWH	EDD	123-4567-8
CA- Disability Employee	State Disability Tax	0.9%	-110,902.00	SDI	EDD	123-4567-8
CA- Unemployment Company	State Unemployment Tax	4.0%	7,000.00	Comp. SUI	EDD	123-4567-8
CA- Employment Training Tax	Other Tax	0.1%	7,000.00	Co. Paid Other Tax	EDD	123-4567-8
Medicare Employee Addl Tax	Other Tax	0.9%		Medicare Addl Tax	United States Treasury	12-3456789

Payroll Item ▼   Activities ▼   Reports ▼   ☐ Include inactive

View the Payroll Item List to see the ITEM NAME, TYPE, AMOUNT, LIMIT, TAX TRACKING, PAYABLE TO, and ACCOUNT ID
- Remember, Limits and Amounts are subject to change so this chart may not match the one you see later.
- As you learned when printing reports, you may resize the columns in the Payroll Item List.

Close the list without printing

CREATE PAYCHECKS

Once the manual payroll option has been selected, paychecks may be created. You may enter hours and preview the checks before creating them, or, if using a payroll service, you may create the checks without previewing. Once the payroll has been processed, checks may be printed.

Since you process the payroll manually, you must enter the payroll data for withholdings and deductions. QBDT will enter other payroll items such as medical and dental insurance deductions, and it will calculate the total amount of the checks.

> **MEMO**
> **DATE:** January 31, 2018
>
> Create and print paychecks for January 31, 2018. Use this date as the pay period ending date and the check date.

   Pay all employees using the hours and deductions listed in the following table:

PAYROLL TABLE: JANUARY 31, 2018					
	Raymond Baker	Kenisha Brown	Cheryl Crown	Rafael Cruz	Vivian Kamaka
HOURS					
REGULAR	160	140	8	72	160
OVERTIME					8
SICK				8	
VACATION		20		0	
DEDUCTIONS OTHER PAYROLL ITEMS: EMPLOYEE					
DENTAL INS.	10.00	10.00			
MEDICAL INS.	50.00	50.00			
DEDUCTIONS: COMPANY					
CA-EMPLOYMENT TRAINING TAX	2.50	1.67	0.00	2.00	2.58
SOCIAL SECURITY	155.00	103.33	7.44	124.00	159.96
MEDICARE	36.25	24.17	1.74	29.00	37.41
FEDERAL UNEMPLOYMENT	15.00	10.00	0.00	12.00	15.48
CA-UNEMPLOYMENT	100.00	66.67	4.80	80.00	103.20
DEDUCTIONS: EMPLOYEE					
MEDICARE EMPLOYEE ADDDL TAX	0.00	0.00	0.00	0.00	0.00
FEDERAL WITHHOLDING	312.00	124.60	0.00	132.50	276.34
SOCIAL SECURITY	155.00	103.33	7.44	124.00	159.96
MEDICARE	36.25	24.17	1.74	29.00	37.41
CA-WITHHOLDING	75.00	34.06	0.00	30.31	42.48
CA-DISABILITY	22.50	15.00	1.08	18.00	23.22

8

Click **Pay Employees** icon in the **Employees** section of the **Home Page**
The **Enter Payroll Information** screen appears
Enter the **PAY PERIOD ENDS** date of **01/31/18**
Enter the **CHECK DATE** of **01/31/18**
The **BANK ACCOUNT** is **Checking** with a **BANK ACCOUNT BALANCE** of **35,840.00**
CHECK OPTIONS should be **Print Paychecks on check stock**
Click the **Check All** button to select all employees

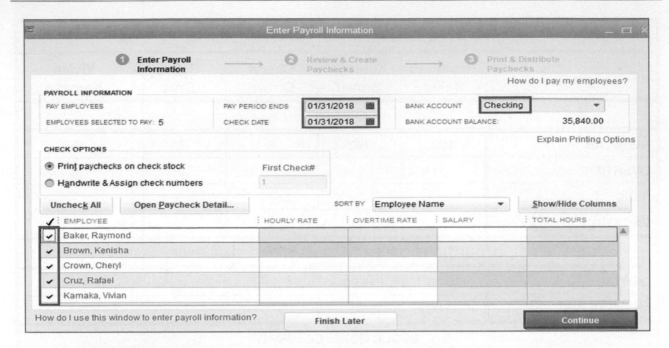

- Notice the check mark in front of each employee name.

Click the **Continue** button

- Notice the amounts given for each employee. There is nothing listed for taxes, employer taxes, contributions, or total hours. This information needs to be entered when preparing payroll manually.
- Remember, if you do subscribe to a QuickBooks payroll service, you will not enter the taxes manually. QBDT will calculate them and enter them for you. Since tax tables change frequently, the taxes calculated by QBDT may not be the same as the amounts listed on the Payroll Table in the text.
- As you record the information for each employee, refer to the payroll chart listed earlier in the chapter.

Click the **Open Paycheck Detail...** button on the Review and Create Paychecks screen

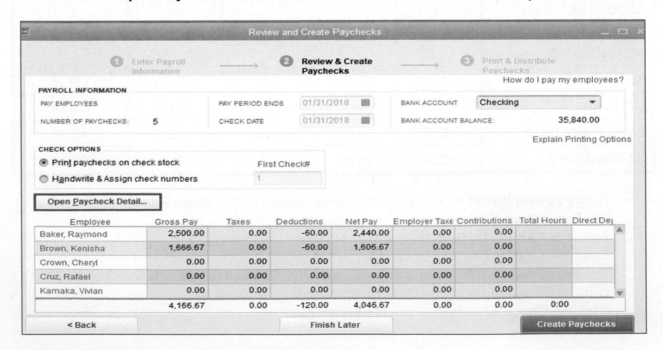

The **Preview Paycheck** screen for Raymond Baker appears.
- Notice that QBDT calculated the monthly salary based on the annual salary.

Tab to or click in the **HOURS** column, enter **160**

The section for Other Payroll Items is automatically completed by QBDT
- Because the deductions for Raymond were already set up, the amounts deducted for Dental and Health Insurance paid by the employee have been entered automatically.

Complete the **Company Summary (adjusted)** information:

Click in the **AMOUNT** column for **CA-Employment Training Tax,** enter **2.50**

Tab to or click in the **AMOUNT** column for **Social Security Company**, enter **155.00**

Tab to or click in the **Medicare Company** line, enter **36.25**

Tab to or click in the **Federal Unemployment** line, enter **15.00**

Tab to or click in the **CA-Unemployment Company** line, enter **100.00**
- You may need to scroll down the list to see this item.

Complete the **Employee Summary (adjusted)** information:
- You will be leaving Medicare Employee Addl Tax at 0.00 for all employees. The additional 0.9% tax is levied on people and/or couples with higher levels of income. Currently, income more $125,000 married filing separately, $200,000 single, and $250,000 married will be taxed.
- QBDT will automatically insert the – in front of the amount.

Click in the **AMOUNT** column for **Federal Withholding**, enter **312.00**

Tab to or click in the **Social Security Employee** line, enter **155.00**

Tab to or click in the **Medicare Employee** line, enter **36.25**

Tab to or click in the **CA-Withholding** line, enter **75.00**

Tab to or click in the **CA-Disability Employee** line, enter **22.50**, press **Tab**
- In the Company Summary for the paychecks, the line for CA – Employment Training Tax is not shown in the screen shot. To view the line, scroll up.

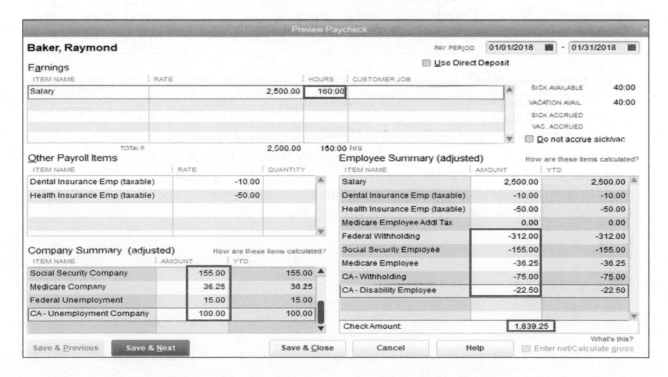

After verifying that everything was entered correctly, click **Save & Next**

Pay **Kenisha Brown** for **140** hours of **Salary**

- Notice that the number of Vacation Hours listed in **Vacation Avail.** is **20.00**.

In the **ITEM NAME** column under **Earnings**, click on the blank line beneath Salary

Click the drop-down list arrow that appears, click **Vacation Salary**, tab to or click the
   Hours column, enter **20**, press **Tab**

- The Vacation Avail. will show 0.00 and the Rates for Salary and Vacation Salary will
   change to reflect the amount paid for vacation.

Complete the paycheck information using the Payroll Table for January 31, 2018

- You may need to use the scroll bar in the Company Summary section to complete the
   information for CA – Employment Training Tax.

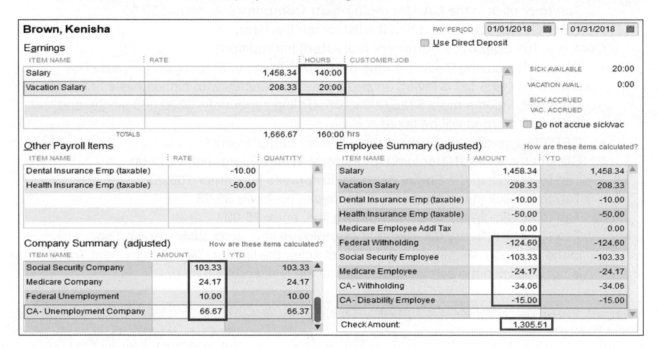

- In the completed Company Summary for the paychecks, the line for CA – Employment
   Training Tax is not shown in the screen shot. To view the line, scroll up.

Click **Save & Next**

The next Preview Paycheck screen should be for **Cheryl Crown**

Tab to or click the **Hours** column next to **Hourly Rate** for **Cheryl Crown**, enter **8**

Refer to the Payroll Table for January 31, 2018, and enter the information

- You may need to use the scroll bar in the Company Summary section to complete the
   information for CA – Employment Training Tax.

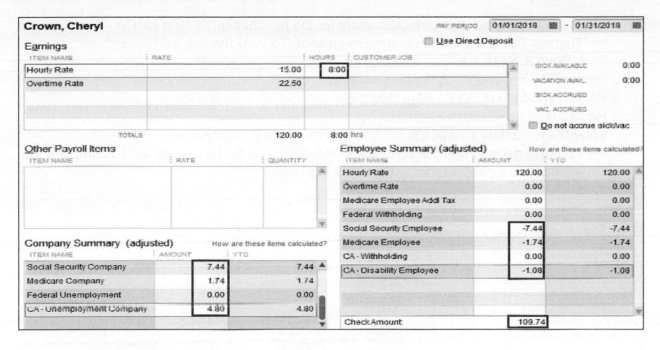

- In the completed Company Summary for the paychecks, the line for CA – Employment Training Tax is not shown in the screen shot. To view the line, scroll up.

Click **Save & Next**

Pay **Rafael Cruz** for **72** hours of **Hourly Regular Rate**

In the **ITEM NAME** column for **Earnings**, click the line below Overtime Rate

Click the drop-down list arrow, click **Sick Hourly Rate**

Enter **8** for the number of hours Rafael was out sick

Enter the company and employee deductions from the Payroll Table for January 31, 2018

- You may need to use the scroll bar in the Company Summary section to complete the information for CA – Employment Training Tax.

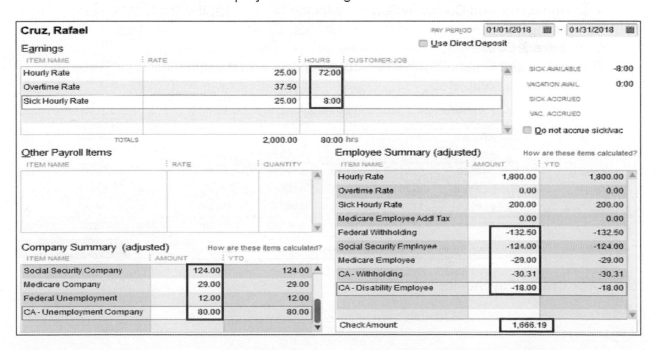

- In the completed Company Summary for the paychecks, the line for CA – Employment Training Tax is not shown in the screen shot. To view the line, scroll up.

Click **Save & Next**

Process the paycheck for **Vivian Kamaka**

Record **160** for her Hourly Rate Hours

Record **8** as her Overtime Rate Hours

Enter the remaining payroll information as previously instructed

- You may need to use the scroll bar in the Company Summary section to complete the information for CA – Employment Training Tax.

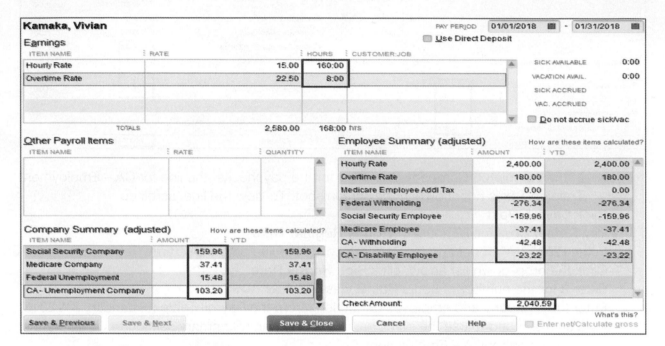

- In the completed Company Summary for the paychecks, the line for CA – Employment Training Tax is not shown in the screen shot. To view the line, scroll up.

Click **Save & Close**

The Review and Create Paychecks screen appears with the information for Taxes and Deductions completed

Employee	Gross Pay	Taxes	Deductions	Net Pay	Employer Taxe	Contributions	Total Hours	Direct De
Baker, Raymond	2,500.00	-600.75	-60.00	1,839.25	308.75	0.00	160:00	
Brown, Kenisha	1,666.67	-301.16	-60.00	1,305.51	205.84	0.00	160:00	
Crown, Cheryl	120.00	-10.26	0.00	109.74	13.98	0.00	8:00	
Cruz, Rafael	2,000.00	-333.81	0.00	1,666.19	247.00	0.00	80:00	
Kamaka, Vivian	2,580.00	-539.41	0.00	2,040.59	318.63	0.00	168:00	
	8,866.67	-1,785.39	-120.00	6,961.28	1,094.20	0.00	576:00	

< Back	Finish Later	Create Paychecks

Click **Create Paychecks**

PRINT PAYCHECKS

Paychecks may be printed one at a time or all at once. You may use the same printer setup as your other checks in QBDT or you may print using a different printer setup. If you use a voucher check, the pay stub is printed as part of the check. If you do not use a voucher check, you may print the pay stub separately. The pay stub information includes the employee's name, address, Social Security number, the pay period start and end dates, pay rate, the hours, the amount of pay, all deductions, sick and vacation time used and available, net pay, and year-to-date amounts.

MEMO
DATE: January 31, 2018

Print the paychecks for all employees using a voucher-style check with 2 parts. Print the company name on the checks.

 Print the January 31 paychecks

> The **Confirmation and Next Steps** screen shows on the screen

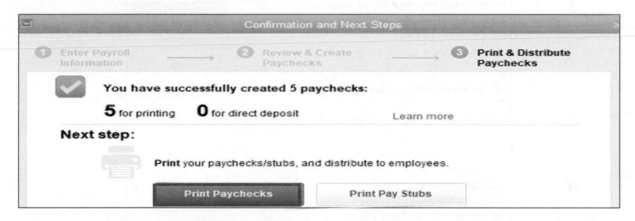

Click the **Print Paychecks** button
On the Select Paychecks to Print screen:

> **Bank Account** should be **Checking**; if it is not, click the drop-down list for Bank Account, and click **Checking**
> **First Check Number** is **1**; if it is not, change it to 1
> All the employees should have a check mark in the √ column, if not click the **Select All** button,

- Notice that there are 5 Paychecks to be printed for a total of $6,961.28.
- QBDT can process payroll for direct deposit or printed paychecks. Even though we are not processing direct deposit paychecks, leave **Show** as **Both**.

Click the **Preferences** button

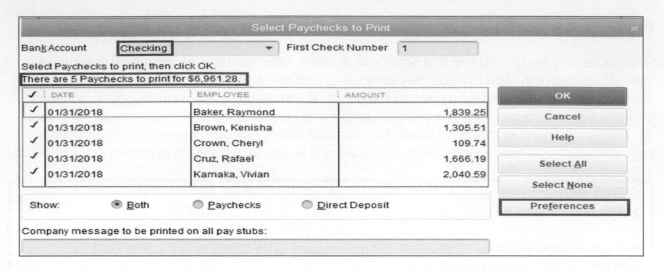

Verify that items for Payroll Printing Preferences for Paycheck Vouchers and Pay stubs have been selected

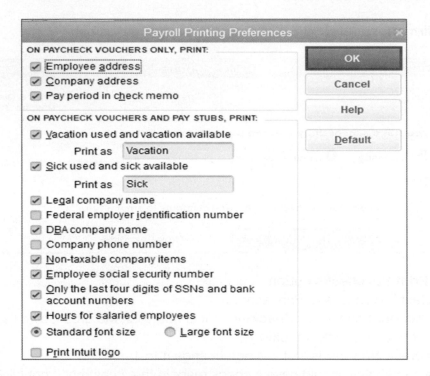

Click **OK**

Click **OK** on the Select Paychecks to Print screen

- Printer Name and Printer Type will be the same as in the earlier chapters.

Click **Voucher Checks** to select as the check style

- If necessary, click **Print company name and address** to select. There should not be a check mark in Use logo. **Number of copies** should be **1**.

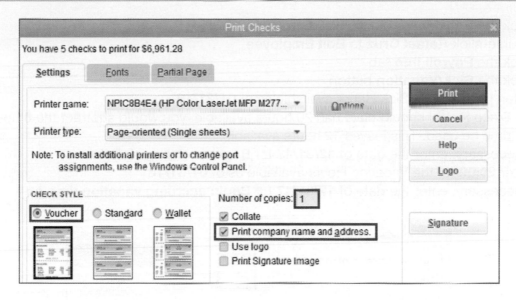

Click **Print**
- *Note*: The pay stub information may be printed on the check two times. This is the way the two-part voucher check is formatted.
- If you print to a pdf file, save the document as **1-Your Name's Cks 1-5 Ch8**.
 If the checks print correctly, click **OK** on the **Print Checks Confirmation** screen
 Click **Close** on the **Confirmation and Next Steps** screen

PREVIEW PAYCHECK DETAIL AND EDIT EMPLOYEE

As in earlier chapters, checks may be viewed individually and printed one at a time. A paycheck differs from a regular check. Rather than list accounts and amounts, it provides a Payroll Summary and an option to view Paycheck Detail at the bottom of the screen. When you are viewing the paycheck detail, corrections may be made. If the corrections do not affect the net pay, they may be made without unlocking the check. If the corrections affect the net pay, the check must be unlocked before you will be allowed to enter the appropriate corrections.

8

MEMO
DATE: January 31, 2018

After reviewing the printed checks, you notice that Rafael Cruz shows -8.00 for Available Sick time. He should have had 20 hours available. Go to his paycheck and view his Paycheck Detail. Open the Employee Center and change his employee information to show 12.00 hours of Available Sick Time and 20 hours of vacation time available as of January 31, 2018. Return to his Paycheck Detail, Unlock the Net Pay, and re-enter the number of Sick and Vacation Hours Available. Reprint his check.

  View the paycheck detail for Rafael Cruz

Click the **Write Checks** icon to open the **Paycheck – Checking** window
Click **Previous** (Back Arrow icon) until you get to the check for Rafael Cruz
Click the **Paycheck Detail** button
Notice the **Sick Available** is **-8:00** and the **Vacation Avail.** is **0:00**
Click **OK** to close the **Paycheck Detail** but leave Rafael's check showing on the screen

Click the **Employees** Menu, click **Employee Center**

Double-click **Rafael Cruz** to **Edit Employee**

Click the **Payroll Info** tab

Click the **Sick/Vacation** button

Enter **12:00** for the Sick Hours available as of **01/31/18**

- Since Rafael should have had 20 hours available, you would subtract the 8 hours of sick time he used. This leaves 12 hours available.

If necessary, enter the date of **12/31/17** for **Begin accruing sick time on**

Enter **20:00** for the Vacation Hours available as of **01/31/18**

If necessary, enter the date of **12/31/17** for **Begin accruing vacation time on**

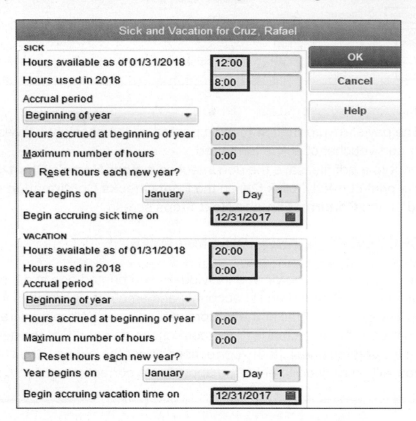

Click **OK** for Sick/Vacation, and click **OK** on the Edit Employee Screen

- If you get a Save message box, click **Yes**.

Close the **Employee Center** and return to Rafael Cruz's check

- The change in sick and vacation hours entered in the Employee Center will be effective for automatic calculation on the next paycheck but will not be updated on the paycheck prepared January 31, 2018.

On the check for **Rafael Cruz** for **01/31/18**, click the **Paycheck Detail**

- Notice that the Sick Available shows 12:00 and Vacation Avail. shows 20:00.
- Even though the correct hours appear, the information for sick and vacation time available must be changed before the correct hours will appear on the paycheck voucher stub.

Even though the correct hours show, delete the hours and re-enter them: Sick Available is **12:00** and Vacation Avail. is **20:00**

Cruz, Rafael

PAY PERIOD 01/01/2018 🗓 - 01/31/2018 🗓

☐ Use Direct Deposit

Earnings

ITEM NAME	RATE	HOURS	CUSTOMER:JOB
Hourly Rate	25.00	72:00	
Overtime Rate	37.50		
Sick Hourly Rate	25.00	8:00	

SICK AVAILABLE	12:00
VACATION AVAIL.	20:00
SICK ACCRUED	

Click **OK** on the Review Paycheck screen

- Even though the amount of the check is not changed by this adjustment, the check should be reprinted so the correct sick leave information is shown.

To reprint Check **4**, click **Print**

- Click **Yes** on the Recording Transaction dialog box to record the changes.

If 4 is not shown as the check number, enter **4** as the Printed Check Number, and click **OK**

Verify the information on the Print Checks screen including the selection of Voucher checks, click **Print**

- If you print to a pdf file, save the document as **2-Your Name Ck 4 Cruz Ch8**.

When the check has printed successfully, click **OK** on the **Print Checks Confirmation** screen

Do <u>not</u> close the Paycheck – Checking window

MAKE CORRECTIONS TO PAYCHECK DETAIL

When you need to make changes to Paycheck Detail that effect the amount of pay, you may do so by unlocking the Net Pay, entering the required changes, and reprinting the check.

MEMO

DATE: January 31, 2018

Vivian Kamaka should have been paid for 10 hours overtime. Change her overtime hours and change her deductions as follows: CA-Employment Training Tax: 2.63, Social Security (Company and Employee): 162.75, Medicare (Company and Employee): 38.06, Federal Unemployment: 15.75, CA-Unemployment: 105.00, Federal Withholding: 330.65, CA Withholding: 45.45, and CA Disability: 23.63. Reprint the check.

 Correct and reprint the paycheck for Vivian Kamaka

Click **Next** (Forward Arrow icon) until you get to **Vivian Kamaka's** paycheck
Click **Paycheck Detail**

- Since paychecks are not distributed to the employees until after they have been reviewed, it is acceptable to change this paycheck rather than void and reissue a new one.

Change the Overtime Rate Hours to **10**
Press the **Tab** key
You will get a message regarding Net Pay Locked

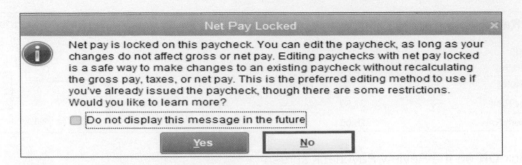

Click **No**

At the bottom of the paycheck, click **Unlock Net Pay**

You will get a **Special Paycheck Situation** screen to allow the paycheck to be changed

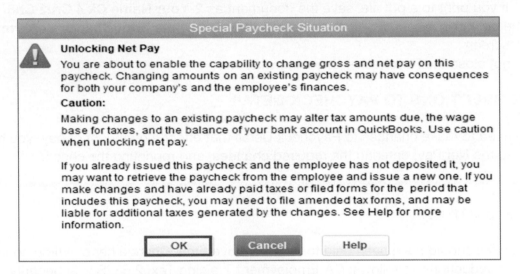

Click **OK** on the **Special Paycheck Situation** screen

Enter the changes to the tax amounts as indicated in the Memo

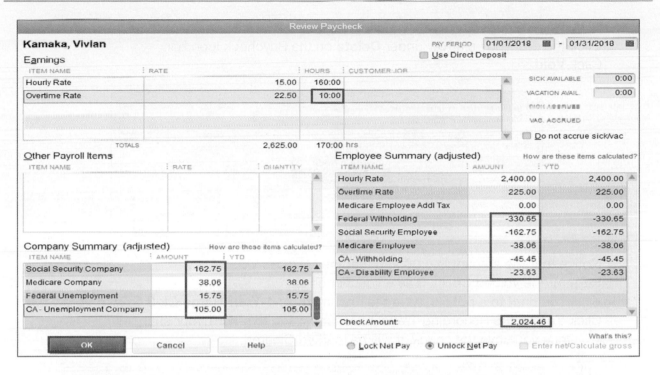

- In the completed Company Summary for the paychecks, the line for CA – Employment Training Tax is not shown in the screen shot. To view the line, scroll up.

Click **OK**, click **Yes** on the Recording Transactions message if necessary

- If you return to the Paycheck Detail, you will find that Lock Net Pay is once again selected.

Reprint Check 5

- If you print to a pdf file, save the document as **3-Your Name Ck 5 Kamaka Ch8**.

Do not close the Paycheck-Checking window

VOID AND DELETE PAYCHECKS

As with regular checks, paychecks may be voided or deleted. A voided check remains as a check, has an amount of 0.00, and a Memo that says VOID. If a check is deleted, it is completely removed from the company records. The only way to have a record of the deleted check is in the Voided/Deleted Transactions reports and the audit trail, which keeps a behind the scenes record of every entry in QBDT. If you have prenumbered checks and the original check is misprinted, lost, or stolen, you should void the check. If an employee's check is lost or stolen and needs to be replaced and you are not using prenumbered checks, it may be deleted and reissued. For security reasons, it is better to void a check than to delete it.

> **MEMO**
>
> **DATE:** January 31, 2018
>
> The checks have been distributed and Cheryl Crown spilled coffee on her paycheck for the January 31 pay period. Void the check, issue and print a new one.

 Void Cheryl's January 31 paycheck and issue a new one

Print the Voucher-style check

- If you print to a pdf file, save the document as **5-Your Name Ck 6 Crown Replacement Ch8**.

After the check has been printed successfully, click **OK**

Close the Confirmation and Next Steps screen

MISSING CHECK REPORT

Since the same account is used for paychecks and regular checks, the Missing Check report will provide data regarding all the checks issued by Your Name's Total Fitness. After entering checks, it is wise to review this report.

 View the Missing Check report

Open the **Report Center**, click **Banking** for the type of report, double-click **Missing Checks**

Specify Account is **Checking**

Your Name's Total Fitness
Missing Checks
All Transactions

Type	Date	Num	Name	Memo	Account	Split	Amount
Paycheck	01/31/2018	1	Baker, Raymond		Checking	-SPLIT-	-1,839.25
Paycheck	01/31/2018	2	Brown, Kenisha		Checking	-SPLIT-	-1,305.51
Paycheck	01/31/2018	3	Crown, Cheryl	VOID:	Checking	-SPLIT-	0.00
Paycheck	01/31/2018	4	Cruz, Rafael		Checking	-SPLIT-	-1,666.19
Paycheck	01/31/2018	5	Kamaka, Vivian		Checking	-SPLIT-	-2,024.46
Paycheck	01/31/2018	6	Crown, Cheryl		Checking	-SPLIT-	-109.74

Review the report and close without printing, do not close the Report Center

PAYROLL SUMMARY REPORT

The Payroll Summary Report shows gross pay; the amounts and hours for salary, hourly, overtime, sick, and vacation; adjusted gross pay; taxes withheld; deductions from net pay; net pay; and employer-paid taxes and contributions for each employee individually and for the company.

 Print the Payroll Summary Report for January

With the Report Center on the screen, click **Employees & Payroll**

Double-click **Payroll Summary**

Enter the report dates from **01/01/18** to **01/31/18**

- View the information listed for each employee and for the company.

Print the report in Landscape orientation, and close the report

- If you print to a pdf file, save the document as **6-Your Name Payroll Sum Ch 8**.
- If you get a Memorize Report screen, click **No**.

Click the **Previous/Back** arrow until Cheryl's paycheck appears on the screen
Click the drop-down arrow under **Delete** on the Paycheck Icon bar
Click **Void**

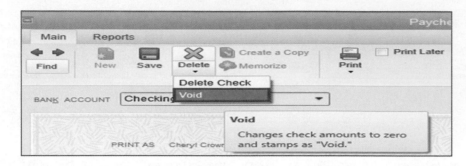

Notice that the amount is **0.00** and that the Memo is **VOID:**.
Re-print the voided Check **3** as a voucher check
* If you print to a pdf file, save the document as **4-Your Name Ck 3 Crown Void Ch8**.
Click **Yes** on the Recording Transactions message to record your changes
* Once you save the check, it will be marked Cleared.

Click **Save & Close** on **Paycheck-Checking** screen
To issue Cheryl's replacement check, click **Pay Employees** in the Employees section of
  the Home Page
The **Pay Period Ends 01/31/18** and the **Check Date** is **01/31/18**
The Bank Account is **Checking**
Click in the check column for **Cheryl Crown** to select her
Click **Continue**, then click the **Open Paycheck Detail** button
Pay Period is **01/01/18 - 01/31/18**
Cheryl worked **8** hours at the **Hourly Regular Rate**
Enter the deductions listed on the Payroll Table for January 31, 2018
Click **Save & Close**
Click the **Create Paychecks** button
Click **Print Paychecks**
Print the replacement check as Check **6**
Click **OK** on the **Confirmation and Next Steps** screen

PREPARE EMPLOYEE EARNINGS SUMMARY REPORT

The Employee Earnings Summary Report lists the same information as the Payroll Summary
Report above. The information for each employee is categorized by payroll items.

 Prepare the Employee Earnings Summary report

Double-click **Employee Earnings Summary** as the report
Use the dates from **01/01/18** to **01/31/18**
Scroll through the report
* Notice the way in which payroll amounts are grouped by item rather than employee.
Close the report without printing

PAYROLL LIABILITY BALANCES REPORT

Another payroll report is the Payroll Liability Balances Report. This report lists the company's
payroll liabilities that are unpaid as of the report date. This report should be prepared prior to
paying any payroll taxes.

 Prepare and print the Payroll Liability Balances report

Double-click **Payroll Liability Balances** in the Employees & Payroll section of the Report
  Center
The report dates should be **01/01/18** to **01/31/18**

Your Name's Total Fitness
Payroll Liability Balances
January 2018

	BALANCE
▼ **Payroll Liabilities**	
Federal Withholding ▶	899.75
Medicare Employee	129.22
Social Security Employee	552.52
Federal Unemployment	52.75
Medicare Company	129.22
Social Security Company	552.52
CA - Withholding	184.82
CA - Disability Employee	80.21
CA - Unemployment Company	356.47
Medicare Employee Addl Tax	0.00
CA - Employment Training Tax	8.80
Dental Insurance Emp (taxable)	20.00
Health Insurance Emp (taxable)	100.00
Total Payroll Liabilities	**3,066.28**

Print the report in Portrait orientation; close the report and the Report Center
* If you print to a pdf file, save the document as **7-Your Name Payroll Liab Bal Ch8**.

PAY PAYROLL TAXES AND LIABILITIES

QBDT keeps track of the payroll taxes and payroll liabilities that you owe. When it is time to make
your payments, QBDT allows you to choose to pay all liabilities or to select individual liabilities for
payment. When the liabilities have been selected, QBDT will consolidate all the amounts by vendor
and prepare one check for a vendor.

> **MEMO**
> **DATE:** January 31, 2018
>
> Based on the information in the Payroll Liabilities Report, pay all the payroll liabilities.

➡ Pay all the payroll liabilities

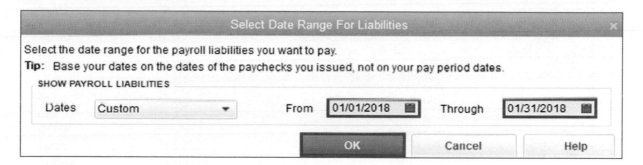

    Click the **Pay Liabilities** icon in Employees section of the Home Page
    Enter the dates From **01/01/18** Through **01/31/18** on the **Select Date Range For Liabilities** screen

    Click **OK**
    On the Pay Liabilities screen, select **To be printed** if necessary
    Bank Account should be **Checking**; if it is not, select it from the drop-down list.
    Check Date is **01/31/18**
    Sort by is **Payable To**
    Select **Create liability check without reviewing**
    Show payroll liabilities from **01/01/18** to **01/31/18**
    Click in the check column to place a check mark next to each liability listed; be sure to scroll through the list to view and mark each liability

8

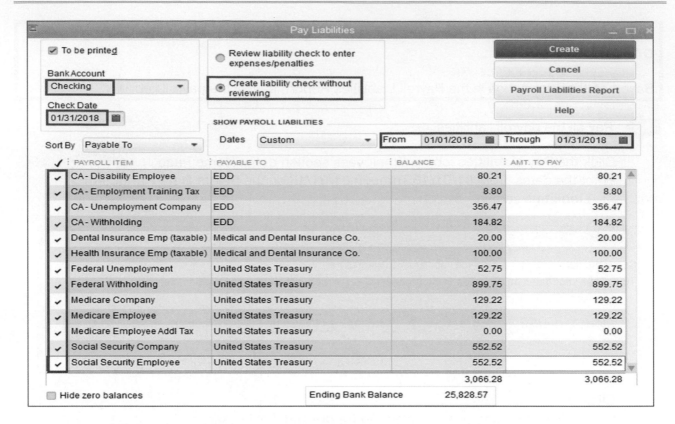

Click **Create**

To print the checks, access **Write Checks** as previously instructed

Click the drop-down list arrow below the **Print** icon at the top of the window

Click **Batch**

On the **Select Checks to Print** screen, the first check number should be **7**

- The names of the agencies receiving the checks and the check amounts should be listed and marked with a check. If not, click the **Select All** button.

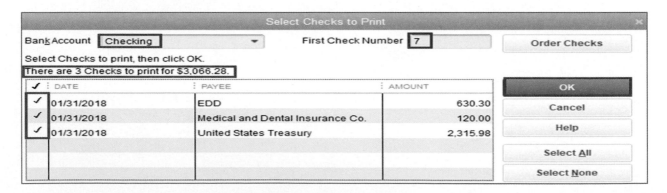

Click **OK**

Change the style of checks to **Standard**, click **Print**

When the checks have printed successfully, click **OK** on the confirmation screen

- Standard style checks print three to a page, so all three checks will print on one page.
- If you wish to have each check printed separately, you would go to each check and print individually as previously instructed.
- If you print to a pdf file, save the document as **8-Your Name Cks 7-9 Ch8**.

Close the Write Check - Checking window

PAYROLL TAX FORMS

Depending on the type of payroll service to which you subscribe, QBDT will prepare, print, and sometimes submit your tax forms for Quarterly Form 941, Annual Form 944, Annual Form 940, Annual Form 943, Annual W-2/W-3, and State SUI Wage Listing

Since we do not subscribe to a payroll service, QBDT will not complete any of these forms. However, at the time of writing, QBDT includes several reports that enable you to link payroll data from QBDT to Excel workbooks. The workbooks provided contain worksheets designed to summarize payroll data collected and to organize data needed to prepare the state and federal tax forms listed above. Many of the worksheets are preset with an Excel Pivot Table. The worksheets may be used as designed or they may be modified to suit your reporting needs. You may only prepare these Excel reports if you have entered payroll data; i.e., paychecks and withholding, in QBDT and have Microsoft Excel 2000 or later installed on your computer with Macros enabled.

To access the various tax forms, click Employees on the menu bar, point to Payroll Tax Forms & W-2s; and then, click Tax Form Worksheets in Excel.

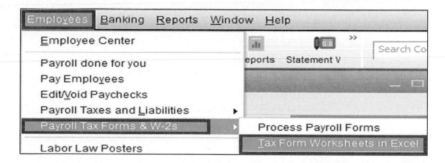

At this point you are taken to Excel where you need to turn on Macros. Once Macros have been enabled, you may select the form being prepared. Data from QBDT will be inserted into the Excel spreadsheet and may be used to manually complete the tax forms. We will not use this feature at this time.

PRINT JOURNAL REPORT

As in the previous chapters, it is always a good idea to print the Journal report to see all the transactions that have been made. If, however, you only want to see the transactions for a specific date or period, you can control the amount of data in the report by restricting the dates.

 Print the Journal report for January 31 in landscape orientation

Prepare the report as previously instructed
Use the dates from **01/01/18** to **01/31/18**
Expand the report
Adjust column widths so the information in each column is displayed in full and print
- If you print to a pdf file, save the document as **9-Your Name Journal Ch8**.

BACK UP

Follow the instructions provided in previous chapters to make a backup file. If you get a message in QBDT about rebuilding your company file, follow the prompts to rebuild.

 Create the Chapter 8 Backup File

SUMMARY

In this chapter, paychecks were generated for employees who worked their Standard number of hours, worked overtime hours, took vacation time, took sick time, and were just hired. Rather than have QBDT calculate the amount of payroll deductions, a table was provided and deductions to paychecks were recorded manually. Changes to employee information were made, and a new employee was added. Payroll reports were printed and/or viewed, and payroll liabilities were paid. Exporting payroll data to Excel workbooks was explored.

END-OF-CHAPTER QUESTIONS

TRUE/FALSE

ANSWER THE FOLLOWING QUESTIONS IN THE SPACE PROVIDED BEFORE THE QUESTION NUMBER.

_____ 8.01. Paychecks may be printed individually or as a batch.

_____ 8.02. When you process payroll manually, QBDT automatically prepares your paychecks and files your payroll tax reports.

_____ 8.03. To edit amounts that affect net pay, you must unlock the paycheck detail on the paycheck.

_____ 8.04. You may change the pay period from semi-monthly to monthly only at the beginning of the year.

_____ 8.05. All payroll reports must be printed before payroll liabilities may be paid.

_____ 8.06. An employee may be added at any time.

_____ 8.07. If several taxes are owed to a single agency, QBDT generates a separate check to the agency for each tax liability item.

_____ 8.08. QBDT will enter the correct amount of earnings to Vacation Salary once the number of vacation hours has been entered for a salaried employee.

_____ 8.09. Processing the Payroll Liabilities Balances Report also generates the checks for payment of the liabilities.

_____ 8.10. A payroll check may not be deleted.

MULTIPLE CHOICE

WRITE THE LETTER OF THE CORRECT ANSWER IN THE SPACE PROVIDED BEFORE THE QUESTION NUMBER.

_____ 8.11. A new employee may be added ___.
A. at any time
B. only at the end of the week
C. only at the end of the pay period
D. only when current paychecks have been printed

_____ 8.12. To change the amount of a deduction entered on an employee's check that has been created but not distributed, you ___.
A. must void the check and issue a new one
B. adjust the next check to include the change
C. unlock and change the Paycheck Detail for the check and reprint it
D. must delete the check

8

_____ 8.13. When the payroll liabilities to be paid have been selected, QBDT will ___.
    A. create a separate check for each liability
    B. consolidate the liabilities paid and create one check for each vendor
    C. automatically process a Payroll Liability Balances Report
    D. all the above

_____ 8.14. When paying tax liabilities, you may ___.
    A. pay all liabilities at one time
    B. select individual tax liabilities and pay them one at a time
    C. pay all the tax liabilities owed to a vendor (medical insurance for example)
    D. all the above

_____ 8.15. When completing paychecks manually, you ___.
    A. provide the information about hours worked
    B. provide the amounts for deductions
    C. provide the number of sick and/or vacation hours used
    D. all the above

_____ 8.16. Pay stub information may be printed ___.
    A. as part of a voucher check
    B. separate from the paycheck
    C. only as an individual employee report
    D. both A and B

_____ 8.17. A voided check ___.
    A. shows an amount of 0.00
    B. has a Memo of VOID
    C. remains as part of the company records
    D. all the above

_____ 8.18. You may void or delete checks by ___.
    A. clicking Void Checks or Delete Checks in the Banking Menu
    B. clicking either the Void icon or the Delete icon in the Write Checks window
    C. clicking the drop-down arrow under the Delete icon in the Write Checks window; then clicking either Void or Delete
    D. all the above

_____ 8.19. The Employee Earnings Summary Report lists payroll information for each employee categorized by ___.
    A. employee
    B. department
    C. payroll item
    D. date paid

_____ 8.20. Changes made to an employee's pay rate will become effective ___.
    A. immediately
    B. at the end of the next payroll period
    C. at the end of the quarter
    D. after a W-2 has been prepared for the employee

FILL-IN

IN THE SPACE PROVIDED, WRITE THE ANSWER THAT MOST APPROPRIATELY COMPLETES THE SENTENCE.

8.21. In the _____, the individual employee's name, address, and telephone number is displayed in the Employee Information area.

8.22. The _____ Report shows the company's unpaid payroll liabilities as of the report date.

8.23. Click the _____ button to add a new employee in the Employee Center.

8.24. The report that lists all transactions in debit/credit format is the _____.

8.25. The _____ and the _____ reports show an employee's gross pay, sick and vacation hours and pay, deductions, taxes, and other details.

SHORT ESSAY

What is the difference between voiding a paycheck and deleting a paycheck? Why should a business prefer to void paychecks rather than delete them?

_____
_____
_____
_____
_____
_____

8

END-OF-CHAPTER PROBLEM

YOUR NAME'S SWIM PROS

You will be working with a company called Your Name's Swim Pros. Transactions for employees, payroll, and payroll liabilities will be completed.

INSTRUCTIONS

For Chapter 8 use the company file, **Swim 2018.qbw.** (Remember, it may be shown as Swim_2018.qbw.) Open the company as previously instructed. If you get a message to update your company file, click Yes. You will select a manual payroll option; record the addition of and changes to employees; create, edit, and void paychecks; pay payroll liabilities; and prepare payroll reports.

RECORD TRANSACTIONS:

January 30, 2018

▶ Add your first and last name to the company name and the legal name. (Add **'s** to your last name.)

▶ Change the owner equity account names to: **First & Last Name, Capital**; **First & Last Name, Drawing**; and **First & Last Name, Investments**. (Use your real first and last name.)

▶ Turn off the Date Prepared, Time Prepared, and Report Basis in the Header/Footer. For instructions, refer to Chapter 5. Check with your professor to see if you should do this.

▶ Select Manual processing for payroll.

▶ Add a new employee, **Nancy Andrews** to help with pool supply sales. Social Security No.: **100-55-2145**; Gender: **Female**, Date of Birth: **03/04/1985**, Marital Status: **Married**, U.S. Citizen: **Yes**, Ethnicity: **Black/African American**, Disability: **No**. Address: **2325 Summerland Road**, **Summerland, CA 93014**, Main Phone: **805-555-9845**. Nancy has a pay frequency of **Monthly**, is an hourly employee with an Hourly Regular Rate of **$12.00** per hour and an Overtime Hourly Rate 1 of **$18.00**. She is <u>not</u> eligible for medical or dental insurance. For Federal Taxes, she is **Married**, exemptions/ allowances: **0**, and is subject to Federal Taxes: **Medicare, Social Security**, and **Federal Unemployment Tax (Company Paid)**, State Taxes: **CA: SUI (Company Paid)**, and **SDI, Married (two incomes)**, Allowances: **0**; Other Taxes: **CA-Employment Training Tax**. Hire Date: **January 30, 2018**, Employment Type: **Regular**. Nancy does <u>not</u> accrue vacation or sick leave.

▶ Gina Rossi changed her last name to **Thomas** and her Main Phone number to **805-555-5111**. Edit the employee in the employee list and record the change.

January 31, 2018

▶ Use the following Payroll Table to prepare and print checks for the monthly payroll. The pay period ends **January 31, 2018** and the check date is also **January 31, 2018**: Checking is the appropriate account to use. (Remember, if you get a screen regarding signing up for QBDT Payroll service, click **No**.)

PAYROLL TABLE: JANUARY 31, 2018				
	Nancy Andrews	Kent James	Ricardo Salazar	Gina Thomas
HOURS				
Regular	8	152	160	120
Overtime			20	
Sick		8		
Vacation				40
DEDUCTIONS OTHER PAYROLL ITEMS: EMPLOYEE				
Dental Ins.		25.00	25.00	25.00
Medical Ins.		25.00	25.00	25.00
DEDUCTIONS: COMPANY				
CA-Employment Training Tax	0.00	2.42	1.71	2.60
Social Security	5.95	149.83	106.00	161.20
Medicare	1.39	35.04	24.80	37.70
Federal Unemployment	.58	14.50	10.26	15.60
CA-Unemployment	3.84	96.67	68.40	104.00
DEDUCTIONS: EMPLOYEE				
Medicare Employee Addl Tax	0.00	0.00	0.00	0.00
Federal Withholding	0.00	188.75	145.90	168.75
Social Security	5.95	149.83	106.00	161.20
Medicare	1.39	35.04	24.80	37.70
CA-Withholding	0.00	39.48	35.96	43.51
CA-Disability	0.86	21.75	15.39	23.40

8

▶ Print the checks.
  ● Verify the Payroll Printing Preferences: make sure the Intuit logo is not printed.
  ● Print the company name and address on the voucher checks.
  ● Checks begin with number 1.
    ▪ If you print to a pdf file, save the document as **1-Your Name Cks 1-4 Ch8**.
▶ Change Ricardo Salazar's check to correct the overtime hours. (Remember to Unlock Net Pay before recording the changes.) He worked **12** hours overtime. Because of the reduction in overtime pay, his deductions change as follows: CA-Employment Training Tax: **1.60**; Social Security Company and Employee: **99.32**; Medicare Company and Employee: **23.23**; Federal Unemployment: **9.61**; CA-Unemployment: **64.08**; Federal Withholding: **129.70**; CA-Withholding: **31.21**; and CA-Disability: **14.42**. Reprint Check **3**.
  ● If you print to a pdf file, save the document as **2-Your Name Ck 3 Salazar Corrected Ch8**.
▶ Nancy spilled coffee on her check. **Void Check 1** for January 31, print the voided check.
  ● If you print to a pdf file, save the document as **3-Your Name Ck 1 Andrews Void Ch8**.
▶ Reissue Nancy's paycheck, and print it using **Check 5**. Remember to use 01/31/18 as the check and pay period ending date. The pay period is 01/01/18 to 01/31/18. Refer to the payroll table for information on hours and deductions.
  ● If you print to a pdf file, save the document as **4-Your Name Ck 5 Andrews Replacement Ch8**.
▶ Prepare and print the **Payroll Summary Report** for **January 1-31, 2018** in <u>Landscape</u> orientation.
  ● If you print to a pdf file, save the document as **5-Your Name Payroll Sum Ch8**.
▶ Prepare and print the **Payroll Liability Balances Report** for **January 1-31, 2018** in <u>Portrait</u> orientation.
  ● If you print to a pdf file, save the document as **6-Your Name Payroll Liab Bal Ch8**.
▶ Pay <u>all</u> the taxes and other liabilities for **January 1-31, 2018**. The Check Date is **01/31/18**. Select: **Create liability check without reviewing**. Print the checks using a Standard check style with the company name and address.
  ● If you print to a pdf file, save the document as **7-Your Name Cks 6-8 Ch8**.
▶ Prepare, expand, and print the **Journal** report for **January 31, 2018** in <u>Landscape</u> orientation.
  ● If you print to a pdf file, save the document as **8-Your Name Journal Ch8**.
▶ Backup your work.

CHAPTER 8 CHECKLISTS

YOUR NAME'S TOTAL FITNESS

The checklist below shows all business forms and reports printed during training. Check each one that you printed. In the document names below, Your Name and Ch8 have been omitted, and report dates are given.

___ 1-Ck 1: Baker	___ 5-Ck 6: Crown Replacement
___ Ck 2: Brown	___ 6-Payroll Sum, January, 2018
___ Ck 3: Crown	___ 7-Payroll Liab Bal, January, 2018
___ Ck 4: Cruz	___ 8-Ck 7: EDD
___ Ck 5: Kamaka	___ Ck 8: Medical and Dental Insurance Co.
___ 2-Ck 4 Cruz	___ Ck 9: United States Treasury
___ 3-Ck 5: Kamaka	___ 9-Journal, January 31, 2018
___ 4-Ck 3: Crown Void	

YOUR NAME'S SWIM PROS

The checklist below shows all business forms and reports printed during training. Check each one that you printed. In the document names below, Your Name and Ch8 have been omitted, and report dates are given.

___ 1-Ck 1: Andrews	___ 5-Payroll Sum, January, 2018
___ Ck 2: James	___ 6-Payroll Liab Bal, January, 2018
___ Ck 3: Salazar	___ 7-Ck 6: Dental and Medical, Ins.
___ Ck 4: Thomas	___ Ck 7: Employment Development Dept.
___ 2-Ck 3: Salazar Corrected	___ Ck 8: United States Treasury
___ 3-Ck 1: Andrews Void	___ 8-Journal, January 31, 2018
___ 4-Ck 5: Andrews Replacement	

8

CREATE A COMPANY IN QUICKBOOKS DESKTOP

LEARNING OBJECTIVES

At the completion of this chapter, you will be able to:

9.01.   Create a new company using the QuickBooks Desktop Setup and the EasyStep Interview.
9.02.   Select a top Icon bar.
9.03.   Customize the Chart of Accounts.
9.04.   Add customers, vendors, and sales items.
9.05.   Enter Sales Tax information.
9.06.   Print an Account Listing.
9.07.   Select Preferences.
9.08.   Add a Company Logo.
9.09.   Select a Payroll Option.
9.10.   Complete QuickBooks Desktop Payroll Set Up for Company, Employees, Taxes, and Year-to-Date Payrolls.
9.11.   Prepare and print a Payroll Item Listing report.
9.12.   Complete employee information.
9.13.   Enter Adjusting Entries.
9.14.   Print a Balance Sheet.

COMPUTERIZING A MANUAL SYSTEM

In previous chapters, QuickBooks Desktop was used to record transactions for businesses that were already set up for use in the program. In this chapter, you will set up a fictitious business, create a chart of accounts, create various lists, add names to lists, add opening balances, and delete unnecessary accounts. QuickBooks Desktop makes setting up a business user-friendly by going through the process using the EasyStep Interview. Once the EasyStep Interview is completed, you will make refinements to accounts and opening balances, add customers, vendors, and sales items. Reports and preferences will be customized, and a company logo will be added. The Payroll Setup will be completed, and employees will be added. Uncategorized Income and Expenses will be transferred to the owner's equity account.

TRAINING TUTORIAL AND PROCEDURES

The following tutorial is a step-by-step guide to setting up the fictitious company Your Name's Canine Club. Company information, accounts, items, lists, and other items must be provided before transactions may be recorded in QuickBooks Desktop. The EasyStep Interview will be used to set up basic company information. After that, the Chart of Accounts will be completed, and some beginning balances will be added. Then, Customers, Vendors, and Sales Items will be added. Preferences will be changed, and a company logo will be added. The Payroll Setup will be completed, and employees will be added. As in earlier chapters, information for the company setup will be provided in memos. Information may also be shown in lists or within the step-by-step instructions provided.

Please note that QuickBooks Desktop is updated on a regular basis. If your screens are not always an exact match to the text, check with your instructor to see if you should select something that is similar to the text. For example, QuickBooks Desktop has been known to change the type of businesses or industries that it uses in the EasyStep Interview. If that happens, your instructor may suggest that you select the company type closest to Your Name's Canine Club. A different company type may result in a different chart of accounts. This would mean adjusting the chart of accounts to match the one given in the text.

PROGRAM NAME AND DATES

As was done in Chapter 8, the program name QuickBooks Accountant Desktop 2018 will be referred to as QBDT. Some descriptions of QuickBooks Desktop screens or dialog boxes may be referred to as QuickBooks or QuickBooks Desktop. Remember all references to QuickBooks Accountant Desktop may be used interchangeably. Throughout the text, the year used for the screen shots is 2018. Check with your instructor to see what year to use for the transactions. Sometimes, the difference in the computer and text dates will cause a slight variation in the way QBDT screens are displayed and they may not match the text exactly. If you cannot change a date that is provided by QBDT, accept it and continue with your training. Instructions are given where this occurs. The main criterion is to be consistent with the year you use throughout the chapter.

COMPANY PROFILE: YOUR NAME'S CANINE CLUB

Your Name's Canine Club is a fictitious company that provides boarding in the Canine Hotel, playtime at Canine Camp, and grooming in the Canine Salon. In addition, Your Name's Canine Club has a Canine Club Boutique that carries collars, leashes, sweaters, treats, and toys for dogs. Your Name's Canine Club is in San Diego, California, and is a sole proprietorship owned by you. You are involved in all aspects of the business. Your Name's Canine Club has one full-time employee who is paid a salary: Oscar Bailey, whose duties include running the Canine Hotel, ordering and managing the Boutique, and completing all paperwork and forms for dog services. There is one full-time hourly employee: Annabelle Williams, who does the grooming in the Canine Salon, supervises Canine Camp, and cares for the dogs staying at the Canine Hotel.

CREATE A NEW COMPANY

Since "Your Name's Canine Club" is a new company, it does not appear as a company file. You may create a new company by clicking New Company on the File menu or the "Create a new company" button on the No Company Open screen.

There are four ways in which to setup a company. You may create a company using Express Start where you give QBDT a company name, the type of industry, type of ownership, tax ID#, legal name, address, telephone, email, and Web site. You may use the Detailed Start to complete the QuickBooks Desktop Setup using the EasyStep Interview, which provides more detailed company information than Express Start. You may use Create to make a new company file based on an existing company. Finally, you may use Other Options to convert a file from another program.

MEMO

DATE: January 1, 2018

Because this is the beginning of the fiscal year for Your Name's Canine Club, it is an appropriate time to set up the company information in QBDT. Use the QuickBooks Desktop Setup and EasyStep Interview to create a new company.

 Open QBDT as previously instructed

Insert a USB drive as previously instructed or use the storage location you have been using throughout the text

Click **File** menu, click **New Company** or click the **Create a new Company** icon on the **No Company Open** dialog box

- The QuickBooks Desktop Setup will appear with the screen "Let's get your business set up quickly!"

QUICKBOOKS DESKTOP SETUP AND EASYSTEP INTERVIEW

The QuickBooks Desktop Setup uses the EasyStep Interview as a step-by-step guide to enter your company information as of a single date called a start date. The EasyStep Interview uses screens with questions that, when answered, enable QBDT to set up the company file, create a Chart of Accounts designed for your specific type of business or industry, and establish the beginning of a company's fiscal year and income tax year.

Once a screen has been read and any required items have been filled in or questions answered, the <u>Next</u> button is clicked to tell QBDT to advance to the next screen. If you need to return to a previous screen, click the <u>Back</u> button. If you need to stop the Setup before completing everything, you may exit by clicking the <u>Leave</u> button in the bottom-left corner of the screen or by clicking the close button at the top-right corner of the EasyStep Interview screen. Depending on where you are in the interview, your data may or may not be saved.

 Begin creating Your Name's Canine Club

Click **Detailed Start**

MEMO

DATE: January 1, 2018

Use the following information to complete the QuickBooks Desktop Setup and EasyStep Interview for Your Name's Canine Club:

Company and Legal Name: **Your Name's Canine Club** (*Key in your actual first and last name*)
Tax ID: **15-9828654**
Address: **3737 Midway Drive, San Diego, CA 92110**
Phone: **760-555-7979**; Fax: **760-555-9797**
E-mail: **YourName@CanineClub.com** (use *your actual name@CanineClub.com*)
Web: **www.CanineClub.com**
Type of Business: **Retail Shop or Online Commerce**
Company Organization: **Sole Proprietorship**
Fiscal year starts in **January**
Administrator Password: **QBDT2018**
File Name: **Your Name's Canine Club**
File Type: **.qbw**
Sell: **Both services and products**
Enter Sales: **Record each sale individually**
Charge sales tax: **Yes**
Estimates, Statements, Progress Invoicing, or Track Time: **No**
Track Customer Orders (Sales Orders) and Inventory: **Yes**
Manage Bills: **Yes**
Employees: **Yes, W-2 Employees**
Date to start tracking finances: **01/01/2018**
Use QBDT to set up the Income and Expense Accounts: Add **Service Sales** and remove
   Merchant Account Fees

 Use the information in the Memo above to create Your Name's Dog Days by completing the EasyStep Interview in QuickBooks Desktop Setup

> Enter the Company Name, **Your Name's Canine Club**, press the Tab key
> - To identify your work, type your own name, not the words "Your Name's" as part of the company name. For example, Sam Moreno would enter **Sam Moreno's Canine Club**.
> - Your Name's Canine Club is entered as the Legal name when the Tab key is pressed.
> Tab to **Tax ID**, enter **15-9828654**
> Enter the Company Address information in the spaces provided, tab to or click in the blanks to move from item to item
> For the state, California, type **C** and QBDT will fill in the rest or click the drop-down list arrow for State and click CA
> - The country is automatically filled in as US.
> Enter the telephone number, fax number, e-mail address, and Web address as given in the Memo

9

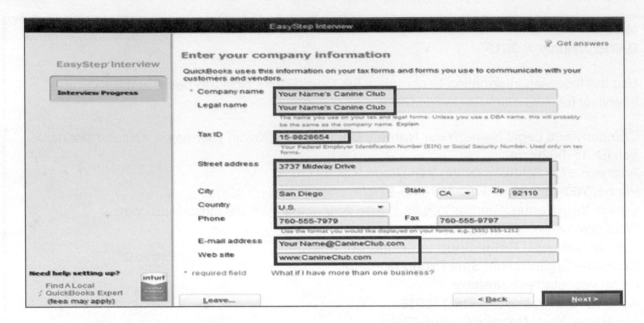

Click **Next**
Scroll through the list of industries
Click **Retail Shop or Online Commerce**, click **Next**

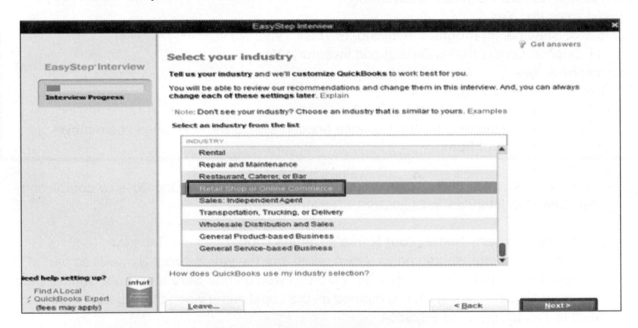

- Notice the Interview Progress in the upper-left side of the EasyStep Interview. This shows how much of the Interview has been completed.
- This Interview Progress portion of the screen will no longer be shown in every screen shot in the text, but it will be shown on your QBDT screen.
- The Next, Back, and Leave buttons will no longer be shown.

The company is a **Sole Proprietorship**, select this, and then click **Next**

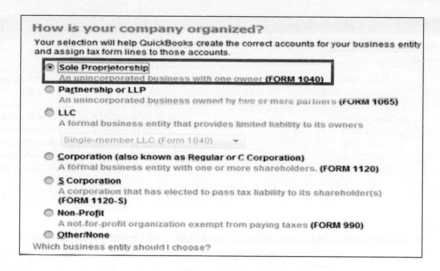

The fiscal year starts in **January**, click **Next**

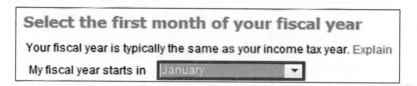

Enter your administrator password, **QBDT2018**

Retype the password **QBDT2018**

- Even though the screen says this is optional, you will not be able to reopen your company file until you enter an Administrator password.

Set up your administrator password (optional)

We recommend you set up a **password to protect your company file**. You will be prompted for this password whenever you open this file. It is optional to set up a password.

Administrator password •••••••••
Retype password •••••••••
Your password is case-sensitive.

What is an "administrator"? Entering a password here sets up the **administrator user**, who has full access to all activities and information in QuickBooks. When you are ready, you can set up **other users** with more limited privileges.

Note: You can also set up or change your administrator password later.

Click **Next**

Read the screen to Create your company file, click **Next**

Click the drop-down list for **Save in:** and click the storage location you have been instructed to use (The example provided shows a USB drive in H: as the storage location.)

The File name is **Your Name's Canine Club**

Save as type: should show **QuickBooks Files (*.QBW, *.QBA)**

- Think: QuickBooks Working file = QBW.

9

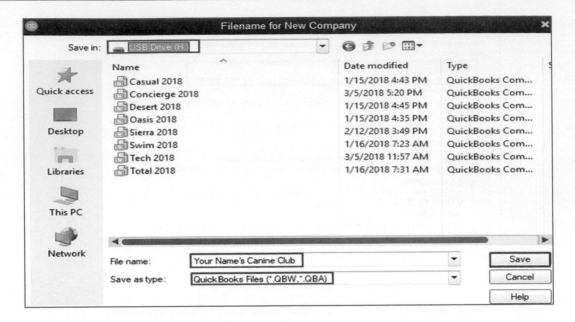

Click **Save**
- If you need to exit the program before finishing the Easy Step Interview, complete the following steps. Otherwise, read them for information only.
  - Once the company file has been saved, you may click **Leave** and then click **OK** to exit the setup without losing the information entered during the EasyStep Interview. Close QBDT as previously instructed.

  - When you resume, you will open QBDT. You must then open the company, Your Name's Canine Club. When you do, QBDT will give you a Welcome Back screen. Simply click **OK** and resume the company setup.

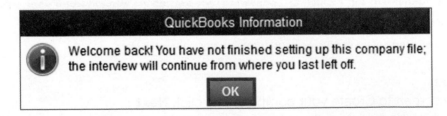

Read the screen regarding Customizing QuickBooks for your business; then click **Next**
- Some screens will require that you click a selection; on others the selection will already be marked.

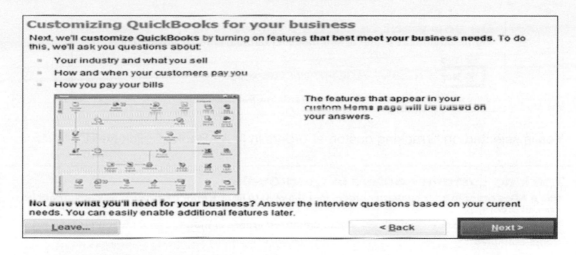

Click **Both services and products** on "What do you sell?" screen; click **Next**

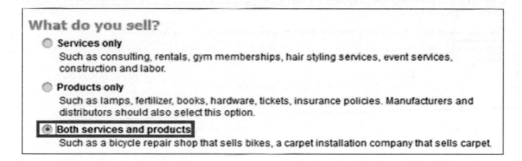

Click **Record each sale individually** on "How will you enter sales in QuickBooks" screen; click **Next**

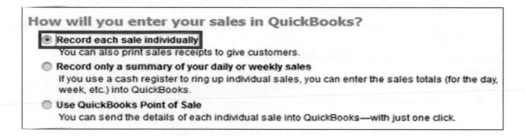

You do charge sales tax, **Yes** is selected for "Do you charge sales tax?"; click **Next**

No is selected on "Do you want to create estimates in QuickBooks?," click **Next**

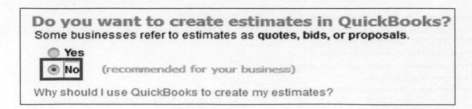

Yes is selected on "Tracking customer orders in QuickBooks," click **Next**

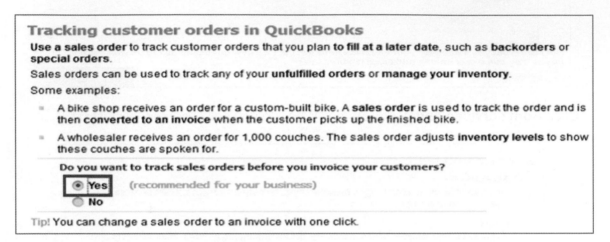

No is selected on "Using statements in QuickBooks," click **Next**

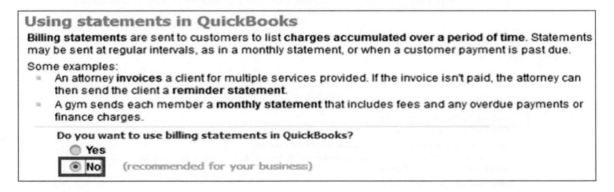

No is selected for "Using progress invoicing," click **Next**

Yes is selected on "Managing bills you owe," click **Next**

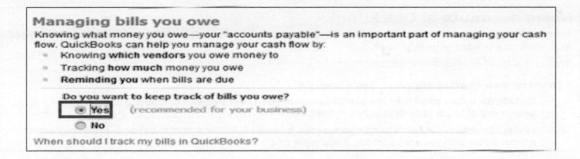

Click **Yes** on "Tracking inventory in QuickBooks," since you have inventory and plan to use QuickBooks to track it; click **Next**

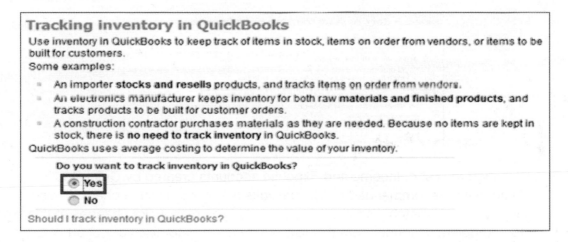

Tracking time is used to keep track of the time spent on a specific job or with a client, which is not done in your company; **No** is selected on "Tracking time in QuickBooks," click **Next**

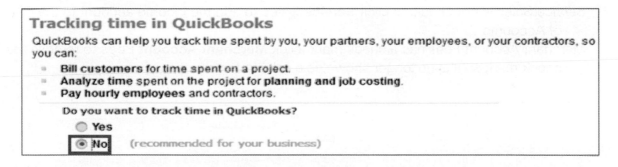

9

There are two employees who work for Canine Club, click **Yes** and click **We have W-2 employees.** on "Do you have employees?," click **Next**

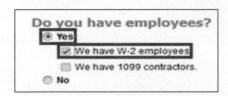

You want to use QuickBooks to set up the Chart of Accounts; read the screen for Using accounts in QuickBooks; click **Next**

Using accounts in QuickBooks

Next, we'll help you set up your **Chart of Accounts**, which are categories of income, expenses and more that you'll use to track your business.

Why is the chart of accounts important?

To set up your chart of accounts, you'll need to:

- Decide on a date to use as the starting point to track your business finances in QuickBooks (e.g., beginning of fiscal year, first of this month, etc.)
- Understand how you want to categorize your business' income and expenses. (You may want to discuss this with your accountant, if you have one.)

Click **Use today's date or the first day of the quarter or month.**
Enter the date **01/01/2018**; click **Next**

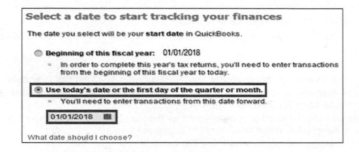

Scroll through the list of Income and Expense accounts created by QuickBooks

- The accounts recommended by QuickBooks are marked with a check. These accounts may or may not match your chart of accounts. You may make changes at this time to add and delete accounts from this list, or you may customize your chart of accounts later.
- To customize the income and expense section of the chart of accounts now, you add an account by clicking the unmarked account name.
- To remove an account that has been marked, click the account name to deselect.

Service Sales is not checked; click **Service Sales** to add the Income account to the Chart of Accounts

Merchant Account Fees has a check mark, click **Merchant Account Fees** to remove the check mark so it is no longer shown as a selected account

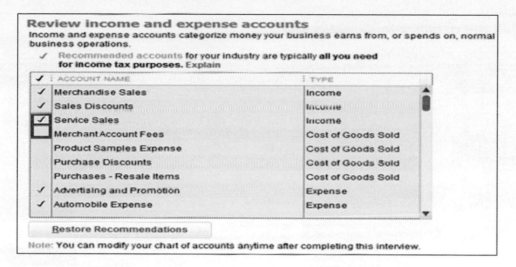

Other changes to the Chart of Accounts will be made later, click **Next**
On the **Congratulations** screen, click the **Go to Setup** button

On the screen for QuickBooks Desktop Setup, read the screen to learn about three sections
- Add the people you do business with: This screen enables you to add information for customers, vendors, and employees.
- Add the products and services you sell: This screen is where you add the information about your sales items. There are three types that may be included: services, inventory parts (items sold), and non-inventory parts (items that would be included as materials for a job).
- Add your bank accounts: This is used to enter your bank account name, account number, opening balance, and opening balance dates for all your bank accounts.

You will be adding customers, vendors, employees, sales items, and bank accounts individually as you work through the chapter, click **Start Working**

9

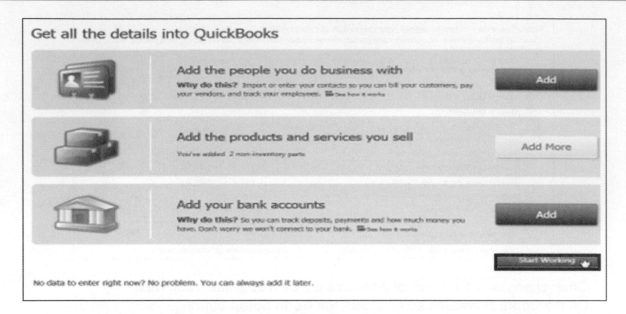

If you get screens showing Quick Start Center or New Feature Tour, close them

SELECT A TOP ICON BAR

Throughout the textbook, the Top Icon Bar has been used. The Left Icon Bar is the default icon and shows when the company setup is complete. QBDT allows you to use either of the icon bars. Since the Left Icon Bar takes up a lot of room on the screen, we will continue to use the Top Icon Bar.

   Select a Top Icon Bar

Click **View** on the Menu Bar
Click **Top Icon Bar**

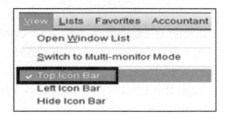

- The Top Icon Bar is now shown in grayscale. We will change to color in Preferences later in the chapter.

CUSTOMIZE CHART OF ACCOUNTS

Using the QuickBooks Desktop Setup to set up a company is a user-friendly way to establish the basic structure of the company. However, the Chart of Accounts created by QBDT may not be the exact Chart of Accounts you wish to use in your business. To customize your chart of accounts, additional accounts need to be created, balances need to be entered for balance sheet accounts, some account names need to be changed, and some accounts need to be deleted or made inactive.

The Chart of Accounts is not only a listing of the account names and balances but also the General Ledger used by the business. As in textbook accounting, the General Ledger/Chart of Accounts is the book of final entry.

At the completion of the QuickBooks Desktop EasyStep Interview and Setup, you will have the following Chart of Accounts, which is not complete. Please be aware that the Chart of Accounts created in the QuickBooks EasyStep Interview may be different from the one shown.

NAME	TYPE	BALANCE TOTAL	ATTACH
◦ Inventory Asset	Other Current Asset	0.00	
◦ Accumulated Depreciation	Fixed Asset	0.00	
◦ Furniture and Equipment	Fixed Asset	0.00	
◦ Security Deposits Asset	Other Asset	0.00	
◦ Payroll Liabilities	Other Current Liability	0.00	
◦ Sales Tax Payable	Other Current Liability	0.00	
◦ Opening Balance Equity	Equity	0.00	
◦ Owners Draw	Equity	0.00	
◦ Owners Equity	Equity		
◦ Merchandise Sales	Income		
◦ Sales Discounts	Income		
◦ Service Sales	Income		
◦ Advertising and Promotion	Expense		
◦ Automobile Expense	Expense		
◦ Bank Service Charges	Expense		
◦ Computer and Internet Exp...	Expense		
◦ Depreciation Expense	Expense		
◦ Insurance Expense	Expense		
◦ Interest Expense	Expense		
◦ Janitorial Expense	Expense		
◦ Meals and Entertainment	Expense		
◦ Office Supplies	Expense		
◦ Payroll Expenses	Expense		
◦ Professional Fees	Expense		
◦ Rent Expense	Expense		
◦ Repairs and Maintenance	Expense		
◦ Telephone Expense	Expense		
◦ Uniforms	Expense		
◦ Utilities	Expense		
◦ Ask My Accountant	Other Expense		

Use the following Chart of Accounts table and balances as a reference while you customize Your Name's Canine Club Chart of Accounts. Information regarding changes, additions, etc. is provided in the Memo that follows the Chart of Accounts. As usual, the steps used in making changes to the Chart of Accounts are detailed after the memo.

As you review the Chart of Accounts, look at the descriptions provided by QBDT. In many instances, the descriptions provided are explanatory and quite lengthy; and, frequently, they are unnecessary for clarification. In these instances, the descriptions should be deleted.

In addition to the changes you will be making in the Chart of Accounts, the Customer List, Vendor List, and Sales Items will also need to have information entered before your Chart of Accounts will match the following:

YOUR NAME'S CANINE CLUB
CHART OF ACCOUNTS

ACCOUNT	TYPE	BALANCE	ACCOUNT	TYPE
Checking	Bank	29,385.00	Sales	Inc.
Accounts Receivable (QB)	Accts. Rec.	***2,950.00	Boarding	Inc.
Inventory Asset	Other C.A.	***33,750.00	Day Camp	Inc.
Office Supplies	Other C.A.	350.00	Grooming	Inc.
Prepaid Insurance	Other C.A.	1,200.00	Merchandise	Inc.
Sales Supplies	Other C.A.	500.00	Sales Discounts	Inc.
Equipment	Fixed Asset	***	Cost of Goods Sold (QB)	COGS
Original Cost	Fixed Asset	8,000.00	Advertising and Promotion	Exp.
Depreciation	Fixed Asset	-800.00	Automobile Expense	Exp.
Fixtures	Fixed Asset	***	Bank Service Charges	Exp.
Original Cost	Fixed Asset	15,000.00	Computer and Internet Expenses	Exp.
Depreciation	Fixed Asset	-1,500.00	Depreciation Expense	
Accounts Payable (QB)	Other C.L.	***5,000.00	Insurance Expense	Exp.
Payroll Liabilities	Other C.L.	0.00	Interest Expense	Exp.
Sales Tax Payable	Other C.L.	0.00	Janitorial Expense	Exp.
Equipment Loan	Long Term L.	2,000.00	Office Supplies Expense	Exp.
Fixtures Loan	Long Term L.	2,500.00	Payroll Expenses	Exp.
First & Last Name, Capital	Equity	***	Professional Fees	Exp.
First & Last Name, Investment	Equity	25,000.00	Rent Expense	Exp.
First & Last Name, Withdrawals	Equity	0.00	Repairs and Maintenance	Exp.
Owner's Equity (QB*)	Equity	***	Sales Supplies Expense	Exp.
			Telephone Expense	Exp.
			Utilities	Exp.
			Other Income	Other Inc
			Other Expenses	Other Exp

Chart Abbreviations:

(QB)=Account Created by QBDT

(QB*)=Account Created by QBDT. Name change required.

Indented Account Names indicate that the account is a subaccount

*** means that QBDT will enter the account balance

C.A.=Current Asset, C.L.=Current Liability; Long Term L.=Long Term Liability; COGS=Cost of Goods Sold, Inc.=Income, Exp.=Expense.

MEMO

DATE: January 1, 2018

Since Your Name's Canine Club's Chart of Accounts/General ledger needs to be customized, make the following changes to the accounts:

Add: **Checking**, Type: **Bank**; Bank Acct. No.: **456114865**, Routing Number: **126735894**, Statement Ending Balance: **$29,385**, Statement Ending Date: **12/31/17**

Delete: **Accumulated Depreciation, Furniture and Equipment, Security Deposits Asset, Uniforms, and Ask My Accountant**

Make inactive: **Meals and Entertainment**

Edit Equity Accounts: Change the name of Opening Balance Equity to **First & Last Name, Capital**; change Owners Equity to **Owner's Equity**, change Owners Draw to **First & Last Name, Withdrawals**, Subaccount of: **First & Last Name, Capital**

Add Equity Accounts: **First & Last Name, Investment,** Subaccount of: **First & Last Name, Capital**; Opening Balance: **$25,000** as of: 01/01/18

Add Income Accounts: Add **Sales**; add **Other Income**; add **Boarding**, Subaccount of: **Sales**; add **Grooming**, Subaccount of: **Sales**

Edit Income Accounts: rename Merchandise Sales to **Merchandise**, Subaccount of: **Sales**; rename Service Sales to **Day Camp**, Subaccount of: **Sales**

Add Expense Accounts: **Sales Supplies Expense**, and **Other Expenses**

Edit Expense Accounts: Rename Office Supplies to **Office Supplies Expenses**

Delete Account Descriptions: Delete the descriptions entered by QBDT for each account

Change Tax-Line Mapping: Select Unassigned for all Tax-Line Mapping

---

 Make the changes indicated above and delete the descriptions in all the accounts

Click **Chart of Accounts** in the Company section of the Home Page
Use the keyboard shortcut **Ctrl+N** to add a new account
Account Type click **Bank**, click **Continue**
Enter Account Name: **Checking**, enter Bank Acct. No: **456114865**, Routing Number: **126735894**
Click **Enter Opening Balance**, enter the Statement Ending Balance: **29,385**
Enter the date of the last bank statement received prior to setting up the company in QBDT for the Statement Ending Date: **12/31/2017**

9

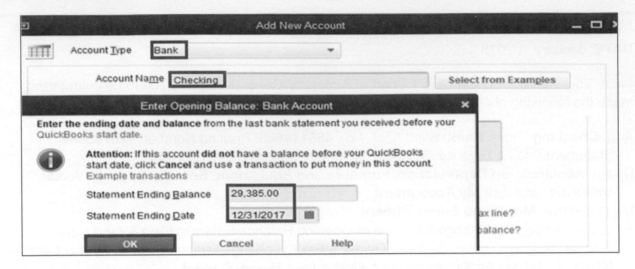

Click **OK** on Enter Opening Balance: Bank Account; then click **Save & Close**

If you get a Set Up Bank Feed message, click **No**

Click the account **Accumulated Depreciation** to highlight, use the keyboard **Ctrl+D** to delete the account, click **OK** to delete

Repeat to delete the other accounts listed in the memo

Position the cursor on the expense account, **Meals and Entertainment**, click the **Account** button, and click **Make Account Inactive**

Position the cursor on **Opening Balance Equity**, click the **Account** button, click **Edit Account** or use **Ctrl+E**, enter **First & Last Name, Capital** as the account name (use your actual first and last name), click **Save & Close**

Edit **Owners Equity** and change the name to **Owner's Equity**, click **Save & Close**

Edit **Owners Draw** and rename it **First & Last Name, Withdrawals** (use your actual first and last name), click **Subaccount of**, click **First & Last Name, Capital**, click **Save & Close**

Click the **Account** button, click **New**, or use **Ctrl+N**, account type is **Equity**, click **Continue**

Enter the account name **First & Last Name, Investment** (use your first and last name), click **Subaccount**, click **First & Last Name, Capital**

Click the **Enter Opening Balance** button, enter **25,000** as of **12/31/17**

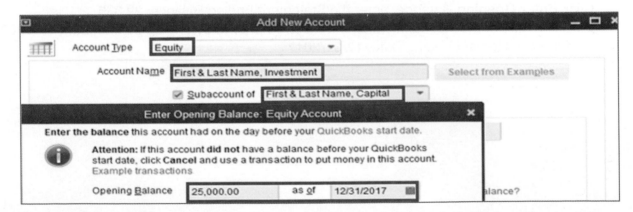

Click **OK**; and then, click **Save & Close**

- If you get a screen warning about a transaction being 30 days in the future or 90 days in the past, click **Yes**.

Use **Ctrl+N**, account type is **Income**, click **Continue**

Account name is **Sales**, click **Save & New**

Add the Income Account: **Boarding**, Subaccount of: **Sales**, click **Save & New**

Add the Income Account: **Grooming**, Subaccount of: **Sales**, click **Save & New**

Click the drop-down list arrow for Account Type, click **Other Income**, the account name is **Other Income**, click **Save & Close**

Click **Merchandise Sales**, use **Ctrl+E** to edit, change the name to **Merchandise**, Subaccount of: **Sales**; click **Save & Close**

Edit **Service Sales** change the name to **Day Camp**, Subaccount of: **Sales**; click **Save & Close**

Use **Ctrl+N** to add a new **Expense** account, Account Name: **Sales Supplies Expense**, click **Save & New**

Change Account Type: **Other Expense**, Account Name: **Other Expenses**, click **Save & Close**

Edit the Expense Account **Office Supplies** change the Account Name to **Office Supplies Expense**, click **Save & Close**

To remove unwanted and lengthy account descriptions and a variety of tax-line mappings, use **Ctrl + E** to edit each account individually, delete descriptions added by QBDT, and change tax-line mapping to **<Unassigned>**, when finished, click **Save & Close**

Since you created Checking, it does not have a description or Tax-Line, so begin with Inventory Asset and repeat for all the accounts

- Lengthy account descriptions are provided by QBDT when it establishes the Chart of Accounts. These descriptions are designed to help those with limited accounting knowledge. They will print on reports so removing them helps to streamline QBDT reports.

- QBDT will include appropriate tax-line mapping for some accounts but not others. Since our focus is not on tax-line mapping, making all tax lines <Unassigned> is appropriate.

Click the **Account** button, click **Show Inactive Accounts**

- Note that the inactive account, Meals and Entertainment, is shown with an **X**.

At this point, the Chart of Accounts appears as follows:

- As you can see, income and expense accounts do not have opening balances. Only some balance sheet accounts—assets, liabilities, and equity accounts—have opening balances.

9

The type of account is still Fixed Asset, Account Name: **Original Cost**, Subaccount of: **Equipment**

Click the **Enter Opening Balance** button, enter **8,000** as of **12/31/17**, click **OK**

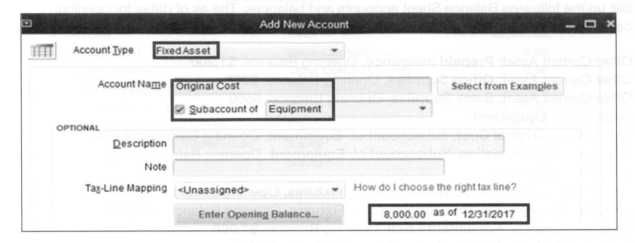

Click **Save & New** and add Account Name: **Depreciation**, Subaccount of: **Equipment** with an Opening Balance of **-800** as of **12/31/17**

- Be sure to use a minus (-) sign in front of the 800. Remember, depreciation reduces the value of the asset.

Click **OK** on the Opening Balance screen

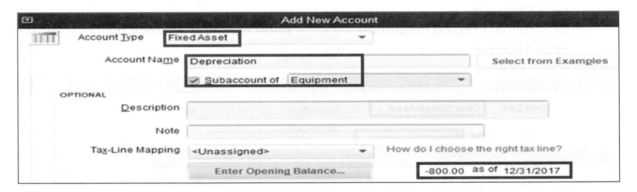

Click **Save & New**

Add the other fixed asset, **Fixtures**

Use the information in the Memo to add the Subaccounts of Fixtures **Original Cost** and **Depreciation** and the Opening Balances listed in the Memo, click **Save & New** after adding each account

Change the account Type to **Long Term Liability**, Account Name: **Equipment Loan**

Click the **Enter Opening Balance** button; enter **2,000** as of **12/31/17**, click **OK**

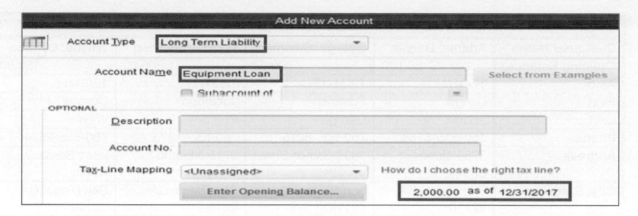

Click **Save & New**

Add the Long-Term Liability Account **Fixtures Loan** and its Opening Balance, click **Save & Close**

Review the Chart of Accounts; then close it

- Note the value of Store Equipment, Store Fixtures, and the two loans.
- You will notice that Accounts Receivable and Accounts Payable are not in the account listing. QBDT will add these accounts when the customers and vendors and their opening balances are added.
- In addition, Inventory Asset has a 0.00 balance. QBDT will calculate the balance once all inventory items and total values are added.
- The Chart of Accounts will be printed once we have added customers, vendors, and sales items.

ADD CUSTOMERS

In accounting, the Customer List is known as the Accounts Receivable Subsidiary Ledger. Whenever a transaction is entered for a customer, it is automatically posted to the General Ledger account and the Accounts Receivable Subsidiary Ledger. Customers and any opening balances need to be added to the Customer List. QBDT allows you to store preferred payment methods for customers. As a result, credit card information may be added to the customer's account. For security reasons, debit card information may not be added.

  As you add customers, enter the information provided in the following chart:

9

CUSTOMERS				
Customer Name	**Adams, Dennis**	**George, Summer**	**Perez, Jonathon**	**Wayne, Cynthia**
Opening Balance	500.00	800.00	1,500.00	150.00
As of	12/31/17	12/31/17	12/31/17	12/31/17
First	Dennis	Summer	Jonathon	Cynthia
Last	Adams	George	Perez	Wayne
Phone	760-555-8763	760-555-8015	760-555-1275	760-555-2594
Address	3750 James Street	3838 Gaines Street	2715 Nipomo Street	2841 Barnard Street
City, State Zip	San Diego, CA 92110	San Diego, CA 92110	San Diego, CA 92106	San Diego, CA 92110
Terms	Net 30	Net 30	Net 30	Net 30
Credit Limit	500.00	1,000.00	1,500.00	500.00
Preferred Delivery Method	Mail	Mail	Mail	Mail
Preferred Payment Method	Visa	Check	Check	Debit Card
Credit Card Information	4123-4907-8901-237			
Exp. Date	02/2020			
Tax Code	Tax	Tax	Tax	Tax
Tax Item	State Tax	State Tax	State Tax	State Tax

Use **Ctrl+J** to open the **Customer Center**, click the **New Customer & Job** button; and then click **New Customer**

Enter **Adams, Dennis**

- Since you want your Customer List to be sorted according to the customer's last name, type the last name first.

Tab to or click in OPENING BALANCE, enter **500**, AS OF enter **12/31/17**

Complete the Address Info tab:

For the FULL NAME, click in **First**, enter **Dennis**, tab to **Last**, enter **Adams**

Click in or tab to **Main Phone**, enter **760-555-8763**

Click at the end of the name in the ADDRESS DETAILS section for INVOICE/BILL TO, press the Enter key

Enter the address **3750 James Street**, press Enter, type **San Diego, CA 92110**

Click the **Payment Settings** tab and complete:

Click the drop-down list arrow for **PAYMENT TERMS**, click **Net 30**

Click in the text box for **CREDIT LIMIT**, enter **500**

Select the PREFERRED DELIVERY METHOD: **Mail**

Select the PREFERRED PAYMENT METHOD: **Visa**

Since Visa is the preferred payment method, enter the CREDIT CARD INFORMATION CREDIT CARD NO. **4123-4907-8901-237**, EXP. DATE **02/2020**

Tab through NAME ON CARD, ADDRESS, and ZIP/POSTAL CODE (QBDT enters the information)

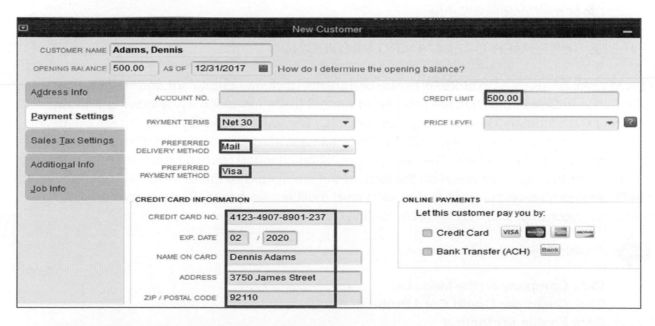

Click the **Sales Tax Settings** tab and complete:

Tax Code should be **Tax**; if not, click the drop-down list arrow and select

Click the drop-down list arrow for **Tax Item**, click **State Tax**

CUSTOMER NAME	Adams, Dennis			
OPENING BALANCE	500.00	AS OF	12/31/2017	How do I determine the opening balance?

Address Info		TAX CODE	Tax	▼	?
Payment Settings		TAX ITEM	State Tax	▼	
Sales Tax Settings		RESALE NO.			

Click **OK**

Use the Customer Chart and enter the information for the remaining customers

- When you enter the information for Cynthia Wayne, remember that you cannot save Debit card information in QBDT.

Click the **Print** icon in the Customer Center, click **Customer & Job List**, print in Portrait orientation

- If you print to a pdf file, save the document as **1-Your Name Cust List Ch9**.

If you get a message for List Reports, click **Do not display this message in the future**, then click **OK**

- The date of your computer will show as the report date and the Date Prepared and Time Prepared will be shown.

Your Name's Canine Club
Customer & Job List
January 1, 2018

Customer	Balance Total	Attach
Adams, Dennis	500.00	No
George, Summer	800.00	No
Perez, Jonathon	1,500.00	No
Wayne, Cynthia	150.00	No

Close the Customer Center

ENABLE CUSTOMER CREDIT CARD PROTECTION

QuickBooks DT users who store, process, or transmit customer debit card and/or credit card information in QuickBooks DT are required to protect that information by complying with the Payment Card Industry Data Security Standard (PCI DSS). To enable QuickBooks DT Customer Credit Card Protection, you must create a complex password for you and all others who view complete credit card numbers. The password must be changed every 90 days, and the three-digit number near the signature panel on the back of the credit card or the four-digit number above the credit card number on the front of the credit card must not be stored. If you do not provide protection, your business may be liable for fines and other damages.

 Enable Credit Card Protection

Click **Company** on the Menu bar
Click **Customer Credit Card Protection...**
Click **Enable Protection**

Complete the **Sensitive Data Protection Setup**

User Name: **Admin** (do <u>not</u> change this)

Current Password: **QBDT2018**

New Password: **2018QBDT**

Confirm New Password: **2018QBDT**

Challenge Question: **Name of your first manager**

Answer: **Enter your professor's last name**

- To keep your company file accessible by the instructor, do <u>not</u> customize or change the Sensitive Data Protection Setup.

Click **OK**

Read the information on the Sensitive Data Protection Enabled screen, click **OK**

- You will now use the password QBDT2018 every time you open the company.

ADD VENDORS

In accounting the Vendor List is known as the Accounts Payable Subsidiary Ledger. Whenever a transaction is entered for a vendor, it is automatically posted to the Accounts Payable account in the Chart of Accounts (also known as the General Ledger) and the Accounts Payable Subsidiary Ledger.

For ease of entry, vendors are divided into two tables. Use these tables as you add Vendors.

VENDORS			
Vendor and Company Name	**Growler Grooming Supplies**	**Pampered Pet Supplies**	**Rover Treats**
Opening Balance	3,000.00	2,000.00	0.00
As of	12/31/17	12/31/17	12/31/17
Main Phone	310-555-6971	760-555-2951	310-555-6464
Fax	310-555-1796	760-555-1592	310-555-4646
Address	10855 Los Angeles Avenue	5787 Western Avenue	1970 Sunset Boulevard
City, State, Zip	Los Angeles, CA 90012	San Diego, CA 92101	Hollywood, CA 90028
Payment Terms	2% 10, Net 30	Net 30	2% 10, Net 30
Credit Limit	10,000	5,000	8,500

9

Open the **Item List**, click the **Item** button; click **New** to begin entering Service items
Click the drop-down list arrow for Type, click **Service**
Enter the Item Name/Number **Canine Hotel**, enter the Description **Boarding**
Enter the Rate **55**, the Tax Code is **Non**
The **Account** is **Boarding**, Subaccount of: **Sales**

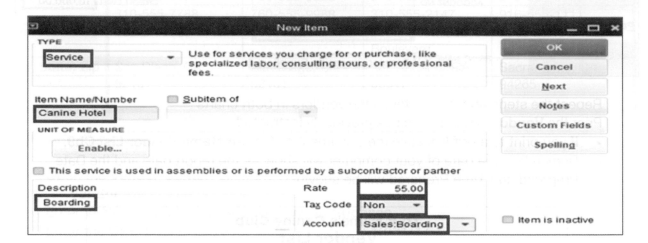

Click **Next** and add the remaining Service Items using the information in the chart
When finished adding service items, click **Next**

  Use the following chart and add the Inventory Items

INVENTORY PART ITEMS				
Item Name	Collars	Leashes	Sweaters	Toys & Treats
Purchase and Sales Description	Collars	Leashes	Sweaters	Toys & Treats
Cost	0.00	0.00	0.00	0.00
COGS Account	Cost of Goods Sold	Cost of Goods Sold	Cost of Goods Sold	Cost of Goods Sold
Preferred Vendor	Pampered Pet Supplies	Pampered Pet Supplies	Pampered Pet Supplies	Rover Treats
Sales Price	0.00	0.00	0.00	0.00
Tax Code	Tax	Tax	Tax	Tax
Income Account	Merchandise	Merchandise	Merchandise	Merchandise
Inventory Asset Account	Inventory Asset	Inventory Asset	Inventory Asset	Inventory Asset
Reorder Point (Min)	100	100	100	100
Max	700	500	375	3500
On-Hand	650	450	325	3,450
Total Value	12,750	6,250	7,500	7,250
As Of	12/31/17	12/31/17	12/31/17	12/31/17

Click the drop-down list arrow for Type, click **Inventory Part**
Enter the Item Name/Number **Collars**
Enter **Collars** as the Description on Purchase Transactions, press **Tab**

- Collars will be entered as the Description on Sales Transactions. The Cost of 0.00 and the COGS Account Cost of Goods Sold is already entered.

Click the drop-down list arrow for **Preferred Vendor**, click **Pampered Pet Supplies**

- The Sales Price of 0.00 and Tax Code of Tax are already entered.

Select the Income Account **Merchandise**, Subaccount of: **Sales**

- The Inventory Asset is already entered as the Asset Account.

Click in the column for Reorder Point (Min) and enter **100**, Tab to Max and enter **700**

- When ordering an item, QBDT will calculate the quantity for the Purchase Order so the item will be at the Maximum amount when the order is received.

Tab to On Hand and enter **650**, enter the Total Value of **12,750**, and enter the date for As of **12/31/17**

Click **Next**

Repeat for each inventory item, click **OK** after all Inventory Part Items have been entered

- Don't forget to enter the max and the reorder point for inventory items.

After the service and inventory items have been added, click **Consignment Item** in the Item list, use **Ctrl+D** to delete the item, click **OK** on Delete Item dialog box

Repeat the procedures to delete the Non-inventory Item; and continue to the next section without closing the Item List

ENTER SALES TAX INFORMATION

As you view the Item List, you will notice that the State Tax shows 0.0%. This should be changed to show the appropriate amount of sales tax deducted for the state. If you also collect local sales tax, this amount needs to be provided as well. In addition to the amount of tax collected, the Tax Agency needs to be identified. The Tax Agency was already added to the company's vendor list.

> **MEMO**
> **DATE**: January 1, 2018
>
> Complete the CA Sales Tax: Tax rate of 8% paid to State Board of Equalization, delete the item for Local taxes.

Enter the amount of sales tax information for CA Sales Tax

Scroll through the Item List until you see State Sales Tax
Click **State Sales Tax** in the Item List; use **Ctrl+E** to edit the Item
Change the Sales Tax Name and Description to **CA Sales Tax**
Enter **8%** as the tax rate
- Since sales tax rates vary and may change at any given time, the rate of 8% is used as an example.

Click the drop-down list arrow for **Tax Agency**, click **State Board of Equalization**

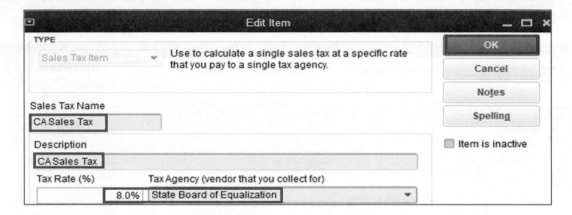

Click **OK** to close the Sales Tax Item
- Note the change to the State Tax on the Item List.

Click **Local Tax**, the use **Ctrl+D** to delete the item as previously instructed
The Item List appears as follows:

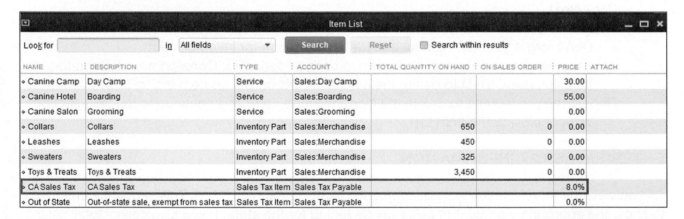

To print the List, click the **Reports** button at the bottom of the Item List
Click **Item Listing**
Click the **Customize Report** button, click the **Header/Footer** tab, change the **Subtitle** to show the report date of **January 1, 2018**, deselect **Date Prepared** and **Time Prepared**, click **OK**
Adjust the column widths to remove extra space and to allow the information to display in full. Since all amounts are zero in the columns for Quantity on Sales Order and Quantity on Purchase Order hide the columns
Click **Print**, click **Landscape**, and click the **Print** button

- If you print to a pdf file, save the document as **3-Your Name Item List Ch9**.
- If you get a Memorize Report message, click **No**.

Close the report and close the Item List

PRINT ACCOUNT LISTING

When customers, vendors, and sales items have been entered, the Chart of Accounts will contain all the beginning balances and should match the complete Chart of Accounts shown earlier in the chapter.

 Print the **Account Listing** in Landscape orientation

Click the **Reports** menu, point to **List**; click **Account Listing**
- Notice the descriptions entered for Accounts Receivable, Accounts Payable, and Uncategorized Income and Uncategorized Expenses. A Tax Line for Uncategorized Income has also been selected by QBDT.

With the Account Listing on the screen, double click on each account that shows a description or tax line; then, delete the Descriptions and change any Tax Lines to <Unassigned>

Close the Chart of Accounts and return to the Account Listing

Resize columns to eliminate extra space, display columns in full, and remove Description and Tax Line from the report
- The Account column shows both the master and the subaccount in the report.

Click the **Customize Report** button, click the **Header/Footer** tab, change the report date to **January 1, 2018**, click **Date Prepared** and **Time Prepared** to remove from the heading, click **OK** (Check with your instructor to see if you should do this.)

Click the **Print** button, select **Portrait** orientation
- If you print to a pdf file, save the document as **4-Your Name Account Listing Ch9**.

9

Your Name's Canine Club
Account Listing
January 1, 2018

Account	Type	Balance Total
Checking	Bank	29,385.00
Accounts Receivable	Accounts Receivable	2,950.00
Inventory Asset	Other Current Asset	33,750.00
Office Supplies	Other Current Asset	350.00
Prepaid Insurance	Other Current Asset	1,200.00
Sales Supplies	Other Current Asset	500.00
Equipment	Fixed Asset	7,200.00
Equipment:Depreciation	Fixed Asset	-800.00
Equipment:Original Cost	Fixed Asset	8,000.00
Fixtures	Fixed Asset	13,500.00
Fixtures:Depreciation	Fixed Asset	-1,500.00
Fixtures:Original Cost	Fixed Asset	15,000.00
Accounts Payable	Accounts Payable	5,000.00
Payroll Liabilities	Other Current Liability	0.00
Sales Tax Payable	Other Current Liability	0.00
Equipment Loan	Long Term Liability	2,000.00
Fixtures Loan	Long Term Liability	2,500.00
First & Last Name, Capital	Equity	81,385.00
First & Last Name, Capital:First & Last Name, Investment	Equity	25,000.00
First & Last Name, Capital:First & Last Name, Withdrawals	Equity	0.00
Owner's Equity	Equity	
Sales	Income	
Sales:Boarding	Income	
Sales:Day Camp	Income	
Sales:Grooming	Income	
Sales:Merchandise	Income	
Sales Discounts	Income	
Uncategorized Income	Income	
Cost of Goods Sold	Cost of Goods Sold	
Advertising and Promotion	Expense	
Automobile Expense	Expense	
Bank Service Charges	Expense	
Computer and Internet Expenses	Expense	
Depreciation Expense	Expense	
Insurance Expense	Expense	
Interest Expense	Expense	
Janitorial Expense	Expense	
Office Supplies Expense	Expense	
Payroll Expenses	Expense	
Professional Fees	Expense	
Rent Expense	Expense	
Repairs and Maintenance	Expense	
Sales Supplies Expense	Expense	
Telephone Expense	Expense	
Uncategorized Expenses	Expense	
Utilities	Expense	
Other Income	Other Income	
Other Expenses	Other Expense	

Close the Report

PREPARE DAILY BACKUP

A backup file is prepared as a safeguard in case you make an error. After the company has been created and customers, vendors, and items have been entered, it is wise to prepare a backup file. In addition, a backup should be made at the end of every work session.

 Prepare the Your Name's Canine Club (Daily Backup).qbb file

Follow the steps presented in Chapter 1 for creating a backup file
Name the file **Your Name's Canine Club (Daily Backup)**
The file type is **QBW Backup (* .QBB)**

SELECT PREFERENCES

Many preferences used by QB DT are selected during the QuickBooks Desktop Setup. However, there may be some preferences you would like to select, change, or delete. The Preferences section has two tabs where you may indicate My Preferences or Company Preferences. The

Preferences that may be customized are: Accounting, Bills, Calendar, Checking, Desktop View, Finance Charge, General, Integrated Applications, Items & Inventory, Jobs & Estimates, Multiple Currencies, Payments, Payroll & Employees, Reminders, Reports & Graphs, Sales & Customers, Sales Tax, Search, Send Forms, Service Connection, Spelling, Tax: 1099, and Time & Expenses. In previous chapters, some of the Preferences were changed. In this chapter, all the Preferences available will be explored and some changes will be made.

MEMO

DATE: January 1, 2018

Open the Preferences screen and explore the choices available for each of the areas. When you get to the following preferences, make the changes indicated below:

Accounting: <u>Company Preferences</u>—Delete the Date Warnings for past and future transactions
Checking: <u>Company Preferences</u>—Select Default Accounts to use should be Checking for Open the Create Paychecks and Open the Pay Payroll Liabilities; <u>My Preferences</u>—Select Default Accounts to Checking for Open the Write Checks, Open the Pay Bills, Open the Pay Sales Tax, and Open the Make Deposits
Desktop View: <u>My Preferences</u>—Select Switch to colored icons/light background on the Top Icon Bar, use Blue-Medium for the Company Color
General: <u>My Preferences</u>—Turn off pop-up messages for products and services
Payroll & Employees: <u>Company Preferences</u>—Deselect Job Costing for paycheck expenses and Display Employee List by Last Name
Reports & Graphs: <u>Company Preferences</u>—Display Report Items by Name only and modify the report Format for the Header/Footer to remove the Date Prepared, Time Prepared, and Report Basis from reports; <u>My Preferences</u>—Refresh reports automatically
Sales & Customers: <u>Company Preferences</u>—select No Custom Pricing
Sales Tax: <u>Company Preferences</u>—Most common sales tax is State Tax

---

 Access Preferences from the Edit menu

- In the following sections the Preferences are shown in the exact order listed on the Preferences screen.
  Click the icons for each category and explore the choices available on both the My Preferences tab and the Company tab
  When you get to a Preference that needs to be changed, make the changes indicated in the Memo above

ACCOUNTING PREFERENCES

Company Preferences tab is accessed to select the use of account numbers. Class tracking may be selected. This screen instructs QBDT to automatically assign general journal entry numbers and to warn when posting a transaction to Retained Earnings. There are two check boxes for warnings when transactions are 90 days within the past or 30 days within the future. The closing date for a period is entered after clicking the Set Date/Password button on this screen. On the My Preferences screen, there is a checkbox that has been selected to Autofill memo in general journal entry.

9

Remove the Date Warnings

Click **Accounting**, and then, if necessary, click the **Company Preferences** tab
Click the check boxes for **Date Warnings** to deselect the two warnings

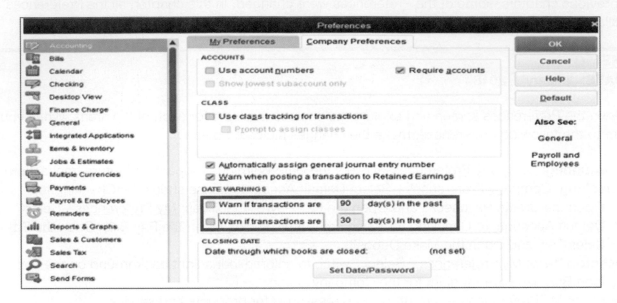

Click **Bills** in the list of **Preferences**
Each time you change a Preference and click on another Preference you get a dialog box
to Save Changes to the Preference, always click **Yes**

BILLS PREFERENCES

Company Preferences has selections for Entering Bills and Paying Bills. You may tell QBDT the
number of days after the receipt of bills that they are due. You may select "Warn about duplicate
bill numbers from the same vendor." When paying bills, you may tell QBDT to use discounts and
credits automatically. There are no selections available for My Preferences.

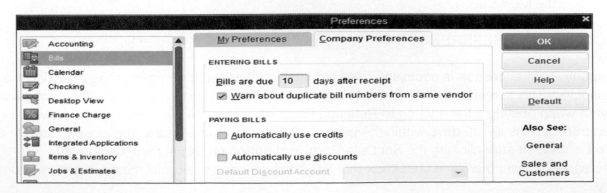

CALENDAR PREFERENCES

QBDT has a calendar that may be used to view transactions entered, transactions that are due, and to do's for a selected day. My Preferences is used to indicate the calendar view, the weekly view, and the types of transactions you wish to appear. You may also select settings for the number of days to display upcoming and past due data. There are no choices available for Company Preferences.

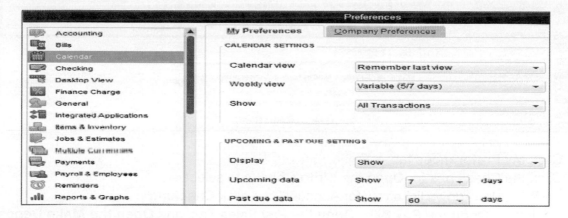

CHECKING PREFERENCES

The Company Preferences listed for checking allows QBDT to print account names on check vouchers, change the check date when a non-cleared check is printed, start with the payee field on a check, warn of duplicate check numbers, autofill payee account number in check memo, set default accounts to use for checks, and to view and enter downloaded transactions in Bank Feeds in either the Express Mode or the Classic (Register) Mode.

 Select Default Accounts to use Checking

Click **Checking** in the **Preferences** list; and, if necessary, click the **Company Preferences** tab
Click the check box for **Open the Create Paychecks**
Click **Checking** on the drop-down list for account
Repeat for **Open the Pay Payroll Liabilities**

9

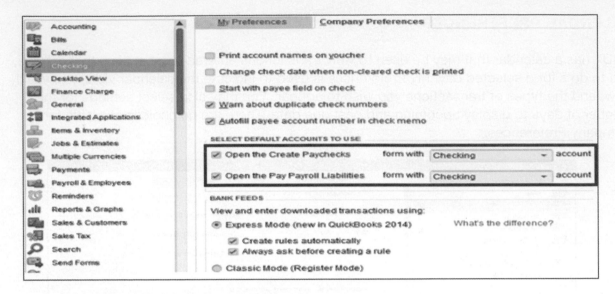

Click **My Preferences** tab

Click the Check box for **Open the Write Checks** to select

Click the drop-down list arrow for Account, and click **Checking**

Repeat for **Open the Pay Bills**, **Open the Pay Sales Tax**, and **Open the Make Deposits**

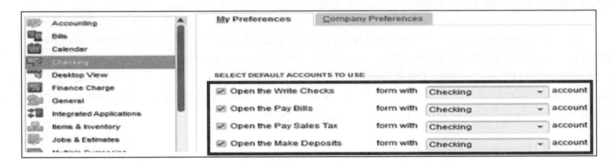

Click the **Desktop View** preference, and then click **Yes** on **Save Changes**

DESKTOP VIEW PREFERENCES

My Preferences has selections to customize your QBDT screens to view one or multiple windows, to display the Home Page, to save the desktop, to switch to colored icons on the Top Icon Bar, to select color schemes and sounds, and to add a Company File Color Scheme. Company Preferences allows you to select features that you want to show on the Home Page and to explore Related Preferences.

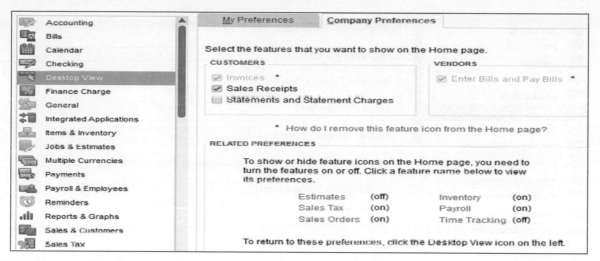

 Select colored icons with light backgrounds for the Top Icon Bar and add a Company File Color Scheme

On the **Desktop View** preference, click **My Preferences Tab**
Click **Switch to colored icons/light background on the Top Icon Bar** to select
Click the drop-down list arrow for **Company File Color Scheme**, click **Blue-Medium**

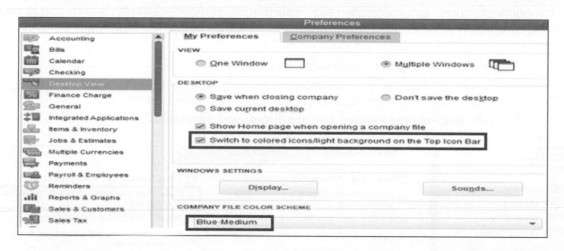

Click **Finance Charge** in the Preferences list, and then click **Yes** on **Save Changes**

FINANCE CHARGE PREFERENCES

The Company Preference allows you to tell QBDT if you want to collect finance charges and to provide information about finance charges. The information you may provide includes the annual interest rate, the minimum finance charge, the grace period, the finance charge account, whether to calculate finance charges from the due date or from the invoice/billed date, and to mark finance charge invoices "To be printed". There are no selections available for My Preferences.

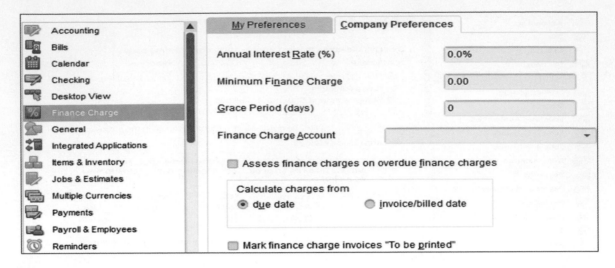

GENERAL PREFERENCES

Use the Company Preferences tab to set the time format, to display the year as four digits, select whether to update name information when saving transactions, and to save transactions before printing. My Preferences tab is used to indicate decimal point placement, set warning screens and beeps, bring back messages, turn off pop-up messages for products and services, keep QBDT running for quick startups, automatically recall information, indicate default date to use in new transactions, and keep custom item information when changing items in transaction.

 Turn off pop-up messages for products and services

> Click **General** in the Preferences list, click the **My Preferences** tab
> Click **Turn off pop-up messages for products and services**

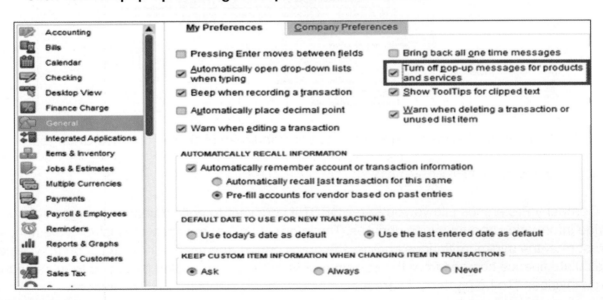

Click **Integrated Applications** in the Preferences list; click **Yes** on Save Changes

INTEGRATED APPLICATIONS PREFERENCES

The Company Preferences are used to manage all the applications that interact with the current QBDT company file. There are no selections available for My Preferences.

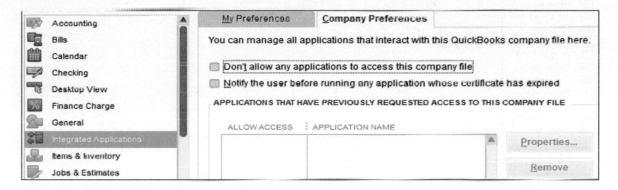

ITEMS & INVENTORY PREFERENCES

The Company Preference is used to activate the inventory and purchase orders features of the program, enable units of measure, provide warnings if there is not enough inventory to sell or there are duplicate purchase order numbers. There are no selections available for My Preferences.

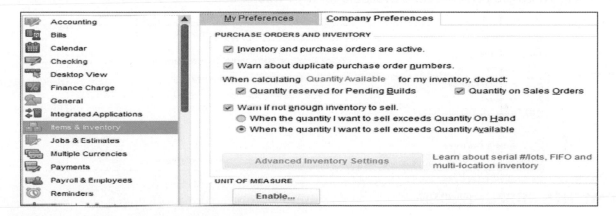

JOBS & ESTIMATES PREFERENCES

The Company Preference allows you to indicate the status of jobs and to choose whether to use estimates. There are no selections available in My Preferences.

9

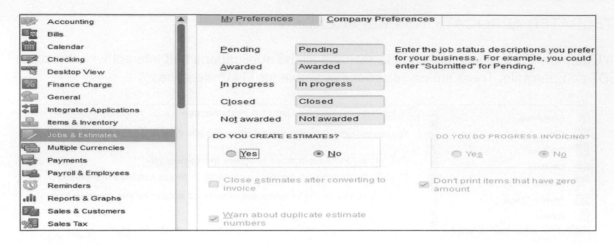

MULTIPLE CURRENCIES PREFERENCES

Using the Company Preferences tab, you may select to use more than one currency. If you use multiple currencies, a currency may be assigned to customers, vendors, price levels, bank and credit card accounts as well as accounts receivable and accounts payable accounts. You must designate a home currency that will be used for income and expense accounts. Once you choose to use multiple currencies, you may not change the preference to discontinue the use of multiple currencies. There are no selections available for My Preferences.

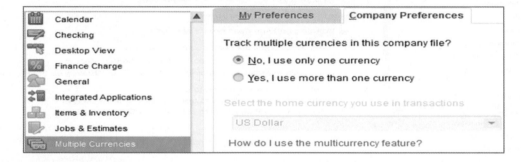

PAYMENTS PREFERENCES

Company Preferences tab for Payments enables you to select tasks for Receive Payments that will automatically apply payments, automatically calculate payments, and use Undeposited Funds as a default deposit to account. If you accept Online Payments, you may select Credit Card and Bank Transfer (ACH) payments. There are no selections available for My Preferences.

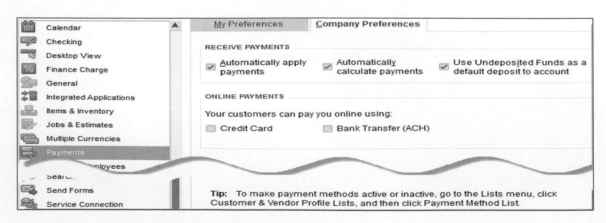

PAYROLL & EMPLOYEES PREFERENCES

Company Preferences include selecting the payroll features, if any, you wish to use. Set Preferences for pay stub and voucher printing, workers compensation, and sick and vacation may be selected. Copying earnings details, recalling quantities and/or hours, and job costing for paycheck expenses may be marked or unmarked. You may choose the method by which employees are sorted. Employee Defaults may be accessed from this screen. Once accessed, the Employee Defaults may be changed and/or modified. There are no selections on My Preferences.

 Change the Display Employee List to Last Name

> Click **Payroll & Employees** Preference; click the **Company Preferences** tab
> Click **Job Costing for paycheck expenses** to deselect
> Click **Last Name** in the section for Display Employee List by

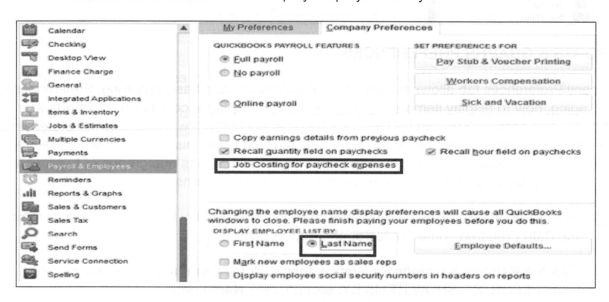

> Click **Reminders** Preference; click **Yes** on the Save Changes dialog box
> Click **OK** on the Warning screen
> • Preferences should reopen automatically. If it does not, click the Edit menu, click Preferences, and click Reminders.

REMINDERS PREFERENCES

In this section you may use My Preferences to select having the Reminders List appear when the QBDT program is started. If you chose to have Reminders displayed, the specific Reminders are selected on the Company Preferences tab.

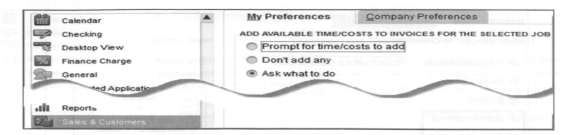

 Change Company Preferences to deselect Enable Price Levels

Click the **Company Preferences** tab; click **No Custom Pricing**

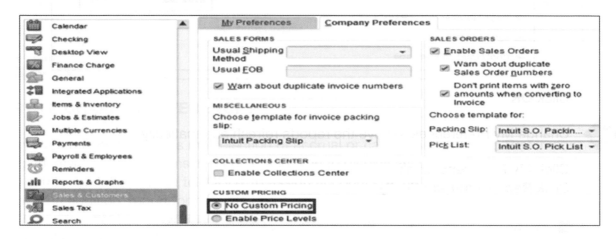

SALES TAX PREFERENCES

Use Company Preferences to indicate whether you charge sales tax. If you do collect sales tax, the default sales tax codes, when you need to pay the sales tax, when sales tax is owed, the most common sales tax, and whether to mark taxable amounts are selected on this screen. My Preferences does not have any selections.

 Change the default for the Most common sales tax to CA State Tax

Click the **Company Preferences** tab for **Sales Tax**
Click the drop-down list arrow for **Your most common sales tax item**
Click **CA State Tax**

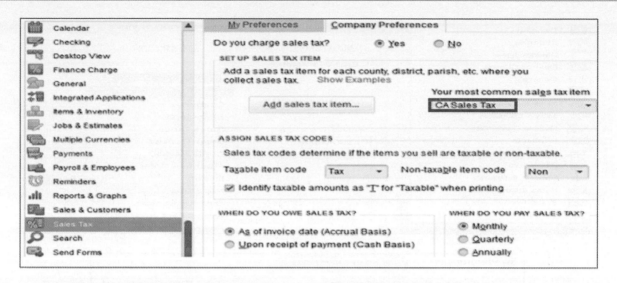

Click **Search** in the Preferences List; then click **Yes** to Save Changes

SEARCH PREFERENCES

Company Preferences include how often to update search information and to use Update Now. My Preferences allows the selection of "Show Search field in the Icon Bar" and of "Choose where to search by default."

SEND FORMS PREFERENCES

Default text is provided for business documents that are sent by email. The text may be changed for invoices, estimates, statements, sales orders, sales receipts, credit memos, purchase orders, reports, pay stubs, overdue invoices, almost due invoices, and payment receipts. My Preferences allows auto-check to determine if the customer's and preferred send method is e-mail. You may also select whether to send e-mail using Web Mail or QuickBooks E-mail. To use QuickBooks E-mail, you must subscribe to Billing Solutions.

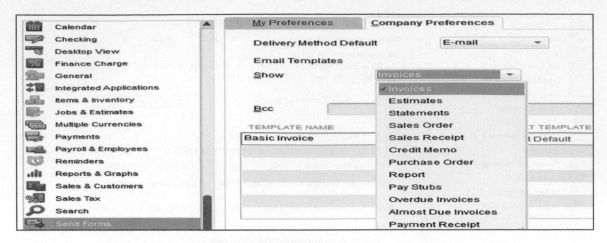

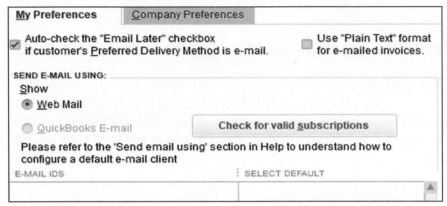

SERVICE CONNECTION PREFERENCES

Company Preferences allows you to specify how you want to handle your connections to QuickBooks Services. You may select to automatically connect without a password or to require a password before connecting. You may also select to allow background downloading of QBDT service messages. My Preferences allows settings for saving a file whenever Web Connect data is downloaded and leaving your browser open after Web Connect is done. (Web Connect is used as a Web browser to connect to financial institutions and is used in online banking.)

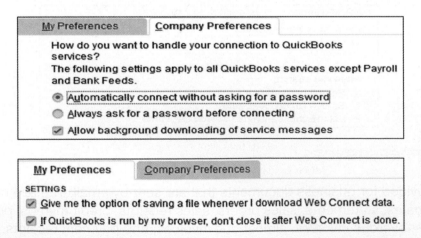

SPELLING PREFERENCES

On the My Preferences tab, you can check the spelling in the fields of most sales forms including invoices, estimates, sales receipts, credit memos, purchase orders, and lists. You can run Spell Checker automatically or change the preference and run the Spell Checker manually. There is also a selection for words to ignore. A list of words added to the dictionary is also shown. These words may be deleted if you do not want them. There are no Company Preferences to select.

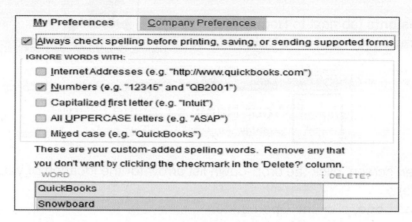

TAX: 1099 PREFERENCES

The only selection is on the Company Preferences screen. This is where you indicate whether you file 1099-MISC forms. There are no selections available for My Preferences.

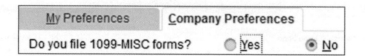

TIME & EXPENSES PREFERENCES

Company Preferences is used to indicate whether you track time, which is useful if you bill by the hour. There are also some Invoicing Options associated with tracking time available. My Preferences does not have any selections available.

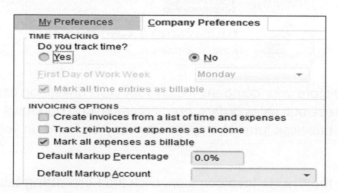

Click **OK** to close Preferences

ADD COMPANY LOGO

To customize your business, you may add a logo to the Insights page and to business forms; such as, invoices, sales receipts, sales orders, and purchase orders. If you store your company file on a USB drive, you may add the logo to Insights, but you may not add it to business forms.

   Add the company logo to the Insights page

Click the **Insights** tab next to Home Page
Click the gray square that says **Upload Logo**

Source: Great19/Shutterstock

On the **Open** screen, click the drop-down list arrow for the location of your USB (H: in the example)
Click **Canine Logo**, click the **Open** button

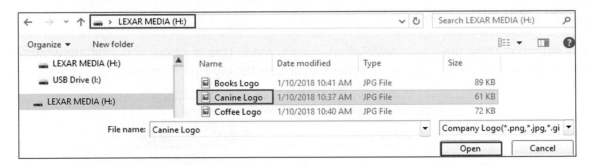

- The screen shot shows only the logo files. It does not show all the company and backup files.

You will see the company logo inserted on Insights

READ ONLY: Since you store your company file on your USB drive, you cannot add the Company Logo to invoices, sales receipts, sales orders, credit memos, and purchase orders. As a result, the steps to add a logo to a business form when your company is stored on your hard drive will be illustrated below.

Click **Home Page**, click the **Create Invoices** icon, click the **Formatting** tab on the Create Invoice icon bar

- The steps to add logos to business forms are the same except that you must use a copy of an invoice, which is illustrated below.

Click **Customize Data Layout**, click **Make a Copy** on the Locked Template message

Click **Basic Customization...** button on the Additional Customization screen
Click **Use logo** to select
Click the drop-down list arrow on the **Select Image** screen; click the location of your hard drive
Click **Canine Logo** to highlight, click the **Open** button

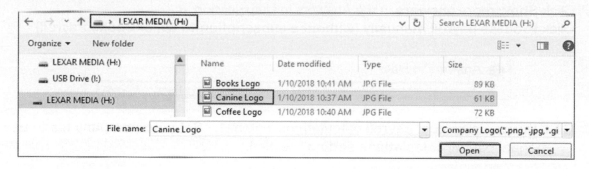

You will get a Warning screen for QBDT to copy your image into Your Name's Canine Club –
  Images, click **OK**
* The next business form you customize will use the logo from the Images folder.
* You will not see the logo unless your preview a business document or print it.
Click **OK** on the Basic Customization screen, then click **OK** on the Additional Customization
  screen
The heading area of the invoice appears as follows:

PREPARE DAILY BACKUP

 Use Create Local Backup and Your Name's Canine Club (Daily Backup).qbb file to update
the backup

PAYROLL

When you completed the tutorial in Chapter 8, you paid the employees who worked for the
company. To use QBDT to process payroll, you need to complete the Payroll Set up and provide
individual information regarding your employees.

SELECT PAYROLL OPTION

Before entering any payroll transactions, QBDT must be informed of the type of payroll service you
are selecting. Once QBDT knows what type of payroll process has been selected for the company,
you will be able to create paychecks. As in you did in Chapter 8, you must go through the Help
menu to designate the selection of the Manual payroll option.

Select a **Manual** payroll option

Open the Employee Center
Press **F1** to access Help
Click **Show more answers** in the Answers in Help section
Click **Process payroll manually (without a subscription to QuickBooks Payroll)**

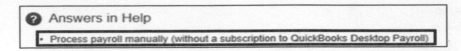

> ? Answers in Help
> • Process payroll manually (without a subscription to QuickBooks Desktop Payroll)

Click the words **manual payroll calculations** in Item 1. **"Set your company file to use the manual payroll calculations setting"** section,

---

Process payroll manually (without a subscription to QuickBooks Desktop Payroll)

What we recommend

We strongly recommend that you sign up for QuickBooks Desktop Payroll to make sure that you have the most current tax tables available. In addition to providing current tax tables, QuickBooks Desktop Payroll provides additional features that take the worry out of doing your payroll.

If you prefer to process your payroll manually

1. Set your company file to use the manual payroll calculations setting.

   Important: When your company file is set up for manual payroll calculations, **QuickBooks inserts a "zero" amount** for each payroll item associated with a tax.

   - What does this mean? ⊞
   - What will happen in QuickBooks if I choose manual calculations? ⊞

2. Set up your payroll using the **Payroll Setup interview.** ⊞

3. ⌗Contact the IRS, your state and local tax agencies, and your professional tax advisor to get the most recent payroll tax information, such as:

   - Tax tables, including mid-year tax changes that can affect your payroll
   - Wage base limits on taxes such as FUTA
   - The frequency with which you pay your payroll taxes. (The frequency can change from year to year, depending on certain conditions in your company.)

4. Then, each pay period use the information you gather in Step 3 to calculate the current and year-to-date federal, state, and local tax information for each employee.

5. Go to the Employees menu and click Pay Employees. On the Enter Payroll Information screen select the employees to pay, open the Paycheck Detail for each employee, and replace the "zero" amounts with the appropriate tax amounts for each paycheck.

6. Pay your payroll tax liabilities using the tax schedules provided by the IRS and your state or local tax agency.

On the screen for Are you sure...? Click **Set my company file to use manual calculations** in the line for "If you are sure you want to manually calculate your payroll taxes in QuickBooks"

Are you sure you want to set your company file to use manual calculations?

Before you click the link below...

- The manual calculations setting is applied immediately. You may not receive a message that indicates the change in your company file.
- If you click this link inadvertently and want to reinstate payroll tax calculations in your company file, you will need to sign up for QuickBooks Desktop Payroll.
- If you already have a QuickBooks Desktop Payroll subscription and click this link inadvertently, contact QuickBooks Desktop Payroll. Clicking this link does **not** cancel your QuickBooks Desktop Payroll subscription.

If you are sure you want to manually calculate your payroll taxes in QuickBooks, click here: Set my company file to use manual calculations

---

Once QBDT processes the selection, you will get a QuickBooks Information message,
   which may be hidden behind the Help screen

Close Help

Click **OK** on the QuickBooks Information screen

GENERAL NOTES ON QUICKBOOKS DESKTOP PAYROLL SETUP

Once the payroll processing method is selected, you must complete the QuickBooks Payroll
Setup. QBDT is setup with Automatic Update turned on. Periodically, Intuit will send out program
updates via the Internet that will be downloaded to your computer. It is important to note that
sometimes information in the program changes. If your screens differ from the ones shown, do not
be alarmed, you will enter the same information; but, perhaps, in a slightly different format or
order.

You may find that some of your screens are different from the ones shown in the text. This is
because the computer date used when writing the text is January 1, 2018 and your computer will
use the current date. If you see a different year on your screen, and you are not able to change it,
just continue with the training and leave the date as it appears.

QUICKBOOKS DESKTOP PAYROLL SETUP

There are six sections in the QuickBooks Payroll Setup that are completed to setup payroll.

The first section is an introductory screen. The second section is the Company Setup for payroll.
This section helps you identify and setup your methods of compensation, benefits your company
offers, and additions and deductions your employees might have.

The third section leads you through adding employee information or setting up individual
employees. When establishing the Employee Defaults, you will specify which payroll items apply to
all or most of the employees of the company. Payroll items are used to identify and/or track the
various amounts that affect a paycheck. These items include salaries and wages, taxes, types of
other deductions, commissions, and company-paid benefits.

The fourth section, Taxes, automatically sets up the payroll items for federal, state, and local taxes.
Payroll tax liabilities and payroll withholding items need to be associated with a vendor to process
tax payments appropriately.

The fifth section, Year-to-Date Payrolls, enter earnings and withholdings for employees and payroll
liability payments for the current year. This is important if you are installing QBDT and have already
made payroll payments during the calendar year.

The final section, Finishing Up, takes companies with a subscription to QuickBooks Payroll to the
Payroll Center. If you are using manual payroll, you are taken to the Home Page.

CAUTION: If you exit the payroll setup before everything is complete, be sure to click the **Finish
Later** button. If you exit the payroll setup by any other method, you may lose all the information
you have entered and will need to re-enter it. Sometimes, QBDT will retain the information and will
re-enter it for you as you click through each of the sections in the QuickBooks Payroll Setup.

9

BEGIN QUICKBOOKS DESKTOP PAYROLL SETUP

 Click the **Employees** menu, click **Payroll Setup**

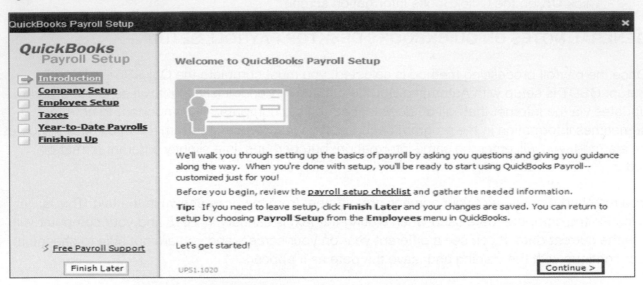

Read the Introduction screen
- If you click <u>payroll setup checklist</u> you will go to an Adobe pdf file that contains information about the data needed to setup your payroll.

Click **Continue**

COMPANY SETUP

In this section of the QuickBooks Payroll Setup, information about the methods of paying employees, deductions, and benefits is entered.

MEMO
DATE: January 1, 2018

Complete the Company portion of the QuickBooks Desktop Payroll Setup:

Methods used to compensate employees: **Salary**, **Hourly wage**, and **Overtime**
Insurance Benefits: **Health Insurance** and **Dental Insurance** both are fully <u>paid by the employee</u> <u>after taxes have been deducted</u>
Retirement Benefits: **None**
Paid Time Off: **Sick Time** and **Vacation Time**
Other Payments and Deductions: **None**

 Complete the Company Setup portion of the QuickBooks Payroll Setup
Read the first screen regarding Company Setup: Compensation and Benefits

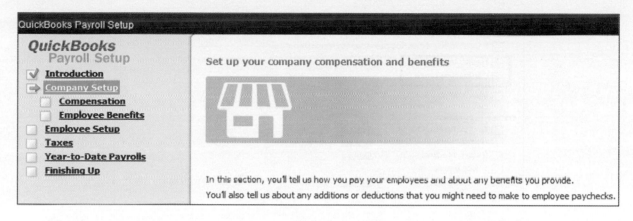

Click the **Continue** button (located in the lower-right corner of the screen)

Click **Bonus, award, or one-time compensation** to unmark

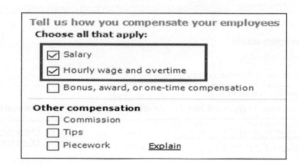

Click **Finish** (located in the lower-right corner of the screen)

Review the Compensation List

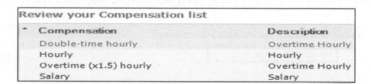

Click **Continue**

Read the screen regarding **Set up employee benefits**

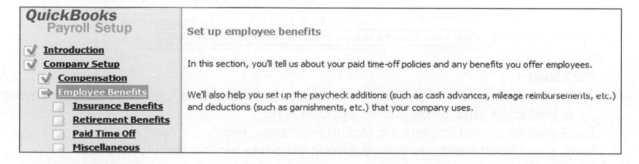

Click **Continue**

Click **Health insurance** and **Dental insurance** to select; then click **Next**

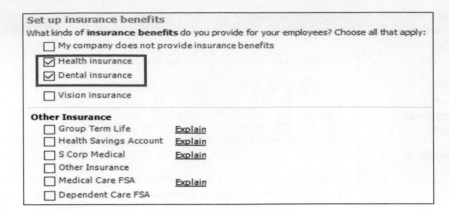

On the Health Insurance screen, click **Employee pays for all of it**

Payment is deducted after taxes should appear and be selected; then click **Next**

Click the drop-down list arrow for **Payee (Vendor)**, click **Health Insurance, Inc.** to select
the Vendor that receives payment for health insurance premiums

Make sure **I don't need a regular payment schedule for this item** is selected

Click **Next**

On the Dental Insurance screen, click **Employee pays for all of it** and verify that **Payment
is deducted after taxes** is checked; click **Next**

The Payee for Dental Insurance is **Health Insurance, Inc.**

Make sure **I don't need a regular payment schedule for this item** is selected

Click **Finish**

Review your Insurance Benefits list

Review your Insurance Benefits list

* Insurance Item	Description
Dental Insurance (taxable)	After-Tax Employee-Paid Dental
Health Insurance (taxable)	After-Tax Employee-Paid Health

Click **Continue**

The next screen allows you to select retirement benefits

We do not provide any retirement benefits for our employees

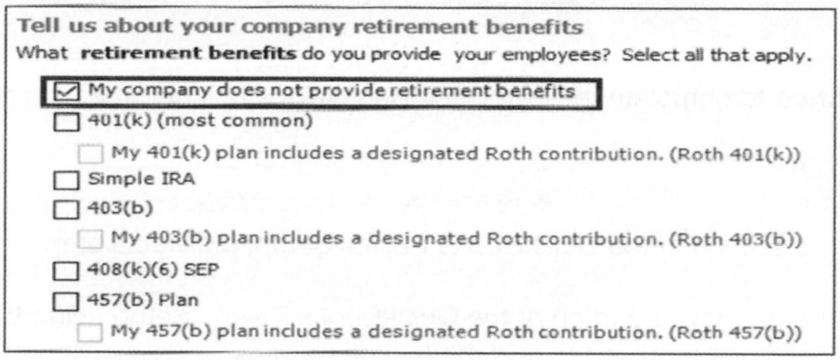

Tell us about your company retirement benefits
What **retirement benefits** do you provide your employees? Select all that apply.

- ☑ My company does not provide retirement benefits
- ☐ 401(k) (most common)
  - ☐ My 401(k) plan includes a designated Roth contribution. (Roth 401(k))
- ☐ Simple IRA
- ☐ 403(b)
  - ☐ My 403(b) plan includes a designated Roth contribution. (Roth 403(b))
- ☐ 408(k)(6) SEP
- ☐ 457(b) Plan
  - ☐ My 457(b) plan includes a designated Roth contribution. (Roth 457(b))

Click **Finish**, and then click **Continue**

For Paid Time Off, we do provide paid time off for Sick Leave and Vacation Leave, click **Paid sick time off** and **Paid vacation time off** to select

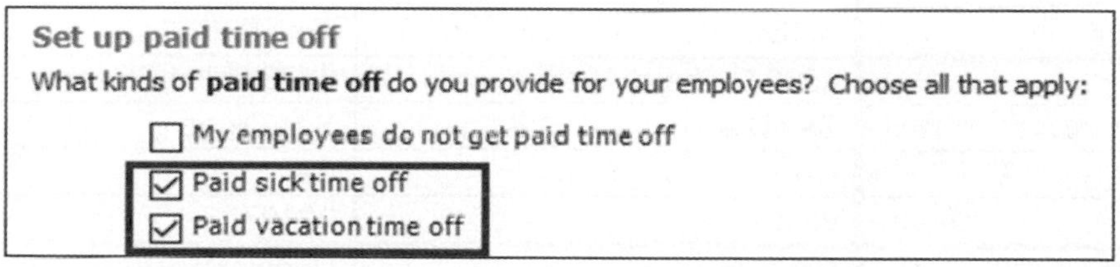

Set up paid time off
What kinds of **paid time off** do you provide for your employees? Choose all that apply:

- ☐ My employees do not get paid time off
- ☑ Paid sick time off
- ☑ Paid vacation time off

Click **Finish**

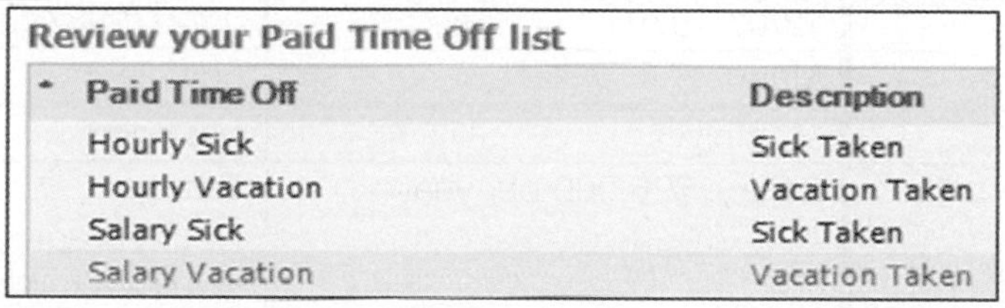

Review your Paid Time Off list

* Paid Time Off	Description
Hourly Sick	Sick Taken
Hourly Vacation	Vacation Taken
Salary Sick	Sick Taken
Salary Vacation	Vacation Taken

9

Review the Paid Time Off list, click **Continue**

We do not have any other Additions or Deductions

Set up additions and deductions

Tell us about **anything else** that affects your employees' paychecks. Choose all that apply:

Additions
- ☐ Cash advance
- ☐ Taxable fringe benefits   Explain
- ☐ Mileage reimbursement   Explain
- ☐ Miscellaneous addition   Explain

Deductions
- ☐ Wage garnishment   Explain
- ☐ Union dues
- ☐ Donation to charity
- ☐ Miscellaneous deduction   Explain

Click **Finish**

Click **Continue** to complete the Employee Benefits section and the Company Setup

EMPLOYEE SETUP

During the Employee section of the QuickBooks Payroll Setup, individual employees are added.

 Complete the Employee portion of the QuickBooks Payroll Setup using the following chart and the instructions provided to add the two employees

EMPLOYEES Oscar Bailey and Annabelle Williams		
Legal Name	Oscar Bailey	Annabelle Williams
Employee Status	Active	Active
Home Address	2062 Orchard Avenue	3875 Milan Street
City	San Diego	San Diego
State	CA	CA
Zip Code	92107	92107
Employee Type	Regular	Regular
Social Security No.	100-55-2525	100-55-9661
Hire Date	04/23/2014	06/30/2015
Birth Date	12/07/1979	09/27/1987
Gender	Male	Female
Pay Period	Monthly	Monthly
Compensation	Salary: $26,000 per year	Hourly: Hourly wage: $15.50 Double-time hourly: $31.00 Overtime (x1.5) hourly: $23.25
Dental Insurance	$30 per month, annual limit $360	$30 per month, annual limit $360
Health Insurance	$250 per month, annual limit $3,000	$250 per month, annual limit $3,000
Sick Time Earns	40:00 at beginning of year	40:00 at beginning of year
Unused Sick Hours	Have an accrual limit	Have an accrual limit
Maximum Hours	120:00	120:00
Earns	Time off currently	Time off currently

EMPLOYEES Oscar Bailey and Annabelle Williams		
Hours Available as of 01/01/18 (Your computer date will show)	20:00	50:00
Hours Used as of 01/01/18 (Your computer date will show)	0:00	0:00
Vacation Time Earns	40:00 at beginning of year	40:00 at beginning of year
Unused Vacation Hours	Have an accrual limit	Have an accrual limit
Maximum Hours	120:00	120:00
Earns	Time off currently	Time off currently
Hours Available as of 01/01/18 (Your computer date will show)	20:00	40:00
Hours Used as of 01/01/18 (Your computer date will show)	0:00	0:00
Payment Method	Check (no Direct Deposit)	Check (no Direct Deposit)
State Subject to Withholding	CA	CA
State Subject to Unemployment Tax	CA	CA
Live or Work in Another State in 2018	No	No
Federal Filing Status	Single	Married
Allowances (Federal)	0	2
Extra Withholding	0.00	0.00
Nonresident Alien Withholding	Does not apply	Does not apply
HIRE Act Exemption	Not a qualified employee	Not a qualified employee
Subject to (Federal)	Medicare Social Security Federal Unemployment	Medicare Social Security Federal Unemployment
State Filing Status	Single	Married (two incomes)
Regular Withholding Allowances (State)	0	2
Subject to (State)	CA-Unemployment CA-Employment Training Tax CA-Disability	CA-Unemployment CA-Employment Training Tax CA-Disability
Local Taxes	No	No
Wage Plan Code	S	S

9

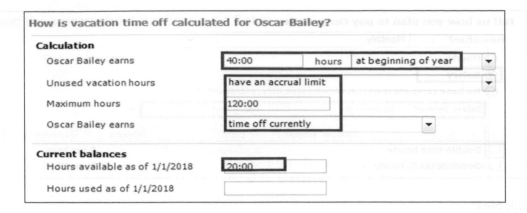

Click **Next**

We do not pay using Direct Deposit, click **Next** on the direct deposit screen

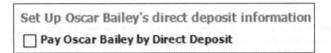

Enter **CA** as the state where Oscar is subject to withholding and unemployment tax. He has not lived or worked in another state in 2018

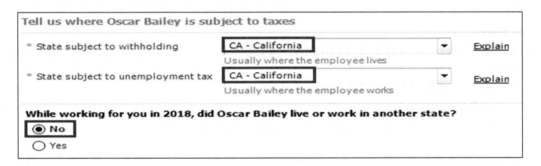

Click **Next**

Use the Employees table and enter the federal tax information for Oscar

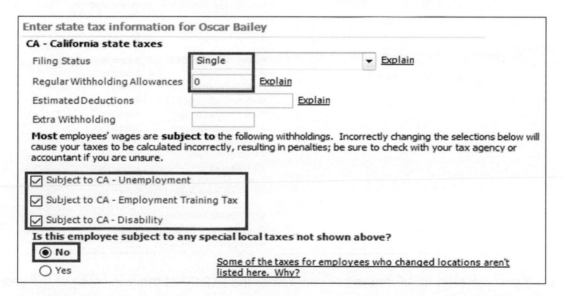

Click **Next**

Use the Employees table and enter the state tax information for Oscar

* Note: If you do not see the section for Subject to CA-Unemployment, Subject to CA-Employment Training Tax, Subject to CA-Disability, or Is this employee subject to any special local taxes not shown above?, click **Next** to go to a separate screen.

Click **Next**

* The California Employment Development Department agency requires employers who file electronically to select a Wage Plan Code.

Since you do participate in the state unemployment and disability insurance programs, select **S** as the code

9

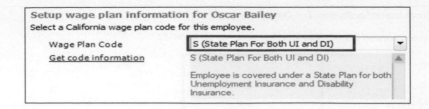

Click **Finish**

Click the **Summary** button to view the information entered for Oscar Bailey

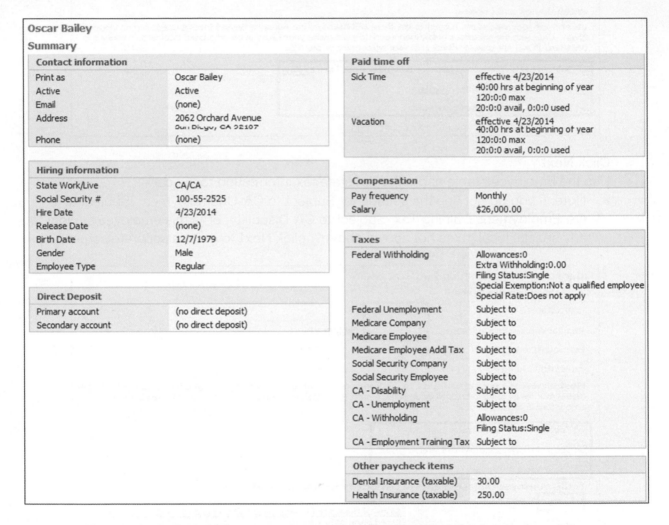

- If you selected 40:00 hours per year rather than 40:00 at the beginning of the year, your summary will show 3:20 per paycheck. If this happens, you may return to the Employee List, click Oscar Bailey to highlight, click the Edit button, then, click through Oscar's Information until you get to the Sick Time and Vacation information. At that point change his information to say Beginning of the year.

Click **Print** on the Summary screen and print Oscar's information

- If you print to a pdf file, save the document as **5-Your Name Oscar Bailey Emp Sum Ch9**.

Close the **Employee Summary** window for Oscar

Click **Add New**, use the Employees table and add the information for **Annabelle Williams** following the steps provided for Oscar Bailey

When you complete the wages and compensation section for Annabelle, after selecting
Monthly for How often?, click **Hourly**, enter **15.50** for Hourly wage
Click, **Double-time hourly** to select, enter **31.00**; click **Overtime (x1.5) hourly** to select,
enter the amount **23.25**

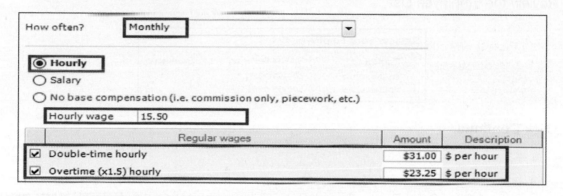

Complete the employee setup for Annabelle Williams
With Annabelle Williams highlighted in the employee list, click the **Summary** button

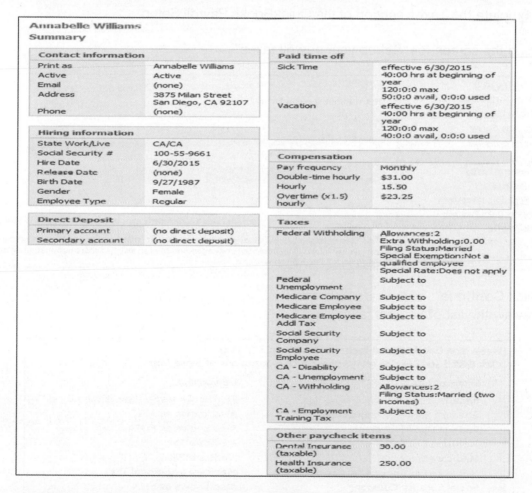

- Sometimes QBDT will use the effective date for sick time and vacation time that was
  used for the last employee. If this happens, disregard the date. Oscar's effective date of
  4/23/2014 was also used for Annabelle. This will be changed when the employee
  information for Annabelle Williams is edited.

Print **Annabelle Williams'** Summary, close the Summary

- If you print to a pdf file, save the document as **6-Your Name Annabelle Williams Emp Sum Ch9**.

Review the Employee List

Click **Continue**

TAXES

The Taxes section of the QuickBooks Payroll Setup allows you to identify federal, state, and local tax payments and agencies. You may also schedule tax payments in this section.

 Complete the Taxes section of the QuickBooks Payroll Setup

Read the screen for "Set up your payroll taxes"

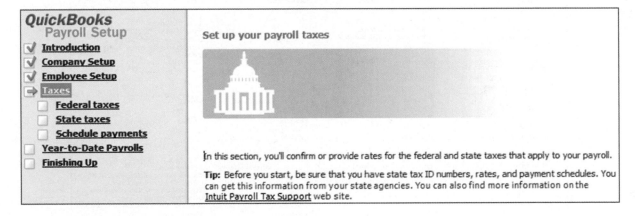

Click **Continue**

Review the list of Federal taxes

Here are the federal taxes we set up for you	
Click **Edit** if you need to review or make changes to any of these taxes.	
Federal Tax	**Description**
Federal Withholding	Also known as Federal Withholding Tax
Advance Earned Income Credit	Also known as AEIC
Federal Unemployment	Also known as FUTA
Medicare Company	Medicare Tax
Medicare Employee	Medicare Tax
Medicare Employee Addl Tax	Medicare Additional Tax
Social Security Company	Also known as FICA
Social Security Employee	Also known as FICA

Click **Continue**

Review your state taxes: complete the following:

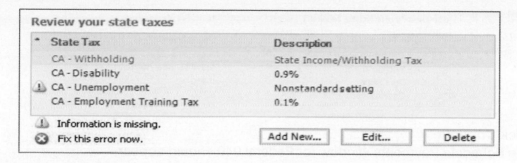

- Notice that CA-Unemployment is marked with the symbol for Information is missing. Click **CA-Unemployment**, click **Edit**

    Make sure your Edit CA-Unemployment screen matches the following; when it does, click **Next**

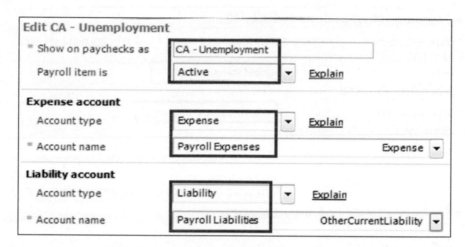

Enter the California-Unemployment Company Rate of **3.4%**; click **Finish**
- California has a variable rate schedule for Unemployment Insurance for companies. A new company will pay 3.4% for the first three years. After that, the rate is determined by a variety of factors and can range from 1.5% to 6.2%.
- Remember, the Tax Year will be shown based on the date of your computer. If it is not 2018, do not worry about trying to change the date.

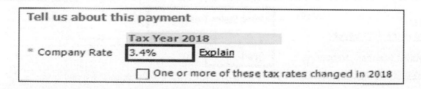

Review your state taxes
- If your State Tax listing appears in a different order, that is not a concern. The important thing is that the correct rates are shown. If the rates are not correct, edit the tax as demonstrated for CA – Unemployment. Since tax rates change on a regular basis, if the rates automatically entered by QBDT are different than shown, change them to match.

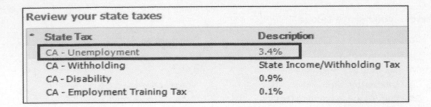

Click **Continue**

The Schedule Payments window for Federal 940 should appear

- If you get a screen to Review your Scheduled Tax Payments list, click Federal 940; and then, click the **Edit** button.
- For Federal Form 940, the Payee should be United States Treasury, the deposit frequency is Quarterly. Enter these if necessary.

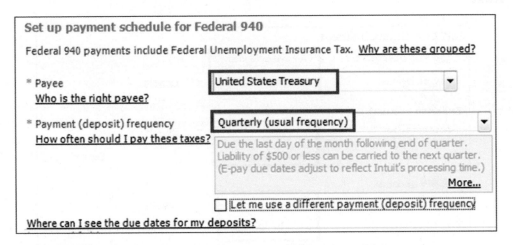

Click **Next** on the Schedule Payments window for Federal 940

- For Federal Form 941/944/943, the Payee should be United States Treasury, enter this if necessary.

Click the drop-down list arrow for Payment (deposit) frequency, click **Quarterly**

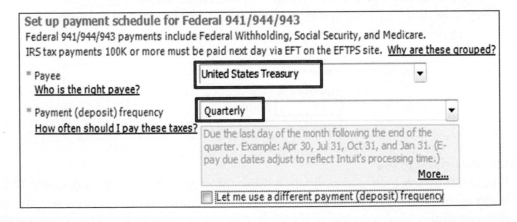

Click **Next**

- If the screens advance by clicking Next, they may be displayed in a different order than shown. If that occurs, enter the information pertinent to the screen and continue until all payment schedule information is complete.

Complete the information for CA UI and Employment Training Tax

Click the drop-down list arrow for Payee, and then click **Employment Development Department**

Employer Acct No. is ~~999-9999-9~~

Deposit Frequency is **Quarterly**

Set up payment schedule for CA UI and Employment Training Tax

CA UI payments include Unemployment Insurance and Employment Training Tax. Why are these grouped?

* Payee
Who is the right payee?
[Employment Development Department] ▼

* CA Employment Development Dept Employer Acct No.
What number do I enter?
[999-9999-9]

* Payment (deposit) frequency
How often should I pay these taxes?
[Quarterly (usual frequency)] ▼

Due the last day of the month following the end of the quarter. Example: Apr 30, Jul 31, Oct 31, and Jan 31. (E-pay due dates adjust to reflect Intuit's processing time.)
More...

☐ Let me use a different payment (deposit) frequency

Where can I see the due dates for my deposits?

Click **Next**

Repeat the steps to enter the information for **CA Withholding and Disability Insurance**, selecting **Employment Development Department** as the Payee, an Employer Acct No. of **999-9999-9**, and a Deposit Frequency of **Quarterly**

Set up payment schedule for CA Withholding and Disability Insurance

CA Withholding payments include Income Tax Withholdings and State Disability Insurance. Why are these grouped?

* Payee
Who is the right payee?
[Employment Development Department] ▼

* CA Employment Development Dept Employer Acct No.
What number do I enter?
[999-9999-9]

* Payment (deposit) frequency
How often should I pay these taxes?
[Quarterly] ▼

Due the last day of the month following the end of the quarter. Example: Apr 30, Jul 31, Oct 31, and Jan 31. (E-pay due dates adjust to reflect Intuit's processing time.)
More...

☐ Let me use a different payment (deposit) frequency

Where can I see the due dates for my deposits?

Click **Finish**, view the finalized **Scheduled Tax Payment List**

Review your Scheduled Tax Payments list

Scheduled Payments	Description
Federal 940	Check\Quarterly (usual frequency)
Federal 941/944/943	Check\Quarterly
CA UI and Employment Training Tax	Check\Quarterly (usual frequency)
CA Withholding and Disability Insurance	Check\Quarterly

• As with previous screens, the Scheduled Tax Payments list may show the Scheduled Payments in a different order than in the text. If the information on the screen is complete, the order displayed is of no concern.

Click **Continue**

9

YEAR-TO-DATE PAYROLLS

The Year-to-Date Payrolls section is completed to enter year-to-date amounts for employees and to identify liability payments you made. Since there have been no payroll payments processed or paid for 2018, there is no payroll history to enter.

 Read the screen, click **Continue**

- Depending on the date of your computer, your screens for Payroll History may not be an exact match for the following screen shots. Your screen may show all four quarters listed under payroll history. This will not affect your setup. (Some examples of screens that you might see appear below.)

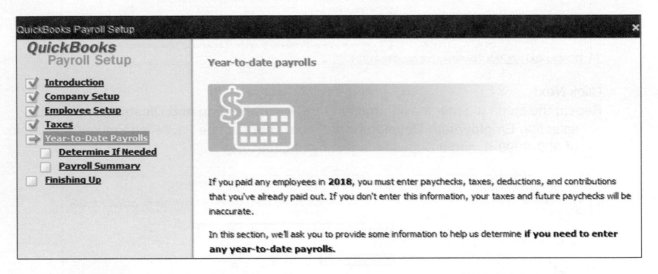

Click **Continue**

On the screen to determine if you need to add payroll history, click **No** for "Has your company issued paychecks this year?"

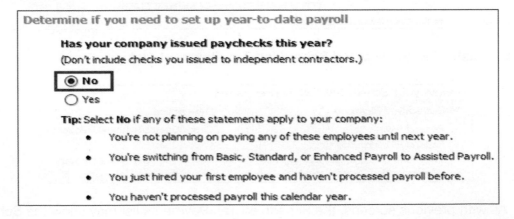

Click **Continue**

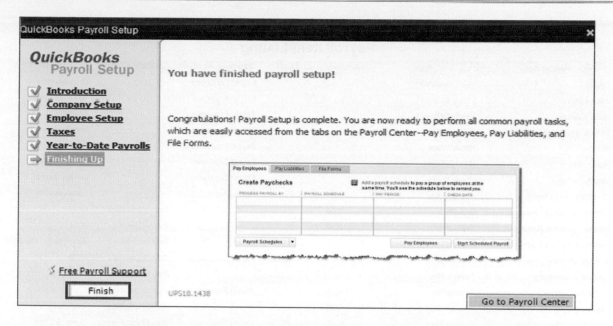

Click the **Finish** button, click **Home** on the Icon Bar to display the Home Page
- If you see the Employee Center, close it. Then, click **Home** on the Icon Bar.

PRINT PAYROLL ITEM LISTING

To verify the payroll items used, it is wise to print a listing of the Payroll Items.

 Print the **Payroll Item Listing** for January 1, 2018

Click the **Reports** menu; point to **List** as the report type, click **Payroll Item Listing**
Adjust the column widths and print the report in **Landscape** orientation
- If you print to a pdf file, save the document as **7-Your Name Payroll Item List Ch9**.

9

Your Name's Canine Club
Payroll Item Listing

Payroll Item	Type	Amount	Limit	Expense Account	Liability Account	Tax Tracking
Salary	Yearly Salary			Payroll Expenses		Compensation
Salary Sick	Yearly Salary			Payroll Expenses		Compensation
Salary Vacation	Yearly Salary			Payroll Expenses		Compensation
Double-time hourly	Hourly Wage			Payroll Expenses		Compensation
Hourly	Hourly Wage			Payroll Expenses		Compensation
Hourly Sick	Hourly Wage			Payroll Expenses		Compensation
Hourly Vacation	Hourly Wage			Payroll Expenses		Compensation
Overtime (x1.5) hourly	Hourly Wage			Payroll Expenses		Compensation
Dental Insurance (taxable)	Deduction	0.00			Payroll Liabilities	None
Health Insurance (taxable)	Deduction	0.00			Payroll Liabilities	None
Advance Earned Income Credit	Federal Tax				Payroll Liabilities	Advance EIC Payment
Federal Unemployment	Federal Tax	0.6%	7,000.00	Payroll Expenses	Payroll Liabilities	FUTA
Federal Withholding	Federal Tax				Payroll Liabilities	Federal
Medicare Company	Federal Tax	1.45%		Payroll Expenses	Payroll Liabilities	Comp. Medicare
Medicare Employee	Federal Tax	1.45%			Payroll Liabilities	Medicare
Social Security Company	Federal Tax	6.2%	127,200.00	Payroll Expenses	Payroll Liabilities	Comp. SS Tax
Social Security Employee	Federal Tax	6.2%	127,200.00		Payroll Liabilities	SS Tax
CA - Withholding	State Withholding Tax				Payroll Liabilities	SWH
CA - Disability	State Disability Tax	0.9%	110,902.00		Payroll Liabilities	SDI
CA - Unemployment	State Unemployment Tax	3.4%	7,000.00	Payroll Expenses	Payroll Liabilities	Comp. SUI
CA - Employment Training Tax	Other Tax	0.1%	7,000.00	Payroll Expenses	Payroll Liabilities	Co. Paid Other Tax
Medicare Employee Addl Tax	Other Tax	0.9%			Payroll Liabilities	Medicare Addl Tax

Close the report

COMPLETE EMPLOYEE INFORMATION

Once the Payroll Setup is complete, there will be a few items that still need to be entered for each employee. At the same time, corrections to employee information may be made.

MEMO

DATE: January 1, 2018

Complete the Employee Information:

Oscar Bailey: Add Marital Status: **Single**, U.S. Citizen: **Yes**, Ethnicity: **White**, Disability: **No**. Main Phone: **760-555-8348**.

Annabelle Williams: Add Marital Status: **Married**, U.S. Citizen: **Yes**, Ethnicity: **Hawaiian/Pacific Islander**, Disability: **No**. Main Phone: **760-555-1386**. Correct the accrual dates for sick and vacation time to **06/30/2015**.

 Open the Employee Center and enter the required information and changes

Open the **Employee Center** as previously instructed
Double-click **Bailey, Oscar** in the Employee List
On the Personal tab, enter his MARITAL STATUS: **Single**; U.S. CITIZEN: **Yes**; ETHNICITY: **White**; DISABILITY: **No**

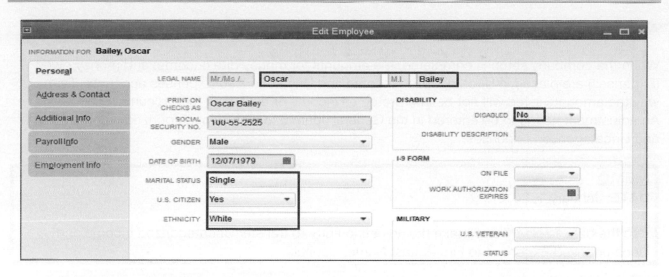

Click the **Address & Contact** tab, enter MAIN PHONE: **760-555-8348**

Click **OK** to save his new information

For Annabelle Williams, complete the information on the Personal and Address & Contact tabs using the information in the memo

When that is complete, click the **Payroll Info** tab; click the **Sick/Vacation** button

Change the Begin accruing dates for sick time and vacation time to her employment date of **06/30/2015**

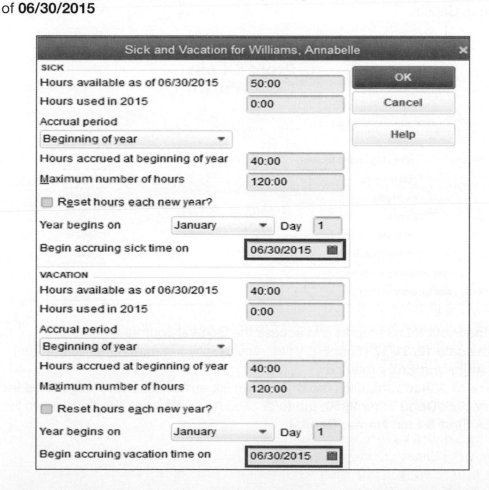

Click **OK** on the Sick and Vacation screen for Williams, Annabelle; click **OK** on the Edit Employee screen; close the Employee Center

ADJUSTING ENTRIES

When the company setup is completed, the amounts for money due (Income) and money owed (Expenses) are placed in Uncategorized Income and Uncategorized Expenses accounts. That way the amounts listed will not be interpreted as income or expenses for the current period. An adjustment needs to be entered in the General Journal to close Uncategorized Income and Uncategorized Expenses.

MEMO
DATE: January 1, 2018

Use the date 12/31/17 and make the adjusting entry to transfer Uncategorized Income and Uncategorized Expenses to First & Last Name, Capital.

     Transfer the Uncategorized Income and Expenses to the owner's capital account

Prepare a Profit & Loss Statement for **12/31/17**
- Note the amount for Uncategorized Income of $2,950.00 and the amount for Uncategorized Expenses of $5,000.00.
- A General Journal entry needs to be made to transfer the two amounts into First & Last Name, Capital.

Your Name's Canine Club
Profit & Loss
December 31, 2017

	Dec 31, 17
▼ Ordinary Income/Expense	
▼ Income	
Uncategorized Income ▶	2,950.00 ◀
Total Income	2,950.00
Gross Profit	2,950.00
▼ Expense	
Uncategorized Expenses	5,000.00
Total Expense	5,000.00
Net Ordinary Income	-2,050.00
Net Income	**-2,050.00**

Close the Profit & Loss report and access the General Journal
Enter the date **12/31/17** (Your Entry No. may or may not match the illustration.)
Leave **Adjusting Entry** marked
Tab to or click **Account**, click the drop-down list arrow, click **Uncategorized Income**, tab to or click **Debit** enter **2950**, tab to or click **Account**, click the drop-down list arrow, click **First & Last Name, Capital**

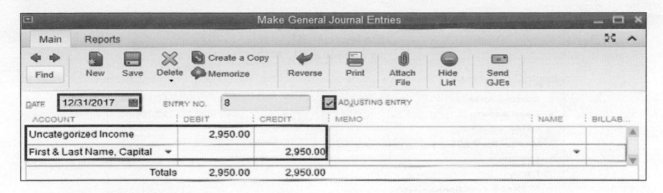

Click **Save & New**

Enter the adjustment to transfer the amount of **Uncategorized Expenses** to **First & Last Name, Capital**

- Remember, you will debit the Capital account and credit the Uncategorized Expenses account.

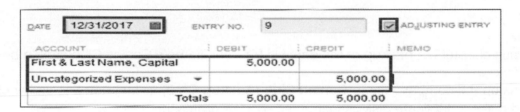

Click **Save & Close**

PRINT BALANCE SHEET

At the completion of the company setup, it is helpful to print a Balance Sheet to confirm that:
Assets = Liabilities + Owner's Equity

 Prepare a **Standard Balance Sheet** for **January 1, 2018**

Total Assets of **$88,835.00** should equal the Total Liabilities + Owners Equities of **$88,835.00**

Print the report in Portrait orientation; then close the report

- If you print to a pdf file, save the document as **8-Your Name Bal Sheet Ch9**.

9

Your Name's Canine Club
Balance Sheet
As of January 1, 2018

	Jan 1, 18
▼ASSETS	
▶ Current Assets	68,135.00
▶ Fixed Assets	20,700.00
TOTAL ASSETS	88,835.00
▼LIABILITIES & EQUITY	
▶ Liabilities ▶	9,500.00 ◀
▼ Equity	
▼ First & Last Name, Capital	
First & Last Name, Investment	25,000.00
First & Last Name, Capital - Other	54,335.00
Total First & Last Name, Capital	79,335.00
Total Equity	79,335.00
TOTAL LIABILITIES & EQUITY	88,835.00

Collapsed Report

BACKUP

As in previous chapters, a backup of the data file for Your Name's Canine Club should be made.

 Back up the company file to **Canine Club (Backup Ch 9)** as instructed in earlier chapters and make a duplicate disk as instructed by your professor

SUMMARY

In this chapter a company was created using the QuickBooks Desktop Setup and the EasyStep Interview. Once the Setup and Interview were complete, the Chart of Accounts/General Ledger was customized. Sales items, customers and vendors were added. Preferences were customized. A company logo was added. The Payroll Setup was completed, and employees were added. Adjusting entries were made.

END-OF-CHAPTER QUESTIONS

TRUE/FALSE

ANSWER THE FOLLOWING QUESTIONS IN THE SPACE PROVIDED BEFORE THE QUESTION NUMBER.

_____ 9.01. The QuickBooks Desktop Payroll Setup is used to add year-to-date earnings for employees.

_____ 9.02. If you create a company using the Direct Interview, you will enter the company name, address, and Tax ID number as part of the Interview.

_____ 9.03. The start date is the date you select to begin tracking financial information for your company in QBDT.

_____ 9.04. You must set up an Administrator Password to have full access to all areas of your company in QuickBooks.

_____ 9.05. Permanently removing the date prepared and time prepared from a report heading is done the first time you complete the report.

_____ 9.06. When the QuickBooks Desktop Setup is complete, the Uncategorized Expenses account contains a balance that reflects the total amount of all receivables accounts.

_____ 9.07. When using the EasyStep Interview to set up income and expenses, you must type in the name of every income and expense account you use.

_____ 9.08. You must use Quick Start to add customers, vendors, and employees.

_____ 9.09. You complete the QuickBooks Desktop Payroll Setup by accessing the Employee Center.

_____ 9.10. Customer credit terms and credit limits are entered into customer accounts in the Customer Center.

MULTIPLE CHOICE

WRITE THE LETTER OF THE CORRECT ANSWER IN THE SPACE PROVIDED BEFORE THE QUESTION NUMBER.

_____ 9.11. To process payroll manually, you must go through the ___ to designate this choice.
  A. Payroll menu
  B. Help menu
  C. QuickBooks Desktop Setup
  D. Company Configuration

9

_____ 9.12. Send Forms preferences contain default text for business documents sent by ___.
   A. Fax
   B. E-mail
   C. Fed-Ex
   D. All the above

_____ 9.13. Adjusting entries that must be made after the company setup are ___.
   A. Close Uncategorized Income to Capital
   B. Close Uncategorized Expenses to Capital
   C. Both A and B
   D. None of the above

_____ 9.14. The Payroll Setup is accessed on the ___.
   A. File Menu
   B. Payroll & Employees Preferences
   C. Employees menu
   D. Employee Center

_____ 9.15. To add a sales tax rate and payee, you edit the sales tax item in the ___.
   A. EasyStep Interview
   B. Sales Tax Preferences
   C. Vendor List
   D. Item List

_____ 9.16. Select to display employee names by last name on the ___.
   A. Payroll & Employees Preferences
   B. Employee List
   C. Employee Center
   D. All the above

_____ 9.17. Colored icons and Company File Color Schemes are selected in the ___ Preference.
   A. General
   B. Customize
   C. Other
   D. Desktop View

_____ 9.18. Employee deductions for medical and dental insurance may be created ___.
   A. during the QuickBooks EasyStep Interview
   B. during the QuickBooks Payroll Setup
   C. by clicking the Reports button at the bottom of the employee list
   D. on the Employee Menu

_____ 9.19. When a(n) ___ account is created, you must provide an opening balance.
   A. Income
   B. Expense
   C. Asset
   D. Posting

_____ 9.20. Sales tax is listed on the ___.
   A. Vendor List
   B. Company List
   C. Banking List
   D. Item List

FILL-IN

IN THE SPACE PROVIDED, WRITE THE ANSWER THAT MOST APPROPRIATELY COMPLETES THE SENTENCE.

9.21.   In the _____ you add vendor information that may include the opening balance, address, phone number, payment terms, and credit limit.

9.22.   In the Chart of Accounts, only _____ accounts have opening balances.

9.23.   The _____ is a step-by-step guide to enter your company information.

9.24.   The asset account used for Inventory sales items is _____.

9.25.   _____ Preferences warns you of duplicate check numbers.

SHORT ESSAY

List the six sections in the Payroll Setup and describe the purpose of each section.

_____

_____

_____

_____

_____

_____

9

END-OF-CHAPTER PROBLEM

YOUR NAME'S COFFEE TIME

Your Name's Coffee Time is a fictitious company located in San Francisco, California, and is a sole proprietorship owned by you. You sell coffee and pastries and provide catering service for meetings and lunches. You are involved in all aspects of the business. There is one full-time employee, Teri Lin, who is paid a salary. She manages the store, is responsible for the all the employees, and keeps the books. There is one full-time hourly employee, Amber Rogers, who works in the shop and provides catering service.

CREATE A NEW COMPANY

▶ Use the following information to complete the QuickBooks Desktop Setup and EasyStep Interview for Your Name's Coffee Time.
  - **Your Name's Coffee Time** *(Use your actual name)* is the Company Name and the Legal Name
  - Federal Tax ID **45-6221346**
  - Address: **1297 6ᵗʰ Avenue**, **San Francisco**, **CA 94122**
  - Phone: 415-555-4646; Fax: 415-555-6464
  - E-mail: **YourName@CoffeeTime.com** *(Use your actual name)*
  - Web: **www.CoffeeTime.com**
  - Type of Business: **Retail Shop or Online Commerce**
  - Company Organization: **Sole Proprietorship**
  - Fiscal year starts in: **January**
  - Password: **QBDT2018**
  - File Name: **Your Name's Coffee Time**
  - File Type: **qbw**
  - Sell: **Both services and products**
  - Enter Sales: **Record each sale individually**
  - Charge sales tax: **Yes**
  - Estimates, Statements, Progress Invoicing, or Track Time: **No**
  - Track Customer Orders (Sales Orders) and Inventory: **Yes**
  - Manage Bills: **Yes**
  - Employees: **Yes, W-2 Employees**
  - Date to start tracking finances (Start Date) is: **01/01/2018** (If your date is not 01/01/18, select "Use today's date or the first day of the quarter" and enter 01/01/18.)
  - Scroll through the list of the income and expense accounts created by QBDT, **remove** check marks for **Merchant Account Fees**, **Uniforms**, and **Ask My Accountant** (New Accounts will be added later.)
  - Click **Go to Setup**
▶ Click **Start Working** on the QuickBooks Desktop Setup screen.

SELECT A TOP ICON BAR

▶ Rather than use the Left Icon Bar, use the View menu to select a **Top Icon Bar**.

CHART OF ACCOUNTS

After QuickBooks Desktop Setup using the EasyStep Interview has been completed, you have created a partial Chart of Accounts. The Chart of Accounts must be customized to reflect the actual accounts used by Your Name's Coffee Time.

▶ Customize the Chart of Accounts provided by QBDI:
  - Add Bank Account: **Checking**, Bank Acct. No.: **5147965513**, Routing Number: **121000273**, Opening Balance/Statement Ending Balance: **35,871**, Statement Ending Date **12/31/17**
  - Delete: **Accumulated Depreciation, Furniture and Equipment**, and **Security Deposits Asset**
  - Make Inactive: **Meals and Entertainment**
  - Edit Equity Accounts:
    - Change the name of Opening Balance Equity to **First & Last Name, Capital** (use your real name) and delete the description
    - Change Owners Equity to **Owner's Equity**, delete the description
    - Change Owners Draw to **First & Last Name, Drawing** (use your real name); Subaccount of First & Last Name, Capital, delete the description
  - Add Equity Accounts:
    - **First & Last Name, Investment** (use your real name); Subaccount of First & Last Name, Capital; Opening Balance **$35,000** as of **12/31/17**
  - Edit Income Accounts:
    - Rename Merchandise Sales to **Sales**, delete the description, Tax-Line **<Unassigned>**
  - Add Income Accounts:
    - Add **Catering Sales**, Subaccount of: Sales
    - Add **Coffee Sales**, Subaccount of: Sales
    - Add **Pastry Sales**, Subaccount of: Sales
  - Add Other Income Account: **Other Income**
  - Add Expense Account: **Store Supplies Expense**
  - Add Other Expense Account: **Other Expenses**
  - Edit Expense Accounts: Rename Office Supplies to **Office Supplies Expense**, Tax-Line **<Unassigned>**
  - Delete: Descriptions for each account
  - Change: Tax-Line Mapping to **Unassigned** for each account
▶ Set up the following Balance Sheet accounts and balances. The Opening Balance date is **12/31/17**.

9

CHART OF ACCOUNTS			
Account Type	Account Name	Sub-Account of	Opening Balance 12/31/17
Other Current Asset	Prepaid Insurance		$1,200.00
Other Current Asset	Office Supplies		$950.00
Other Current Asset	Store Supplies		$1,800.00
Fixed Asset	Store Fixtures		
Fixed Asset	Original Cost	Store Fixtures	$18,000.00
Fixed Asset	Depreciation	Store Fixtures	$-1,800.00
Long-Term Liability	Store Fixtures Loan		$2,000.00

▶ Close the Chart of Accounts without printing.

ADD CUSTOMERS

▶ Access the Customer Center and enter the information provided in the following chart.

CUSTOMERS		
Customer Name	Mary Davis, Inc.	Impact Training, Inc.
Opening Balance	1,500.00	5,245.00
As of	12/31/17	12/31/17
Company Name	Mary Davis, Inc.	Impact Training, Inc.
Main Phone	415-555-1248	415-555-8762
Address	1325 5ᵗʰ Avenue	602 Hugo Street
City, State Zip	San Francisco, CA 94122	San Francisco, CA 94122
Payment Terms	Net 30	Net 30
Credit Limit	2,000.00	8,000.00
Preferred Delivery Method	Mail	Mail
Preferred Payment Method	Check	Visa
Credit Card Information		4175-7880-3245-7211
Exp. Date		02/20
Name on Card		Impact Training, Inc.
Address		602 Hugo Street
Zip		94122
Tax Code	Tax	Tax
Tax Item	State Tax	State Tax

▶ Print the Customer & Job List in Portrait orientation.
  • If you print to a pdf file, save the document as **1-Your Name Customer List Ch9**.
  • Remember, once a credit card number is entered in QBDT, you need to **Enable** Customer Credit Card Protection and change the company password to **2018QBDT**. Use the question: **Name of your first manager**. The answer should be the last name of your professor.

ADD VENDORS

► Access the Vendor Center and enter the information provided in the following two charts.

VENDORS		
Vendor and Company Name	Coffee Magic	Deluxe Pastries
Opening Balance	1,000.00	500.00
As of	12/31/17	12/31/17
Main Phone	415-555-3614	415-555-8712
Fax	415-555-4163	415-555-2178
Address	195 N. Market Street	671 7th Street
City, State, Zip	San Francisco, CA 94103	San Francisco, CA 94122
Payment Terms	2% 10, Net 30	2% 10, Net 30
Credit Limit	3,000.00	2,500.00

VENDORS				
Vendor and Company Name	Employment Development Department	SF Bank	Insurance Org of CA	State Board of Equalization
Main Phone	415-555-5248	415-555-9781	415-555-2347	916-555-0000
Fax	415-555-8425	415-555-1879	415-555-7432	916-555-1111
Address	1027 Canyon Street	1205 Irving Street	20751 Oak Street	7800 State Street
City, State, Zip	San Francisco, CA 94117	San Francisco, CA 94122	San Francisco, CA 94117	Sacramento, CA 94265

► Print the Vendor List in Portrait orientation.
  • If you print to a pdf file, save the document as **2-Your Name Vendor List Ch9**.

ADD SALES ITEMS

► Use the information in the following chart to add the Service Item.

SERVICE ITEM	
Item Name	Catering
Description	Catering
Rate	50.00
Tax Code	Non
Income Account	Catering Sales

► Use the information in the following chart to add the Inventory Items.

9

INVENTORY ITEMS		
Item Name	Coffee	Pastry
Purchase and Sales Description	Coffee	Pastry
Cost	0.00	0.00
COGS Account	Cost of Goods Sold	Cost of Goods Sold
Preferred Vendor	Coffee Magic	Deluxe Pastries
Sales Price	0.00	0.00
Tax Code	Tax	Tax
Income Account	Coffee Sales	Pastry Sales
Inventory Asset Account	Inventory Asset	Inventory Asset
Reorder Point (Min)	500	600
Max	1,550	1,800
On-Hand	1,500	1,750
Total Value	12,000	1,750
As Of	12/31/17	12/31/17

▶ Delete the following sales items: **Consignment Item**, **Non-Inventory Item**, and **Local Tax**.

▶ Edit the State Tax item. The name and description: **CA Sales Tax**, Tax rate: **8.75%**, paid to: **State Board of Equalization**.

▶ Print the Item Listing in Landscape orientation. Resize the columns; do not display columns for **Quantity on Sales Order** and **Quantity on Purchase Order**. Customize the report to use the date of **January 1, 2018** as the Subtitle and to remove Date and Time Prepared.

   • If you print to a pdf file, save the document as **3-Your Name Item List Ch9**.

PRINT AN ACCOUNT LISTING

▶ Prepare the Account Listing; then open the Chart of Accounts and delete the account descriptions and change all Tax Lines to <Unassigned>.

▶ Print an Account Listing in Portrait orientation. Customize the report to use the date of **January 1, 2018** as the Subtitle and to remove Date and Time Prepared. Resize columns and do not include the Description or Tax Line columns in your report.

   • If you print to a pdf file, save the document as **4-Your Name Account Listing Ch9**.

Your Name's Coffee Time
Account Listing
January 1, 2018

Account	Type	Balance Total
Checking	Bank	35,871.00
Accounts Receivable	Accounts Receivable	6,745.00
Inventory Asset	Other Current Asset	13,750.00
Office Supplies	Other Current Asset	950.00
Prepaid Insurance	Other Current Asset	1,200.00
Store Supplies	Other Current Asset	1,800.00
Store Fixtures	Fixed Asset	16,200.00
Store Fixtures:Depreciation	Fixed Asset	-1,800.00
Store Fixtures:Original Cost	Fixed Asset	18,000.00
Accounts Payable	Accounts Payable	1,500.00
Payroll Liabilities	Other Current Liability	0.00
Sales Tax Payable	Other Current Liability	0.00
Store Fixtures Loan	Long Term Liability	2,000.00
First & Last Name, Capital	Equity	67,771.00
First & Last Name, Capital:First & Last Name, Drawing	Equity	0.00
First & Last Name, Capital:First & Last Name, Investment	Equity	35,000.00
Owner's Equity	Equity	
Sales	Income	
Sales:Catering Sales	Income	
Sales:Coffee Sales	Income	
Sales:Pastry Sales	Income	
Sales Discounts	Income	
Uncategorized Income	Income	
Cost of Goods Sold	Cost of Goods Sold	
Advertising and Promotion	Expense	
Automobile Expense	Expense	
Bank Service Charges	Expense	
Computer and Internet Expenses	Expense	
Depreciation Expense	Expense	
Insurance Expense	Expense	
Interest Expense	Expense	
Janitorial Expense	Expense	
Office Supplies Expense	Expense	
Payroll Expenses	Expense	
Professional Fees	Expense	
Rent Expense	Expense	
Repairs and Maintenance	Expense	
Store Supplies Expense	Expense	
Telephone Expense	Expense	
Uncategorized Expenses	Expense	
Utilities	Expense	
Other Income	Other Income	
Other Expenses	Other Expense	

CUSTOMIZE PREFERENCES

▶ Make the following changes to Preferences:
- Accounting: Company Preferences—Deselect: **Date Warnings for past and future transactions**
- Checking: Company Preferences—Select Default Accounts for Open the Create Paychecks and Open the Pay Payroll Liabilities: **Checking**
- Checking: My Preferences—Select Default Accounts for Open the Write Checks, Open the Pay Bills, Open the Pay Sales Tax, and Open the Make Deposits: **Checking**
- Desktop View: My Preferences—Select: **Switch to colored icons/light background on the Top Icon Bar** and select a Company File Color Scheme: **Orange**
- Payroll & Employees: Company Preferences—Deselect: **Job Costing for paycheck expenses**. For Display Employee List by: Select **Last Name**
- Reports & Graphs: Company Preferences— For Reports-Show Items By: Select **Name only**, Deselect: **Default formatting for reports**, Modify the report Format for the Header/Footer: Remove the **Date Prepared**, **Time Prepared**, **Report Basis** (Verify this with your instructor)

9

- <u>Reports & Graphs</u>: My Preferences—Select: **Refresh automatically**
- <u>Sales & Customers</u>: Company Preferences—Select: **No Custom Pricing**
- <u>Sales Tax</u>: Company Preferences—Most common sales tax: **CA Sales Tax**

ADD COMPANY LOGO

▶ Add the company logo for Coffee Time to the Insights page (Remember to look for the logo you downloaded to your USB drive.)

Source: Findriyani/Shutterstock

SELECT MANUAL PAYROLL

▶ Prior to completing the QuickBooks Payroll Setup, select **Manual Payroll**.
▶ Begin the QuickBooks Payroll Setup.

QUICKBOOKS PAYROLL SETUP

▶ Complete the **Company** portion of the QuickBooks Payroll Setup:
- <u>Compensation List</u>: Select: **Salary, Hourly wage and overtime**; deselect: **Bonus, award, or one-time compensation**
- <u>Insurance Benefits</u>: Select: **Health Insurance, Dental Insurance**; for both insurances, select: **Employee pays for all of it** and **Payment is deducted after taxes**; for both insurances Payee (Vendor): **Insurance Org of CA**; Select: **I don't need a regular payment schedule for this item**
- <u>Retirement Benefits</u>: None
- <u>Paid Time Off</u>: Sick Time and Vacation Time
- <u>Additions and Deductions</u>: None

▶ Use the following information to add the two employees. Print a Summary Report for each employee.

EMPLOYEES Teri Lin and Amber Rogers		
Legal Name	Teri Lin	Amber Rogers
Employee Status	Active	Active
Home Address	2477 Moraga Street	1088 17th Avenue
City	San Francisco	San Francisco
State	CA	CA
Zip Code	94122	94122
Employee Type	Regular	Regular
Social Security No.	100-55-9107	100-55-5201
Hire Date	02/19/2010	06/30/2012
Birth Date	09/29/1985	07/17/1980
Gender	Female	Female
Pay Period	Monthly	Monthly
Compensation	Salary: $21,000 per year	Hourly wage: $15.50 Double-time hourly: $31.00 Overtime (x1.5) hourly: $23.25
Dental Insurance	$25 per month, annual limit $300	$25 per month, annual limit $300

EMPLOYEES		
Teri Lin and Amber Rogers		
Health Insurance	$325 per month, annual limit $3,900	$325 per month, annual limit $3,900
Sick Time Earns	40:00 at beginning of year	40:00 at beginning of year
Unused Sick Hours	Have an accrual limit	Have an accrual limit
Maximum Hours	120:00	120:00
Earns	Time off currently	Time off currently
Hours Available as of 01/01/2018 (your computer date will show)	30:00	20:00
Hours Used as of 01/01/18 (Your computer date will show)	0:00	0:00
Vacation Time Earns	40:00 at beginning of year	40:00 at beginning of year
Unused Vacation Hours	Have an accrual limit	Have an accrual limit
Maximum Hours	120:00	120:00
Earns	Time off currently	Time off currently
Hours Available as of 01/01/18 (Your computer date will show)	40:00	20:00
Hours used as of 01/01/18 (Your computer date will show)	0:00	0:00
Payment Method	Check (no Direct Deposit)	Check (no Direct Deposit)
State Subject to Withholding	CA	CA
State Subject to Unemployment Tax	CA	CA
Live or Work in Another State in 2018	No	No
Federal Filing Status	Single	Married
Allowances (Federal)	0	2
Extra Withholding	0.00	0.00
Nonresident Alien Withholding	Does not apply	Does not apply
HIRE Act Exemption	Not a qualified employee	Not a qualified employee
Subject to	Medicare Social Security Federal Unemployment	Medicare Social Security Federal Unemployment
State Filing Status	Single	Married (two incomes)
Regular Withholding Allowances	0	2
Subject to	CA-Unemployment CA-Employment Training Tax CA-Disability	CA-Unemployment CA-Employment Training Tax CA-Disability
Special Local Taxes	No	No
Wage Plan Code	S	S

▶ Print the Summary for each employee.
  • If you print to a pdf file, save the documents as **5-Your Name Teri Lim Emp Sum Ch9** and **6-Your Name Amber Rogers Emp Sum Ch9**.
▶ Complete the **Taxes** section of the QuickBooks Payroll Setup:
  • State Payroll Tax Rates—CA-Disability Employee Rate: **0.9%**; CA-Employment Training Tax Company: **0.1%;** California-Unemployment Company Rate: **3.4%**
  • Federal Payroll Taxes—Schedules 940 and 941/944/943: Payee: **United States Treasury**, Frequency: **Quarterly**
  • State Payroll Taxes—Payee: **Employee Development Department**; Employer Account No.: **999-9999-9**, Payment frequency: **Quarterly**
▶ Complete the **Year-to-Date Payrolls** section of the QuickBooks Payroll Setup. For "Has your company issued paychecks this year," select: **No**.
▶ After completing the Payroll Setup, print the Payroll Item Listing in Landscape orientation using the Report menu or Report Center.
  • If you print to a pdf file, save the document as **7-Your Name Payroll Item Listing Ch9**.

COMPLETE EMPLOYEE INFORMATION

▶ Open the Employee Center; enter additional employee information in the table below:

EMPLOYEES		
Employee Name	Lin, Teri	Rogers, Amber
Marital Status	Single	Married
U.S. Citizen	Yes	Yes
Ethnicity	Asian	Black/African American
Disability	No	No
Main Phone	415-555-7801	415-555-7364

▶ Check the accrual dates for sick and vacation for Amber Rogers; if the date is 02/19/10 change it to her hire date of 06/30/12.

ADJUSTMENTS, BALANCE SHEET, AND BACKUP

▶ Record the adjusting entry to transfer Uncategorized Income and Uncategorized Expenses to Your Name's, Capital. Date the entry 12/31/17.
▶ Print the Balance Sheet for January 1, 2018 in Portrait orientation.
  • If you print to a pdf file, save the document as **8-Your Name Bal Sheet Ch9**.
▶ Backup your company file to **Your Name's Coffee Time (Backup Ch. 9)**.

CHAPTER 9 CHECKLISTS

YOUR NAME'S CANINE CLUB

The checklist below shows all the business forms printed during training. Check each one that you printed. In the document names below, Your Name and Ch9 have been omitted, and report dates are given.

___ 1-Customer List
___ 2-Vendor List
___ 3-Item Listing
___ 4-Account Listing
___ 5-Oscar Bailey Emp Sum
___ 6-Annabelle Williams Emp Sum
___ 7-Payroll Item Listing
___ 8-Bal Sheet, January 1, 2018

YOUR NAME'S COFFEE TIME

The checklist below shows all the business forms printed during training. Check each one that you printed. In the document names below, Your Name and Ch9 have been omitted, and report dates are given.

___ 1-Customer List
___ 2-Vendor List
___ 3-Item Listing
___ 4-Account Listing
___ 5-Teri Lin Emp Sum
___ 6-Amber Rogers Emp Sum
___ 7-Payroll Item Listing
___ 8-Bal Sheet, January 1, 2018

9

PRACTICE SET 3 COMPREHENSIVE

YOUR NAME'S MADISON AVENUE BOOKS

Source: Paulista/Shutterstock

The following is a comprehensive practice set that includes all the elements of QuickBooks Desktop that were studied throughout the text. In this practice set you will set up a company and keep the books for January 2018 (or the year that your instructor specifies). You will use the QuickBooks Desktop Setup/EasyStep Interview to create Your Name's Madison Avenue Books. Once the company has been created, you will add customers, vendors, and sales items, finalize the Chart of Accounts, and select Preferences. The QuickBooks Payroll Setup will be completed, and employees will be added. Adjustments will be made to accounts and various items, transactions will be recorded, and reports will be prepared.

YOUR NAME'S MADISON AVENUE BOOKS

Your Name's Madison Avenue Books is a fictitious company that provides keyboarding services and sells books and educational supplies. Your Name's Madison Avenue Books is in Sacramento, California, and is a sole proprietorship owned by you. You do all the purchasing and are involved in all aspects of the business. The company has one full-time employee who is paid a salary, Ms. Sherry Compton, who manages the store, is responsible for the all the employees, and keeps the books. Devon Peterson is a full-time hourly employee who works in the shop. The store is currently advertising for a part-time employee who will provide keyboarding services.

CREATE A NEW COMPANY

▶ Use the following information to complete the QuickBooks Desktop Setup:
  ○ Company and Legal Name: **Your Name's Madison Avenue Books** (*Key in your actual name*)
  ○ Federal Tax ID: **46-6521446**
  ○ Address: **4748 Madison Avenue, Sacramento, CA 95841**
  ○ Phone: **916-555-9876**; Fax: **916-555-6789**
  ○ E-mail: **YourName@MABooks.com** (don't forget to use your real name)
  ○ Web: **www.MadisonAvenueBooks.com**
  ○ Type of Business: **Retail Shop or Online Commerce**
  ○ Company Organization: **Sole Proprietorship**
  ○ Fiscal Year Starts: **January**
  ○ Passwords: **QBDT2018**
  ○ File Name: **Your Name's Madison Avenue Books.qbw** (don't forget to use your real name)

- o Sell **Both Services and Products**, record each sale **individually**
- o Charge Sales tax: **Yes**
- o Estimates, statements, progress invoicing, or track time: **No**
- o Track customer orders (sales orders), track inventory: **Yes**
- o Manage bills: **Yes**
- o Employees: **Yes, W-2 Employees**
- o Date to start tracking finances: **01/01/18** (If your date is not 01/01/18, select "Use today's date or the first day of the quarter or month" and enter 01/01/18.)
- o Use QBDT to set up the **Income and Expense Accounts**
  - ▪ Review Income and Expense Accounts provided by QBDT:
    - • Remove: Merchandise Sales, Merchant Account Fees, Automobile Expense, Meals and Entertainment, Uniforms, and Ask My Accountant by clicking the √ column to remove the checkmark
    - • Add: Purchase Discounts, Equipment Rental, Miscellaneous Expense, Postage and Delivery, Printing and Reproduction, and Interest Income
- ▶ Click **Go to Setup**, click Start Working

SELECT A TOP ICON BAR (OPTIONAL)

▶ If you wish to use a Top Icon Bar, use the View Menu to change from the Left Icon Bar.

DATES

▶ The year used in the text is 2018. As usual, check with your instructor to determine the year you should use. When creating a new company, all As of dates and dates for Opening Balances are **12/31/17**.

CHART OF ACCOUNTS

▶ Use the following chart of accounts and balances to customize the chart of accounts for Your Name's Madison Avenue Books:
- o To save space when printing, delete account descriptions for all accounts
- o Use <Unassigned> for tax line mapping for all accounts
- o Add Bank Account: Name: **Checking**; Bank Acct. No.:**123-456-10987**; Routing Number: **123025987**; Statement Ending Balance: **130,870.25**; Statement Ending Date: **12/31/17**
- o Delete: Security Deposits Asset
  - ▪ If you did not delete the listed income and expense accounts during the company setup, do so now.
- o Edit Equity Accounts:
  - ▪ Change Opening Balance Equity to **First & Last Name, Capital** (use your real name)
  - ▪ Change Owners Equity to **Owner's Equity**
  - ▪ Change Owners Draw to **First & Last Name, Withdrawals**, Subaccount of: **First & Last Name, Capital**
- o Add Equity Accounts: **First & Last Name, Investment**; Subaccount of: **First & Last Name, Capital**; Opening Balance: **75,000** as of **12/31/17**

PS
3

ADD CUSTOMERS

▶ Access the Customer Center and enter the information provided in the following chart:

CUSTOMERS				
Customer Name	Complete Training, Inc.	Slater, Abby	Sacramento Schools	Kim, Binh
Opening Balance, 12/31/2017	1,400.00	100.00	1,000.00	350.00
As of	12/31/17	12/31/17	12/31/17	12/31/17
Company Name	Complete Training, Inc.		Sacramento Schools	
First Name		Abby		Binh
Last Name		Slater		Kim
Main Phone	916-555-8762	916-555-8961	916-555-1235	916-555-2264
Main Email	CompleteTraining@ skills.com	AbbyS@abc.com	SacramentoSchools@ Sac.edu	BinhK@xyz.com
Address	212 Harvard Street	8025 Richmond Street	1085 2nd Street	5311 College Oak Dr., Apt. B
City, State, Zip	Sacramento, CA 95815	Sacramento, CA 95825	Sacramento, CA 95814	Sacramento, CA 95841
Payment Terms	Net 30	2% 10, Net 30	2% 10, Net 30	Net 30
Credit Limit	1,500.00	500.00	5,000.00	350.00
Preferred Delivery Method	Mail	Mail	Mail	Mail
Preferred Payment Method		Check	Visa	Check
Credit Card Information			4929 4970 3749 8670	
Exp. Date			06/2021	
Name on Card			Sacramento Schools	
Address			1085 2nd Street	
Zip			95814	
Tax Code	Tax	Tax	Tax	Tax
Tax Item	State Tax	State Tax	State Tax	State Tax

○ Remember, once a credit card number is entered in QBDT, when you close the program, you will get a Customer Credit Card Protection screen the next time you open QBDT. Click **Enable Protection**. Complete Sensitive Data Protection Setup.
  ▪ User Name: **Admin** (DO NOT CHANGE THIS)
  ▪ Current Password: **QBDT2018**

- New Password: **2018QBDT**
- Confirm New Password: **2018QBDT**
- Challenge Question: **Name of your first manager**
- Answer: **Your instructor's last name**

ADD VENDORS

▶ Access the Vendor Center and enter the information provided in the following two charts:

VENDORS			
Vendor and Company Name	Textbook Co.	Pens Aplenty	Supplies Co.
Opening Balance	1,000.00	500.00	800.00
As of	12/31/17	12/31/17	12/31/17
Main Phone	916-555-2788	415-555-3224	916-555-5759
Main Email	Textbook@Texts.com	PensAplenty@abc.com	Supplies@123.com
Fax	916-555-8872	415-555-4223	916-555-9575
Address	559 4th Street	8572 Market Street	95 8th Street
City, State, Zip	Sacramento, CA 95814	San Francisco, CA 94103	Sacramento, CA 95814
Payment Terms	2% 10, Net 30	2% 10, Net 30	2% 10, Net 30
Credit Limit	25,000.00	5,000.00	15,000.00

VENDORS				
Vendor and Company Name	State Board of Equalization	Employment Development Department	Capitol State Bank	Insurance, Inc.
Main Phone	916 555-0000	916-555-8877	916-555-6446	415-555-2369
Fax	916-555-1111	916-555-7788	916-555-6464	415-555-9632
Address	7800 State Street	1037 California Street	5255 Hemlock Street	20865 Oak Street
City, State, Zip	Sacramento, CA 95814	Sacramento, CA 95814	Sacramento, CA 95841	San Francisco, CA 94101

ADD SALES ITEMS

PS 3

▶ Use the following chart to add the Service Item.

SERVICE ITEM	
Name	Keyboarding
Description	Keyboarding Services
Rate	0.00
Tax Code	Non
Income Account	Keyboarding Services

▶ Use the information in the following chart to add the Inventory Part Items.

INVENTORY ITEMS					
Item Name	Paper	Paperback Books	Pens, etc.	Stationery	Textbooks
Purchase and Sales Description	Paper Supplies	Paperback Books	Pens, etc.	Stationery	Textbooks
Cost	4.00	5.00	3.00	7.50	50.00
COGS Account	Cost of Goods Sold	Cost of Goods Sold	Cost of Goods Sold	Cost of Goods Sold	Cost of Goods Sold
Preferred Vendor	Supplies Co.	Textbook Co.	Pens Aplenty	Supplies Co.	Textbook Co.
Sales Price	0.00	0.00	0.00	0.00	0.00
Tax Code	Tax	Tax	Tax	Tax	Tax
Income Account	Supplies Sales	Book Sales	Supplies Sales	Supplies Sales	Book Sales
Subaccount of	Sales and Services Income	Sales and Services Income	Sales and Services Income	Sales and Services Income	Sales and Services Income
Asset Account	Inventory Asset	Inventory Asset	Inventory Asset	Inventory Asset	Inventory Asset
Reorder Point (Min)	150	30	50	25	2,000
Max	200	40	60	35	2,010
On-Hand	200	45	50	30	2,000
Total Value	1,000.00	180.00	250.00	225.00	100,000.00
As of Date	12/31/17	12/31/17	12/31/17	12/31/17	12/31/17

- o Delete: **Local Tax** (If **Consignment** or **Non-inventory Part** items appear, delete them as well.)
- o Edit: **State Sales Tax** Item, change the name and description to **CA Sales Tax**, tax rate of **8.0%,** paid to **State Board of Equalization**

FINALIZE CHART OF ACCOUNTS

- o Edit a Cost of Goods Sold Account: Change Purchase Discounts to **Merchandise Discounts**, Subaccount of: **Cost of Goods Sold**

CUSTOMIZE PREFERENCES

▶ Change the following preferences:
- o **Accounting**: Deselect the **Date Warnings** for past and future transactions
- o **Checking**: My Preferences—Default Accounts to use is **Checking** for Open the Write Checks, Open the Pay Bills, Open the Pay Sales Tax, and Open the Make Deposits; Company Preferences—Select Default Accounts to use is **Checking** for Open the Create Paychecks and Open the Pay Payroll Liabilities
- o **Desktop View**: My Preferences—Switch to **colored icons/light background** on the Top Icon Bar (if using). The Company File Color Scheme should be **Blue-Gray**
- o **Payroll & Employees**: Company Preferences—Display Employee List by **Last Name**; deselect "Job Costing for paycheck expenses"

- o **Reports & Graphs**: <u>My Preferences</u>—**Refresh** reports automatically; <u>Company Preferences</u>—Reports – Show Items By: **Name only**; Reports – Show Accounts By: **Name only**; modify the report Format for the Header/Footer to remove the **Date Prepared, Time Prepared, and Report Basis** from reports (Verify this with your instructor.)
- o **Sales & Customers**: <u>Company Preferences</u>—select **No Custom Pricing**
- o **Sales Tax**: <u>Company Preferences</u>—Most common sales tax is **CA Sales Tax**

ADD COMPANY LOGO

▶ Add the company logo for Books to the Insights page.

PAYROLL

▶ Select Manual as the payroll option.
▶ Complete the Payroll Setup. (Remember that on some screens QBDT will show you the current computer date or current year. This should not make a difference if you use the same year as the one you used in the QuickBooks Desktop Setup whenever you enter a date.)
- o Complete the Company portion of the setup:
  - ▪ <u>Compensation List</u>: **Salary**, **Hourly Wage**, and **Overtime**
  - ▪ <u>Insurance Benefits</u>: **Health Insurance** and **Dental Insurance**. Both are **Employee pays for all of it** and **Payment is deducted after taxes**. The Payee/Vendor is **Insurance, Inc.**, you do not need a payment schedule
  - ▪ <u>Retirement Benefits</u>: **None**
  - ▪ <u>Paid Time Off</u>: **Sick Time** and **Vacation Time**
  - ▪ <u>Additions and Deductions</u>: **None**
- o Use the Employee List below to add Employees
  - ▪ Print the Summary for <u>each</u> employee. If you print to a pdf file, save the documents as **1-Your Name Emp Sum Peterson PS3**, and **2-Your Name Emp Sum Compton PS3**.

EMPLOYEES Devon Peterson and Sherry Compton		
Legal Name	Peterson, Devon	Compton, Sherry
Employee Status	Active	Active
Home Address	383 Oak Avenue	3763 Lily Street
City	Sacramento	Sacramento
State	CA	CA
Zip Code	95814	95838
Employee Type	Regular	Regular
Social Security No.	100-55-6886	100-55-5244
Hire Date	04/03/96	02/17/10
Birth Date	12/07/75	11/28/85
Gender	Male	Female
Pay Period	Monthly	Monthly
Compensation	Hourly: $10.00 per hour $20.00 Double-time hourly $15.00 Overtime (x1.5) hourly	Salary: $26,000.00 per year

PS
3

EMPLOYEES Devon Peterson and Sherry Compton		
Dental Insurance	$20 per month, annual limit $240	$30 per month, annual limit $360
Health Insurance	$20 per month, annual limit $240	$30 per month, annual limit $360
Sick Time Earns	40:00 at beginning of year	40:00 at beginning of year
Unused Sick Hours	Have an accrual limit	Have an accrual limit
Maximum Hours	120:00	120:00
Earns	Time off currently	Time off currently
Hours Available as of 01/01/18	40:00	40:00
Vacation Time Earns	40:00 at beginning of year	40:00 at beginning of year
Unused Vacation Hours	Have an accrual limit	Have an accrual limit
Maximum Hours	120:00	120:00
Earns	Time off currently	Time off currently
Hours Available as of 01/01/18	40:00	40:00
Payment Method	Check (no Direct Deposit)	Check (no Direct Deposit)
State Subject to Withholding	CA	CA
State Subject to Unemployment Tax	CA	CA
Live or Work in Another State in 2018	No	No
Federal Filing Status	Married	Single
Allowances (Federal)	1	0
Extra Withholding	0.00	0.00
Nonresident Alien Withholding	Does not apply	Does not apply
HIRE Act Exemption	Not a qualified employee	Not a qualified employee
Subject to	Medicare Social Security Federal Unemployment	Medicare Social Security Federal Unemployment
State Filing Status	Married (one income)	Single
Regular Withholding Allowances	1	0
Subject to	CA-Unemployment CA-Employment Training Tax CA-Disability	CA-Unemployment CA-Employment Training Tax CA-Disability
Special Local Taxes	No	No
Wage Plan	S	S

- Did you print each employee's summary? If you print to a pdf file, save the documents as **1-Your Name Emp Sum Peterson PS3** and **2-Your Name Emp Sum Compton PS3**.
- ○ Enter Payroll Tax information:
  - State Payroll Tax Rates: CA-Disability Employee Rate: **.9%**; CA-Employment Training Tax Company: **0.1%**; California-Unemployment Company Rate: **3.4%**
  - Federal Payroll Taxes: Schedules 940 and 941/944/943: Payee **United States Treasury**, Frequency: **Quarterly**
  - State Payroll Taxes: Payee: **Employment Development Department**, Employer Account No. **999-9999-9**, Payment frequency: **Quarterly**

▶ Complete the **Year-to-Date Payrolls** section of the QuickBooks Payroll Setup.
  ○ Has your company issued paychecks this year? **No.**

COMPLETE EMPLOYEE INFORMATION

▶ Open the Employee Center, enter additional employee information in the table below:

EMPLOYEES		
Employee Name	Devon Peterson	Sherry Compton
Marital Status	Married	Single
U.S. Citizen	Yes	Yes
Ethnicity	White	Two or More Races
Disability	No	No
Main Phone	916-555-7862	916-555-1222

▶ Check the accrual dates for sick and vacation for Sherry Compton; if the date is 04/03/96 change it to her hire date of 02/17/10.

MAKE ADJUSTMENTS

▶ Transfer the Uncategorized Income and Uncategorized Expenses to Your First & Last Name, Capital account. Date the General Journal entry **12/31/17**.

PRINT

▶ Compare your Chart of Accounts with the one shown earlier in the practice set. When everything matches, prepare the Account Listing; then open the Chart of Accounts to the accounts in that have descriptions and Tax Lines that are not <Unassigned>. Delete the descriptions and change the tax line. Customize the report to use the date of **January 1, 2018** as the Subtitle. Resize the columns to display the names in full and remove the Description and Tax Line columns. Print an Account Listing in Portrait orientation. If you print to a pdf file, save the document as **3-Your Name Acct List PS3**.

▶ Delete the Out of State Sales Tax Item. Prepare an Item Listing report and resize columns to display information in full and remove columns for Quantity on Sales Order and Quantity on Purchase Order. Customize the report subtitle to use the date **January 1, 2018**. Print the report in Landscape orientation. If you print to a pdf file, save the document as **4-Your Name Item List PS3**.

▶ Use the Report menu or Reports Center to print a Transaction List by Customer. Use the dates From December 31, 2017 To January 1, 2018. Resize the columns to display information in full. Print in Landscape orientation. If you print to a pdf file, save the document as **5-Your Name Trans List by Cust PS3**.

▶ Use the Report menu or Reports Center to print a Transaction List by Vendor. Use the dates From December 31, 2017 To January 1, 2018. Resize the columns to display information in full. Print in Landscape orientation. If you print to a pdf file, save the document as **6-Your Name Trans List by Vend PS3**.

▶ Print a Balance Sheet as of January 1, 2018. If you print to a pdf file, save the document as **7-Your Name Bal Sheet PS3**.

PS 3

CUSTOMIZE

▶ Customize business forms: Make the default title all capital letters, use Layout Designer to make the area for the company name wide enough for your name on Sales Receipts, Credit Memos, Sales Orders, and Purchase Orders. Then, create a duplicate of a Product Invoice. Customize the Copy of Product Invoice the same as the other business forms. The Column Order is 1 Quantity 2 Item Code, 3 Description, and 4 Price Each. Plus, use Basic Customization and click Print Past Due Stamp to select.

ENTER TRANSACTIONS

▶ During the month, add new customers, vendors, employees, items, and accounts as necessary.

▶ Create a Customer message for Credit Memos: **Your return has been processed.**

▶ You determine which memos to include in transactions.

▶ Unless otherwise specified, the terms for each sale or bill will be the one specified in the Customer or Vendor List.

▶ The transaction date will be the date the entry is made unless instructed otherwise.

▶ If a customer's order exceeds the established credit limit, accept the order.

▶ If the terms allow a discount for a customer, make sure to apply the discount if payment is received in time for the customer to take it. Remember, the discount period starts with the date of the invoice. If an invoice or bill date is not provided, use the transaction date to begin the discount period.

▶ Use Sales Discounts as the discount account for sales.

▶ If a bill or customer payment is eligible for a discount and a return has been made, subtract the amount of the credit from the amount due and recalculate the discount based on the actual amount owed.

▶ If a customer has a credit and a balance on the account, apply the credit to the invoice used for the sale. If there is no balance for a customer and a return is made, issue a credit memo and a refund check.

▶ Always pay bills in time to take advantage of purchase discounts.

▶ Most reports will be printed in Portrait orientation; however, if the report (such as the Journal) will fit across the page using Landscape orientation, use Landscape.

▶ Whenever possible, adjust the column widths so that reports fit on one-page wide <u>without</u> selecting Fit report to one page wide.

▶ If a report format is changed and you prepare the report frequently, memorize the report.

▶ Print invoices, sales receipts, purchase orders, checks, and other items as they are entered in the transactions. Check with your instructor to see what should be printed. If you print your documents to a pdf file, save the documents using the same naming format that you used in the chapters. For example, 1-Your Name Report Name PS3 or 1-Your Name Business Form Name and Number and Last or Company Name PS3.It is your choice whether to print lines around each field.

▶ Use the customized Copy of Product Invoice for all invoices (except those prepared from sales orders). Use the customized Credit Memo for customer returns, Voucher Checks for payroll, Standard Checks for all other checks, and the customized Purchase Order, Sales Order, and Sales Receipts forms.

▶ Prepare an Inventory Stock Status by Item Report every five days as the last transaction of the day to see if anything needs to be ordered. Print the report and hide the For Assemblies column. (This would be a good report to memorize.) Unless instructed otherwise, if anything is less than the Reorder Point (Min), order enough of the item so you will have the Max on hand. (For example, if you needed to order an item and the Reorder Point (Min) is 100, and the Max Is 110, you would order enough to have 110 available. If sales orders have been recorded, the number of items available may be less than the number of items on hand so base your order on the number <u>available</u>. If you have 100 items on hand and 75 items available, order 35 items to reach the 110 Max Reorder Point.) For each item, use the Cost in the Item List.

▶ Full-time employees usually work 160 hours during a payroll period. Hourly employees working more than 160 hours in a pay period are paid overtime.

▶ Create a new report called Unpaid Bills with Terms Detail. Prepare an Unpaid Bills Detail report; then customize it by adding a column for Terms. When the report is memorized, use it every five days to determine which bills are eligible for discounts if they are paid within the discount period given in the transaction. If any bills qualify for payment, make comments on the report; such as, "Pay this bill." If there is a credit that should be applied, make a comment; such as, "Use this credit." Print the commented report. Remember, an opening balance is not eligible for a discount.

▶ In addition to preparing the Unpaid Bills with Terms report to determine bill payment, there will be some bills where payment instructions will be given in the transactions.

▶ Backup the company file every five days. Create your first backup file before recording transactions. Name the file **Your Name's Madison Avenue Books (Backup Company)**, name subsequent files with the date. For example, your first backup that includes transactions would be named **Your Name's Madison Avenue Books (Backup 01-05-18)**. The final backup should be made at the end of the practice set. Name it **Your Name's Madison Avenue Books (Backup Complete)**.

<u>January 1:</u>
▶ Create a backup file and name it **Your Name's Madison Avenue Books (Backup Company)**
▶ Add a new part-time hourly employee:
  ○ Personal Info:
    ▪ Mary Delgado
    ▪ Social Security No.: 100-55-3699
    ▪ Gender: Female
    ▪ Birthday: 1/3/90
    ▪ Marital Status: Single
    ▪ U.S. Citizen: Yes
    ▪ Ethnicity: Hispanic/Latino
    ▪ Disability: No
  ○ Address & Contact
    ▪ Address: 4811 Wheat Street
    ▪ City: Sacramento
    ▪ State: CA
    ▪ Zip: 95821
    ▪ Main Phone: 916-555-7766
  ○ Payroll Info:
    ▪ Pay Frequency: Monthly
    ▪ Hourly: $8.00, Overtime (x1.5) hourly: $12.00, Double-time hourly: $16.00

PS
3

- Dental and Health Insurance: None
- Federal Taxes:
  - Filing Status and Allowance: Single, 0
  - Subject to: Medicare, Social Security, Federal Unemployment
- State Taxes:
  - State Worked and State Subject to Withholding: California
  - Subject to, CA Unemployment (SUI), CA Disability taxes (SDI)
  - Filing Status and Allowance: Single, 0
- Other Taxes:
  - CA Employment Training Tax
  - Medicare Employee Addl Tax
- Employment Info:
  - Hire Date: 01/01/18
  - Type: Regular
- On the Exit Message regarding Sick and Vacation Hours, click Leave as is

January 2:

▶ Mary typed a five-page paper @ $5 per page, sold one textbook @ $80, and three paperback books @ $6.99 each to a Cash Customer. Received Check 2951 for the full payment. (QBDT may give you a variety of messages, mark so they do not display in the future.) If you print to a pdf file, save the document as **8-Your Name SR 1 Cash Cust PS3**.

▶ Complete Training, Inc. purchased 30 copies of a textbook on account @ $95 each. (Accept transactions that are over the established credit limit.) (Did you use your customized invoice? Make sure the Print Past Due Stamp was selected.) If you print to a pdf file, save the document as **9-Your Name Inv 1 Complete Training PS3**.

▶ Received Check 1096 from Abby Slater for $100 as payment in full on her account. (An opening balance is not eligible for a discount.) If you print to a pdf file, save the document as **10-Your Name Rcv Pmt Slater PS3**.

▶ Received a telephone call for a Sales Order from Sacramento Schools for 25 pens @ $8.99 each and five reams of paper @ $6.99 per ream. If you print to a pdf file, save the document as **11-Your Name SO 1 Sacramento Schools PS3**.

▶ Sold one textbook @ $79.99, one textbook @ $95.99, one textbook @ $125.00, one textbook @ $139.95, and one textbook @ $145.00 for the new quarter to a student using Visa # 4485 5122 7321 1912, Expiration 02/2023. If you print to a pdf file, save the document as **12-Your Name SR 2 Cash Cust PS3**.

▶ Prepare an Inventory Stock Status by Item report for January 1-2, 2018 to see if anything needs to be ordered. After resizing the columns and removing the column "For Assemblies," memorize the report, fit on 1-page wide, then print in Landscape. (Are pens and textbooks marked to order?) If you print to a pdf file, save the document as **13-Your Name Stock Status by Item PS3**.

▶ Prepare and print Purchase Orders for any merchandise that needs to be ordered. Check the number available and refer to the Reorder Qty column in the Inventory Stock Status by Item report. Use this information to calculate the number of items to order. (Hint: Pens have a Max of 60 and because there are 25 pens on sales order, 25 are available. You will need to order more than the number shown in Reorder Qty column.) If you print to a pdf file, save the documents as **14-Your Name PO 1 Pens Aplenty PS3** and **15-Your Name PO 2 Textbook Co. PS3**.

January 3:

▶ Memorize a transaction for the bill for rent. Add it to my Reminders List, How Often: Monthly, Next Date: 01/15/18. The bill will be recorded on the 15th and will be paid on January 30. The amount is $1,200 and is paid to Sacramento Rental, Main Phone: 916-555-1234, Fax: 916-555-4321, 5322 Auburn Boulevard, Sacramento, CA 95841, Payment Terms: Net 15, Account Setting: Rent Expense.

▶ Sacramento Schools picked up the merchandise from Sales Order 1. Create the invoice dated January 2, 2018 from the Sales Order. (Even though the "Product Invoice" was customized earlier in the practice set, the Sales Order Invoice was not. Once you create the invoice from the sales order, you should customize the Sales Order Invoice so that the default title, INVOICE, is all capital letters; use Basic Customization to select Print Past Due Stamp; use Layout Designer to make room for your full name to print. If you print to a pdf file, save the document as **16-Your Name Inv 2 Sacramento Schools PS3**.

▶ Received Check 915 for $350 from Binh Kim for the full amount due on his account. If you print to a pdf file, save the document as **17-Your Name Rcv Pmt Kim PS3**.

▶ Sold two pens on account @ $12.99 each and five boxes of stationery @ $10.99 per box to Abby Slater. If you print to a pdf file, save the document as **18-Your Name Inv 3 Slater PS3**.

▶ Received payment of $1,400 as payment in full for the opening balance from Complete Training, Inc., Debit Card # 5179 6633 9480 2309, Expiration: 06/2021. If you print to a pdf file, save the document as **19-Your Name Rcv Pmt Complete Training PS3**.

January 5:

▶ Sold two textbooks on account @ $125 each to a new customer: Hector Gonzalez, Main Phone: 916-555-6841, Main E-mail: **HGonzalez@email.com**, 4694 Norris Avenue, Sacramento, CA 95841, Payment Terms: Net 10 (Do you need to add a new Standard Term for Net 10?), Credit Limit: $500, Delivery Method: Mail, Taxable, CA Sales Tax. If you print to a pdf file, save the document as **20-Your Name Inv 4 Gonzalez PS3**.

▶ Received the pens ordered from Pens Aplenty with the bill. (Did you date the transaction 01/05/18?) If you print to a pdf file, save the document as **21-Your Name Bill Pens Aplenty PS3**.

▶ Received the textbooks ordered from Textbook Co. without the bill. If you print to a pdf file, save the document as **22-Your Name Item Rct Textbook Co. PS3**.

▶ Prepare and print Inventory Stock Status by Item Report for January 1-5, 2018. (Did you use your memorized report?) If you print to a pdf file, save the document as **23-Your Name Stock Status by Item PS3**.

▶ Order any items indicated. (Stationery) on the Inventory Stock Status by Item Report. If you print to a pdf file, save the document as **24-Your Name PO 3 Supplies Co. PS3**.

▶ Prepare an Unpaid Bills with Terms Detail report.
  ○ If the Terms column shows a discount percentage, calculate the discount date for the bill.
  ○ If a bill is eligible for a discount but can be paid on or after January 10 and still get the discount, do <u>not</u> pay it now.
  ○ If a bill qualifies for a discount between January 5-9, add the comment "Pay this bill" to the report.
  ○ If a bill qualifying for a discount has a credit, add the comment "Use this credit" to the report.
  ○ If you make comments on the report, print it. Otherwise, close the report <u>without</u> printing. Do not save the commented report.

PS 3

▶ Pay any bills and credits marked in the commented report. Remember, if a credit is shown, apply it; and then, recalculate the discount. (Amount Due – Credit * Discount % = Discount) Remember, no discounts are available for opening balances.

▶ Deposit all cash, checks, debit card, and credit card payments received. If you print to a pdf file, save the document as **25-Your Name Dep Sum PS3**.

▶ Backup the company file. Name it **Your Name's Madison Avenue Books (Backup 01-05-18)**.

January 7:

▶ Abby Slater returned the two pens purchased on January 3. She did not like the color. Apply the credit to the invoice and print after you apply the credit to the invoice. (Did you use your Customer Message for Credit Memos?) If you print to a pdf file, save the document as **26-Your Name CM 5 Slater PS3**.

▶ Received the bill for the textbooks ordered from Textbook Co. Use the transaction date January 5, 2018. If you print to a pdf file, save the document as **27-Your Name Bill Textbook Co. PS3**.

▶ The nonprofit organization, Capitol Schools, bought a classroom set of 30 computer training textbooks on account @ $110.00 each and 15 reams of paper @ $4.99 each. Add the new customer: Capitol Schools, Main Phone: 916-555-8787, Main Email: **CapitolSchools@caps.edu**, Fax: 916-555-7878, 2407 J Street, Sacramento, CA 95816, Payment Terms: Net 30, Credit Limit: $5,000, Preferred Delivery Method: Mail, Preferred Payment Method: Check, Taxable, CA Sales Tax. Include a subtotal for the sale and apply a 10% sales discount for a nonprofit organization. (Create any new sales items necessary. Use Sales Discounts as the account for the nonprofit discount.) If you print to a pdf file, save the document as **28-Your Name Inv 6 Capitol Schools PS3**.

▶ Add a new inventory part sales item for Gift Ware, Purchase Description: Gift Ware, Cost: 5.00, COGS Account: Cost of Goods Sold, Preferred Vendor: Brilliant Gifts (Main Phone: 916-555-5384, Main E-mail: **gifts@abc.com**, Fax: 916-555-4835, 125 Oak Street, Sacramento, CA 95814, Payment Terms: Net 30, Credit Limit: $1,500), Sales Description: Gift Ware, Sales Price: 0.00, Tax Code: Tax, Income Account: Supplies Sales, Asset Account: Inventory Asset, Reorder Point (Min): 15; Max: 25, Quantity on Hand: 0, Value: 0.00, as of 01/07/2018.

▶ Order 15 gift ware items from Brilliant Gifts. If you print to a pdf file, save the document as **29-Your Name PO 4 Brilliant Gifts PS3**.

January 8:

▶ Mary typed a 15-page report @ $5.00 per page and sold ten reams of paper @ $5.99 per ream on account to Abby Slater. If you print to a pdf file, save the document as **30-Your Name Inv 7 Slater PS3**.

▶ Use Pay Bills to pay Textbook Co. the full amount owed on the opening balance of $1,000. Print Check 1 using Standard Checks. (Remember, no discounts are available for opening balances.) If you print to a pdf file, save the document as **31-Your Name Ck 1 Textbook Co. PS3**.

▶ Received a telephone order for eight additional computer textbooks on account to Sacramento Schools @ $110 each. If you print to a pdf file, save the document as **32-Your Name SO 2 Sacramento Schools PS3**.

January 10:

▶ Sold three pens @ $14.95 each, two sets of stationery @ $14.99 each, and three paperback books @ $6.99 each to a cash customer using cash as the payment method. If you print to a pdf file, save the document as **33-Your Name SR 3 Cash Cust PS3**.

▶ Sacramento Schools picked up the merchandise on sales order. (Use January 10, 2018 for the invoice date.) If you print to a pdf file, save the document as **34-Your Name Inv 8 Sacramento Schools PS3**.

▶ Received Visa payment (card on file) from Sacramento Schools for the 01/02/18 Invoice for $274.87, the full amount due, less discount. (Did you use Sales Discounts as the Discount Account?) If you print to a pdf file, save the document as **35-Your Name Rcv Pmt Sacramento Schools PS3**.

▶ Received $1,000 as partial payment on account from Complete Training, Inc., MasterCard # 5275 2607 2325 1366, Expiration: 03/2020. If you print to a pdf file, save the document as **36-Your Name Rcv Pmt Complete Training PS3**.

▶ Deposit all cash, checks, debit card, and credit card receipts. If you print to a pdf file, save the document as **37-Your Name Dep Sum PS3**.

▶ Prepare Inventory Stock Status by Item Report for January 1-10, 2018.) If you print to a pdf file, save the document as **38-Your Name Stock Status by Item PS3**.

▶ Order any items indicated on the Inventory Stock Status by Item report. (If an item is marked to order but a purchase order has already been prepared, do not order any more of the item. Since Gift Ware was ordered on 01/07/18, it does not need to be ordered.) If you print to a pdf file, save the document as **39-Your Name PO 5 Textbook Co. PS3**.

▶ Prepare an Unpaid Bills with Terms Detail report.
  ○ If the Terms column shows a discount percentage, calculate the discount date for the bill.
  ○ If a bill is eligible for a discount but can be paid on or after January 15 and still get the discount, do <u>not</u> pay it now.
  ○ If a bill qualifies for a discount between January 10-14, add the comment "Pay this bill" to the report.
  ○ If a bill qualifying for a discount has a credit, add the comment "Use this credit" to the report.
  ○ If you make comments on the report, print it. Otherwise, close <u>without</u> printing. Do not save the commented report.

▶ Pay any bills and credits marked in the commented report. Remember, if a credit is shown, apply it; and then, recalculate the discount. (Amount Due – Credit * Discount % = Discount) Remember, no discounts are available for opening balances.

▶ Backup the company file. Name it **Your Name's Madison Avenue Books (Backup 01-10-18)**.

January 11:

▶ Sold fifteen paperback books @ $8.99 each and two pens @ $35.99 each to Cash Customer using MasterCard # 5242 8521 5925 6842, Expiration: 02/2023. If you print to a pdf file, save the document as **40-Your Name SR 4 Cash Cust PS3**.

▶ Sold ten reams of paper @ $5.99 each, one pen @ $8.99, and one box of stationery @ $12.99 to Cash Customer. Received Debit Card # 4024 0071 5548 3695, Expiration: 04/2024. If you print to a pdf file, save the document as **41-Your Name SR 5 Cash Cust PS3**.

January 12:

▶ Mary typed a one-page letter with an envelope on account for Binh Kim @ $8.00 (Qty 1). If you print to a pdf file, save the document as **42-Your Name Inv 9 Kim PS3**.

▶ Received gift ware ordered from Brilliant Gifts. A bill was not included with the order. If you print to a pdf file, save the document as **43-Your Name Item Rct Brilliant Gifts PS3**.

PS
3

January 13:

- ▶ Received Check 1265 from Abby Slater in payment for full amount due for Invoice 3 after discounts, $58.15. (Since the invoice has a return, subtract the amount of the Credit from the Amount Due; and, then, recalculate the discount.) Payment date is 01/13/2018. If you print to a pdf file, save the document as **44-Your Name Rcv Pmt Slater PS3**.
- ▶ Received the textbooks and the bill from Textbook Co. for Purchase Order 5. Date the bill January 13, 2018. If you print to a pdf file, save the document as **45-Your Name Bill Textbook Co. PS3**.
- ▶ Received a notice from the bank that Check 915 for $350.00 from Binh Kim was marked NSF and returned. Record the NSF check, the bank's $25 fee for the bad check, and Your Name's Madison Avenue Books fee of $40. Use the items created by QBDT for the bounced check charges. Use the Copy of the Intuit Product Invoice for Invoice 10 and the Opening Balance Invoice, Terms: Due on Receipt, and the Customer Message: Please Remit to above address. Print both invoices. If you print to a pdf file, save the documents as **46-Your Name Inv 10 Kim PS3** and **47-Your Name Opening Bal Inv Kim PS3**.

January 14:

- ▶ Received Check 10283 for $270.00 from Hector Gonzalez in payment of Invoice 4. If you print to a pdf file, save the document as **48-Your Name Rcv Pmt Gonzalez PS3**.
- ▶ Received Binh Kim's Debit Card # 4916 0740 7266 0525, Expiration: 03/2022 for payment in full for $398.00. (Record this just like you would record a regular payment on account.) If you print to a pdf file, save the document as **49-Your Name Rcv Pmt Kim PS3**.
- ▶ Received seven boxes of stationery ordered from Supplies Co. The bill was included with the stationery and the three missing boxes are on back order. (Was your original Purchase Order to Supplies Co. for 10 boxes of stationery?) If you print to a pdf file, save the document as **50-Your Name Bill Supplies Co. PS3**.

January 15:

- ▶ Use your memorized transaction to record the bill for rent. If you print to a pdf file, save the document as **51-Your Name Bill Sacramento Rentals PS3**.
- ▶ Received Check 1278 from Abby Slater in payment for full amount due for Invoice 7 after discounts $136.90. If you print to a pdf file, save the document as **52-Your Name Rcv Pmt Slater PS3**.
- ▶ Deposit all cash, checks, debit card, and credit card receipts. If you print to a pdf file, save the document as **53-Your Name Dep Sum PS3**.
- ▶ Prepare an Unpaid Bills with Terms Detail report.
  - ○ If the Terms column shows a discount percentage, calculate the discount date for the bill.
  - ○ If a bill is eligible for a discount but can be paid on or after January 20 and still get the discount, do <u>not</u> pay it now.
  - ○ If a bill qualifies for a discount between January 15-19, add the comment "Pay this bill" to the report.
  - ○ If a bill qualifying for a discount has a credit, add the comment "Use this credit" to the report.
  - ○ If you make comments on the report, print it. Otherwise, close without printing. Do not save the commented report.
  - ○ If you print to a pdf file, save the document as **54-Your Name Comment Unpaid Bills with Terms PS3**.

▶ Pay any bills and credits marked in the commented report. Remember, if a credit is shown, apply it; and then, recalculate the discount. (Amount Due – Credit * Discount % = Discount) Remember, no discounts are available for opening balances. (Did you use Merchandise Discounts for the Discount Account?) If you print to a pdf file, save the document as **55-Your Name Cks 2-3 PS3**.

▶ Received the bill from Brilliant Gifts for the gift ware ordered January 7 and received January 12. Date the bill January 15. If you print to a pdf file, save the document as **56-Your Name Bill Brilliant Gifts PS3**.

▶ Prepare and print an Inventory Stock Status by Item Report for January 1-15 in Landscape orientation. If you print to a pdf file, save the document as **57-Your Name Stock Status by Item PS3**.

▶ Prepare Purchase Orders for all items marked Order on the Inventory Stock Status by Item Report. Use the Reorder Qty column to determine the number of items to order. Place all orders with preferred vendors. If you print to a pdf file, save the documents as **58-Your Name PO 6 Brilliant Gifts PS3** and **59-Your Name PO 7 Textbook Co. PS3**.

▶ Backup the company file. Backup the company file. Name it **Your Name's Madison Avenue Books (Backup 01-15-18)**.

January 17:

▶ Sold eight textbooks on account @ $125 each to Capitol Schools, a nonprofit organization. If you print to a pdf file, save the document as **60-Your Name Inv 11 Capitol Schools PS3**.

▶ Hector Gonzalez returned one textbook he had purchased for $125. Prepare a refund, then print the credit memo. Finally, print the check. If you print to a pdf file, save the documents as **61-Your Name CM 12 Gonzalez PS3**, and **62-Your Name Ck 4 Gonzalez PS3**.

▶ Received Credit Memo 721 from Supplies Co. for the return of five boxes of stationery at 7.50 each. (Apply the credit to the bill dated 01/14/18 when you pay the bill.) If you print to a pdf file, save the document as **63-Your Name Bill Credit Supplies Co. PS3**.

January 20:

▶ A cash customer purchased four textbooks @ $109.99 each, one textbook @ $89.95, and one gift ware item @ $15.90 using Debit Card # 4539 2566 9981 8084, Expiration: 04/2024. If you print to a pdf file, save the document as **64-Your Name SR 6 Cash Cust PS3**.

▶ Received Visa payment (card on file) from Sacramento Schools for $931.39 for payment in full of Invoice 8—not the beginning balance. If you print to a pdf file, save the document as **65-Your Name Rcv Pmt Sacramento Schools PS3**.

▶ Change the Reorder Point (Min) for Textbooks to 1,500 and Pens to 45.

▶ Prepare Inventory Stock Status by Item Report for January 1-20, 2018. Prepare Purchase Orders for marked items. (If nothing is marked, do not print the report.)

▶ Prepare an Unpaid Bills with Terms Detail report.
   ○ If the Terms column shows a discount percentage, calculate the discount date for the bill.
   ○ If a bill is eligible for a discount but can be paid on or after January 25 and still get the discount, do not pay it now.
   ○ If a bill qualifies for a discount between January 20-24, add the comment "Pay this bill" to the report.
   ○ If a bill qualifying for a discount has a credit, add the comment "Use this credit" to the report.

PS
3

- o If you make comments on the report, print it. Otherwise, close without printing. Do not save the commented report.
- o If you print to a pdf file, save the document as **66-Your Name Comment Unpaid Bills with Terms PS3**.
- ▶ Pay any bills and credits marked in the commented report. Remember, if a credit is shown, apply it; and then, recalculate the discount. (Amount Due – Credit * Discount % = Discount) Remember, no discounts are available for opening balances. If you print to a pdf file, save the document as **67-Your Name Cks 5-6 PS3**.
- ▶ Record the bank deposit on January 20. Deposit all cash, checks, debit card, and credit card receipts. If you print to a pdf file, save the document as **68-Your Name Dep Sum PS3**.
- ▶ Backup the company file. Name it **Your Name's Madison Avenue Books (Backup 01-20-18)**.

January 21:

- ▶ Mary typed an eight-page exam @ $5 per page for Hector Gonzalez on account. Hector also purchased 2 pens @ 12.99 each and one box of stationery @ $14.99. If you print to a pdf file, save the document as **69-Your Name Inv 13 Gonzalez PS3**.

January 22:

- ▶ Sold five gift ware items @ $19.99 each, three paperback books @ $8.99 each, and three pens @ $8.99 each to Abby Slater on account. If you print to a pdf file, save the document as **70-Your Name Inv 14 Slater PS3**.

January 25:

- ▶ Received Check 127 for $162.88 as payment in full from Abby Slater. If you print to a pdf file, save the document as **71-Your Name Rcv Pmt Slater PS3**.
- ▶ Increase the Credit Limit for Complete Training, Inc. to $20,000.00.
- ▶ Received a telephone order for 60 textbooks @ $99.95 each and 45 textbooks @ 119.95 each on account to Complete Training, Inc. If you print to a pdf file, save the document as **72-Your Name SO 3 Complete Training PS3**.
- ▶ Prepare Inventory Stock Status by Item Report. Print only if an item needs to be ordered.
- ▶ Prepare an Unpaid Bills with Terms Detail report.
  - o If the Terms column shows a discount percentage, calculate the discount date for the bill.
  - o If a bill is eligible for a discount but can be paid on or after January 30 and still get the discount, do <u>not</u> pay it now.
  - o If a bill qualifies for a discount between January 25-29, add the comment "Pay this bill" to the report.
  - o If a bill qualifying for a discount has a credit, add the comment "Use this credit" to the report.
  - o If you make comments on the report, print it. Otherwise, close without printing. Do not save the commented report.
- ▶ Pay any bills and credits marked in the commented report. Remember, if a credit is shown, apply it; and then, recalculate the discount. (Amount Due – Credit * Discount % = Discount) Remember, no discounts are available for opening balances.
- ▶ Deposit all cash, checks, debit card, and credit card receipts. If you print to a pdf file, save the document as **73-Your Name Dep Sum PS3**.
- ▶ Backup the company file. Name it **Your Name's Madison Avenue Books (Backup 01-25-18)**.

January 29:
- ▶ Received Check 4325 for $84.25 from Hector Gonzalez as payment on his account. If you print to a pdf file, save the document as **74-Your Name Rcv Pmt Gonzalez PS3**.
- ▶ Received $2,078.00 from Complete Training as payment on account using Debit Card # 5525 3362 8698 6925, Expiration: 06/2023. If you print to a pdf file, save the document as **75-Your Name Rcv Pmt Complete Training PS3**.
- ▶ Received the back order of three boxes of stationery and the bill from Supplies Co. Date the bill January 29, 2018. If you print to a pdf file, save the document as **76-Your Name Bill Supplies Co. PS3**.
- ▶ Received bills and items ordered from Textbook Co. (paperback books ordered) and from Brilliant Gifts (gift ware ordered). Date the bills January 29, 2018. If you print to a pdf file, save the document as **77-Your Name Bill Textbook Co. PS3** and **78-Your Name Bill Brilliant Gifts PS3**.
- ▶ Complete Training, Inc. picked up the merchandise ordered by telephone. (Did you prepare an invoice from the sales order?) If you print to a pdf file, save the document as **79-Your Name Inv 15 Complete Training PS3**.

January 30:
- ▶ Prepare Inventory Stock Status by Item Report. If nothing is marked to order, do not print.
- ▶ Deposit all checks, cash, debit card, and credit card receipts. If you print to a pdf file, save the document as **80-Your Name Dep Sum PS3**.
- ▶ Use Pay Bills to pay:
  - ○ Both bills due to Supplies Co. (Be sure to take discounts if eligible.)
  - ○ Rent
    - ▪ If you print to a pdf file, save the document as **81-Your Name Cks 7-8 PS3**.
- ▶ Prepare an Unpaid Bills with Terms Detail report.
  - ○ If the Terms column shows a discount percentage, calculate the discount date for the bill.
  - ○ If a bill is eligible for a discount but can be paid on or after February 5 and still get the discount, do <u>not</u> pay it now.
  - ○ If a bill qualifies for a discount between January 30 and February 4, add the comment "Pay this bill" to the report.
  - ○ If a bill qualifying for a discount has a credit, add the comment "Use this credit" to the report.
  - ○ If you make comments on the report, print it. Otherwise, close without printing. Do not save the commented report.
- ▶ Pay any bills and credits marked in the commented report. Remember, if a credit is shown, apply it; and then, recalculate the discount. (Amount Due – Credit * Discount % = Discount) Remember, no discounts are available for opening balances.
- ▶ Add a new vendor CA Utilities & Telephone, Main Phone: 916-555-8523, Main Email: **CAUtilTel@CAUT.com**, 8905 Richmond, Sacramento, CA 95825, Payment Terms: Net 30. Then, use Write Checks to pay the utility and telephone bill. The amount of the utilities portion of the bill is $257 and the amount of the telephone portion of the bill is $189. (Did you write just one check?) If you print to a pdf file, save the document as **82-Your Name Ck 9 CA Utilities PS3**.
- ▶ Backup the company file. Name it **Your Name's Madison Avenue Books (Backup 01-30-18)**.

PS
3

January 31:

► Sherry Compton just got married. Change her last name to **Nunez** and her Marital Status to **Married**. Do not change her Federal or State Tax Filing Status. Verify her Sick and Vacation Time and change anything that does not agree with the following. Sick time should be: Hours available 01/31/18: **40:00**, Hours used in 2018: **0:00** (If it shows 2010 as the year, that is her Hire Date. You cannot change this.), Accrual period: **Beginning of year**, Hours accrued at beginning of year: **40:00**, Maximum number of hours: **120:00**, Year begins on **January 1**, Begin accruing sick time on **02/17/2010**. Vacation time should be: Hours available 01/31/28: **40:00**, Hours used in 2018: **0:00** (If it shows 2010 as the year, that is her Hire Date. You cannot change this.), Accrual period: **Beginning of year**, Hours accrued at beginning of year: **40:00**, Maximum number of hours: **120:00**, Year begins on **January 1**, Begin accruing sick time on **02/17/2010**.

► Prior to processing the first payroll, verify the Sick and Vacation Time for Devon Peterson and change anything that does not agree with the following. Sick time should be: Hours available 01/31/28: **40:00**, Hours used in 2018: **0:00** (If it shows 1996 as the year, that is his Hire Date. You cannot change this.), Accrual period: **Beginning of year**, Hours accrued at beginning of year: **40:00**, Maximum number of hours: **120:00**, Year begins on **January 1**, Begin accruing sick time on **04/03/1996**. Vacation time should be: Hours available 01/31/18: **40:00**, Hours used in 2018: **0:00** (If it shows 1996 as the year, that is his Hire Date. You cannot change this.), Accrual period: **Beginning of year**, Hours accrued at beginning of year: **40:00**, Maximum number of hours: **120:00**, Year begins on **January 1**, Begin accruing sick time on **04/03/1996**.

► Pay the payroll: The pay period is 01/01/18 through 01/31/18. The check date is 01/31/18. Use the information in the following table to prepare the checks.

PAYROLL TABLE, JANUARY 31, 2018			
	Mary Delgado	**Sherry Nunez**	**Devon Peterson**
HOURS			
Regular	80	158	144
Overtime (x1.5)			3
Sick			16
Vacation		2	
DEDUCTIONS OTHER PAYROLL ITEMS: EMPLOYEE			
Dental Ins.		30.00	20.00
Medical Ins.		30.00	20.00
DEDUCTIONS: COMPANY			
CA Employment Training Tax	.64	1.27	1.65
Social Security	39.68	78.53	101.99
Medicare	9.28	31.42	23.85
Federal Unemployment	3.84	7.60	9.87
CA-Unemployment	21.76	43.07	55.93

PAYROLL TABLE, JANUARY 31, 2018			
	Mary Delgado	**Sherry Nunez**	**Devon Peterson**
DEDUCTIONS: EMPLOYEE			
Medicare Employee Addl Tax	0.00	0.00	0.00
Federal Withholding	46.10	126.90	65.53
Social Security	26.88	53.20	69.09
Medicare	9.28	31.42	23.85
CA-Withholding	7.39	56.06	22.50
CA-Disability	6.40	12.67	16.45

▶ Print the paychecks using a **voucher**-style check. (If the voucher prints two times, it is fine.) Be sure to remove the Intuit logo from the Payroll Printing Preferences. If you print to a pdf file, save the document as **83-Your Name Cks 10-12 PS3**.

▶ Before distributing paychecks, you realize that the Social Security Employee Deductions for each employee are incorrect. Go to the checks, unlock them and change the amount of Social Security Employee Deductions for Mary to 39.68, for Sherry to 78.53, and for Devon to 101.99. Reprint the checks using Voucher style. If you print to a pdf file, save the document as **84-Your Name Ck 10 Delgado Corrected PS3**, **85-Your Name Ck 11 Nunez Corrected PS3**, and **86-Your Name Ck 12 Peterson Corrected PS3**.

▶ Prepare and print the Payroll Summary Report for January in Landscape orientation. (Adjust column widths and fit the report to print on one page.). If you print to a pdf file, save the document as **87-Your Name Payroll Sum PS3**.

▶ Prepare and print the Payroll Liabilities Balances Report for January in Portrait orientation. If you print to a pdf file, save the document as **88-Your Name Payroll Liab Bal PS3**.

▶ Pay all the payroll liabilities for January 1-31, 2018. Print the standard checks. You may print the checks individually or as a batch. If you print to a pdf file, save the document as **89-Your Name Cks 13-15 PS3**.

▶ Prepare Sales Tax Liability Report for January 1-31, 2018. Print in Landscape orientation. Adjust column widths so the report fits on one page, maintains the same font, and has column headings shown in full. If you print to a pdf file, save the document as **90-Your Name Sales Tax Liab PS3**.

▶ Pay Sales Tax for January 31, 2018 and print the check. If you print to a pdf file, save the document as **91-Your Name Ck 16 State Board of Equal PS3**.

▶ Print a Sales by Item Summary Report for January 1-31 in Landscape orientation. Adjust column widths so the report fits on one-page wide. If you print to a pdf file, save the document as **92-Your Name Sales by Item Sum PS3**.

▶ Print a Trial Balance for January 1-31 in Portrait orientation. If you print to a pdf file, save the document as **93-Your Name Trial Bal PS3**.

▶ Enter adjusting entries: Depreciation—Store Equipment & Fixtures $266.66. Supplies used—$400.00. Insurance used a total of $100—$50 Fire Insurance, $50 Liability Insurance. (Use a compound entry to record insurance adjustment.)

PS 3

▶ Record the owner withdrawal for the month $2,000.00. (Did you use QuickAdd to add your name to the Other Names list?) If you print to a pdf file, save the document as **94-Your Name Ck 17 Your Name PS3**.

▶ Prepare a bank reconciliation and record any adjustments. Be sure to use the date of 01/31/18 for the bank statement date, service charges, and interest earned.

CAPITOL STATE BANK			
5255 Hemlock Street Sacramento, CA 95841 (916) 555-9889			
Your Name's Madison Avenue Books 4748 Madison Avenue Sacramento, CA 95814	Acct. # 91-1132-7022		January, 2018
Beginning Balance, January 1, 2018			$130,870.25
1/5/2018, Deposit	2,616.85		133,487.10
1/10/2018, Check 1		1,000.00	132,487.10
1/10/2018, Deposit	1,378.33		133,865.43
1/13/2018, Check 6 NSF Binh Kim		350.00	133,515.43
1/13/2018, NSF Bank Charge Binh Kim		25.00	133,490.43
1/15/2018, Deposit	1,174.86		134,665.29
1/15/2018, Check 2		102.90	134,562.39
1/15/2018, Check 3		2,254.00	132,308.39
1/18/2018, Check 4		135.00	132,173.39
1/20/2018, Deposit	1,520.86		133,694.25
1/20/2018, Check 5		14.70	133,679.55
1/20/2018, Check 6		1,960.00	131,719.55
1/25/2018, Deposit	162.88		131,882.43
1/31/2018, Service Charge		15.00	131,867.43
1/31/2018, Store Equipment & Fixtures Loan Pmt.: Interest $124.71, Principal $22.65		147.36	131,720.07
1/31/2018, Interest	1,976.10		133,696.17
Ending Balance, January 31, 2018			**$133,696.17**

▶ When the reconciliation is complete, print the Detail Reconciliation Report. If you print to a pdf file, save the document as **95-Your Name Bank Rec PS3**.

▶ After printing the Reconciliation Detail Report, close the Drawing account.

▶ Transfer the Net Income/Owner's Equity into the capital account.

▶ Adjust the Merchandise Item of Gift Ware for 1 Gift Set that was damaged. (Use the expense account Merchandise Adjustments.)

▶ Correct the Amount of Net Income to reflect the merchandise adjustment.

▶ Print a Standard Profit & Loss Statement for January 1-31, 2018. If you print to a pdf file, save the document as **96-Your Name P & L PS3**.

▶ Print a Standard Balance Sheet As of January 31, 2018. If you print to a pdf file, save the document as **97-Your Name Bal Sheet PS3**.

▶ Make an Archive Copy backup of the company. Name it **Your Name's Madison Avenue Books (Archive 01-31-18)**.

▶ Close the period with a closing date of **01/31/18**. (Do not use passwords.)

▶ Print the Journal, expand the columns, use the dates from **12/31/2017** to **01/31/2018**, adjust columns, and print in Landscape orientation. (If necessary, select Fit report to 1 page(s) wide.) The order in which your transactions appear may be different from any answer keys provided. If all the transactions have been entered, the order of entry does not matter. If you print to a pdf file, save the document as **98-Your Name Journal PS3**.

▶ Backup the company file. Name it **Your Name's Madison Avenue Books (Backup Complete)**.

PRACTICE SET 3 CHECKLIST

YOUR NAME'S MADISON AVENUE BOOKS

Check the items below as you complete and/or print them; then attach the documents and reports in the order listed when you submit them to your instructor. Printing is optional for Payment Receipts and Bills (unless your instructor requires them to be printed); however, they are included in the checklist, so they can be checked as they are completed.

(Note: When paying bills and printing a batch of checks, your checks may be in a different order than shown below. If you print the checks to the correct people or company and have the correct amounts, do not be concerned if your check numbers are not an exact match.)

Set Up
___ 1-Emp List Peterson
___ 2-Emp Sum Compton
___ 3-Acct List
___ 4-Item List
___ 5-Trans List by Cust
___ 6-Trans List by Vend
___ 7-Bal Sheet

January 1-5, 2018
___ 8-SR 1 Cash Cust
___ 9-Inv 1 Complete Training
___ 10-Rcv Pmt Slater
___ 11-SO 1 Sacramento Schools
___ 12-SR 2 Cash Cust
___ 13-Stock Status by Item
___ 14-PO 1 Pens Aplenty
___ 15-PO 2 Textbooks Co.
___ 16-Inv 2 Sacramento Schools
___ 17-Rcv Pmt Kim
___ 18-Inv 3 Slater
___ 19-Rcv Pmt Complete Training
___ 20-Inv 4 Gonzalez
___ 21-Bill Pens Aplenty
___ 22-Item Rct Textbook Co.
___ 23-Stock Status by Item
___ 24-PO 3 Supplies Co.
___ 25-Dep Sum

January 6-10, 2018
___ 26-CM 5 Slater
___ 27-Bill Textbook Co.
___ 28-Inv 6 Capitol Schools
___ 29-PO 4 Brilliant Gifts
___ 30-Inv 7 Slater
___ 31-Ck 1 Textbook Co.
___ 32-SO 2 Sacramento Schools
___ 33-SR 3 Cash Cust

___ 34-Inv 8 Sacramento Schools
___ 35-Rcv Pmt Sacramento Schools
___ 36-Rcv Pmt Complete Training
___ 37-Dep Sum
___ 38-Stock Status by Item
___ 39-PO 5 Textbook Co.

January 11-15, 2018
___ 40-SR 4 Cash Cust
___ 41-SR 5 Cash Cust
___ 42-Inv 9 Kim
___ 43-Item Rct Brilliant Gifts
___ 44-Rcv Pmt Slater
___ 45-Bill Textbook Co.
___ 46-Inv 10 Kim
___ 47-Opening Bal Inv Kim
___ 48-Rcv Pmt Gonzalez
___ 49-Rcv Pmt Kim
___ 50-Bill Supplies Co.
___ 51-Bill Sacramento Rentals
___ 52-Rcv Pmt Slater
___ 53-Dep Sum
___ 54-Comment Unpaid Bills with Terms
___ 55-Cks 2-3
___ 56-Bill Brilliant Gifts
___ 57-Stock Status by Item
___ 58-PO 6 Brilliant Gifts
___ 59-PO 7 Textbooks Co.

January 16-20, 2018
___ 60-Inv 11 Capitol Schools
___ 61-CM 12 Gonzalez
___ 62-Ck 4 Gonzalez
___ 63-Bill Credit Supplies Co.
___ 64-SR 6 Cash Cust
___ 65-Rcv Pmt Sacramento Schools
___ 66-Comment Unpaid Bills with Terms
___ 67-Cks 5-6
___ 68-Dep Sum

January 21-15, 2018
___ 69-Inv 13 Gonzalez
___ 70-Inv 14 Slater
___ 71-Rcv Pmt Slater
___ 72-SO 3 Complete Training
___ 73-Dep Sum

January 26-30, 2018
___ 74-Rcv Pmt Gonzalez
___ 75-Rcv Pmt Complete Training
___ 76-Bill Supplies Co.
___ 77-Bill Textbooks Co.
___ 78-Bill Brilliant Gifts
___ 79-Inv 15 Complete Training
___ 80-Dep Sup
___ 81-Cks 7-8
___ 82-Ck 9 CA Utilities
___ 83-Cks 10-12

January 31, 2018
___ 84-Ck 10 Delgado Corrected
___ 85-Ck 11 Nunez Corrected
___ 86-Ck 12 Peterson Corrected
___ 87-Payroll Sum
___ 88-Payroll Liab Bal
___ 89-Cks 13-15
___ 90-Sales Tax Liab
___ 91-Ck 16 State Board of Equal
___ 92-Sales by Item Sum
___ 93-Trial Bal
___ 94-Ck 17 Your Name
___ 95-Bank Rec
___ 96-P & L
___ 97-Bal Sheet
___ 98-Journal

PS
3

QUICKBOOKS DESKTOP: PROGRAM INTEGRATION

A

QuickBooks Desktop is integrated to work in conjunction with Microsoft Word and Excel to prepare many different types of letters or send QuickBooks Desktop reports directly to an Excel workbook. To use the integration features of the program, you must have Microsoft® Word 2010 (or higher) and Microsoft® Excel 2010 (or higher) installed on your computer.

This appendix will use the sample company, Larry's Landscaping & Garden Supply, to provide information regarding program integration with QuickBooks Desktop. Since saving the demonstration transactions will make permanent changes to the sample company, you will not need to do the demonstration transactions unless they are assigned by your instructor. Because the material presented in the appendix is for illustration purposes only, memo boxes and detailed data for entry are not included.

QUICKBOOKS DESKTOP LETTERS

There are many times in business when you need to write a letter of one type or another to your customers. This is an important feature because QuickBooks Desktop will insert information, from your customer files directly into a letter.

To prepare a letter to Active Customers, Click **Open a sample file**, and the click the type of sample company you wish to explore—**Sample service-based business**
- If you get an Update Company File message, click **Yes**.
A notification regarding QuickBooks Information appears

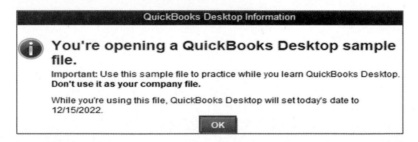

Click **OK** on the QuickBooks Information screen
Open the Customer Center
Click the **Word** button
Click **Prepare Customer Letters**
- If you get a screen regarding the lack of available templates, click **Copy**.
For "Include names that are:" click **Active**
For "Create a letter for each:" click **Customer**

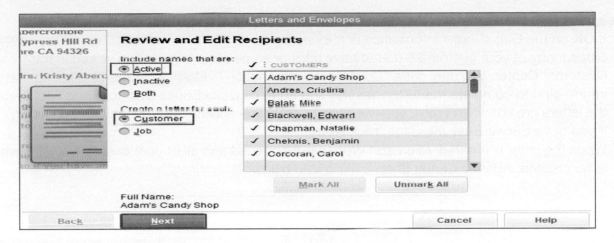

Click **Next**

Scroll through the list of Letter Templates

Click **Thanks for business (service)**

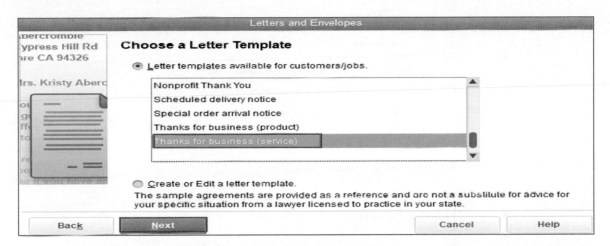

- If you do not find a template that is appropriate or you want to make permanent changes to one of the existing letter templates, you may do so by clicking Create or Edit a letter template.

Click **Next**

Enter **Your First and Last Name** (your actual name not the words your name) for the name at the end of the letter

Enter your title as **President**

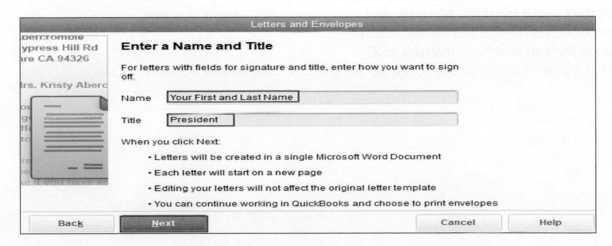

A

Click **Next**

Click **OK** on the QuickBooks Information Is Missing screen

- Since many of your customers do not have titles or some other information stored in the Customer Center, you may get a "QuickBooks Information Is Missing" screen indicating that information to complete this letter was missing from the QuickBooks Desktop Data File. Once the letters are shown in Word, you will need to enter the missing information for each letter.

- If you get a Server Busy message, click **Retry**.

- When the letter is created, Microsoft Word will be opened and all of your customers will have a letter created. Adam's Candy Shop is illustrated below:

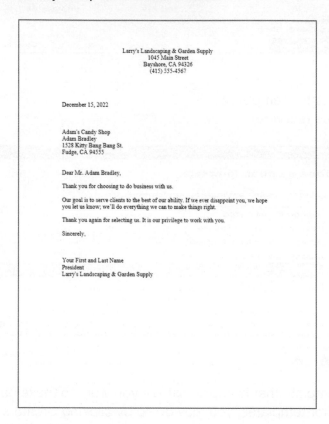

- The letters are not technically correct with formats and spacing so may need some adjustment on your part. However, it is much easier to edit letters prepared for you than it is to create a letter for each customer.

To make the short letter appear more balanced:

Click the **Layout** tab, click **Margins**, and click the words **Custom Margins**

Change the Top and Bottom margins to **1"**

Change the Left and Right margins to **2"**

Click the drop-down list arrow for **Apply to:** and then click **Whole document**

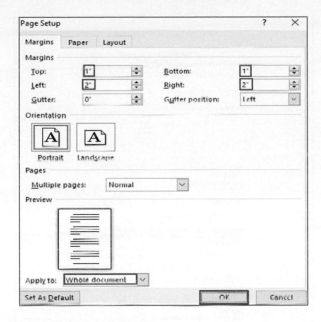

Click **OK**

Position the cursor between the date and the letter address

Press the **Enter** key **5 times**

- There will be 8 blank lines between the date and the letter address.

Delete one of the blank lines between the letter address and the salutation (Dear Mr. Adam Bradley,)

The appropriate salutation is: Dear Mr. Bradley:

Delete his first name and the comma following his last name

- A formal business letter does not use a first name or a comma in the greeting (salutation). The first name and a comma may be used for an informal letter when you know the person, not a business letter.

Click the **View** tab; and then, click **Print Layout**

- Your letter should look like the following. Notice how much more balanced the letter appears.
- Notice that Adam's Candy Shop address information was automatically inserted in the letter.

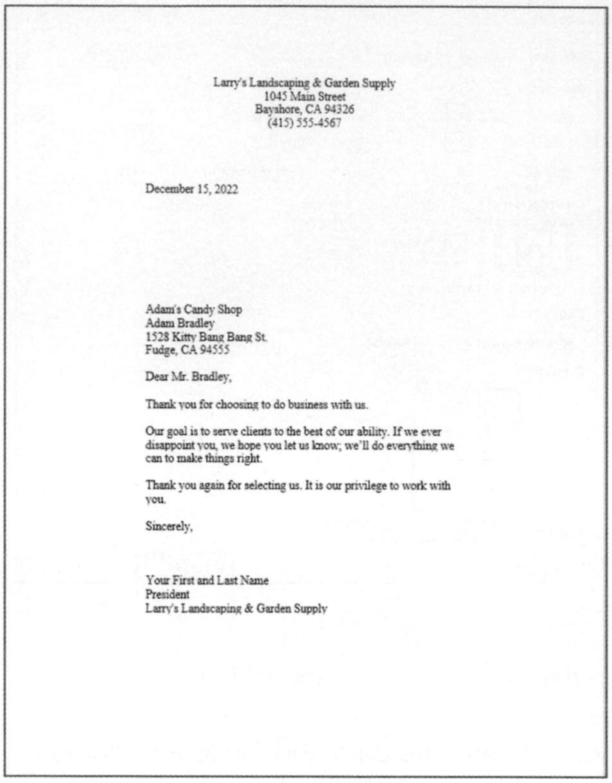

Larry's Landscaping & Garden Supply
1045 Main Street
Bayshore, CA 94326
(415) 555-4567

December 15, 2022

Adam's Candy Shop
Adam Bradley
1528 Kitty Bang Bang St.
Fudge, CA 94555

Dear Mr. Bradley,

Thank you for choosing to do business with us.

Our goal is to serve clients to the best of our ability. If we ever
disappoint you, we hope you let us know; we'll do everything we
can to make things right.

Thank you again for selecting us. It is our privilege to work with
you.

Sincerely,

Your First and Last Name
President
Larry's Landscaping & Garden Supply

On the View tab, click **Draft** to return to the original display
Close **Word** without saving the letter
On the Print Letters and Envelopes screen, click **Cancel** to cancel the Letters to Customers
Do <u>not</u> close the Customer Center

EXPORTING INFORMATION TO EXCEL

Many of the reports prepared in QuickBooks Desktop can be exported to Microsoft Excel. This allows you to take advantage of extensive filtering options available in Excel, hide detail for some but not all groups of data, combine information from two different reports, change titles of columns, add comments, change the order of columns, and experiment with *what if* scenarios. Exporting reports to Excel from within a report was demonstrated within the chapters. Information may also be exported from the Customer, Vendor, and Employee Centers.

To export a Customer List to Excel, click the **Excel** button in the **Customer Center**, and click
    Export Customer List
On the Export dialog box click **Create new worksheet** and **in new workbook**
Click the **Export** button

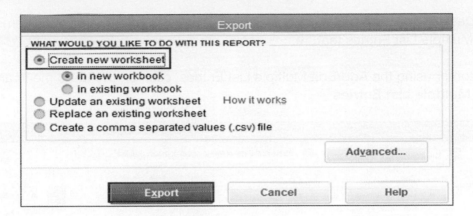

- A detailed Customer List will be displayed in Excel.

	Active Status	Customer	Balance	Balance Total	Company	Mr./Ms./...	First Name	M.I.	Last Name	Primary Contact	Main Phone	Fax
2	Active	Adam's Candy Shop	40.00	40.00	Adam's Candy Shop	Mr.	Adam		Bradley	Adam Bradley	707 555 5734	
3	Active	Andres, Cristina	0.00	0.00			Cristina		Andres	Cristina Andres	415-555-2174	
4	Active	Balak, Mike	0.00	180.00			Mike		Balak	Mike Balak	415-555-6453	none
5	Active	Balak, Mike:330 Main St	180.00	180.00	Hair, Nails and Supply		Mike		Balak	Mike Balak	415-555-6453	none
6	Active	Balak, Mike:Residential	0.00	0.00			Mike		Balak	Mike Balak	415-555-6453	none

Partial Report

Click the **Close** button in the upper right corner of the Excel title bar to close **Excel**
Click **Don't Save** to close **Book2** without saving
- Depending on the number of documents opened in Excel previously, your Book number may not be 2.

Close the **Customer Center**

IMPORTING DATA FROM EXCEL

Another feature of QuickBooks Desktop is the ability to import data from Excel into QuickBooks Desktop. You may have Excel or .csv (comma separated value) files that contain important business information about customers, vendors, sales items, and other lists that are not contained in your QuickBooks Desktop Company File. That information can be imported directly into QuickBooks Desktop and customized as desired. An import file must conform to a specific structure for QuickBooks Desktop to interpret the data in the file correctly.

You may import your data from Excel in three ways. First, you may use an advanced import method to modify and use an existing Excel or CVS file, use a specially formatted spreadsheet and then add it to QuickBooks Desktop, or you may copy and paste your data from Excel directly into QuickBooks Desktop using the Add/Edit Multiple List Entries window.

Since importing data is not reversible, a backup should be made prior to importing data. An example of procedures to follow when using a spreadsheet to import a customer is shown below:

A

QuickBooks Desktop makes it possible to import customers, vendors, and sales items by using the Add/Edit Multiple List Entries feature.

To add a customer using the Add/Edit Multiple List Entries, click on the **Lists** menu and choose **Add/Edit Multiple List Entries**

Partial List

Verify that the List is **Customers** and the View is **Active Customers**
- To import and export customer information between QuickBooks Desktop and Excel, you will need to make sure the column headings and the order in which the columns are listed in QuickBooks Desktop matches your Excel spreadsheet.

Click **Adam's Candy Shop** in the Name column
- If you get a Time Saving Tip regarding Copy Down, click **OK**.

Right-click **Adam's Candy Shop**, and then click **Insert line**

Enter the customer information for **Acme Rentals** on the blank line (or copy and paste from an existing Excel spreadsheet)

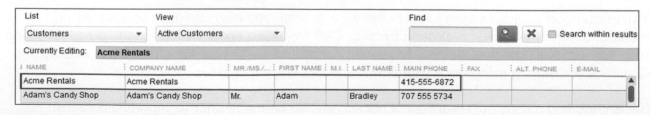

Click the **Save Changes** button

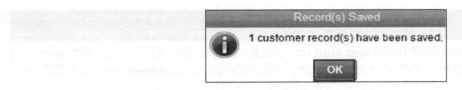

Click **OK** on the Record(s) Saved screen; and then, click **Close** on the Add/Edit Multiple List
Entries Screen

The following information shows an <u>alternate method</u> of adding customers:
In the Customer Center, click the drop-down list arrow for the Excel menu, and click **Import from
Excel**.
Click **No** on the Add/Edit Multiple List Entries
Complete the **Wizard**

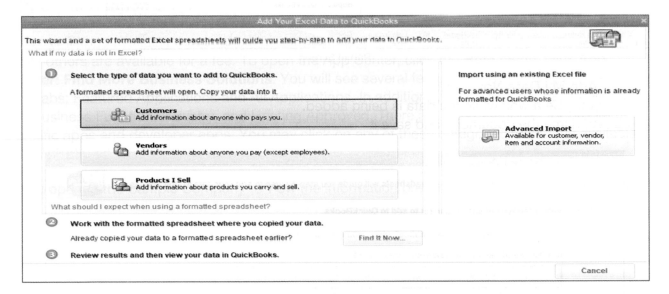

Click **Customers**
Click **Yes** on the Import textbox.
You are taken to a pre-formatted spreadsheet that is ready for data entry.
Click in the Company Name column in Row 8 on the QuickBooks Desktop screen
Enter the customer data for **Able, Sandra** (or, if you were using your own company, copy it from
an existing Excel document)
● Notice the Coach Tips as you go from field to field as you enter all of the customer data.
● Since you want your customers shown alphabetically by last name, Display should be Able,
Sandra.
When you have entered the data,
Click the **Disk** icon to **save** the file and give the file a name and a location

QUICKBOOKS DESKTOP: ADDITIONAL FEATURES

B

The QuickBooks Desktop Program contains many areas that were not explored during the training chapters of the text. Some of these areas are portable company files, calendar, time tracking, job costing and tracking, price levels, and notes. Features such as Client Data Review, batch invoicing, the Document Center, attaching documents, and customizing the icon bar are also addressed in this appendix.

When possible, the Sample Product-Based Business, Rock Castle Construction, will be used to explore these features. As was done in the chapters, the Top Icon bar will be used.

Since saving the demonstration transactions will make permanent changes to the sample company, you will <u>not</u> need to do the demonstration transactions unless they are assigned by your instructor. Since the material presented in the appendix is for illustration purposes only, memo boxes and detailed data for entry are not included.

PORTABLE COMPANY FILES

During training in the text, you used Company (.QBW) files, made Backup (.QBB) files, and restored a Backup file to a Company file. In addition to these types of files, QuickBooks Desktop also has a Portable Company (.QBM) file, which is a compact version of your company file that contains only financial data. A portable file is small enough to be emailed and saved to portable media. It cannot be used to record transactions and, just like a Backup file, must be restored to a Company (.QBW) file before use. Data entered and then saved to a portable file cannot be merged into an existing company file because a portable file that is restored overwrites data just like restoring a backup file. In order to restore a portable file, you must have an Administrator password.

NEW BUSINESS CHECKLIST

Many businesses use QuickBooks Desktop from the time they begin operations. There is a **New Business Checklist** provided in QuickBooks Desktop. It is accessed from the Help menu. This checklist helps a new business work through all the details involved in starting a business. Even existing businesses may profit from working through the checklist to make sure nothing was forgotten during the business setup. Of course, a business may have special items that are very specific in nature that are not on the checklist. When you complete the **Steps to Startup Success** on the New Business Checklist, there are categories for

1. Conceive your business
2. Structure your business
3. Prepare all necessary forms, permits, and licenses
4. Fund your business
5. Taxes and insurance

Within each category, there will be topics with check boxes that may be marked when the topic is completed. Help opens with an explanation for each topic provided when you click the topic.

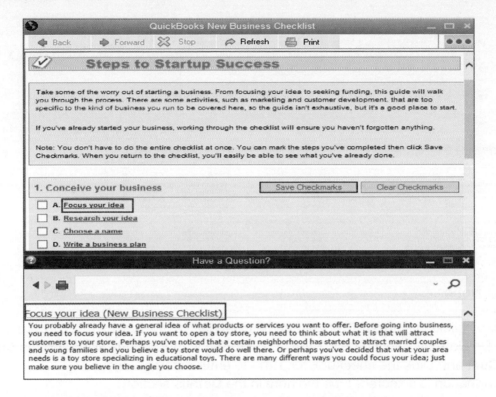

The checklist does not have to be completed all at once. After you finish a topic, click it to mark it. When leaving the QuickBooks Desktop New Business Checklist, click Save Checkmarks. When you return to the checklist, you will see where you left off.

QUICKBOOKS DESKTOP CALENDAR

QuickBooks Desktop Calendar is an easy way to view transactions that have been entered, transactions that are due, and tasks that are shown on the To Do list. You may view the calendar for an entire month, a week, or a day. You may choose which types of transactions appear on the calendar. You may decide whether to show or hide detail and may double-click a transaction to view or edit it.

Open the Calendar

Click the **Calendar** icon in the Company Section of the Home Page, on the Icon bar, or click
    Calendar on the drop-down menu for Company to open the Calendar
The Monthly Calendar for December, 2022 is shown
 The "current" date of **15** is highlighted with the note of **Entered (40)**
- This tells you the number of transactions entered that day.
On the right-side of the Calendar is a list of **Upcoming: Next 7 days** and **Due: Past 60 days**
- This lets you know about transactions that need to be completed.
Beneath the Calendar is a list of **Transactions Entered**
- This shows you exactly what transactions were entered on the selected date of December 15.

B

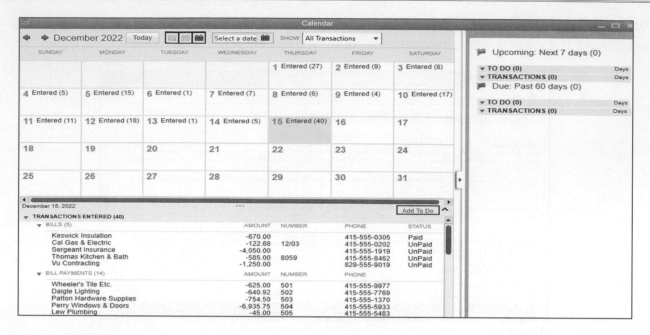

Add a To Do Note:

Add a To Do by clicking **Add To Do** beneath the calendar

Create a To Do Note by selecting the **Type** and **Priority**; if appropriate, **With** and the **Customer Name**; **Due**, and click the checkbox for **Time** to enter different times.

Once the information is selected, type the note in the **Details** section

Click **OK** and the To Do is added to the Calendar, in the listing for Upcoming Next 7 days, and below the calendar

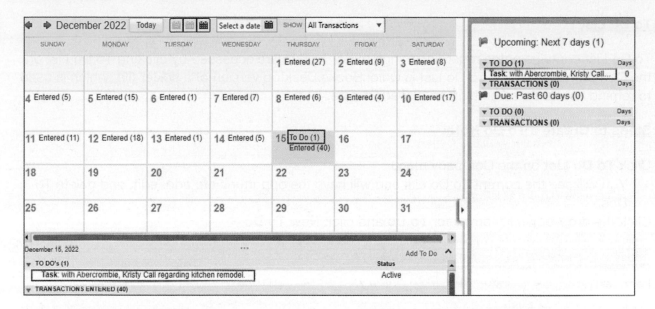

Change Calendar Views

To change the view click one of the icons at the top of the calendar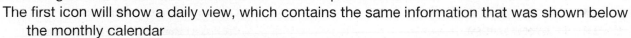
The first icon will show a daily view, which contains the same information that was shown below the monthly calendar
The middle icon will show you the five-day weekly view
- In the screen shot for the week of December 11-17, the Upcoming, Past Due, and Transactions Entered information is not shown.

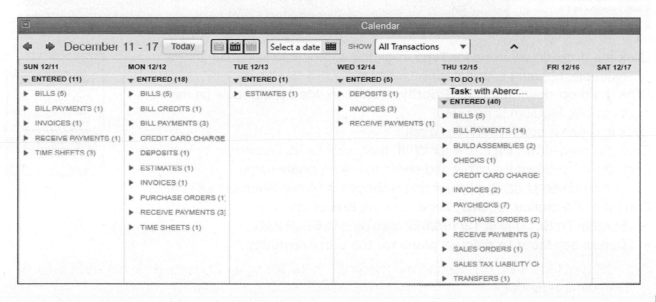

Close the Calendar

QUICKBOOKS DESKTOP NOTES

QuickBooks Desktop allows you to use several types of notes. These are To Do List, Customer notes, Vendor notes, Employee notes, and Time Tracking notes.

B

To Do List

To Do List contains notes regarding things to do. To Dos are accessed by clicking To Do List on the Company menu. The To Do List is QuickBooks Desktop version of a tickler file, which is used to remind you to do something on a specific date.

Steps to Create a To Do Note:

Click **To Do List** on the Company menu
- You will see the current To Do List and will have the opportunity to add, edit, and delete To Dos.

Click the drop-down list arrow for **To Do** and click **New To Do**

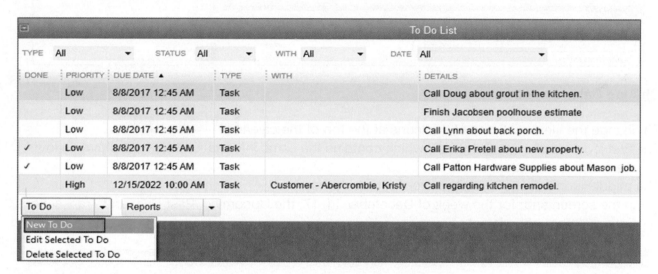

Click the **drop**-down arrow for **Type**, click the appropriate selection (in the example, Meeting is selected)

Click the drop-down arrow for **Priority**, click High, Medium, or Low (in the example, Medium is selected)

Click in the text box for WITH to mark

Click the drop-down list arrow for **With**, then click Lead, Customer, or Vendor

Click the drop-down list arrow and select the appropriate name
- In the screen shot, **Customer** and **Babcock's Music Shop** are selected.

Enter the information for **Due**, **Time**, and the **text** of the note
- For this To Do, Due is **12/19/2022** and Time is **09:00 AM**.
- Details say **Meet to discuss plans for the store remodel**.

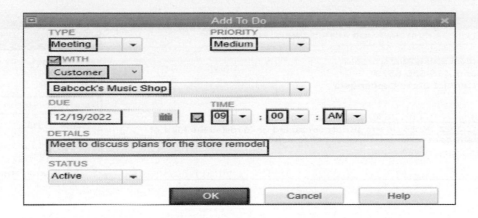

Click **OK**

- The note will be added to the list of To Do notes and will appear in the Calendar.

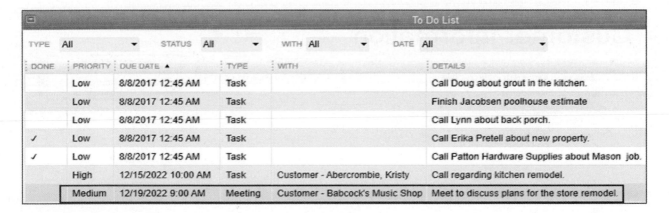

Close the **To Do List**

<u>**Customer Notes**</u>

In the Customer Center, QuickBooks Desktop provides a notepad for recording notes about each customer or job. Approximately ten windows worth of text can be displayed on each customer's notepad. You can also write on the customer notepad when viewing a customer's record or when entering a transaction. When using the customer notepad, an entry may be date stamped, To Do notes may be accessed, and the note may be printed.

<u>**Steps to Create Customer or Job Notes**</u>

Open the **Customer Center**
Click on the Customer you wish to view or add notes (Kristy Abercrombie)
To access the Customer Notepad, click the **Notes** tab
- In the section below Customer Information, there are tabs for Transactions, Contacts, To Do's, Notes, and Sent Email.
Click the **Manage Notes** button at the bottom of the list of notes, click **Add New**
Click the **Date/Time Stamp** button and QuickBooks Desktop will enter the date and time of the note (the current date and time of your computer), then type the note

B

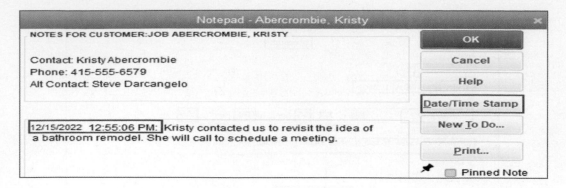

Click **OK** to save

The note is added to her list of notes and displayed in full on the right side of the notes tab

If you want to add the note to her Customer Information dashboard, click the Note in the list of notes to mark (Pin). The note will be shown in the Note section of the Customer Information

- All the Notes are shown on the Notes Tab. Be sure to use the Notes tab to view, create, pin, and manage notes.

Exit the notepad, close the **Customer Center**

Vendor, Employee, and Other Names Notes

Vendor notes are recorded on the notepad for individual vendors in the Vendor Center. As with customer notes, this is where important conversations and product information would be recorded. The vendor notepad can be accessed from the Vendor Center. When using the vendor notepad, an entry may be date stamped, To Do notes may be accessed, and the note may be printed. Each entry on your Vendor, Employee, and Other Names lists has its own notepad where you can keep miscellaneous notes to yourself about that vendor, employee, or name. The procedures followed for vendors, employees, or other names are the same as those illustrated for customers.

Notes for Time Tracking

The Timer is a separate program that is installed and works in conjunction with QuickBooks Desktop. Notes regarding the time spent working on a task are entered when using the stopwatch. Time Tracking in QuickBooks Desktop will be demonstrated later in this appendix.

Steps to Create Notes for Time Tracking

Click the **Employees** menu and click **Enter Time**
Click **Time/Enter Single Activity**
Click the drop-down list arrow for **Name** and select the employee (Elizabeth N. Mason)
Click the drop-down list arrow for **Customer:Job** and select the customer (Abercrombie, Kristy: Kitchen)
Click the drop-down list arrow for **Service Item**, click the item (Blueprint Changes)
Click in the **Notes** section of the window
Enter the note: **Revise plan for kitchen remodel.**

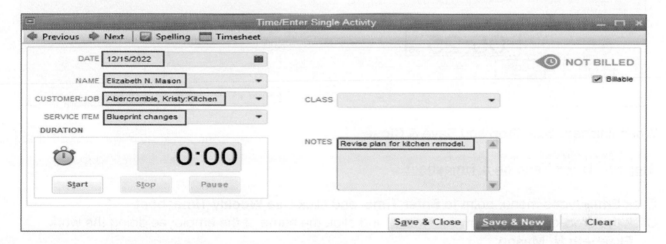

Do <u>not</u> close the Time/Enter Single Activity screen

TRACKING TIME

Many businesses bill their customers or clients for the actual amount of time they spend working for them. In this case you would be tracking billable time. When you complete the invoice to the customer, you can add the billable time to the invoice with a few clicks. In other situations, you may not want to bill for the time; but you may want to track it. For example, you may want to find out how much time you spend working on a job that was negotiated at a fixed price. This will help you determine whether or not you estimated the hours for the job correctly. Also, you may want to track the amount of time employees spend on various jobs, whether or not you bill for the time.

QuickBooks Desktop comes with a separate Timer program. You have a choice between tracking time via the Timer (not shown) and then importing the time data to QuickBooks Desktop, using the Stopwatch on the Time/Enter Single Activity window to time an activity while you are performing it, or entering time directly into QuickBooks Desktop manually on the Weekly Timesheet window or the Time/Enter Single Activity window.

B

Steps to Track Time as a Single Activity

With the **Time/Enter Single Activity** screen showing the time for Elizabeth N. Mason and the blueprint changes for Kristy Abercrombie, indicate whether or not the time recorded is billable
- A check in the billable box means that this is recorded as billable time. No check means that the time is being tracked but not billed.

Click **Start** on the timer, and when finished with the work, click **Stop** on the timer
- If work is stopped at any time, you may click Pause when stopping and click Start when resuming work.

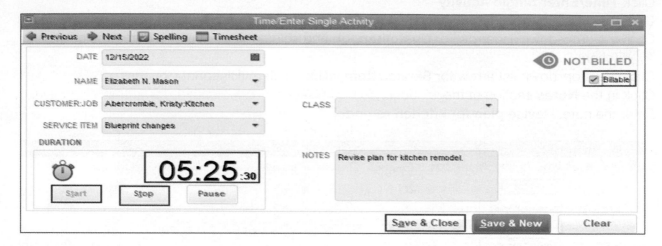

When finished, click **Stop** and **Save & Close**

Steps to Track Time on a Timesheet

Click **Employees** menu, point to **Enter Time**, and click **Use Weekly Timesheet**
Click the drop-down list arrow for **Name**, and click the name of the employee doing the work:
  Elizabeth N. Mason
- Accept the date the computer provides.
  ○ If you want to change the date of the time sheet, click the calendar button, and click the date for the time sheet.
- Any work completed as a Single Activity will appear on the time sheet. Notice the time and note entered for Abercrombie, Kristy.

To enter information for a time period directly on the time sheet, click the next available blank line, then click the drop-down list arrow for **Customer:Job** in the Customer:Job column
Click the name of the customer for whom work is being performed: **Babcock's Music Shop: Remodel**
Click the drop-down list arrow for **Service Item**, click the name of the service item: **Blueprint Changes**
Enter any notes regarding the work: **Correct Blueprints**
Click in the appropriate columns for the days of the week: **TU 13** enter the number of hours worked **2:15** and **W 14** enter **8:00**

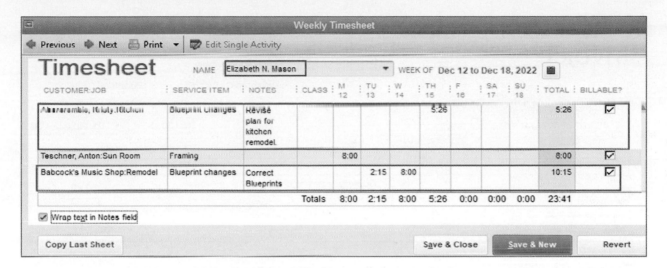

- If the information is the same for the current week is the same as the previous timesheet, click Copy Last Sheet.
  - ○ The information for the previous timesheet will be entered for this time period.

Indicate whether or not the hours are billable

- QuickBooks Desktop Timer records all hours as billable unless otherwise indicated.
- Notice the Blueprint changes for Abercrombie Kristy:Kitchen were recorded when using the Timer and the information for Babcock's Music Shop:Remodel were added manually. The information for Teschner, Anton: Sun Room was previously added.

When the timesheet is complete, click **Save & Close**

Prepare an Invoice Using Billable Hours

Click the **Create Invoices** icon on the Home Page

Enter the name of the **Customer:Job: (Abercrombie, Kristy: Kitchen)**

The Billable Time/Costs screen appears

"Select the outstanding billable time and costs to add to this invoice?" should be selected, click **OK**.

- If the Billable Time/Costs screen does not appear, click the Add Time/Costs button on the Invoice Icon Bar.

Scroll through the list of Time and Costs for the customer

Click the time you wish to bill

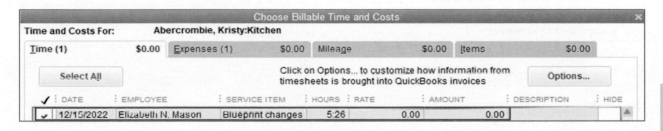

Click **OK**

- The time will be entered on the invoice.

The invoice would be completed as previously instructed

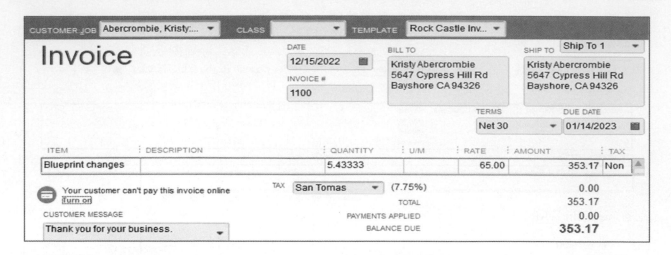

- The time clock keeps time in minutes but enters time on the invoice in tenths of an hour.
Click **Save & Close**

REMINDERS

Reminders is a list that gives you alerts and reminds you of tasks that need to be completed. It is accessed by clicking the clock on the Menu bar ⏰11 or by clicking Reminders on the Company menu. The dashboard for Reminders shows several categories in collapsed mode. On the left side of the Reminders list are alerts and today's tasks. When you click a category, it is expanded and the individual tasks/alerts are shown. If a task is overdue, it appears in red. If you click the Plus icon ➕ , you may add a To Do. If you click the Gear icon ⚙ , you go to Preferences where you may choose reminders to include for tasks and the number of days to give a reminder. If you double-click an alert, transaction, or To Do, you will open it.

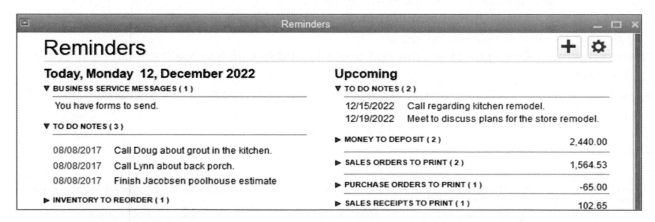

JOB COSTING AND TRACKING

Many companies complete work based on a job for a customer rather than just the customer. In QuickBooks Desktop, a job is a project done for a customer; for example, a kitchen remodel. You must always associate a job with a customer. This is very useful to organize and track work you perform for a client. Adding a job to a customer's account enables you to view each project for the customer individually. Once you add a job for a customer, you use the Job Info tab to track the status of the job, the Start Date, the Projected End Date, and the End Date. You may track several jobs for one customer.

When tracking jobs, there are four categories of reports that may be prepared. These are listed in the Jobs, Time & Mileage section of the Report Center. These report categories are Jobs & Profitability, Job Estimates, Time, and Mileage. The reports prepared use the information provided when tracking the jobs to display data that may help you answer questions about how well you estimate jobs, how much time you spend on jobs, how profitable jobs are, and mileage costs for the jobs.

Some of the available reports are:

Job Profitability Summary: This report summarizes how much money your company has made or lost on each job.

Job Profitability Detail: This report shows how much money your company has made to date on the customer or job whose name you entered. The report lists costs and revenues for each item you billed to the customer so you can see which parts of the job were profitable and which parts were not.

Profit & Loss by Job: Shows how much money you are making or losing on each job.

Job Estimates vs. Actuals Summary: This report summarizes how accurately your company estimated the job-related costs and revenues. The report compares estimated cost to actual cost and estimated revenue to actual revenue for all customers.

Job Estimates vs. Actuals Detail: This report shows how accurately your company estimated costs and revenues for the customer or job whose name you entered. The report compares estimated and actual costs and estimated and actual revenues for each item that you billed. That way, you can see which parts of the job you estimated accurately and which parts you did not.

Time by Job Summary: This report shows how much time your company spent on various jobs. For each customer or job, the report lists the type of work performed (service items). Initially, the report covers all dates from your QuickBooks Desktop records, but you can restrict the period covered by choosing a different date range from the Dates list.

Time by Job Detail: This report lists each time activity (that is, work done by one person for a particular customer or job on a specific date) and shows whether the work is billed, unbilled, or not billable. The report groups and subtotals the activities first by customer and job and then by service item.

Mileage by Job Detail: This report shows the miles for each trip per Customer:Job and includes the trip date, billing status, item, total miles, sales price and amount.

B

Steps to Create a Job for a Customer

Open the **Customer Center**
Select the customer for whom you want to add a job
* In this example, it is **Abercrombie, Kristy**.
Click the **New Customer & Job** button, click **Add Job**

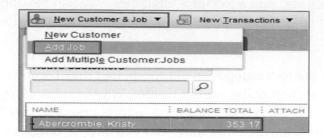

In the New Job window, enter a name for this job **Master Bedroom Remodel**
Click the Job Info tab and select from the following:
* (Optional) Enter a **Job Description** and a **Job Type**.
Select a **Job Status** (Pending, Awarded, In progress, etc.) from the drop-down list
* (Optional) Enter a **Start Date**, a **Projected End** date, and/or an **End Date** for the job.

Click **OK** to record the new job
* The job is added to the customer or the Customer List.

NAME	BALANCE TOTAL	ATTACH
◆ Abercrombie, Kristy	353.17	
◆ Master Bedroom Remodel	0.00	
◆ Family Room	0.00	
◆ Kitchen	353.17	
◆ Remodel Bathroom	0.00	

Close the **Customer Center**

Steps to Create a Bill Received for Job Expenses and Purchases

Enter the bill information as instructed in Chapter 6
Enter the date and amount of the bill

Enter the expense on the Expenses tab
* In the example, the expense account **54520: Freight & Delivery** is used.

Click the drop-down list arrow for Customer:Job in the Customer:Job column on the Expenses tab

Click the appropriate Customer:Job
* In the example, the Customer:Job is **Babcock's Music Shop: Remodel**.

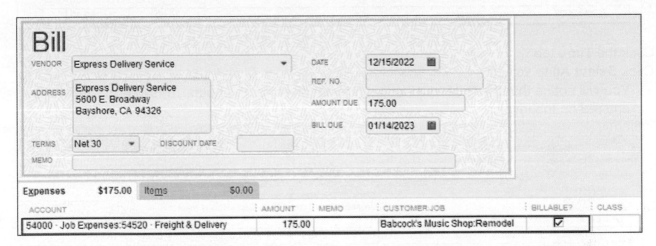

If a bill was for both expenses and items and expenses have been entered, you would then click the Items tab and enter the appropriate information for the Items including the Customer:Job

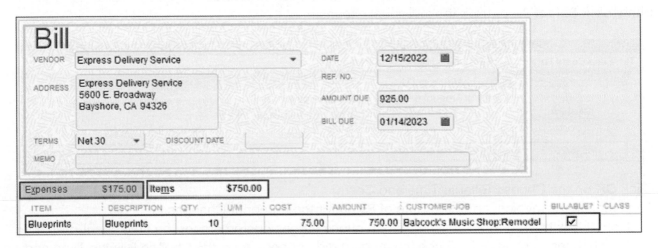

Click **Save & Close**

Steps to Create an Invoice for Items and Time Billed for a Job

Open an Invoice, select the Customer:Job
* In the example, the Customer:Job is **Babcock's Music Shop: Remodel**.

The Billable Time/Costs screen appears

"Select the outstanding billable time and costs to add to this invoice?" should be selected, click **OK**
* If the Billable Time/Costs screen does not appear, click the **Add Time/Costs** icon on the Invoice Icon Bar.

Click the **Items** tab

Click **Select All**
* Blueprints will be marked and $750.00 will be shown on the Items (1) tab.

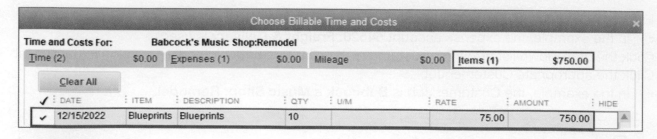

Click the **Time** tab

Click **Select All** to select

- You will notice that the Rate and Amount are not given for the hours. This information will be entered on the invoice.

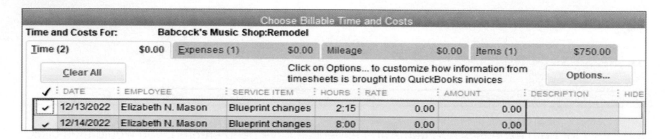

Click the **Expenses** tab to add the cost of the Delivery to the invoice

Either click **Select All** or click the individual expense

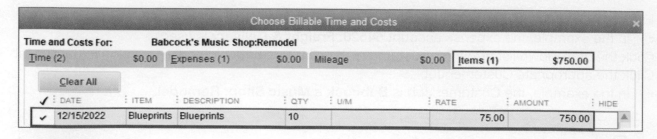

Click **OK** on the Choose Billable Time and Costs

To complete the invoice, enter the Rate of **85.00** for the Blueprint Changes

- Note this is the rate Rock Castle Construction charges customers for the time spent preparing the changes to blueprints. Since the amount did not appear on the Choose Billable Time and Costs screen, it must be entered manually. It is not the amount paid to the employee.
- The $750 was the cost of the changed Blueprints from Express Delivery (in the earlier example) and was entered by QuickBooks Desktop after choosing billable time and costs.

Add the Description **Delivery** to the $175 charge for Express Delivery Service

- The amount was entered by QuickBooks Desktop after choosing billable time and costs.

Complete the Invoice

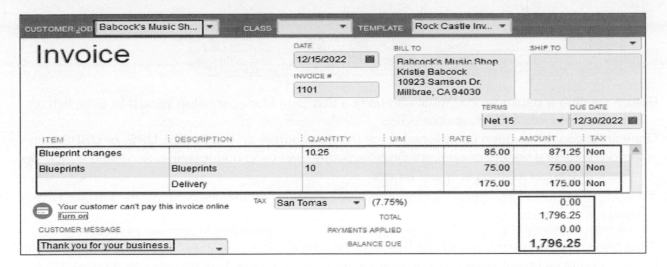

Notice that the Balance Due includes the amount for the delivery, the blueprints, and time billed for blueprints

Click **Save & Close**

Creating Reports Using Jobs and Time

Use **Report Center** or the Reports Menu
Click **Jobs, Time & Mileage**
Click the report you wish to prepare (The example shown is the Job Profitability Summary.)
If preparing the report from the menu, enter the Dates as a range or enter the **From** and **To** dates at the top of the report and Tab

Rock Castle Construction
Job Profitability Summary
All Transactions

	Act. Cost	Act. Revenue	($) Diff.
▼ **Abercrombie, Kristy**			
Family Room	2,150.00 ◄	2,961.05	811.05
Kitchen	2,645.00	5,145.17	2,500.17
Remodel Bathroom	5,416.23	6,749.50	1,333.27
Total Abercrombie, Kristy	10,211.23	14,855.72	4,644.49

Partial Report

Scroll through the report to evaluate the information
Close the report

SENDING MERCHANDISE USING QUICKBOOKS DESKTOP SHIPPING MANAGER

QuickBooks Desktop has a shipping manager that works in conjunction with FedEx, UPS, or USPS. To send merchandise to a customer, you must set up the shipping manager and have an account with the shipping company. Since we are working for a fictitious company we are unable to do this.

To set up the Shipping Manager, you would click the **Send/Ship** tab at the top of an invoice

B

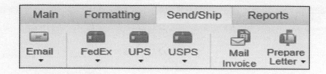

Before sending a package, you must complete a Shipping Manager setup wizard to establish an account for FedEx, UPS, and/or USPS

Once an account has been established, click the down arrow on the **FedEx**, **UPS**, or **USPS** icon and you have a variety of choices: Ship Package, Find drop off locations, Schedule a Pick Up, Track or Cancel a Shipment, and others

PRICE LEVELS

Price levels are created to increase or decrease inventory, non-inventory, and service item prices. For each price level you create, you assign a name and percentage of increase or decrease. You can use price levels on invoices, sales receipts, or credit memos. When you apply a price level to an item on a sales form, the adjusted price appears in the Rate column. You can assign price levels to customers and jobs. Then, whenever you use that customer and job on a sales form, the associated price level is automatically used to calculate the item price.

Create a Price Level List

From the Lists menu, choose **Price Level List**

Click the **Price Level** button, choose **New**

In the New Price Level window, enter the name of the new price level (Valued Customer in the example below)

Select the Price Level Type

In the area for **This price level will**, select either **increase** or **decrease** for **item prices by**

In the Percentage % field, enter the number and the % sign for the percentage by which the item price will be increased or reduced

Indicate whether QuickBooks Desktop should round numbers

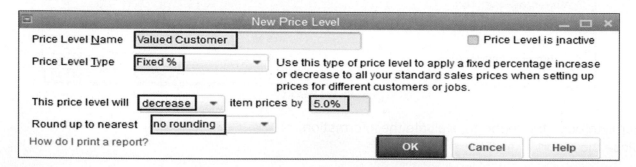

Click **OK** to go back to the Price Levels list, and close the **Price Level List**

Apply a Price Level on an Invoice

Fill out the invoice as previously instructed (shown on the next page)

Click the drop-down list arrow for **Rate**, and click a price level to apply to the item (Valued Customer in this example)

- The amount shown next to each price level is the adjusted rate for the item.

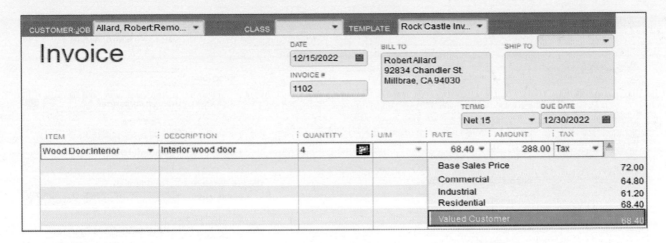

Save & Close the invoice

Associate a Price Level with a Customer

Access the **Customer Center**, select the **Customer**
Click the **Edit Customer** icon or double-click the Customer
Click the **Payment Settings** tab
From the Price Level drop-down list, select the price level you want to associate with the customer
    (Valued Customer in the example)

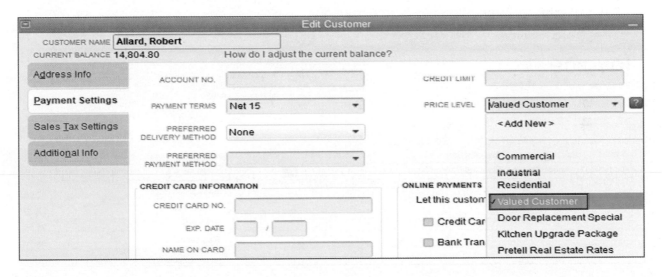

Click **OK**

Associate a Price Level with a Job

To apply a Price Level to a Job, click the **Job** listed beneath the customer in the Customer Center
Click the **Edit Job** icon or double-click the Job
Click the appropriate **price level** on the **Payment Settings** tab
In this example, **Valued Customer** is selected as the Price Level, click **OK**

B

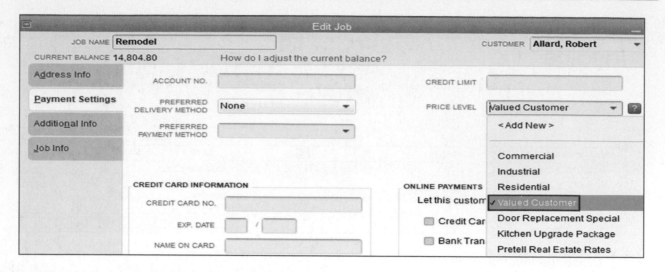

Prepare an Invoice Using Selected Price Levels

When preparing an invoice, items will automatically appear at the price level selected for the customer or job

To verify this, create a new invoice, and then click the drop-down list arrow for Rate

- Notice that Robert Allard is identified as a Valued Customer and that the price for the Standard Doorknobs in the example below has been entered at the price level selected for the customer (Valued Customer).

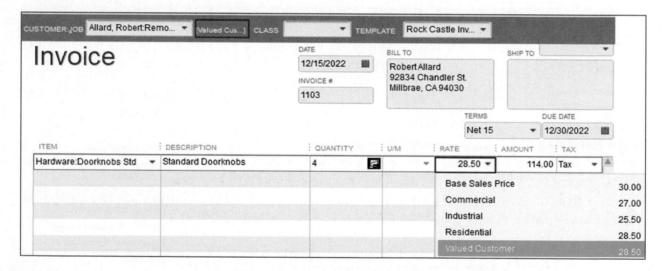

CLASSES

QuickBooks Desktop allows you to create classes that you assign to transactions. This lets you track account balances in various segments of your business. Reports may be prepared for the different classes you track. For example, in a construction company like Rock Castle Construction, you may want reports that itemize account balances for each construction division on your jobs. This lets you know how well you managed income and expenses. You may want to track your subcontractors by setting up a subset of the construction divisions; i.e. Rough Electrical and Finish Electrical to distinguish one segment of construction from the other.

To use class tracking, you must select the feature on the Company Preferences tab for Accounting Preferences.

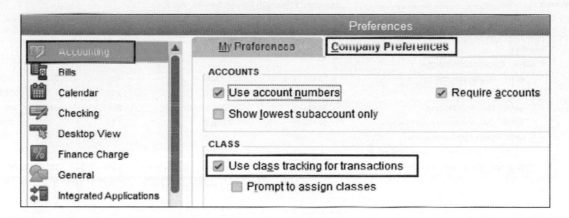

To use or create a Class, click **Class List** on the Lists menu
Click the **Class** button, and then click **New**; or use the Ctrl + N shortcut
To complete the following example, you would enter **Advertising** as the Class Name
Click **Subclass of**, and then click **New Construction**

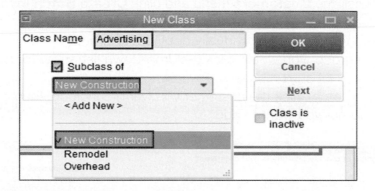

Click **OK** to save the New Class, close the Class List

* To use class tracking, every income and expense transaction should have a class assigned. To do this click the **Class** drop-down list and choose a class for every Item.
* For example, once the Customer:Job name has been entered on an invoice for work on Kristy Abercrombie's Kitchen, the class of Remodel should be assigned to the invoice.

Several reports, such as, a Balance Sheet by Class and a Profit & Loss by Class, etc. are available when working with classes. The example below shows the Construction income section of Rock Castle Construction's Profit & Loss by Class report. This report shows the income earned, the cost of goods sold, and expenses incurred for each account categorized by class; i.e. New Construction, Remodel, Overhead, and Unclassified. The report includes a Totals column so you can see the total amounts for each account and each section of the report.

B

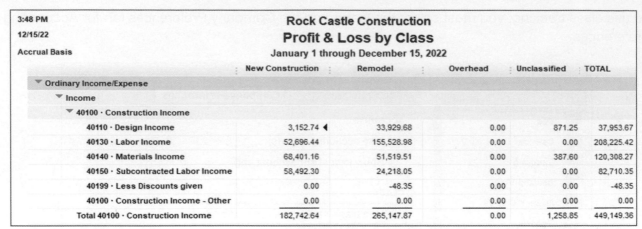

3:48 PM	Rock Castle Construction				
12/15/22	**Profit & Loss by Class**				
Accrual Basis	January 1 through December 15, 2022				
	New Construction	Remodel	Overhead	Unclassified	TOTAL
▼ Ordinary Income/Expense					
▼ Income					
▼ 40100 · Construction Income					
40110 · Design Income	3,152.74 ◄	33,929.68	0.00	871.25	37,953.67
40130 · Labor Income	52,696.44	155,528.98	0.00	0.00	208,225.42
40140 · Materials Income	68,401.16	51,519.51	0.00	387.60	120,308.27
40150 · Subcontracted Labor Income	58,492.30	24,218.05	0.00	0.00	82,710.35
40199 · Less Discounts given	0.00	-48.35	0.00	0.00	-48.35
40100 · Construction Income - Other	0.00	0.00	0.00	0.00	0.00
Total 40100 · Construction Income	182,742.64	265,147.87	0.00	1,258.85	449,149.36

Partial Report

BATCH INVOICING

If you have an invoice that you want to send to multiple customers, you may create a single batch of invoices rather than an invoice for each individual customer.

To do this, you would click the **Customers** menu and click **Create Batch Invoices**
Click **OK** on the "Is your customer info set up correctly?" message box
You may add customers to the batch individually or by billing group.

- If you were adding a group, you would click the drop-down list arrow for **Billing Group**, and click the group name. (Not shown.)

To add customers to the batch, click the customer you want to include, then click the **Add** button; repeat for each customer you want to add

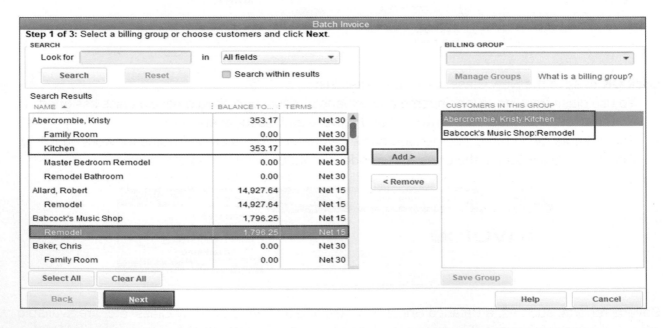

Click **Next**, select the Items used in the invoices, enter the quantity, select the message

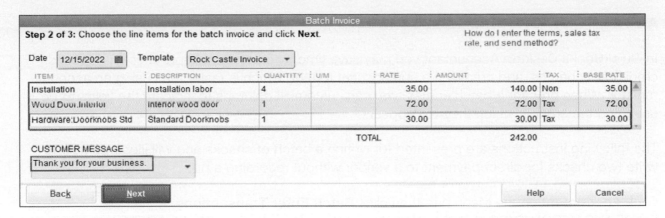

Click **Next** , review the list

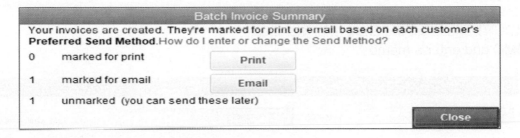

Click **Create Invoices**

On the Batch Invoices Summary you will see how many invoices are being emailed, printed, or need to be sent later

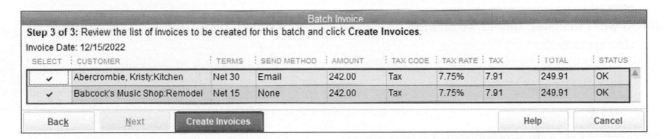

Click **Close**

Look at the invoices for Kristy Abercrombie, and Babcock's Music Shop

* Except for the amount of sales tax charged, both invoices should be the same.

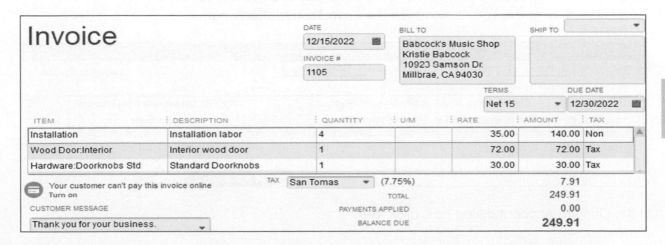

B

ACCOUNTANT BATCH ENTRIES

In QuickBooks Desktop Accountant you may save time by entering multiple checks, deposits, credit card charges, and credits in a spreadsheet format, which is faster than using an account register. When preparing batch entries, you can customize columns to indicate the fields to be used and the order in which they will appear.

The following instructions are presented for writing a batch of checks and will illustrate how to write two checks for direct payment to a vendor without recording a bill.

Click **Accountant** on the Menu bar, then click **Batch Enter Transactions**
For TRANSACTION TYPE click the drop-down list arrow and select **Checks**
BANK ACCOUNT should be : **10100 – Checking**, if not, click the drop-down arrow and select the account
If you want to insert, delete, or change the display order of the columns, click the **Customize Columns** button

To pay Cal Oil Company for gasoline you would:
Click in the DATE column and enter the date
NUMBER is automatically completed with the next available check
Click the drop-down arrow for PAYEE (the company receiving the check) and click **CalOil Company**
Click the drop-down arrow for ACCOUNT and click **60100 Automobile:60110- Fuel**
Tab to AMOUNT and enter the amount of the check
Tab to MEMO and enter a memo

Repeat the steps to enter a payment of $185.00 to City of Bayshore for water
When finished, note the TOTAL and click the **Save Transactions** button

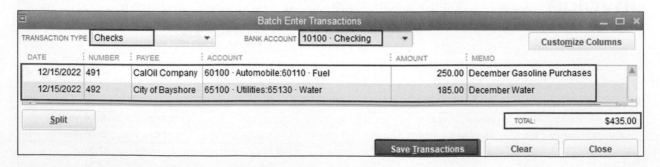

On the Confirm Account dialog box, click **Yes**

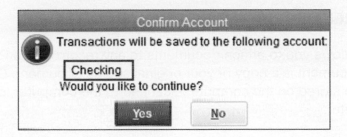

Click **OK** on the Transactions(s) Saved dialog box

To verify the payment, open Write Checks – Checking and scroll through or use find to view the checks written by QuickBooks Desktop

DOCUMENT CENTER

The Doc Center keeps track of documents you use with QuickBooks Desktop. You may add a document from your computer, scan a document, or drag and drop a document from Outlook or Explorer to the Doc Center. The documents may then be attached to QuickBooks Desktop records such as invoices, customers, etc.

Click the **Docs** icon on the Top Icon bar to open the Doc Center

To add a document from your computer, click the **Add a Document Folder** icon, find the document, click it to select, click **Open**

The document is added to the Doc Center

To scan a document, click the **Scanner** icon; place the document on your scanner; click **Scan**; on the "What do you want to scan?" screen; select the option for the type of picture or document; click **Scan**; when finished, click **Done Scanning**; give the document a name; click **OK**

To drag and drop a document on the desktop, point to the document icon, hold down the primary mouse button, drag the document to the section that says Drop documents from Outlook, your desktop, or folders here, release the mouse button

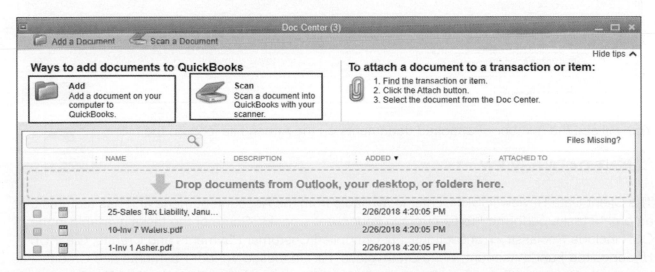

The number of documents in the Doc Center is shown in parentheses on the Doc Center title bar

You may view the details, open, or remove the document by clicking one of the buttons at the bottom of the Doc Center

Click the **Close** button to close the Doc Center

ATTACHED DOCUMENTS

QuickBooks Desktop allows you to attach documents to any record with a Paperclip Attach button. An attached document is a copy of your original source document. Documents may be attached when they are stored on the computer, scanned to the computer, copied by drag and drop, or in the Doc Center.

To attach a document from the Doc Center to a transaction, open and complete the business form
* In the example, a Bill from Thomas Kitchen & Bath was selected.
Click the icon for Attach File on the Enter Bills Main icon bar

Select the **Doc Center** for the document location
Click the document to select, click the **Attach** button
The document is attached to the business document
To view the attached document, simply click on the attachment and click the **Open** button
When finished attaching documents from the Doc Center, click **Done**

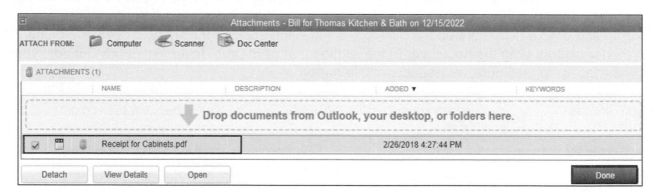

You will see the number of attached documents on the Attach File icon on the bill

CLIENT DATA REVIEW

The Client Data Review (CDR) Center is available from the Accountant menu and has features that automate tasks performed to fix errors in your client's books. Some of the tasks available in the CDR include Reclassify Transactions, Fix Unapplied Customer Payments and Credits, Clear Up Undeposited Funds Account, Write Off Invoices, Fix Unapplied Vendor Payments and Credits, Fix Incorrectly Recorded Sales Tax, Compare Balance Sheet and Inventory Valuation, Troubleshoot Inventory, Find Incorrectly Paid Payroll Liabilities, and Merge Vendors.

Click the **Accountant** menu, point to Client Data Review, and then click **Client Data Review** in the side menu

Enter the Date Range, Review Basis, and click **Start Review**

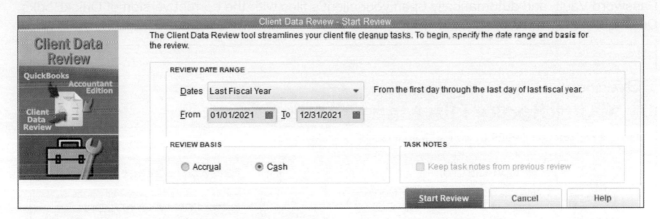

The Client Data chart appears with the tasks listed. As you work on the different review areas, you can indicate the Status of the review, add Task Notes, and add Review Notes

Task areas include: Account Balances, Review List Changes, Accounts Receivable, Accounts Payable, Sales Tax, Inventory, Payroll, Bank Reconciliation, and Miscellaneous

The Review may be printed or saved as a PDF file. You may obtain an Audit Trail of Review, and when finished, mark the review as complete

Close the Client Data Review when finished

FILE MANAGER

QuickBooks Desktop File Manager is accessed from the Accountant menu. File Manager enables you to open and manage clients' QuickBooks Desktop files. This is a very helpful component of QuickBooks Accountant Desktop and QuickBooks Enterprise Accountant; especially if you manage company files from multiple years.

When using QuickBooks Desktop File Manager, you may build a client list that organizes QuickBooks Desktop files by client, create client groups that will display files for specific types of clients, upgrade clients' QuickBooks Desktop files in batches, store client passwords in the Password Vault, and automatically open your client's files with the correct version of QuickBooks Desktop.

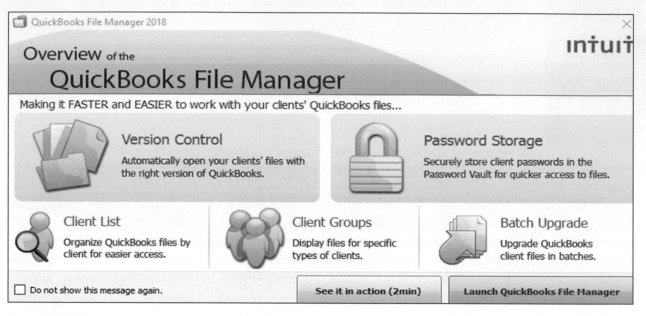

SEND AND IMPORT GENERAL JOURNAL ENTRIES

Using the Accountant menu, you may use the Make General Journal Entries to enter General Journal entries and then click the icon **Send GJEs** to add them to a list of entries to be sent from the accountant to the client. Once the entries have been selected, click Send General Journal Entries on the Accountant menu to select which entries to send. You will send the entries as either an email attachment to send the entries now or as a saved .QBJ file, which you can attach to an email or store on a USB drive.

After the accountant has sent the General Journal entries, the client opens the .QBJ file from email or Windows Explorer and the Add General Journal Entries to Your File window opens in QuickBooks Desktop. At this point, the client clicks Add GJEs to import the transactions into your company file. You then get a GJEs Import Summary window, which lists the imported journal entries.

STATEMENT WRITER

The QuickBooks Statement Writer (QSW) allows you to create customized financial reports from a QuickBooks Desktop company file. The QuickBooks Statement Writer contains a library of templates that may be used for statements and supporting documents; in addition, a template may be created. The QSW uses data directly from the QuickBooks Desktop company file. You can set preferences, formats, and styles for all of your reports. You may combine accounts and subaccounts automatically or by specification. Supporting documents may also be prepared using the same look as the one used in statements.

To use this feature, select QuickBooks Statement Writer on the Accountant menu
- There may be a fairly lengthy and detailed install update required in order to use the Statement Writer.

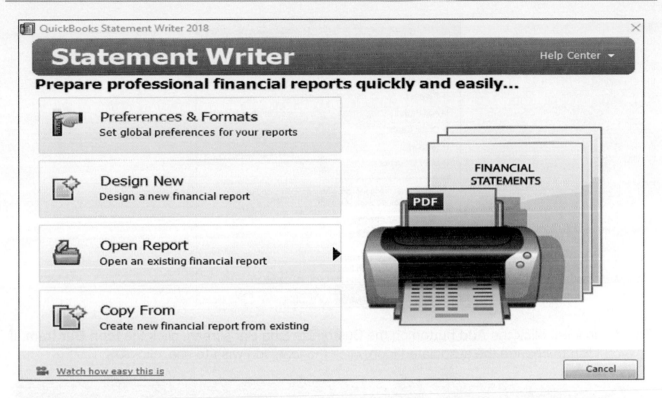

When QuickBooks Statement Writer is on the screen, there are buttons available that allow you to select General Preferences for Reports and Templates, Design New financial reports, Open Reports to select existing reports, and Copy From to create new financial report from existing reports reports.

CUSTOMIZE THE ICON BAR(S)

As previously demonstrated within the text, you may use the default Left Icon Bar or the Top Icon Bar. Both the Left and Top Icon Bars may be customized to display Centers and frequently used Commands. If you do not use an icon or shortcut shown on the Icon Bar, you may delete it.

If you are using the Left Icon Bar, right-click anywhere on it to get Customize Shortcuts; and then click **Customize Shortcuts**

If you are using the Top Icon Bar, right-click anywhere on it to get Customize Icon Bar; and then, click the **Customize Icon Bar** button

Either method takes you to the Customize Icon Bar screen, where you may Add, Edit, Delete, or Add Separator to the Icon Bar Content. You may also choose to display icons and text or icons only. The final selection is whether to Show Search Box in Icon Bar

To delete an icon, you would click the icon and then click the Delete button

B

To add an icon, click the **Add** button on the Customize Icon Bar screen, click the **Icon Bar Item**; if you wish to change the associated icon, click the icon you wish to use, click **OK**

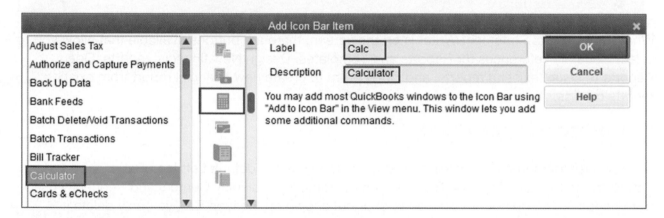

To position an added icon, drag the icon's diamond up or down within the icon bar content on the Customize Icon Bar screen

Click **OK** to close Customize Icon Bar

You will see the Icon for Calc in the Top Icon Bar

If you are using the Left-Icon Bar, you will see the Icon in the list of My Shortcuts

QUICKBOOKS DESKTOP: ONLINE FEATURES

C

QuickBooks Desktop uses the Internet as an integral part of the program. Subscribers to the Payroll Services can receive online updates to tax tables and forms. Online banking and vendor payments can be performed within the program. You can order supplies, obtain product support, access training resources, find a QuickBooks expert in your area, send feedback online, get suggestions for resources for your business, and access Live Community (where you may post questions, give advice, and participate in Webinars). The browser requirement to use QuickBooks Desktop's Online features is Internet Explorer 11 (32-bit).

In addition to the included online items, there are several online subscription programs that may be used in conjunction with QuickBooks Desktop. These include Payroll Services, Online Bill Pay, QuickBooks Payments (Merchant Service), Billing Solutions, Direct Deposit, Intuit Data Protect, QuickBooks Point of Sale, and many others.

Use QuickBooks' App Center to access free and for fee Apps that work with QuickBooks Desktop and bring together both mobile and web-based applications that companies have created to integrate their software products with QuickBooks Premier Desktop and QuickBooks Enterprise Solutions.

Intuit makes frequent changes to the applications, programs, and services that are available to work with or through QuickBooks Desktop. This appendix explores some of those features that were available at the time of writing.

Since many of the features listed above, may not be completed unless you have an active Intuit Account and subscribe to the services, they cannot be illustrated. Thus, this Appendix will explore only some of the online options available. And, as with the other appendices, you should just read the information presented and not try to complete what is illustrated.

INTUIT AND THE INTERNET

At Intuit's Web site you may get up-to-date information about QuickBooks Desktop and other products by Intuit. You can access the Intuit Web site at **www.Intuit.com**.

CONNECTING TO INTUIT IN QUICKBOOKS DESKTOP

Before connecting to Intuit's Web Site using QuickBooks Desktop, you must have the QuickBooks Desktop program and a company open. In addition, you modem for your computer, and the modem must be connected to a telephone line or cable. Once the modem is connected and QuickBooks Desktop and a company are open, you may establish your Internet connection. You may also use a wireless Internet connection.

QuickBooks Desktop has a step-by-step tutorial that will help you connect to the Internet through QuickBooks Desktop. Clicking Internet Connection Setup on the Help menu allows you to identify an internet connection and complete the setup. The first screen you see informs QuickBooks Desktop of your choice for your Internet connection. You may select one of three connection options: you have an Internet connection that you identify; you plan to use your computer's Internet connection; or you want to sign up for an Internet account with limited access.

The three choices and their accompanying screens are shown in the following:

Click the **Help** menu, click **Internet Connection Setup**
Click on one of the three options

To Use Other Internet Connection

Click **Use the following connection**, click **Other Internet connection**, and click the **Next** button
    at the bottom of the screen
Verify the information provided, click the **Done** button at the bottom of the screen

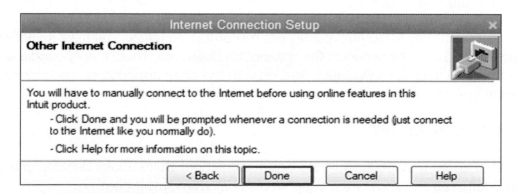

To Use a Computer's Internet Connection

Click the **Help** menu, click **Internet Connection Setup**
If you have a direct Internet connection, select **Use my computer's Internet connection settings to establish a connection when this application accesses the Internet**, click the **Next** button at the bottom of the screen

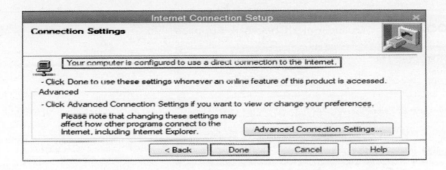

Verify the information; click the **Done** button at the bottom of the screen

To Establish an Internet Provider and Connection

If you do not have an Internet provider, click **I do not have a way to connect to the Internet.**
   Please give me more information on setting up an Internet account
Click **Next**
The screen will tell you that you must sign up with an Internet Service Provider

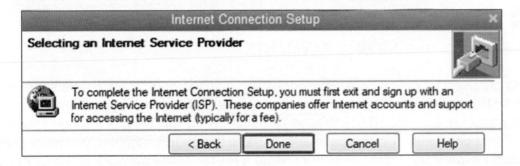

Click **Done**

ACCESS QUICKBOOKS DESKTOP'S ONLINE FEATURES

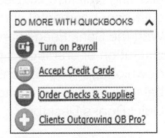

When you see a section on the Home Page or the Left Icon Bar that says "Do More with QuickBooks Desktop," clicking one of the items will take you to the areas requested if you have a direct Internet connection. You may also access the items listed at the bottom of the Insights tab.

For example, Order Checks & Supplies in the Do More with QuickBooks Desktop section of the Home Page was clicked. QuickBooks Desktop connected to the Web and brought up a screen describing QuickBooks Desktop Checks and Supplies that are designed to work with QuickBooks Desktop and that may be ordered.

C

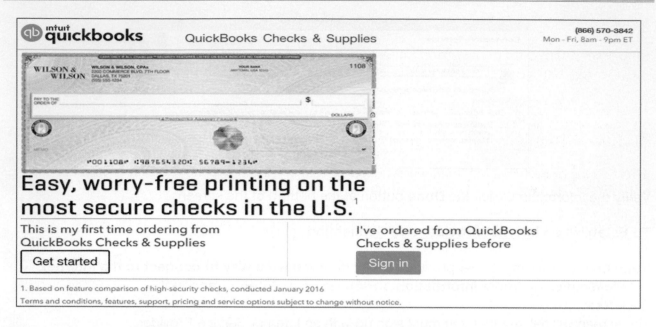

Apps are another example of online access through QuickBooks Desktop and were previously discussed.

BANK FEEDS AND ONLINE BILL PAYMENTS

Bank Feeds are used for online banking services and management. Bank Feeds are offered through QuickBooks Desktop in conjunction with a variety of financial institutions. This is also called online account access. To use this, you must apply for this service through your financial institution. If you bank with or make payments to more than one institution, you must sign up with each institution separately. Most banks will charge a fee for online services and may not offer both online banking and online payment services. Some institutions provide enhanced services, such as allowing QuickBooks Desktop to transfer money between two online accounts, accepting online customer payments, and accepting eChecks that have been processed by telephone or scanned. With the Bank Feeds service, you can download electronic statements from your financial institution or credit card provider into QuickBooks Desktop. Once statements have been downloaded, you can see what transactions have cleared your account, find out your current balance, and add transactions that have been processed but have not been entered in QuickBooks Desktop.

Some financial institutions allow you to pay bills from your vendor electronically. Once you set up the service with your bank, you use QuickBooks Desktop to send payment instructions to your financial institution. If your bank does not use electronic payments, QuickBooks Desktop has an online bill payment service that you may access on a subscription basis. For a monthly fee, you may write checks or pay bills as you would normally; then select Online Bank Payment and the date on which you would like the payment delivered. You then send the payments from the Online Banking Center within QuickBooks Desktop and they will be made by the delivery date. It is suggested that you allow up to four business days for processing.

Bank Feeds

Bank Feeds allow you to download transactions from your financial institution or credit card provider into QuickBooks Desktop.

To use the Bank Feeds services for account access or payment, you need access to the Internet and an account at a participating financial institution. You must also apply for the service through QuickBooks Desktop or through a participating financial service.

To see a list of participating financial institutions, click the **Banking** menu, point to **Bank Feeds**, and click **Participating Financial Institutions**

QuickBooks Desktop connects to the Internet and a list of financial institutions appears

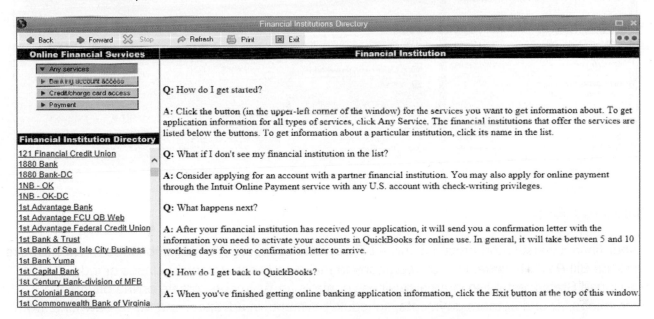

To provide security and confidentiality in online services, QuickBooks Desktop uses state-of-the-art encryption and authentication security features. All of your online communications with your financial institution require a Personal Identification Number (PIN) or password, which only you possess. You may also use passwords within QuickBooks Desktop.

Set Up Bank Feeds

Since we do not have an actual company, we are unable to setup an online banking account. However, to create an online banking account for your own business, click the **Banking** menu, point to **Bank Feeds**, and click **Set Up Bank Feeds for an Account**. Complete the Online Setup Interview. Once you have setup online banking, the Checking account and any other bank accounts that are setup for online banking will have a second screen for Bank Feed Settings that is accessible when you edit the account.

Using Bank Feeds

Bank Feeds allow you to download current information from and send messages to your financial institution. This can include transactions, balances, online messages, and transfer of funds. To use online banking, click **Banking** on the menu bar, point to Online Banking, and click **Bank Feeds Center**.

Because we do not have actual companies, we will not be able to use the Bank Feeds Center; however, note on the following screen, that you may update the account, download transactions, send items to your bank, and create new items for your bank. On the left of the screen, you will see a list of bank accounts and current information for them.

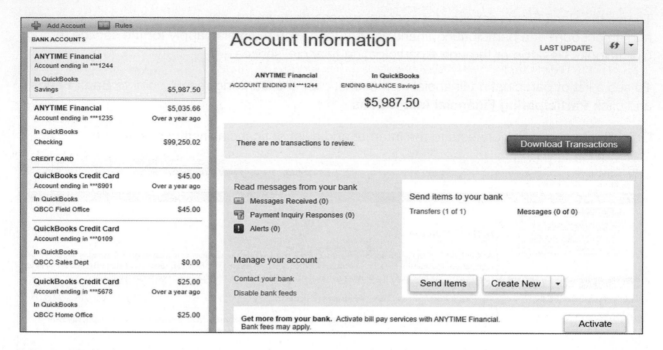

Online Payments

If your financial institution provides online bill payment services, you may subscribe to QuickBooks Desktop Bill Pay. This enables your company to make payments to any business or individual in the United States, establish internal business controls for payments, create online payment instructions for one or more payments, schedule payments in advance, and make payments from up to ten different accounts. You may schedule a payment to arrive on a certain date, inquire about online payments, and cancel them if need be. You can record and pay your bills at the same time, all from within QuickBooks Desktop. Online banking through QuickBooks Desktop uses state-of-the-art encryption technology and requires a PIN to send transactions. You can use online payments with any U.S. bank account with check-writing privileges.

To use online payments, you need to set up a payee. Once the payee is set up, you may either send an electronic funds transfer (EFT) to the payee's institution or have your financial institution print a check and send it to the payee. An electronic funds transfer deducts money from your account and transfers it into the payee's account electronically. This usually takes one or two business days; however, payments should be scheduled four days before they are due. This is called lead time and must be considered when sending online payments.

You may prepare an online payment by:
- Writing a check in Write Checks.
- Paying a bill in Pay Bills.
- Or clicking Write Checks or Pay Bills in the Bank Feeds (Online Banking) Center.

Prepare the check or bill using these methods the same way you always do, except that you designate the transaction as an online transaction and send the payment instructions to your financial institution.

For a check, record the check in QuickBooks Desktop, click **Online Payment**, and then select the date you want the check delivered.

When using Pay Bills to pay your bill, click the drop-down list arrow for **Method**, click **Online Bank Pmt**, and then select the date you want your payment delivered.

After the Check or the Bill Payment has been prepared, you send the payments from the Online Banking Center within QuickBooks Desktop and the payment will be made by the delivery date selected. You need to allow up to four business days for processing.

The Bank Feeds Preference was changed to Classic Mode in order to show the online payments recorded.

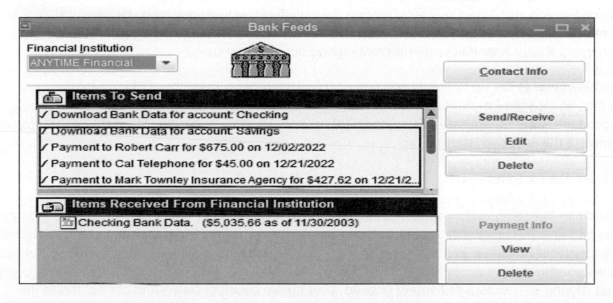

QUICKBOOKS PAYMENTS

QuickBooks Desktop offers a variety of services to help with processing Customer Payments. With QuickBooks Payments, you may accept online credit card payments, scan and/or accept telephone eChecks, swipe credit cards, and your money will be auto-deposited into your bank account.

To accept online credit card payments from customers, a subscription to QuickBooks Payments is required. Then, invoices may be enabled for online payment by clicking the "Allow online payment" checkbox on the Create Invoices window. Customers may pay for invoices and statements online by entering their credit card information in the Customer Account Center, which is a secure Web site hosted by Intuit. Charges to your company for this service are processed through QuickBooks Merchant Service. Because we do not use actual companies within the text and are unable to sign up for a Merchant Services account, these features cannot be demonstrated.

ACH/eCheck payment options allow you to accept electronic checks by telephone or by scanning paper checks into QuickBooks Desktop. QuickBooks Payments was designed to support check scanning but also allows you to accept checks by telephone. Whether you scan checks or accept checks by phone, you are required to follow certain procedures.

To process customer credit card payments by swiping or inserting an EMV chip credit card, you will need to purchase a card reader from Intuit. Currently, a chip reading card processor is not available for QuickBooks DT; however, there is an EMV chip reader available for your smartphone or tablet when using the GoPayment App. In addition, the QuickBooks Point of Sale has the EMV reader and will integrate with QuickBooks Desktop. Depending on the method chosen, a card reader attaches to your phone, tablet, or computer, so your transactions can be recorded in QuickBooks DT automatically. Each of these options will incur charges from Intuit.

DIRECT DEPOSIT

Rather than mail or give paychecks to your employees, you may sign up for Direct Deposit if you have a subscription to QuickBooks Payroll. You will go to the Employees menu and click My Payroll Service and Activate Direct Deposit. To activate direct deposit, you will need the company's legal name and address, contact information for one of your company owners or officers, and your financial institution routing and account numbers.

You also need to set up those employees who wish to receive their checks by direct deposit. To do this, access the Employee Center, double-click the employee you want to set up for direct deposit, click the Payroll Info tab in the Edit Employee window, click the Direct Deposit button and complete the required information.

INTUIT DATA PROTECT

In addition to having a backup stored in the office, having an offsite backup copy of your company data files is extremely important. This is necessary in case something happens to your computer or your office. For a fee, you may subscribe to Intuit Data Protect. Files are automatically backed up once a day on a predetermined schedule. Bank-level security encryptions and safeguards are used. During the Intuit Data Protect backup, your computer must be on and connected to the Internet. Since the backup runs in the background, you may continue to use QuickBooks Desktop while the backup is being made. In addition to data, everything you need to re-create your company file and QuickBooks Desktop environment is backed up. Each backup is stored for 45 days.

INDEX

I

I

I

I